The Right to Erasure in EU Data Protection Law

OXFORD DATA PROTECTION AND PRIVACY LAW

Series Editors
CHRISTOPHER KUNER
Professor of Law, VUB Brussel

GRAHAM GREENLEAF
Professor of Law and Information Systems,
University of New South Wales

The aim of this series is to publish important and original books on legal issues of data protection and privacy. This includes many different areas of law, including comparative law, EU law, human rights law, international law, privacy on the Internet, and others.

Prospective authors are welcome to submit proposals for the series, as outlined on the series website: global.oup.com/academic/content/series/o/oxford-data-protection-and-privacy-law-odppl/

The Right to Erasure in EU Data Protection Law

From Individual Rights to Effective Protection

JEF AUSLOOS

OXFORD
UNIVERSITY PRESS

OXFORD
UNIVERSITY PRESS

Great Clarendon Street, Oxford, OX2 6DP,
United Kingdom

Oxford University Press is a department of the University of Oxford.
It furthers the University's objective of excellence in research, scholarship,
and education by publishing worldwide. Oxford is a registered trade mark of
Oxford University Press in the UK and in certain other countries

First Edition published in 2020

Published in the United States of America by Oxford University Press
198 Madison Avenue, New York, NY 10016, United States of America

British Library Cataloguing in Publication Data

Data available

Library of Congress Control Number: 2019954550

ISBN 978–0–19–884797–7

Foreword

The technological and economic forces characterising modern society have thoroughly disrupted the constitutional status quo in the west which grew from the lessons of the Second World War, fascism and communism. Today again, human autonomy and democracy are in peril. Not a day goes by without us having to confront how technology developers and users, big and small, are challenging not just our privacy, but also core European principles such as equality, information freedoms, liberty and democracy itself. The key catalyst in these developments is the hunger to generate profits with *personal* data and the readiness to put profits over individual autonomy and freedom. Al Gore called this business model the "stalker economy".

Jef Ausloos explores ways to safeguard individual autonomy in this brave new world. He investigates this through the lens of EU data protection law and the legal tools it contains to empower individuals in their efforts to exercise control over their personal data. The right to erasure ('right to be forgotten') constitutes the centrepiece of the GDPR in this endeavour.

Readers should not be misled by the title of the study, which is more than an analysis of Article 17 GDPR. Jef Ausloos rather positions this provision as a central junction in the GDPR and skilfully uses it as a starting point to go deeper into EU data protection law in its entirety.

The book could not be more timely. It is based on the author's PhD research, defended in 2018, the year that data protection went mainstream. The GDPR entered into force, Convention 108+ of the Council of Europe was adopted, and perhaps most importantly the Facebook / Cambridge Analytica scandal signified the tipping point in public opinion on the issues of democracy and individual freedom emerging from data-driven power asymmetries. These modern-day cautionary tales—from psychological manipulation in the gig economy and political microtargeting on social media, to arbitrary visibility on search engines and the problematic practices of so-called 'virtual assistants'—feature throughout the book, offering valuable illustrations of practical operation of data protection law.

Article 17 GDPR is not such a complex provision. Its purpose is clear. But as so often in texts of law which are the result of a democratic compromise, a closer reading raises a number of issues. Jef Ausloos structures all of these issues in clear terms, under three questions: Does the right to erasure apply in the first place? If it applies, how should we go about balancing the different rights, freedoms and interests at stake? If the right applies, and *if* a balance can be found, how should this right be made effective in practice?

To answer these questions, the book sets out a case-law analysis of fundamental rights balancing, focusing specifically on Articles 7 (right to private life), 8 (data protection), 11 (information freedoms), and 16 (freedom to conduct a business) of the EU Charter of Fundamental Rights.

The author does not shy away from taking a swing at some of the broader societal issues of increasingly datafied—and thus controllable—actions, relationships and environments. He dissects complex data processing operations and thus successfully seeds doubts against the dominant tech sector arguments in defending their practices which put in question individual autonomy.

His key theme throughout the book is the power asymmetries as catalysed by *technological* and *economic* forces and how to address them through law which empowers individuals. For Ausloos, empowerment and autonomy play two roles: They are a goal in themselves, as a manifestations of freedom and dignity of men, which we need to fight to preserve in the age of AI. Secondly, they are tools to achieve informational self-determination through legal institutions, namely GDPR.

Paul Nemitz
Principal Adviser at the European Commission and
Visiting Professor of Law at the College of Europe

Series Editors' Preface

The Internet raises numerous challenges for the protection of personal data, such as the simultaneous desire of individuals to make their personal data public while retaining control over their processing; the global nature of data transfers, which brings challenges for effective enforcement of data protection rights; and the lack of transparency and accountability that surround much data processing.

These issues have gained particular attention in light of recent developments concerning application of the right to erasure (also known as the 'right to be forgotten') to global online networks. The right first gained notoriety when the EU General Data Protection Regulation (GDPR) was proposed in 2012, and then became even more famous following the 2014 judgment of the Court of Justice of the European Union in the case *Google Spain SL*, in which the Court affirmed the application of the right in the context of online search engines. Since then, questions surrounding the right to erasure have provoked international controversy about the proper balance between data protection rights and other rights and freedoms, the extraterritorial scope of EU law, and the threats to individual rights posed by data processing on the Internet.

These issues are all dealt with in detail in the present volume by Dr. Jef Ausloos. The author, who has examined the legal and technical implications of the right to erasure since it first gained attention, has produced a monograph which is a superb work of scholarship. It focuses on the right to erasure under the EU data protection framework, particularly the GDPR, but also recognizes that the right to erasure has become an international phenomenon that has received legal responses in non-European countries as disparate as Argentina, Japan, Qatar, Russia, Madagascar, Turkey, and Brazil.

A particular strength of this book is that, while the author provides a meticulous examination of the legal issues surrounding the right to erasure under the GDPR, he also puts the legal issues into a wider context. Thus, he considers the tensions between the right and other important values (such as freedom of expression), and examines the important question of how the right works in practice. Perhaps most significantly, he recognizes that the issues surrounding the right to erasure serve as a paradigm for a broader discussion about informational self-determination in online data processing.

We are thus pleased to include this important book in our series. We believe that it makes a significant contribution to data protection scholarship, both in EU law and with regard to questions of online data processing more generally.

Christopher Kuner and Graham Greenleaf

Acknowledgements

Of the many metaphors that exist to describe the process of writing a PhD, I prefer the one linking it to climbing a mountain. You start in the valley, looking at the summit full of wonder and eager anticipation. But as you move your eyes downwards and downwards, following a meandering path over icy rocks, steep cliffs, and through dark forests, you quickly realize the ascent will be no walk in the park. I am therefore incredibly grateful to have been surrounded by such great people all along the way to the top.

First of all, there is my wonderful advisory committee, without whom I would never have embarked on this journey in the first place. Prof Dr Peggy Valcke defines, and exceeds, the term 'promotor'. Her unwavering enthusiasm and support were not just vital in reaching the summit, but also enabled many fascinating excursions along the way. I am also incredibly grateful to my co-promotors: Prof Dr Eleni Kosta for being the lighthouse I often needed when losing sight of the summit, and Dr Seda Gürses reminding me to take a step back, breath, and look at the broader picture. This trinity of (co-)promoters was complemented by three people whose insights and encouragement have made this dissertation worthwhile. Thank you Prof Dr Serge Gutwirth, Prof Dr Jo Pierson, and Prof Dr Nico van Eijk. Thank you also to jury members Prof Dr Geert van Calster, Prof Dr Elise Muir, and chair Em Prof Dr Jacques Herbots for meeting me at the top.

Climbing a mountain never happens in a straight line. You encounter many challenges and distractions along the way, resulting in numerous detours. I was lucky enough to have (had) wonderful colleagues with whom I shared parts of the path to the summit. In particular, Brendan Van Alsenoy who not only helped me achieve new heights, but also taught me the importance of academic integrity and humility. Aleksandra Kuczerawy, for being a great writing-buddy and the best roomie one could wish for. Damian Clifford for always-inspiring conversations and being a partner-in-crime for many PhD discussion days. Pieter-Jan, Amandine, and Valerie for putting a huge smile on my face throughout most of the journey. And of course so many other CiTiP colleagues that have made 'going to the office' a true joy throughout the years!

My journey would never have been successful without two major detours along the way. I am very grateful to the wonderful people at the Institute for Information Law at the University of Amsterdam—and in particular Nico van Eijk, Natali Helberger, Kristina Irion, and Frederik Zuiderveen Borgesius—for a productive research stay in the fall of 2015. Thank you also to everyone at the Center for Intellectual Property and Information Law at Cambridge University for a very inspiring four months in the winter of 2017. Especially David Erdos for being such a great host and never shy for some intellectual sparring. Julia Powles and Christina Angelopoulos, thank you as well for all the stimulating discussions.

At the risk of forgetting many names, I would also like to thank the following truly amazing people for the inspiring conversations and/or collaborations without which I would not be where I am today: Günes Acar, Paul Bernal, Reuben Binns, Ian Brown, Lorenzo Dalla Corte, Paul-Olivier Dehaye, Lilian Edwards, Gloria González Fuster, Kirsten Gollatz, Edina Harbinja, Rob Heyman, Paulan Korenhof, Ronald Leenes, Meg Leta Jones, Orla Lynskey, Nora Ní Loideain, Marcelo Thompson, Joris van Hoboken, Michael Veale, and Nicolo Zingales. Thank You.

Reaching the top of Mount PhD would not have been possible without the warm support and understanding of family and friends. I am particularly grateful to my mother for instilling me with that sense of awe and wonder that makes life so fascinating. Thank you to both of my grandmothers who I admire for being the rebels and artists they are. And of course, thank you Laura, without whom I would have been long lost in the woods. You walked by me all along, enduring yet encouraging me while I was spiralling around the top for years and actively supporting me during the last stretch straight to the top. You make everything possible.

Jef Ausloos
September 2018

Table of Contents

Table of Cases

EUROPEAN COURT OF HUMAN RIGHTS

EUROPEAN UNION

NATIONAL

Austria

Belgium

France

Switzerland

Germany

Ireland

Italy

Netherlands

Table of Legislation

INTERNATIONAL

Council of Europe

TREATIES

'SOFT LAW' INSTRUMENTS

European Union

PRIMARY LAW

REGULATIONS

National

FRANCE

GERMANY

List of Abbreviations

29WP	Article 29 Working Party
ASHRS	Archiving in the Public Interest, Scientific or Historical Research, or Statistical Research? Purposes?
Charter	Charter of Fundamental Rights of the European Union
CJEU	Court of Justice of the European Union
CNIL	Commission Nationale de l'Informatique et des Libértes
Convention 108	Convention for the Protection of Individuals with regard to Automatic Processing of Personal Data'
CoE	Council of Europe
Directive 95/46	Data Protection Directive 95/46/EC
ECHR	European Convention of Human Rights
ECtHR	European Court of Human Rights
EDPB	European Data Protection Board
EDPS	European Data Protection Supervisor
EU	European Union
FRA	European Union Agency for Fundamental Rights
GDPR	General Data Protection Regulation 2016/679
ICO	Information Commissioner's Office
ICT	Information Communication Technology
IoT	Internet of Things
ISS	Information Society Service
JAAL	Journalistic, Academic, Artistic or Literary expression
OECD	Organisation for Economic Co-operation and Development
OECD Guidelines	OECD 'Guidelines on the Protection of Privacy and Transborder Flows of Personal Data
PETs	Privacy Enhancing Technologies
TFEU	Treaty on the Functioning of the European Union

Note to the Readers

The field of data protection law is burgeoning. The amount of scholarship, policy work, and landmark cases coming out of the EU and elsewhere seems to increase exponentially every year. Any work in this field is therefore destined to age from the moment the author finishes their last sentence. That being said, important scholarship stands the test of time because it manages to connect current issues with more established notions and traditions. This book aims to do exactly this. It is the product of research completed in pursuit of my PhD, defended at the Law Faculty of the University of Leuven in October 2018 (new cases, regulatory guidance, and academic work have been added up until June 2019). While it is grounded in contemporary issues, for example by using real-life examples of high societal relevance at the time of writing, the book's main contribution to the field stems from the analyses and reframing of core notions in EU data protection law. As such, I hope readers will still find it useful in guiding and informing their own work for many years to come.

1
Introduction

Section 1. The Tolling Giant

An old Belgian folkloristic fable, tells the story of the giant Druon Antigoon

> Once upon a time, in a castle on the riverbanks of the Scheldt river, there lived a giant called Druon Antigoon. Because of the castle's location near the river's estuary, all ships sailing up or down the river had to pass by Antigoon's castle. Taking advantage of this privileged position, as well as his giant-powers, Druon Antigoon became greedier and started asking for higher and higher tolls from passing ships. As the giant was always on full alert and nothing escaped his steady gaze, it was impossible to sneak through. People who did try to pass by unnoticed, or simply refused to pay the exorbitant taxes, were captured and had their hands cut off without any sense of reason or mercy. One day, a brave young man called Silvius Brabo stood up to the giant. When Antigoon approached to seize his ship, Brabo skilfully threw a knife into the giant's eye. While Antigoon swung around his arms in disarray, Brabo chopped of Antigoon's hand and threw it in the river. Upon the grounds of this epic battle—legend goes—the city of Antwerp emerged.

The tale of Brabo and Antigoon can be recounted as follows. A superhuman, very powerful entity controls one of the central nodes in a communication network. Due to its position, this entity is virtually impossible to avoid when trying to reach a certain destination. Driven by (financial) self-interest, this entity requests exorbitant tolls from anyone who wants to pass. No specific safeguards or promises are offered in return (eg safe passage). Moreover, due to its superhuman powers and all-seeing eye, deviant behaviour is made impossible and even severely punished. In short, you have a powerful tyrant constraining individual freedom for its own self-interest.

Sounds familiar? Fast-forward and one does not need to make a giant mental leap to draw parallels with the current ecosystem of online consumer services. Today's Antigoons are also driven by self-interest and, because of their position, effectively control today's main communication and information channels. Virtually impossible to avoid, these entities charge huge—though arguably more stealthily than Antigoon—tolls and provide little assurances in return. Opposite these present-day Antigoons, a new Brabo has emerged as well. Even though he has not

The Right to Erasure in EU Data Protection Law. First Edition. Jef Ausloos. Oxford University Press (2020). © Jef Ausloos
DOI: 10.1093/oso/9780198847977.001.0001

chopped of any hands yet—let alone defeated any of them altogether—his actions have had a tremendous impact so far.

The story begins in June 2011. What started as a simple access request under European data protection law, quickly turned into a transatlantic David-and-Goliath battle. Most will know the story of Max Schrems and his civil society organization NOYB.eu (formally Europe-v-Facebook). Back in 2011, Max was still just an Austrian law student on exchange at Santa Clara University in Northern California. After a presentation by a Facebook representative during one of his classes, Max decided to file an official data access request with the company. Relying on the EU Data Protection Directive, he asked Facebook to send him what information the company held about him and what purposes they were processing it for. Back in Austria, Schrems received a CD-ROM, straight from California, with a 1,222-page-long PDF document containing all data the social network allegedly kept on him. Not only was he surprised by the amount (and categories) of information in the file, but also the fact the company so openly shared this.[1] As it turned out, Facebook not only processed data specifically disclosed to them (eg birthday, name, address, shares), but also inferred data (eg location, facial recognition) and general interactions (eg with advertisement, like button tracking, searches).[2] The file even contained information that had been deleted years before (eg likes, pokes, pictures). Startled by this—and with much more ardour than your average law student—Schrems decided to file sixteen complaints[3] with the Irish[4] Data Protection Commissioner (DPC). These various complaints related inter alia to so-called shadow profiles (of non-Facebook users and/or substituting existing profiles); various issues with its privacy policy and data security; as well as the continued storage of data after users explicitly requested erasure. The Irish DPA started investigations with a swiftness seldom seen in such administrative bodies. In December of the same year, it published a report of its audit into Facebook's privacy practices, a first in the EU.[5]

Overall, the Irish DPC was quite lax, issuing some broad recommendations and suggesting that Schrems and Facebook come to an 'amicable solution'. Unsurprisingly, such a compromise was not reached, not in the least due to the substantial imbalance in bargaining positions between the two parties. After some parallel back and forth with the DPC, the social network did implement a new global privacy policy mid-2012. As it turned out, however, this change primarily

[1] When later asked why they shared so much information with Mr Schrems, a Facebook representative said there were 'internal communication problems'.

[2] A full list of the categories shared with Max Schrems can be found at: <http://europe-v-facebook.org/fb_cat1.pdf>

[3] Six more were submitted later on, each targeting a particular issue. For the full list, see: <www.europe-v-facebook.org/EN/Complaints/complaints.html>

[4] At the time, Facebook Ireland was the company's headquarters for all non-North-American users.

[5] Irish Data Protection Commissioner, 'Report of Audit (Facebook Ireland Ltd)' (2011) <http://europe-v-facebook.org/Facebook_Ireland_Audit_Report_Final.pdf> accessed 1 June 2019.

consisted of inscribing many of the contested and/or undesired practices in the privacy policy. Henceforth, Facebook explicitly allowed itself far-reaching data collection and processing as part of the 'deal' with its users.[6]

Later in 2012, the Irish DPC published a report of its follow-up audit, assessing whether the social network had implemented all recommendations. The report was primarily positive regarding the measures taken by Facebook and its commitments to tackle the problematic practices that remained. Neither of the two audits constituted 'formal decisions' by the DPC, leaving the ball in a potential complainant's court to take action. Aiming to do exactly this—and considering his fruitless attempts at engaging with either the DPC or Facebook in response to the re-audit—Schrems decided to take legal action. So far, Schrems's different court cases have resulted in one huge success,[7] a minor failure,[8] several pending cases,[9] and ongoing initiatives.[10]

Schrems's actions were but the first ripples of a growing wave of criticism and protest against Internet behemoths more broadly.[11] They are emblematic of a broader issue in today's information society: the lack of (meaningful) control over the collection and use of one's personal data. This absence of control becomes particularly evident in an online environment dominated by a handful of private companies that find themselves at the central nerve points through which most (personal) data flows online. Google,[12] to name but another such company, collects and uses personal data on an even bigger scale than Facebook. With an

[6] Terminology used both by the DPC and Facebook when talking about its contract terms and privacy policy.

[7] The invalidation of the so-called Safe Harbor Agreement, validating data transfers between the EU and the US. *Maximillian Schrems v Data Protection Commissioner* [2015] Court of Justice of the European Union C-362/14.

[8] Early 2018, the CJEU ruled Schrems could not file a class action lawsuit against Facebook Ireland before a court in Vienna. See: *Maximilian Schrems v Facebook Ireland Limited* [2018] Court of Justice of the European Union C-498/16; Mark Scott, 'Europe's Highest Court Sides with Facebook in Privacy Class-Action Lawsuit' *Politico* (25 January 2018) <www.politico.eu/article/facebook-ecj-european-court-justice-max-schrems-austria-lawsuit-classaction-privacy-data protection-max-schrems> accessed 13 February 2018.

[9] A follow up case involving Facebook's current data-transfer mechanisms. Conor Humphries, 'Ireland Asks Europe's Top Court to Rule on EU–U.S. Data Transfers' Reuters (3 October 2017) <www.reuters.com/article/us-eu-privacy-facebook/ireland-refers-key-eu-u-s-data-transfer-mechanism-to-europes-top-court-idUSKCN1C80XQ> accessed 13 February 2018.

[10] Notably the crowdsourced NOYB.eu initiative, which aims to offer a platform for European data protection enforcement.

[11] eg after Facebook's Data Use Policy update in January 2015, a number of European data protection authorities initiated actions against the company, in Belgium even leading to a court case. One of the main allegations related to Facebook's extensive browsing behaviour tracking of non-users, as well as logged-out users and users who deliberately opted out of being tracked in the first place. For an overview of this 'European Task Force' and the analysis underlying the Belgian case, see: Brendan Van Alsenoy and others, 'From Social Media Service to Advertising Network—A Critical Analysis of Facebook's Revised Policies and Terms' (KU Leuven & VUB 2015) 1.3 <www.law.kuleuven.be/icri/en/news/item/icri-cir-advises-belgian-privacy-commission-in-facebook-investigation>.

[12] Due to a corporate restructuring in 2015, Alphabet Inc. officially became the parent company of Google and several of its former subsidiaries.

incredibly varied assortment of services, this Internet giant collects data related to virtually every aspect of our lives. From its search engine, email, and mapping service to browsers, operating systems, and the management of our music and photo libraries. Not to mention its involvement in the Internet of Things (IoT) (thermostats, cars, smart homes, etc). All these services and/or products generate tremendous amounts of personal data, which are then processed and reapplied to shape our lives and reality.

The lack of control over personal data in today's information society will occupy a central role throughout this book. More specifically, this book will assess how the right to erasure—as an important extension of control over personal data—can meaningfully safeguard the fundamental right to data protection. In doing so, it will first investigate the underlying rationale for giving individuals a right to control and erase their personal data (Chapter 2). Subsequently, it will analyse *when, how*, and against *whom* the right to erasure can be applied exactly (Chapters 3 and 4). In Part II, the book will also look at the often-complex balancing issues arising in the context of data subject empowerment measures such as the right to erasure. The book will end with a critical evaluation of the merits of data subject empowerment and the requirements for its effectiveness (Part III).

Section 2. How We Got Here

LACK OF CONTROL—Max Schrems's ongoing story is emblematic of a broader crisis we are facing today: the loss of control over personal data. In this highly dynamic information-hungry society, individuals cannot possibly keep track of the extent to which their data is being captured and processed, let alone anticipate all potential impacts of such processing on themselves and society more broadly. Defining this lack of control over personal data is particularly difficult. The goal of this book is to approach this problem statement from a data protection point of view.[13] More specifically, it aims to identify the principal causes of this lack of control, frame them in legal terms, and clarify how empowerment measures in data protection law can remedy the main concerns. Because of its apparent potency and overall controversial nature, the right to erasure will be the focal point through which this book analyses data empowerment in the face of online power asymmetries. In order to do so, it is useful to consider four real-life stories or 'vignettes' that have made international headlines and are emblematic of the broader concerns that instigated the research behind this book.

[13] As a result, other relevant legal frameworks such as consumer protection or non-discrimination law will not be covered (in detail).

Vignettes

Uber's Psychological Manipulation

In 2017, a story broke on how the ride-hailing company Uber was putting a lot of resources into psychologically manipulating its drivers. As summarized in the *New York Times*: 'Employing hundreds of social scientists and data scientists, Uber has experimented with video game techniques, graphics and noncash rewards of little value that can prod drivers into working longer and harder—and sometimes at hours and locations that are less lucrative for them.'[14] As Rosenblat and Stark had observed 'Uber's digitally and algorithmically mediated system of flexible employment builds new forms of surveillance and control into the experience of using the system, which result in asymmetries around information and power for workers.'[15] Of course the company is hardly the only one using advanced psychological inducement methods in pursuit of its commercial interests.[16] Insights from social sciences, combined with modern data-processing techniques, however, are increasingly affecting fundamental rights such as human dignity and individual freedom. When done by a company such as Uber, it may directly impact an individual's health, income, and social life.[17]

Facebook's Emotion Contagion and Political Advertisement

In March 2018 a huge media storm erupted around Facebook and political consulting company Cambridge Analytica on data-driven voter manipulation in the 2016 US presidential elections and Brexit.[18] As a matter of fact, Facebook

[14] Noam Scheiber, 'How Uber Uses Psychological Tricks to Push Its Drivers' Buttons' *New York Times* (2 April 2017) <www.nytimes.com/interactive/2017/04/02/technology/uber-drivers-psychological-tricks.html> accessed 25 October 2017.

[15] Alex Rosenblat and Luke Stark, 'Algorithmic Labor and Information Asymmetries: A Case Study of Uber's Drivers' Data & Society, 15 October 2015 <https://datasociety.net/output/ubers-drivers-information-asymmetries-and-control-in-dynamic-work> accessed 21 June 2018; Natali Helberger, Jo Pierson, and Thomas Poell, 'Governing Online Platforms: From Contested to Cooperative Responsibility' (2018) 34 Information Society 1, 5.

[16] Ralph Schroeder, 'Big Data and the Brave New World of Social Media Research' (2014) 1 Big Data & Society 2053951714563194; Valerie Verdoodt, Damian Clifford, and Eva Lievens, 'Toying with Children's Emotions, the New Game in Town? The Legality of Advergames in the EU' (2016) 32 Computer Law & Security Review 599.

[17] For a more comprehensive analysis, see inter alia: Ryan Calo and Alex Rosenblat, 'The Taking Economy: Uber, Information, and Power' (2017) 117 Columbia Law Review 1623; Gemma Newlands, Christoph Lutz, and Christian Fieseler, 'Power in the Sharing Economy' (BI Norwegian Business School 2017) <https://papers.ssrn.com/abstract=2960938> accessed 1 June 2019.

[18] For an overview, see: <www.theguardian.com/news/series/cambridge-analytica-files> At the time of writing, the UK's Information Commissioner has already released two reports following its ongoing investigations: Information Commissioner's Office, 'Investigation into the Use of Data Analytics in Political Campaigns' (2018) <https://ico.org.uk/media/action-weve-taken/2259371/investigation-into-data-analytics-for-political-purposes-update.pdf> accessed 23 July 2018; Information Commissioner's Office, 'Democracy Disrupted? Personal Information and Political Influence' (2018) <https://ico.org.uk/media/action-weve-taken/2259369/democracy-disrupted-110718.pdf> accessed 23 July 2018.

had already been experimenting with influencing voters (turnout) since at least 2010.[19] In 2014, Facebook was also in the news for covertly influencing the emotions of more than half a million of its users.[20] While it is no secret that the company can relatively easily infer individuals' emotional state from seemingly innocuous data, its active exploitation of such knowledge does raise some serious concerns, eg taking advantage of user vulnerabilities to keep them hooked,[21] or allowing advertisers to 'target teens who feel worthless'.[22] Facebook's capacity for emotional manipulation (the result of social sciences progress in understanding emotions, combined with unprecedented abilities to capture and monitor data, as well as the company's vast reach and ability to interact with individuals) in combination with its business model (enabling advertisers incredibly detailed ways for targeting people) raises significant questions with regard to basic principles of a democratic society, as well as a range of fundamental rights and freedoms.

Google Spain or the Right to Be Delisted

Search engines play a crucial role in navigating the information society. As with any other search term, entering a personal identifier (eg name) in its search box may prompt Google to auto-suggest specific words to add to the search; list certain websites; and/or compile a profile from different sources about the respective search term. In light of the company's market position, its decisions on what (not) to include as a result, auto-suggest, or how it compiles a profile, may have a considerable impact on the person searched for.[23] This impact can easily extend beyond that person's private life and also affect job/education prospects for example, in turn triggering a variety of fundamental rights and freedoms. This is also why in 2014, the Court of Justice of the European Union

[19] Robert M Bond and others, 'A 61-Million-Person Experiment in Social Influence and Political Mobilization' (2012) 489 Nature 295; Zeynep Tufekci, 'Engineering the Public: Big Data, Surveillance and Computational Politics' (2014) 19 First Monday <http://firstmonday.org/ojs/index.php/fm/article/view/4901> accessed 1 June 2019; Jonathan Zittrain, 'Facebook Could Decide an Election without Anyone Ever Finding Out' [2014] New Republic <www.newrepublic.com/article/117878/information-fiduciary-solution-facebook-digital-gerrymandering> accessed 1 June 2019.

[20] Chris Chambers, 'Facebook Fiasco: Was Cornell University's Study of "Emotional Contagion" a Breach of Ethics?' *The Guardian* (1 July 2014) <www.theguardian.com/science/head-quarters/2014/jul/01/facebook-cornell-study-emotional-contagion-ethics-breach> accessed 1 June 2019.

[21] Richard Freed, 'The Tech Industry's Psychological War on Kids' (12 March 2018) <https://medium.com/@richardnfreed/the-tech-industrys-psychological-war-on-kids-c452870464ce> accessed 20 April 2018.

[22] Sam Machkovech, 'Report: Facebook Helped Advertisers Target Teens Who Feel "Worthless" [Updated]' Ars Technica, 1 May 2017 <https://arstechnica.com/information-technology/2017/05/facebook-helped-advertisers-target-teens-who-feel-worthless> accessed 30 October 2017.

[23] For a list of relevant case law, see inter alia: Aleksandra Kuczerawy and Jef Ausloos, 'NoC Online Intermediaries Case Studies Series: European Union and Google Spain' (2015) <http://ssrn.com/abstract=2567183> accessed 1 June 2019.

(CJEU) confirmed that individuals have a 'right to be delisted' under certain circumstances.[24]

Apple Siri and the Perverse Effects of Data Protection by Design

Smart/voice assistants are commonplace in a range of devices and are becoming increasingly popular. Their interfaces (ie often without a screen and/or keyboard) are meant to invite more natural and personalized interactions. Their very purpose generally is to be a central access point for all kinds of services, and therefore they may have a holistic perspective on their users. Indeed, in order to function properly, smart assistants will generally have to combine many different data streams and perform complex processing. In light of how these 'smart assistants' will increasingly constitute the first points of access for people to interact with any online service, their impact on individuals as well as society at large will be enormous. Yet, their actual operation often still remains a black box. Quite worryingly, therefore, recent academic research demonstrated that exercising basic data subject rights appear to be blocked under the veil of so-called 'privacy-by-design' measures.[25] Indeed, access requests to personal data stored (eg voice recordings) are blocked by Apple because, they argue, it is too difficult to retrieve that personal data due to certain security measures they undertook (such as using different sets of identifiers).

Before continuing, it is important to delineate the scope of this book. Indeed, the 'lack of control over personal data' can be investigated from multiple different angles. For example, this book will not deal with the many complex data protection issues emerging from the asymmetric relationship between individuals and the state. Instead, its focus is on power asymmetries over personal data in a commercial setting.[26] As will become apparent in the following chapters, with virtually every aspect of modern society being 'digitized', data protection law becomes increasingly relevant in virtually all (inter)actions. In an attempt at narrowing down

[24] *Google Spain SL, Google Inc v Agencia Española de Protección de Datos (AEPD), Mario Costeja González* [2014] Court of Justice of the European Union C-131/12.

[25] Jef Ausloos and Pierre Dewitte, 'Shattering One-Way Mirrors—Data Subject Access Rights in Practice' (2018) 8 International Data Privacy Law 4; Michael Veale, Reuben Binns, and Jef Ausloos, 'When Data Protection by Design and Data Subject Rights Clash' (2018) 8 International Data Privacy Law 4; Jef Ausloos, 'Paul-Olivier Dehaye and the Raiders of the Lost Data' (*CITIP blog*, 10 April 2018) <www.law.kuleuven.be/citip/blog/paul-olivier-dehaye-and-the-raiders-of-the-lost-data> accessed 23 April 2018.

[26] It should be recognized that surveillance by commercial entities versus by the state is increasingly hard to distinguish. See in this regard, for example: Neil M Richards, 'The Dangers of Surveillance' (2013) 126 Harvard Law Review 1934, 1958.

the scope, this book will focus on one particular kind of entity: information society services (ISS).[27] Over the past one and a half decades, these actors have permeated many facets of our daily lives, effectively defining the social fabric of society.[28] To many, they are no longer considered as 'services', but rather as logical extensions of the ways we interact with information and other people. To paraphrase Bruce Sterling, without these services, and the devices that make their use possible, people effectively become 'non-persons'.[29] On top of this, there is a general lack of awareness and underestimation of risks of data processing in the online environment.[30] Yet, it is important to keep in mind these services are run by commercial entities, each with their own goals and interests. Hence, it is the purpose of this book to investigate the relationship between these ISS providers and individuals from a data protection law perspective. More specifically, it will zoom in on how 'control over personal data' is distributed between the relevant actors and what the role of data subject rights are in this context. Eventually, the findings may be extrapolated to different kinds of situations and entities that are characterized by a lack of control over personal data.

STRUCTURE—This introductory chapter will set the scene for what is to come. The present section will touch on two major trends that seem to lie at the source of the lack of control over personal data. First, it will highlight the key characteristics—relevant to the book—of today's data deluge. Building on this, second, this chapter will elaborate on the power asymmetry that pervades the relationships between individuals and ISS providers. The following section will look at the importance of data autonomy and how data protection law contributes to this. The last section finally will provide the blueprint for the rest of this book, describing the research question, structure, and methodology.

[27] As defined in Article 1(1) of Directive (EU) 2015/1535 of the European Parliament and of the Council of 9 September 2015 laying down a procedure for the provision of information in the field of technical regulations and of rules on Information Society services, and referred to in Article 4(25) GDPR.

[28] eg Carolin Gerlitz and Anne Helmond, 'The Like Economy: Social Buttons and the Data-Intensive Web' (2013) 15 New Media & Society 1348; Paul Bernal, *Internet Privacy Rights: Rights to Protect Autonomy* (CUP 2014).

[29] Bruce Sterling, 'Dispatches from the Hyperlocal Future' (*Wired*, 26 June 2007) <www.wired.com/2007/06/local> accessed 18 July 2017.

[30] European Commission, 'Commission Staff Working Paper: Impact Assessment Accompanying the Proposals for General Data Protection Regulation and Directive on Data Protection in Police and Judicial Matters' (European Commission 2012) Commission Staff working Paper SEC (2012) 72 final 21ff. The lacking awareness regarding the extent of data processing in commercial settings is also considered in other legislative initiatives, see for example: European Commission, 'Green Paper: Preparing for a Fully Converged Audiovisual World: Growth, Creation and Values' (2013) COM(2013) 231 final <https://ec.europa.eu/digital-single-market/sites/digital-agenda/files/convergence_green_paper_en_0.pdf> accessed 1 June 2019.

2.1 Data Deluge

INTRODUCTION—The pdf file sent to Max Schrems in response to his data access request was over 1,200 pages long (0.5 gigabyte) and did not even include *all* personal data Facebook held on him.[31] This was back in 2011, for an account of barely a few years old. Fast-forward to today, and it is not hard to imagine how much bigger such a file would be. As illustrated by the Uber and Facebook vignettes, many ISS providers are capturing and processing vast amounts of data, extending far beyond what individuals may consciously be providing directly themselves. This notably includes detailed information relating to interaction with the service (eg mouse movements, unfinished/deleted posts, location data),[32] which in turn is then used to infer mood, shape environments, and nudge people into performing certain actions. Turning to the third vignette, the reason why the right to be delisted was proclaimed by the CJEU in the first place is because of the seemingly bottomless pit of (often random) information available on individuals, and easily accessible by search engines.

The explosion of 'data' precipitates growing information and power asymmetries. Indeed, most of our day-to-day activities involve capturing, generating, or processing data in one way or another: browsing or searching the web, using location-based apps, making phone calls, reading, streaming audio or video content, interacting and communicating with others and our environment more broadly. For the purposes of this book, at least three important factors can be identified that lie at the source of this 'data deluge': (a) ubiquity of sensors; (b) limitless storage capacity; (c) instant and global communication capabilities.[33] All three factors enable exponential advancements in data sciences (and, as a result, many other disciplines), providing novel and improved value propositions, from credit card fraud detection; improving spellcheckers; credit scoring; content recommenders; disease prediction; traffic management; crime prevention; and environmental protection. Perhaps more cynically, however, all these 'big data' benefits have generated a vicious circle in the shape of an increasingly voracious data ecosystem.

[31] <www.europe-v-facebook.org>

[32] eg Steven Englehardt, 'No Boundaries: Exfiltration of Personal Data by Session-Replay Scripts' (*Freedom to Tinker*, 15 November 2017) <https://freedom-to-tinker.com/2017/11/15/no-boundaries-exfiltration-of-personal-data-by-session-replay-scripts> accessed 1 December 2017.

[33] It goes without saying that many other characteristics explain the data deluge as well as information asymmetries more broadly. For example: the move to service architectures as referred to in: Seda Gürses and Joris van Hoboken, 'Privacy after the Agile Turn' in Jules Polonetsky, Omer Tene, and Evan Selinger (eds), *Cambridge Handbook of Consumer Privacy* (CUP 2017) <https://osf.io/preprints/socarxiv/9gy73> accessed 1 June 2019. But also miniaturization, ubiquity, and automation as referred to in: European Group on Ethics in Science and New Technologies, 'Ethics of Security and Surveillance Technologies' (European Commission 2014) Opinion 28 26ff.

2.1.1 Ubiquity of Sensors

Zittrain candidly describes three important (successive) shifts in technology from the early 1970s onwards: cheap processors; cheap storage; and cheap sensors.[34] The latter, he explains, 'has opened the doors to new and formidable privacy invasions'. Sensors should be broadly understood as pieces of equipment or software that capture information and they can be found everywhere. Today's smartphones are jampacked with sensors capturing all kinds of information. In 2020, the average smartphone at the very least has a microphone; two HD cameras; a GPS antenna; and an accelerometer.[35] Max Schrems's story too is a healthy reminder that many (mobile) apps eagerly tie in to all these sensors to provide 'added value'. Facebook, for example, enables its users to check in at certain locations, geo-tag images, and receive 'place tips'. Users are also invited to give the social network access to their microphone in order to identify songs playing or television being watched.[36] But Facebook does not just capture information through your smartphone. The company tracks its users (and even non-users) across the web.[37] Its algorithms also scan uploaded pictures in order to identify people, even when their faces are not visible.[38] Of course, Facebook is not the only entity engaging in this level of data collection. Smart assistants such as Apple's Siri or Google's Assistant allegedly require as much data input as possible in order to maximize their utility. This is not even mentioning how society's physical infrastructure is increasingly being equipped with very detailed sensor technology.

It is not the purpose of this section to provide an exhaustive list or taxonomy of ways to capture (personal) data, but simply to emphasize how sensors are becoming more diverse, numerous, and accurate. They can capture online behaviour[39] (eg web browsing[40] and search[41] behaviour; reading patterns;[42] mouse

[34] Jonathan Zittrain, *The Future of the Internet—And How to Stop It* (Yale UP 2008) 205.

[35] The latest iPhone model at the time of writing, also includes a variety of additional location sensors; a barometer; three-axis gyro; proximity sensor; ambient light sensor; and an advanced facial ID sensor, capturing detailed traits and movements <www.apple.com/iphone-x/specs>

[36] Kashmir Hill, 'Facebook Wants to Listen in on What You're Doing' *Forbes* (22 May 2014) <www.forbes.com/sites/kashmirhill/2014/05/22/facebook-wants-to-listen-in-on-what-youre-doing> accessed 1 June 2019.

[37] See Van Alsenoy and others (n 11).

[38] Aviva Rutkin, 'Facebook Can Recognise You in Photos Even If You're Not Looking' *New Scientist* (22 June 2015) <www.newscientist.com/article/dn27761-facebook-can-recognise-you-in-photos-even-if-youre-not-looking.html#.VYkeo0a4HEIcc> accessed 1 June 2019.

[39] Lawrence Lessig, *Code: Version 2.0* (Basic Books 2006) 216.

[40] Gunes Acar and others, 'The Web Never Forgets: Persistent Tracking Mechanisms in the Wild' (ACM Press 2014) <http://dl.acm.org/citation.cfm?doid=2660267.2660347> accessed 1 June 2019; Samuel Gibbs, 'Facebook "Tracks All Visitors, Breaching EU Law"' *The Guardian* (31 March 2015) <www.theguardian.com/technology/2015/mar/31/facebook-tracks-all-visitors-breaching-eu-law-report> accessed 1 June 2019.

[41] Article 29 Working Party, 'Opinion 1/2008 on Data Protection Issues Related to Search Engines' (2008) WP 148 <http://ec.europa.eu/justice/article-29/documentation> accessed 1 June 2019.

[42] Margot Kaminski, 'Reading Over Your Shoulder: Social Readers and Privacy Law' *Wake Forest Law Review* (9 March 2012) <http://wakeforestlawreview.com/2012/03/reading-over-your-shoulder-social-readers-and-privacy-law> accessed 1 June 2019; Alexandra Alter, 'Your E-Book Is Reading You' *Wall Street Journal* (29 June 2012) <https://www.wsj.com/articles/SB10001424052702304870304577490950051438304> accessed 1 June 2019.

movements;[43] and emotions),[44] as well as offline behaviour (eg surveillance cameras;[45] thermal imagers;[46] biometric scanners;[47] and a wide variety of fitness and health trackers).[48] As a side note, it should be said that data *production* may be a more appropriate term than data *collection*. The latter suggests data is simply to be picked up, whereas in reality it is created by means of technology. Indeed, 'data does not just exist—it needs to be generated'.[49] This observation pierces the perceived 'neutrality/objectivity' of data and emphasizes how any 'big data' process (and its impact on fundamental rights/freedoms) inherently depends on the decisions made by their architects.[50]

Essentially all activities that are mediated by a computer—understood in the broadest sense—generate data that can be captured. Schneier aptly explains that data is a by-product of computing.[51] In other words, each (inter) action that involves a computer can generate a data trail. With computers now mediating the ways we read, write, think, and communicate, this data trail is

[43] Nan Zheng, Aaron Paloski, and Haining Wang, 'An Efficient User Verification System via Mouse Movements' Proceedings of the 18th ACM conference on Computer and communications security (ACM 2011) <http://dl.acm.org/citation.cfm?id=2046725> accessed 1 June 2019.

[44] Federal Trade Commission, 'Facing Facts—Best Practices for Common Uses of Facial Recognition Technologies' (2012) 3–4 <www.ftc.gov/os/2012/10/121022facialtechrpt.pdf>; George Lawton, 'Emerging Technologies Promise to Quantify Emotions' (*Torque*, 15 September 2014) <http://torquemag.io/emerging-technologies-promise-quantify-emotions> accessed 1 June 2019 . In 2010, Microsoft even filed a patent for 'Targeting Advertisements Based on Emotion'. Wook Jin Chung, Pritesh Patwa, and Martin Miroslavov Markov, 'United States Patent Application: 0120143693—Targeting Advertisements Based on Emotion' A1.

[45] The UK alone has a reported 6 million CCTV cameras nationwide. In: Matthew Weaver, 'UK Public Must Wake up to Risks of CCTV, Says Surveillance Commissioner' *The Guardian* (6 January 2015) <www.theguardian.com/world/2015/jan/06/tony-porter-surveillance-commissioner-risk-cctv-public-transparent> accessed 1 June 2019.

[46] Jonathan Todd Laba, 'If You Can't Stand the Heat, Get Out of the Drug Business: Thermal Imagers, Emerging Technologies, and the Fourth Amendment' (1996) 84 California Law Review 1437.

[47] Such as fingerprint devices; iris scanners; facial recognition. For an extensive overview of the data protection and privacy aspects involved with biometrics, see: Els J Kindt, *Privacy and Data Protection Issues of Biometric Applications: A Comparative Legal Analysis* (Springer 2013).

[48] See the many examples, as well as privacy implications in: Scott R Peppet, 'Regulating the Internet of Things: First Steps toward Managing Discrimination, Privacy, Security and Consent' (2014) 93 Texas Law Review 85, 87–104. It is also worth referring, in this context, to the whole 'self-tracking' movement. For more, see the work by Elsden and in particular: Chris Elsden and others, 'Fitter, Happier, More Productive: What to Ask of a Data-Driven Life' (2016) 23 Interactions 45; Chris Elsden, David S Kirk, and Abigail C Durrant, 'A Quantified Past: Toward Design for Remembering with Personal Informatics' (2016) 31 Human–Computer Interaction 518.

[49] Lev Manovich, *The Language of New Media* (MIT Press 2002) 198. Gitelman and Jackson explain '[d]ata need to be imagined *as* data to exist and function as such, and the imagination of data entails an interpretive base'. In: Lisa Gitelman and Virginia Jackson, 'Introduction' in Lisa Gitelman, *'Raw Data' Is an Oxymoron* (MIT Press 2013) 3. Similarly, see: Oscar H Gandy, 'Toward a Political Economy of Personal Information' (1993) 10 Critical Studies in Mass Communication 70, 76.

[50] For more extensive explorations, see notably: Cathy O'Neil, *Weapons of Math Destruction: How Big Data Increases Inequality and Threatens Democracy* (Penguin 2017); John Cheney-Lippold, *We Are Data: Algorithms and the Making of Our Digital Selves* (New York UP 2017).

[51] This is particularly relevant given the fact that '[w]ith a few specific exceptions, computers are now everywhere we engage in commerce and most places we engage with our friends'. Bruce Schneier, *Data and Goliath: The Hidden Battles to Capture Your Data and Control Your World* (Norton 2015) pt 1.

becoming significantly larger every day.[52] Put briefly, the exponential growth (in new kinds) of sensors has enabled what has been called the 'datafication of everything'.[53]

2.1.2 Limitless Storage

> Quite obviously, remembering has become the norm, and forgetting the exception.[54]

Half a gigabyte might not seem a huge amount of data today. Nonetheless, the file size of the response to Max Schrems's access request was definitely substantial back in 2011. Especially when considering the fact that it only related to a profile of around four years old and considerable portions of personal data were still missing. Schrems was very surprised, though, to discover information in his file that he had asked to be deleted before. Facebook defended itself, explaining to the Irish DPC, that it is operating 'large, distributed computing systems, where information necessarily is stored in many places at once',[55] not rendering the deletion process a sinecure. This anecdote illustrates the marginal cost of storing data has become near to zero.[56] Indeed, one of the driving forces behind today's 'big data' age is the plummeting price of data storage,[57] combined with the perceived benefits of maximizing storage.[58] Cheap storage has rendered futile detailed selection criteria for *collecting* data and, at the very best, pushed such decisions to being mere afterthoughts

[52] Neil Richards, *Intellectual Privacy: Rethinking Civil Liberties in the Digital Age* (OUP 2015) 2.

[53] Viktor Mayer-Schönberger and Kenneth Cukier, *Big Data: A Revolution That Will Transform How We Live, Work and Think* (Houghton Mifflin Harcourt 2013). This especially holds true against the backdrop of the switch to service architectures, with a continuous need for user feedback loops to make incremental changes to the system (see Gürses and van Hoboken (n 33)).

[54] Viktor Mayer-Schönberger, *Delete: The Virtue of Forgetting in the Digital Age* (1st edn, Princeton UP 2009) 52. See also: Lawrence Lessig, 'The Architecture of Privacy' (1999) 1 Vanderbilt Journal of Entertainment & Technology Law 56, 60.

[55] Ensuring redundancy and preventing data losses. See: Irish Data Protection Commissioner (n 5) 71.

[56] Mayer-Schönberger (n 54) 62–72. Cheap data storage is also implied in Zittrain's three technological shifts opening the door to formidable privacy invasions: 'cheap processors, cheap networks, and cheap sensors' (Zittrain (n 34) 205).

[57] For a visualization of the decreasing costs of data storage, see: Andy Klein, 'The Cost of Hard Drives over Time' (*Backblaze Blog/Cloud Storage & Cloud Backup*, 11 July 2017) <www.backblaze.com/blog/hard-drive-cost-per-gigabyte> accessed 20 February 2018. Importantly, these plummeting data storage prices do not account for certain externalities, such as the growing environmental cost of data storage centres. The carbon footprint of data centres is expected to soon overtake that of air travel. John Harris, 'Our Phones and Gadgets Are Now Endangering the Planet' *The Guardian* (17 July 2018) <www.theguardian.com/commentisfree/2018/jul/17/internet-climate-carbon-footprint-data-centres> accessed 30 August 2018.

[58] ISS providers have an incentive to 'invest in the storage of trivial information, hoping to reap benefits in the future'. Tal Zarsky, 'Mine Your Own Business: Making the Case for the Implications of the Data Mining of Personal Information in the Forum of Public Opinion' (2002) 5 Yale Journal of Law & Technology 1, 3.

(further precipitating the need for entities helping to sift through the data). Put differently, data storage strategies have evolved from calculated a priori decisions to a posteriori eventualities.

The growing ability to record every (inter)action of an individual's life, combined with the ability to permanently store this data, leads to what one could call a 'loss of the ephemeral'.[59] As explained by Lessig in 1999 already, digital memory eliminates the transient nature of monitored data, which, in turn, conflicts with our traditional understanding of privacy.[60] The permanent and detailed nature of digital records sharply contrasts with the fluid nature of human memory and often clashes with prevailing social norms. Not to mention the way in which this trend precipitates massive information asymmetries between those who hold the data and those to whom the data pertain. Mayer-Schönberger famously wrote about the virtue of forgetting[61] and Schneier wittily pondered whether his relationship 'would be improved by the ability to produce transcripts of old arguments'.[62] In short, digital memory's lack of transience constitutes both one of its biggest strengths, as well as one of its key threats to fundamental rights and freedoms.[63]

2.1.3 Instant and Global Communication

> Our infrastructures are increasingly networked and dominated by computation.[64]

Schrems would never have entered the limelight without the Internet. After all, without it, Facebook—a quintessential online service—could not exist. By its very nature, the social network is aimed at connecting sensors, stored information, and individuals across the globe. It is, essentially, a platform for transferring and extracting value from information. Being a proprietary platform, Facebook has full control over what, when, and how exactly information flows. Taking advantage of its dominant position, the company also stretched out its reach to millions of third-party websites and services (eg collecting information via social plug-ins).[65] As such, Facebook skilfully makes use of the Internet's basic feature—being a 'network

[59] 'Big data initiatives mean that we're saving everything we can about our customers on the remote chance that it might be useful later. Everything is now digital, and storage is cheap—why not save it all?' In: Bruce Schneier, 'The Security of Data Deletion' (*Schneier on Security*, 15 January 2015) <www.schneier.com/blog/archives/2015/01/the_security_of_10.html> accessed 1 June 2019.

[60] Lessig (n 54) 58–59.

[61] Mayer-Schönberger (n 54).

[62] Schneier (n 51).

[63] Niloufer Selvadurai, 'Not Just a Face in the Crowd: Addressing the Intrusive Potential of the Online Application of Face Recognition Technologies' (2015) 23 International Journal of Law and Information Technology 187, 5.

[64] Christian Sandvig and others, 'Can Algorithms Be Unethical?' (2015) 23. Paper presented to the 65th annual meeting of the International Communication Association, San Juan, Puerto Rico, USA. May 2015. Available at: http://social.cs.uiuc.edu/papers/pdfs/ICA2015-Sandvig.pdf.

[65] Van Alsenoy and others (n 11);Günes Acar and others, 'Facebook Tracking Through Social Plug-Ins. Technical Report Prepared for the Belgian Privacy Commission' (KU Leuven–COSIC 2015) <https://securehomes.esat.kuleuven.be/~gacar/fb_tracking>.

of networks'—to track individuals across, interconnecting information without spatial restraints. It is this vast dragnet, combined with Facebook's primary business model that triggered some of Schrems's complaints, as well as investigations by several EU (data protection) authorities.[66]

Modern communication technologies—and the Internet in particular—enable instant, frictionless, and global transference of information. In this regard, the Internet essentially democratizes the ability to communicate, share, and access information, regardless of frontiers. Instant and global accessibility massively amplifies the impact of information, for better or worse. In 1978, it was still said that information was destined to oblivion shortly after being published.[67] Technology today, however, enables information to be perpetually accessible from anywhere.[68] One of the key flipsides of these invaluable virtues is that they may have enormous negative repercussions for individuals,[69] communities,[70] and society at large.[71]

A symbiosis exists between the Internet, sensors, and data storage; enhancements to one will boost the others. Most significantly, this upwards spiral has given rise to a whole new industry (commonly referred to as 'cloud computing') and has enabled a paradigm shift in software development (ie agile software development). Growing bandwidth and declining connection fees make us all increasingly rely on third parties, better equipped to store and process the information generated by sensor-loaded 'smart' devices and environments. Apart from cloud computing, the sensor–storage–Internet symbiosis has also enabled the so-called 'platform economy',[72] as well as the 'Internet of Things' (IoT).[73] It is this instant, global

[66] See: <www.theguardian.com/technology/facebook>

[67] Norman Lindop, *Report of the Committee on Data Protection, Chairman: Norman Lindop* (HMSO 1978) 270.

[68] At least in theory. In practice, the 'permanency' of information online is far from evident. See: Wallace Koehler, 'A Longitudinal Study of Web Pages Continued: A Consideration of Document Persistence' (2004) 9 Information Research <www.informationr.net/ir/9-2/paper174.html> accessed 9 January 2017; Meg L Ambrose, 'It's About Time: Privacy, Information Life Cycles, and the Right to Be Forgotten' (2013) 16 Stanford Technology Law Review 371.

[69] Inter alia recognized by the CJEU on at least two occasions: *Joined Cases eDate Advertising GmbH v X and Olivier Martinez and Robert Martinez v MGN Limited* [2011] Court of Justice of the European Union C-509/09 and C-161/10; *Google Spain* (n 24). See also: Hielke Hijmans, *The European Union as Guardian of Internet Privacy: The Story of Art 16 TFEU* (Springer 2016) 232ff.

[70] See the examples in: Anita L Allen, *Unpopular Privacy: What Must We Hide?* (OUP 2011).

[71] eg fake news, which can spread much more quickly in this new environment (often proactively aided by ISS providers in pursuit of commercial interests such as generating more clicks). See inter alia: Evgeny Morozov, 'Moral Panic over Fake News Hides the Real Enemy—The Digital Giants' *The Guardian* (8 January 2017) <www.theguardian.com/commentisfree/2017/jan/08/blaming-fake-news-not-the-answer-democracy-crisis> accessed 8 January 2017; Jack M Balkin, 'Free Speech in the Algorithmic Society: Big Data, Private Governance, and New School Speech Regulation' (2017) Working Draft 25ff <https://papers.ssrn.com/abstract=3038939> accessed 20 September 2017; and more broadly: Tim Wu, *The Attention Merchants: From the Daily Newspaper to Social Media, How Our Time and Attention Is Harvested and Sold* (Atlantic Books 2017).

[72] Consisting of 'matchmaking services'—from dating to transport and accommodation—that inherently depend on large networks and economies of scale.

[73] Defined by WP29 as: 'an infrastructure in which billions of sensors embedded in common, everyday devices [...] are designed to record, process, store and transfer data and [...] interact with

communication ability which is the *sine qua non* for all of the companies referred to in the vignettes, and effectively enables generating a permanently accessible repository for every aspect of a person's life.[74]

All trends described above have led to the de facto loss of practical obscurity, emphasizing the importance of privacy and data protection as fundamental rights. Even though written in 1969, the following words ring very true today:

> Informational privacy has been relatively easy to protect in the past for a number of reasons: (1) large quantities of information about individuals have not been collected and therefore have not been available; (2) the available information generally has been maintained on a decentralized basis; (3) the available information has been relatively superficial in character and often has been allowed to atrophy to the point of uselessness; (4) access to the available information has been difficult to secure; (5) people in a highly mobile society are difficult to keep track of; and (6) most people are unable to interpret and infer revealing information from the available data. But a casual perusal of the testimony elicited by various congressional subcommittees and brief reflection on the intrusive capabilities of the new surveillance devices and information technologies leads to the conclusion that these traditional safeguards on informational privacy no longer are reliable.[75]

2.2 Power Asymmetry

The previous section made clear that, increasingly so, every human (inter)action is—or at least *can* be—captured and 'datafied' in one way or another. Moreover, growing data storage capabilities have resulted in all of this data being stored by default. Because of the Internet, finally, sensors and storage no longer need to be in the same location. Put differently, modern technology enables ever-expanding

other devices or systems using networking capabilities'. Article 29 Working Party, 'Opinion 8/2014 on Recent Developments on the Internet of Things' (2014) Opinion WP 223 <http://ec.europa.eu/justice/article-29/documentation> accessed 1 June 2019. The US Federal Trade Commission defines the concept broadly: 'The Internet of Things ("IoT") refers to the ability of everyday objects to connect to the Internet and to send and receive data.' Federal Trade Commission, 'Internet of Things—Privacy & Security in a Connected World' (Federal Trade Commission 2015) FTC Staff Report i <www.ftc.gov/system/files/documents/reports/federal-trade-commission-staff-report-november-2013-workshop-entitled-internet-things-privacy/150127iotrpt.pdf>.

See also: Julia Powles and Jat Singh, 'Why the Internet of Things Favours Dominance' *The Guardian* (24 July 2015) <www.theguardian.com/technology/2015/jul/24/internet-of-things-centralisation-dominance> accessed 1 June 2019; Marie-Helen Maras, 'Internet of Things: Security and Privacy Implications' (2015) 5 International Data Privacy Law 99, 5.

[74] As observed by Zarsky, this new environment is a 'data miner's paradise' (n 58) 16.

[75] Arthur R Miller, 'Personal Privacy in the Computer Age: The Challenge of a New Technology in an Information-Oriented Society' (1969) 67 Michigan Law Review 1089, 1108–09.

information piles to transcend both time and space. This, in turn, has precipitated the 'dataveillance society';[76] obliterated 'contextual integrity';[77] and have enabled what has been referred to as 'surveillance capitalism'.[78] It has resulted in a fertile environment for new economic actors, which have quickly evolved into the Antigoons of our times. The following quote—remarkably coming from then Google's Executive Chairman Eric Schmidt—illustrates this last point very well:

> We believe that modern technology platforms, such as Google, Facebook, Amazon and Apple, are even more powerful than most people realize, and our future world will be profoundly altered by their adoption and successfulness in societies everywhere. These platforms constitute a true paradigm shift [. . .] Almost nothing short of a biological virus can spread as quickly, efficiently or aggressively as these technology platforms, and this makes the people who build, control and use them powerful too.[79]

Put briefly, in the last few decades technology has thoroughly shaken up the socioeconomic terrain. Initial optimism as to the Internet's potential for democratizing knowledge and realizing human freedom has faded in the face of today's reality.[80] This reality is characterized by powerful economic actors occupying practically unavoidable nodes in today's information society.[81] Capitalizing on the data deluge described above, these actors play a central role in the commodification of data and, as a result, of those to whom the data pertain. This brave new world brings about growing asymmetries of various kinds between individuals and economic actors. Two are particularly relevant in the context of this book: information and control asymmetries.

[76] '*Dataveillance* is the systematic use of personal data systems in the investigation or monitoring of the actions or communications of one or more persons.' The risks it poses to the individual include, inter alia: acontextual use of data; lack of subject knowledge and/or consent; blacklisting; denial of redemption; arbitrariness; complexity and incomprehensibility of data; *ex ante* discrimination and guilt prediction; inversion of the onus of proof; denial of due process. In: Roger Clarke, 'Information Technology and Dataveillance' (1988) 31 Communications of the ACM 498.

[77] Helen Nissenbaum, *Privacy in Context: Technology, Policy, and the Integrity of Social Life* (Stanford UP 2009).

[78] Shoshana Zuboff, 'Big Other: Surveillance Capitalism and the Prospects of an Information Civilization' (2015) 30 Journal of Information Technology 75; Shoshana Zuboff, *The Age of Surveillance Capitalism: The Fight for a Human Future at the New Frontier of Power* (Profile 2019). Similarly, see: Frank Pasquale, 'Two Narratives of Platform Capitalism' (2016) 35 Yale Law & Policy Review 309.

[79] Eric Schmidt and Jared Cohen, *The New Digital Age: Reshaping the Future of People, Nations and Business* (Knopf 2013).

[80] See in this regard: Oren Bracha and Frank Pasquale, 'Federal Search Commission? Access, Fairness, and Accountability in the Law of Search' (2008) 93 Cornell Law Review 1149.

[81] SE Peacock, 'How Web Tracking Changes User Agency in the Age of Big Data: The Used User' (2014) 1 Big Data & Society 1 <https://doi.org/10.1177/2053951714564228> accessed 1 June 2019.

2.2.1 Information Asymmetry

The technological developments described in the previous section have resulted in a considerable information gap between individuals and ISS providers. This is routinely demonstrated by the headlines these entities make when new findings are made on the extent to which they collect and/or use personal data. From Google's StreetView cars capturing Wi-Fi data,[82] to pervasive online and offline tracking technologies,[83] and a whole array of other 'creepy'[84] apps and services. The psychological/emotional manipulation in the Uber and Facebook vignettes, as well as smart assistants in the third vignette hinge on user engagement, maximizing data input to improve accuracy, efficiency, and profitability. Individuals, on the other hand, are often unaware of the full extent of data processing.

Information asymmetries[85] stem from the large gaps in awareness about *what* personal data is captured and processed (eg nature and amount) and *how* it is processed (eg purposes and identity of those holding the data). This distinction—between what and how—will also appear relevant in the following chapters, one determining the applicability of the General Data Protection Regulation (GDPR), the other lawfulness and fairness of processing that data. For now, it is worth briefly exploring the key drivers behind the growing information asymmetries between individuals and economic actors.

a) Complexification

Sensors, storage, and communication technology, as explained before, precipitate an ever-complexifying data processing ecosystem. With data no longer bound by temporal or spatial restraints, it is impossible to fully apprehend *who* exactly processes *what* data, *why*, and *when*. Today, personal data-processing operations often involve an indeterminate and permanently changing number of controllers, processors, and/or third parties.[86] This is especially true 'after the agile turn', described by Gürses and van Hoboken as the culmination of three shifts: 'waterfall to agile development methodologies; shrink-wrap software to services; and, from software running on personal computers to functionality being carried out in cloud'.[87]

[82] Joseph Menn, 'Google Admits That Street View Project Cars Accidentally Gathered WiFi Data from Homes' *Financial Times* (London, 15 May 2010).

[83] Acar and others (n 40). Also see the Web Transparency & Accountability Project at Princeton University, at: <https://webtap.princeton.edu>

[84] Omer Tene and Jules Polonetsky, 'A Theory of Creepy: Technology, Privacy and Shifting Social Norms' (2013) 16 Yale Journal of Law & Technology 59, 61–71.

[85] The term information asymmetry is used in its broadest sense, also including what Hildebrandt calls 'knowledge asymmetry'. Mireille Hildebrandt, 'The Dawn of a Critical Transparency Right for the Profiling Era' Digital Enlightenment Yearbook 2012 (IOS Press 2012) 48 <https://works.bepress.com/mireille_hildebrandt/40> accessed 1 June 2019.

[86] See notably: Jatinder Singh and others, 'Big Ideas Paper: Policy-Driven Middleware for a Legally-Compliant Internet of Things' Proceedings of the 17th International Middleware Conference (ACM 2016) 2 <http://doi.acm.org/10.1145/2988336.2988349> accessed 1 June 2019.

[87] Gürses and van Hoboken (n 33).

Against this backdrop, both the number of actors potentially having access to (part of) sets of personal data as well as the use(s) of said data are never fixed.[88] This complexification makes it particularly hard to install preventive safeguards (for protecting fundamental rights and freedoms in the face of data processing), but also complicates individuals wishing to determine vis-à-vis *which* entity they can exercise *what* rights and to what *extent*.[89] A useful illustration can be found in an individual uploading a 'group-selfie' to a social network site:

- The picture itself contains personal data of several individuals: faces, potentially 'sensitive data' (Arts 9–10 GDPR), metadata including timestamp and location, type of camera. Once uploaded, all of this information is accessible by the social network operator, by the uploader's 'friends', by connected third-party apps, advertisers, etc. Each of these entities pursues different interests and might further process the personal data in many different ways. Other individuals, for example, might reshare the picture; the social network operator might perform facial recognition on the pictures, identifying and linking the people in it and use it for fine-tuning its search algorithms and profile templates. Connected apps might use the picture (and/or its metadata) to infer data that could then be repackaged and transferred to yet other parties. And so on.

b) Data Begets Data

The previous section explained that today, virtually all of our (inter)actions generate data, particularly online. ISS providers eagerly gather all of this information, which only grows more valuable when aggregated.[90] Through what is commonly referred to as 'data mining',[91] ISS providers incessantly try to extract value from the data they collect. Indeed, data is not just 'provided' and 'observed', but also 'derived' and 'inferred'.[92] It is often exactly the further processing and

[88] See in this regard also: Lokke Moerel and Corien Prins, 'Privacy for the Homo Digitalis: Proposal for a New Regulatory Framework for Data Protection in the Light of Big Data and the Internet of Things' 13 <http://papers.ssrn.com/abstract=2784123> accessed 1 June 2019. The authors explain that 'the scope and nature of data usage does not follow a grand design. Almost by definition, the playing field is determined by a complex set of interactions and interdependent (public and private) actors.'

[89] Lee A Bygrave, *Data Protection Law: Approaching Its Rationale, Logic and Limits* (Kluwer 2002) 96–97; Bert-Jaap Koops, 'The Trouble with European Data Protection Law' (2014) 4 International Data Privacy Law 250, 252.

[90] Lessig (n 39) 216.

[91] 'The general practice of amassing and saving all kinds of data is called "Big Data", and the science and engineering of extracting useful information from it is called "data mining"' Schneier (n 51). Also see: Zarsky (n 58); Manon Oostveen, 'Protecting Individuals Against the Negative Impact of Big Data: The Potential and Limitations of the Privacy and Data Protection Law Approach' (PhD Thesis, University of Amsterdam 2018).

[92] Martin Abrams, 'The Origins of Personal Data and Its Implications for Governance' OECD Expert Roundtable Discussion Protecting Privacy in a Data-Driven Economy: Taking Stock of Current Thinking (2014) <http://informationaccountability.org/wp-content/uploads/Data-Origins-Abrams.pdf> accessed 1 June 2019. See also: Joe McNamee, 'Is "Privacy" Still Relevant in a World of Bastard

interpretation of data that produces added value to the ISS provider.[93] This process of data mining generates a vicious circle of more data generating more data. For example:

- **Age.** Imagine an age-restricted website asking for your birth date. You might not feel like you are giving up much privacy by doing so. Even if the website would track your browsing behaviour, it seems unlikely the website could link it to your person. However, in a seminal 2000 paper, it was demonstrated that almost 90 per cent of the US population could uniquely be identified by simply combining birth date, zip code, and sex.[94] This website can infer the user's zip code via his/her IP address. The sex can often be inferred from other elements (eg the accessed content). Once the user is identified, it becomes even easier to expand his/her profile with information from other sources.
- **Face.**[95] Once entities like Google and Facebook become cognizant of the link between a name and a face,[96] doors open to a wealth of information about that individual. Having access to a bottomless pit of images, these companies can henceforth look and/or identify that individual in each of them and learn a lot more about him/her.[97]
- **Online Presence.** Consider the 'Crystal'-app, promising to show you the 'best way to communicate with any co-worker, prospect, or customer based on their unique personality'.[98] Examining their online data trail (information that is publicly available to anyone), Crystal generates a 'personality profile, offering you suggestions on how best to communicate with that person'.[99]
- **Likes.** Finally, researchers at Cambridge University demonstrated that 'Facebook Likes, can be used to automatically and accurately predict a range of highly sensitive personal attributes including: sexual orientation, ethnicity, religious and political views, personality traits, intelligence, happiness,

Data?' (10 March 2016) <www.ocl.org/articles/3616-is-privacy-still-relevant-in-a-world-of-bastard-data> accessed 22 February 2018.

93 See in this regard: Gandy (n 49) 75.

94 Oostveen (n 85). For more recent work, see the ongoing research at Princeton's Center for Information Technology Policy: <https://citp.princeton.edu/research> and <https://freedom-to-tinker.com>

95 Investigating facial recognition capabilities of Facebook, Microsoft, Apple, Google, and more: Selvadurai (n 63) 5–6.

96 This can happen, for example, because the individual tags him/herself, or because a third party does so.

97 Notably from the picture's metadata (eg time and place) as well as from the content itself (eg other people in the picture).

98 <www.crystalknows.com> A very similar service is provided by <https://www.sharecare.com/static/employers>

99 Evan Selinger, 'Opinion: If Predictive Algorithms Craft the Best e-Mails, We're All in Big Trouble' [2015] Christian Science Monitor <www.csmonitor.com/World/Passcode/Passcode-Voices/2015/0427/Opinion-If-predictive-algorithms-craft-the-best-e-mails-we-re-all-in-big-trouble> accessed 1 June 2019.

> use of addictive substances, parental separation, age, and gender.'[100] The same researchers also argued that a computer algorithm is more accurate than humans in (a) assessing personality, simply by looking at Facebook Likes;[101] and (b) identifying sexual orientation from facial images.[102]

All these examples clearly illustrate the vicious circle of data generating more data. With Moore's law over 50 years old,[103] there are virtually no (technological) limits to how data might be used once collected, rendering the concept of anonymity meaningless in practice.[104] Aggregated, many seemingly innocuous pieces of data can reveal a detailed picture and have a profound impact on both individuals and society at large.[105] Indeed, as demonstrated by the Uber and Facebook vignettes, even if individuals could manage to keep track of all the data these companies collect about them, it would still be impossible to know the inferences and categorization made on the basis of that data. The 'right of access', as will be clarified later in Chapter 8, might remedy this in theory but is often significantly impaired in practice.[106] Finally, in light of the power law underlying data collection, it is nearly

[100] Michal Kosinski, David Stillwell, and Thore Graepel, 'Private Traits and Attributes Are Predictable from Digital Records of Human Behavior' (2013) 110 Proceedings of the National Academy of Sciences 5802.

[101] Wu Youyou, Michal Kosinski, and David Stillwell, 'Computer-Based Personality Judgments Are More Accurate Than Those Made by Humans' [2015] Proceedings of the National Academy of Sciences 201418680; Issie Lapowsky, 'How Facebook Knows You Better Than Your Friends Do' (*Wired*, 13 January 2015) <www.wired.com/2015/01/facebook-personality-test> accessed 1 June 2019. 'In the end, the researchers found that with information on just ten Facebook "Likes", the algorithm was more accurate than the average person's colleague. With 150 "Likes", it could outsmart people's families, and with 300 "Likes", it could best a person's spouse.'

[102] Yilun Wang and Michal Kosinski, 'Deep Neural Networks Are More Accurate than Humans at Detecting Sexual Orientation from Facial Images' [2017] *Open Science Framework* <https://osf.io/zn79k> accessed 22 February 2018; 'Advances in AI Are Used to Spot Signs of Sexuality' [2017] The Economist (9 September 2017) <www.economist.com/news/science-and-technology/21728614-machines-read-faces-are-coming-advances-ai-are-used-spot-signs> accessed 22 February 2018. This research has been the subject of considerable criticism, see inter alia: Alan Burdick, 'The A.I. "Gaydar" Study and the Real Dangers of Big Data' [2017] *New Yorker* (15 September 2017) <www.newyorker.com/news/daily-comment/the-ai-gaydar-study-and-the-real-dangers-of-big-data> accessed 24 July 2018; Andrew Gelman, Greggor Mattson, and Daniel Simpson, 'Gaydar and the Fallacy of Decontextualized Measurement' (2018) 5 Sociological Science 270.

[103] Arik Hesseldahl, 'Moore's Law Hits 50, But It May Not See 60' (*Re/code*, 15 April 2015) <http://recode.net/2015/04/15/moores-law-hits-50-but-it-may-not-see-60> accessed 1 June 2019.

[104] Solon Barocas and Helen Nissenbaum, 'Big Data's End Run around Anonymity and Consent' in Julia Lane and others (eds), *Privacy, Big Data, and the Public Good: Frameworks for Engagement* (CUP 2014); P Ohm, 'Broken Promises of Privacy: Responding to the Surprising Failure of Anonymization' (2010) 57 UCLA Law Review 1701.

[105] Explanatory Report to: Council of Europe—Committee of Ministers, 'Resolution (73) 22 on the Protection of the Privacy of Individuals vis-à-vis Electronic Data Banks in the Private Sector' <https://rm.coe.int/CoERMPublicCommonSearchServices/DisplayDCTMContent?documentId=0900001680502830> in fine; Lindop (n 67) 141–43; Daniel J Solove, 'A Taxonomy of Privacy' (2006) 154 University of Pennsylvania Law Review 477, 506; Article 29 Working Party, 'Opinion 06/2014 on the Notion of Legitimate Interests of the Data Controller under Article 7 of Directive 95/46/EC' (European Commission 2014) Opinion WP 217 37 <http://ec.europa.eu/justice/article-29/documentation> accessed 1 June 2019.

[106] See notably: Ausloos and Dewitte (n 25); Veale, Binns, and Ausloos (n 25).

impossible to (technologically and/or economically) surpass those having access to the largest data sets.[107] Pasquale refers to this as the 'self-reinforcing data advantage of dominant firms'.[108] Indeed, the Silicon Valley mantra of growing one's user base as quickly as possible, and the high prices paid in data-rich mergers/acquisitions clearly demonstrate this very point.[109]

c) Incomprehensibility

The data deluge combined with the increasing complexity of the data-processing ecosystem leave even the most diligent individuals in the dark as to how their personal data is being processed.[110] Legally required documentation such as terms of service or privacy policies are notoriously unread(able).[111] These documents usually consist of hypothetical and vague language rather than clear statements regarding the actual use of data.[112] More than ten years ago, researchers calculated that reading privacy policies would take the average individual over 200 hours per year.[113] Others have demonstrated that communicating such policies is often impossible in environments where there are no interfaces to show them in in the first place.[114] Academic debate on the so-called right to an explanation has emphasized such information may not always be straightforward to provide in the first place.[115] Indeed, the growing complexification of data-processing

[107] For an illustrative example—ie in the context of health-related data—see: Julia Powles and Hal Hodson, 'Google DeepMind and Healthcare in an Age of Algorithms' (2017) 7 Health and Technology 351.

[108] Frank Pasquale, 'Privacy, Antitrust, and Power' (2013) 20 George Mason Law Review 1009, 1015. See also: Orla Lynskey, 'Regulating "Platform Power"' (LSE 2017) Working Paper 1/2017 19ff <https://papers.ssrn.com/abstract=2921021> accessed 1 June 2019.

[109] Inge Graef, *EU Competition Law, Data Protection and Online Platforms: Data as Essential Facility* (Kluwer 2016).

[110] Simone Fischer-Hübner and others, 'Online Privacy: Towards Informational Self-Determination on the Internet' in Mireille Hildebrandt and others (eds), *Digital Enlightenment Yearbook 2013: The Value of Personal Data*, vol 1 (IOS Press 2013) 127 <http://ssrn.com/abstract=2468200> accessed 1 June 2019.

[111] Alex Hern, 'I Read All the Small Print on the Internet and It Made Me Want to Die' *The Guardian* (15 June 2015) <www.theguardian.com/technology/2015/jun/15/i-read-all-the-small-print-on-the-internet> accessed 1 June 2019; Joel R Reidenberg and others, 'Disagreeable Privacy Policies: Mismatches between Meaning and Users' Understanding' (2015) 30 Berkeley Technology Law Journal 1; Jamila Venturini and others, *Terms of Service and Human Rights: An Analysis of Online Platform Contracts* (Revan 2016) <http://internet-governance.fgv.br/sites/internet-governance.fgv.br/files/publicacoes/terms_of_services_06_12_2016.pdf> accessed 1 June 2019; Joel R Reidenberg and others, 'Ambiguity in Privacy Policies and the Impact of Regulation' (2016) 45 Journal of Legal Studies S163.

[112] See, eg: Van Alsenoy and others (n 11) 10; Venturini and others (n 111).

[113] Aleecia M McDonald and Lorrie Faith Cranor, 'The Cost of Reading Privacy Policies' (2008) 4 I/S: A Journal of Law and Policy for the Information Society 543.

[114] eg, 'smart public spaces' and many 'Internet of Things' products. See: Meg Leta Jones, 'Privacy without Screens & the Internet of Other People's Things' (2014) 51 Idaho Law Review 639, 647.

[115] See eg: Sandvig and others (n 64) 26; Bryce Goodman and Seth Flaxman, 'EU Regulations on Algorithmic Decision-Making and a "Right to Explanation"' (2016) <http://arxiv.org/pdf/1606.08813v1.pdf> accessed 1 June 2019; Sandra Wachter, Brent Mittelstadt, and Luciano Floridi, 'Why a Right to Explanation of Automated Decision-Making Does Not Exist in the General Data Protection Regulation' (2017) 7 International Data Privacy Law 76; Menaka Narayanan and others, 'How Do Humans Understand Explanations from Machine Learning Systems? An Evaluation of the Human-Interpretability of Explanation' [2018] arXiv:1802.00682 [cs] <http://arxiv.org/abs/1802.00682> accessed 11 February 2018; Andrew D Selbst and Solon Barocas, 'The Intuitive Appeal of Explainable Machines' (2018) 87 Fordham Law Review 1085.

ecosystems also makes it harder for controllers to comprehend the full extent of data processing. Even the most well-intentioned companies might experience great difficulties in trying to communicate their data practices in an accurate *and* intelligible way.[116]

d) Conclusion

The complexification of the data-processing ecosystem, combined with data-mining's power law and the lack of adequate transparency have shaped the data deluge into a growing information asymmetry. As demonstrated by Schrems's story, while many individuals might have some notion of how their data is being collected and processed in the abstract, 'the depth and the scale [...] remains opaque and inaccessible to the ordinary person'.[117] Especially in light of many ISS providers' own inability to describe the details of their 'data operations'[118] as well as the fact that most data often resides with only a handful of economic actors.[119] Moreover, sensors and data-processing technology more broadly, are becoming more subliminal as they 'weave themselves into the fabric of everyday life until they are indistinguishable from it'.[120] Such invisibility makes the underlying algorithms and design choices more resistant to scrutiny.[121]

In summary, there is a growing information asymmetry between individuals and ISS providers. This asymmetry materializes both in the amount of personal data being collected and generated, as well as the (lack of) information on how the data is processed. It is further amplified by surveillance being the Internet's de facto business and software development model as well as the broader 'algorithmic culture' that characterizes modern society.[122] In this context, Solove has

[116] Frank Pasquale, *The Black Box Society: The Secret Algorithms That Control Money and Information* (Harvard UP 2014) 8; Ausloos and Dewitte (n 25).

[117] Tufekci (n 19).

[118] Koops (n 89) 252; Veale, Binns, and Ausloos (n 25). According to Sandvig et al., the lack of transparency in this context is at least partly due to 'corporate secrecy and the complexity and unfamiliarity of math and computer code', Sandvig and others (n 64) 26.

[119] Angela Daly, *Private Power, Online Information Flows and EU Law: Mind the Gap* (Hart 2016); Graef (n 109); Evgeny Morozov, 'To Tackle Google's Power, Regulators Have to Go after Its Ownership of Data' *The Guardian* (2 July 2017) <www.theguardian.com/technology/2017/jul/01/google-european-commission-fine-search-engines> accessed 1 June 2019.

[120] Mark Weiser, 'The Computer for the Twenty-First Century' *Scientific American* (September 1991) 94 et seq. As referred to in: European Group on Ethics in Science and New Technologies (n 33) 29.

[121] Marlia E Banning, 'Shared Entanglements—Web 2.0, Info-Liberalism & Digital Sharing' (2016) 19 Information, Communication & Society 489, 494.

[122] Referring to the ways in which 'computers, running complex mathematical formulae, engage in what's often considered to be the traditional work of culture: the sorting, classifying, and hierarchizing of people, places, objects, and ideas'. In: Giuseppe Granieri, 'Algorithmic Culture. "Culture Now Has Two Audiences: People and Machines"— Futurists' Views' (*Medium*, 30 April 2014) <https://medium.com/futurists-views/algorithmic-culture-culture-now-has-two-audiences-people-and-machines-2bdaa404f643> accessed 1 June 2019. See also: Schneier (n 51) ch 4.

compared individuals to Josef K. (in Kafka's *Der Prozess*): unknowledgeable—or even unaware—of the underlying reasoning of data-driven decision-making that impacts him.[123]

2.2.2 Control Asymmetry

> Information gives the watcher increased power of the watched that can be used to persuade, influence, or otherwise control them.[124]

Information asymmetries enable control asymmetries.[125] The one-way mirrors between ISS providers and individuals leave the latter naked and the former in charge. In this context, one can think of Foucault's *le regard* (the gaze),[126] which is described as a technique enabling 'administrators to manage their institutional populations by creating and exploiting a new kind of visibility [...] organizing these populations so that they could be seen, known, surveyed, and thus controlled'.[127] According to Foucault, modern power therefore 'replaces violence and force of arms with the "gentler" constraint of uninterrupted visibility'.[128] Today, this is at least as true in individuals' horizontal relationships with ISS providers, as it is in vertical relationships with the state.[129] In this regard, it is also worth referring to the 'Panoptic Sort'.[130] Gandy describes this as a 'system of power and disciplinary surveillance that identifies, classifies, and assesses' and is connected to what Lyon refers to as 'social sorting'.[131] Indeed, 'measuring the social and the human is also to shape and discipline the social and the human'.[132]

With ever more interconnected sensors, generating ever more data, we increasingly (need to) rely on ISS providers to help make sense of the world. Indeed, the role of ISS providers as information intermediaries cannot be underestimated.[133]

[123] Daniel Solove, *The Digital Person: Technology and Privacy in the Information Age* (New York UP 2004) 47. Cited in: Bart W Schermer, 'The Limits of Privacy in Automated Profiling and Data Mining' (2011) 27 Computer Law & Security Review 45, 47.

[124] Richards (n 26) 1956.

[125] See in this regard, for example: Serge Gutwirth, *Privacy and the Information Age* (Raf Casert tr, Rowman & Littlefield 2002) 16.

[126] Michel Foucault, *Surveiller et punir: naissance de la prison* (Gallimard 2004) 172ff.

[127] Nancy Fraser, 'Foucault on Modern Power: Empirical Insights and Normative Confusions' in Stuart Henry (ed), *Social Control: Aspects of Non-State Justice* (Dartmouth 1994) 22; Wendy Hui-Kyong Chun, *Control and Freedom: Power and Paranoia in the Age of Fiber Optics* (MIT Press 2006) 6ff.

[128] Fraser (n 127) 23.

[129] See eg: Marisol Sandoval, 'A Critical Empirical Case Study of Consumer Surveillance on Web 2.0' in Christian Fuchs and others (eds), *Internet and Surveillance: The Challenges of Web 2. 0 and Social Media* (Routledge 2012).

[130] Oscar H Gandy, *The Panoptic Sort: A Political Economy of Personal Information* (Westview 1993).

[131] ibid 15; David Lyon, *Surveillance as Social Sorting: Privacy, Risk, and Digital Discrimination* (Routledge 2003). Cited in: Fuchs and others (n 129) 6–7.

[132] David Beer, *Metric Power* (Palgrave Macmillan UK 2016) 182 <http://link.springer.com/10.1057/978-1-137-55649-3> accessed 24 February 2018; Wendy Nelson Espeland and Mitchell L Stevens, 'A Sociology of Quantification' (2008) 49 European Journal of Sociology 401, 414.

[133] Miller (n 75) 1108.

Their key position in today's information society does warrant further examination of (inter alia) their power over the (personal) data they process.[134] One of the most important features characterizing the ISS landscape is that it has gradually become an oligarchy of powerful corporate entities.[135] Similarly to Antigoon, these quasi-monopolies[136] control the main communication channels we use to interact online.[137] Examining the causes of the rise to power of these entities largely goes beyond the scope of this section (and book overall). Suffice to say that the technological trends described in subsection 2.1, combined with the information asymmetry and complexification of the data-processing landscape all contribute considerably. From an economics perspective, factors such as network externalities and lock-in effects also contribute significantly to the growth and further concentration of ISS providers' power.[138]

From a privacy and data protection point of view, the powerful position of ISS providers has one very important ramification. In full control over the channels, network, and/or platforms they operate, they are generally also aware of how they are used (whether by end users, developers or any other entity interacting with the provider).[139] This entails that most ISS providers will at least have access to vast amounts of behavioural data (eg metadata such as timestamps, location, or mouse clicks) and often to content data as well (eg media posted on a social network).[140] As a matter of fact, they are often designed in a way that requires access to most of this information in order to provide services in the first place. Facebook, for example, would not work the way it does without knowing who their users' friends are, or what content they post on someone's wall. Uber cannot operate as it does, without having access to the real-time location of riders *and* drivers. Search

[134] Martin Moore, 'Tech Giants and Civic Power' (King's College (Policy Institute) 2016) <www.kcl.ac.uk/sspp/policy-institute/CMCP/Tech-Giants-and-Civic-Power.pdf>.

[135] In 2012, *The Economist* cleverly visualized the constellation of the Internet's corporate giants on a map. See: 'Another Game of Thrones' [2012] *The Economist* <www.economist.com/news/21567361-google-apple-facebook-and-amazon-are-each-others-throats-all-sorts-ways-another-game> accessed 1 June 2019. More recently, see: 'How to Tame the Tech Titans' [2018] *The Economist* <www.economist.com/news/leaders/21735021-dominance-google-facebook-and-amazon-bad-consumers-and-competition-how-tame> accessed 22 February 2018.

[136] '[T]he leading Internet players may be new, but they dominate their markets at least as much as Wal-Mart or Intel dominate theirs'. In: Kevin Werbach, 'Centripetal Network: How the Internet Holds Itself Together, and the Forces Tearing It Apart' (2009) 42 UC Davis Law Review 343, 352.

[137] Schneier described this as a return to Feudalism: Schneier, *Data and Goliath* (n 51). See also: Bracha and Pasquale (n 80) 1161.

[138] See: Werbach (n 136) 393ff; Justus Haucap and Ulrich Heimeshoff, 'Google, Facebook, Amazon, eBay: Is the Internet Driving Competition or Market Monopolization?' (Düsseldorf Institute for Competition Economics 2013) www.dice.hhu.de/fileadmin/redaktion/Fakultaeten/Wirtschaftswissenschaftliche_Fakultaet/DICE/Discussion_Paper/083_Haucap_Heimeshoff.pdf accessed 1 June 2019; Graef (n 109); Ariel Ezrachi, *Virtual Competition: The Promise and Perils of the Algorithm-Driven Economy* (Harvard UP 2017) <https://doi.org/10.4159/9780674973336> accessed 22 February 2018.

[139] This book will focus on the end users' perspective in particular.

[140] In the last few years, end-to-end encryption has prevented these actors from access to data in transit.

engines, by definition, analyse a great deal of information too (from your individual queries to the whole World Wide Web). Looking for a specific message in one's ever-expanding Gmail or Hotmail account would also not be as easy without Google or Microsoft being able to read through your emails. What is more, the current software development paradigm is focused on constant optimization through continued user surveillance. The data gathered in this way is constantly fed back into the system in order to make incremental changes to the software/services. As eloquently explained by Gürses:

> Optimisation systems treat the world as one large logistics enterprise. They do not only collect, store, process and transfer information, but they leverage information to optimise the world in the interest of some stakeholders' value proposition. Optimisation systems differ from information systems since they treat the world not as a static place that can be known, but as a place to sense and co-create. [. . .] Optimisation systems are concerned with maximum extraction of economic value through the capture and manipulation of people's activities and their environments at scale. And here the agile turn comes in handy too. With concepts like permanent bèta, combined with continuous experimentation on users, and exploration on populations and environments allows optimisation systems to be continuously fitted into our everyday.[141]

Once collected, individuals have little to no control over how their personal data is further processed by ISS providers. Indeed, from a practical perspective, individuals have no *physical* control over the medium (and channels) on (through) which their personal data is located (flows) once it leaves their devices.[142] In this paradigm, the notion of 'control' becomes more abstract and dependent on artificial constructions such as data protection law and/or technical measures such as Privacy Enhancing Technologies (PETs). Without these, individuals are essentially left to the goodwill of ISS providers. Today, many of these service providers do offer a more or less elaborate privacy-settings panel to their users.[143] However, these 'privacy dashboards' generally only enable users to control third party access (eg what information 'friends', advertisers, or connected services such as games can see). Rarely do these settings allow meaningful control over how the ISS provider itself processes the data. In practice, users are typically left with a binary

[141] Seda Gürses *Data Justice Conference: Keynote Plenary I* <https://cardiff.cloud.panopto.eu/Panopto/Pages/Viewer.aspx?id=547383b2–9d0a-4966-a4aa-a8e50178e2cf> accessed 16 June 2018 01:29:35; Gürses and van Hoboken (n 33).

[142] Kristina Irion, 'Your Digital Home Is No Longer Your Castle: How Cloud Computing Transforms the (Legal) Relationship between Individuals and Their Personal Records' [2015] International Journal of Law and Information Technology 9 <http://ijlit.oxfordjournals.org/content/early/2015/09/25/ijlit.eav015> accessed 28 September 2015.

[143] eg <www.google.com/settings/dashboard; www.facebook.com/settings?tab=privacy>

take-it-or-leave-it option. As farcical as this 'choice' may seem,[144] it is crippled even more by the information asymmetry mentioned before. Without knowing when/what data is processed and what for, how can one effectively 'control' personal data? Moreover, these dashboards are generally only available to actual registered users of the service. Hence, non-Facebook users being tracked across the Net;[145] people without a Google account using the search engine or emailing a Gmail user; non-Apple or Amazon customers reading an e-book, all have little recourse to prevent—or control in any meaningful way—how their personal data is captured and further processed.

These asymmetries of 'data control' (ie the ability to manipulate data) in turn lead to power asymmetries, where those who control the data, can control the individuals behind that data. Technology-driven (information) power asymmetries—whether between consumers and companies or citizens and their government—are nothing new.[146] They are exactly what triggered the first data protection laws in the twentieth century.[147] The past two decades, however, have been characterized by an unusually prodigious rise and concentration of a new kind of corporate power. One that inherently hinges on the commodification (and maximum value extraction) of personal data.[148] As described before, these entities control the growing information flows of our lives. Indeed, their control over personal data—and hence 'power'—only increases as more and more of our (inter)actions occur on their quasi-monopolistic[149] platforms and/or networks.[150] Such control becomes more convoluted and hard to identify as these services subtly infiltrate the fabric of our lives, disappearing into the background (eg Uber vignette,[151] Apple vignette).[152] The unstoppable information tsunami also makes individuals increasingly dependent on these providers. As a result, opting out of this ecosystem has become virtually impossible.[153] It is this growing dependence and lack of control

[144] To what extent can individuals truly avoid ever passing by ISS providers such as Google (owning the dominant search engine, video platform, online maps service, etc) or Facebook (hosting an increasing number of pictures, videos, event- and company-pages, etc)?

[145] Acar and others (n 65); Van Alsenoy and others (n 11).

[146] Nissenbaum (n 77) 43.

[147] Viktor Mayer-Schönberger, 'Generational Development of Data Protection in Europe' in Philip E Agre and Marc Rotenberg (eds), *Technology and Privacy: The New Landscape* (MIT Press 1998).

[148] Zuboff (n 78); Julie E Cohen, 'The Biopolitical Public Domain: The Legal Construction of the Surveillance Economy' (2017) 31 Philosophy & Technology 213.

[149] The high market share of many ISS providers can partially be explained by the mutually reinforcing relationship with the service's quality. Increase in either market share or quality, results in an increase of the other. See: Christian Fuchs and others (eds), 'Critique of the Political Economy of Web 2.0 Surveillance' in Fuchs and others (n 129) 66; Schneier (n 46).

[150] 'Every message we write, every video we post, every item we buy or view, our time-space paths and patterns of social interaction all become data points in algorithms for sorting, predicting, and managing our behaviour.' In: Mark Andrejevic, 'Exploitation in the Data Mine' in Fuchs and others (n 129) 85–86.

[151] Calo and Rosenblat (n 17).

[152] See in this regard: Jones (n 114).

[153] Julia Angwin, *Dragnet Nation: A Quest for Privacy, Security, and Freedom in a World of Relentless Surveillance* (Times Books, Henry Holt 2014) ch 11.

that lies at the basis of the power asymmetry. Here, again, a parallel can be drawn with Antigoon's story: sailors (and everyone down their communication/demand/supply chain) are dependent on Druon the giant if they want to pass by, though have no control over the conditions. Asymmetry of power, in this context, stems from the ability of one actor to control the behaviour of others.[154] This power asymmetry—shaped by information and control asymmetries—constitutes the starting point of this book.[155]

Section 3. The Control Conundrum

> As everything becomes datafied, everything we do becomes controllable.[156]

The data deluge described in subsection 2.1 has led to an important information asymmetry, described in section 2. This information asymmetry, in turn, has contributed considerably to the power asymmetry—in terms of control over personal data—between individuals and ISS providers. Power asymmetries are unavoidable, but become problematic when growing too large.[157] The law plays an essential role in safeguarding against excesses of power, whether stemming from the state or economic actors. In light of what was described above, regulation of the latter through data protection law appears particularly prescient today.

3.1 Data (dis)Empowerment

Today, individuals' ability to 'control' (the processing of) their personal data in relation to ISS providers is largely hypothetical. This is problematic for a variety of reasons. From a data protection perspective, control over personal data is closely linked to concepts such as human dignity, individual freedom and informational self-determination. This principle—construed by the German Federal Constitutional Court in the 1983 *Population Census* case—has been described as

[154] See in this regard: Titus Stahl, 'Indiscriminate Mass Surveillance and the Public Sphere' (2016) 18 Ethics and Information Technology 33, 35–36.

[155] While recognizing the important body of work on power (asymmetries), it would go beyond the scope of this book to dedicate much space to the philosophical and normative literature on this topic. Useful references are: Joseph Raz, *The Morality of Freedom* (Clarendon Press 1986); Joseph Raz, *From Normativity to Responsibility* (OUP 2011); Philip Pettit, *Republicanism: A Theory of Freedom and Government* (Clarendon Press 2002); Manuel Castells, *Communication Power* (OUP 2009) 10; Christian Fuchs, *Social Media: A Critical Introduction* (Sage 2014) 72–73; Daly (n 119).

[156] Cheney-Lippold (n 50) 262.

[157] Serge Gutwirth, 'De Toepassing van Het Finaliteitsbeginsel van de Privacywet van 8 December 1992 Tot Bescherming van de Persoonlijke Levenssfeer Ten Opzichte van de Verwerking van Persoonsgegevens' [The Application of the Purpose Specification Principle in the Belgian Data Protection Act of 8 December 1992] (1993) 1993 Tijdschrift voor Privaatrecht—TPR 1409, 1420.

a precondition for a free and democratic society.[158] Others have also pointed out how control asymmetries over personal data may affect individual autonomy;[159] innovation;[160] non-discrimination;[161] intellectual freedom;[162] and a broad scale of other ethical[163] and fundamental values.[164] The public sphere has effectively been privatized and co-opted by market forces.[165] There is research demonstrating the many problems stemming from how (personal) data mining is used for political,[166] commercial,[167] and/or emotional,[168] manipulation.[169] In this 'big data' environment, people have virtually no control over how their personal data is impacting their reputation;[170] is used for (price) discrimination;[171] and a whole range of other

[158] Gerrit Hornung and Christoph Schnabel, 'Data Protection in Germany I: The Population Census Decision and the Right to Informational Self-Determination' (2009) 25 Computer Law & Security Review 84.

[159] Bernal (n 28) 24ff; Zarsky (n 58); Nissenbaum (n 77) 81ff.

[160] Julie Cohen, 'What Privacy Is for' (2013) 126 Harvard Law Review 1904; European Data Protection Supervisor, 'Opinion on Coherent Enforcement of Fundamental Rights in the Age of Big Data' (EDPS 2016) Opinion 8/2016 3 <https://secure.edps.europa.eu/EDPSWEB/webdav/site/mySite/shared/Documents/EDPS/Events/16-09-23_BigData_opinion_EN.pdf> accessed 25 October 2016.

[161] Mireille Hildebrandt, 'Who Is Profiling Who? Invisible Visibility' in Serge Gutwirth and others (eds), *Reinventing Data Protection?* (Springer 2009) <www.springerlink.com/index/P7710R0760613778.pdf> accessed 12 February 2013; Bart Schermer, 'Risks of Profiling and the Limits of Data Protection Law' in Bart Custers and others (eds), *Discrimination and Privacy in the Information Society—Data Mining and Profiling in Large Databases* (Springer 2013).

[162] Richards (n 52).

[163] Chun (n 127); European Group on Ethics in Science and New Technologies (n 33) 20.

[164] Paul De Hert and Serge Gutwirth, 'Data Protection in the Case Law of Strasbourg and Luxembu rg: Constitutionalisation in Action' in Serge Gutwirth and others (eds), *Reinventing Data Protection?* (Springer Science 2009).

For critical research on the political economy of these new data-driven ISS providers such as social networks, see notably: Robert Waterman McChesney, *Digital Disconnect: How Capitalism Is Turning the Internet against Democracy* (New Press 2013); Fuchs (n 155) 14; Arvind Arvidsson, 'Facebook and Finance: On the Social Logic of the Derivative' (2016) 33 Theory, Culture & Society 3.

[165] Stephen Metcalf, 'Neoliberalism: The Idea That Swallowed the World' *The Guardian* (18 August 2017) <www.theguardian.com/news/2017/aug/18/neoliberalism-the-idea-that-changed-the-world> accessed 6 September 2017.

[166] Tufekci (n 19).

[167] Ryan Calo, 'Digital Market Manipulation' (2014) 82 George Washington Law Review 995; Zarsky (n 58) 16, 30.

[168] Kashmir Hill, 'Ok Cupid Lied to Users about Their Compatibility as an Experiment' [2014] *Forbes* <www.forbes.com/sites/kashmirhill/2014/07/28/okcupid-experiment-compatibility-deception> accessed 1 August 2014; Michelle Meyer, 'Everything You Need to Know about Facebook's Controversial Emotion Experiment' (*Wired*, 30 June 2014) <www.wired.com/2014/06/everything-you-need-to-know-about-facebooks-manipulative-experiment> accessed 1 July 2014; Evgeny Morozov, 'Facebook Invades Your Personality, Not Your Privacy' *Financial Times* (10 August 2014) <www.ft.com/intl/cms/s/2/dd5e5514-198d-11e4-8730-00144feabdc0.html> accessed 19 May 2015.

[169] 'When the system seems to know what you want better and earlier than you do, how can you know where these desires really come from?' In: Lessig (n 39) 220. See also: Bracha and Pasquale (n 80); Forbruker Rådet, 'Deceived by Design. How Tech Companies Use Dark Patterns to Discourage Us from Exercising Our Rights to Privacy' (2018) <https://fil.forbrukerradet.no/wp-content/uploads/2018/06/2018-06-27-deceived-by-design-final.pdf> accessed 28 June 2018.

[170] eg: Brendan Van Alsenoy, Aleksandra Kuczerawy, and Jef Ausloos, 'Search Engines after "Google Spain": Internet@Liberty or Privacy@Peril?' (2013) <http://papers.ssrn.com/abstract=2321494> accessed 21 January 2014.

[171] Nicholas Diakopoulos, 'Algorithmic Accountability Reporting: On the Investigation of Black Boxes' 9 <http://www.nickdiakopoulos.com/wp-content/uploads/2011/07/Algorithmic-Accountability-

undesirable purposes,[172] not to mention the many externalities resulting from technology-mediated processes.[173] Indeed, these trends are increasingly affecting the social, economic, and political fabric of society more broadly. The vignettes described above, all illustrate problematic components of unbridled corporate data processing as well (ie profit-driven psychological manipulation by Uber and Facebook, or opportunistic republishing of personal data by Google). Chapter 2 will further expand on the importance of safeguarding data autonomy against the backdrop of data-driven power asymmetries.

Without adequate safeguards, the processing of personal data by ISS providers will further exacerbate the power asymmetry and ensuing perils to fundamental rights, freedoms, and interests.[174] One part of the solution—according to an emerging research field—would be to open up and critically assess data-mining black boxes in order to ensure 'algorithmic accountability'.[175] Who exactly would be burdened to enforce such accountability is unclear. After all, it is questionable to what extent lawyers and/or policymakers (traditionally involved in assessing legality of business processes) are capable of properly assessing this complex data-processing ecosystem.[176] Hence, even though *ex ante* safeguards such as transparency are crucial, they are no magic potions. There is a clear need for empowering individuals as well. Data protection rights in particular seem to offer a helpful toolbox for individuals to maintain some level of control over their data over time.

3.2 Data Protection Law's Toolbox

The right to the protection of personal data (henceforth: 'right to data protection') has been granted fundamental right status (Art 8) with the entry into force of the

Reporting_final.pdf>; Executive Office of the President, 'White House Report on Big Data and Differential Pricing' (2015) <https://obamawhitehouse.archives.gov/sites/default/files/whitehouse_files/docs/Big_Data_Report_Nonembargo_v2.pdf>

[172] Tene and Polonetsky (n 84).

A useful and elaborate exploration of key challenges to individuals, raised by corporate data processing, can be found in: Wolfie Christl, 'How Companies Use Personal Data Against People' (*Cracked Labs* 2017) <http://crackedlabs.org/dl/CrackedLabs_Christl_DataAgainstPeople.pdf> accessed 12 October 2017.

[173] Nick Couldry and Andreas Hepp, *The Mediated Construction of Reality* (Polity Press 2017).

[174] The 'vast asymmetries of information coupled with the unilateral power to design the legal and visual terms of the transaction could alter the consumer landscape'. In: Calo (n 167) 1006.

[175] See, inter alia: Diakopoulos (n 171); Pasquale (n 116).

[176] In other words, the lack of algorithmic accountability is not just a result of organizations not being transparent, but also an insufficient understanding of how their functioning by lawyers and policymakers, Schermer (n 123) 50. It should be said, though, that very thorough investigations into Facebook's practices are currently conducted in the UK. See inter alia: Digital, Culture, Media and Sport Committee, 'Disinformation and "Fake News": Interim Report' (HC 2018) 5.

EU Charter.[177] Control constitutes the central tenet of this fundamental right, as will be discussed in the next chapter. Similar to the fact that controlling one's body is crucial to ensure physical freedom, controlling one's data is crucial to ensure digital freedom.[178] The GDPR lays down a secondary law framework that is aimed at safeguarding *all* fundamental rights and freedoms in the Charter, and the right to data protection in particular.[179] Perhaps the best way to look at the GDPR is as a toolbox for safeguarding Charter provisions whenever personal data is processed.

Among the many tools within the GDPR's toolbox, data subject *rights* most clearly safeguard the control prerogative in Article 8 Charter. That is also why they might be most appropriate to mitigate power asymmetries between individuals and ISS providers. Indeed, while certainly valuable in their own right, many other 'GDPR tools' may fail to 'empower' individuals effectively in today's complex data-processing ecosystem. While the value of *ex ante* measures such as the data quality principles in Article 5, or the conditions for lawfulness in Article 6 certainly cannot be underestimated, they are insufficient in a highly dynamic environment, characterized by enormous power imbalances. *Ex post* empowerment tools such as the rights of access (Art 15), erasure (Art 17), portability (Art 20), or object (Art 21) offer an effective opportunity to permanently (re-)evaluate the use of data and take action where needed. They are aimed at empowering data subjects throughout the data-processing lifecycle. This book focuses on perhaps one of the most controversial and radical of these rights in particular: the right to erasure.

Section 4. Structure and Approach

4.1 Guiding Questions

This book aims to formulate an answer to the following question:

> Does the right to erasure in the GDPR meaningfully contribute to safeguarding the fundamental right to data protection in the face of online power asymmetries?

The primary rationale behind the fundamental right to data protection is massively under threat by growing power asymmetries in the context of ISS. Data subject rights in the GDPR constitute the most straightforward tools in secondary law that explicitly empower individuals in the face of such asymmetries. In the past,

[177] Gloria González Fuster, *The Emergence of Personal Data Protection as a Fundamental Right of the EU* (Springer 2014).

[178] See Stefano Rodotà, 'Data Protection as a Fundamental Right' in Serge Gutwirth and others (eds), *Reinventing Data Protection?* (Springer 2009) 80 <http://link.springer.com/10.1007/978-1-4020-9498-9> accessed 6 April 2015.

[179] For more on this, see: Orla Lynskey, *The Foundations of EU Data Protection Law* (OUP 2016).

under the national implementations of Directive 95/46, these rights have been criticized for being vague, ineffective, and underused. With the GDPR reinvigorating data subject rights, it is worth reassessing their potential. In order to scope this book, it was decided to focus on one right in particular: the right to erasure (Art 17). This can easily be justified by at least two reasons. First, if successful, the right arguably has the most 'extreme' or radical effect, ie the obliteration of the respective personal data. Second, Article 17 on the right to erasure effectively constitutes a central node in the overall data protection framework, packed with cross-references. As such, an analysis of this provision will in fact help elucidate most other key data subject empowerment measures as well. Whereas in theory, the right to erasure might appear as the epitome of individual empowerment under data protection law, many issues arise when looked at in practice. Three central questions—each corresponding to a major part—will be tackled:

Part I When, why, and how does the right to erasure apply? Sub-questions include: What is the history and rationale of the right to erasure? How does it relate to the fundamental right to data protection? What is the scope of application of the right to erasure? What are the requirements for (and exemptions to) applying the right to erasure?

Part II How to ensure applying the right to erasure does not unduly interfere with other fundamental rights and freedoms, and in particular freedom of expression (Art 11 Charter) and freedom to conduct a business (Art 16 Charter)? Sub-questions include: How does fair balancing between Charter provisions relate to fair balancing within the GDPR? How does the GDPR ensure and operationalize fair balancing? How to perform right to erasure-induced fair balancing involving economic interests and/or information freedoms and/or security interests? Does the GDPR effectively ensure *fair* balancing in the ISS context?

Part III Does the right to erasure effectively contribute to mitigating power asymmetries in the ISS context? Sub-questions include: What are the main challenges for the right to erasure to achieve its purpose and how can they be tackled? What are the requirements for ensuring effective data subject empowerment?

4.2 Roadmap

The objective of this book is to unravel the right to erasure's role in meaningfully protecting the fundamental right to data protection without undue interference with other fundamental rights. In order to accomplish this feat, the scope of the underlying research has been limited to a context in which the power asymmetry (over personal data) is most evident today: the relationship between individuals and ISS providers. Tackling the main research question will require three consecutive steps, each dependent on the one before it. Part I will provide a comprehensive, in-depth analysis of the central subject matter of this book: the right to erasure in EU data protection law. This part is subdivided into three chapters. The first one (Chapter 2) explores the history and rationale of the right to erasure and how it should be positioned in the broader data protection framework. The second Chapter (3) lays out the scope of application for data subject rights, with specific attention to some contentious issues of particular relevance in the context of the right to erasure (eg sensitive data, intermediary liability exemptions). The last Chapter (4) in Part I will provide a detailed analysis of how the right to erasure itself operates, ie its requirements, reach, and exemptions. In sum, Part I therefore provides answers to the *why* (Chapter 2), *when* (Chapter 3), and *how* (Chapter 4) of the right to erasure.

Invoking the right to erasure will generally have an impact on the rights, freedoms, and interests of others, even if minimally. The goal of Part II is to clarify, again in three chapters, how such balancing should operate. This is not an easy task in the context at hand, where many different actors use personal data for a variety of purposes. Indeed, the Google vignette illustrates a complex clashing of interests between the individual, the search engine, as well as the search engine users and website publishers. The GDPR purports to resolve such conflicts via fair balancing acts. With this in mind, Part II's first Chapter (5) critically dissects how exactly balancing features throughout the GDPR, *ex ante* and *ex post*, with the 'legitimate interests' provision (Art 6(1)f GDPR) at its epicentre. The following Chapter (6) will then do a deep dive into three particularly widespread 'balancing scenarios' in the ISS context, ie (a) commercial interests, (b) information freedoms, and (c) security or research interests. Part II ends with a short Chapter (7) that explores, criticizes, and nuances central issues emerging from balancing within data protection law.

Part III, finally, will tackle the central research question of this book, ie does the right to erasure meaningfully contribute to safeguarding the fundamental right to data protection in the face of online power asymmetries? In other words, is the right to erasure a boon for data subject empowerment, or rather an empty promise? The answer to this question will of course build on the insights gained throughout Parts I and II, but will also be inspired by the broader landscape in which it is set. Indeed, even if the GDPR will be the main reference point for investigating key challenges and how to mitigate them, Part III will also allude to other laws and take a broader perspective, incorporating technical and socioeconomic considerations as well.

All chapters eventually lead to clarifying and determining how the right to erasure can achieve its underlying rationale in practice, with due regard to the fundamental rights it might impact.

4.3 Method

As a whole, the objective of this book is explanatory and normative in nature. It is aimed at giving concrete guidance on how the right to erasure *should* be interpreted and implemented in pursuit of mitigating online power asymmetries between individuals and ISS providers. In order to achieve this normative goal, considerable preliminary research is required. Three key methodological strands can be identified: (a) descriptive/explanatory; (b) evaluative; and (c) normative. First, a legal–historical and systematic analysis of the relevant legal concepts sets out their respective meaning, rationale, scope, and preconditions. The underlying research primarily consisted of classic legal desk research, looking at: legal scholarship; (preparatory) legislative documents; EU level case law; and documents issued by public institutions. This method is central to Chapters 2 to 3 and 5 to 6. The second methodological strand consisted of evaluating the (interaction between) legal concepts explained before. These evaluations are primarily based on internal legal criteria drawn from the descriptive phases (eg stemming from the rationale of the relevant legal concepts). Vignettes will reappear throughout in order to illustrate and facilitate the evaluations. With regard to evaluating the impact of the right to erasure on fundamental Charter rights (notably information and economic freedoms in Arts 11 and 16), CJEU case law constitutes an important source as well. Moreover, the book also incorporates the findings of legal–empirical research conducted in 2017, assessing the level of compliance with data subject rights of access and erasure with around sixty ISS providers. This second methodological strand is issued in Chapters 3 to 4, 6 to 7, and Chapter 8. Finally, the explanatory and evaluative research strands lead to normative—or recommendatory—suggestions and conclusions. The key reference framework for this will be Part II on fair balancing and Chapter 2 setting out the normative underpinnings of the fundamental right to data protection (Art 8 Charter) as well as the right to erasure (Art 17 GDPR). This approach will be key in Chapter 7 and especially Chapter 8.

The research should be situated at a European Union level. The two central legal documents being researched—ie the GDPR and the Charter of Fundamental Rights—are of an EU level nature. With this in mind, the European Convention of Human Rights (ECHR) only features tangentially, notably when its provisions and case law contribute to interpreting the key questions at hand (see Art 52(3) Charter). The focus on EU, rather than Member State, level is further justified by the context in which the main research question is situated: the information society, inherently transcending national borders.

The four vignettes in Section 2 will be referred to throughout the book. Their primary purpose is to illustrate otherwise quite theoretical points in a practical manner. Rooted in reality, they will also enable us to flesh out and identify issues that else might have remained unnoticed or too abstract. These *vignettes* find themselves in between fully fledged case studies/use cases and mere examples.

In other words, they are not aimed at emulating the work traditionally done by practitioners, ie providing in-depth assessments of the legal regime governing the respective actors. But neither do they constitute gratuitous examples that only contribute superficially to the overall research. Instead, they plot concrete, real-life situations that are emblematic of the landscape against which this book was written and lay bare specific complexities that appear throughout. They pave the yellow brick road leading up to this book's main conclusions.

Even though all four vignettes will be useful throughout all chapters, each of them is selected because of their particular relevance with regard to specific key points. The *first vignette* (Uber's psychological manipulation) is helpful in better understanding (a) the need for a granular and functional approach to data protection (Chapters 3 and 4); and (b) balancing commercial interests with the data subject's interests (Chapter 6). The *second vignette* (Facebook's emotion contagion and political advertisement) is useful to almost all chapters, in particular to (a) practically investigate issues regarding the GDPR's personal scope of application—ie who is responsible for what—and scope exemptions (Chapter 3); (b) the reach of the right to erasure (Chapter 4); (c) the interaction between fundamental rights balancing and the GDPR (Chapter 5); and (d) untangle concepts such as responsibility and liability (Part III). The *third vignette* (Google Spain or the right to be delisted) is useful to illustrate and flesh out (a) issues at the intersection of data protection and intermediary liability (Chapter 3); (b) the balancing scenario involving information freedoms (Chapter 6); as well as (c) questions relating to fair balancing performed by private entities (Chapter 7). The *fourth vignette* (Apple Siri and the perverse effects of data protection by design), finally is useful to (a) demonstrate issues relating to the right to erasure's applicability (Chapter 4); (b) particularize the first and last balancing scenarios (Chapter 6); and (c) evaluate how protective and empowerment measures interact in the GDPR (Chapter 8).

PART I

THE RIGHT TO ERASURE IN EU DATA PROTECTION LAW

2

Foundations of Data Protection Law

Section 1. Introduction

The purpose of this book is to unravel the right to erasure—and data subject empowerment more broadly—in the General Data Protection Regulation (GDPR). In particular, it is aimed at clarifying and determining *if* and *how* the right to erasure can achieve its underlying rationale in the highly asymmetrical relationships between individuals and information society service providers. In light of this overall goal, the present chapter will lay the groundwork for further analyses and evaluations. The first section sets out the origins story of the right to data protection, its emergence as a *fundamental* right in the Charter, and its main rationale. This will constitute the necessary backdrop against which the second section will draw the contours of the right to erasure. More specifically, this section will position the right to erasure in the broader data protection framework, describe its legislative history, and articulate its main rationale. The chapter ends with a short section, delineating frequent conceptual misunderstandings.

Section 2. The Fundamental Right to Data Protection

CHARTER OF FUNDAMENTAL RIGHTS OF THE EUROPEAN UNION

Article 8—Protection of Personal Data

(1) Everyone has the right to the protection of personal data concerning him or her.
(2) Such data must be processed fairly for specified purposes and on the basis of the consent of the person concerned or some other legitimate basis laid down by law. Everyone has the right of access to datawhich has been collected concerning him or her, and the right to have it rectified.
(3) Compliance with these rules shall be subject to control by an independent authority.

The Right to Erasure in EU Data Protection Law. First Edition. Jef Ausloos. Oxford University Press (2020). © Jef Ausloos
DOI: 10.1093/oso/9780198847977.001.0001

2.1 History

The 'protection of personal data' was declared a fundamental right in the European Union (EU) at the dawn of this millennium.[1] Article 8 of the Charter of Fundamental Rights of the EU (the Charter)[2]—proclaimed in December 2000—unambiguously declares: '*[e]veryone has the right to the protection of personal data*'. It took another nine years for the Charter to become legally binding.[3] Still, the importance of the right to data protection precedes its formal recognition in the Charter. In fact, the Charter's preamble emphasizes that it *reaffirms*[4] and strengthens rights in light of 'changes in society, social progress and scientific and technological developments by making those rights more visible in a Charter'.[5] Indeed, the right to data protection can be traced back to many pre-existing legal sources.[6] The 1970 Data Protection Act of the German state of Hesse is generally considered to be the first legislative document and symbolic starting point of data protection in the EU.[7] This Act, and several others, will briefly be expounded in the following pages.

The overall purpose of this section (and chapter) is to provide the essential background and context for the book's main focus: the right to erasure. Rather than duplicating the extensive work that has been done already on the emergence of data protection laws and the fundamental right to data protection, it will pinpoint key threads in the birth and further development of data protection law in the EU, relevant in order to better understand the right to erasure today. Put yet differently, this section will paint the necessary backdrop against which the following section will portray the main character of this book.

[1] Even though they can be interpreted in different ways, for the purposes of this book 'data protection' and 'protection of personal data' will both be used as synonyms. For more on conceptual issues, see: Gloria González Fuster, *The Emergence of Personal Data Protection as a Fundamental Right of the EU* (Springer 2014) 254ff; Eleni Kosta, *Consent in European Data Protection Law* (Martinus Nijhoff 2013) 46. Hondius explained that the term 'data protection' is not quite etymologically correct, though its meaning is clear. Frits W Hondius, *Emerging Data Protection in Europe* (North-Holland 1975) 1.

[2] Charter of Fundamental Rights of the European Union [2000] OJ C364/01 and [2010] OJ C83/389.

[3] Through the Treaty of Lisbon amending the Treaty on European Union and the Treaty establishing the European Community, signed at Lisbon [2007] OJ C306/1. The Charter had slightly been adjusted in the meantime: Charter of Fundamental Rights of the European Union [2007] OJ C303/1. Definitive version: [2010] OJ C83/389.

[4] In particular those resulting from 'the constitutional traditions and international obligations common to the Member States, the Treaty on European Union, the Community Treaties, the European Convention for the Protection of Human Rights and Fundamental Freedoms, the Social Charters adopted by the Community and by the Council of Europe and the case-law of the Court of Justice of the European Communities and of the European Court of Human Rights.'

[5] Preamble to the Charter.

[6] See also: González Fuster, *The Emergence of Personal Data Protection as a Fundamental Right of the EU* (n 1) 2–3.

[7] ibid 4; Kosta (n 1) 13.

2.1.1 A Dark Past

Unsurprisingly, the protection of personal data only became relevant when data started being processed. Systematic processing of personal data only really took off in the 20th century. Similar to several other (fundamental) rights and laws, the right to data protection's origin story contains some dark elements. As a matter of fact, early tabulation technology—underlying modern-day 'data processing'—contributed in no small part to the Holocaust.[8] So-called '*Hollerith* machines'[9] constituted a vital component in the vast data-processing apparatus of Nazi-Germany.[10] Stasi practices in the German Democratic Republic over the course of the following decades have certainly amplified concerns related to the processing of personal data.[11]

Undoubtedly, these bleak examples were in the back of people's minds when confronted with the incessant and exponential growth of data capturing, storing, and processing technologies.[12] In the 1960s—when computers really began to enter daily administration—these technological developments began to affect individuals more palpably.[13] It is in this context that the post-Westin notion of 'privacy as control over personal information' emerged.[14] Interestingly—from today's point of view—the first legislative discussions and activities concerning computers, privacy, and control over personal information can be traced back to the USA.[15]

[8] David Martin Luebke and Sybil Milton, 'Locating the Victim: An Overview of Census-Taking, Tabulation Technology and Persecution in Nazi Germany' (1994) 16 IEEE Annals of the History of Computing 25.

[9] Named after its inventor (and IBM founder) Herman Hollerith, who is generally regarded as the father of automated data processing.

[10] See NB: Edwin Black, *IBM and the Holocaust. The Strategic Alliance between Nazi Germany and America's Most Powerful Corporation* (Crown Publishers 2001). The machines being used by the Nazis, were managed by German IBM subsidiary *Dehomag*, the director of which was recorded saying: 'We are recording the individual characteristics of every single member of the nation onto a little card.... We are proud to be able to contribute to such a task, a task that makes available to the physician of our German body-social [ie Adolf Hitler] the material for his examination, so that our physician can determine whether, from the standpoint of the health of the nation, the results calculated in this manner stand in a harmonious, healthy relation to one another, or whether unhealthy conditions must be cured by corrective interventions .... We have firm trust in our physician and will follow his orders blindly, because we know that he will lead our nation toward a great future. Hail to our German people and their leader!' Cited in: Luebke and Milton (n 8) 27.

[11] A telling account of the Stasi's data processing practices can be found in: Timothy Garton Ash, *The File* (Atlantic Books 2009).

For the data protection implications after the fall of the Iron Curtain, see: Angela Kolb, 'Data Protection—Germany: The Creation of Legislation for Data Protection in the New States of the Federal Republic of Germany' (1991) 7 Computer Law & Security Review 123.

[12] Lee A Bygrave, *Data Protection Law: Approaching Its Rationale, Logic and Limits* (Kluwer 2002) 93ff; Lucas Bergkamp, 'EU Data Protection Policy: The Privacy Fallacy: Adverse Effects of Europe's Data Protection Policy in an Information-Driven Economy' (2002) 18 Computer Law & Security Review 31, 36.

[13] Hondius (n 1) 3.

[14] González Fuster, *The Emergence of Personal Data Protection as a Fundamental Right of the EU* (n 1) 48; Alan F Westin, *Privacy and Freedom* (Atheneum 1967).

[15] González Fuster, *The Emergence of Personal Data Protection as a Fundamental Right of the EU* (n 1) 27–36.

These debates served as major sources of inspiration for the first data protection legislations in Europe.

2.1.2 First Nations

HESSE—In light of the previous paragraphs, it may not come as a surprise that the first fully-fledged[16] data protection law in Europe was of German make. More specifically, in October 1970, the federal state of Hesse proclaimed its '*Hessisches Datenschutzgesetz*'.[17] This Act regulated the Land's use of personal information and was primarily put in place to counter what was seen as the 'inherent centralizing power of the machine'.[18] The drafting of the Act was preceded by a thorough study of the US system, where technological developments had prompted legislative action for longer already.[19] Being the first of its kind, the '*Hessisches Datenschutzgesetz*' defined some of the basic themes that would return in later (inter)national data protection legislation. Most notably in this regard are: (a) the negative default rule (data processing always constitutes an interference requiring legitimization); (b) data subject rights (notably access, without the need for motivation); and (c) the omnibus approach (ie a generic, sector-agnostic legislative framework).[20]

SWEDEN—In 1973, Sweden was the first country to enact national data protection legislation.[21] Whereas the '*Hessisches Datenschutzgesetz*' only applied to data processing in the public sector, the Swedish Data Act (*Datalagen*) was the first to apply to private sector use of 'computer techniques'.[22] The initial goal of this legislation though was to prevent undue invasions of individuals' 'personal integrity' and restore 'trust and confidence between the State and citizens'.[23] At the time, Sweden was pioneering the development of registers and automated data banks, where public authorities stored the information of citizens.[24] The country also has

[16] Prior to 1970, data protection(-like) provisions had only appeared incidentally in other legal documents. See: ibid 56ff.

[17] Simply translatable as: the 'Data Protection Act of Hesse'. Hessisches Datenschutzgesetz vom 7 oktober 1970 GVBl II 300-10, published at Wiesbaden, 12 October 1970, in *Gesetz-und Verordnungsblatt für das Land Hessen* [Laws and Regulations Journal], Part I, No 41. Referenced in: ibid.

[18] Local communities were particularly concerned their 'traditional power and influence would shift to the Land [state]'. Herbert Burkert, 'Privacy-Data Protection: A German/European Perspective', *2nd Symposium of the Max Planck Project Group on the Law of Common Goods and the Computer Science and Telecommunications Board of the National Research Council* (1999) 45 <http://www.coll.mpg.de/sites/www/files/text/burkert.pdf> accessed 1 June 2019.

[19] The Hesse legislator paid particular attention to Congressional hearings and reports, such as the one on 'Privacy and the National Data Bank Concept'. Spiros Simitis, 'Privacy—An Endless Debate' (2010) 98 California Law Review 1989, 1995–1996.

[20] Burkert (n 18) 46.

[21] The Data Act (*Datalagen*). Kosta (n 1) 35–36; González Fuster, *The Emergence of Personal Data Protection as a Fundamental Right of the EU* (n 1) 58–59.

[22] Jan Freese, 'The Swedish Data Act' (1973) 4 Current Sweden 3 (reprint). Cited in: Kosta (n 1) footnote 97.

[23] González Fuster, *The Emergence of Personal Data Protection as a Fundamental Right of the EU* (n 1) 58–59.

[24] Lars Ilshammar, 'When Computers Became Dangerous: The Swedish Computer Discourse of the 1960s' (2007) 9 Human IT 6.

one of the most liberal traditions of granting public access to official records.[25] In this 'Transparent Society'[26] *avant la lettre*, private companies could go and copy massive amounts of citizens' data, process, and subsequently market it.[27] A compromise between privacy interests, publicity, and the benefits of computing technology was eventually achieved through the creation of a dedicated data protection act.[28] Overall, the Swedish *Datalagen* was not so much aimed at empowering individuals, rather than simply to 'prevent undue invasions on personal integrity'.[29]

GERMANY—Seven years after Hesse—and meanwhile several other *Länder*—Germany enacted a federal '*Act on Protection Against the Misuse of Personal Data in Data Processing*'.[30] This Act had been in the works since the early 1970s already and was (also) heavily influenced by the writings of American scholars.[31] What was innovative about the federal Act was that—contrary to the state-level legislations—it applied to the private sector as well. One of the key features in this new piece of legislation was the importance given to consent.[32] In its 1983 *population census* case, the German Constitutional Court famously proclaimed the 'right to informational self-determination', which anchored data protection in the German Constitution.[33] The concept of 'informational self-determination' can be described as the legal manifestation of the German view on data protection and has been (and remains) tremendously influential throughout Europe. Informational self-determination not only emphasizes data protection's role in shielding individuals from interference in personal matters, but is also 'a precondition for citizens' unbiased participation in the political processes of the democratic constitutional state'.[34]

FRANCE—France's data protection law was enacted in 1978.[35] It followed a long legislative process, with initial proposals dating back as far as 1970. In 1974, the

[25] Kosta (n 1) 36ff.

[26] David Brin, *The Transparent Society: Will Technology Force Us To Choose Between Privacy And Freedom?* (1st edn, Basic Books 1999). The author pleads for a society with (near) absolute transparency, where even 'the watchers are being watched'.

[27] Ilshammar (n 24) 22. Cited in: Kosta (n 1) 40.

[28] In combination with alterations to existing legislation. See: Ilshammar (n 24) 24ff.

[29] González Fuster, *The Emergence of Personal Data Protection as a Fundamental Right of the EU* (n 1) 70.

[30] *Gesetz zum Schutz vor mißbrauch personenbezogener Daten bei der Datenverarbeitung (Law on protection against the misuse of personal data in data processing) (Bundesdatenschutzgesetz—BDSG) (Federal Data Protection Act) of 27 January 1977, Bundesgesetzblatt (BGBl) 1 S 201.* Cited in: ibid 59–61.

[31] Especially Westin and Miller. Burkert (n 18) 49; González Fuster, *The Emergence of Personal Data Protection as a Fundamental Right of the EU* (n 1) 60.

[32] At the time, consent was the only ground legitimating the processing of personal data, apart from those specifically authorized by law. Kosta (n 1) 49ff; González Fuster, *The Emergence of Personal Data Protection as a Fundamental Right of the EU* (n 1) 60–61.

[33] Gerrit Hornung and Christoph Schnabel, 'Data Protection in Germany I: The Population Census Decision and the Right to Informational Self-Determination' (2009) 25 Computer Law & Security Review.

[34] ibid 86.

[35] *Loi n° 78-17 du 6 janvier 1978 relative à l'informatique, aux fichiers et aux libertés.* (*Loi Informatique et Libertés*)

Commission informatique et libertés was established, with the mandate to devise appropriate (legislative) measures 'for protecting citizens against dangers arising from electronic data processing in the public and private sector'.[36] Its first article clearly established that computers (*l'informatique*) should serve the citizen and may not harm human identity, human rights, privacy (*vie privée*), or individual and public liberties.[37] Indeed, the *Loi Informatique et Libertés* really positioned itself against the loss of humanity (dignity) and reducing individuals to mere numbers in a machine.[38] Importantly, the French law was one of the first to put considerable emphasis on data subject rights (notably the right of access (Arts 34–40), right to rectification (Art 27), and a right to object (Art 38)).[39] Moreover, it also introduced the idea of reinforced protection for particular kinds of personal data (ie sensitive data) and stressed the need for regulating 'automated decision-making'. Though innovative in some parts, the French data protection law is arguably also one of the first examples where a national legislator was significantly influenced by pre-existing legislations and policy developments. In light of this, it can also be situated among the last pioneering data protection legislations in Europe.

2.1.3 International Level

While a critical mass of national legislations was emerging, data protection was also being debated at the international level. Indeed, by the end of the 1970s, there was growing concern that the surfacing of many 'European regulations would be impractical, bureaucratic, and detrimental to the free flow of information'.[40] Organizations such as the Council of Europe (CoE) and the Organisation for Economic Co-operation and Development (OECD) played an important role in facilitating the cross-fertilization and interoperability of data protection frameworks at the state-level.[41] Both of these organizations adopted data protection instruments themselves in 1980 (OECD '*Guidelines on the Protection of Privacy and Transborder Flows of Personal Data*')[42] and 1981 (CoE's '*Convention for the Protection of Individuals with regard to Automatic Processing of Personal Data*'[43] or simply: 'Convention 108') respectively.

[36] Hondius (n 1) 34.

[37] *Article 1 of Loi informatique et libertés 1978: 'Elle (l'informatique) ne doit porter atteinte ni à l'identité humaine, ni aux droits de l'homme, ni à la vie privée, ni aux libertés individuelles ou publiques'.* See: André Holleaux, 'La Loi Du 6 Janvier 1978 Sur l'informatique et Les Libertés-I' (1978) 31 la Revue administrative 31; González Fuster, *The Emergence of Personal Data Protection as a Fundamental Right of the EU* (n 1) 64.

[38] Holleaux (n 37) 31–32.

[39] González Fuster, *The Emergence of Personal Data Protection as a Fundamental Right of the EU* (n 1) 70.

[40] Herbert Burkert, 'Institutions of Data Protection—An Attempt at a Functional Explanation of European National Data Protection Laws' (1981) 3 Computer/LJ 167, 169.

[41] Hondius (n 1) 5–6.

[42] OECD, Guidelines on the Protection of Privacy and Transborder Flows of Personal Data (23.09.1980). The Guidelines were updated on 11 July 2013.

[43] Council of Europe, *Convention for the Protection of Individuals with regard to Automatic Processing of Personal Data* (ETS 108) (28.01.1981).

OECD GUIDELINES—The OECD started investigating the issues emerging from the use of computers, electronic databanks and telecoms in the late 1960s already.[44] In 1972, the organization put in place a group specifically dealing with the 'regulation of the processing of information about individuals in automated databases'.[45] One of the key motivations for the OECD to get involved in this debate was the fear for 'data protectionism': nation-states installing barriers to the free flow of data.[46] Influenced by data protection discussions taking place at different (inter) national bodies, the OECD adopted its '*Guidelines on the Protection of Privacy and Transborder Flows of Personal Data*' in 1980.[47] The Guidelines emphasized the importance of reconciling 'fundamental but competing values such as privacy and the free flow of information'.[48] They also further solidified the conception of data protection as a necessary instrument to protect privacy.[49] The Guidelines constitute one of the first documents clearly specifying a duality of goals in data protection regulation: on the one hand to protect privacy, and on the other hand facilitating 'a full exploitation of the potentialities of modern data processing technologies in so far as this is desirable'.[50] Put differently, the OECD Guidelines marked the first time (at this level) that data protection was seen as an instrument reconciling international trade/economic interests with privacy and individual liberties. Both the intrinsic linking of data protection to the right to privacy, as well as the duality of the Guidelines' aims, would considerably influence the Data Protection Directive, adopted 15 years later.

COUNCIL OF EUROPE (ECHR)—The European Convention of Human Rights, adopted in 1950, proclaims '*the right to respect for private and family life*' (Art 8). It is noteworthy that the term 'privacy' is not used once in the Convention (contrary to the Universal Declaration of Human Rights, Art 12)[51] and has consistently been avoided by the European Court of Human Rights (ECtHR).[52] It is only since the late 1960s that Article 8 of the Convention started being referred to as a general

44 Hondius (n 1) 57–59; González Fuster, *The Emergence of Personal Data Protection as a Fundamental Right of the EU* (n 1) 76; Kosta (n 1) 27ff.

45 González Fuster, *The Emergence of Personal Data Protection as a Fundamental Right of the EU* (n 1) 76ff.

46 Michael Kirby, 'The History, Achievement and Future of the 1980 OECD Guidelines on Privacy' (2011) 1 International Data Privacy Law 6, 8; González Fuster, *The Emergence of Personal Data Protection as a Fundamental Right of the EU* (n 1) 77–78.

47 Kirby (n 46).

48 Explanatory Memorandum to the Guidelines.

49 Even though originally intended to be a 'data protection instrument', the eventual text of the OECD Guidelines gives preference to the terminology 'privacy protection', bolstering the entanglement of both concepts. See: González Fuster, *The Emergence of Personal Data Protection as a Fundamental Right of the EU* (n 1) 79.

50 Explanatory Memorandum to the Guidelines.

51 It has been argued that the term 'privacy' was lost in translation from French to English. The French language versions of both the UDHR and ECHR both consistently refer to *vie privée*. See: González Fuster, *The Emergence of Personal Data Protection as a Fundamental Right of the EU* (n 1) 81–82.

52 ibid 82.

right to privacy.[53] Since the mid-1980s, the ECtHR has accorded some level of protection over 'information relating to private life'.[54] In subsequent years, the Court has interpreted Article 8 as 'containing various guarantees to personal autonomy, personal privacy, personal identity, personal integrity, personal development, personal identification and similar concepts linked to the individual notion of personhood'.[55] Notably, there have been several cases involving the erasure of certain information on the basis of privacy grounds (more on this, later).[56] Still, the ECtHR has only recognized a partial level of 'data protection' under Article 8.[57]

Council of Europe (Convention 108)—From the late 1960s onwards already, Article 8 ECHR was considered to offer insufficient safeguards to protect individuals from technological developments.[58] Not coincidentally in parallel to the emerging national data protection frameworks, the Council appointed a Committee of Experts on Human Rights to investigate the impact of technological developments on Article 8 ECHR.[59] Emphasizing the Convention only applies to public authorities, the Committee clarified Article 8 lacks safeguards to tackle 'the issue of computers' between private entities and explained urgent action was needed.[60] Whereas public sector processing was already subject to parliamentary supervision and many specific regulatory frameworks, private sector data processing was not. Private entities could also easily avoid scrutiny in one country by transferring to another.[61] In 1981, these concerns culminated into the

[53] ibid 83; Kosta (n 1) 17–18. Not coincidentally, the timing corresponds with the growing concerns over technological developments that led to the first data protection frameworks mentioned before.

[54] Particularly since its ruling in: *Leander v Sweden* [1987] Series A No 116, App No 9248/81. See: González Fuster, *The Emergence of Personal Data Protection as a Fundamental Right of the EU* (n 1) 96ff; Paul De Hert and Serge Gutwirth, 'Data Protection in the Case Law of Strasbourg and Luxemb urg: Constitutionalisation in Action' in Serge Gutwirth and others (eds), *Reinventing Data Protection?* (Springer Science 2009) 18.

[55] Pieter Van Dijk et al., *Theory and Practice of the European Convention on Human Rights* (4th edn Intersentia, Antwerpen—Oxford 2006) 665. Cited in: Kosta (n 1) 18. Also see: De Hert and Gutwirth (n 54) 18ff.

[56] eg *Von Hannover v Germany* [2004] European Court of Human Rights 59320/00; *Von Hannover v Germany (No2)* [2012] European Court of Human Rights 40660/08 and 60641/08.

[57] De Hert and Gutwirth (n 54) 19; 24ff; European Court of Human Rights—Research Division, 'Internet: Case-Law of the European Court of Human Rights' (European Court of Human Rights 2011) 6–10 <www.echr.coe.int/Documents/Research_report_internet_ENG.pdf> accessed 1 June 2019.

[58] In 1968, for example, the CoE Parliamentary Assembly explained that 'newly developed techniques such as phone-tapping, eavesdropping, surreptitious observation, the illegitimate use of official statistical and similar surveys to obtain private information, and subliminal advertising and propaganda are a threat to the rights and freedoms of individuals and, in particular, to the right to privacy which is protected by Article 8 of the European Convention on Human Rights'. Council of Europe—Parliamentary Assembly, 'Recommendation 509 (1968)—Human Rights and Modern Scientific and Technological Developments'; Council of Europe, 'Recommendation on the Protection of Individuals with Regard to Automatic Processing of Personal Data in the Context of Profiling CM/Rec(2010)13' para 7.

[59] Council of Europe—Parliamentary Assembly, 'Recommendation 509 (1968)—Human Rights and Modern Scientific and Technological Developments', n 8. Also see: Kosta (n 1) 20ff.

[60] Hondius (n 1) 66–67; González Fuster, *The Emergence of Personal Data Protection as a Fundamental Right of the EU* (n 1) 84.

[61] Hondius (n 1) 67.

enactment of a dedicated '*Convention for the Protection of Individuals with regard to Automatic Processing of Personal Data*' (or: Convention 108). This Convention marks the first time the term 'data protection' is used in a legally binding international document.[62] Its focus on *automated* data processing also emphasizes the technological concerns underlying the Convention's rationale. Contrary to the OECD Guidelines' duality of goals—reconciling economic with data protection and privacy considerations—Convention 108's primary purpose is the protection of individuals' data.[63] Similarly to other frameworks, the purpose of data protection in the Convention extends beyond securing the right to privacy, but aims to safeguard respect for every individual's 'rights and fundamental freedoms' more broadly (Article 1). Since its adoption, the Convention has influenced many national data protection frameworks.[64] In May 2018, a modernized version of the Convention was proclaimed.[65]

2.1.4 Data Protection Directive

In 1990, the European Commission issued a proposal for a 'Council Directive concerning the protection of individuals in relation to the processing of personal data'.[66] The Commission pointed out that nine years after the enactment of Convention 108, there were still considerable disparities between Member-State level data protection frameworks.[67] In light of European integration, the Commission's goals in proposing a Data Protection Directive were twofold: (a) 'to protect the fundamental rights of individuals, and in particular the right to privacy'[68] and; (b) 'prevent restrictions to the free flow of personal data between Member States'.[69] This duality of objectives—which can be traced back to the

[62] González Fuster, *The Emergence of Personal Data Protection as a Fundamental Right of the EU* (n 1) 89; 254.

[63] It is recognized, however, that the facilitation of transborder data-flows is also an implicit goal of Convention 108. Kirby (n 46) 8; González Fuster, *The Emergence of Personal Data Protection as a Fundamental Right of the EU* (n 1) 78; 89; European Union Agency for Fundamental Rights (FRA) and Council of Europe, *Handbook on European Data Protection Law* (Publications Office of the European Union 2018) 16 <http://www.coe.int/t/dghl/standardsetting/dataprotection/TPD_documents/Handbook.pdf>.

[64] González Fuster, *The Emergence of Personal Data Protection as a Fundamental Right of the EU* (n 1) 92–94.

[65] Council of Europe, 'Modernisation of the Data Protection "Convention 108"' (May 2018) <https://www.coe.int/en/web/portal/28-january-data-protection-day-factsheet> accessed 22 June 2018.

[66] European Commission, Proposal for a Council Directive concerning the protection of individuals in relation to the processing of personal data 1990 [COM(90)314 final-SYN 287].

[67] Right after the adoption of Convention 108 in 1981, the European Commission had urged Member States to sign and ratify the Convention. Kosta (n 1) 83–85; González Fuster, *The Emergence of Personal Data Protection as a Fundamental Right of the EU* (n 1) 125.

[68] Borrowed from Convention 108. See also: González Fuster, *The Emergence of Personal Data Protection as a Fundamental Right of the EU* (n 1) 156.

[69] Article 1, European Commission Proposal for a Council Directive concerning the protection of individuals in relation to the processing of personal data (n 245). See: González Fuster, *The Emergence of Personal Data Protection as a Fundamental Right of the EU* (n 1) 125–26; 129–30.

OECD Guidelines (and to a lesser extent, Convention 108)[70]—was maintained in the eventual Directive[71] when adopted in 1995.[72] The Directive's second objective is clearly consonant with pre-existing EC (now EU) freedoms such as free movement of goods, services, capital, and persons.[73] Aiming for the 'free flow of data' also signals the economic grounding of EU (data protection) law more broadly. The general idea is that a high level of protection in *all* Member States will nullify any potential objections one might have to the free flow of personal data on the basis of fundamental or human rights.[74] Indeed, with Directive 95/46 a seed was planted that slowly but firmly took root in all EU Member States. For the next two decades national regimes gradually grew towards each other. This progress was in no small part fostered by the Article 29 Working Party (WP29),[75] called into life by the Directive (Article 29). The Working Party regularly issued Opinions,[76] aiming to develop a common understanding and interpretation of key data protection concepts.

Directive 95/46, for the first time harmonized approaches to data protection rules throughout the EU. According to Lynskey, this shared approach (still valid today) has four main characteristics: (a) an omnibus regime;[77] (b) a legitimizing regime;[78] (c) a rights-based regime;[79] (d) with a considerable extraterritorial impact.[80] Indeed, the very wide scope of application constitutes a core feature of EU data protection law (initiated by Directive 95/45).[81] With the aim of protecting individuals 'against *misuse* of personal data',[82] the Directive casts its nets widely, but

[70] Hustinx explains that indeed, '[t]he Directive used Convention 108 as a starting point, but specified it in many respects and also added new elements'. Peter Hustinx, 'Data Protection in the European Union' (2005) 2 Privacy & Informatie 62, 63.

[71] Directive 95/46/EC of the European Parliament and Council of 24 October 1995 on the protection of individuals with regard to the processing of personal data and on the free movement of such data [1995] OJ L281/31. Hereafter referred to as 'Directive 95/46' or 'Data Protection Directive'.

[72] '[B]y mentioning both elements in its opening Article, Directive 95/46/EC reinforced the significance of each, as well as their configuration as rival values.' González Fuster, *The Emergence of Personal Data Protection as a Fundamental Right of the EU* (n 1) 130. De Hert and Gutwirth further explain that '[t]he Commission itself conceded that although both objectives are said to be equally important, in legal terms the economic perspective and internal market arguments prevailed.' De Hert and Gutwirth (n 54) 8.

[73] González Fuster, *The Emergence of Personal Data Protection as a Fundamental Right of the EU* (n 1) 135.

[74] Orla Lynskey, *The Foundations of EU Data Protection Law* (OUP 2016) 8.

[75] Since the entry into force of the General Data Protection Regulation on 25 May 2018, this entity is now called the European Data Protection Board (EDPB). In this book, WP29 will be used to refer to all documents/activities of this body dating back from before 25 May 2018.

[76] http://ec.europa.eu/justice/data-protection/article-29/index_en.htm.

[77] Or at least, *aspires* to be one. Lynskey explains that '[w]hile data protection continues to be subject to completely independent oversight, it is inaccurate to suggest that the EU regime is sector-neutral and applies equally to public and private actors' (n 74).

[78] ie processing of personal data requires a justification.

[79] Both meaning 'rights-conferring', as well as 'giving expression to a fundamental right'.

[80] Lynskey, *The Foundations of EU Data Protection Law* (n 74) ch 2.

[81] This will become evident in Chapter 3 .

[82] Peter Blume, 'The Inherent Contradictions in Data Protection Law' (2012) 2 International Data Privacy Law 26, 28.

allows for some flexibility in its application.[83] A broadly defined scope of application ensures (or at least, aims to ensure) the future-proof nature of the data protection framework. Flexibility in its application is required to ensure the law can efficiently be applied to new and/or unforeseen processing operations impacting data protection. Mayer-Schönberger, finally, identifies two main approaches to data protection in the Directive (and other frameworks of its 'generation').[84] On the one hand it sets out certain non-negotiable principles that need to be complied with. On the other hand, it strengthens the bargaining position of individuals by granting them certain data protection rights.[85] It is all of these attributes that have contributed to making Directive 95/46 the *de facto* 'international data protection metric against which data protection adequacy is measured'.[86]

2.1.5 Charter of Fundamental Rights

The *Charter of Fundamental Rights of the European Union* (the Charter) was signed into law in December 2000.[87] It was the legislator's intention to consolidate the patchwork of pre-existing fundamental rights[88] and firmly establish them into EU primary law.[89] It was considered necessary to complement and reinforce this catalogue of fundamental rights with a specific EU list of rights in light of contemporary needs.[90] The fundamental right to the protection of personal data is one such right (Art 8 of the Charter).[91] Even though several Member States had related rights in place already, there was no 'common constitutional tradition in EU member States in relation to the right to the protection of personal data'.[92] Little is known on the motivation for its inclusion in the Charter, which is generally ascribed to the importance of safeguarding rights and freedoms (the right to privacy in particular)

[83] See, inter alia: *Lindqvist* [2003] Court of Justice of the European Union C-101/01 [83]. Here the CJEU explains that Directive 95/46's provisions 'are necessarily relatively general since [they have] to be applied to a large number of very different situations. […] the directive quite properly includes rules with a degree of flexibility'.

[84] Viktor Mayer-Schönberger, 'Generational Development of Data Protection in Europe' in Philip E Agre and Marc Rotenberg (eds), *Technology and Privacy: The New Landscape* (MIT Press 1998) 232–35.

[85] As will appear later on (subsection 2.3.3), this dichotomy bears strong resemblances to the (slightly broader) distinction between 'protective' and 'empowerment' approaches to (data protection) regulation.

[86] Paul De Hert and Vagelis Papakonstantinou, 'The Proposed Data Protection Regulation Replacing Directive 95/46/EC: A Sound System for the Protection of Individuals' (2012) 28 Computer Law & Security Review 130, 131.

[87] The Charter did not became legally binding until 2009.

[88] The most important sources being the ECHR and national constitutional traditions. See: González Fuster, *The Emergence of Personal Data Protection as a Fundamental Right of the EU* (n 1) 170–74.

[89] ibid 206.

[90] ibid.

[91] Also: Article 16 TFEU. For an official list of sources Article 8 Charter was based on, see: European Parliament, Council and Commission, 'Explanations Relating to the Charter of Fundamental Rights (2007/C 303/02)' <http://eur-lex.europa.eu> accessed 1 June 2019.

[92] González Fuster, *The Emergence of Personal Data Protection as a Fundamental Right of the EU* (n 1) 185; Gloria González Fuster and Raphaël Gellert, 'The Fundamental Right of Data Protection in the European Union: In Search of an Uncharted Right' (2012) 26 International Review of Law, Computers & Technology 73, 75.

against the backdrop of technological progress.[93,94] However, dedicating a separate provision to this right liberated the protection of personal data from being a mere subservient right to a fully-fledged *sui generis* right in itself, contrary to the framing of the right in Convention 108 and Directive 95/46 for example.[95] It was the first time for a supranational legal instrument to put in place a right to data protection (Art 8) next to the right to privacy (Art 7). Importantly, the right to the protection of personal data in Article 8 is not absolute and needs to be interpreted in light of article 52 Charter (see Chapter 5).[96]

Codifying the protection of personal data into the Charter,[97] Article 8 consists of three paragraphs. The first paragraph sets out in a general manner that '[e]veryone has the right to the protection of personal data concerning him or her'. Whereas this first paragraph comprises the actual fundamental right to data protection, the second and third paragraphs specify the conditions for limitations of the right (to be read in conjunction with Article 52(1) of the Charter).[98] The third paragraph foresees independent oversight in order to ensure compliance. The second paragraph enumerates the key principles of data protection: fair processing; purpose specification; legitimate basis; right of access and to correction. It is worth noting at this stage that a right to erasure (or rather 'to delete') had almost made it into this list. The suggestion to include such a right—made by the European Group on Ethics in Science and New Technologies (Commissioned by EC President Prodi)—was still considered until the last few months leading up the final text but evidently did not make the final cut.[99]

2.1.6 CJEU Takes the Limelight

Even before Directive 95/46 was adopted, the Court of Justice of the European Union had already decided on cases concerning the processing of personal information. Yet, it had never (overtly) connected 'the regulation of the processing of

[93] And the threats these developments create for fundamental rights and freedoms. See, for example: Comité des Sages, *For a Europe of Civic and Social Rights* (Office for Official Publications of the European Communities 1996) 15–16; 41; European Group on Ethics in Science and New Technologies, 'Citizens Rights and New Technologies: A European Challenge. Report on the Charter on Fundamental Rights Related to Technological Innovation as Requested by President Prodi (Reproduced in: Draft Charter of Fundamental Rights of the European Union, CHARTE 4370/00)' (European Commission 2000) CONTRIB 233 26–27; González Fuster, *The Emergence of Personal Data Protection as a Fundamental Right of the EU* (n 1) 190.

[94] González Fuster, *The Emergence of Personal Data Protection as a Fundamental Right of the EU* (n 1) 206.

[95] ibid 199.

[96] Fuster and Gellert (n 92) 75.

[97] Some authors have argued the qualification of 'data protection' as a fundamental right in the Charter is a mere codification of pre-existing conceptions of the right. Especially: De Hert and Gutwirth (n 54) 7; Lynskey, *The Foundations of EU Data Protection Law* (n 74) 38–40.

[98] González Fuster explains that the last two paragraphs of Article 8 can either be understood as they are here (as detailing the requirements applicable to limitations of the right), or as further substantiating the content of the first paragraph. González Fuster, *The Emergence of Personal Data Protection as a Fundamental Right of the EU* (n 1) 203.

[99] European Group on Ethics in Science and New Technologies (n 273) 26; González Fuster, *The Emergence of Personal Data Protection as a Fundamental Right of the EU* (n 1) 194–95.

information about individuals to any right to privacy, to respect for private life, or to personal data protection.'[100] In the period between the enactment of the Directive (1995) and the entering into force of the Charter (2009), the CJEU only ruled in a handful of data protection related cases. This phase was characterized by the Court—as well as WP29[101]—cautiously tracing the scope and extent of the data protection framework.[102]

In the 'first data protection case' to come before the Court (2003),[103] it was ruled that the provisions in Directive 95/46 must 'be interpreted in the light of fundamental rights'.[104] In the same ruling, the CJEU confusingly linked the proportionality principle in Directive 95/46 to Article 8(2) of the ECHR (regulating interferences with the general right to privacy).[105] From 2003 onwards, the CJEU has interpreted the Directive's material,[106] personal,[107] and territorial[108] scope of application in a notoriously broad manner.[109] The Court also got the opportunity to interpret specific, more substantial provisions such as legitimacy of processing;[110] the right of access;[111] and the rights to object and erase.[112]

[100] González Fuster, *The Emergence of Personal Data Protection as a Fundamental Right of the EU* (n 1) 131–32.

[101] Especially through the publication of 'Opinions' on how to interpret certain key principles in the data protection framework. See notably http://ec.europa.eu/justice/data-protection/article-29/index_en.htm. Since the entry into force of the GDPR on 25 May 2018, this body is now called the European Data Protection Board (EDPB).

[102] On the potential reasons for this cautiousness (eg uncertainty about the 'competence issue' regarding enforcing v legislating fundamental rights), see inter alia: Claus Dieter Classen, 'Case C-139/01 *Österreichischer Rundfunk and Others*: Case-note' (2004) 41 *Common Market Law Review* 1377, 1381. Referred to in: Lynskey, *The Foundations of EU Data Protection Law* (n 74) 60–61.

[103] ibid 51–52.

[104] Not further specifying what fundamental rights exactly. *Österreichischer Rundfunk and others* [2003] Court of Justice of the European Union Joined Cases C-465/00, C-138/01 and C-139/01 [68].

[105] Rendering the relationship between the right to data protection and the right to privacy more complex and unclear. See notably: (n 74) 90–91; Fuster and Gellert (n 92) 79–80.

[106] Especially: *Tietosuojavaltuutettu v Satakunnan Markkinapörssi & Satamedia* [2008] Court of Justice of the European Union C-73/07; *Google Spain SL, Google Inc v Agencia Española de Protección de Datos (AEPD), Mario Costeja González* [2014] Court of Justice of the European Union C-131/12, para 21ff. More recently, the Court has somewhat narrowed the scope of what constitutes 'personal data': *YS v Minister voor Immigratie, Integratie en Asiel and Minister voor Immigratie, Integratie en Asiel (C-372/12) v M and S* [2014] Court of Justice of the European Union Joined Cases C-141/12 and C-372/12; Lynskey, *The Foundations of EU Data Protection Law* (n 74) 123.

[107] Especially: *Google Spain* (n 106) para 32ff. On the so-called 'household exemption', see: *Lindqvist* (n 83); *František Ryneš v Úřad pro ochranu osobních údajů* [2014] Court of Justice of the European Union C-212/13; Brendan Van Alsenoy, 'The Evolving Role of the Individual Under EU Data Protection Law' (KU Leuven—CiTiP 2015) Working Paper 23 <http://papers.ssrn.com/abstract=2641680> accessed 1 June 2019.

[108] Especially: *Google Spain* (n 106) para 42ff; *Weltimmo* [2015] Court of Justice of the European Union C-230/14; Brendan Van Alsenoy and Marieke Koekkoek, 'Internet and Jurisdiction after Google Spain: The Extraterritorial Reach of the "Right to Be Delisted"' (2015) 5 International Data Privacy Law 105.

[109] '[T]he Directive [is] to be applied as a general rule and its non-application should represent an exception to be considered narrowly.' In: De Hert and Gutwirth (n 54) 30–31.

[110] *Österreichischer Rundfunk and others* (n 104); *Huber v Germany* [2008] Court of Justice of the European Union C-524/06.

[111] *College van burgemeester en wethouders van Rotterdam v MEE Rijkeboer* [2009] Court of Justice of the European Union C-553/07.

[112] *Google Spain* (n 106) para 62ff.

It is only *after* the Charter became legally binding in 2010, that the CJEU finally seemed confident enough (as to its competence) to explicitly refer to Article 8 on the protection of personal data.[113] The first time the CJEU did so, was partly due to a national court explicitly referring to Article 8—and thus forcing the CJEU's hand—in a 2010 request for preliminary ruling.[114] Still quite reticent, the CJEU highlighted the close connection between Article 8 and the right to privacy in Article 7 Charter (§47).[115,116] This resulted in an awkward—and criticized—hybrid between Articles 7 and 8 of the Charter *and* Article 8 ECHR: the '*Right to respect for private life with regard to the processing of personal data*'.[117,118] Interestingly enough, it took two copyright infringement cases for the CJEU to refer to Article 8 Charter in a straightforward manner and independently from Article 7 Charter.[119] It was also only in 2011 that the CJEU for the first time unambiguously declared that the purpose of Directive 95/46 is to ensure the right to protection of personal data (indirectly referring to Article 8 Charter).[120] Even though the CJEU has repeatedly specified this right is not absolute,[121] its case law has reinforced the right to data protection ever since. Particularly since 2014, the CJEU has taken a particularly strong stance in a growing number of high-profile cases,[122] clearly

[113] With one insignificant exception (*Promusicae v Telefónica* [2008] Court of Justice of the European Union C-275/06) where the CJEU recognized the existence of Article 8 Charter, immediately after which it connected it with the general right to privacy. See: Fuster and Gellert (n 92) 76. See also: Christopher Docksey, 'Four Fundamental Rights: Finding the Balance' (2016) 6 International Data Privacy Law 195, 198.

[114] *Volker und Markus Schecke GbR and Hartmut Eifert v Land Hessen* [2010] Court of Justice of the European Union Joined Cases C-92/09 and C-93/09.

[115] ibid.

[116] Fuster and Gellert (n 92) 77.

[117] Grand Chamber, Joined Cases Volker und Markus Schecke GbR and Hartmut Eifert v Land Hessen, InfoCuria, 52 (Court of Justice of the EU 2010) echoed in: *Joined ASNEF and FECEMD Cases* [2011] Court of Justice of the European Union Joined Cases C-468/10 and C-469/10 [42].

[118] Fuster and Gellert (n 92); González Fuster, *The Emergence of Personal Data Protection as a Fundamental Right of the EU* (n 1) 234ff.

[119] *Scarlet Extended v Sabam* [2011] Court of Justice of the European Union C-70/10; *SABAM v Netlog* [2012] Court of Justice of the European Union C-360/10. Cited in: González Fuster, *The Emergence of Personal Data Protection as a Fundamental Right of the EU* (n 1) 236–39.

[120] *Deutsche Telekom AG v Bundesrepublik Deutschland* [2011] Court of Justice of the European Union C-543/09 [49–50]. In its pre-Lisbon Treaty case law, the Court still argued data protection's purpose was the protection of individuals' *privacy*. Fuster and Gellert, 'The Fundamental Right of Data Protection in the European Union', 76, referring to: *Promusicae v Telefónica* (n 113); *Satamedia* (n 106); *College van burgemeester en wethouders van Rotterdam v MEE Rijkeboer* (n 111).

[121] Especially: *Volker und Markus Schecke GbR and Hartmut Eifert v Land Hessen* (n 294) para 48; *Deutsche Telekom AG v Bundesrepublik Deutschland* (n 120) para 51.

[122] Especially: *Digital Rights Ireland Ltd* [2014] Court of Justice of the European Union Joined Cases C-293/12 and C-594/12 invalidating the Data Retention Directive (2006/24/EC); *Google Spain* (n 106) proclaiming a so-called right to be delisted; *Maximillian Schrems v Data Protection Commissioner* [2015] Court of Justice of the European Union C-362/14 invalidating the EU-US Safe Harbor Agreement.

establishing data protection as a fundamental pillar in today's information society.[123]

2.1.7 General Data Protection Regulation

SECONDARY LEGISLATION—Throughout the 2000s, the European Commission issued several communications reporting on Directive 95/46's implementation.[124] By the beginning of the 2010's, the Commission made clear its intentions to revise the legal framework for data protection in the EU.[125] The Lisbon Treaty already laid down the mandate to do so in Article 16 of the Treaty on the Functioning of the European Union (TFEU).[126] On 25 January 2012, the European Commission proposed a comprehensive reform package, notably including the General Data Protection Regulation.[127] Driven *inter alia* by the need for more legal certainty and harmonization in the internal market in light of technological change,[128] the Regulation gives shape to the—still fresh—fundamental right to data protection in the Charter.[129] The proposal marked a departure from the intrinsic link between data protection and privacy, still central in Directive 95/46.[130] Not only did a stand-alone fundamental right to data protection (Article 8 Charter) emerge in the meantime, the GDPR was also explicitly positioned as safeguarding much more than simply one or two Charter provisions. Indeed, as will appear later in this chapter, the GDPR is a legal instrument that protects *all* rights and freedoms that

[123] Gloria González Fuster, 'Beyond the GDPR, Above the GDPR' (*Internet Policy Review*, 30 November 2015) <http://policyreview.info/articles/news/beyond-gdpr-above-gdpr/385> accessed 1 June 2019.

[124] Article 33 of Directive 95/46 requires such regular reporting. See: González Fuster, *The Emergence of Personal Data Protection as a Fundamental Right of the EU* (n 1) 240ff.

[125] European Commission, 'Communication from the Commission to the European Parliament, the Council, the European Economic and Social Committee and the Committee of the Regions A Comprehensive Approach on Personal Data Protection in the European Union' (2010) COM(2010) 609 final.

[126] This dedicated mandate to legislate liberated data protection rules from internal market objectives and reinvigorated its link with fundamental rights protection. See: González Fuster, *The Emergence of Personal Data Protection as a Fundamental Right of the EU* (n 1) 230–34; Lynskey, *The Foundations of EU Data Protection Law* (n 74) ch 3. See more generally: Hielke Hijmans, *The European Union as Guardian of Internet Privacy: The Story of Art 16 TFEU* (Springer 2016).

[127] '[S]etting out a general EU framework for data protection' but also a 'Directive on protecting personal data processed for the purposes of prevention, detection, investigation or prosecution of criminal offences and related judicial activities.' European Commission, 'Press Release: Commission Proposes a Comprehensive Reform of Data Protection Rules to Increase Users' Control of Their Data and to Cut Costs for Businesses' <http://europa.eu/rapid/press-release_IP-12-46_en.htm?locale=en> accessed 1 June 2019. The choice for two separate legal instruments has been criticized for being schematic and artificial. See De Hert and Papakonstantinou (n 86) 132.

[128] European Data Protection Supervisor, 'Opinion of the European Data Protection Supervisor (EDPS) on the Data Protection Reform Package' 2–3 <www.edps.europa.eu/EDPSWEB/webdav/site/mySite/shared/Documents/Consultation/Opinions/2012/12-03-07_EDPS_Reform_package_EN.pdf> accessed 1 June 2019.

[129] As well as Article 16 TFEU. For a full account see (references) of the process leading up to the European Commission's proposal, see: González Fuster, *The Emergence of Personal Data Protection as a Fundamental Right of the EU* (n 1) 240ff.

[130] ibid 5; 242ff.

are affected by data processing.[131] Even though the GDPR protects the right to the protection personal data *in particular* (Art. 1(2)), it should not be confused with Article 8 Charter, neither in scope or mission (see amply Sections 2.2.2 and 2.3.1). Put very briefly, Article 8 Charter is a fundamental right with a singular and independent goal (ie control), whereas the GDPR is a secondary piece of legislation aimed at ensuring a responsible and fair data processing ecosystem.

STRONG EMPHASIS ON DATA SUBJECT RIGHTS—The GDPR has elaborated on two things which are particularly relevant in the context of this book;[132] data subject rights and freedom of expression. As to the former, one of the three key problems the European Commission identified in its evaluation of the EU data protection framework prior to 2012, related to the growing '[d]ifficulties for individuals to stay in control of their personal data'.[133] Citing several examples and surveys, the Commission explained that it is often very difficult, or even impossible, to exercise one's data subject rights effectively.[134] Unsurprisingly, therefore, one of the key goals put forward by the GDPR Proposal, related to 'strengthening and detailing the rights of data subjects'.[135] With data protection having achieved fundamental right status, it has become crucial to ensure effective, credible, and easily accessible tools are available to validate that right.[136] In a free and democratic society,

[131] For example: 'Freedom of thought, freedom of expression, freedom of assembly and association, but also the freedom to conduct a business will not be exercised fully by all citizens in an environment where the individual feels that each of her or his moves, acts, expressions and transaction is subject to scrutiny by others trying to control him or her.' European Commission, 'Commission Staff Working Paper: Impact Assessment Accompanying the Proposals for General Data Protection Regulation and Directive on Data Protection in Police and Judicial Matters' (European Commission 2012) Commission Staff working Paper SEC (2012) 30.

[132] Obviously, the GDPR contained many more important new characteristics which are not, or only tangentially, relevant to this book's main focus (eg principle of accountability, the stronger position accorded to data protection authorities and the threat of high pecuniary penalties). For more, see inter alia: De Hert and Papakonstantinou (n 86); Christopher Kuner, 'The European Commission's Proposed Data Protection Regulation: A Copernican Revolution in European Data Protection Law' (2012) 11 Privacy & Security Law Report 15.

[133] When the European Commission considers a legislative proposal that is expected to have a considerable (economic, social, or other) impact, it is customary to have an impact assessment prepared. As part of this assessment, a public consultation is organized. European Commission, 'Impact Assessment (Explanation)' <http://ec.europa.eu/smart-regulation/impact/index_en.htm> accessed 1 June 2019 in particular page 21ff. The other two related to (a) legal fragmentation resulting in legal uncertainty, inconsistent enforcement, and barriers for business; and (b) gaps and inconsistences in data protection in the field of police and judicial matters. See: European Commission, 'Commission Staff Working Paper: Impact Assessment Accompanying the Proposals for General Data Protection Regulation and Directive on Data Protection in Police and Judicial Matters' (n 30).

A 2015 Eurobarometer on data protection underlined the lack of control over personal data is still a prominent general concern among EU citizens. European Commission, 'Special Eurobarometer: Data Protection' (European Commission 2015) 431.

[134] The Commission highlighted in particular difficulties relating to (a) access one's own data; (b) having one's own data deleted; (c) withdraw and transfer one's personal data from an application or service; and (d) access effective remedies.

[135] '... and the obligations of those who process and determine the processing of personal data.' Recital 9, still present in the final version of the GDPR.

[136] Crucially, and as will be explained later on, this does not mean the data subject rights in the GDPR are to be equated to Article 8 Charter. Data subject rights are merely tools that *can* be used to achieve Article 8 Charter protection, but are not *necessary* in themselves.

the Commission explains, 'the individual must have reassurance that fundamental rights are respected'.[137] The Regulation has sharpened the requirements for consent as a legitimate ground for processing[138] and dedicates a chapter (including 11 lengthy articles) specifically to data subject rights. The introduction of two separate provisions on the right to erasure (Art 17) and the right to data portability (Article 20) further confirm the aim of strengthening the individual's position as much as possible.[139] Whether or not these rights can/will achieve their desired purpose is more controversial[140] and will be analysed in the following sections and chapters.

Heightened Attention to Freedom of Expression—The exponential rise of 'Web 2.0' has amplified the potential for clashes between freedom of expression and data protection online. Article 9 in Directive 95/46, aimed at tackling the conflict between these two rights, has been criticized for inadequately/insufficiently safeguarding freedom of expression interests.[141] It is not surprising, therefore, that the Regulation's drafters paid more attention to this conflict.[142] Several recitals emphasize the need to reconcile data protection rules with the fundamental right to freedom of expression. Article 17 on the right to erasure even contains an explicit exemption clause for situations where the 'processing of personal data is necessary for exercising the right of freedom of expression and information'. Article 23(1)i GDPR allows Member States to restrict the scope of data subject rights in the name of freedom of expression (subject to certain conditions), and Article 85 GDPR contains a general provision aiming to reconcile both fundamental rights. Even though in the proposed draft it was still phrased quite narrowly, after amendments, the provision now is much broader than the one in Directive 95/46.[143] Conflicts

137 European Commission, 'Commission Staff Working Paper: Impact Assessment Accompanying the Proposals for General Data Protection Regulation and Directive on Data Protection in Police and Judicial Matters' (n 131) 30.

138 Colette Cuijpers, Nadezhda Purtova, and Eleni Kosta, 'Data Protection Reform and the Internet: The Draft Data Protection Regulation' in Andrej Savin and Jan Trzaskowski (eds), *Research Handbook on EU Internet Law* (Edward Elgar Publishing 2014) 5–6

139 De Hert and Papakonstantinou (n 86) 136–37.

140 Bert-Jaap Koops, 'The Trouble with European Data Protection Law' (2014) 4 International Data Privacy Law 250, 252.; Blume, 'The Inherent Contradictions in Data Protection Law' (n 82) 6.

141 In particular because the provision had a seemingly narrow scope (solely for journalistic purposes or the purpose of artistic or literary expression) and left it up to Member States to devise exemptions or derogations (leading to considerable fragmentation). See, inter alia: David Erdos, 'From the Scylla of Restriction to the Charybdis of Licence? Exploring the Scope of the "Special Purposes" Freedom of Expression Shield in European Data Protection' (2015) 52 Common Market Law Review 119; David Erdos, 'Confused? Analysing the Scope of Freedom of Speech Protection Vis-à-Vis European Data Protection' (Oxford University 2012) 48/2012 <http://papers.ssrn.com/abstract=2119187> accessed 1 June 2019. More on this in Part III.

142 The European Commission's evaluation of Directive 95/46's implementation also brought to light issues related to the Directive's attempt at reconciling data protection with freedom of expression. European Commission, 'Commission Staff Working Paper: Impact Assessment Accompanying the Proposals for General Data Protection Regulation and Directive on Data Protection in Police and Judicial Matters' (n 131) Annex 2, page 23ff.

143 The initial proposal very much resembled the wording of the Directive, leading even the European Data Protection Supervisor to plead for a substantive opening up of the provision. European Data Protection Supervisor, 'Opinion of the European Data Protection Supervisor (EDPS) on the Data Protection Reform Package' (EDPS 2016) Opinion 8/2016 3 46–47 <https://secure.edps.europa.

involving information freedoms, as triggered by the right to erasure, will be discussed in detail in Chapter 6.

2.2 Rationale of the Fundamental Right to Data Protection in Article 8 of the Charter

The stated objective of the Charter as a whole is the reaffirmation and strengthening of the protection of fundamental rights 'in the light of changes in society, social progress and scientific and technological developments'.[144] How and why exactly the right to the protection of personal data contributes to this objective is not specified.[145] As the historical context in the previous section made clear, the rationale behind data protection has been debated for decades already. Justification(s) for data protection may take different shapes depending on one's perspective, though *control*—interpreted broadly—is considered its central tenet here.[146] This book does not call into question the merits of having data protection as a standalone fundamental right, but instead takes it as a given. Even more, it actively recognizes the importance of this fundamental right status, as will become clear in the following pages. But, before looking at how control constitutes the main rationale for the fundamental right to data protection, this section will first briefly elaborate on the reason explaining the right's urgency.

2.2.1 Power Asymmetries

Gatekeepers—It is widely acknowledged that the information society environment is dominated by power asymmetries. Chapter 1 (introductory chapter, Section 2.2, paragraphs 27 to 49) already explained how information and control (over data) asymmetries precipitate power asymmetries online.[147] Exactly trying to qualify these asymmetries in legal terms does not seem to be as easy as it might

eu/EDPSWEB/webdav/site/mySite/shared/Documents/EDPS/Events/16-09-23_BigData_opinion_EN.pdf> accessed 1 June 2019.

144 Preamble to the Charter.

145 Though the explanations to the Charter refer to other legal instruments that inspired the inclusion of Article 8: Especially Article 16 TFEU; Directive 95/46; Article 8 ECHR; and Convention 108. European Parliament, Council, and Commission (n 271).

146 It would go beyond the scope of this book to dissect the rationale of the fundamental right to data protection in full. Especially because it is such a contested notion, still very much in motion. For a more elaborate discussion on the matter, see the extensive analyses in: Bygrave (n 12); Paul Bernal, *Internet Privacy Rights: Rights to Protect Autonomy* (CUP 2014); González Fuster, *The Emergence of Personal Data Protection as a Fundamental Right of the EU* (n 1); Lynskey, *The Foundations of EU Data Protection Law* (n 74); Hijmans, *The EU as Guardian of Internet Privacy* (n 126).

147 NEMITZ identifies four relevant sources of power, which can be summarized as (a) money; (b) control over the infrastructure of public discourse; (c) (personal) data business; and (d) domination of the development and systems integration into usable AI services. Paul Nemitz, 'No Reason for AI and GAFAM to Escape Democratic Oversight' (2019) 11 The Progressive Post 50.

appear however. Competition law—the go-to framework for dealing with *market* power—has already proven to be particularly ill-equipped to tackle important issues stemming from power asymmetries online.[148] Unsatisfied with existing legal definitions, Lynskey proposes her own framing. She does so by tweaking Laidlaw's 'internet information gatekeeper' or IIG, which is an entity that 'because of the role it takes on, the type of business it does, or the technology with which it works, or a combination thereof, has the capacity to impact democracy in a way traditionally reserved for public institutions'.[149] Lynskey adds to this two caveats: Firstly, the scope should not be limited to actions that 'influence democratic culture', but should also entail actions by IIGs that may hinder individual autonomy or dignity. Secondly, it is not just control over information flows that matter, but also control over access to individuals. In sum, this functional approach focuses on gatekeepers' 'role in controlling the flow and accessibility of information and structuring the digital environment'.[150]

VIGNETTES—It is Lynskey's understanding of IIGs that also underlies the notion of power asymmetries in this book. Indeed, it is clear how each of the vignettes as set out in the Introduction, would qualify within her conceptualization of gatekeeper. *Uber* actively exploits its gatekeeper position in order to induce behavioural modification, which (due to its size) may in turn have spill-over effects on a city's traffic-control for example. *Facebook* and *Google* effectively control the information (from news, to social interactions and media) the majority of internet users consume, but also control access to those consumers (mainly for targeting ads). The capacity for behavioural modification (eg economic and political nudging) of smart assistants such as *Apple*'s Siri, finally, is disconcerting.

Whether it is access to information or access to individuals, what these gatekeepers control generally takes the form of (computing) *data*. As a result, their activities will commonly affect the fundamental right to data protection in Article 8 Charter. This is not surprising. Information and power asymmetries have been central to data protection rules from the very start.[151] Even more so, data protection

[148] Frank Pasquale, 'Privacy, Antitrust, and Power' (2013) 20 George Mason Law Review 1009, 1015; Angela Daly, *Private Power, Online Information Flows and EU Law: Mind the Gap* (Hart 2016); Angela Daly, *Private Power, Online Information Flows and EU Law: Mind the Gap* (Hart 2016); Orla Lynskey, 'Regulating "Platform Power"' (LSE 2017) Working Paper 1/2017 19ff <https://papers.ssrn.com/abstract=2921021> accessed 1 June 2019.

[149] Emily Laidlaw, 'A Framework for Identifying Internet Information Gatekeepers' (2010) 24 International Review of Law, Computers & Technology 263, 268.

[150] 'This echoes Zuboff's claim that if "power was once identified with the ownership of the means of production, it is now identified with the ownership of the means of behavioural modification".' Lynskey, 'Regulating "Platform Power"' (n 148) 10–11. Referring to: Shoshana Zuboff, 'Big Other: Surveillance Capitalism and the Prospects of an Information Civilization' (2015) 30 Journal of Information Technology 75 82.

[151] Serge Gutwirth, 'De Toepassing van Het Finaliteitsbeginsel van de Privacywet van 8 December 1992 Tot Bescherming van de Persoonlijke Levenssfeer Ten Opzichte van de Verwerking van Persoonsgegevens' [The Application of the Purpose Specification Principle in the Belgian Data Protection Act of 8 December 1992] (1993) 1993 Tijdschrift voor Privaatrecht—TPR 1424; Antoinette Rouvroy and Yves Poullet, 'The Right to Informational Self-Determination and the Value

emerged from 'a perception of a dangerous loss of control and lack of awareness suffered by citizens due to the advent of computerisation'.[152] The exponential growth of power asymmetries is characterized by two catalysts in particular: technology and commercialization. It is worth, therefore, expanding briefly on both of these elements, as they will play a central role throughout the rest of this book.

a) Technology

Data protection rules are a reaction to technological developments.[153] As a matter of fact, the German term *Datenschutz* from which the notion 'data protection' derives,[154] was conceived to specifically designate information being processed by computers.[155] For the purposes here, however, an important precision should be made. Rather than the emergence of information technology per se, it is the power asymmetries enabled and amplified by technology,[156] that explain the emergence of data protection rules.[157] Indeed, information technology exponentially increases the scope and scale of these asymmetries,[158] leaving the 'captured' increasingly at the mercy of the 'capturers'.[159] Put differently, information technology

of Self-Development: Reassessing the Importance of Privacy for Democracy' in Serge Gutwirth and others (eds), *Reinventing Data Protection?* (Springer Netherlands 2009) 68 <http://link.springer.com/10.1007/978-1-4020-9498-9> accessed 1 June 2019; AG Opinion in: *Rīgas satiksme* [2017] Court of Justice of the European Union C-13/16 [95].

[152] Gloria González Fuster, 'How Uninformed Is the Average Data Subject? A Quest for Benchmarks in EU Personal Data Protection' [2014] IDP. Revista de Internet, Derecho y Política 94. See in this regard also: Synthesis Report by Hans Peter Gassmann and G Russel Pipe (OECD Secretariat): *Policy Issues in Data Protection and Privacy: Concepts and Perspectives: Proceedings of the OECD Seminar, 24th to 26th June 1974* (Paris: Organisation for Economic Co-operation and Development 1976) 14; Hondius (n 1) 59–60.

[153] Hondius (n 1) 18; Burkert (n 40); Colin J Bennett, *Regulating Privacy: Data Protection and Public Policy in Europe and the United States* (Cornell UP 1992) 3ff; Comité des Sages (n 93) 15–16; 41; Mayer-Schönberger (n 84); Bygrave (n 12) 93ff; Ilshammar (n 24); Simitis (n 19) 1995; González Fuster, *The Emergence of Personal Data Protection as a Fundamental Right of the EU* (n 1) 190; 264.

[154] First coined in the Hessian Data Protection Act, or '*Datenschutzgesetz*'. See NB: Kosta (n 1) 45–47.

[155] Hondius (n 1) 84; González Fuster, *The Emergence of Personal Data Protection as a Fundamental Right of the EU* (n 1) 57.

[156] International Commission of Jurists, 'The Protection of Privacy' (1972) XXIV International Social Science Journal 413, 427–28; 'Privacy, Privatisation and Self-Determination', in John Young and Christopher GA Bryant, *Privacy* (Wiley 1978) 62; Solove, 'A Taxonomy of Privacy' (n 287) 506; Helen Nissenbaum, *Privacy in Context: Technology, Policy, and the Integrity of Social Life* (Stanford UP 2009)43.

Also see: Recital 4 Directive 95/46.

[157] Burkert (n 40) 170; Gutwirth, 'De Toepassing van Het Finaliteitsbeginsel van de Privacywet' (n 151) 1424ff; Peter Blume, 'The Data Subject' (2015) 1 European Data Protection Law Review 258, 258. In order to get a sense of anxieties relating to the emergence of information technology in 1970's France, see: Simon Nora and Alain Minc, *L'informatisation de la société: rapport a M. le President de la Republique* (La Documentation française 1978).

[158] González Fuster, *The Emergence of Personal Data Protection as a Fundamental Right of the EU* (n 1) 40ff.

[159] See in this regard, eg International Commission of Jurists (n 156) 428–29. Similarly, see: Explanatory Report to: Council of Europe—Committee of Ministers, 'Resolution (73) 22 on the Protection of the Privacy of Individuals vis-à-vis Electronic Data Banks in the Private Sector' para 3 <https://rm.coe.int/CoERMPublicCommonSearchServices/DisplayDCTMContent?documentId=0900001680502830>. The Article 29 Working Party also explains that modern technology enables

allows the construction of what Cohen refers to as architectures of control; 'configurations that define in a highly granular fashion ranges of permitted conduct'.[160] The more society operates through a digital spectrum, the more important Lessig's *Code = Law* becomes. To put it yet differently, when every interaction is mediated through technology, the architect of that technology has considerable power over its users. Many of these architects are private actors, driven by economic interests, rather than the values and norms of a liberal democracy.

b) Privatization and Commercialization

Public v Private Power—Originally, technology-fuelled power asymmetries primarily played out between individuals and public authorities.[161] At least until several decades ago, the nation state was the dominant actor in society in many ways. Unsurprisingly, they were the first to adopt large-scale information technology infrastructures (even if with the help of corporations).[162] Right after two world wars and with the Iron Curtain still up, concerns over government use of increasingly powerful technologies to collect, process and share citizens' information naturally grew.[163] But, a multitude of factors—notably including ceaseless technological/economic progress, globalization, and more generally, the rise of neo-liberalism—have resulted in corporations substituting the state (or at least rising to the same level) when it comes to today's information asymmetries[164,165] Importantly, corporations are not traditionally subject to the same checks and balances (eg democratic oversight) as states are. Indeed, they often invoke an arsenal of legal (eg trade secrecy, IP rights) and practical (eg burdensome interactions) hurdles reinforcing—and preventing to counter—information power asymmetries.[166]

large imbalances, regardless of the monopolistic/dominant position of the company-controller. Article 29 Working Party, 'Opinion 03/2013 on Purpose Limitation' (Article 29 Working Party 2013) WP 03/2013 46 <http://ec.europa.eu/justice/article-29/documentation> accessed 1 June 2019.

160 Julie E Cohen, *Configuring the Networked Self: Law, Code, and the Play of Everyday Practice* (Yale UP 2012) ch 7.

161 Hondius (n 1) 23.

162 See notably IBM's collaboration with the Nazis in: Black (n 10).

163 Mayer-Schönberger (n 84); Kirby (n 16) 9; Kosta (n 1) 12–13. Even when also applicable to private actors, data protection rules were initially still mostly targeted at preventing government misuse of (private sector) data. See: Holleaux (n 37) 35; Bergkamp (n 12) 36.

164 Gutwirth, 'De Toepassing van Het Finaliteitsbeginsel van de Privacywet' (n 151) 1419–20; Eleni Frantziou, 'The Horizontal Effect of the Charter of Fundamental Rights of the EU: Rediscovering the Reasons for Horizontality' (2015) 21 European Law Journal 657, 674–75.

165 In practice, there are also many different forms of public-private partnerships, which may be harder to qualify and are also outside the scope of this book. For more on the blurring of corporate and bureaucratic power, see for example: Michael D Birnhack and Niva Elkin-Koren, 'The Invisible Handshake: The Reemergence of the State in the Digital Environment' (2003) 8 Virginia Journal of Law and Technology 57; Lawrence Quill, *Secrets and Democracy from Arcana Imperii to Wikileaks* (Palgrave Macmillan 2014) 109.

166 This will also appear from the empirical research on compliance with data subject rights in Part III. See also: Hildebrandt and Gutwirth, LSTS Response to the Non-Paper on 'Data Collection, Targeting and Profiling of Consumers for Commercial Purposes in Online Environments Brussels, 10th May, 2009'. Cited in: Paul De Hert, 'Consumer Protection and Personal Data Protection' (Data

They are not driven by the same goals often attributed to states such as general (social) welfare, nor are they similarly bound by national borders.[167] In light of all this, it seems increasingly hard to maintain the traditional distinction in fundamental human rights law, between 'vertical' and 'horizontal' relationships.[168]

Scholarship on Corporate Information/Power Asymmetries—There is a growing body of multi-disciplinary research, aimed at qualifying the nature, scope, and effects of powerful economic actors online. There is Laidlaw's definition of Internet Information Gatekeepers mentioned before, aimed at highlighting the impact on human rights in particular. Graef explores the role of market power over data from a competition law perspective, in particular focusing on the essential facilities doctrine.[169] Wu takes a more policy oriented perspective and pleads for a constitutional approach to constrain and divide power stemming from control over information.[170] Gräf assesses the impact of automated profiling on individual freedom,[171] through the lens of Pettit's 'liberty as non-domination'.[172] It is also worth referring to Fuch's Marxist analysis of value extraction through data processing[173] and Arvidsson's comparison of Facebook's data processing operations to the logic of derivatives in the financial sector.[174] Zuboff famously categorized the contemporary information economy as surveillance capitalism; a 'new form of information capitalism [that] aims to predict and modify human behavior as a means to produce revenue and market control'.[175] This theory builds on previous critiques such as 'digital labour'[176] and 'economic surveillance',[177] and is also

Protection Conference (organised by the European commission as part of its open consultation), 20 May 2009) <http://ec.europa.eu/justice/newsroom/data-protection/events/090519_en.htm>. See also: Lynskey, 'Regulating "Platform Power"' (n 148) 18.

[167] See for example: Ian Kerr, Valerie Steeves, and Carole Lucock (eds), *Lessons from the Identity Trail Anonymity, Privacy, and Identity in a Networked Society* (OUP 2009) 9–10.

[168] Gutwirth, 'De Toepassing van Het Finaliteitsbeginsel van de Privacywet' (n 151) 1425–27.

[169] Graef (n 148).

[170] Specifically, he argues for a separations principle, requiring major functions and layers in the information economy to remain under separate control. See: Tim Wu, *The Master Switch* (Atlantic Books 2011) ch 21.

[171] Eike Gräf, 'When Automated Profiling Threatens Our Freedom: A Neo-Republican Perspective' (2017) 3 European Data Protection Law Review 441.

[172] According to Pettit, 'someone has dominating power over another, someone dominates or subjugates another, to the extent that: (1) they have the capacity to interfere; (2) on an arbitrary basis; (3) in certain choices that the other is in a position to make'. Philip Pettit, *Republicanism: A Theory of Freedom and Government* (Clarendon Press 2002) 52; see subsection 2.2.2.b).

[173] Christian Fuchs, *Social Media: A Critical Introduction* (Sage 2014) 14.

[174] Adam Arvidsson, 'Facebook and Finance: On the Social Logic of the Derivative' (2016) 33 Theory, Culture & Society 3.

[175] Zuboff, 'Big Other' (n 150) 75.

[176] ie the idea that people are not paying online services financially, but through value-extraction from their data. See: Trebor Scholz, *Digital Labor: The Internet as Playground and Factory* (Routledge 2013); Daly (n 148) 20.

[177] Marisol Sandoval, 'A Critical Empirical Case Study of Consumer Surveillance on Web 2.0' in Christian Fuchs and others (eds), *Internet and Surveillance: The Challenges of Web 2. 0 and Social Media* (Routledge 2012).

related to the work of Cohen, who critiques narratives focusing too much on the economics of data power.[178] The least that can be concluded from this burgeoning field of research is that the dramatic expansion (and centralization)[179] of corporate power in the information economy, challenges fundamental values, norms, and rights.[180] The right to data protection is one such right, particularly at risk in this brave new world.

c) *Out of Control*

CONTROL-ASYMMETRY OVER DATA—Recall the Uber vignette, described in Chapter 1. In contrast to a 'traditional taxi company' its control over drivers does not (yet) take the form of an employment contract (even if *de facto* the relationship could be qualified as such). Instead, Uber effectively controls drivers' behaviour through data-driven psychological inducements. The company's 'actual' employees include 'hundreds of social scientists and data scientists, experimenting with video game techniques, graphics and noncash rewards of little value that can prod drivers into working longer and harder — and sometimes at hours and locations that are less lucrative for them'.[181] This revelation—akin to the Facebook vignette on emotion contagion and political manipulation—illustrates how information technology and centralized commercial power significantly impact individual autonomy.[182] Indeed, control over personal data implies power over (groups of) individuals, especially when combined with control over individuals' environment and lived experiences.[183] The relevant asymmetries are not simply about who has access to the most information, but rather who has the most (actionable) knowledge inferred from that information.[184] As appears from the data deluge

178 See notably: Julie E Cohen, 'The Biopolitical Public Domain: The Legal Construction of the Surveillance Economy' (2017) 31 Philosophy & Technology.

179 A number of centripetal forces (eg network effect, lock-in, etc) have resulted in the centralization of information power into a handful of actors. For more, see: Graef (n 148).

180 Mikkel Flyverbom, Ronald Deibert, and Dirk Matten, 'The Governance of Digital Technology, Big Data, and the Internet: New Roles and Responsibilities for Business' [2017] Business & Society 6.

181 Noam Scheiber, 'How Uber Uses Psychological Tricks to Push Its Drivers' Buttons' *New York Times* (2 April 2017) <www.nytimes.com/interactive/2017/04/02/technology/uber-drivers-psychological-tricks.html> accessed 1 June 2019.

182 'Measures that initially may have been designed to describe behavior can easily be used to judge and control it.' Wendy Nelson Espeland and Mitchell L Stevens, 'A Sociology of Quantification' (2008) 49 European Journal of Sociology 414. See also: Shoshana Zuboff, 'Google as a Fortune Teller: The Secrets of Surveillance Capitalism' *Frankfurter Allgemeine Zeitung* (5 March 2016) <http://www.faz.net/aktuell/feuilleton/debatten/the-digital-debate/shoshana-zuboff-secrets-of-surveillance-capitalism-14103616-p2.html?printPagedArticle=true#pageIndex_2> accessed 1 June 2019; Martin Moore, 'Tech Giants and Civic Power' (King's College (Policy Institute) 2016) <www.kcl.ac.uk/sspp/policy-institute/CMCP/Tech-Giants-and-Civic-Power.pdf>.

183 William Bogard, 'Welcome to the Society of Control: The Simulation of Surveillance Revisited' in Richard Victor Ericson and Kevin D Haggerty (eds), *The New Politics of Surveillance and Visibility* (University of Toronto Press 2006) 60; Titus Stahl, 'Indiscriminate Mass Surveillance and the Public Sphere' (2016) 18 Ethics and Information Technology 33, 35–36.

184 Mireille Hildebrandt, 'The Dawn of a Critical Transparency Right for the Profiling Era' *Digital Enlightenment Yearbook 2012* (IOS Press 2012) 49 <https://works.bepress.com/mireille_hildebrandt/40> accessed 1 June 2019.

trends described in the Introduction, datafication effectively creates 'measurable types' which can then be modulated by those in control over the data, in pursuit of their own interests. This is also referred to as 'computational politics'[185] or 'algorithmic governmentality'.[186,187]

Asymmetries' Impact—In light of the trends described before, the scale of ensuing power asymmetries has increased dramatically.[188] The notion of 'power'—for the purposes of this book and vastly simplified—is understood as the ability to control individuals. Most relevant here, power asymmetries are composed of information asymmetries and (data) control asymmetries. The former referring to both the distribution of (personal) data as well as knowledge about the respective operations and ecosystem more broadly. The latter referring to the actual ability to manipulate (personal) data. Having said all that, power asymmetries of course have many more significant characteristics and manifestations (eg political economic power) that will interact with how it is understood here. Apart from the many concrete ways in which they may negatively affect individuals (eg price discrimination, employment opportunities) and society at large (eg shaping democratic debate), power asymmetries as such are inherently problematic from a fundamental human rights perspective. Against this backdrop, the right to data protection's main goal is to reign in disproportionate power and ensure control is not usurped, so as to safeguard individual autonomy, freedom, and human dignity.

2.2.2 Individual Control over Personal Data

Placing Control at the Centre of the Right to Data Protection—Several normative values are often said to underlie the fundamental right to data protection: autonomy, informational self-determination, balance of powers, integrity, and dignity.[189] Within the Charter, the right to data protection is framed as a *freedom* (Title II of the Charter) and significantly does *not* hinge on a notion

[185] Zeynep Tufekci, 'Engineering the Public: Big Data, Surveillance and Computational Politics' (2014) 19 First Monday <http://firstmonday.org/ojs/index.php/fm/article/view/4901> accessed 1 June 2019.

[186] Antoinette Rouvroy, 'The End(s) of Critique: Data-Behaviourism vs. Due-Process' in Mireille Hildebrandt and Katja de Vries, *Privacy, Due Process and the Computational Turn: The Philosophy of Law Meets the Philosophy of technology* (Routledge 2013); Antoinette Rouvroy, '"Of Data and Men": Fundamental Rights and Freedoms in a World of Big Data' (Council of Europe 2016) T-PD-BUR(2015)09REV <www.coe.int/t/dghl/standardsetting/DataProtection/TPD_documents/T-PD-BUR(2015)09REV_Big%20Data%20report_A%20%20Rouvroy_Final_EN.pdf> accessed 1 June 2019.

[187] John Cheney-Lippold, *We Are Data: Algorithms and the Making of Our Digital Selves* (New York UP 2017) ch 2: Control.

[188] See generally in this regard: Cheney-Lippold (n 187). More specifically in the consumer context, see: Eliza Mik, 'The Erosion of Autonomy in Online Consumer Transactions' (2016) 8 Law, Innovation and Technology 1.

[189] And more. See: Paul De Hert and Serge Gutwirth, 'Data Protection in the Case Law of Strasbourg and Luxemburg: Constitutionalisation in Action' in Serge Gutwirth and others (eds), *Reinventing Data Protection?* (Springer Science 2009) 5; Lynskey, *The Foundations of EU Data Protection Law* (n 74) 210ff.

of harm (in whatever shape or form).[190,191] This is important as it demonstrates that the right does not (merely) occupy a protective role, safeguarding individuals' interests and ensuring fair processing, but a more proactive empowerment role too. As explained by Lynskey, 'there is a general interest in conferring control over personal data to individuals even in the absence of tangible or intangible harm. [. . .] harms are not a prerequisite for the recognition of control as an aspect of EU data protection law; individual control is a liberal objective which is pursued for liberal aims'.[192] This 'control' component also constituted a predominant narrative in the leading up to the adoption of (Article 8 in) the Charter.[193] Indeed, when reporting on the draft Charter in 2000, the European Group of Ethics in Science and New Technologies explicitly linked the right to data protection to informational self-determination and considered it to refer to identity, autonomy, and an 'active' right to information.[194]

Control as an Independent Core of the Right to Data Protection—*Control* over one's personal data not only constitutes a central tenet of the right to data protection,[195] it constitutes its essence.[196] A minimum level of control over one's personal data can be deemed a prerequisite for ensuring core values in the EU such as autonomy, freedom, and human dignity.[197] In light of data processing pervading every aspect of modern life, the right to data protection is also permanently on the line. Control, in this context, is not limited to individuals' ability to manage their data, but more broadly as an infrastructure that regulates disproportionate power in an attempt at safeguarding the aforementioned values. Article 8 in the Charter is not an 'instrumental' right, merely at the service of other fundamental rights and freedoms. At least not beyond the extent to which all Charter provisions

[190] Nadezhda Purtova, *Property Rights in Personal Data: A European Perspective*, vol 24 (Kluwer Law International 2012) 44; Lynskey, *The Foundations of EU Data Protection Law* (n 74) 192ff; Yvonne McDermott, 'Conceptualising the Right to Data Protection in an Era of Big Data' (2017) 4 Big Data & Society 2053951716686994, 2. The CJEU also confirmed that simply processing personal data, as a general rule, already affects Article 8(1) in the Charter. See: *Michael Schwarz v Stadt Bochum* [2013] Court of Justice of the European Union C-291/12.

[191] Which is not to say, of course, that it does not protect against harm stemming from data processing. For some illustrations, see: Wolfie Christl, 'How Companies Use Personal Data Against People' (*Cracked Labs* 2017) <http://crackedlabs.org/dl/CrackedLabs_Christl_DataAgainstPeople.pdf> accessed 1 June 2019); Frederike Kaltheuner and Elettra Bietti, 'Data Is Power: Towards Additional Guidance on Profiling and Automated Decision-Making in the GDPR' (2018) 2 Journal of Information Rights, Policy and Practice <https://jirpp.winchesteruniversitypress.org/articles/abstract/10.21039/irpandp.v2i2.45/> accessed 11 February 2018.

[192] Lynskey, *The Foundations of EU Data Protection Law* (n 74) 195–96.

[193] González Fuster, *The Emergence of Personal Data Protection as a Fundamental Right of the EU* (n 1) 194ff.

[194] European Group on Ethics in Science and New Technologies (n 273) 26–27.

[195] See Lynskey, *The Foundations of EU Data Protection Law* (n 74) 11.

[196] Damian Clifford and Jef Ausloos, 'Data Protection and the Role of Fairness' (2018) 37 Yearbook of European Law 130; European Group on Ethics in Science and New Technologies (n 33) 45.

[197] Stefano tà, 'Data Protection as a Fundamental Right' in Serge Gutwirth and others (eds), *Reinventing Data Protection?* (Springer 2009) 80 <http://link.springer.com/10.1007/978-1-4020-9498-9> accessed 1 June 2019.

interact and support each other.[198] The right to data protection in Article 8 represents an independent core value in today's information society. Indeed, mass-scale data processing and the power asymmetries it precipitates raise unique concerns which cannot be reduced to for example 'privacy' (Art 7 Charter) or 'non-discrimination' (Art 21) violations.[199] This has been confirmed by the CJEU, *inter alia* in its *Google Spain* ruling, where the ability to control one's personal data, and the responsibilities in function of such control, were approached independently from a potential infringement of the right to privacy.[200]

ARCHITECTURES OF CONTROL *FOR*, NOT AGAINST, INDIVIDUALS—The fundamental right to data protection purports to install an 'architecture of control' in function of data subjects.[201] The need for this right grew out of power asymmetries as facilitated by technology that have emerged since the first half of the 20th century.[202] In other words, data protection requires a reconfiguration of existing architectures of control (described by Cohen as structures unilaterally exercising power over individuals),[203] so as to ensure data subjects maintain a level of control over their personal data throughout its lifetime. Such control, Lynskey explains, 'strengthens the hand of the individual when faced with power and information asymmetries and, second, it proactively promotes the individuals' personality rights which are threatened by personal data processing'.[204] The concept of informational self-determination captures this notion of control as the essence of Article 8 in the Charter to a large extent.

a) *Informational Self-Determination*

BACKGROUND—Called into life by the German constitutional Court (*Bundesverfassungsgericht*) in the 1983 'Population Census' case,[205] the right of informational self-determination (*Recht auf informationelle Selbstbestimmung*) has been very influential in the development of European data protection law.[206]

[198] See in this regard, for example: McDermott (n 190) 2.

[199] Lynskey, *The Foundations of EU Data Protection Law* (n 74) 131ff; 144–46; Christopher Docksey, 'Articles 7 and 8 of the EU Charter: Two Distinct Fundamental Rights' in Alain Grosjean (ed), *Enjeux européens et mondiaux de la protection des données personnelles: Ouvrage de synthèse* (Primento Digital Publishing 2016) 74–75; Zuboff, 'Google as a Fortune Teller' (n 182).

[200] *Google Spain* (n 106); Lynskey, *The Foundations of EU Data Protection Law* (n 74) 149.

[201] Lynskey, *The Foundations of EU Data Protection Law* (n 74).

[202] Norman Lindop, *Report of the Committee on Data Protection, Chairman: Norman Lindop* (HMSO 1978) paras 2.10–11; Gutwirth, 'De Toepassing van Het Finaliteitsbeginsel van de Privacywet' (n 151) 1419; Lynskey, *The Foundations of EU Data Protection Law* (n 74) 213.

[203] Cohen, *Configuring the Networked Self* (n 160) ch 7.

[204] Orla Lynskey, 'Deconstructing Data Protection: The "Added-Value" of a Right to Data Protection in the EU Legal Order' (2014) 63(3) International & Comparative Law Quarterly 569, 573–74.

[205] *Volkszaehlungsurteil* [1983] BVerfGE BvR 209/83.

[206] Kosta (n 1) 51ff; References in: Brendan Van Alsenoy, Eleni Kosta, and Jos Dumortier, 'Privacy Notices versus Informational Self-Determination: Minding the Gap' (2013) 28 International Review of Law, Computers & Technology 185, 4. Lynskey explains the importance of the concept should not be overstated either, as it would not be desirable to 'impose the values of one Member State onto the Union as a whole.' Lynskey, *The Foundations of EU Data Protection Law* (n 74) 178–79.

The underlying principle of the right to informational self-determination is *control* over one's data. More specifically, the ability for the individual to 'decide for him/herself which personal information is to be disclosed in his/her social environment'.[207] This 'individual decisional power' has been described as 'a dimension of the free development of personality according to which subjects need to have the capacity to decide autonomously and take free decisions'.[208] The right has been considered critical in order to ensure other values such as personal development, dignity, and democracy.[209] In light of this, the right is not just important from an individual point of view, but also from the perspective of the individual's participation in society.[210]

Countering Critics—Some have denounced the fact that informational self-determination would constitute an underlying rationale—let alone the 'essence'—of the right to data protection. Among the most prominent critics, Hijmans,[211] Kranenborg,[212] and Docksey[213] all wrote in different publications that the concept of informational self-determination hinges on *ex ante* consent and therefore is narrower than the right to data protection. It is noteworthy that all of these authors only refer to each other to make this point.[214] The only other source that is referred to is a paper and speech given by their former employer, ex-European Data Protection Supervisor Peter Hustinx.[215] In this paper, the

[207] Hornung and Schnabel (n 33) 87.

[208] González Fuster, *The Emergence of Personal Data Protection as a Fundamental Right of the EU* (n 1) 177.

[209] Yves Poullet and Thierry Léonard, 'Les libertés comme fondement de la protection des données nominatives' in François Rigaux, *La vie privée: une liberté parmi les autres?* (Larcier 1992) 234; Hornung and Schnabel (n 33); Rouvroy and Poullet (n 151); González Fuster, *The Emergence of Personal Data Protection as a Fundamental Right of the EU* (n 1) 177.

[210] González Fuster, *The Emergence of Personal Data Protection as a Fundamental Right of the EU* (n 1) 177.

[211] Hijmans, *The EU as Guardian of Internet Privacy* (n 126) 54ff.

[212] Herke Kranenborg, 'Protection of Personal Data' in Steve Peers and others (eds), *The EU Charter of Fundamental Rights: A Commentary* (Hart 2014) 229 <https://www.bloomsburycollections.com/book/the-eu-charter-of-fundamental-rights-a-commentary/>.

[213] Docksey (n 199) 79.

[214] It should be said that Hijmans also makes the argument more broadly that *control* cannot be the essence of Article 8 Charter, because this would imply Article 6(1) of the GDPR would be in violation of Article 52(1) Charter. Article 6(1) GDPR foresees several lawful grounds for processing that are palpably outside of the control of the data subject, but depend on *necessity* for compliance with a legal obligation or protection of vital interests, for example. If data can be lawfully collected and processed outside of the data subject's initial power, Hijmans claims, how can control constitute the *essence* of the fundamental right to data protection. This argument is erratic, as it is nonsensical to look at specific provisions in the GDPR in isolation. Also, and as will appear later on in this book, control can still be exercised *ex post*, notably through data subject rights. As a whole therefore, the GDPR does respect the 'control' *essence* of the right to data protection in light of Article 52(1) Charter. See: Clifford and Ausloos (n 196) 17ff.

[215] Peter Hustinx, 'EU Data Protection Law: The Review of Directive 95/46 EC and the Proposed General Data Protection Regulation' <https://secure.edps.europa.eu/EDPSWEB/webdav/site/mySite/shared/Documents/EDPS/Publications/Speeches/2014/14-09-15_Article_EUI_EN.pdf>. Speech of P Hustinx (EDPS) of 10 May 2012, 'The EU Data Protection Reform: New Fundamental Rights Guarantees' 4. As referred to in: Kranenborg (n 212) n 31.

latter indeed states that following the approach of the German Constitutional Court, 'any processing of personal data is in principle regarded as an interference with the right to informational self-determination, unless the data subject has consented'.[216] This remark not only misconceptualizes the concept of control itself, but also misreads the underlying 'Population Census' case. First of all, the *Bundesverfassungsgericht* does not limit the concept of control to consent only. Indeed, it explicitly recognizes that control extends beyond merely deciding when data is disclosed but also continues throughout its further use. Secondly, and related to this, Hustinx's remark is emblematic of a very persistent misunderstanding about how 'control' (over data) manifests itself. It is not because personal data can be processed without obtaining the data subject's consent first, that the latter has no 'control' anymore. Neither does it mean that control cannot be the essence of Article 8. Consent is not a sine qua non for being 'in control' over one's personal data. Instead, control is a fluid concept that can manifest itself to different degrees at different stages of the data processing lifecycle.

Positive and Negative Control—As will amply appear throughout this book, individual control can be constrained, promoted, or even substituted depending on the circumstances at hand. What is important to keep in mind is that control as the essence of the right to data protection should be interpreted broadly. This can either have a positive or negative dimension. In a positive sense, control implies a proactive manifestation of individual autonomy, for example through consenting, objecting, or requesting the erasure of one's data. The negative dimension of control implies data subjects are protected from their autonomy being subverted and/or being under disproportionate power of those who process their data.[217] In other words, it is not because the right to data protection contains components installing protective measures (not requiring proactive action to be taken by the data subject), that control cannot be its essence. The right to data protection simply implies an environment that fosters and safeguards the ability of individuals to maintain some level of control—positive or negative—over their personal data throughout its lifecycle.[218]

[216] Hustinx, 'EU Data Protection Law: The Review of Directive 95/46 EC and the Proposed General Data Protection Regulation' (n 215) 8.

[217] These two facets of control were also recognized by the European Commission when announcing its plan for revising the data protection framework. 'Two important preconditions for ensuring that individuals enjoy a high level of data protection are the limitation of the data controllers' processing in relation to its purposes (principle of data minimisation) and the retention by data subjects of an effective control over their own data.' European Commission, 'Communication from the Commission to the European Parliament, the Council, the European Economic and Social Committee and the Committee of the Regions A Comprehensive Approach on Personal Data Protection in the European Union' (n 125) 7.

[218] See in this regard also: Cécile de Terwangne, *The Right to Be Forgotten and the Informational Autonomy in the Digital Environment* (Publications Office 2013) 4ff<http://dx.publications.europa.eu/10.2788/54562> accessed 1 June 2019.

Informational Self-Determination as Part of the Essence—In light of the above, informational self-determination—ie the ability to remain master over one's datafied/digital representation[219]—can still be seen as a key component of Article 8's essence.[220] The 'protection of personal data' ensures individuals maintain final control over what happens with their data, without necessitating their active and constant engagement.[221] It safeguards the *capacity* to decide the faith of one's personal data.[222] As will appear later-on, this separates the right to data protection from the GDPR, the latter pursuing a much wider array of values, rights, and interests. For now, it is useful to still dig one level deeper into the rationale of the right to data protection itself. Informational self-determination, after all, could be seen as a derivation from a more abstract, fundamental value: autonomy.

b) *Autonomy*

What is Autonomy?—Individual autonomy is one of the central normative goals (or 'values')[223] pursued by the fundamental right to data protection, and underlying the Charter as a whole.[224] In today's information society, data protection can be described as a necessary precondition for ensuring a minimum level of autonomy.[225] Referring to Raz's *Morality of Freedom*,[226] Bernal describes autonomy as the ability to make meaningful choices. Such choices have to be present and the individual 'needs to be given the opportunity to make those choices, appropriately informed and free from coercion, restraint, or excessive or undue influence'.[227] Without autonomy, Bernal continues, people are not really free.[228] Others have associated individual autonomy to other fundamental values such as liberty (positive or negative), dignity, integrity, individuality, independence, responsibility

[219] Hornung and Schnabel (n 33) 86.

[220] Poullet and Léonard (n 209) 233–34; de Terwangne (n 218) 5.

[221] Volker Boehme Neßler, 'Privacy: A Matter of Democracy. Why Democracy Needs Privacy and Data Protection' (2016) 6 International Data Privacy Law 222, 224.

[222] Marion Albers, 'Realizing the Complexity of Data Protection' in Serge Gutwirth, Ronald Leenes, and Paul De Hert (eds), *Reloading Data Protection—Multidisciplinary Insights and Contemporary Challenges* (Springer 2014) 217–20 <http://www.springer.com/law/international/book/978-94-007-7539-8> accessed 1 June 2019.

[223] Autonomy itself can be considered a fundamental value, but not as a 'legal right'. See: Valeria Ferraris, Francesca Bosco, and Elena D'Angelo, 'The Impact of Profiling on Fundamental Rights' (2013) 16 <http://profiling-project.eu/wp-content/uploads/2013/10/PROFILINGproject_WS1_Fundamental_1110.pdf> referring to Rouvroy and Poullet (n 151) 59.

[224] See Hondius (n 1) 2; Jeroen van den Hoven, 'Information Technology, Privacy, and the Protection of Personal Data', *Information Technology and Moral Philosophy* (CUP 2008) 315–19; De Hert and Gutwirth (n 54) 14–15; 24–26; Rouvroy and Poullet (n 151).

[225] Hondius (n 1) 2; Rouvroy and Poullet (n 151); Purtova, *Property Rights in Personal Data* (n 190) 46–47; Julie E Cohen, 'Examined Lives: Informational Privacy and the Subject as Object' (2000) 52 Stanford Law Review 1373, 1423ff.

[226] Joseph Raz, *The Morality of Freedom* (Clarendon Press 1986); Joseph Raz, *From Normativity to Responsibility* (OUP 2011).

[227] Bernal (n 146) 24ff.

[228] ibid 30.

and self-knowledge, self-assertion, critical reflection, and many more.[229] An autonomous person shapes his/her own biography; he/she is the 'author and experimenter of his or her own moral career'.[230]

Free From Coercion—Autonomy is jeopardized when an individual's choices are limited to options defined and/or a context controlled by others.[231] It is threatened (to a lesser or greater extent) whenever others attempt to (in)directly engineer, shape, or influence the individual.[232] As explained by Raz, '[a]utonomy is opposed to a life of coerced choices. It contrasts with a life of no choices, or of drifting through life without ever exercising one's capacity to choose'.[233] The information asymmetry resulting from data gathering, affects the power dynamic between individual and data gatherer.[234] This power asymmetry manifests itself in the ability of the 'watcher' to (in)directly influence the individual based on the information collected.[235] A great illustration of this point is presented in Zarsky's 'autonomy trap'[236] and Lessig's related contemplation: '[w]hen the system seems to know what you want better and earlier than you do, how can you know where these desires really come from?'[237]

Data Protection Safeguards Autonomy—In order to safeguard autonomy in today's information society, one would need what Richards calls *Intellectual Privacy*: 'a zone of protection that guards our ability to make up our minds

[229] See, inter alia: Gerald Dworkin, *The Theory and Practice of Autonomy* (CUP 1988); Rouvroy and Poullet (n 151) notably the many references in footnote 17; Ben Colburn, *Autonomy and Liberalism* (Routledge, Taylor & Francis Group 2010); Kosta (n 1) 130ff.

[230] van den Hoven (n 224) 315; 317.

[231] Gutwirth, 'De Toepassing van Het Finaliteitsbeginsel van de Privacywet' (n 151) 1424; Lynskey, *The Foundations of EU Data Protection Law* (n 74) 212; Mireille Hildebrandt, 'Legal and Technological Normativity: More (and Less) than Twin Sisters' (2008) 12 Techné: Research in Philosophy and Technology 169, 174; Purtova, *Property Rights in Personal Data* (n 190) 205; Sheri B Pan, 'Get to Know Me: Protecting Privacy and Autonomy under Big Data's Penetrating Gaze Notes' (2016) 30 Harvard Journal of Law & Technology (Harvard JOLT) 239.

[232] van den Hoven (n 224) 317.

[233] Raz, *The Morality of Freedom* (n 267) 371.

[234] Serge Gutwirth, *Privacy and the Information Age* (Raf Casert tr, Rowman & Littlefield 2002) 16. Gutwirth explains 'the processing of information about individuals always opens the door to some sense of control'. With this in mind, it is of course not the goal of data protection law, nor the right to data protection, to prevent any kind of data processing whatsoever.

[235] Lynskey, *The Foundations of EU Data Protection Law* (n 74) 212. Referring to: Neil M Richards, 'The Dangers of Surveillance' (2013) 126 Harvard Law Review 1953. Leese offers a perspective from surveillance studies: 'This is essentially the practice that Haggerty and Ericson (2000) later identified as the 'surveillant assemblage' of a digitized era—the underlying mechanism of contemporary surveillance that disassembles individuals into 'dividuals' (Deleuze, 1992) that consist of separate data points, in order to scrutinize, calculate, circulate, and reassemble them for distinct purposes.' In: Matthias Leese, 'The New Profiling: Algorithms, Black Boxes, and the Failure Of Anti-Discriminatory Safeguards in the European Union' (2014) 45 Security Dialogue 494, 500.

[236] '[T]he ability of content providers to influence the opinions and conceptions of individuals by providing them with tailored content based on the provider's agenda and the individual's personal traits.' Tal Z Zarsky, 'Desperately Seeking Solutions: Using Implementation-Based Solutions for the Troubles of Information Privacy in the Age of Data Mining and the Internet Society' (2004) 56 Maine Law Review 13; Zarsky (n 236) 37–40. Referring to Paul M Schwartz, Internet Privacy and the State, 32 CONN L REV 815, 821–28 (2000).

[237] Lawrence Lessig, *Code: Version 2.0* (Basic Books 2006) 220. Also see: Purtova, *Property Rights in Personal Data* (n 190) 50.

freely'.[238] Arguably, the right to data protection strives exactly for this goal. In fact, data protection safeguards individual autonomy on two levels. Firstly, it protects individuals against information-based actions that (in)directly affect them (eg manipulation,[239] targeting,[240] etc). Secondly, it empowers individuals to actively control how, why, and when their data is used.[241] The former protects individuals from their autonomy being (disproportionately) affected, while the latter celebrates autonomy by giving individuals the tools to be autonomous actors in society (see positive and negative control, as explained above). Stefano Rodotà, one of the authors of Article 8 in the Charter, compares the right to data protection to the right to the integrity of the person in Article 3 of the Charter; one protecting individuals' *physical* body, the other protecting their *electronic* body.[242]

AUTONOMY, FREEDOM, AND LIBERTY—In the context of data protection, autonomy is also closely related to liberty and personal freedom.[243] Indeed, autonomy can be 'considered an expression of a constitutionally guaranteed human freedom'.[244] Human freedom and liberty are especially under threat in situations characterized by power asymmetries, not least those being discussed within this book.[245] An interesting interpretation of liberty comes from Pettit, who describes it as freedom from domination, the latter having three cumulative criteria: (a) capacity to interfere; (b) on an arbitrary basis; (c) in certain choices that the other is in a position to make.[246] In other words, '[o]ne agent dominates another if and only if they have a certain power over that other, in particular a power of interference on an arbitrary basis'.[247] This is the case today, with Rouvroy's 'algorithmic

238 Neil Richards, *Intellectual Privacy: Rethinking Civil Liberties in the Digital Age* (OUP 2015) 95. See Westin's work from half a century before: Westin, Alan F. *Privacy and Freedom*. New York: Atheneum. 1967.

239 Lessig, *Code* (n 237) 220; Audrey Watters, 'Pigeons, Operant Conditioning, and Social Control' (*Hack Education*, 15 June 2018) <http://hackeducation.com/2018/06/15/pigeons> accessed 18 June 2018.

240 Frederik Zuiderveen Borgesius, 'Improving Privacy Protection in the Area of Behavioural Targeting' (PhD Thesis, University of Amsterdam 2014) <http://hdl.handle.net/11245/1.434236>.

241 Rouvroy and Poullet explain these two facets as: 'freedom from unreasonable constraints (from the State or from others) in the construction of one's identity and control over (some) aspects of the identity one projects to the world'. In: Rouvroy and Poullet (n 151) 75.

242 Rodotà (n 197) 80.

243 As well as human dignity (which arguably underlies all of the Charter rights and freedoms). ibid 81; European Group on Ethics in Science and New Technologies (n 33) 71–72; McDermott (n 190) 3.

244 Guido Comparato and Hans-W Micklitz, 'Regulated Autonomy between Market Freedoms and Fundamental Rights in the Case Law of the CJEU' in Ulf Bernitz, Xavier Groussot, and Felix Schulyok (eds), *General Principles of EU Law and European Private Law* (Kluwer Law International 2013) 121.

245 Power, here, can be understood as the ability of one agent (eg large ISS providers) to control the behaviour of another agent (eg users). See the many references in: Stahl (n 183) 35–36; Steven Livingston, 'Book Review: Communication Power by Manuel Castells' (2010) 27 Political Communication 471, 474.

246 Pettit (n 172); Sarah Song, 'Multiculturalism' in Edward N Zalta (ed), *The Stanford Encyclopedia of Philosophy* (Spring 2017, Metaphysics Research Lab, Stanford University 2017) <https://plato.stanford.edu/archives/spr2017/entries/multiculturalism/> accessed 18 January 2017; Gräf (n 171) Song.

247 Pettit (n 172) 52 referring to Max Weber (1978) Economy and Society, (ed) Günther Roth and Claus Wittich (Berkeley, CA: University of California Press) and William Connolly (1983), The Terms of Political Discourse (Princeton, NJ: Princeton UP).

governmentality';[248] Cohen's 'architectures of control'[249] or Gürses' 'optimisation systems'[250] for example. As illustrated by the vignettes, it is fair to say that the respective ISS providers at least have some level of 'domination' over individuals affected.[251] Individuals are effectively constrained to the options as presented to them by the ISS providers (see code is law).[252] And as the Facebook and Uber vignettes illustrate, even when different options are available, individuals are increasingly and subliminally pushed into certain directions. This clearly erodes and undermines values such as liberty and autonomy. Despite the very rich body of literature on autonomy and liberty,[253] further exploration would distract too much from this book's overall goal. It is seen here, as a core component of the right to data protection and as a key value in society more broadly.[254]

2.2.3 Summary

This subsection aimed to briefly establish the rationale and core essence of the right to the protection of personal data in Article 8 Charter. It became clear that the right only found its *raison d'être* with the emergence of information technology, enabling (mass-scale) automated data processing.[255] Another catalyst for the increased relevance of the fundamental right to data protection relates to the privatization and commercialization of data processing. Though the latter is not a sine qua non for the right to data protection per se, given its scope and impact on individuals, it does constitute a central component to the right's added value today. This added value is composed of core principles aimed at parrying (negative ramifications of) power asymmetries in every liberal democracy; from human dignity, to freedom and liberty, to autonomy and (informational) self-determination. All of these can be concentrated into one core component, which forms the essence and key rationale of the right to data protection: control over personal data. Control, in this context, should be understood broadly, as an architecture of control designed in function of individuals. Indeed, a narrow interpretation of *control* risks justifying the subversion of autonomy under the guise of

[248] Rouvroy, 'The End(s) of Critique: Data-Behaviourism vs. Due-Process' (n 186); Rouvroy, '"Of Data and Men": Fundamental Rights and Freedoms in a World of Big Data' (n 186).

[249] Cohen, *Configuring the Networked Self* (n 160) ch 7.

[250] Seda Gürses *Data Justice Conference: Keynote Plenary I* <https://cardiff.cloud.panopto.eu/Panopto/Pages/Viewer.aspx?id=547383b2-9d0a-4966-a4aa-a8e50178e2cf> accessed 16 June 2018; Gürses and van Hoboken (n 33); Seda Gürses, Rebekah Overdorf, and Ero Balsa, 'POTs: The Revolution Will Not Be Optimized?' [2018] arXiv:1806.02711 [cs] <http://arxiv.org/abs/1806.02711> accessed 11 June 2018.

[251] See Gräf (n 171).

[252] Lessig, Lawrence. *Code: And Other Laws of Cyberspace*. (New York: Basic Books. 1999).

[253] For further reading (on top of the many references before), see inter alia: John Stuart Mill, *On Liberty* (Dover Publications 2002); Isaiah Berlin and Henry Hardy, *Liberty: Incorporating Four Essays on Liberty* (OUP 2008); Dworkin (n 229); Hildebrandt, 'The Dawn of a Critical Transparency Right for the Profiling Era' (n 184) 46; Kosta (n 1) 130ff.

[254] See in this regard also: Boehme-Neßler (n 221) 228.

[255] See Rodotà (n 197) 80.

empowering individuals.[256] The right to data protection aims to prevent control over personal data from being subsumed in relationships characterized by massive power asymmetries. It purports to do so by ensuring a minimum level of individual control over personal data. Importantly, the right to data protection is not about the protection of data, but about 'the individuals to whom the data refer'.[257]

With *control* as the 'essence' of the right to data protection, any processing of personal data interferes with this right. Therefore, any processing of personal data constitutes a limitation to the right, required to satisfy the conditions contained in Article 8(2) in conjunction with Article 52(1) of the Charter. Enter the GDPR. The GDPR can be seen as a manifestation of Article 52(1), in that it lays down a legal framework to regulate legitimate interferences with fundamental rights and freedoms. Importantly, and as will be made clear later on in this book, the right to data protection should clearly be separated from the GDPR. Article 8 Charter has a singular goal which is ensuring a minimum level of control over personal data (in light of safeguarding core values such as autonomy, liberty, and human freedom). It constitutes a crucial value in and on itself. The GDPR, on the other hand has as its main goal to ensure the protection of *all* interests, fundamental rights and freedoms that are affected in any context where personal data is being processed. Individual control is only one, albeit important, element within the broader GDPR scheme.

2.3 From the Fundamental Right to Data Protection to the General Data Protection Regulation

> The [GDPR] must be regarded as seeking to ensure 'effective and complete protection' of all the fundamental rights and freedoms of natural persons, and actually not just any protection, but 'a high level of protection' of these rights and freedoms.[258]

It has been said before, Article 8 Charter should clearly be differentiated—in scope, reach, and rationale—from the GDPR. Whereas the former is a fundamental freedom with *control* as its essence, the latter is a secondary piece of legislation aimed at safeguarding all Charter provisions whenever personal data is being processed. The core of the GDPR, one might claim, is to ensure a *fair* data processing ecosystem, considerate of all interests, rights, and freedoms at stake.

256 See Woodrow Hartzog, *Privacy's Blueprint: The Battle to Control the Design of New Technologies* (HU Press 2018).

257 Albers (n 222) 222.

258 González Fuster, 'Beyond the GDPR, above the GDPR' (n 303). González Fuster, Gloria. "Beyond the GDPR, above the GDPR." Academic Journal. *Internet Policy Review*, November 30, 2015. http://policyreview.info/articles/news/beyond-gdpr-above-gdpr/385.

Put yet differently, the GDPR recognizes the inevitability—and benefits—of data processing but aims to prevent disproportionate impacts on the individual and society.[259] This is evident throughout the Regulation, which installs strict obligations of fairness and lawfulness on controllers' shoulders, provides individuals with a set of 'micro-rights',[260] and foresees independent oversight throughout. In light of all this, the GDPR creates a legal infrastructure that introduces fairness into informational power asymmetries.[261]

It is worth emphasizing at this stage already that the GDPR's wide prerogative needs to be taken with a grain of salt. In light of the 'datafication of everything', the GDPR risks becoming the 'law of everything'.[262] Be that as it may, in practice, other legal frameworks (or even non-legal alternatives) will be much more adequate to tackle a given situation. Put differently, it is not because a conflict or issue can be expressed in terms of personal data processing, that it *should* be resolved through the GDPR. Even the GDPR itself recognizes this by making explicit references to other laws and requiring/enabling legislators to regulate specific issues in other frameworks (eg Arts 23 and 85). This note of nuance will become more apparent throughout this book.

2.3.1 From Control to Fair Balancing

Separating the Right to Data Protection from the GDPR—Fundamental rights and freedoms each strive individually for a specific core value in society.[263] Looked at in isolation, they each univocally push one particular value, regardless of other rights/freedoms.[264] In that sense, they are quite egotistical, ignoring an overall sense of fairness. Of course, it does not make sense to look at these provisions as silos. They interact in different ways—both supporting and conflicting (with) one another—and jointly pursue a common mission. This requires compatibility and coordination between the individual provisions, which is achieved through modalities as laid down in Articles 8(2)–(3)[265] or Article 52(1) Charter,[266]

[259] In Ferretti's words, data protection law regulates 'an accepted exercise of power'. See (the many references in): Federico Ferretti, 'Data Protection and the Legitimate Interest of Data Controllers: Much Ado about Nothing or the Winter of Rights?' (2014) 51 Common Market Law Review 843, 849.

[260] Christophe Lazaro and Daniel Le Métayer, 'Control over Personal Data: True Remedy or Fairytale?' (2015) 12 SCRIPTed <http://script-ed.org/?p=1927> accessed 1 June 2019.

[261] See in this regard: Lynskey, *The Foundations of EU Data Protection Law* (n 74) 213; Hustinx, 'EU Data Protection Law: The Review of Directive 95/46 EC and the Proposed General Data Protection Regulation' (n 395) 50; Rouvroy and Poullet (n 151) 69; Hondius (n 1) 23 (also referring to the Hesse [35–36] and Swedish [89] Data Protection Acts as specifically aimed at balancing power).

[262] Nadezhda Purtova, 'The Law of Everything. Broad Concept of Personal Data and Overstretched Scope of EU Data Protection Law' (2017) <https://papers.ssrn.com/abstract=3036355> accessed 1 June 2019.

[263] This subsection builds on an argument made in: Clifford and Ausloos (n 196).

[264] Having said that, all provisions strive to achieve the overarching notion or value of human dignity and support one another to some extent.

[265] Laying down the conditions for limitations to the right to data protection as laid down in Article 8(1).

[266] Article 52 concerns the scope and interpretation of rights and principles, and its first paragraph is aimed at delineating the requirements for limitations on the exercise of rights and freedoms in the Charter. These elements will be discussed in more detail in Chapter 5.

and more importantly via secondary law frameworks. The reason for explaining this is because it helps to understand the interaction between the fundamental right to data protection in Article 8 Charter and the GDPR. The essence of Article 8 is *not*, as some have claimed,[267] to install a system of checks and balances instilling a fair data processing environment. Such reasoning confuses Article 8 with the GDPR. Rather, it univocally defends a minimum level of *control* over one's personal data (see Section 2.2.2). The GDPR aims to ensure Article 8 Charter is safeguarded in harmony with other interests, fundamental rights, and freedoms.

GDPR Extends Beyond the Right to Data Protection—The expansive scope of the GDPR is indicative of a broader rationale that extends beyond that of the right to data protection. This was also recognized by the European Commission (EC) when officially announcing it would prepare a reform package. Indeed, the EC specified that the new legal framework would, on the one hand, give high priority to the fundamental right to data protection and on the other hand enhance the internal market dimension associated with the free flow of personal data.[268] In doing so, the EC recognizes the focused nature of the right to data protection, and the fair balancing nature of the secondary law framework. This is also reflected in Article 1(2) GDPR which states that '[t]his Regulation protects fundamental rights and freedoms of natural persons and in particular their right to the protection of personal data'. Recital 4 of the GDPR further specifies this intention and states that,

> [t]he processing of personal data should be designed to serve mankind. The right to the protection of personal data is not an absolute right; it must be considered in relation to its function in society and be balanced against other fundamental rights, in accordance with the principle of proportionality. This Regulation respects all fundamental rights and observes the freedoms and principles recognised in the Charter as enshrined in the Treaties, in particular the respect for private and family life, home and communications, the protection of personal data, freedom of thought, conscience and religion, freedom of expression and information, freedom to conduct a business, the right to an effective remedy and to a fair trial, and cultural, religious and linguistic diversity.

As a consequence, although the framework is designed to protect the fundamental right to data protection 'in particular', this is not the sole right at stake. Indeed, the GDPR as a secondary framework has a more expansive prerogative. As will appear in the following subsection, the Regulation may provide useful tools for

[267] Notably: Hijmans, *The EU as Guardian of Internet Privacy* (n 126) 54–62.

[268] European Commission. *Communication from the Commission to the European Parliament, the Council, the European Economic and Social Committee and the Committee of the Regions A Comprehensive Approach on Personal Data Protection in the European Union*. Brussels, COM(2010)609 final. November 4, 2010.

individuals wishing to safeguard a variety of interests, rights, and freedoms in the face of information power asymmetries, not least including their rights to privacy, freedom of expression, and non-discrimination.

THE GDPR AS AN INFRASTRUCTURE FOR FAIR BALANCING—Safeguarding the right to data protection 'in particular', the GDPR does comprise a number of measures specifically aimed at ensuring *control* (see amply below, Section 2.3.3). It is important, however, not to look at them in isolation, but jointly, as part of the broader system of checks and balances laid down by the GDPR. This is important to stress, as it clarifies why processing personal data on another ground than individuals' consent, does not mean data subjects lose control over their personal data.[269] *Ex post* empowerment measures such as the right to erasure and to object actively safeguard a minimum level of control in situations where *ex ante* control might be lacking. Individually, none of these 'empowerment' measures (eg consent or erasure) is *necessary* to safeguard the essence of Article 8. Put differently, it is possible that some empowerment tools are *not* available, while the individual still maintains a minimum level of 'control' over personal data (hence still safeguarding the *essence* of the right to data protection). Combined, and in light of the GDPR as a whole, they install an infrastructure of fair balancing, aimed at regulating acceptable power over information.[270]

SUMMARY—In sum, fair balancing is entrenched throughout data protection law.[271] Indeed, data protection law 'does not protect us from data processing but from unlawful and/or disproportionate data processing'.[272] The CJEU has made clear that the framework should be interpreted in a way that minimizes conflicts with other fundamental rights and/or general EU law principles.[273] This can also be seen as a necessary corollary of the framework's broad scope and its general rationale (see amply below). Balancing enables the required flexibility when applying data protection law (see Chapter 3 *in fine*). Indeed, as a primarily 'technology-oriented law' the GDPR 'does not contemplate deciding all possible conflicts in advance, each specific law has to provide a mechanism by which different interests can be sufficiently discussed, balanced, and then decided'.[274] Even the provisions within the GDPR specifically aimed at empowering data subjects such as the data subject rights in Chapter III of the Regulation, are more or less perfused with fair

[269] And therefore also annuls the argument that *control* can not constitute the essence of the right to data protection, as claimed by Hijmans, building on Kranenborg, Docksey, and Hustinx (see previous pages, notably subsection 2.2.2.a).

[270] See in this regard: Ferretti (n 259) 849. Referring to: De Hert and Gutwirth (n 54).

[271] See notably Recital 4 GDPR. *Joined ASNEF and FECEMD Cases* (n 117) para 43; *Promusicae v Telefónica* (n 113) para 68.

Also see: Paolo Balboni and others, 'Legitimate Interest of the Data Controller New Data Protection Paradigm: Legitimacy Grounded on Appropriate Protection' (2013) 3 International Data Privacy Law 244.

[272] De Hert and Gutwirth (n 54) 3.

[273] *Joined ASNEF and FECEMD Cases* (n 117) para 68.

[274] Burkert (n 40) 173.

balancing. But this might already be running ahead too much. Things will become clearer in the following chapters.

2.3.2 The GDPR's Pluralism

Overview—Contrary to the right to data protection in Article 8 of the Charter, the GDPR has a primarily enabling or instrumental role. The framework contributes to the effective protection and enjoyment of all interests, rights, and freedoms that are challenged or affected by data processing operations: eg human dignity; integrity; privacy; protection of personal data; freedom of thought and expression; economic freedoms; equality and non-discrimination; and democracy (see Art 1 of the GDPR).[275] The GDPR has become one of the most crucial pieces of legislation to safeguard these elements, in the face of increased reliance on ISS providers whose entire modus operandi is based on the processing of data.[276] Four fundamental rights warrant a closer look in light of this book: Data Protection (Art 8 Charter), Privacy (Art 7 Charter), Freedom of Expression (Art 11 Charter), and Non-Discrimination (Art 21 Charter). All four are significantly impacted by current data processing practices, as illustrated by the vignettes.[277] They are all particularly relevant in light of data protection's vocation to empower data subjects, *inter alia* through the right to erasure.

a) Data Protection

Separating the Right to Data Protection from Data Protection Law—The most evident fundamental right which the GDPR safeguards and fosters is the right to data protection in Article 8 Charter. Even though many still conflate both and/or seem to approach them as almost interchangeable, hopefully the previous pages made clear there are substantial differences between Article 8 Charter and the GDPR. The following excerpt from de Andrade is quite illustrative of the confusion among scholars:

> it is important to acknowledge and qualify the right to data protection as a procedural right while the right to privacy and identity as substantive ones. Substantive rights are created to ensure the protection and promotion of interests

[275] See also: Hondius (n 1) 96; De Hert and Gutwirth (n 54) 10; Rouvroy and Poullet (n 151) 46, 57; Hornung and Schnabel (n 33) 86; González Fuster, *The Emergence of Personal Data Protection as a Fundamental Right of the EU* (n 1) 255; Ferretti (n 259) 848ff; Boehme-Neßler (n 221). It is worth reiterating at this stage that most of these fundamental rights have an 'instrumental' component, interacting and safeguarding each other in a symbiotic relationship. But this does not take away that each of them—including the right to data protection—has an inherent core not subservient to the others.

[276] Luca Belli and Jamila Venturini, 'Private Ordering and the Rise of Terms of Service as Cyber-Regulation' (2016) 5 Internet Policy Review <https://policyreview.info/articles/analysis/private-ordering-and-rise-terms-service-cyber-regulation> accessed 1 June 2019.

[277] See also: European Commission, 'Commission Staff Working Paper: Impact Assessment Accompanying the Proposals for General Data Protection Regulation and Directive on Data Protection in Police and Judicial Matters' (n 30) 30; 39–40.

> that the human individual and society consider important to defend and uphold. Procedural rights operate at a different level, setting the rules, methods and conditions through which substantive rights are effectively enforced and protected. Data protection, as such, does not directly represent any value or interest per se, it prescribes the procedures and methods for pursuing the respect of values embodied in other rights.[278]

ARTICLE 8 CHARTER IS SUBSTANTIVE, THE GDPR IS PROCEDURAL—This quote clearly demonstrates the confusion of the *right to data protection* (Art 8 Charter) and data protection *law*, ie the GDPR. As made clear above, the right to data protection is a substantive right, just like the right to privacy. It clearly pursues its own independent values; ie control over one's personal data, one's digital representation or body if you will. Not 'in order to safeguard other rights or freedoms', but simply for the sake of having that control (in line with the values underlying the Charter such as autonomy and freedom). When de Andrade talks about *procedural* rights, what he should be referring to is the GDPR. Not the 'right to data protection'. Indeed, the GDPR operates at a different level (it is a secondary piece of legislation, not a primary) and it sets the 'rules, methods and conditions through which substantive rights are effectively enforced and protected'.

CONFUSING DIFFERENT FRAMEWORKS—Docksey makes a similar logical leap, when he says that 'the underlying idea for creating the right to data protection as a separate concept was [...] to protect everyone's fundamental rights and freedoms, and notably their right to privacy'.[279] In order to substantiate his argument, he refers to a WP29 Opinion,[280] which does not talk about the right to data protection but instead discusses the adoption of Convention 108. This legal document does not install a fundamental right, but rather puts in place a framework for protecting human rights in the context of data processing, just like the GDPR does.

THE GDPR'S ENABLING FUNCTION—Even if their main reasoning still seems to confound the right to data protection with data protection laws, Oostveen and Irion still implicitly support the argument made here. They claim that Article 8 in the Charter is not an end in itself, but rather 'inherently contributes to furthering other individual fundamental rights and freedoms', which they call 'data protection's enabling function'.[281] Again, this reasoning is somewhat misguided, especially

[278] Norberto Andrade, 'Oblivion: The Right to Be Different from Oneself—Reproposing the Right to Be Forgotten' (2012) 13 Revista de Internet, Derecho Y Política 122, 125.

[279] Docksey (n 113) 198.

[280] Article 29 Working Party, 'Opinion 06/2014 on the Notion of Legitimate Interests of the Data Controller under Article 7 of Directive 95/46/EC' (n 105) 6.

[281] Manon Oostveen and Kristina Irion, 'The Golden Age of Personal Data: How to Regulate an Enabling Fundamental Right?' in Bakhoum and others (eds), *Personal Data in Competition, Consumer Protection and IP Law—Towards a Holistic Approach?* (Springer 2017) 3 <https://papers.ssrn.com/abstract=2885701> accessed 19 January 2017.

considering that when the authors go on to explain this 'enabling function' they almost exclusively refer to secondary law (ie the GDPR). In doing so, however, they do support the claim being made here, which is that the GDPR has an enabling function, ie protecting many fundamental rights and freedoms. Indeed, the GDPR *enables* the right to data protection (Art 8 Charter) most of all.

SECONDARY LAW DOES NOT DEFINE PRIMARY LAW—Finally, the interpretation proposed here would also seem to resolve much of van der Sloot's issues with 'control' and data protection. The author criticizes what he observes as an increasing prominence of informational self-determination as the basic philosophy behind the GDPR.[282] As so many others, van der Sloot does not appear to differentiate between Article 8 Charter and the GDPR, even though it would dissipate much of his concerns. Indeed, he effectively equates the content of the GDPR to Article 8 Charter, in order to then criticize the 'fundamental right's character' of the latter.[283] Yet, it is wrong to define the content of a fundamental right by simply copy/pasting a secondary law framework. Such an interpretation creates a straw man, as it will of course raise issues but starts from a misinformed premise. Distinguishing the two would make clear that the GDPR does not have as its aim to ensure individual control, but instead puts in place an infrastructure of checks and balances to ensure fairness. This infrastructure does contain components granting individual control, but never absolute and always against a broader backdrop of responsible fair processing.

In sum, the GDPR sets the parameters for legitimate processing of personal data in light of the Charter as a whole. Having said that, it still protects the right to data protection (Art 8 Charter) *in particular*. This means that the GDPR gives special attention to ensuring the empowerment of data subjects. It does so through constraining the power of controllers as well as through a range of data subject rights for example. It is this empowerment strand—exemplified in the right to erasure and to object—that will constitute the focus of the rest of this book.

282 Bart van der Sloot, 'Do Data Protection Rules Protect the Individual and Should They? An Assessment of the Proposed General Data Protection Regulation' (2014) 4 International Data Privacy Law 307.

283 For instance: 'On the one hand, it could be pointed out that there are certainly data protection rules and cases that qualify as fundamental. For example, the rules in the Directive and the upcoming Regulation on the processing of sensitive personal data, such as those revealing a person's sexual or political orientation, medical conditions or race, qualify as fundamental and essential in a democratic society. [...] On the other hand, however, there are also data protection rules and cases which seem less obvious candidates for fundamental rights protection, because they protect more ordinary interests. [...] there are at least certain provisions in the data protection instruments and certain cases on data protection principles that intuitively do not qualify as (part of) a fundamental (human) right.' Bart van der Sloot, 'Legal Fundamentalism: Is Data Protection Really a Fundamental Right?' in Ronald Leenes and others (eds), *Data Protection and Privacy: (In)visibilities and Infrastructures* (Springer 2017) 20–21 <https://link-springer-com/chapter/10.1007/978-3-319-50796-5_1> accessed 12 March 2018.

b) Privacy

WHAT IS PRIVACY—Article 7 of the Charter (and Art 8(1) of the ECHR) declares that *everyone has the right to respect for his or her private and family life, home and communications*. Privacy protects 'the interiority of the person, the intimacy of the person, in fact the very ability of the individual to form his/her decisions'.[284] It is a freedom, necessary for democracy and the rule of law.[285] Privacy is a notoriously elusive concept 'with a variable content which touches all aspects of life linked to individual freedom'.[286,287] The relationship between privacy and the right to data protection is equally hard to define.[288] Indeed, the CJEU has often referred to both of them in one breath, without clearly separating one from the other (see notably Part II).[289] In the 1978 Lindop Report, the difference between data protection and privacy was illustrated as follows:

> There are aspects of privacy which have no immediate connection with the handling of personal data in information systems, such as the intrusion into the home, powers of entry and search, and embarrassing publicity in the media. There are also aspects of data protection which have no immediate connection with privacy. For example, the use of inaccurate or incomplete information for

[284] Christina Akrivopoulou and Nicolaos Garipidis (eds), *Human Rights and Risks in the Digital Era: Globalization and the Effects of Information Technologies* (Information Science Reference 2012) xvii.

[285] Gutwirth, *Privacy and the Information Age* (n 234); Hildebrandt, 'The Dawn of a Critical Transparency Right for the Profiling Era' (n 85) 48; Boehme-Neßler (n 221) 222.

[286] Gutwirth, *Privacy and the Information Age* (n 234) 34. Gutwirth explains that 'legal scholars have given up hope to find a conclusive and coherent description of privacy and rely on classification, categorizing, or listing of the different sub-areas'.

[287] Aside from protecting the individual, the right to privacy also has a vocation to safeguard societal and democratic values. Priscilla M Regan, *Legislating Privacy: Technology, Social Values, and Public Policy* (University of North Carolina Press 1995); Sami Coll, 'Power, Knowledge, and the Subjects of Privacy: Understanding Privacy as the Ally of Surveillance' (2014) 17 Information, Communication & Society 1250, 1260–61; Daniel J Solove, 'A Taxonomy of Privacy' (2006) 154 University of Pennsylvania Law Review 477, 506.

[288] An in-depth discussion on this complex relationship would reach greatly beyond the scope of this book. For more in-depth analyses, see inter alia: De Hert and Gutwirth (n 54); Raphaël Gellert and Serge Gutwirth, 'The Legal Construction of Privacy and Data Protection' (2013) 29 Computer Law & Security Review 522; Juliane Kokott and Christoph Sobotta, 'The Distinction between Privacy and Data Protection in the Jurisprudence of the CJEU and the ECtHR' (2013) 3 International Data Privacy Law 222; Ferraris, Bosco, and D'Angelo (n 300) 18; Maria Tzanou, 'Data Protection as a Fundamental Right Next to Privacy? "Reconstructing" a Not so New Right' (2013) 3 International Data Privacy Law 88; Lynskey, 'Deconstructing Data Protection: The "Added-Value" Of A Right To Data Protection In The EU Legal Order' (n 204); González Fuster, *The Emergence of Personal Data Protection as a Fundamental Right of the EU* (n 1) 21ff; CJEU case law analysis in: Docksey (n 113 or 199) 201ff; Gloria González Fuster and Hielke Hijmans, 'The EU Rights to Privacy and Personal Data Protection: 20 Years in 10 Questions' https://brusselsprivacyhub.eu/events/20190513.Working_Paper_González_Fuster_Hijmans.pdf.

[289] *Joined ASNEF and FECEMD Cases* (n 117) para 41; Ferretti (n 259) 859–60.

taking decisions about people is properly a subject for data protection, bit it may not always raise questions of privacy.[290]

Informational Privacy Protection—What is important for the purposes here, is that the GDPR clearly supports and fosters the right to privacy. The empowerment measures directly connect to the notion of 'informational privacy'.[291] The protective measures—ie not requiring proactive action by data subjects—instil a broader culture of responsible information practices, conscious of individuals' and society's interests in the protection of privacy. The Google vignette is a clear example of this, where the GDPR fosters the privacy of individuals who might be unreasonably exposed on the basis of a simple name search on Google.

The GDPR Offers Tools For Privacy—More broadly, the GDPR safeguards society's interest in the protection of privacy to the extent it shields disproportionate 'panopticism' (ie the unverifiable sense of being under permanent surveillance). The general idea is that the increased technological capabilities of collecting and processing personal information pose a significant threat to individual privacy.[292] Hence, to the extent data protection law acts as a check on disproportionate power over individuals' information, it contributes to the protection of privacy. One might say, in this regard, that the GDPR constitutes a *tool* to ensure the protection of individual privacy (and more). In sum, the GDPR ensures 'privacy in data processing by providing a checklist of safeguards to be respected. As such, it is a valuable tool to thwart the erosion of privacy in the digital age'.[293]

c) Freedom of Expression

What is Freedom of Expression?—The fundamental right to freedom of expression can be found in Article 11 of the Charter (and Art 10 ECHR). The right includes the *freedom to hold opinions and to receive and impart information and ideas without interference by public authority and regardless of frontiers*.[294] Often represented as an important counter-force to data protection (below, Part II),

[290] Lindop (n 202) 9.

[291] González Fuster, *The Emergence of Personal Data Protection as a Fundamental Right of the EU* (n 1) 27ff. In the discussions leading up to the OECD Guidelines, it was said that 'privacy can be assured by control as to the use of personal data'. Synthesis Report by Hans Peter Gassmann and G Russel Pipe (OECD Secretariat): *Policy Issues in Data Protection and Privacy: Concepts and Perspectives: Proceedings of the OECD Seminar, 24th to 26th June 1974* (n 332) 13. For the ECtHR's interpretation of *informational* privacy (as comprised within the ECHR's Article 8 on the protection of private life), see also: *Vukota-Bojić v Switzerland* [2016] European Court of Human Rights 61838/10 [52].

[292] González Fuster, *The Emergence of Personal Data Protection as a Fundamental Right of the EU* (n 1) 40ff; Gutwirth, *Privacy and the Information Age* (n 234) 113.

[293] Ironically, this is a quote from Docksey. Whereas the author is talking about the fundamental right to data protection (misguidedly, in my opinion), it is used here in reference to the GDPR. See: Docksey (n 113 or 199) 198.

[294] The right will be discussed in-depth in Chapter 6.

freedom of expression actually greatly depends on the GDPR. In his 2013 Report, UN special rapporteur La Rue emphasized the strong interdependence between privacy and data protection on the one hand and freedom of expression on the other hand.[295]

Freedom of Expression Needs the GDPR—Richards' whole concept of 'intellectual privacy' builds on the premise that in order to freely speak, think, and access information in today's digital society, individuals need to be able to do so without being watched.[296] The ability to freely express oneself and access information interacts considerably with the fundamental value of individual autonomy. Indeed, information processing-based erosions of individual autonomy will also have an impact on the enjoyment of one's right to freedom of expression.[297] Growing corporate control over communication channels and platforms—and particularly the (personal) information that flows through it—considerably impacts how individuals receive and impart information today. Indeed, the power these actors effectively exert over information freedoms should be seen in light of their commercial motives (ie maximizing attention and clicks),[298] and are generally not governed by values traditionally desired from the public sphere (eg quality, independence, and institutional legitimacy). Information asymmetries (online) lead to 'corporate censorship';[299] 'filter bubbles';[300] fake news[301] as well as commercial,[302] emotional,[303] and political[304] manipulation.[305] Moreover, one of the key concerns fuelling the mass-surveillance backlash is that it effectively creates 'a

295 Frank La Rue, 'Report of the Special Rapporteur on the Promotion and Protection of the Right to Freedom of Opinion and Expression' (United Nations (Human Rights Council) 2013) A/HRC/23/40 particularly paragraphs 24–27; 79. In 1975 already, Hondius recognized the complex interaction between data protection and information freedoms, the former both reinforcing and restricting the latter. Hondius (n 1) 126.

296 '[I]ntellectual privacy has three essential elements—freedom of thought, the right to read freely, and the right to communicate in confidence'. Richards (n 235).

297 Bernal (n 146) 269–70.

298 Wu (n 170); Stephen Metcalf, 'Neoliberalism: The Idea That Swallowed the World' *The Guardian* (18 August 2017) <www.theguardian.com/news/2017/aug/18/neoliberalism-the-idea-that-changed-the-world> accessed 1 June 2019; John Naughton, 'Extremism Pays. That's Why Silicon Valley Isn't Shutting It Down | John Naughton' (*the Guardian*, 18 March 2018) <http://www.theguardian.com/commentisfree/2018/mar/18/extremism-pays-why-silicon-valley-not-shutting-it-down-youtube> accessed 18 March 2018.

299 Rebecca MacKinnon, *Consent of the Networked: The Worldwide Struggle for Internet Freedom* (Basic Books 2012) ch 8; Jef Ausloos and others, *How Internet Censorship Works* (2012) <https://youtu.be/HfS_2oXVch0> accessed 1 June 2019.

300 Eli Pariser, *The Filter Bubble: What The Internet Is Hiding From You* (Penguin Books 2012).

301 Morozov, Evgeny Morozov, 'Moral Panic over Fake News Hides the Real Enemy—The Digital Giants' *The Guardian* (8 January 2017) <www.theguardian.com/commentisfree/2017/jan/08/blaming-fake-news-not-the-answer-democracy-crisis> accessed 1 June 2019.

302 Ryan Calo, 'Digital Market Manipulation' (2014) 82 Geo Wash L Rev 995; Zarsky (n 236) 16; 30.

303 Evgeny Morozov, 'Facebook Invades Your Personality, Not Your Privacy' *Financial Times* (10 August 2014) <http://www.ft.com/intl/cms/s/2/dd5e5514-198d-11e4-8730-00144feabdc0.html> accessed 1 June 2019.

304 Tufekci (n 185).

305 See References made in the Introduction.

panopticon beyond anything Bentham ever imagined'.[306,307] The inhibiting effect of mass surveillance on information freedoms has also been explicitly recognized by the CJEU as an argument to strike down the so-called data retention directive.[308]

ILLUSTRATION—As a brief illustration, it is worth referring to the last two vignettes. The Google vignette alludes to the importance of search engines in finding information today. Through increased personalization, and complexification of the underlying algorithms to achieve that personalization, it is rare that two persons will see the exact same (order of) results for a given search term. While this is not negative per se, it does emphasize the impact search engines may have on society's perspectives on the world. The Apple vignette similarly concerns an intermediary between individuals and information they want to access or share. On the one hand, when asking smart home assistants to read the headlines, play a cheerful song, or upload a video, individuals are effectively at the mercy of this device to do so in their best interest (rather than, for example, on the basis of sponsored headlines, contracted artists, or partnered social media). A final example can be drawn from Kaiser's research on right-wing populist movements and polarization on social media.[309] For example, Kaiser demonstrates how YouTube's recommender algorithms (for related videos, channels, or users) push far-right content to 'conservatives'. As such, these recommender algorithms may have a considerable impact on freedom of expression/information and democracy more broadly. Data protection law offers important tools to gain insights into this impact, as well as how to mitigate it.

In sum, an environment without data protection—where people's every action can be monitored, anticipated, and/or acted upon—poses great threats to the fundamental right to freedom of expression and information

d) Non-Discrimination

EQUALITY THREATENED BY DATA PROCESSING—Article 21 of the Charter—located within Chapter III on Equality—proclaims the principle of non-discrimination, particularly on grounds such as *sex, race, colour, ethnic or social origin, genetic features, language, religion or belief, political or any other opinion, membership of a*

306 Lessig, *Code* (n 237) 208. The panopticon was a prison structure designed by Jeremy Bentham—effectively erecting one-way mirrors, where guards can see many prisoners simultaneously but not vice versa—and became the crucial diagram for Foucault's work on surveillance (Michel Foucault, *Surveiller et punir: naissance de la prison* (Gallimard 2004) 201ff). This model has amply been applied to and analysed in the digital environment. See notably: Oscar H Gandy, *The Panoptic Sort: A Political Economy of Personal Information* (Westview 1993); David Lyon, *Theorizing Surveillance: The Panopticon and Beyond* (Willan Publishing 2006).

307 Glenn Greenwald, *No Place to Hide: Edward Snowden, the NSA, and the Surveillance State* (Hamish Hamilton 2014) 174–77.

308 *Digital Rights Ireland Ltd* (n 122) para 28.

309 See: The Berkman Klein Center for Internet & Society, *Jonas Kaiser on The Dark Side of the Networked Public Sphere* <https://www.youtube.com/watch?v=bhiA6pg4ohs> accessed 7 February 2018.

national minority, property, birth, disability, age or sexual orientation (similarly to Art 14 ECHR).[310] In light of the data deluge (see Introduction), data processing activities performed by ISS providers entail an inherent risk of unequal treatment.[311] Because the underlying processes are increasingly complex and opaque,[312] it also becomes harder to apprehend *how* and *why* differential treatment occurs.[313] Indeed, modern-day data processing enables and facilitates differential treatment on the basis of much more than just the 'protected grounds' in Article 21 Charter.[314] As a result, traditional non-discrimination rules may not offer solace when these widespread practices generate undesired consequences.[315]

Illustration—Data protection law's broad scope of application (see Chapter 3), combined with the datafication of every aspect of life, makes it an increasingly interesting route to counter undesirable differential treatments.[316] Whereas the right to data protection (Art 8 Charter) focuses on ensuring processing activities are 'under control' and is agnostic to its outcome being discriminatory or not, the GDPR aims to safeguard equality and non-discrimination in

[310] For a general introduction, see: European Union Agency for Fundamental Rights (FRA) and Council of Europe, *Handbook on European Non-Discrimination Law* (Publications Office of the European Union 2011).

[311] See generally: Lyon (n 307); Oscar H Gandy, 'Data Mining, Surveillance, and Discrimination in the Post-9/11 Environment' in Richard Victor Ericson and Kevin D Haggerty (eds), *The New Politics of Surveillance and Visibility* (University of Toronto Press 2006); Bart W Schermer, 'The Limits of Privacy in Automated Profiling and Data Mining' (2011) 27 Computer Law & Security Review 46; Lynskey, *The Foundations of EU Data Protection Law* (n 74) 197–202; O'Neil (n 50); Safiya Umoja Noble, *Algorithms of Oppression: How Search Engines Reinforce Racism* (New York UP 2018) <https://www.overdrive.com/search?q=50344CBA-F46F-46D8-AED3-8E55ACCAEC93> accessed 16 March 2018; Virginia Eubanks, *Automating Inequality: How High-Tech Tools Profile, Police, and Punish the Poor* (St Martin's Press 2018). On 'economic zoning' (idea of unaccountable data collection and processing rule-sets promoting distinctions based on social and/or economic criteria), see: Lessig, *Code* (n 237) 220.

[312] The fact that most of these practices are veiled in (corporate) secrecy, further adds to the complexity and information/power asymmetry. See: Frank Pasquale, *The Black Box Society: The Secret Algorithms That Control Money and Information* (Harvard UP 2014); Oren Bracha and Frank Pasquale, 'Federal Search Commission? Access, Fairness, and Accountability in the Law of Search' (2008) 93 Cornell Law Review 1149; Danielle Keats Citron and Frank Pasquale, 'The Scored Society: Due Process for Automated Predictions' (2014) 89 Washington Law Review 1, 7.

[313] 'The power to treat people differently' Richards explains 'can bleed imperceptibly into the power of discrimination.' Richards (n 235) 1957; Lynskey, *The Foundations of EU Data Protection Law* (n 74) 198.

[314] ie sex, race, colour, ethnic or social origin, genetic features, language, religion or belief, political or any other opinion, membership of a national minority, property, birth, disability, age or sexual orientation. See: Raphaël Gellert and others, 'A Comparative Analysis of Anti-Discrimination and Data Protection Legislations' in Bart Custers and others (eds), *Discrimination and Privacy in the Information Society—Data Mining and Profiling in Large Databases* (Springer 2013); Lynskey, *The Foundations of EU Data Protection Law* (n 74) 199.

[315] Even more so when taking into account that non-discrimination rules require intervention by a third-party 'endowed with the legitimacy to undertake the legal hermeneutics to decide about the discriminatory nature of the consequences of the contested action'. Gellert and others (n 314) 70.

[316] Clearly illustrated in the Huber Case (*Huber v Germany* (n 110)). In this case the CJEU ruled on the basis of data protection law, whereas 'discrimination' is what was actually at the core of the case. Gellert and others (n 314) 61–63; 76–79. See also: Rouvroy and Poullet (n 151) 70.

From a US (non-data protection) perspective, Pasquale worries that '[w]ithout a society-wide commitment to fair data practices, digital discrimination will only intensify.' In: Pasquale, *The Black Box Society* (n 312) 21.

the face of automated data processing. For example, the Uber vignette brings to the surface how the differential treatment of both riders and drivers is based on complex data processing. An important factor relates to the ratings riders and drivers give each other. Many have argued how this system—which by the way remains very opaque—reinforces discriminatory practices.[317] Similar concerns can be raised with regard to predictive data processing, for instance in the context of policing, banking, or marketing.[318] Data protection law is aimed at constraining such processing and instilling fairness through a system of checks and balances. Having said that, the GDPR may not be the most well-suited legal framework to tackle discriminatory practices in given situations (eg employment context).

Interaction GDPR and Non-Discrimination—The important role for data protection law in tackling differential treatment and discrimination is recognized in the GDPR[319] and confirmed by the CJEU in its Huber ruling.[320] It is also no coincidence that the special categories of data covered in Article 9 GDPR largely overlap with the protected grounds under Article 21 Charter.[321] Processing such information is prohibited by default as it inherently risks infringing the non-discrimination principle (see Chapter 3).[322] Yet, data protection law is no silver bullet to tackle discriminatory practices (or undesirable differential treatments) either.[323] It is designed to regulate actions, whereas non-discrimination rules target a specific legal outcome.[324] With this in mind, it is fair to say that data protection law

317 Yanbo Ge and others, 'Racial and Gender Discrimination in Transportation Network Companies' (National Bureau of Economic Research 2016); Oscar H Gandy, 'Engaging Rational Discrimination: Exploring Reasons for Placing Regulatory Constraints on Decision Support Systems' (2010) 12 Ethics and Information Technology 29; Alex Rosenblat and others, 'Discriminating Tastes: Customer Ratings as Vehicles for Bias' [2016] Data & Society <https://datasociety.net/output/discriminating-tastes-customer-ratings-as-vehicles-for-bias/> accessed 27 July 2018; Newlands, Lutz, and Fieseler Newlands, Gemma, Christoph Lutz, and Christian Fieseler. *Power in the Sharing Economy*. Norway. EU H2020 Research Project Ps2Share: Participation, Privacy, and Power in the Sharing Economy. BI Norwegian Business School. April 30, 2017. https://papers.ssrn.com/abstract=2960938. 20–21.

318 McDermott, Yvonne, 'Conceptualising the Right to Data Protection in an Era of Big Data' (1 June 2017) 4, no. 1 Big Data & Society 5; Crawford, Kate, and Jason Schultz, 'Big Data and Due Process: Toward a Framework to Redress Predictive Privacy Harms' (29 January 2014) 55, no. 1 Boston College Law Review 93; O'Neil, Cathy, *Weapons of Math Destruction: How Big Data Increases Inequality and Threatens Democracy*. (Penguin Books 2017).

319 ie Recitals 71 and 75 and Article 35 GDPR. Lynskey, *The Foundations of EU Data Protection Law* (n 74) 197.

320 *Huber v Germany* (n 110).

321 European Union Agency for Fundamental Rights (FRA), 'Opinion on the Proposed Data Protection Reform Package' (2012) FRA Opinion 2/2012 5–6. In 1973 already, the CoE stressed that 'information relating to the intimate private life of persons or information which might lead to unfair discrimination should not be recorded or, if recorded, should not be disseminated'. Council of Europe—Committee of Ministers (n 159) para 1; Council of Europe—Committee of Ministers, 'Resolution (74) 29 on the Protection of the Privacy of Individuals Vis-a-Vis Electronic Data Banks in the Public Sector' Explanatory Memorandum para 24.

322 Gutwirth, *Privacy and the Information Age* (n 234) 105.

323 Schermer (n 311); Lynskey, *The Foundations of EU Data Protection Law* (n 74) 202.

324 Gellert and others (n 493) 70–71.

is instrumental in safeguarding against undesirable differential treatments (online) and as such, complements existing anti-discrimination rules.[325]

2.3.3 Operationalization of Data Protection Law

Aim of the GDPR—In the European Union, the General Data Protection Regulation lays down the general framework, the rules of the game if you will, for processing personal data. As mentioned before, its aim is to safeguard all fundamental rights and freedoms in the context of data processing operations. Put differently, it constitutes the procedural infrastructure for tackling conflicts between the many different interests, rights, and freedoms at stake in data processing.

Like other regulatory frameworks, the GDPR comprises different approaches to achieve its goal(s). For the purpose of this book, two main distinctions can be made in the operationalization of data protection: *ex ante* v *ex post* measures and protective v empowerment measures. Combined, these categories can be projected onto a matrix which will be discussed below. But first, it is important to briefly elaborate on the distinction between *responsibility* and *liability* in the GDPR's approach to regulating the protection of personal data. After all, this distinction will appear relevant at different instances throughout this book.

a) Responsibility v Liability

A Responsibility Framework—The GDPR is a framework that aims to instil the responsible use of data processing. This is especially evident in other languages where the concept 'controller' (explained in Chapter 3), is referred to as '*Verwerkingsverantwoordelijke*' (Dutch), '*Verantwortlicher*' (German), and '*Responsable du traitement*' (French). Under certain circumstances, the GDPR also imposes liability, perhaps most prominently in Articles 82 (right to compensation and liability) and 83 (administrative fines). One could say that liability is the stick behind the door, to ensure responsibility is taken seriously. It is hard to find any writing putting the finger on the distinction between these two concepts in the context of data protection law.[326] Yet, as will be explained here, separating the two is important when reading the GDPR. This subsection will not elaborate on broader legal theory concerning these concepts, but simply focus on their distinction as relevant within the confines of this book.

Obligations Of Means—In simple terms, the GDPR allocates responsibility to comply with certain obligations. If those obligations are not followed, liability might arise. Straightforward as this may seem from a distance, things are a lot more complicated when looked at up close. Nearly all provisions in the GDPR are subject

[325] ibid 81; Lynskey, *The Foundations of EU Data Protection Law* (n 74) 210.

[326] Though not analysing the distinction per se, Van Alsenoy does meticulously flesh out how data protection law deals with *liability*. See: Brendan Van Alsenoy, 'Liability under EU Data Protection Law: From Directive 95/46 to the General Data Protection Regulation' (2017) 7 JIPITEC <http://www.jipitec.eu/issues/jipitec-7-3-2016/4506>.

to considerable interpretative flexibility. The reason for this is that most obligations are framed as obligations of means, rather than obligations of results.[327] Indeed, as will become clear throughout the rest of this book, the applicability and extent of obligations within the GDPR will almost always be debatable. Especially how they are complied with, will almost always be a question of degree, depending on the specific circumstances at hand.[328] This makes it very hard to define liability, which will only be clear-cut in case of blatant disrespect of certain obligations. In this way, one could very loosely compare the distinction between liability and responsibility, with that between rules and principles.[329] Rules are binary, they are syllogisms and either apply or do not. Principles, on the other hand, are open-ended and have a weight-dimension that depends on the context. It is said that rules are preferable in homogenous situations, whereas principles are to be preferred in situations 'where the primary behaviour is heterogeneous, evolves rapidly over time, or occurs infrequently'.[330]

A Question of Degree—The GDPR is first and foremost an instrument aimed at instilling responsibility, not control, nor liability. It is aimed at ensuring data is processed responsibly, which explains the centrality of the notion of fairness.[331] Similarly to 'principles' therefore, the extent of its obligations is a question of degree. It is no surprise that its core provision, Article 5, is indeed titled (and composed of) *principles* relating to processing of personal data. More than two decades of experience with Directive 95/46 have demonstrated that compliance with principles such as purpose limitation, data minimization, and storage limitation are not yes or no questions. The same is true with regard to data subject rights, where the extent to which (and way in which) they are accommodated will virtually always be open to debate as well.

Relevance of Distinction—Why is it important to make this distinction between responsibility and liability here? The previous paragraphs illustrate that while responsibility may be relatively easy to establish, liability is not. Van Alsenoy

[327] ibid. See also Article 5.1.4 in: International Institute for the Unification of Private Law, *Unidroit Principles of International Commercial Contracts* (2010) <https://www.unidroit.org/english/principles/contracts/principles2010/integralversionprinciples2010-e.pdf> accessed 15 March 2018; Gabriela Zanfir, 'Tracing the Right to Be Forgotten in the Short History of Data Protection Law: The "New Clothes" of an Old Right' in Serge Gutwirth, Ronald Leenes, and Paul de Hert (eds), *Reforming European Data Protection Law* (Springer Netherlands 2015) 235–39 <http://link.springer.com/chapter/10.1007/978-94-017-9385-8_8> accessed 1 June 2019.

[328] For example, Article 24(1) GDPR explains the controller shall implement appropriate technical and organizational measures to ensure processing complies with the Regulation, 'taking into account the nature, scope, context and purposes of processing as well as the risks of varying likelihood and severity of the rights and freedoms of natural persons'.

[329] For more, see: Sébastien Van Drooghenbroeck, *La proportionnalité dans le droit de la Convention européenne des droits de l'Homme: prendre l'idée simple au sérieux* (FUSL 2001) 624ff; NE Simmonds, 'Dworkin', in *Central Issues in Jurisprudence: Justice, Law and Rights* (Sweet & Maxwell 2006) ch 6..

[330] Brendan Van Alsenoy, *Data Protection Law in the EU: Roles, Responsibilities and Liability* (Intersentia 2019) 612ff.

[331] Clifford and Ausloos (n 196).

explains how the burden of proof for demonstrating liability on data subjects' shoulders remains quite onerous, even despite some presumptions in their favour.[332] In other words, data subjects wishing to validate their rights, or data protection authorities trying to ensure a secure data processing environment, may find it hard to effectively enforce this in practice.

Vignette Illustration—For example, Apple refuses to accommodate data subject access requests to Siri voice data (ie the recordings of a user's voice when asking a question to Siri), because they argue not to have the technology in place to retrace that information.[333] In short, when a user asks Siri a question, the voice-recording is uploaded to Apple's servers, but then the link with the device (and user-account) is cut. This 'privacy-by-design measure' makes it impossible, the company claims, to send users their voice recordings, even if these evidently constitute personal data (see Chapter 3). Where does this leave data subjects? How far does Apple's responsibility go in accommodating the right of access? What about erasure? What if ensuring these rights can be accommodated comes at the cost of reduced security? Would a strict liability regime (to accommodate rights) be preferable?

Bigger Picture—The focus on responsibility may promote a broader sense of fairness, extending beyond individual relationships with data subjects, to the data processing eco-system more broadly. The second vignette illustrates that although it may be clear that Facebook is responsible for influencing elections and emotional manipulation, determining liability for those activities might not be as straightforward. The underlying processing operations effectively trigger broader policy questions that may more adequately be tackled through concepts such as diligence, responsibility, and fairness, than through liability regimes.[334]

Intermediary Liability v Responsibility—The distinction between responsibility and liability will also appear relevant in the discussion on so-called intermediaries later on. These actors do not create content themselves but help distribute it (eg video hosting platforms). While these entities may be exempted from liability over unlawful content shared on their platform (under certain conditions),

[332] The fact that most obligations are framed as obligations of means, and the difficulty, for individuals to truly comprehend the actual processing activities, render it particularly hard to make one's claim or counter arguments of the organization processing personal data. See: Van Alsenoy, 'Liability under EU Data Protection Law' (n 326).

The same will also appear with the right to erasure for example (see Chapter 4).

[333] This example will feature more prominently in Part III and is derived from the following Article: Michael Veale, Reuben Binns, and Jef Ausloos, 'When Data Protection by Design and Data Subject Rights Clash' (2017) ID 3081069 <https://papers.ssrn.com/abstract=3081069> accessed 9 February 2018.

[334] For example, WP29 also advocates for a continued dialogue with major industry players when interpreting the household exemption so that it is workable and fair. Article 29 Working Party, 'Annex 2: Proposals for Amendments Regarding Exemption for Personal or Household Activities' 7 <http://ec.europa.eu/justice/article-29/documentation> accessed 1 June 2019.

this does not imply they do not bear any responsibility. Indeed, the 'sliding scales' nature of responsibility under the GDPR implies the more powerful or impactful an actor processing personal data is, the more responsibility will rest on its shoulders.[335] This is also the underlying idea behind increased policy pressure on these actors to do more about illegal content circulating on their platforms.[336] This discussion merits a book in its own right and will only be referred to where relevant throughout the following chapters.[337]

Accountability and Responsibility—A key notion in data protection law which captures the above discussion is that of 'accountability'.[338] This provision was introduced in an attempt to translate data protection into practice. It is also meant to facilitate an increased reliance on 'decentred regulation', ie counting on actors to self-regulate to some extent and only have regulatory/administrative intervention when there is an indication of a breach.[339] The 'new' accountability principle constitutes a central component in data protection law and can be found in Article 5(2), which should be read together with Article 24 (responsibility of the controller). It essentially requires entities subject to data protection law, to (be able to) demonstrate necessary steps have been taken to ensure compliance with the relevant obligations. The GDPR recognizes these obligations are scalable and need to be interpreted in light of factors such as contractual asymmetries or riskiness of processing for example.[340] Thus, the accountability principle is a vehicle to render responsibility and fairness more grounded and durable.[341] Liability, ideally, should not even feature in this debate.

335 See notably the CJEU, which stated that a search engine processing personal data must ensure compliance with data protection law 'within the framework of its responsibilities, powers and capabilities'. *Google Spain* (n 106) paras 35–38; 83. A similar conclusion can be drawn from Article 24(1) GDPR. All of this will amply be elaborated on throughout the rest of this book.

336 See for example: European Commission, 'Communication on Tackling Illegal Content Online—Towards an Enhanced Responsibility of Online Platforms' (2017) COM(2017) 555 final; Committee of Experts on Internet Intermediaries (MSI-NET), 'Draft Recommendation CM/Rec(2017)Xxx of the Committee of Ministers to Member States on the Roles and Responsibilities of Internet Intermediaries' <https://rm.coe.int/draft-recommendation-on-internet-intermediaries-7th-revised version-/1680770c37> accessed 10 March 2018.

337 See also: Aleksandra Kuczerawy and Jef Ausloos, 'NoC Online Intermediaries Case Studies Series: European Union and Google Spain' (2015) <http://ssrn.com/abstract=2567183> accessed 1 June 2019.

338 For a general introduction and broader perspective, see: Brendan Van Alsenoy and others, 'Cultures of Accountability: A Cross-Cultural Perspective on Current and Future Accountability Mechanisms' (University of Leuven—CiTiP 2014) Report of Expert Workshop <www.law.kuleuven.be/citip/en/news/item/coa-workshop-report.pdf>.

339 Article 29 Working Party, 'Opinion 3/2010 on the Principle of Accountability' (European Commission 2010) Opinion WP 173 <http://ec.europa.eu/justice/article-29/documentation> accessed 1 June 2019; European Data Protection Supervisor, 'Opinion on Coherent Enforcement of Fundamental Rights in the Age of Big Data' (n 160) 7.

340 European Data Protection Supervisor, 'Opinion on Coherent Enforcement of Fundamental Rights in the Age of Big Data' (n 160) 7.

341 In the words of WP29, accountability's 'emphasis is on showing how responsibility is exercised and making this verifiable.' Article 29 Working Party, 'Opinion 3/2010 on the Principle of Accountability' (n 339) 7.

Responsibility v Liability—In sum, the main drawback of data protection law's focus on responsibility, rather than liability, is the vagueness it engenders. From a corporate perspective, it is easier to express compliance in terms of liabilities rather than open-ended responsibilities. The interpretative flexibility that comes with obligations of means, reduces legal certainty. Yet, such legal certainty may still be found in other (sector-specific) legal frameworks, or through codes of conducts and guidance issued by data protection authorities. The main advantage is that it purports to install a broader perspective. Rather than focusing on legal checklists to prevent liability, a framework of responsibility forces to consider the implications of one's actions in the broader data processing eco-system, and match compliance accordingly. Having said that, the practical reality is that such call for responsibility will often only be taken seriously when there is a sword of Damocles in the shape of liabilities, which explains the GDPR's introduction of considerable fines (Arts 82–84).[342] Concluding, this subsection is not aimed at providing a detailed analysis of the concepts and interaction between responsibility and liability. It rather aims to put the finger on the fact that these are different concepts and that difference does have an important impact when interpreting the GDPR, as will clearly appear at several instances throughout this book.

b) Data Protection Matrix

The dimensions of EU data protection law have dramatically increased with the introduction of the GDPR. The number of Articles in Directive 95/46 (34) almost tripled when compared to the GDPR (99). Add to this the 173 Recitals and pervasive cross-references between Articles, and it is easy to see how getting a grasp on all these interactions can become quite complex. In an attempt to simplify so as to better comprehend the GDPR, this subsection proposes a rough categorization of provisions. Two *summa divisios* are made—*ex ante* v *ex post* measures and protective v empowerment measures—that jointly form a matrix with four quadrants. While not absolute or foolproof, this matrix constitutes a useful conceptualization of the main provisions in the GDPR, and allows to clearly position the rights to erasure and to object vis-à-vis other provisions.

i. *Ex Ante v Ex Post* The division between *ex ante* and *ex post* measures is quite straightforward. Data protection law provides for measures at different stages throughout a data processing operation's lifecycle. Some of these measures can be situated at a specific moment in time (eg data subject rights). Other measures rather take place over a more or less extended period of time (eg security

[342] Indeed, as a 2016 empirical research report demonstrated, responsible data processing behaviour in the ISS context pre-GDPR is often hard to find. Jamila Venturini and others, *Terms of Service and Human Rights: An Analysis of Online Platform Contracts* (Revan 2016) 61–74 <http://internet-governance.fgv.br/sites/internet-governance.fgv.br/files/publicacoes/terms_of_services_06_12_2016.pdf> accessed 29 December 2016.

obligations). Categorizing these measures will depend on the moment when they are triggered: *before* or *after* the relevant processing operation initiates. For example, when Alice signs up to a social networking site (SNS), *ex ante* measures will include the SNS-provider's transparency obligations and requirement to have a lawful ground; while the *ex post* measures include Alice's rights to object to certain uses of her data.

It is often argued that the data protection framework primarily relies on *ex ante* measures.[343] An approach that becomes increasingly hard to maintain in an age of data deluge (see Introduction). This also explains the—primarily industry-initiated—discussions on collection-based v use-based regulation,[344] as well as the (revived)[345] debate on accountability already alluded to above. Arguably, the latter principle transcends the *ex ante* v *ex post* division. Regardless, these concepts and debates do not constitute the focus of this book and will therefore only return tangentially.

ii. Protective v Empowerment Measures DICHOTOMY—The second divide that can be made in the way data protection law aims to achieve its goals, is the one between protective v empowerment measures.[346] This distinction is more profound than the one between (controller) obligations and (data subject) rights (which only describes specific kinds of implementation). The basic idea is simple: *empowerment* measures are aimed at providing individuals with the tools to control their data and protect themselves; and *protective* measures aim to offer protection without the individual having to be proactive. In other words, the empowerment approach presupposes an *active* role by the individual, whereas the protective approach allows the individual to be more *passive*. The merits and drawbacks of both regulatory approaches have been amply written about.[347] It is not the goal of this section to provide a comprehensive overview of this debate. Nor does this section want to present the dichotomy as absolute.[348] Instead, it is aimed at providing a conceptual structure that will facilitate a better understanding and contextualization of the central subject matter of this book: the right to erasure.

343 Schermer (n 311) 49.

344 Especially: Daniel J Weitzner and others, 'Information Accountability' (2008) 51 Commun. ACM 82; Fred H Cate, Peter Cullen, and Viktor Mayer-Schönberger, 'Data Protection Principles for the 21st Century—Revising the 1980 OECD Guidelines' <https://www.repository.law.indiana.edu/facbooks/23>.

345 The concept was already introduced in the 1980 OECD Guidelines (Principle 14).

346 A compelling, in-depth analysis and comparison of this dichotomy can be found in: Claudia Quelle, 'Not Just User Control in the General Data Protection Regulation', *Privacy and Identity Management. Facing up to Next Steps* (Springer International Publishing 2016) <https://link-springer-com/chapter/10.1007/978-3-319-55783-0_11> accessed 27 February 2018. The author maps the distinction onto the distinction between will-based and interest-based theories of rights.

347 See inter alia: Ryan Calo, 'Code, Nudge, or Notice?' (2014) 99 Iowa L Rev 773; the many references mentioned in: Frederik Zuiderveen Borgesius, 'Improving Privacy Protection in the Area of Behavioural Targeting' (PhD Thesis, University of Amsterdam 2014) 242ff.

348 It will appear later on in this book that data protection provisions can be considered both empowering *and* protective simultaneously. See also in this regard: Zuiderveen Borgesius, 'Improving Privacy Protection in the Area of Behavioural Targeting' (n 347) 162.

EMPOWERMENT—For the purposes of the discussion here, *empowerment* can also be qualified as 'data subject control' in its more narrow interpretation (see Section 2.2.2).[349] Underlying this approach is the libertarian value of empowering individuals so they can take measures into their own hands.[350] The main way in which this approach materializes in the current data protection framework is through data subject *rights* (notably the rights to object, erase, rectify).[351] Consent (as a lawful ground) is another example of an empowerment measure that is *not* a data subject right *stricto sensu*. The underlying rationale is that increasing the ability to control one's data tilts 'the scales in favour of the data subject'[352] and as such contributes to the GDPR's overall mission of fairness and countering (the negative aspects of) power asymmetries. Having said that, empowerment measures are also criticized for over-responsibilizing and overburdening individuals.[353]

EMPOWERMENT MEASURES V ARTICLE 8 CHARTER—It is important not to confuse these empowerment measures within the GDPR, with the right to data protection (Art 8 Charter) that has been described before. Data subject control within the GDPR only serve as instruments for the data subject to pursue their interests, rights, or freedoms in general. When scholars talk about the 'enabling' function of data protection,[354] what they are really talking about is these empowerment measures within the GDPR. They intend to effectively *enable* individuals to defend themselves from being discriminated against, censored, or spied upon, but do not have an inherent value in themselves. The distinction is important, as empowerment measures within the GDPR can be overridden (eg because of an exemption or derogation), whereas the right to data protection in the Charter cannot be entirely overridden.[355] Put differently, the data subject rights in the GDPR do not

[349] See Westin (n 193); Bygrave (n 12) 63; González Fuster, *The Emergence of Personal Data Protection as a Fundamental Right of the EU* (n 1) 5; Lynskey, *The Foundations of EU Data Protection Law* (n 74) 179.

[350] See in this regard also Recital 7 GDPR.

[351] Lazaro and Le Métayer call these specific provisions 'micro-rights'. Lazaro and Le Métayer (n 260); Lynskey, *The Foundations of EU Data Protection Law* (n 74) 180–81.

[352] Lynskey, *The Foundations of EU Data Protection Law* (n 74) 180.

[353] Mayer-Schönberger (n 84) 229; 232 suggesting that relying too much on empowerment would require individuals to turn into digital hermits; Laura Brandimarte and Alessandro Acquisti, 'The Economics of Privacy' in Martin Peitz and Joel Waldfogel (eds), *The Oxford Handbook of the Digital Economy* (OUP 2012) 564 explaining the difficulty to think long-term; Jef Ausloos, 'The "Right to Be Forgotten"—Worth Remembering?' (2012) 28 Computer Law & Security Review 143, 144 on the impossibility be fully informed and in control; Daniel J Solove, 'Introduction: Privacy Self-Management and the Consent Dilemma' (2013) 126 Harvard Law Review 1880, 1883–88 on the cognitive disconnect; Judith Rauhofer, 'Of Men and Mice: Should the EU Data Protection Authorities' Reaction to Google's New Privacy Policy Raise Concern for the Future of the Purpose Limitation Principle?' (2015) 1(1) EDPL 5–15 explaining that individuals 'may have neither the skill nor the bargaining power to resist commercial demands for their data'; Lynskey, *The Foundations of EU Data Protection Law* (n 74) 13 highlighting the difficulties in this age of data proliferation.

[354] eg Manon Oostveen and Kristina Irion, 'The Golden Age of Personal Data: How to Regulate an Enabling Fundamental Right?' in Mor Bakhoum, Beatriz Conde Gallego, Mark-Oliver Mackenordt, and Gintarė Surblytė-Namavičienė Surblyte (eds), *Personal Data in Competition, Consumer Protection and IP Law* (Springer 2017).

[355] Article 52(1) allows for limitations, but requires that the *essence* of the right to data protection—ie control—remains intact.

constitute the 'essence' of Article 8 Charter.[356] The latter understands control more broadly than simply in the form of empowerment measures that require individuals to be proactive.

PROTECTIVISM—Protective measures, as used in this book, are closely connected to the concept of paternalism. Paternalistic approaches to regulation are generally characterized by the following three features: (a) interference with the individual's liberty; (b) primarily with benevolence toward the individual; (c) without the individual's consent.[357] Several provisions within the data protection framework fulfil these three requirements.[358] They are the provisions that set certain non-negotiable limitations to how data can be processed (notably data quality principles[359] and data protection authorities[360]). The justification behind such protective (dare one say 'paternalistic') measures largely stems from the considerable (power and information) asymmetries that exist between the respective parties.[361] These imbalances also explain (part of) the inadequacies/insufficiencies of the empowerment approach. As a matter of fact, the first data protection laws were primarily protective in nature. They were aimed at keeping in check large centralized data banks in the hands of powerful governmental/corporate agencies.[362] Today, the regulatory approach to data protection seems to be more nuanced. Protective measures also come in different tastes and degrees.[363] Fairly recently, so-called 'soft-paternalism' measures (eg nudging, education) have gained traction in both Europe and the US.

iii. The Data Protection Matrix Putting together the *ex ante* v *ex post* and the empowerment v protective axes, a matrix can be drawn up with four fields: (a) *ex*

[356] Clifford and Ausloos (n 196) 21.

[357] P Cserne, *Freedom of Contract and Paternalism: Prospects and Limits of an Economic Approach (PhD thesis University of Hamburg)* (Academic version 2008) http://ediss.sub.uni- hamburg.de/volltexte/2008/3765/pdf/edisscserne.pdf; CJ Hoofnagle et al., 'Behavioral Advertising: The Offer You Cannot Refuse' (2012) 6(2) Harvard Law & Policy Review 273. Both cited in: Zuiderveen Borgesius (n 347) 243. Importantly, consent here should not be confused with consent in the GDPR (see Arts 6(1)(a) and 7).

[358] ibid 243–47.

[359] Requiring among others, data to be processed fairly and lawfully and imposing the purpose specification and use limitation principles. See, inter alia, ibid 161.

[360] Which also find normative foundation in the Charter (Art 8(3)) and TFEU (Art 16(2)) and whose role/importance only increased with the GDPR.

[361] This also holds true (to some extent) for example in: consumer protection law, and environmental protection regulation. '[B]y making "principal matters non-negotiable" data protection regulation corrects power imbalances.' Lynskey, *The Foundations of EU Data Protection Law* (n 74) 215. Referring to: Purtova, *Property Rights in Personal Data* (n 190) 205. Critical of this approach for data protection law: Bergkamp (n 12) 37.

[362] 'Complex and rich procedures to control and regulate the use of technology took precedence over the protection of individual privacy rights.' In: Mayer-Schönberger (n 84) 223–25.

[363] Looking at the data protection framework in particular, some measures may seem more vague (eg data minimization principle or requirement for fair and lawful processing) than others (eg purpose specification).

Table 2.1 Data protection matrix (incl examples)

	Ex Ante	*Ex Post*
Protective Measures	eg Data Quality Principles	eg DPA Enforcement
Empowerment Measures	eg Consent	eg Right to Erasure

ante protective measures; (b) *ex post* protective measures; (c) *ex ante* empowerment measures; (d) *ex post* empowerment measures (see Table 2.1). None of these four categories constitute absolutes in themselves. Moreover, as is so often the case in law, most adequate solutions in any given case lie somewhere in the middle. This particularly holds true in light of the complexity of today's information society, where there is no one-size-fits-all solution. From the 1970s onwards already, it has been recognized that in a dynamic and 'complex societal environment', it is necessary to both place 'conditions on information content' *and* enable 'control over dissemination and use of personal data'.[364]

HYBRIDS—The four categories should not be seen as mutually exclusive. In reality, data protection provisions can often be labelled with several of these categories. One such 'hybrid' is the transparency principle, which is both protective (requiring controllers to communicate certain information) and empowering (being a precondition for individuals to exercise control over their data). The measure might also evolve over time (certain information needs to be provided *ex ante*, but additional information might be requested *ex post*). As will become clear in Chapter 3 (see Chapter I.2, Section 4.2.2. Muddy Waters), the complexification of the data processing landscape—with a constantly morphing constellation of interacting operators—further complicates a neat division. Conscious of this, the purpose of the matrix is to enable conceptual clarity and provide the necessary structure and context in which to situate the 'right to erasure'.

The right to erasure can be located in field (d), ie as an *ex post* empowerment measure. Nowadays individual control over personal data is often said to have failed, particularly because of the data deluge trends described before (Introduction). Still, most of the empowerment criticism pivots around the thorny 'notice-and-consent/choice' issue.[365] As becomes clear in the data protection matrix, *consent* is but one form of empowerment. *Ex post* measures become particularly important in an environment where it is impossible to foresee all potential uses of personal data (both from an individual's or regulator's standpoint). Given

[364] Synthesis Report by Hans Peter Gassmann and G Russel Pipe (OECD Secretariat): *Policy Issues in Data Protection and Privacy: Concepts and Perspectives: Proceedings of the OECD Seminar, 24th to 26th June 1974* (n 332) 13. Proposing both empowerment measures (eg access rights) as well as paternalistic measures (eg regulatory authorities).

[365] See especially: Solove (n 353). Referred to in: Meg Leta Jones, 'Privacy without Screens & the Internet of Other People's Things' (2014) 51 Idaho Law Review 646.

this complexity, it is also not realistic to rely entirely on protective measures to keep data processing in check over time.[366] Hence, it is important to put at the disposal of individuals a data protection 'toolbox', in order for them to be able to also undertake action themselves. This toolbox includes several more or less powerful 'tools' that effectively put individuals in control throughout time.

Section 3. The Right to Erasure: Ultimate Power Tool?

Chapter 1 described how data protection—in no small part—emerged from the ruins of World War II. The Nazis' massive use of automated citizen registries to detect and capture 'Jews and other undesirables' may well be the first major example of the dangerous potential of automated data processing.[367] Unsurprisingly, the right to erasure can also be traced back to this dark era in European history.

Amsterdam, March 1943. One Saturday night, a small group of the resistance approached the local population registry office, dressed as police officers. The guards on duty outside the building were asked to join in searching for suspicious people on the premises. Once inside, the fake police officers sedated the guards and 'laid them to rest' in the zoological gardens next door. Back inside, the men entered the wooden attic where they emptied many drawers of ID cards. The registry contained such 'person-cards' on hundreds of thousands of Dutchmen, with detailed information such as birthday, family situation, occupation, religion and so on. These cards even contained the picture and fingerprints of the respective individuals. After drenching the piles of cards in fuel and installing timed explosives, the men quietly left the building. The explosion and fire that ensued destroyed most of the attic, and in fact the whole building. The fire-brigade slowly deployed its gear and then lavishly extinguished the fire, aiming to create as much water damage as possible. The goal was straightforward: prevent the German occupier from using this vast wealth of personal data for undesirable purposes.[368]

This anecdote might be one of the most striking historical examples where individuals seized control and enforced the erasure of (systematically processed) personal data. At the time, there were no data protection—let alone fundamental—rights that could be relied upon and people empowered

[366] Quelle (n 346).

[367] Black (n 10).

[368] Unfortunately, however, the main storage-hall remained largely intact. The majority of cards were tightly packed together in metal boxes and did not suffer (much) damage from the fire. Still, the attack generated a lot of chaos and rendered the register *de facto* unusable for almost a year. For a full account of the story, as well as more context to the coming into being of the Register and its role throughout the war, see: JT Veldkamp, *Het Amsterdamse Bevolkingsregister in Oorlogstijd (on File with the Author)*. (Unpublished monograph available at the Amsterdam Resistance Museum 1954).

themselves. But this makes the anecdote even more compelling. It clearly illustrates the normative underpinnings for the control over personal data and a 'right to erasure' in particular.[369] Section 3 is aimed specifically at investigating the origins and rationale of the right to erasure (and *ex post* empowerment measures in the GDPR more broadly).

3.1 History

3.1.1 Coming of Age

The previous section pinpointed some of the key hallmarks in data protection history generally. In light of this book's overall aim, this subsection zooms into the right to erasure in particular. It describes the coming of age of this seemingly exemplary individual 'empowerment measure' in data protection law. Unfortunately, a comparative analysis of the growing number of 'right to erasure' lookalikes in other jurisdictions (eg Argentina,[370] Japan,[371] Qatar,[372] Russia,[373] Madagascar,[374] Turkey,[375] and Brazil[376]) would far exceed the scope of this book, let alone this subsection.[377] With that caveat, the following pages will explore *when*, *where*, and *how* the right to erasure surfaced in EU data protection legislation, and as such provide the required context for the next sections and chapters. Indeed, the following subsection will briefly explain and evaluate the apparent key benefits and drawbacks of the right to erasure (and *ex post* empowerment measures more broadly).

[369] As an interesting side-note, the Belgian law regulating the national identity register (Rijksregister) contains a provision specifically mandating the destruction of the register in times of war. Article 14 wet tot regeling van een Rijksregister van de natuurlijke personen, *BS* 21 April 1984, 5247. Also, much more recently in the USA, a country with no GDPR (or Art 8 Charter) equivalent, the city of New York decided to purge information from some of their databases in order to prevent the Trump administration from using it for mass deportations. See: Cory Doctorow, 'NYC Will Cease Retaining Data That Trump Could Use for Mass Deportations' (*Boing Boing*, 8 December 2016) <https://boingboing.net/2016/12/08/nyc-will-cease-retaining-data.html> accessed 1 June 2019.

[370] Article 16, Personal Data Protection Law 25,326, Enacted on 30/10/2000.

[371] Article 26, Act No 57 on the Protection of Personal Information, 30/05/2003.

[372] Article 15, Regulation No 6 of 2005 on QFC Data Protection Regulations, Enacted on 17/10/2005.

[373] Article 14, Federal Law on Personal Data (No 152-FZ), Enacted on 27/07/2006.

[374] Article 25, Law No 2014-038 relating to protection of personal data is the main regulatory framework in Madagascar, Enacted on 16/12/2014.

[375] Article 11, Turkish Personal Data Protection Law No 6698, Enacted on 24/3/2016.

[376] Article 18, Federal Law No 13,709/2018, Enacted on 15/08/2018.

[377] See Efforts to map international data protection laws by: Graham Greenleaf, 'Global Data Privacy Laws: 89 Countries, and Accelerating' SSRN eLibrary <http://papers.ssrn.com/sol3/papers.cfm?abstract_id=2000034> accessed 1 June 2019; Graham Greenleaf, 'Global Data Privacy Laws 2017: 120 National Data Privacy Laws, Including Indonesia and Turkey' (Social Science Research Network 2017) SSRN Scholarly Paper ID 2993035 <https://papers.ssrn.com/abstract=2993035> accessed 12 June 2019; DLA Piper, 'Data Protection Laws of the World' <https://www.dlapiperdataprotection.com/index.html?t=world-map> accessed 12 June 2019; United Nations Conference on Trade and Development, 'Data Protection and Privacy Legislation Worldwide' <https://unctad.org/en/Pages/DTL/STI_and_ICTs/ICT4D-Legislation/eCom-Data-Protection-Laws.aspx> accessed 12 June 2019.

Section 4 will finally provide important conceptual clarifications as to the meaning of related—but different—rights, such as the right to be forgotten, the *droit à l'oubli*, right to erasure, right to be delisted, etc.

a) Council of Europe

The first noteworthy appearance of a 'right to erasure' can be found in a 1973 Council of Europe Resolution (on the '*Protection of the Privacy of Individuals vis-à-vis Electronic Data Banks in the Private Sector*').[378] Indeed, the explanatory report, specifically mentioned that 'it seems advisable to adopt a rule which would halt unbridled hoarding of data'.[379] This Resolution contained ten principles, which would later return in Convention 108 as well as the EU data protection framework. Principle 7 specifies 'Every care should be taken to correct inaccurate information and to erase obsolete information or information obtained in an unlawful way.' This principle was phrased as an obligation for 'those responsible for data banks [. . .] to pay attention not only to the ageing of data after their storage in the computer, but also to storage of data which were already obsolete from the outset'.[380]

For the first time an international document of this significance specified circumstances under which personal data should be deleted. A year later,[381] the CoE emphasized that 'in the private sector, individuals have a legitimate interest in seeing certain kinds of information concerning them, particularly that which is harmful to them, wiped off or rendered inoperative after a certain time has passed'.[382]

The absence of a formal right to erasure in the 1973 Resolution (on private sector use) was a deliberate decision. As noted in the Explanatory Report, 'the committee of experts [*authors of the Resolution*] did not wish to go so far as to recognise a formal "right to oblivion"'.[383] Their intention was solely to protect individuals from 'unreasonably long retention of data that could be harmful'.[384] Still, even though it does not confer an explicit data subject right, the provision certainly lays the groundwork for what is now known as *the right to erasure*. Importantly, the shadow of the right to erasure can also be found in several other principles in the Resolution. Principle 1 specifies that 'information stored should be accurate and [. . .] kept up to date'; Principle 2 states that 'information should be appropriate and relevant with regard to the purpose'; and Principle 4 explains '[r]ules should be laid down to specify the periods beyond which certain categories of information

378 Council of Europe—Committee of Ministers (n 159). This Resolution is usually cited together with: Council of Europe—Committee of Ministers (n 321).

379 Explanatory Report to: Council of Europe—Committee of Ministers (n 159) para 21.

380 Explanatory Report to: ibid 33.

381 When adopting: Council of Europe—Committee of Ministers (n 321).

382 Explanatory Report to: ibid 21.

383 Explanatory Report to: Council of Europe—Committee of Ministers (n 159) para 24.

384 Hondius (n 1) 218–19 citing the Explanatory Report.

should no longer be kept or used'.[385] These are all provisions—still present in todays' data protection framework—which (in a more or less subtle manner) incorporate or imply a right to erasure.[386]

b) *An Embryonic Right*

As illustrated by the CoE Resolution from 1973, most early data protection frameworks did not include explicit right to erasure provisions. Instead, the right was implied in other provisions, specifically those related to access and data quality.[387] For example, most early data protection frameworks already contained provisions obliging data to be 'accurate and kept up-to-date'. Most even included additional provisions requiring inaccurate information to be corrected and obsolete information to be erased.[388] Similarly, the first data protection frameworks already contained a purpose limitation principle, requiring information to be appropriate and relevant with regard to the purpose it is stored for.[389] Policy makers were also conscious of the time-dimension in factors such as 'relevance' and 'appropriateness'. Data—even if correct—that is no longer needed in order to achieve a specified purpose should be erased.[390]

The pioneering French and German data protection acts incorporated the first iterations of a right to erasure. Section 4(4) of the 1977 German *Bundesdatenschutzgesetz (BDSG)* explicitly stated that 'in accordance with this law, everyone has a right to [...] 4. Erasure of his personal data when its storage was not permitted, or, optionally in addition to the right to blocking, when the original purpose has expired.'[391] Section 14(3) of the same Act specified that personal data (a) *can* (*können*) be erased when

[385] In its Resolution directed at *public* sector data banks, the CoE specified a carve-out to obligatory time-limits 'if the use of the information for statistical, scientific or historical purposes requires its conservation for an indefinite duration'. Council of Europe—Committee of Ministers (n 321) principle 4(2).

[386] As they constrain the conditions under which the controller can process personal data. *A contrario*, if these conditions are *not* fulfilled, the erasure of the data can be requested. This will extensively be explained in Chapter 4. Similarly, see: Hondius (n 1) 112–13.

[387] In the same year as the CoE Resolution (73) was adopted, erasure was also being proposed as a subset of access principles in the USA. See: Caspar Weinberger, 'Records, Computers and the Rights of Citizens' (US Department of Health, Education and Welfare 1973).

[388] Especially Principles 1 and 7 in: Council of Europe—Committee of Ministers (n 159). Also: the 1973 Swedish (Sections 8–9) 1973 German (Sections 12(1), (21(1), (27(1)) and 1974 Austrian (Section 11(1)) Data Protection Bills. The Norwegian Private Registers Bill interestingly defines a legal presumption of obsoleteness 'of any personal credit information of an unfavorable kind which dates back more than five years.' All cited in: Hondius (n 1) 112–15.

[389] References to early national legislation in: Hondius (n 1) 115–20. CoE's Resolution (73) 22, Principle 2. Given the vague and abstract nature of these requirements (as compared to 'correct' and 'up-to-date'), private sector legislation was spelled out in terms of 'exceptions to the freedom of data gathering' rather than general interdictions. ibid 116–17.

[390] CoE's Resolution (73) 22 Principles 4 and 7. Also see: Explanatory Memorandum to 1980 OECD Guidelines, Paragraph 9: Purpose Specification; and European Union Agency for Fundamental Rights (FRA) and Council of Europe (n 242) 75.

[391] Loose translation by the author of *Jeder hat nach Maßgabe dieses Gesetzes ein Recht auf*

> [...] 4. Löschung der zu seiner Person gespeicherten Daten, wenn ihre Speicherung unzulässig war oder—wahlweise neben dem Recht auf Sperrung—nach Wegfall der ursprünglich erfüllten Voraussetzungen für die Speicherung.

the data is not necessary *anymore* to achieve the specified purpose and there is no reason to believe that the interests of the data subject would be thereby jeopardized and (b) *must* be erased if it was stored inadmissibly *or* when the data subject prefers erasure instead of blocking after the purpose has expired.[392] The BDSG also dictated the erasure of what would now be called 'sensitive data' (ie data concerning health, criminal offences, offences against public order, and religious or political opinions), unless the one holding the data could demonstrate their accuracy.[393]

The 1978 French *Loi relative à l'informatique, aux fichiers et aux libertés (Loi Informatique et Libertés)* can be seen as the first national data protection law to position individual empowerment very prominently. Indeed, its Article 26 granted every natural person a right to object, for legitimate reasons, to any processing of their personal data.[394] The *Loi Informatique et Libertés* also devoted a whole chapter (V), with six articles to an elaborate right of access.[395] Within that chapter, Article 36 provides for a right to erasure not unlike the one that would be incorporated into Directive 95/46. Specifically, it gives anyone who has a valid right of access, the right to demand for their personal data to be corrected, completed, clarified, updated, or erased, when that data is inexact, incomplete, ambiguous, expired, or when the collection, use, communication, or storage of that data is prohibited.[396] In case the entity receiving the request disagrees, the provision also puts the burden of proof on that entity rather than the data subject.[397] It is interesting to note that even though the French recognized the importance of a 'right to be forgotten' (*droit à l'oubli*), they did not in relation to the explicit right to erasure in Article 36. Instead the *droit à l'oubli* was seen as comprised within the purpose/storage limitation principle in Article 28.[398]

In sum, it seems that throughout the 1970s empowering individuals to exert their data protection interests themselves was not a policy goal.[399] In this 'first

See also: ACM Nugter, *Transborder Flow of Personal Data within the EC: A Comparative Analysis of the Privacy Statutes of the Federal Republic of Germany, France, the United Kingdom and The Netherlands and Their Impact on the Private Sector* (Kluwer Law and Taxation Publ 1990) 62.

392 In the case of purpose expiration, the processing should first be *blocked* (Section 14(2)), after which the data subject can request erasure.

393 Nugter (n 391) 62.

394 Author's translation of '*Toute personne physique a le droit de s'opposer, pour des raisons légitimes, à ce que des informations nominatives la concernant fassent l'object d'un traitement.*'

395 Indeed, it was said that even just the right of access alone justified the law as a whole. '*Cette partie de la loi est fondamentale. A elle seule, elle la justifie.*' André Holleaux, 'La Loi Du 6 Janvier 1978 Sur Informatique et Les Libertés — II —' (1978) 31 La Revue administrative 160, 160.

396 Author's translation of '*Le titulaire du droit d'accès peut exiger que soient rectifies, complètes, clarifies, mises à jour ou effaces les informations le concernant qui sont inexactes, incompletes, équivoques, périmées ou don't la collecte, ou l'utilisation, la communication ou la conservation est interdite.*' For a detailed description, see: Holleaux (n 395).

397 Unless the personal data have been shared by the data subject him/herself, or are obtained with their consent.

398 Holleaux (n 37) 38–39.

399 See: Mayer-Schönberger (n 84) 221–25.

generation' of data protection norms, it was primarily data protection commissioners (or their equivalents) who were expected to enforce the rules.[400] Given the still relatively high cost of data storage, erasure also often appeared to be somewhat of a non-issue (see language in several laws saying that personal data *may* be erased, unless harmful to the respective individual).[401] Indeed, the erasure of data in particular was thought to be potentially detrimental to the individual (see notably the first situation under Section 14(3) of the 1977 German BDSG).[402] Gradually, the primarily 'protective' approach to data protection of the first generation was complemented by more empowerment measures in the second generation towards the late 1970s.[403] Individuals were given a more prominent role through specific data protection *rights*. For the first time, *consent* was introduced as a proper ground for lawful processing.[404] The rights of access[405] and to correct personal data constitute the first meaningful *ex post* empowerment measure in the data protection context.[406] The rights to erasure and to object seemed to only appear later on. Erasure in particular was generally seen as part of the broader 'right of access' (also including the right to rectification, bring up to date, etc).

c) *From Duty to Right*

By 1980, the right to erasure had changed from being an implicit element in data protection norms to an explicit right. The OECD guidelines notably included a paragraph on Individual Participation,[407] providing *inter alia* that:

[400] ibid.

[401] Nugter (n 391).

[402] It was suggested that the erasure of personal data should require a Court ruling. This would exclude, of course, situations in which there is a legal obligation to remove certain personal data (eg after a certain time or if other conditions are fulfilled). H Auernhammer (Federal Ministry of the Interior—Germany), 'Legislation on Data Processing and Particularly on Data Transmission and Deletion' *Policy Issues in Data Protection and Privacy: Concepts and Perspectives: Proceedings of the OECD Seminar, 24th to 26th June 1974* (n 332) 161; 166–67; Kosta (n 1) 29; on the dangers of data alteration, deletion and potential decontextualization from a computer scientist's point of view (in the 1970s), see: Ruth M Davis, 'Technologist's View of Privacy and Security in Automated Information Systems, A' (1974) 4 Rutgers J Computers & L 264, 276.

[403] Which can be situated in French, Austrian, Danish, and Norwegian legislation. Mayer-Schönberger (n 84) 226–29.

[404] ibid 227. As an interesting side-note, the Commission's initial proposal for Directive 95/46 mentioned *consent* under the heading of data subject *rights*. This was later changed, as it would have meant that consent would be required whenever personal data is processed (not just as one ground among several). See: Kosta (n 1) 91–92.

[405] The right of access to information traditionally had quite an important role. See especially Article 18 of the 1989 Declaration of fundamental rights and freedoms. See also: González Fuster, *The Emergence of Personal Data Protection as a Fundamental Right of the EU* (n 1) 188–89.

[406] Mayer-Schönberger acknowledges that such a right was already present in the first generation of data protection norms. He explains, however, that in these first frameworks, the right to access and correct was merely there to support 'accuracy requirements'. Mayer-Schönberger (n 84) 226–27. Also see: Hondius (n 1) 112–15; Burkert (n 18) 45; Bennett (n 153) 103–06; 156–58.

[407] Paragraph 13. The Explanatory Memorandum to the Guidelines explained that this principle 'is generally regarded as perhaps the most important privacy protection safeguard. It has been explained above that in the discussions preceding the OECD guidelines (notably the 1974 OECD Seminar), there was agreement at that stage already on the fact that preventive protection should be extended

> individuals should have the right: [...] (d) to challenge data relating to them and, if the challenge is successful to have the data erased [...].

A year later, the CoE's Convention 108 (Article 8) specified that:

> [a]ny person shall be enabled (c) to obtain, as the case may be, rectification or erasure of such data if these have been processed contrary to [...] domestic law [...].

With the adoption and subsequent implementation of Directive 95/46, the right to erasure was now framed (more or less) identically throughout the EU. Five years later, in the running up to the Charter, the European Group on Ethics (see 'Charter of Fundamental Rights'), strongly advised for including a *right to delete* in the Charter, but to no avail.[408] Still, one might argue the Charter indirectly includes such a right through explicit reference to data quality principles and data subject rights of access and to rectification. After all, up until the GDPR, the right to erasure was still a subset of the right of access.

Ever since the adoption of Directive 95/46, *ex post* empowerment measures—actively enabling participation through individual rights—have played a pivotal role in EU data protection frameworks.[409] Yet, from the 1980s already, such 'data subject rights' have been criticised as 'toothless paper tigers'. Mayer-Schönberger characterizes the paradoxical effect of endowing individuals with too much responsibility to exercise their rights[410] as 'contractual devaluation of data protection'.[411] Even before the breakthrough of the Internet, people routinely contracted away their rights and/or did not appear willing to exercise them in the first place.[412] Indeed, it took almost two decades since Directive 95/46 reaffirmed the existence of a right to erasure, before the right's first notable application at an EU level.

Quite some eyebrows were raised when the CJEU issued its landmark ruling of 13 May 2014, in which it firmly established data subjects' rights to erasure and to object are a direct extension of their fundamental right to data protection under the Charter.[413] This clearly signalled the right to erasure should not be considered

with control over information once recorded (Synthesis Report in: *Policy Issues in Data Protection and Privacy: Concepts and Perspectives: Proceedings of the OECD Seminar, 24th to 26th June 1974* (n 332) referred to in; Kosta (n 1) 28–29). Put differently, in 1974 already, there was agreement on the need for *ex post* empowerment measures.

408 European Group on Ethics in Science and New Technologies (n 273) 26–27. The Group acknowledged the strong influence of the German concept of Informational Self-Determination.

409 Mayer-Schönberger (n 84) 235.

410 Typifying the 'third generation of data protection norms', which followed the German Population Census (or informational self-determination) Case.

411 Mayer-Schönberger (n 84) 232. Similarly see: Koops (n 140).

412 Mayer-Schönberger (n 84) 229–32.

413 *Google Spain* (n 106). The Ruling will amply be discussed throughout the rest of this book.

subordinate to the right of access (anymore). Indeed, in 2009 already, the CJEU had explained that the 'right of access is necessary to enable the data subject to exercise' his/her right to erasure.[414] In 2015, the Court further solidified the importance of the right to erasure, establishing that 'legislation not providing for any possibility for an individual to pursue legal remedies in order to [...] obtain the [...] erasure of such data, does not respect the essence of the fundamental right to effective judicial protection, as enshrined in Article 47 of the Charter'.[415] In this relatively short period, the Court of Justice clearly paved the way for the right to erasure's emancipation in the GPDR.

3.1.2 Legislative History of Article 17 GDPR

On 25 January 2012, the European Commission[416] published its proposal for a General Data Protection Regulation.[417] As anticipated, it comprised a specific provision titled the 'Right to be forgotten and to erasure', which was described as giving individuals 'the right to have their data deleted if they withdraw their consent and if there are no other legitimate grounds for retaining the data'.[418] A helicopter view of the whole legislative process suggests two scenarios played a particularly important role in proposing and adopting the provision: search engines and social networks.[419] Several Member States had already been experimenting with similar ideas in the late 2000s.[420] Despite a wave of criticism,[421] and four years of fierce

[414] *College van burgemeester en wethouders van Rotterdam v MEE Rijkeboer* (n 111) para 51.

[415] *Maximillian Schrems v Data Protection Commissioner* (n 122) para 95.

[416] This section refers to key data protection concepts such as *controller* and *data subject* that will be explained in more detail in Chapter 3.

[417] COM(2012) 11 final.

[418] European Commission, 'Communication from the Commission to the European Parliament, the Council, the European Economic and Social Committee and the Committee of the Regions Safeguarding Privacy in a Connected World. A European Data Protection Framework for the 21st Century,' COM(2012)9 final January 25, 2012.

[419] Most, if not all, examples mentioned to illustrate the right either refer to the *Google Spain* vignette or users wishing to remove information from a social network. Edwards even claimed that if social networks would have been more accommodating and actually enabled data to be removed (which was often not possible around 2010), the right to be forgotten might even not have made it into the proposal in the first place. See: Lilian Edwards, 'Keynote Address on the Right to Be Forgotten' (Bileta, Hertfordshire, UK, 12 April 2016).

[420] For example, France (Premier Ministre de la République Française, 'Charte Du Droit a l'Oubli Dans Les Sites Collaboratifs et Les Moteurs de Recherche'), and Spain (Artemi Rallo Lombarte and Centro de Estudios Políticos y Constitucionales (Espanya), *El Derecho al olvido en Internet: Google versus España* (Centro de Estudios Políticos y Constitucionales 2014).) See also: De Hert and Papakonstantinou (n 86) 137.

[421] Particularly across the Atlantic many commentators reacted panicky: Mike Masnick, 'Why Can't Europe Just Forget The Ridiculous Idea Of A "Right To Be Forgotten"' (*Techdirt*, 31 January 2012) <www.techdirt.com/articles/20120129/23085517583/why-cant-europe-just-forget-ridiculous-idea-right-to-be-forgotten.shtml> accessed 1 June 2019; Adam Thierer, 'Europe's "Right to Be Forgotten": Privacy as Internet Censorship' (*The Technology Liberation Front*, 23 January 2012) <http://techliberation.com/2012/01/23/europes-right-to-be-forgotten-privacy-as-internet-censorship/> accessed 1 June 2019; Jane Yakowitz, 'More Crap From the E.U.' (*Info/Law*, 25 January 2012) <http://blogs.law.harvard.edu/infolaw/2012/01/25/more-crap-from-the-e-u/> accessed 1 June 2019; Jeffrey Rosen, 'The Right to Be Forgotten' (2012) 64 Stanford Law Review Online 88. Others were more nuanced: Meg

lobbying[422] and negotiations, the provision still stands and is now undeniably part of EU data protection law. Given the centrality of this provision to this book overall, its current form will be elaborately analysed later on (Chapter 4). This sub-section will pinpoint some of the most important alterations the article underwent throughout the legislative process.

Build Up—In July 2009, the European Commission (EC) launched a public consultation on 'the future legal framework for protecting personal data'. This consultation showed that citizens were demanding more control over their personal data.[423] Businesses on the other hand, raised concerns over potentially unreasonable and disproportionate exercise of data subject rights.[424] In the same consultation, WP29 called for greater empowerment of data subjects and strengthening the responsibility of controllers.[425] When officially announcing its plans for drafting a data protection reform in 2010, the EC's first key objective was to strengthen individuals' rights. One of the main components for doing so, was through 'enhancing control over one's data' and indeed by 'improving the modalities for the actual exercise of the right [...] to erasure' and 'clarifying the so-called "right to be forgotten", i.e. the right of individuals to have their data no longer processed and deleted when they are no longer needed for legitimate purposes'.[426] This was said to be mainly a German and French suggestion.[427] Once the ball had started to roll, individual empowerment and the 'right to be forgotten' quickly became central themes leading

Leta Ambrose, 'You Are What Google Says You Are: The Right to Be Forgotten and Information Stewardship' (2012) 17 International Review of Information Ethics 07; Steven C Bennett, 'The Right to Be Forgotten: Reconciling EU and US Perspectives' (2012) 30 Berkeley J Int'l L 161; John Hendel, 'Why Journalists Shouldn't Fear Europe's "Right to Be Forgotten"' (*The Atlantic*, 25 January 2012) <http://www.theatlantic.com/technology/archive/2012/01/why-journalists-shouldnt-fear-europes-right-to-be-forgotten/251955/> accessed 1 June 2019. In Europe, see inter alia: Joris Van Hoboken, '9 Reasons Why a "Right to Be Forgotten" Is Really Wrong' (8 December 2011) <http://www.jorisvanhoboken.nl/?m=201112> accessed 19 September 2012; Koops (n 140); Christiana Markou, 'The "Right to Be Forgotten": Ten Reasons Why It Should Be Forgotten' in Serge Gutwirth, Ronald Leenes, and Paul de Hert (eds), *Reforming European Data Protection Law* (Springer Netherlands 2015) <http://link.springer.com/chapter/10.1007/978-94-017-9385-8_8> accessed 1 June 2019.

422 See, for example: Monica Horten, *Closing of the Net* (Polity Press 2016); Carole Cadwalladr and Duncan Campbell, 'Revealed: Facebook's Global Lobbying against Data Privacy Laws' *The Observer* (2 March 2019) <https://www.theguardian.com/technology/2019/mar/02/facebook-global-lobbying-campaign-against-data-privacy-laws-investment> accessed 5 March 2019. And the work by LobbyPlag.eu.

423 DG Justice, 'Summary of Replies to the Public Consultation about the Future Legal Framework for Protecting Personal Data.' (European Commission 2010) 2–3.

424 ibid 9.

425 ibid 13.

426 European Commission, 'Communication from the Commission to the European Parliament, the Council, the European Economic and Social Committee and the Committee of the Regions—A Comprehensive Approach on Personal Data Protection in the European Union' (n 305) 5–8.

427 Council of the European Union, 'Council Conclusions on the Communication from the Commission to the European Parliament and the Council—A Comprehensive Approach on Personal Data Protection in the European Union' <http://www.statewatch.org/news/2011/feb/eu-council-draft-conclusion-dp-17923-rev1-11.pdf> accessed 16 March 2018.

up to the EC's eventual proposal in 2012. A Eurobarometer in June 2011 highlighted inter alia that 75 per cent of Europeans wanted a strong right to erasure.[428] The impact assessment accompanying the official proposal also highlighted the practical difficulties in effectively exercising the right to erasure already present in Directive 95/46.[429] Indeed, it is fair to say the right to erasure and to be forgotten was one of the pet notions of then Commissioner Viviane Reding, who was the driving force behind the reform.[430]

From Two to One—Zooming into (the different iterations of) the actual text of the 'right to be forgotten and to erasure', a number of observations can be made. First of all, it seems the two were first seen as separate data subject rights. A draft of the EC proposal that was leaked on 10 November 2011,[431] suggests that what is now known as Article 17, initially consisted of two provisions: the 'right to erasure' (Art 15) and the 'right to be forgotten' (Art 16). The 'right to erasure' was said to spell out more clearly and explicitly what was already found in Directive 95/46. The 'right to be forgotten' was considered more innovative, because it (a) dictated erasure upon withdrawal or expiration of consent or after the right to object was successfully invoked; and (b) renders the right 'effective also in relation to search engines, etc. (sic)'. However, in another leaked draft less than three weeks later (29 November 2011), the two provisions had already been merged into one Article.

Right to Be Forgotten—Perhaps the most noteworthy innovation relates to the right's second paragraph. Today, this paragraph essentially puts in place a duty on the shoulders of controllers to inform others about received erasure requests when it has made that data public.[432] The leaked draft from 10 November 2011 made very clear the intended target were search engines and other 'publicly available communication service which allows or facilitates the search of or access to this data' (references that were later removed). It is clear from the different iterations of the EC's proposal that this second paragraph is what was meant with the terminology 'right to be forgotten'. The explanation accompanying the EC's proposal still implied the distinction between the right to erasure and right to be

[428] European Commission, 'Special Eurobarometer 359: Attitudes on Data Protection and Electronic Identity in the European Union' (European Commission 2011) 158–59 <http://ec.europa.eu/public_opinion/archives/ebs/ebs_359_en.pdf>.

[429] European Commission, 'Commission Staff Working Paper: Impact Assessment Accompanying the Proposals for General Data Protection Regulation and Directive on Data Protection in Police and Judicial Matters' (n 30) 27–28.

[430] Viviane Reding, 'Building Trust in the Digital Single Market: Reforming the EU's Data Protection Rules (SPEECH/11/814)' (Conference organized by the Industry Coalition for Data Protection—American Chamber of Commerce to the European Union, Brussels, 28 November 2011).

[431] On file with the author.

[432] The full text reads: 'Where the controller has made the personal data public and is obliged pursuant to paragraph 1 to erase the personal data, the controller, taking account of available technology and the cost of implementation, shall take reasonable steps, including technical measures, to inform controllers which are processing the personal data that the data subject has requested the erasure by such controllers of any links to, or copy or replication of, those personal data.' This paragraph will be analysed extensively in Chapter 4.

forgotten, stating that: 'Article 17 provides the data subject's right to be forgotten and to erasure. It further elaborates and specifies the right of erasure provided for in Article 12(b) of Directive 95/46/EC and provides the conditions of the right to be forgotten, including the obligation of the controller which has made the personal data public to inform third parties on the data subject's request to erase any links to, or copy or replication of that personal data.' This was further confirmed in Recital 54 of the 2012 Proposal, which explained that the right to erasure should be extended in order to strengthen the right to be forgotten in the online environment. As will appear later on (Chapter 4), this motivation has largely remained the same in the final version of Article 17(2).

Obligation of Means v Obligation of Result—Tracing the evolution of Article 17's second paragraph, it is worth going back to the draft version of the Commission's initial proposal, that was leaked on 29 November 2011.[433] Recital 47 of this leaked draft required that 'any publicly available copies or replications in websites and search engines should also be deleted by the controller who has made the information public'.[434] The actual provision itself obliged controllers who have made personal data public, to 'ensure the erasure of any public Internet link to, copy of, or replication of the personal data relating to the data subject contained in any publicly available communication service which allows or facilitates the search of or access to this personal data'. Presumably attenuating concerns, the EC had converted this far-reaching obligation of result into an obligation of means in the official proposal of January 2012. Controllers having made personal data public, were now expected to 'take all reasonable steps, including technical measures, [. . .] to inform third parties' about erasure requests. Importantly however, a second sentence was added which appeared to introduce a quasi-strict liability regime for controllers who authorized a third party to publish personal data (in which case, the original controller was considered responsible for that publication). This second sentence was removed after the European Parliament's first reading. As a matter of fact, many MEPs had (unsuccessfully) suggested to remove the second paragraph altogether.[435]

Requirements—A second component that changed considerably relates to the requirements for invoking the right to erasure (which will be discussed in detail in Chapter 4). The list of situations in which the right to erasure can be invoked evolved from three (earliest leaked draft, 10 November 2011), to four (official EC

433 Available at: http://statewatch.org/news/2011/dec/eu-com-draft-dp-reg-inter-service-consultation.pdf.

434 This had already changed from the earlier leaked draft (from 10 November 2011), which did not yet narrow the scope to controllers who have made the data public.

435 Committee on Civil Liberties, Justice and Home Affairs (Rapporteur Albrecht JP), 'Report on the Proposal for a Regulation of the European Parliament and of the Council on the Protection of Individuals with Regard to the Processing of Personal Data and on the Free Movement of Such Data (General Data Protection Regulation)' (European Parliament (Committee on Civil Liberties, Justice and Home Affairs) 2013) A7-0402/2013 Amendments 1411–1414.

proposal, 25 January 2012), to five (Council General Approach, 11 June 2015), to six in the final version.[436] Yet, when looked at more closely, the changes seem to be more of a cosmetic rather than substantive in nature. Indeed, the gist of the six 'right to erasure triggers' in current Article 17(1) were mostly present since the EC's first leaked drafts already. Some were simply grouped together (eg 'withdrawal of consent and unlawful processing') or already alluded to in the introductory sentence (eg data made available while the data subject was a child). The only 'new' trigger that was not included until the Council General Approach in June 2015, grants a right to erasure when 'the personal data have to be erased for compliance with a legal obligation (currently Art 17(1)e).

Last Six Paragraphs—The original right to be forgotten and to erasure provision contained nine paragraphs. Only the first three were retained in the final version, so what happened to the other six? Paragraphs 4 to 6 related to the right to restriction of processing, ie the personal data is not erased, but can only be processed for very narrowly specified purposes. These paragraphs were not removed from the final GDPR text altogether but were rather given their own independent Article (18). The seventh paragraph essentially applied the accountability principle (current Art 6(2)), data protection by design (current Art 25), and the obligation for record keeping (current Art 30) to the right to erasure.[437] It is therefore not surprising that it did not make the final cut. The same can be said with regard to the eighth paragraph, which was even more redundant, declaring '[w]here the erasure is carried out, the controller shall not otherwise process such personal data'. The ninth paragraph in the EC's proposal, finally, empowered the Commission to adopt delegated acts on some of the modalities of the right to be forgotten, erasure, and restriction of processing. This provision was partially subsumed by Article 92 in the final version of the GDPR. The drafting of guidance on the problematic second paragraph, however, was assigned to the European Data Protection Board (Art 70(1)d).

Title—Finally, it is worth to point out the oscillating terminology used in the title of Article 17. The original title (in leaked drafts and) in the EC's official proposal was still 'Right to be forgotten and to erasure'. After the first reading of the European Parliament, this was changed to 'Right to erasure'. Among the justifications for shortening the title were that it was misleading and overpromising, as the GDPR allegedly did not provide a 'right to be forgotten'.[438] After the Council

[436] All official documents and iterations of the GDPR can be found at: http://eur-lex.europa.eu/procedure/EN/2012_11.

[437] The provision stated that '[t]he controller shall implement mechanisms to ensure that the time limits established for the erasure of personal data and/or for a periodic review of the need for the storage of the data are observed'.

[438] See Amendments 1380–1383 in: Committee on Civil Liberties, Justice and Home Affairs (Rapporteur Albrecht JP), 'Draft Report on the Proposal for a Regulation of the European Parliament and of the Council on the Protection of Individual with Regard to the Processing of Personal Data and on the Free Movement of Such Data (General Data Protection Regulation). Amendments (4)

general approach, the title was changed again, now reading *Right to erasure and 'to be forgotten'*. The introduction of quotation marks seems to try and walk the line between on the one hand acknowledging the contested nature of the term, and on the other hand recognizing the important connotation it has. Making things even more odd, the finally adopted Article 17 is now titled *Right to erasure ('right to be forgotten')*. Adding parentheses on top of the quotation marks confuses readers even further as to the meaning. It appears that the legislator decided to maintain the political slogan because it had become the nom de plume for the right to erasure in popular parlance.

In sum, the final version of Article 17 GDPR essentially spells out and strengthens principles that were already implied in Directive 95/46.[439] The provision is primarily aimed at empowering individuals, rendering more effective their ability to have personal data removed 'if there are no legitimate grounds for retaining it'.[440] The main added value of Article 17 GDPR is that it removes (or at least, drastically reduces) uncertainty as to the existence and conditions for applying such a right as well as explicitly recognizes potential conflicts, notably with information freedoms. Both are particularly thorny issues in today's information society and will be examined in detail in the following two parts of this book. Chapter 4 will extensively dissect Article 17 and provide the required insights into the legislative history of each specific element in the provision.

3.1.3 Interim Conclusion

It took quite a while for the right to erasure in EU data protection law to come of age. Even though it made its way into policy/legal documents as early as in the 1970s, not much importance was given to the right to erasure. It was generally subsumed by the right of access and mentioned in relation to the right to rectification. This emphasizes the right to erasure was primarily seen in function of the accuracy of 'data banks'. Admittedly, the right was also implied in other—more 'protective'—provisions such as 'purpose limitation' and 'lawful ground'. Laying down these principles into law entails that when they are not complied with, data should not (or no longer) be kept. The right to erasure, in other words, was mainly a by-product of other data protection principles/provisions. It is only

1189–1492' (European Parliament (Committee on Civil Liberties, Justice and Home Affairs) 2013) 2012/0011(COD). Axel Voss (MEP and member of the European Parliament's LIBE committee) even called the 'right to be forgotten' illusionary.

[439] This will become clear throughout the following parts of this book. See, in particular, Chapters 3–4 on the application of the right to erasure.

[440] Viviane Reding, 'The EU Data Protection Reform 2012: Safeguarding Privacy in a Connected World' (Press Conference on the Presentation of the new Proposals, Brussels, 25 January 2012) <http://ec.europa.eu/archives/commission_2010-2014/reding/pdf/speeches/data-protection-reform2012_en.pdf> accessed 1 June 2019.

since around 2010 that one could say the right to erasure has been elevated to a more prominent position in the broader data protection framework. Most notably through the European Commission's introduction of a dedicated provision in the GDPR in 2012 and the CJEU Ruling in *Google Spain*. With the adoption of the GDPR in 2016, the right to erasure has finally embarked on adulthood. Standing on its own feet now, the right is put forward as a crucial empowerment measure serving the control rationale behind the right to data protection in the Charter.

3.2 The Right to Erasure Today

With the right to erasure being one of the prototypical *ex post* empowerment measures in the data protection framework, it is worth reiterating the key merits and drawbacks of such an approach to data protection.

3.2.1 The Case for *Ex Post* Empowerment Measures

Protection through empowerment clearly corroborates the right to data protection's underlying rationale of control and (personal) autonomy.[441] In order to be a free and autonomous citizen, at least some level of control over one's information is required.[442] This liberal ideology also entails a reluctance to overregulate the collection and use of personal data (through protective measures). Empowering individuals with a right to erasure has pragmatic justifications too. As a matter of fact, the current data-processing eco-system as described in the Introduction has become too complex to adequately regulate through protective measures only.[443]

The value of *ex post* empowerment measures in particular, is that they are designed with *time* in mind. They inherently enable control throughout the personal data's lifecycle. Data protection does not stop at the moment it is collected.[444] Enabling individuals to control (the use of) their personal data over time is important for a variety of reasons. Today, it is practically impossible to predict (all) (negative) consequences of the use of personal data.[445] Even if one can foresee a

[441] See above and: Ausloos, 'The "Right to Be Forgotten"—Worth Remembering?' (n 353) 147–48.

[442] Which is a central idea throughout: Bernal (n 146).

[443] eg Ausloos, 'The "Right to Be Forgotten"—Worth Remembering?' (n 353) 145; Lokke Moerel and Corien Prins, 'Privacy for the Homo Digitalis: Proposal for a New Regulatory Framework for Data Protection in the Light of Big Data and the Internet of Things' <http://papers.ssrn.com/abstract=2784123> accessed 1 June 2019.

[444] Emphasized once again by WP29 with regard to the Internet of Things: 'users must remain in complete control of their personal data throughout the product lifecycle'. Article 29 Working Party, 'Opinion 8/2014 on the on Recent Developments on the Internet of Things' (n 73) 3.

[445] Reconfirmed in: European Commission, 'Commission Staff Working Paper: Impact Assessment Accompanying the Proposals for General Data Protection Regulation and Directive on Data Protection in Police and Judicial Matters' (n 30).

few, they are very abstract, distant, and uncertain. They are abstract because the harms or impact is often of an intangible societal or psychological nature.[446] They are distant, as they do not generally present themselves right away. And they are uncertain because they might never occur, or at least not in a predictable way. So, even if an individual might know intellectually that the usage may have negative consequences, this is not going to change behaviour that much.[447] In many cases, the individual will not even be aware that personal data is being collected and/or used in the first place (let alone the extent to which this happens).[448] The few technical efforts people can make in order to protect their data online, are often ignored or circumvented.[449]

Against this backdrop, *ex ante* data protection empowerment measures are not sufficient to enable an adequate—persistent through time—level of control over data. In isolation, consent can hardly be seen as 'the main means of empowerment of the data subject'.[450,451] This is particularly true given the increasing ambiguity regarding the data protection framework's material scope (see Chapter 3).[452] *Ex post* measures—and the rights to erasure and to object in particular—offer people an effective opportunity to permanently (re-)evaluate the use of their data for ever-changing purposes in dynamic contexts.[453]

Today, the right to erasure is one of the key *ex post* empowerment measures in the data protection framework. As Bernal explains: 'wherever and however data

[446] eg The panopticon effect (Oscar H Gandy, *The Panoptic Sort: A Political Economy of Personal Information* (Westview 1993)); comprehensive and permanent digital 'remembering' would undermine human reasoning, preventing people from generalizing and conceptualizing (Viktor Mayer-Schönberger, *Delete: The Virtue of Forgetting in the Digital Age* (1st edn, Princeton UP 2009) 118–19); decontextualization (Nissenbaum (n 156)); and digital market manipulation (Ryan Calo, 'Digital Market Manipulation' (2014) 82 Geo Wash L Rev 995).

[447] On cognitive biases, see (the references in): Ian Brown, 'The Economics of Privacy, Data Protection and Surveillance' (2013) 6–7 <http://papers.ssrn.com/abstract=2358392> accessed 1 June 2019.

[448] Only very motivated individuals will take the time to read privacy policies. But even if they do, these documents rarely give a full and detailed picture of all potential uses. Moreover, researchers calculated in 2008 already, that it would take an average of 76 working days to read all privacy policies a user encounters over the period of a year. McDonald and Cranor (n 113); Meg Leta Jones, *Ctrl + Z: The Right to Be Forgotten* (New York UP 2016) 86–87; Brendan Van Alsenoy and others, 'From Social Media Service to Advertising Network—A Critical Analysis of Facebook's Revised Policies and Terms' (KU Leuven & VUB 2015) 1.3 <www.law.kuleuven.be/icri/en/news/item/icri-cir-advises-belgian-privacy-commission-in-facebook-investigation>.

[449] eg Mika Ayenson and others, 'Flash Cookies and Privacy II: Now with HTML5 and ETag Respawning' <ssrn.com/abstract=1898390> accessed 1 June 2019; Van Alsenoy and others (n 448); Dan Goodin, 'Beware of Ads That Use Inaudible Sound to Link Your Phone, TV, Tablet, and PC' (*Ars Technica*, 13 November 2015) <http://arstechnica.com/tech-policy/2015/11/beware-of-ads-that-use-inaudible-sound-to-link-your-phone-tv-tablet-and-pc/> accessed 1 June 2019.

[450] Kosta (n 1) 140.

[451] Koops speaks of the 'mythology of consent'. See: Koops (n 140) 251.

[452] The notion of 'personal data' has become very ambiguous and should not be seen as a static concept. Information can be (un)linked to a person over time, vis-à-vis different actors and in different contexts. A flexible and casuistic approach is required, taking into account the constant transformation of 'data' as such.

[453] See in this regard also: *College van burgemeester en wethouders van Rotterdam v MEE Rijkeboer* (n 111) paras 51–54.

exists, it is vulnerable, in many different ways. Conversely, [...] if data does not exist, it cannot be vulnerable.'[454] This may seem quite self-evident in theory but raises questions from a practical point of view. The technological trends described in the Introduction explain how 'the default of forgetting has shifted to one of remembering'.[455] There are no (more) technical or economic constraints to the pervasiveness of (personal) data[456] and there is a lot of randomness as to what is (not) 'remembered'.[457] This permanent memory generates vulnerability to individuals ranging from frequent data breaches,[458] to unforeseen and/or undesirable future uses. Indeed, simply 'liking' pages or content on Facebook might reveal your sexual or political orientation,[459] information which in turn may be used for a variety of different ends. The ephemerality, spontaneity, and whimsical nature of human behaviour contrasts sharply with economic incentives to datafy and valorize that behaviour.[460] Digital abstention or refusing to consent is increasingly unrealistic. Protective measures imposing (automatic) deletion that have been around since the first data protection legislations already have clearly proven to be insufficient in addressing these concerns as well. The rights to erasure and to object do empower concerned individuals, without the negative externalities of protective or even paternalistic measures that are too prescriptive. On a macro level, the rights also contribute to sustain 'semantic discontinuity'. A counter-intuitive, but societally desirable goal, Cohen explains, making it difficult to assemble and maintain comprehensive personal data records.[461] Indeed, *ex post*

[454] Bernal (n 146) 177.

[455] Mayer-Schönberger (n 84) 2.

[456] Today, it is fair to say the opposite is true. It has become costlier to erase personal data than to store it. See (references in) de Terwangne (n 218) 3–4. On the economic incentives to maximize data collection and storage, see notably the work of big data evangelists such as Mayer-Schönberger and Cukier (Ch 1 n 53).

[457] Meg L Ambrose, 'It's About Time: Privacy, Information Life Cycles, and the Right to Be Forgotten' (2013) 16 Stanford Technology Law Review 371.

[458] eg Sebastian Anthony, 'Ashley Madison, an Online Dating Website for Cheaters, Gets Hacked [Updated]' (*Ars Technica*, 21 July 2015) <https://arstechnica.com/information-technology/2015/07/ashley-madison-an-dating-website-for-cheaters-gets-hacked/> accessed 18 March 2018; Lee Mathews, 'Equifax Data Breach Impacts 143 Million Americans' (*Forbes*, 7 September 2017) <https://www.forbes.com/sites/leemathews/2017/09/07/equifax-data-breach-impacts-143-million-americans/> accessed 18 March 2018.

[459] Michal Kosinski, David Stillwell, and Thore Graepel, 'Private Traits and Attributes Are Predictable from Digital Records of Human Behavior' (2013) 110 Proceedings of the National Academy of Sciences 5802.

[460] Wilfred McClay, 'On the Need for Erasure' (2015) 17 The Hedgehog Review <http://www.iasc-culture.org/THR/THR_article_2015_Spring_McClay.php> accessed 1 June 2019.

[461] 'Semantic discontinuity helps to separate contexts from one another, thereby enabling personal boundary management.' Julie Cohen in: Wouter De Been, Payal Arora, and Mireille Hildebrandt (eds), *Crossroads in New Media, Identity, and Law: The Shape of Diversity to Come* (Palgrave Macmillan 2015) 78. Similarly see Hildebrandt (with references to Morozov and Brownsword) who explains that human freedom depends on mistakes, ambiguity, opportunities to disobey, and so on. These are all elements that 'big data' tries to halt. Mireille Hildebrandt, 'Slaves to Big Data. Or Are We?' (2013) 16 IDP Revista de Internet, Derecho Y Política 18 <http://works.bepress.com/mireille_hildebrandt/52> accessed 1 June 2019.

empowerment measures in data protection law facilitate civil disobedience in the information age.

In sum, the durability and decontextualization of (personal) data overrides individual autonomy and deeply affects relationships, affordances, and (legal) status. *Ex post* empowerment measures are absolutely necessary to restore some level of autonomy and safeguard fundamental rights.

3.2.2 Drawbacks

Ex post empowerment measures—and the right to erasure in particular—are no silver bullet for data protection overall. Some of the key concerns with regard to empowerment measures in general pertain to the overburdening of individuals; the (over)reliance on transparency, and equal bargaining positions.[462] In 1992 already, Bennett pointed out that '[s]ubject control entails some enormous disadvantages, relying as it does on very unrealistic assumptions about the participatory inclinations and abilities of the average citizen'.[463] More recently, Koops challenged the effectiveness of empowerment measures against the backdrop of practices which 'involve multiple data controllers and processors sharing sets of data, for multiple, not seldom fuzzy, purposes, and increasingly with automated operations on data—think of cloud computing and profiling—that data controllers themselves do not fully understand or know the details of'.[464] Due to individuals' bounded rationality, leaving them too much 'in control', is also said to potentially lead them to take decisions that are contrary to their own stated preferences, or even long-term interests.[465] Indeed, overreliance on data subject empowerment shifts the responsibility of data protection onto the shoulders of individuals, 'who, in many cases, may have neither the skill nor the bargaining power to resist commercial demands for their data'.[466]

The right to erasure specifically raises some additional concerns. It could be seen as merely postponing the 'illusion of choice' offered by consent.[467] Indeed, is one truly free to fully delete all personal data from Facebook, if that also entails losing a great deal of social interactions? More fundamentally, attaching too much importance to data subject empowerment measures risks occluding 'the true problems which rest in societal power relations and institutions as much as the software

[462] For a useful taxonomy of issues with 'self-management' in this context, see: Tuukka Lehtiniemi and Yki Kortesniemi, 'Can the Obstacles to Privacy Self-Management Be Overcome? Exploring the Consent Intermediary Approach' (2017) 4 Big Data & Society 1.

[463] Bennett (n 153) 157–58.

[464] Koops (n 140) 252.

[465] Brandimarte and Acquisti (n 353) 564.

[466] Rauhofer (n 172) 14.

[467] Referring to the many concerns with regard to the 'consent' regime. See: Ausloos, 'The "Right to Be Forgotten"—Worth Remembering?' (n 353) 147; Solove, 'Introduction' (n 353); Frederik Zuiderveen Borgesius, 'Consent to Behavioural Targeting in European Law—What Are the Policy Implications of Insights from Behavioural Economics?' (2013) <http://papers.ssrn.com/abstract=2300969> accessed 1 June 2019.

tools employed'.[468] Besides, the right to erasure has also been called unworkable in practice, not just technically, but also conceptually.[469] How should it apply to group profiles, for example? And does it really make a difference when the processing only/primarily relates to real-time personal data processing and not historical data (eg WiFi-tracking in a smart-city)?

Crucial in light of this book, is that invoking the right to erasure will virtually always result in a conflict of interests. A request to erase personal data will generally impact one or more other actors that are storing, using, sharing, accessing, or otherwise relying on that personal data. Indeed, even if no use is made of the data whatsoever, the mere technical action of erasing itself still requires (economic, time, and technical) resources, impacting the one who receives the request. Conflicts resulting from a request for removal might take any shape or form, involving a plethora of different clashing interests, values, rights, and/or norms. Some of them will be easy to resolve, whereas others will be incredibly hard to resolve. In the context of ISS providers particularly, two pivotal conflicts involve information freedoms and/or economic freedoms.[470] Both will be analysed extensively in Part II.

3.2.3 Ultimate Power-Tool?

A number of (technological, economic, legal) factors seem to be rendering *ex post* empowerment measures increasingly important. They are crucial means in the effective realization of the fundamental right to data protection (Art 8 Charter). Moreover, they constitute a fail-safe to ensure compliance with *ex ante* and/or protective measures. At first sight, one might look at the right to erasure as the GDPR's ultimate power-tool. It is a straightforward measure—or 'tool'—that can directly be invoked by individuals to enforce their data protection interests.[471] The right to erasure is also irreversible. When accommodated, it results in the obliteration of the actual subject-matter of data protection rules. When looked at more closely however, this ultimate power-tool qualification may be called into question. Does the right to erasure actually ensure that individuals retain control over (the use of) their data throughout time? This will be one of the guiding questions throughout the following chapters. Indeed, to answer it the following sub-questions will be investigated: when does the right to erasure apply? (Chapters 3–4) and if so, how should the conflict of interests that is likely to ensue be resolved? (Chapters 5–7)?

[468] Lilian Edwards and Michael Veale, 'Slave to the Algorithm: Why a Right to an Explanation Is Probably Not the Remedy You Are Looking For' (2017) 16 Duke Law & Technology Review 18, 67.

[469] Peter Druschel, Michael Backes, and Rodica Tirtea, 'The Right to Be Forgotten—Between Expectations and Practice' (ENISA 2012) 8ff <https://www.enisa.europa.eu/activities/identity-and-trust/library/deliverables/the-right-to-be-forgotten/> accessed 1 June 2019. Also see Part III of this book.

[470] For a more granular breakdown of these two main categories, see: Bernal (n 146) 202–03.

[471] Subject to certain conditions which will be described in Chapter 4.

Section 4. Conceptualizing the Right to Erasure

So far, most discussions on the right to erasure and right to be forgotten are shrouded in terminological chaos. The aim of this chapter's last section is to delineate the different concepts that are often talked about in the context of the right to erasure so as to prevent misunderstandings throughout the rest of this book.

4.1 The Right to Be Forgotten

Before the GDPR had even been officially proposed, Koops already observed that while the right to be forgotten 'may be conceived as a legal right (*de lege lata* or *de lege ferenda*), it can also be seen as a value or interest worthy of protection or a policy goal to be achieved by some means or other, whether through law or through other regulatory mechanisms'.[472] It is this ideological connotation of the term which has turned it into a political slogan and explains much of the polemic surrounding the right today. Looked at more closely, the right to be forgotten is an evocative, rhetorical device devoid of legal substance. Like a balloon, it appears grandiose at first, but is easily pierced when looked at more closely. It obtains meaning, only by what people make of it. Google's Global Privacy Counsel once compared the term to a Rorschach test: 'people can see in it what they want'.[473] Perhaps because of this very reason, the term penetrated popular parlance so profoundly.

Once the European Commission explicitly referred to it in its proposal for a GDPR in 2012,[474] the right to be forgotten brought about a slew of criticism.[475] Across the Atlantic, people called the right 'a ridiculous idea',[476], 'more crap from the EU',[477] and even 'the biggest threat to free speech on the Internet in the coming decade'.[478] Aside from the plethora of fears—some less well-founded than others—the right to be forgotten idiom also creates overblown hopes with enthusiasts.[479]

[472] Bert-Jaap Koops, 'Forgetting Footprints, Shunning Shadows: A Critical Analysis of the "Right to Be Forgotten" in Big Data Practice' (2011) 8 SCRIPTed 229, 3. The author differentiates between three 'guises' of the right to be forgotten: a right to have data deleted in due time, a claim on a clean slate, and the right to unrestrained individual expression here and now.

[473] Peter Fleischer, 'Peter Fleischer: Privacy ... ?: The Right to Be Forgotten, or How to Edit Your History' (*Peter Fleischer*, 29 January 2012) <http://peterfleischer.blogspot.com/2012/01/right-to-be-forgotten-or-how-to-edit.html> accessed 23 June 2018.

[474] In fact, use of the term dates back to at least as early as 1972. See: Klaus Lenk, *The First International Oslo Symposium on Data Banks and Society, Presented by Klaus Lenk* (Oslo: Universitetsforlaget 1972) 146–47.

[475] Sait Shahin, 'Right to Be Forgotten How National Identity, Political Orientation, and Capitalist Ideology Structured a Trans-Atlantic Debate on Information Access and Control' (2016) 93 Journalism & Mass Communication Quarterly 360.

[476] Masnick (n 421).

[477] Yakowitz (n 421).

[478] Rosen (n 421).

[479] eg Tom Brewster, 'CIA Security Luminary: "Right to Be Forgotten Is Not Enough"' *The Guardian* (15 August 2014) <http://www.theguardian.com/technology/2014/aug/15/cia-security-dan-geer-right-to-be-forgotten> accessed 1 June 2019; Mayer-Schonberger (n 446).

The term suggests the legal enforceability of a cerebral process. It ambiguously suggests encroaching on other individuals' 'right to remember'. This ambiguity and lack of legal substance might also explain why the CJEU avoided the term in its *Google Spain* dictum, even though the referring Court explicitly asked about it.[480] Still, the right to be forgotten made it into the final version of the GDPR,[481] albeit between parentheses *and* quotation marks. Maintaining this political slogan could be seen as a deliberate choice by the EU legislator to clearly signal the framework's strong aim of data subject empowerment.

The rhetorical power of the term 'right to be forgotten' is further amplified *and* also influenced much academic work and policy discussions across the globe. Indeed, the term has eagerly been adopted by scholars and journalists in different jurisdictions.[482] Yet, as a reading of any random sample of these texts will quickly demonstrate, each commentator has a slightly different perspective or interpretation on the meaning of this concept. In an effort to map international case law on '*Google Spain*-like' cases, Van Calster et al. also point out the lack of uniformity in how the 'right to be forgotten' has been interpreted by courts.[483]

Zooming in on the GDPR in particular, the preparatory works suggest that the term 'right to be forgotten' specifically refers to Article 17(2). Yet, in practice, it is effectively used as an umbrella term encapsulating many different concepts.[484] Among the legal concepts that it has been used to refer to are: the *droit à l'oubli*; expungement laws (eg relating to credit history, criminal records); as well as the data protection rights to object, to erase, and to delist. For the purposes of this

[480] Contrary to the Opinion by Advocate General Jääskinen.

[481] Though not without some bumps along the road. See above and Zanfir (n 327) 231.

[482] eg Bennett (n 421); Rosen (n 421); Andrade (n 278); Meg L Ambrose and Jef Ausloos, 'The Right to Be Forgotten Across the Pond' (2012) 3 Journal of Information Policy 1; Joris van Hoboken, 'The Proposed Right to Be Forgotten Seen from the Perspective of Our Right to Remember' <www.law.nyu.edu/sites/default/files/upload_documents/VanHoboken_RightTo%20Be%20Forgotten_Manuscript_2013.pdf> accessed 1 June 2019; Paulan Korenhof, 'Forgetting Bits and Pieces: An Exploration of the "Right to Be Forgotten" as Implementation of "Forgetting" in Online Memory Processes' (TILT 2013) Paper for the IFIP Summer School 4/2013 <http://papers.ssrn.com/abstract=2326475> accessed 1 June 2019; Meg Leta Ambrose, 'Speaking of Forgetting: Analysis of Possible Non-EU Responses to the Right to Be Forgotten and Speech Exception' (2014) 38 Telecommunications Policy 800; Allyson Haynes Stuart, 'Google Search Results: Buried If Not Forgotten' (2014) 15 North Carolina Journal of Law & Technology 463; Julia Powles and Luciano Floridi, 'A Manifesto for the Future of the "Right to Be Forgotten" Debate' *The Guardian* (22 July 2014) <http://www.theguardian.com/technology/2014/jul/22/a-manifesto-for-the-future-of-the-right-to-be-forgotten-debate> accessed 1 June 2019; Michael L Rustad and Sanna Kulevska, 'Reconceptualizing the Right to Be Forgotten to Enable Transatlantic Data Flow' (2015) 28 Harv J Law & Tec 349; W Gregory Voss and Céline Castets-Renard, 'Proposal for an International Taxonomy on the Various Forms of the Right to Be Forgotten: A Study on the Convergence of Norms' (2015) 14 J on Telecomm & High Tech L 281.

[483] Geert Van Calster, Alejandro Gonzalez Arreaza, and Elsemiek Apers, 'Not Just One, but Many "Rights to Be Forgotten"' (2018) 7 Internet Policy Review <https://policyreview.info/articles/analysis/not-just-one-many-rights-be-forgotten> accessed 27 July 2018. The authors discuss cases in the following jurisdictions: Belgium, The Netherlands, the United Kingdom, France, Germany, Poland, Argentina, Chile, Mexico, Colombia, Brazil, and Peru.

[484] A noteworthy attempt at devising a taxonomy for the different mutations of the 'right to be forgotten' can be found in: Voss and Castets-Renard (n 482).

book, it is useful to briefly elucidate the main conceptual differences between data protection rights and the *droit à l'oubli*.

4.2 Droit à l'Oubli

For the purposes of this book, the *droit à l'oubli* can best be described as a policy goal aimed at protecting individuals from disproportionate media attention. The classic example is an ex-convict about whom a newspaper article appears decades after the facts. Societal values dictate that in certain cases, individuals should be able to start with a clean slate, not perpetually being pursued by their past. The *droit à l'oubli* does not imply actual erasure, but 'rather means to stop bringing back data from the past' and 'is conditioned by the elapsing of time and concerns information (re)made publicly available'.[485] In that sense, the *droit à l'oubli* is better qualified as a policy goal, rather than a right *stricto sensu*. Indeed, the goal that is pursued by the *droit à l'oubli*—ie shield against disproportionate publicity[486]—can be achieved through a variety of different legal frameworks (from general tort law; defamation law;[487] personality rights;[488] and intellectual property law to privacy[489] and data protection law). In other words, the *droit à l'oubli* does not have a dedicated provision in law, but has rather emerged as a legal construct in continental European case law.

As a result of this wide variety of potential legal sources (and underlying facts),[490] it is difficult to pinpoint a specific jurisdiction where the *droit à l'oubli* first emerged. Things are further complicated by the fact that the term[491] is often not explicitly referred to in the first place. It seems, however, that a considerable amount

485 de Terwangne (n 218) 1.

486 Hans Graux, Jef Ausloos, and Peggy Valcke, 'The Right to Be Forgotten in the Internet Era' in Jorge Pérez, Enrique Badía, and Rosa María Sáinz Peña (eds), *The Debate on Privacy and Security over the Network: Regulation and Markets*, vol 36 (Ariel 2012) <publicpolicy.telefonica.com/blogs/wp-content/uploads/2011/01/net_privacy.pdf> accessed 18 April 2013.

487 *Cour de Cassation, Chambre criminelle, du 22 mars 1966, 65-90914, Publié au bulletin*.

488 Jennifer Granick, 'Convicted Murderer To Wikipedia: Shhh!' (*Electronic Frontier Foundation*, 10 November 2009) <https://www.eff.org/deeplinks/2009/11/murderer-wikipedia-shhh> accessed 1 June 2019; John Schwartz, 'Two German Killers Demanding Anonymity Sue Wikipedia's Parent' *The New York Times* (12 November 2009) <http://www.nytimes.com/2009/11/13/us/13wiki.html> accessed 1 June 2019.

489 *Von Hannover v Germany* (n 56). In another case, the ECtHR did not recognize the (libel law based) *droit à l'oubli*, inter alia because of the public interest in online news-archives: *Case of Times Newspapers Ltd (Nos 1 and 2) v The United Kingdom* [2009] European Court of Human Rights 3002/03 and 23676/03. The preparatory works to the GDPR also show that some 'delegations thought that the right to be forgotten was rather an element of the right to privacy than part of data protection'. See: Council of the European Union, 'Note to the Working Party on Information Exchange of Data Protection. Council Revised Version of the Proposal for a Regulation of the European Parliament and of the Council on the Protection of Individuals with Regard to the Processing of Personal Data and on the Free Movement of Such Data (General Data Protection Regulation)' n 138.

490 For examples, see: Mayer-Schönberger (n 84) Introduction.

491 Or its equivalent in other languages.

of case-law can be traced back to French-language jurisdictions,[492] also explaining the choice of words: *droit à l'oubli*. According to Weber, the first relevant case in Switzerland already dates back to as early as July 1944.[493] In this case a widow had objected to the public display of a painting of her late husband on his deathbed.[494] This 1944 ruling has been complemented with cases *inter alia* in Switzerland,[495] France,[496] Belgium,[497] and Italy[498] since at least the 1960s. The ECtHR as well, implicitly recognized the existence of, though not necessarily granted, a *droit à l'oubli* in a number of cases.[499]

Because the *droit à l'oubli* inherently relates to disproportionate (re-) publications,[500] its application will inevitably result in a conflict with information (including press) freedoms. Even though traditional media outlets have established best practices and deontological guidelines in this regard already,[501] there is still a

[492] Which is not to say, of course, that other European countries have similar case law. For a representative sample of Italian cases since 1979 onwards, see: Alessandro Mantelero, 'The EU Proposal for a General Data Protection Regulation and the Roots of the "Right to Be Forgotten"' (2013) 29 Computer Law & Security Review 229, 229. In Germany, apart from the Sedlmayr Case (Schwartz (n 312)), Defreyne mentions the 'Lebach' Case: Federal Constitutional Court, 5 June 1973, 1 BvR 536/72 (Elise Defreyne, 'Le droit à l'oubli et les archives journalistiques' (2013) 2013 Revue Du Droit Des Technologies De L'Information 75, 81–82).

[493] Rolf H Weber, 'The Right to Be Forgotten More Than a Pandora's Box?' (2011) 2 jipitec 121 <http://www.jipitec.eu/issues/jipitec-2-2-2011/3084>. It is possible to go even further back than that, if one considers laws regulating expungement of criminal records as well. Karst discusses a 1909 Californian Statute in: Kenneth L Karst, '"The Files": Legal Controls over the Accuracy and Accessibility of Stored Personal Data' (1966) 31 Law and Contemporary Problems 342, 369.

[494] *Kaspar v veuve Hodler* [1944] Tribunal Federal BGE 70 II 127.

[495] See cases mentioned in: Franz Werro, 'The Right to Inform v. The Right to Be Forgotten: A Transatlantic Clash' in Aurelia Colombi Ciacchi, *Haftungsrecht im dritten Millennium—Liability in the Third Millennium* (Nomos 2009) 290ff <http://papers.ssrn.com/sol3/papers.cfm?abstract_id=1401357> accessed 1 June 2019.

[496] *Cour de Cassation, Chambre criminelle, du 22 mars 1966, 65-90.914, Publié au bulletin* (n 487). Also see the many references in: Defreyne (n 492); Mantelero, 'The EU Proposal for a General Data Protection Regulation and the Roots of the "Right to Be Forgotten"' (n 496); Maryline Boizard, 'Le Droit Au Respect de La Vie Privée, Un Instrument Effectif Du Droit à l'oubli?' (2015) 1 Montesquieu Law Review 8.

[497] Court of First Instance of Brussels, 20 September 2001, Auteurs & Media 2002/1, 77. Also see: Defreyne (n 492); Etienne Montero and Quentin Van Enis, 'Les métamorphoses du droit à l'oubli sur le net' (2016) 2016 Tijdschrift voor Belgisch Burgerlijk Recht 243. In Belgium, a non-exhaustive list of criteria has been devised for dealing with requests related to re-publications of old newspaper articles: (a) original publication is legal; (b) judicial information; (c) no current interest in dissemination; (d) no historical interest in the underlying facts; (e) lapse of time between two publications; (f) individual does not have a public life; (g) there's a rehabilitation interest and the individual has 'paid his debt'. See NB: *Le Soir v X* (2014) 314 Nieuw Juridisch Weekblad 26 (Court of Appeals Liege).

[498] Giusella Finocchiaro and Annarita Ricci, 'Quality of Information, the Right to Oblivion and Digital Reputation' in Bart Custers and others (eds), *Discrimination and Privacy in the Information Society—Data Mining and Profiling in Large Databases* (Springer 2013) 296.

[499] eg *Peck v the United Kingdom* [2003] European Court of Human Rights 44647/98; *Wegrzynowski and Smolczewski v Poland* [2013] European Court of Human Rights 33846/07.

[500] See generally: Maryline Boizard, 'Le Droit A L'Oubli' (Faculté de droit et de science politique, Rennes 1 2015) IODE UMR CNRS 6262 193.

[501] See, for example: Conseil de déontologie journalistique, 'Code de Déontologie Journalistique' (16 October 2013) <http://codededeontologiejournalistique.be/> accessed 17 November 2015; 'BBC Editorial Guidelines' ch 7 <www.bbc.co.uk/editorialguidelines/guidelines> accessed 17 November 2015.

high potential for conflicts. It is these kinds of conflicts that will be looked at more closely in Part II of this book, at least for those situations where the *droit à l'oubli* is invoked on the basis of data protection law. With the 'datafication/digitisation of everything' in mind—and ever more situations falling within data protection law's scope of application—this is a substantially growing number of potential cases.[502]

4.3 Data Protection Rights

Contrary to the *droit à l'oubli*, data protection rights are not inherently aimed at preventing or limiting publications about an individual's (private) life. Rather, they are of a procedural nature, aimed at *empowering* individuals over how personal data is used. The *control* offered by data protection rights can be utilized in all kinds of situations. In light of the 'datafication of everything' (see Introduction), more and more '*droit à l'oubli* cases' fall within data protection law's scope of application, and thus potentially targetable with data protection rights. Still, it is important to realize this is but one option to achieve the *droit à l'oubli*'s goal.

The focus of this book is on data protection rights, and the right to erasure in particular. Whereas the exact scope and criteria for applying them will be set out in Chapter 4, this section will simply delineate the main conceptual differences between these rights.

4.3.1 Right to Object (Article 21 GDPR)

The right to object is an *ex post* empowerment measure in the data protection framework. Put simply, the right to object enables individuals to oppose specific processing operations if certain conditions are met (see Chapters 4 and 8). It offers a concrete way to still oppose to certain data processing operations when the withdrawal of consent is not possible (because another lawful ground in Art 6(1) is relied on). The key difference with the right to erasure is that the right to object targets a processing operation rather than the underlying data. This means that when one successfully invokes the right to object, (one or more) particular processing operation(s) cannot be performed anymore. It goes without saying, however, that today the same data is processed in many different ways. As a result, a right to object will not necessarily prevent the data being used in other ways. It does not automatically result in the erasure of the data.

4.3.2 Right to Erasure (Article 17)

Similarly to the right to object, the right to erasure is an *ex post* empowerment measure in the data protection framework. The right to erasure enables individuals

502 A case in point being the digitization and online publication of newspaper archives. See: Defreyne (n 492).

to have their data removed if certain conditions are complied with (which will be elaborated upon in Chapter 3). Contrary to the right to object—but similarly to the right to rectification[503] (Art 16)—the right to erasure targets personal data itself. If successfully exercised, the data cannot be used for any other purpose anymore. It has been erased. Its goal is not to silence the media as some critics like to argue, but to place 'more effective, better controlled and realisable limitations on the [...] commercial holding of data [...] it is about control and autonomy'.[504] With this in mind, the right to erasure does not necessarily prevent the same data still being stored and processed by other (unrelated) entities, in different contexts. As data processing eco-systems further complexify, it can become a particularly contentious issue to determine when erasure in one system should result in the erasure in other systems (see Art 17(2)).[505] This issue—and many more related to the erasure of personal data—will thoroughly be analysed in the following Chapter(s).

4.3.3 Right to Restriction of Processing (Article 18)

The right to restriction of processing is the successor to the ambiguous right to blocking of data in Directive 95/46.[506] As mentioned before, this right was initially incorporated into paragraphs 4 to 6 of the proposed right to erasure and to be forgotten in Article 17 GDPR. In short, it requires the controller to preserve the respective personal data, and strictly constrains the options for processing to a narrow set of purposes (Art 18(2)).[507] Recital 67 clarifies such 'restriction of processing' might consist of 'temporarily moving the selected data to another processing system, making the selected personal data unavailable to users, or temporarily removing published data from a website. In automated filing systems, the restriction of processing should in principle be ensured by technical means in such a manner that the personal data are not subject to further processing operations and cannot be changed.' The first paragraph of Article 18 essentially lists four situations in which the right to the restriction of processing can be invoked: (a) when the controller needs to verify the accuracy after it has been contested; (b) when processing is deemed unlawful, but the data subject opposes erasure; (c) upon purpose expiration but the data subject still needs the data for the establishment, exercise or

[503] Which depends on the incorrect nature of the data, contrary to the right to erasure.

[504] Bernal (n 146) 201. Elsewhere, the author explains the right 'should not be seen as a way to rewrite or conceal history or as a tool for celebrities or politicians: it is rather a basic and pragmatic right available to all.' ibid 177.

[505] Even the meaning of erasure or 'expungment' has been the subject of misunderstandings between computer scientists and lawyers since at least the 1970s (Davis (n 402) 269–70) until more recently (Druschel, Backes, and Tirtea (n 469)) already.

[506] European Commission, 'Leaked Proposal for a General Data Protection Regulation' November 29, 2011.

[507] Notably: 'personal data shall, with the exception of storage, only be processed with the data subject's consent or for the establishment, exercise or defence of legal claims or for the protection of the rights of another natural or legal person or for reasons of important public interest of the Union or of a Member State'.

defence of legal claims; and (d) pending the evaluation of a data subject's right to object. It can be concluded, from this list, that the right to restriction of processing is primarily an auxiliary clause, that will only be relevant *after* another data protection provision is invoked.

4.3.4 Right to Be Delisted

Finally, it is worth clarifying one of the latest additions to the 'data protection toolbox': the right to be delisted. Not explicitly mentioned in the GDPR but constructed by the CJEU,[508] the 'right' is a hybrid between the right to erasure (Art 17) and right to object (Art 21). The right to be delisted enables individuals to obtain the removal of the link between a specific search result and their name used as a search term, if certain conditions are complied with.[509] The hybrid nature of the right can be explained by it merely targeting the *link* between two sets of information. On the one hand, linking a search term to a search result can be seen as a specific processing operation (right to object). On the other hand, the link itself can be qualified as personal data as such (right to erasure). One could even say the right to be delisted overlaps with the *droit à l'oubli* too, as it is generally invoked in order to prevent disproportionate publicity.[510] The scope of application of this 'new' right to be delisted is still unclear,[511] but will be analysed later on in this book.[512]

Section 5. Conclusion

This chapter provided the context in which the right to erasure came about. The first half was dedicated to fleshing out the fundamental right to data protection in Article 8 of the Charter. After a brief historical overview, it was made clear how the core rationale of the right to data protection is control over one's personal data,

[508] More specifically, in the *Google Spain* case. Even though the CJEU did not explicitly use this term in its Ruling, 'the right to be delisted' has become the accepted terminology in this context (see, notably: Article 29 Working Party, 'Guidelines on the Implementation of the Court of Justice of the European Union Judgment on "Google Spain and Inc v Agencia Española de Protección de Datos (AEPD) and Mario Costeja González" C-131/12' (Article 29 Working Party 2014) Guidelines WP 225 <http://ec.europa.eu/justice/article-29/documentation>.)

[509] Particularly when the *link* between search term and search result appears 'inadequate, irrelevant or excessive in relation to the purposes of the processing' (*Google Spain SL, Google Inc v Agencia Española de Protección de Datos (AEPD), Mario Costeja González* (n 106) [Especially §§92–94].

[510] If the *droit à l'oubli* is the individual's goal in this context, it is important to keep in mind that different routes remain open. Clear examples of this can be found in the many so-called 'auto-suggest' or 'auto-complete' cases against search engines (often based on defamation law). See notably: Stavroula Karapapa and Maurizio Borghi, 'Search Engine Liability for Autocomplete Suggestions: Personality, Privacy and the Power of the Algorithm' (2015) 23 International Journal of Law and Information Technology 261.

[511] To what extent, for example, can the right to be delisted be applied more broadly to any kind of link/linking between personal data (eg a name) and other information?

[512] See also: Aleksandra Kuczerawy and Jef Ausloos, 'From Notice-and-Takedown to Notice-and-Delist: Implementing Google Spain' (2016) 14 Colorado Technology Law Journal 219.

interpreted broadly. Not as an enabling force for other rights, freedoms or interests, but as an inherent value in itself. Core EU values such as dignity and individual autonomy dictate that every individual is master over their (digital) selves. Spelling this out was crucial in order to differentiate the Charter from the GDPR, which *does* constitute an *enabling* framework. The GDPR provides the tools for safeguarding interests, rights and freedoms whenever personal data is being processed. It is a system of checks and balances, with both protective as well as empowering measures. The second part of this chapter zoomed in on the right to erasure in particular. How did it come about exactly, what are its main benefits and drawbacks, and how does it relate to similar concepts? Now that the scene is set, it is possible to have a closer look at the practical operation of the right to erasure. First by looking at the relevant scope of application (Chapter 3), then by looking at the mechanics of the right itself (Chapter 4).

3

Scope of the Right to Erasure

Section 1. Introduction

In light of this book's overall goal—ie assessing the role of the General Data Protection Regulation (GDPR)'s right to erasure in the relationship between individuals and the information society services (ISS) providers—the following two chapters are aimed at clearly delineating the situations in which the right applies. Before determining the actual requirements for invoking the right to erasure itself, one needs to take a step back and look at the scope of application of EU data protection law more broadly. This chapter aims to do precisely that; delineating the scope of application of EU data protection law in light of the right to erasure. In other words, *under what circumstances* and vis-à-vis *whom* does the right to erasure apply under EU data protection law? The chapter will consecutively set out the GDPR's territorial, material, and personal scope, and end with an overview of the key exemptions and derogations to the framework overall. This structure will be complemented by excursions into the specific issues that are relevant with regard to the book's subject matter. These will particularly relate to data protection law's material and personal scope of application. Territorial scope of application questions are undoubtedly interesting in the online environment, but not unique to the right to erasure in particular.

Section 2. Territorial Scope

Before investigating the GDPR's material and personal scope of application, one needs to ask whether EU data protection law applies in the first place. When can the GDPR's right to erasure be invoked against a non-EU ISS provider?

The question of the territorial scope of application of legal frameworks in the online realm has already been the subject of debate for decades. Despite some strong 'cyber exceptionalism' narratives by the likes of Barlow,[1] and Johnson, and Post[2]

[1] Notably: John Perry Barlow, 'A Declaration of the Independence of Cyberspace' (*Electronic Frontier Foundation*, 8 February 1996) <https://www.eff.org/cyberspace-independence> accessed 1 June 2019.

[2] David R Johnson and David Post, 'Law and Borders: The Rise of Law in Cyberspace' (1996) 48 Stanford Law Review 1367. Also see: Lawrence Lessig, 'The Zones of Cyberspace' (1996) 48 Stanford

The Right to Erasure in EU Data Protection Law. First Edition. Jef Ausloos. Oxford University Press (2020). © Jef Ausloos
DOI: 10.1093/oso/9780198847977.001.0001

in the 1990s, it has become clear that today, the Internet does not escape the cloak of national regulatory frameworks. As pointedly phrased by Kohl: '[t]he debate has moved on from the question of whether States should regulate the transnational Internet to the question of how it can be done'.[3]

Data protection law is emblematic of the complexity and difficulty in regulating borderless flows of information in the online environment. Even so, Article 3 GDPR is aimed to do exactly that, tracing the Regulation's territorial scope of application. Similarly to its predecessor (Art 4(1) Directive 95/46), it does so very broadly and flexibly in order to prevent circumvention of the law that would leave data subjects unprotected.[4] In light of this same reasoning, the territorial scope of data protection law was also updated (by the GDPR), accounting for the exponential growth/adoption of data processing and especially communication technologies (ie the Internet) since Directive 95/46's adoption.[5] By virtue of it being a Regulation (instead of a Directive), one of the major changes brought about by the GDPR is that henceforth, the territorial scope is determined on an EU-wide level instead of 27 Member-State levels. In other words, questions relating to which *national* law applies have become significantly less important. That being said, it should be recognized that the GDPR does allow for derogations in Member-State law (notably Article 23). Moreover, investigative, judicial, and enforcement jurisdiction also remains a question of Member-State law, rather than something resolved in the GDPR. Interesting as they are, these components would distract too much from the core of this book and they will therefore not be further discussed here. Finally, it is also important to separate questions of scope of application from the *reach* of data protection law. The question of extraterritorial reach has presented itself in delisting cases for example, where Google notoriously refused to also delist links when people use the respective search terms from outside the EU for example.[6] This very contentious issue is also not

Law Review 1403; Uta Kohl, *Jurisdiction and the Internet: A Study of Regulatory Competence over Online Activity* (CUP 2007) 12 et seq.

3 Kohl (n 2) 12.

4 Recital 23 GDPR. Also see: Article 29 Working Party, 'Opinion 8/2010 on Applicable Law' (Article 29 Working Party 2010) WP 179 28 <http://ec.europa.eu/justice/article-29/documentation> accessed 1 June 2019; Dan Jerker B Svantesson, *Extraterritoriality in Data Privacy Law* (Ex Tuto Publishing 2013) 95–96. Citing COM(92) 422 final, SYN 287, 15 October 1992, 13 and Recital 20 DPD.

5 Douwe Korff, 'Data Protection Laws in the EU: The Difficulties in Meeting the Challenges Posed by Global Social and Technical Developments' (European Commission—DG Justice 2010) Working Paper No 2 21 et seq <http://ssrn.com/abstract=1638949> accessed 1 June 2019. Also see Recital 6 GDPR.

6 The CJEU was asked to resolve this very question, but has not issued a ruling at the time this book went to press. Advocate General Szpunar argued that the reach of delisting should not be global, but search engines should take all steps available to them to ensure effective and complete de-listing with regard to anyone searching from within the EU (notably through geo-blocking). See: AG Opinion in: *Google (Portée territoriale du déréférencement)* Court of Justice of the European Union C-507/17 [79];

specific to the right to erasure in particular (but equally relevant in the context of any type of takedown, notably also for copyright reasons) and will therefore not be discussed in detail here.[7]

A clear definition of the GDPR's territorial scope of application shall, quite obviously, be critical in determining the applicability of the right to erasure (Art 17). Be that as it may, the *ratio loci* of data protection law can be qualified as more of a 'generic' scope question, rather than a specific issue related to data protection law's *ex post* empowerment measures (data subject rights). It is a question that is relevant for determining the applicability of any of the GDPR's provisions indiscriminately. Hence, this section limits itself to briefly highlighting the key elements in determining data protection law's territorial scope of application in light of exercising data subject rights (focusing on situations involving non-EU entities that are processing personal data). More elaborate accounts on data protection's *ratio loci* will be referenced throughout. In light of the intended continuity between Directive 95/46 and the GDPR, documents interpreting/referring to the former largely remain valid.[8]

The GDPR's territorial scope of application is defined—and interpreted—very broadly.[9] Article 3 GDPR subdivides the territorial reach in three situations (summarized and simplified as):

a) when the processing occurs (in the context of the activities of an establishment of a controller or a processor)[10] in the EU;
b) when the processing targets data subjects in the EU (either by offering goods/services *or* monitoring their behaviour);
c) when Member State law applies by virtue of public international law.

Article 19 and others, 'Written Observations in Case C-507/17 Google, Inc. v CNIL' <https://cippic.ca/uploads/C507_17-A19-CJEU_EN.pdf> accessed 28 May 2018.

[7] For more on the extra-territorial reach of EU data protection law, see: Brendan Van Alsenoy and Marieke Kockkoek, 'Internet and Jurisdiction after Google Spain: The Extraterritorial Reach of the "Right to Be Delisted"' (2015) 5 International Data Privacy Law 105; Dan Jerker B Svantesson, 'Extraterritoriality and Targeting in EU Data Privacy Law: The Weak Spot Undermining the Regulation' (2015) 5 International Data Privacy Law 226; Mistale Taylor, 'The EU's Human Rights Obligations in Relation to Its Data Protection Laws with Extraterritorial Effect' (2015) 5 International Data Privacy Law 246; Geert Van Calster, Alejandro Gonzalez Arreaza, and Elsemiek Apers, 'Not Just One, but Many "Rights to Be Forgotten"'(2018) 7 Internet Policy Review <https://policyreview.info/articles/analysis/not-just one many-rights-be-forgotten> accessed 27 July 2018.

[8] Svantesson, *Extraterritoriality in Data Privacy Law* (n 4) 106.

[9] Article 29 Working Party, 'Opinion 8/2010 on Applicable Law' (n 4); Article 29 Working Party, 'Update of Opinion 8/2010 on Applicable Law in Light of the CJEU Judgment in Google Spain' (Article 29 Working Party 2015) Opinion WP 179 update <http://ec.europa.eu/justice/article-29/documentation> accessed 1 June 2019.

[10] The concepts of 'controller' and 'processor' will be explained in Section 4 of this chapter.

2.1 In the Context of the Activities of an Establishment in the EU

> **Article 3—Territorial Scope**
> (1) This Regulation applies to the processing of personal data in the context of the activities of an establishment of a controller or a processor in the Union, regardless of whether the processing takes place in the Union or not.

Article 3(1) sets out the default rule for determining the territorial applicability of EU data protection law.[11] Following this provision, the GDPR's applicability is triggered when processing activities occur in the context of the activities of an establishment of either a controller or processor in the EU.[12] Simplified, four situations can be envisaged: (a) all parties (data subject, controller/processor, and establishment(s)) are located within the EU; (b) only the controller/processor is located *outside* the EU; (c) only the data subject is located *outside* the EU; (d) both controller/processor and data subject are located *outside* the EU, with only the establishment(s) located within the EU.[13] Whereas the first scenario rather clearly falls within the GDPR's territorial scope of application, this is not as straightforward for the other three. Importantly, neither the nationality of the data processing entities (or data subject(s) for that matter), nor the locale of the processing activities themselves is determinative.[14]

Establishment in the EU—The GDPR (Recital 22) explains the concept of establishment as 'the effective and real exercise of [an] activity through stable arrangements', regardless of the legal form of such arrangements.[15] The CJEU defends a flexible definition of 'establishment' in order to prevent forum-shopping:[16] 'both the degree of stability of the arrangements and the

[11] Lokke Moerel, 'The Long Arm of EU Data Protection Law: Does the Data Protection Directive Apply to Processing of Personal Data of EU Citizens by Websites Worldwide?' (2011) 1 International Data Privacy Law 28, 29–30.

[12] Whereas Directive 95/46 only made mention of the controller in this provision, the GDPR now mentions the processor as well, sidestepping a number of potential issues that might emerge from such a distinction. Lokke Moerel, 'Back to Basics: When Does EU Data Protection Law Apply?' (2011) 1 International Data Privacy Law 92, 98 et seq.

[13] A fifth situation can be imagined—where there is no link with the EU whatsoever (ie no establishment in the EU and controller, processor, and data subject outside of EU)—but will not be considered further as the GDPR will not apply here.

[14] Because, *factually*, the actual processing itself might well be performed outside of the EU, Moerel calls this provision a 'virtual' version of the territoriality principle. Moerel (n 11) 29–30.

[15] Even though Directive 95/46 contained a similar provision in Recital 19, the concept of establishment was defined variably in the member states. See, notably: Svantesson, *Extraterritoriality in Data Privacy Law* (n 4) 97 et seq. The Regulation does define the concept of '*main* establishment in the EU' (Art 4(16) *juncto* Recital 36), which will be particularly relevant in light of questions relating to judicial and enforcement jurisdiction. For more, see: Article 29 Working Party, 'Opinion 8/2010 on Applicable Law' (n 4) 11 et seq.

[16] Article 29 Working Party, 'Update of Opinion 8/2010 on Applicable Law in Light of the CJEU Judgment in Google Spain' (n 15) 7.

effective exercise of activities [...] must be interpreted in the light of the specific nature of the economic activities and the provision of services concerned'.[17] Indeed, the notion of establishment, according to the Court, 'extends to any real and effective activity, even a minimal one, exercised through stable arrangements'.[18] The actual form or size of the establishment, or the number of potential other establishments (in or outside the Union) are all irrelevant.[19] A flexible approach, the Court explains, is essential with regard to Internet services (ie ISS providers).

In the Context of Activities—The inclusion of 'in the context of the activities' clearly emphasizes the legislator's intentions to define a broad (territorial) scope of application. Indeed, both WP29 *and* the Court of Justice of the European Union (CJEU) have explained this terminology implies that the EU establishment does not itself have to factually process personal data (an element now explicitly included in Article 3(1) GDPR). It does not even have to be directly involved in the processing of personal data at all. Moerel explains that personal data is processed 'in the context of the activities of an EU establishment' when 'the establishment is responsible for relations with the users in the relevant EU country; [or] the website is promoted by the establishment by means of local targeted advertisements to the inhabitants of that state'.[20] The CJEU did specify that mere accessibility of a service in a Member State is *not* sufficient.[21] But, as explained by Caspar, it *is* 'sufficient if the activity of [the] establishment fosters economically the data processing of the holding company'.[22] In its *Google Spain* Ruling, the CJEU explained that it is sufficient for the activities of the establishment in the EU to be *inextricably linked* to the data processing activities of a controller/processor outside of the EU.[23] This 'inextricably linked' criterion,[24] confirms the functional approach to interpreting data protection's territorial scope of application. In the same vein, WP29 underlines the importance of considering the establishment's degree of involvement, the nature of

[17] *Weltimmo* [2015] Court of Justice of the European Union C-230/14 para 29. Also see: Orla Lynskey, 'In the Shadows of the Data Protection Juggernaut: Bara and Weltimmo' (*European Law Blog*, 28 January 2016) <http://europeanlawblog.eu/?p=3083> accessed 1 June 2019.

[18] *Verein für Konsumenteninformation v Amazon EU Sàrl* [2016] Court of Justice of the European Union C-191/15 [75].

[19] Article 29 Working Party, 'Opinion 8/2010 on Applicable Law' (n 4) 11 et seq.

[20] Moerel (n 11) 31.

[21] *Verein für Konsumenteninformation v Amazon EU Sàrl* (n 18) para 76.

[22] Johannes Caspar, 'The CJEU Google Spain Decision' (2015) 39 Datenschutz und Datensicherheit—DuD 589, 589.

[23] Concretely, the 'activities carried out by Google [a search engine managed in the US] cannot be separated from the generation of advertising revenue [managed by a Google-subsidiary in Spain]'. Article 29 Working Party, 'Update of Opinion 8/2010 on Applicable Law in Light of the CJEU Judgment in Google Spain' (n 15) 3–5. Importantly, this was one of the only points the CJEU followed the Opinion of Advocate General Jääskinen (notably paragraph 64). *Google Spain SL, Google Inc v Agencia Española de Protección de Datos (AEPD), Mario Costeja González* [2014] Court of Justice of the European Union C-131/12, para 56.

[24] Article 29 Working Party, 'Update of Opinion 8/2010 on Applicable Law in Light of the CJEU Judgment in Google Spain' (n 15) 7 et seq.

its activities; and data protection law's aim of *effective* protection.[25] In conclusion, whether or not a processing activity occurs within the context of the activities of an establishment in the EU will have to be determined on a case-by-case basis.[26]

SUMMARY—Overall, Article 3(1) GDPR sets out the default territorial scope determination of EU data protection law. The provision makes clear that the context in which the processing is carried out is determinative, rather than where the personal data is physically located and/or processed.[27] This functional interpretation professed by the legislator has been confirmed by both the WP29 and the CJEU.[28] Indeed, a restrictive interpretation would thwart 'the effective and complete protection of the fundamental rights and freedoms of natural persons'[29] and give a tremendous competitive advantage to data-processing entities without a formal establishment within the EU. Conversely, WP29 also advised against interpreting *too* broadly, considering any establishment with even the remotest link to be captured by Article 3(1) GDPR.[30] In the end, '[e]ach scenario must be assessed on its own merits, taking into account the specific facts of the case'.[31]

With the above in mind, it is now possible to turn back to the three scenarios mentioned at the beginning of this subsection, examining when the GDPR applies and the right to erasure can be invoked. The most commonly occurring scenario (b) concerns a controller/processor located *outside* the EU, with both data subject and establishment (of the controller/processor) located within the EU. Under these circumstances, the classic test explained in previous pages will apply, ie does the processing of personal data take place 'within the context of the activities of the establishment in the EU'. The last two scenarios rather atypically concern situations where the data subject—the person potentially invoking the right to erasure—is located *outside* the EU. As mentioned before, EU data protection law does not discriminate between EU and non-EU citizens (see personal scope). In theory, anyone located outside the EU (member-state citizen or not) could invoke data subject rights under the GDPR. Key in assessing the territorial applicability

[25] Article 29 Working Party, 'Opinion 8/2010 on Applicable Law' (n 4) 14.

[26] Article 29 Working Party, 'Update of Opinion 8/2010 on Applicable Law in Light of the CJEU Judgment in Google Spain' (n 15) Annex 1.

[27] Not in the least to prevent circumvention by mere relocation of the controller/processor's corporate seat for example. See also: Article 29 Working Party, 'Opinion 8/2010 on Applicable Law' (n 4) 16.

[28] *Google Spain* (n 23) para 58. In this landmark case, the CJEU explicitly stated that considering Google Inc (based in the US) outside the scope of EU data protection law would compromise its effectiveness and the effective and complete protection of the fundamental rights and freedoms of natural persons. Also see: *Weltimmo* (n 108) para 25.

[29] *Google Spain* (n 23) paras 53, 54, and 58. Cited in: Article 29 Working Party, 'Update of Opinion 8/2010 on Applicable Law in Light of the CJEU Judgment in Google Spain' (n 15) 4.

Similarly, see: Moerel (n 11) 29–30. The author explains that '[i]f location were to be decisive, this would easily facilitate by-passing the national data protection laws, for instance by relocating the servers to another jurisdiction'.

[30] Article 29 Working Party, 'Update of Opinion 8/2010 on Applicable Law in Light of the CJEU Judgment in Google Spain' (n 15) 5.

[31] ibid.

in these situations will be whether or not the actual processing activities that are being challenged, occur 'within the context of the activities of the (establishment of the) controller/processor within the EU'. The more entities involved in the processing *in casu* are located outside the EU (potentially controller(s), processor(s), and/or data subject), the harder it will be to claim the GDPR applies by virtue of its Article 3(1).

2.2 Targeting Data Subjects in the EU

Article 3—Territorial Scope

(2) This Regulation applies to the processing of personal data of data subjects who are in the Union by a controller or processor not established in the Union, where the processing activities are related to:

(a) the offering of goods or services, irrespective of whether a payment of the data subject is required, to such data subjects in the Union; or

(b) the monitoring of their behaviour as far as their behaviour takes place within the Union.

Article 3(2) of the GDPR sets out the situations in which EU data protection law might apply even though the controller/processor has no establishment inside the Union. Emblematic of the GDPR's extra-territorial reach, this provision also constitutes the biggest change in the framework's territorial scope of application when compared to Directive 95/46. Put briefly, Article 3(2) GDPR ensures that data subjects in the EU can still invoke their right to erasure vis-à-vis non-EU entities that are targeting them in one way or another, ie by (a) offering goods/services to such data subjects; or (b) monitoring these data subjects' behaviour in the EU. It was conceived with the aim of preventing data subjects within the EU from being left unprotected by the mere fact that the controller/processor is located outside the Union (particularly relevant in the online environment). As a matter of fact, the idea of focusing on the 'targeting of individuals' was already defended and recommended in the WP29's 2010 Opinion on applicable law.[32] Indeed, such a criterion has been used in many different European legal frameworks already.[33]

[32] WP29 even alluded to such an approach in 2002 already, when looking at the applicability of EU data protection law to non-EU based websites. See: Article 29 Working Party, 'Working Document on Determining the International Application of EU Data Protection Law to Personal Data Processing on the Internet by Non-EU Based Web Sites' (Article 29 Working Party 2002) WP 56 <http://ec.europa.eu/justice/article-29/documentation>. Later, WP29 described it as a more specific connecting factor, complementing the old 'equipment/means' criterion in Directive 95/46. Article 29 Working Party, 'Opinion 8/2010 on Applicable Law' (n 4) 24.

[33] WP29 refers specifically to: Article 15(1)(c) of Council Regulation (EC) No 44/2001 of 22 December 2000 on jurisdiction and the recognition and enforcement of judgments in civil and commercial matters (OJ L 12, 16.1.2001, 1), interpreted by Advocate General Trstenjak in 18 May 2010, in

In late 2015, WP29 reiterated its defence for such an 'effects principle' complementing the territoriality principle in the then-almost-finalized GDPR.[34] In sum, the new provision definitely fits in the rationale of the fundamental right to data protection. Interpreting the right's (territorial) scope of application needs to be done in light of the effective and complete protection of data subjects.[35] With this in mind, it is useful to provide some more context on how to interpret the two situations mentioned in Article 3(2).

Offering of Goods or Services—Controllers and processors established *outside* the EU are still covered by the GDPR when they process personal data in relation to goods or services—free or not[36]—offered to data subjects within the EU. This means that the right to erasure can still be invoked against controllers *not* based in the EU. Determining whether or not a controller/processor is actually offering goods/services to data subjects in the EU requires a functional approach, looking at the particular circumstances of the individual case. In light of this, the GDPR specifies that the mere accessibility of their website and/or contact details from within the EU will not be sufficient.[37] Using the language and/or currency of one or more Member States on the other hand, constitute strong indicators of the controller envisaging offering goods or services to data subjects in the EU.[38] Years before Article 3(2) even saw the light of day, and inspired by the field of consumer protection,[39] WP29 already listed several more criteria: explicitly accessible within Member-States; delivery to Member-States; requiring the use of an EU credit card; or advertising in the language of users in the EU.[40]

C-144/09, *Hotel Alpenhof*; some national laws transposing Directive 2000/31/EC on electronic commerce. The WP29 also cites US legislation on the protection of Children: COPPA, 16 CFR 312.2, available at http://www.ftc.gov/os/1999/10/64fr59888.pdf, 59912. More examples are given in: Korff, 'New Challenges to Data Protection Study-Working Paper No. 2' (n 695) 32.

[34] Article 29 Working Party, 'Update of Opinion 8/2010 on Applicable Law in Light of the CJEU Judgment in Google Spain' (n 15) 5–6.

[35] Caspar (n 712) 591; referring to: Brendan Van Alsenoy and Marieke Koekkoek, 'Internet and Jurisdiction after Google Spain: The Extraterritorial Reach of the "Right to Be Delisted"' (2015) 5 International Data Privacy Law 4.

[36] Explicitly mentioned in Article 3(2), this element has also been emphasized by the WP29 in 2015: 'Depending on the facts of the case and the role which the local establishment plays, the judgement [*Google Spain, C-131/12*] may apply to other non-EU companies whose business model relies on offering "free services" within the EU, which are then financed by making use of the personal data collected from the users (such as for advertising purposes).' Article 29 Working Party, 'Update of Opinion 8/2010 on Applicable Law in Light of the CJEU Judgment in Google Spain' (n 15) 5.

[37] See in this regard also: *Verein für Konsumenteninformation v Amazon EU Sàrl* (n 18) para 76.

[38] Recital 23, GDPR.

[39] Svantesson, 'Extraterritoriality and Targeting in EU Data Privacy Law' (n 7) 231. Referring to *Joined cases Peter Pammer v Reederei Karl Schlüter GmbH & Co KG (C-585/08) and Hotel Alpenhof GesmbH v Oliver Heller (C-144/09)* [2010] Court of Justice of the European Union C-585/08 & C-144/09.

[40] Article 29 Working Party, 'Opinion 8/2010 on Applicable Law' (n 4) 31. WP29 even went as far as stating that 'applying it in a data protection context would bring additional legal certainty to controllers as they would have to apply the same criterion for activities which often trigger the application of both consumer and data protection rules'.

Monitoring of Behaviour—The GDPR also applies to controllers/processors established *outside* the EU, when they monitor the behaviour of data subjects within the EU. As a result, following Article 3(2), data subjects may invoke their right to erasure vis-à-vis a foreign controller that is tracking their web-surfing behaviour. Importantly, Article 3(2) only covers the data subject's behaviour taking place in the EU.[41] The GDPR clarifies that 'monitoring of behaviour' encompasses the online tracking of natural persons, especially—but not exclusively—when done for profiling purposes (in light of, for example, analysing or predicting their personal preferences, behaviours and attitudes).[42]

Conclusion/1—In conclusion, it is fair to say Article 3(2) considerably extends the GDPR's extra-territorial reach. Well aware of potential overreach, the drafters did include some level of flexibility as to the interpretation of this provision. As mentioned before, both situations envisaged by Article 3(2) are further elaborated in the Recitals. The GDPR also foresees and mitigates the consequences of its extra-territorial reach from an enforcement perspective. Article 27 (*j* Recital 80), for instance, requires the designation of a representative in the EU whenever Article 3(2) applies.[43] How exactly this will be enforced is a different question.

Conclusion/2—The new targeting provision has been criticized extensively. Acknowledging its appeal in the abstract, Svantesson explains that the provision is conducive of legal uncertainty and will be useless in practice,[44] undermining the legitimacy of the Regulation itself.[45] Regardless of what one might

[41] Originally, the provision did not specify the behaviour itself had to take place within the EU. As a result, an EU citizen's shopping behaviour in an Australian clothing store, for example, would also be captured by the GDPR's extra-territorial reach. Svantesson, *Extraterritoriality in Data Privacy Law* (n 4) 107; Svantesson, 'Extraterritoriality and Targeting in EU Data Privacy Law' (n 7) 230.

[42] Recital 24 GDPR.

[43] Foreign controllers/processors will be relieved from this obligation when they are a public authority/body or when they only process personal data occasionally, and it 'does not include, on a large scale, processing of special categories of data as referred to in Article 9(1) or processing of personal data relating to criminal convictions and offences referred to in Article 10, and is unlikely to result in a risk to the rights and freedoms of natural persons, taking into account the nature, context, scope and purposes of the processing'.

[44] The interpretative factors mentioned in relation to the 'offering of goods and services' provision' (eg currency, language), Svantesson argues, will often not be present or relevant in practice. He continues to say that 'for a large number of parties involved in the handling of personal data, courts are going to have to conclude either that they target just about every country in the world or no countries at all'. In: Dan Jerker B Svantesson, 'The (Uncertain) Future of Online Data Privacy' (2015) 9 Masaryk University Journal of Law and Technology 129, 138.

[45] He describes the 'targeting approach' quite sharply as 'the legislator's (and some academics') dream, but the judge's (and indeed lawyer's) nightmare'. In: Svantesson, 'Extraterritoriality and Targeting in EU Data Privacy Law' (n 7) 232.

Svantesson argues for a more objective approach (ensuring certainty and fairness), focusing on the eventual outcome, rather than the intention of whether a controller/processor has directed its activities towards the EU (in: ibid.). Elsewhere, the author also argued for a more layered approach (instead of

think about Article 3(2), it is here to stay. Therefore, at least in theory, the right to erasure can be invoked vis-à-vis ISS providers without an establishment in the EU, if they target people in the EU or simply monitor their (eg reading, surfing, search) behaviour.

2.3 Public International Law

Article 3—Territorial Scope

(3) This Regulation applies to the processing of personal data by a controller not established in the Union, but in a place where Member State law applies by virtue of public international law.

The third and final set of situations where EU data protection law extends to foreign entities, is when these are established 'in a place where Member State law applies by virtue of public international law'. Such a provision already existed in Directive 95/46 and is much more narrow than one might expect at first glance.[46] It primarily covers situations where an international treaty or custom dictates the applicability of EU law, such as in relation to national embassies outside the EU, or ships, or airplanes.[47] In light of this, a data subject could invoke his/her data subject rights vis-à-vis an EU Member -State consulate in Hong Kong for example. The reverse, invoking EU data protection rights vis-à-vis the Hong Kong consulate within the EU, will not be possible.[48] Though a necessary provision, its practical relevance—particularly in the context of this book—is marginal[49] and will therefore not be further discussed.[50]

all-or-nothing) to territorial scope determinations. After all, it could be considered unreasonable to hold an SME in Venezuela accountable to the same extent as a huge, multinational online social network. In: Dan Jerker B Svantesson, 'A "Layered Approach" to the Extraterritoriality of Data Privacy Laws' (2013) 3 International Data Privacy Law 278.

[46] Article 29 Working Party, 'Opinion 8/2010 on Applicable Law' (n 4) 17.

[47] ibid 18; Van Alsenoy and Koekkoek (n 35) n 16; Svantesson, *Extraterritoriality in Data Privacy Law* (n 4) 98–99; Dan Jerker B Svantesson, 'The Extraterritoriality of EU Data Privacy Law—Its Theoretical Justification and Its Practical Effect on U.S. Businesses' (2013) 50 Stanford Journal of International Law 53, 66.

[48] Article 29 Working Party, 'Opinion 8/2010 on Applicable Law' (n 4) 18.

[49] Kuner also emphasizes this provision has little business relevance. In: Christopher Kuner, *European Data Protection Law: Corporate Compliance and Regulation* (OUP 2007) 128.

[50] For a more elaborate account of the interaction between (public) international law and the GDPR's extraterritorial reach, see: Svantesson, Dan Jerker B. 'The Extraterritoriality of EU Data Privacy Law—Its Theoretical Justification and Its Practical Effect on U.S. Businesses' (2013) 50, no. 1 Stan. J. Int 75 (n 737) 75 et seq.

Section 3. Material Scope

Article 2—Material Scope

This Regulation applies to the processing of personal data wholly or partly by automated means […].

The EU data protection framework has a notoriously wide scope of application.[51] Article 2 GDPR—which defines the material scope—illustrates this point most palpably. Three distinctive elements can be identified in the Regulation's definition of material scope: (a) personal data; (b) processing; (c) fully or partly by automated means.[52] Given this book's focus on online service providers, the third characteristic will not be discussed further. After all, the processing of personal data in the online realm will, by definition, occur 'by automated means'.

3.1 What is the 'Data' in Data Protection?

The GDPR covers an increasingly wide array of 'data' under the common denominator of *personal* data. In light of the 'data deluge' described in the Introduction (Chapter 1), qualifying data as being 'personal' or not is increasingly difficult (Section 3.1.1). In spite of that, the regulatory framework further differentiates between different kinds of personal data. So-called 'sensitive data' can be considered one particular sub-category of personal data, subject to a more protective regime (Section 3.1.2) and several other relevant data categories can be discerned (Section 3.1.3) as well. Given the fact that—at least from the perspective of the data protection right to erasure—no data categorization can be entirely comprehensive and/or satisfactory, this section ends with an alternative perspective: the personal data equalizer (Section 3.1.4).

3.1.1 Personal Data

Article 3—Definitions

(1) 'personal data' means any information relating to an identified or identifiable natural person 'data subject'; an identifiable person is one who can be identified, directly or indirectly, in particular by reference to an identifier such as a name, an

[51] This has also been recognized by the CJEU since at least the early 2000s: *Österreichischer Rundfunk and others* [2003] Court of Justice of the European Union Joined Cases C-465/00, C-138/01 and C-139/01 [68] para 43; *College van burgemeester en wethouders van Rotterdam v MEE Rijkeboer* [2009] Court of Justice of the European Union C-553/07 para 59; *Peter Nowak v Data Protection Commissioner* [2017] Court of Justice of the European Union C-434/16 [33].

[52] Going beyond the scope of Convention 108 before it, which only covers automated data processing (Art 1). Gloria González Fuster, *The Emergence of Personal Data Protection as a Fundamental Right of the EU* (Springer 2014) 136.

> identification number, location data, online identifier or to one or more factors specific to the physical, physiological, genetic, mental, economic, cultural or social identity of that person.

The EU data protection framework is a data-centric piece of legislation.[53] Personal data constitutes the central building block in the GDPR, forming the actual subject matter of most data subject rights and controller obligations. The right to erasure in particular, fundamentally depends on a clearly delineated definition of 'personal data'. Without such a demarcation, it would not be possible to determine what data actually needs to be deleted. In a 2007 Opinion,[54] the Article 29 Working Party dissected the concept of 'personal data' into four main components: (a) any information; (b) relating to; (c) an identified or identifiable; (d) natural person.[55]

ANY INFORMATION—A priori, the Regulation is agnostic to the kind (eg true/false, objective/subjective),[56] or format (eg audiovisual, binary) of information.[57] As to the content of the information, it is not required that this directly concerns an individual's private or family life.[58] For example, information 'concerning working relations or the economic or social behaviour of the individual'[59] are all considered personal data, without necessarily falling within the realm of one's *private and family life*. This 'information-agnosticism' is a clear illustration of how the right to data protection (Art 8 Charter) differs from the general right to privacy (Art 7 Charter).[60]

[53] Joris van Hoboken and Frederik Zuiderveen Borgesius, 'Scoping Electronic Communication Privacy Rules: Data, Services and Values' (2015) 6 JIPITEC 204ff <http://www.jipitec.eu/issues/issue.2016-01-12.5219458400/4316> et seq. For a selection of different interpretations of 'personal data' across three Member States (Italy, France, and the UK), see: Mario Viola de Azevedo Cunha, 'Review of the Data Protection Directive: Is There Need (and Room) For a New Concept of Personal Data?' in Serge Gutwirth and others (eds), *European Data Protection: In Good Health?* (Springer 2012).

[54] Article 29 Working Party, 'Opinion 4/2007 on the Concept of Personal Data' (Article 29 Working Party 2007) WP 136 <http://ec.europa.eu/justice/article-29/documentation> accessed 1 June 2019.

[55] Even though this Opinion was written in light of the definition of personal data in Directive 95/46, it is still relevant with regard to the GDPR's definition of the concept (which remained virtually identical). For a more detailed account of how the concept is understood in the member states, see: Korff, 'New Challenges to Data Protection Study-Working Paper No. 2' (n 33) 53 et seq; Viola de Azevedo Cunha (n 53).

[56] *Peter Nowak v Data Protection Commissioner* (n 51) para 34.

[57] Article 29 Working Party, 'Opinion on Personal Data' (n 54) 7. Even though this indifference as to the kind or form of information seems straightforward, complications might arise when the information is recorded in a proprietary and/or restricted format. In the context of biometric data, see for example: Els J Kindt, *Privacy and Data Protection Issues of Biometric Applications: A Comparative Legal Analysis* (Springer 2013) 87 et seq .

[58] Article 29 Working Party, 'Opinion on Personal Data' (n 54) 6–7.

[59] ibid 6. Later confirmed in: *Worten* [2013] Court of Justice of the European Union C-342/12 [22].

[60] The right to data protection applies, regardless of there being an impact on the right to privacy. See, inter alia: Lynskey, Orla Lynskey, *The Foundations of EU Data Protection Law* (OUP 2016) 11; Kokott and Sobotta (n 466); Bart van der Sloot, 'Do Privacy and Data Protection Rules Apply to Legal Persons and Should They? A Proposal for a Two-Tiered System' (2015) 31 Computer Law & Security Review 26, 27–28; Frederik Zuiderveen Borgesius, 'Improving Privacy Protection in the Area of Behavioural Targeting' (PhD Thesis, University of Amsterdam 2014) 165 et seq <http://hdl.handle.net/11245/1.434236>.

Relating to—Quite obviously, the information still needs to *relate to* an individual. This requirement also needs to be interpreted very broadly. Even facts about a certain object or process might (indirectly) reveal information about an individual.[61] It is therefore important to take into account the circumstances under which the information is generated and used. According to WP29, for example, 'the unique number contained in a [RFID] tag can also serve as a means to remotely identify the nature of items carried by a person, which in turn may reveal information about social status, health, or more'.[62] Similarly, location data of a car or phone; pictures of houses;[63] tracking-cookies;[64] e-reading behaviour patterns;[65] computer mouse movements;[66] a smartphone's battery;[67] accelerometer;[68] or camera[69] information, can all be considered to involve personal data, even though *stricto sensu* the data only relates to an object or process.[70] Ubiquitous computing and the expanding 'Internet of Things' generate troves of data that can increasingly

[61] WP29 cites the example of real estate value. The price of a house indirectly reveals information about the owner of that property. Article 29 Working Party, 'Opinion on Personal Data' (n 54) 9 et seq. See also: Korff, 'New Challenges to Data Protection Study-Working Paper No. 2' (n 5) 42–43.

[62] 'Thus, even in those cases where a tag contains solely a number that is unique within a particular context, and no additional personal data, care must be taken to address potential privacy and security issues if the tag is going to be carried by persons.' Article 29 Working Party, 'Opinion 5/2010 on the Industry Proposal for a Privacy and Data Protection Impact Assessment Framework for RFID Applications' (2010) WP 175 8 <http://ec.europa.eu/justice/article-29/documentation> accessed 1 June 2019.

[63] Belgian Privacy Commission, 'Frequently Asked Questions—Google Street View' <https://www.dataprotectionauthority.be/faq-themes/the-internet/google-street-view> accessed 1 June 2019; dpa, 'Google Street View: Bilder Aus "Blurmany"' *Die Zeit* (Hamburg, 18 November 2010) <http://www.zeit.de/digital/internet/2010-11/start-google-street-view> accessed 1 June 2019; Jeff Jarvis, *Public Parts: How Sharing in the Digital Age Improves the Way We Work and Live* (Simon & Schuster 2011) 25 et seq.

[64] Tracking cookies are one of the most commonly used technologies for personalized advertisement. It would be a *contradicio in terminis* to claim that such cookies would not 'relate' to an individual, while at the same time using them to target specific individuals with personalized advertisement. For a specific example, see the Dutch DPA's investigation into Google's practices: College Bescherming Persoonsgegevens, 'Investigation into the Combining of Personal Data by Google—Report of Definitive Findings' (Dutch Data Protection Authority 2013) z2013-00194 54 <https://cbpweb.nl/sites/default/files/downloads/mijn_privacy/en_rap_2013-google-privacypolicy.pdf>.

[65] Margot Kaminski, 'Reading Over Your Shoulder: Social Readers and Privacy Law' *Wake Forest Law Review* (9 March 2012) <http://wakeforestlawreview.com/2012/03/reading-over-your-shoulder-social-readers-and-privacy-law> accessed 1 June 2019.

[66] Jose Carlos Norte, 'Advanced Tor Browser Fingerprinting' (6 March 2016) <http://jcarlosnorte.com/security/2016/03/06/advanced-tor-browser-fingerprinting.html> accessed 1 June 2019.

[67] Alex Hern, 'How Your Smartphone's Battery Life Can Be Used to Invade Your Privacy' *The Guardian* (4 August 2015) <http://www.theguardian.com/technology/2015/aug/03/privacy-smartphones-battery-life> accessed 1 June 2019.

[68] Samuli Hemminki, Petteri Nurmi, and Sasu Tarkoma, 'Accelerometer-Based Transportation Mode Detection on Smartphones', *11th ACM Conference on Embedded Networked Sensor Systems* (ACM Press 2013) <http://dl.acm.org/citation.cfm?doid=2517351.2517367> accessed 1 June 2019.

[69] Ryan Whitwam, 'Facebook Developing Way to Fingerprint the Camera You Used to Take a Photo' (*@geekdotcom*, 20 September 2015) <http://www.geek.com/news/facebook-developing-way-to-fingerprint-the-camera-you-used-to-take-a-photo-1634542/> accessed 1 June 2019.

[70] Paul De Hert and Vagelis Papakonstantinou, 'The Proposed Data Protection Regulation Replacing Directive 95/46/EC: A Sound System for the Protection of Individuals' (2012) 28 Computer Law & Security Review 133.

easily be tied back to specific individuals.[71] In light of this, WP29 summarized that data can 'relate' to an individual because (a) of its actual content; (b) the purpose it is used for; (c) the result or impact it has on an individual.[72] For example, anonymous 'consumer profiles' or 'group profiles' may not constitute personal data in isolation.[73] A company like Facebook generates models (eg people who like cars) on the basis of large amounts of their userbase-data. Once sucked into the model, data appears to lose its 'personal' nature. Though even this has been called into question by researchers, suggesting that some models may be vulnerable to inversion attacks, enabling the (re-) identification of individuals whose personal data was used to create those models in the first place.[74] Yet, such profiles will often only generate value or usefulness when linked back to a specific individual (eg for advertisement or credit rating). In such particular cases, these profiles—or at least the link between that profile and a specific individual—will constitute personal data and hence be subject to data protection law.[75] Importantly, and as was confirmed by the CJEU, some information can *relate to* several individuals at the same time.[76] This may raise conflicts with regard to the exercise of the right to erasure.

Identifiable Natural Person—In order to qualify as 'personal data', information needs to relate to an *identified* or *identifiable* natural person. Even if only limited to *natural* persons,[77] it was clearly the legislator's intention to ensure a wide scope of application. The mere possibility to single out or distinguish one individual from others already suffices to meet this requirement.[78] This may be easier than one might think today; for example 'in a dataset where the location of an

[71] Korff, 'New Challenges to Data Protection Study-Working Paper No. 2' (n 5) 43.

[72] Article 29 Working Party, 'Opinion on Personal Data' (n 54) 10–12.

[73] Ira S Rubinstein, 'Big Data: The End of Privacy or a New Beginning?' (2013) 3 International Data Privacy Law 74, 80; Mireille Hildebrandt, 'Who Is Profiling Who? Invisible Visibility' in Serge Gutwirth and others (eds), *Reinventing Data Protection?* (Springer 2009) <www.springerlink.com/index/P7710R0760613778.pdf> accessed 1 June 2019.

[74] Michael Veale, Reuben Binns, and Lilian Edwards, 'Algorithms That Remember: Model Inversion Attacks and Data Protection Law' [2018] arXiv:1807.04644 [cs] <http://arxiv.org/abs/1807.04644> accessed 17 August 2018.

[75] Mireille Hildebrandt, 'The Dawn of a Critical Transparency Right for the Profiling Era' *Digital Enlightenment Yearbook 2012* (IOS Press 2012) 47 <https://works.bepress.com/mireille_hildebrandt/40> accessed 1 June 2019.

[76] *Peter Nowak v Data Protection Commissioner* (n 51) paras 44–45.

[77] During the first wave of data protection legislations, it was still considered to include legal entities as well. See: Frits W Hondius, *Emerging Data Protection in Europe* (North-Holland 1975) 96–97. Complementing the general data protection framework in the context of the electronic communications sector, the so-called ePrivacy Directive (2002/58/EC) also provides 'for protection of the legitimate interests of subscribers who are legal persons' (Art 1(2)).

[78] In *Ryneš*, for example, the CJEU considers personal data 'the image of a person recorded by a camera [...] inasmuch as it makes it possible to identify the person concerned', regardless of the fact that the owner of the camera can him/herself identify the relevant individuals. *František Ryneš v Úřad pro ochranu osobních údajů* [2014] Court of Justice of the European Union C-212/13 para 22. Later, the CJEU also answered affirmatively the long-debated question whether dynamic IP addresses can be considered personal data in the hands of someone who does not hold all the information necessary to identify the individual behind it (such as an Internet access provider would have). *Patrick Breyer v Bundesrepublik Deutschland* [2016] Court of Justice of the European Union C-582/14 [31–49].

individual is specified hourly, and with a spatial resolution equal to that given by the carrier's antennas, four spatio-temporal points are enough to uniquely identify 95% of the individuals'.[79] Article 4(1) GDPR explains a person can either be identified directly or indirectly and gives a non-exhaustive list of so-called 'identifiers'.[80] The Working Party explains that even when '*prima facie* the extent of the identifiers available does not allow anyone to single out a particular person, that person might still be 'identifiable' because that information combined with other pieces of information (whether the latter is retained by the data controller or not) will allow the individual to be distinguished from others'.[81,82] This is particularly the case, for example, for so-called online identifiers associated with devices, applications, tools, and protocols.[83] Hence, '[d]ata which has undergone pseudonymization, which could be attributed to a natural person by the use of additional information, should be considered personal data'.[84] It is also worth mentioning that there is 'no requirement that all the information enabling the identification of the data subject must be in the hands of one person'.[85]

Reasonable Means—Determining the identifiability of data requires taking into account the specific circumstances[86] and all 'reasonable means' to be used, either by the controller *or by any other person*.[87] *A contrario*, mere hypothetical

[79] Yves-Alexandre de Montjoye and others, 'Unique in the Crowd: The Privacy Bounds of Human Mobility' (2013) 3 Scientific Reports <http://www.nature.com/srep/2013/130325/srep01376/full/srep01376.html> accessed 1 June 2019.

[80] Recital 24 further cites examples of online identifiers which 'may leave traces which, in particular when combined with unique identifiers and other information received by the servers, may be used to create profiles of the individuals and identify them'.

From a technical perspective, it is worth highlighting that 'any information that distinguishes one person from another can be used for re-identifying data'. Arvind Narayanan and Vitaly Shmatikov, 'Myths and Fallacies of "Personally Identifiable Information"' (2010) 53 Communications of the ACM 24, 24.

[81] Article 29 Working Party, 'Opinion on Personal Data' (n 54) 13.

[82] The ease with which data can be (cross-)combined was already recognized in the first data protection legislations as a reason for not including a quantitative requirement in the personal data definition. Hondius (n 77) 90–91. It has also been recognized by the CJEU in: *Patrick Breyer v Bundesrepublik Deutschland* (n 78) para 41.

[83] Recital 30 GDPR, referring among others to Internet Protocol addresses; cookie identifiers; and Radio Frequency Identification Tags. *Patrick Breyer v Bundesrepublik Deutschland* (n 78) para 49.

[84] Recital 26 GDPR.

[85] *Patrick Breyer v Bundesrepublik Deutschland* (n 78) para 43; *Peter Nowak v Data Protection Commissioner* (n 51) para 31.

[86] A common family name alone, might not be sufficient to identify one specific person in a country's population, but will often allow for the identification of a person within a small group (eg class, workplace, sports club).

[87] Recital 23 of the Regulation specifies that 'means which are reasonably likely to be used to identify an individual' include objective factors 'such as the costs of and the amount of time required for identification, taking into consideration both available technology at the time of the processing and technological development'. The CJEU explains that as long the entity has the legal means enabling the identification, the data should be considered personal data. Citing the AG's Opinion, the CJEU further elaborates that the 'reasonable means' requirement would not be fulfilled when 'the identification of the data subject was prohibited by law or practically impossible on account of the fact that it requires a disproportionate effort in terms of time, cost and man-power, so that the risk of identification appears in reality to be insignificant'. *Patrick Breyer v Bundesrepublik Deutschland* (n 78) paras 46; 49.

identifiability will not be sufficient to consider a person 'identifiable' under the Regulation.[88] As specified by the AG in his Opinion in the *Breyer* Ruling, this reasonable means criterion is not met when (approaching third parties who have the necessary information to identify the individual is) 'very costly in human and economic terms, or practically impossible or prohibited by law'.[89] Exceptionally, the same data set might be considered personal data within one processing-context but not within another. According to WP29, this might be the case when appropriate technical and organisational measures are taken to prevent (re) identification. Key-coded medical research data, for example, would be considered identifiable—and thus personal—data vis-à-vis anyone having access to it, *unless* it is transferred to a third party (eg a pharmaceutical company) having no possibility whatsoever of accessing the key.[90] Put briefly, the identifiability test is a dynamic one, leaving flexibility to take into account a variety of factors, such as the state of technology, cost, the controller's purpose and potential benefits, risks, and the duration of storage (Recital 26).[91]

NATURAL PERSON—Finally, to be considered 'personal data', the information needs to relate to a 'natural person' or a 'human being'. The Regulation applies regardless of the natural person's nationality, status, or capacity (eg patient, consumer, employee).[92] In principle, data ceases to be 'personal' when the individual dies.[93] Depending on the circumstances, however, the data might still be considered personal with regard to surviving relatives.[94] Data relating to legal persons a priori fall outside the scope of the GDPR.[95] Still, information concerning legal

[88] Article 29 Working Party, 'Opinion 5/2010 on the Industry Proposal for a Privacy and Data Protection Impact Assessment Framework for RFID Applications' (n 62) 15.

[89] AG Opinion in: *Patrick Breyer v Bundesrepublik Deutschland* (n 78) para 68.

[90] See: Article 29 Working Party, 'Opinion on Personal Data' (n 54) 19–21. Recitals 12 GDPR. The inability to access the key should be interpreted strictly. The mere fact that two databases (one of which contains anonymous data, and the other containing the same data linked to identities) are controlled by different entities, does not render the data unidentifiable. In the context of biometric data, see: Kindt (n 57) 113.

[91] Directive 95/46 was criticized for lacking criteria to determine whether there were 'reasonable means'. See notably: Viola de Azevedo Cunha (n 53) 281. On the dynamic nature of 'personal data' in the context of cloud computing, see: W Kuan Hon, Christopher Millard, and Ian Walden, 'The Problem of "Personal Data" in Cloud Computing: What Information Is Regulated?—The Cloud of Unknowing' (2011) 1 International Data Privacy Law 211, 214.

[92] See also: Korff, 'New Challenges to Data Protection Study-Working Paper No. 2' (n 33) 41.

[93] Recital 27 GDPR specifies that although the Regulation 'does not apply to data of deceased persons. Member States may provide for rules regarding the processing of data of deceased persons'. Before, the adoption of the GDPR, several member states did have protections in place for the deceased. See notably: Lilian Edwards and Edina Harbina, 'Protecting Post-Mortem Privacy: Reconsidering the Privacy Interests of the Deceased in a Digital World' (2013) 32 Cardozo Arts & Entertainment Law Journal 83, 130–33.

[94] eg data relating to a hereditary decease. Article 29 Working Party, 'Opinion on Personal Data' (n 54) 22–23.

[95] Contrary to Convention 108, which explicitly left open the possibility of extending protection to 'information relating to groups of persons, associations, foundations, companies, corporations and any other bodies consisting directly or indirectly of individuals, whether or not such bodies possess legal personality' (Art 3(2)(b)). González Fuster, *The Emergence of Personal Data Protection as a Fundamental Right of the EU* (n 52 136–37.

persons might be considered 'personal data' to the extent it can be connected to a natural person (eg the owner of a small and medium-sized enterprise (SME); addressees and/or content in email traffic).[96]

3.1.2 Sensitive Data

Recital 51

> Personal data which are, by their nature, particularly sensitive in relation to fundamental rights and freedoms, deserve specific protection as the context of their processing may create important risks for the fundamental rights and freedoms. [. . .]

Description—The GDPR sets out a more protective regime for the processing of so-called 'special categories of personal data' (Art 9). Put simply, the processing of such 'sensitive data' is prohibited by default (Art 9(1)), *unless* special conditions are complied with (Art 9(2)). As will become apparent in Chapter 4, this stricter regime will considerably impact the ability to invoke a right to erasure with regard to sensitive data. Similar to its predecessor Directive 95/46 (Art 8), the GDPR does not offer a definition of what constitutes sensitive data.[97] Instead, it lists a number of data-types that are deemed to be of a more sensitive nature to the data subject, ie 'personal data, revealing racial or ethnic origin, political opinions, religious or philosophical beliefs, trade-union membership, and the processing of genetic data, biometric data in order to uniquely identify a person or data concerning health or sex life and sexual orientation'.[98] In 2003, the CJEU confirmed that 'reference to the fact that an individual has injured her foot and is on half-time on medical grounds' constitutes 'sensitive data' within the meaning of the data protection framework.[99]

Permitted Use—Although the first paragraph of Article 9 provides a general processing prohibition, the second paragraph lists a limited number of situations in which such 'sensitive data' may still be processed. Most of these cover very narrowly scoped situations that generally fall outside of the focus in this book. Some of them *are* relevant however: (a) the data subject has given explicit

[96] The CJEU has explicitly stated that legal persons can invoke data protection rights when 'the official title of the legal person identifies one or more natural persons'. *Volker und Markus Schecke GbR and Hartmut Eifert v Land Hessen* [2010] Court of Justice of the European Union Joined Cases C-92/09 and C-93/09 paras 52–54.

Article 29 Working Party, 'Opinion on Personal Data' (n 54); van der Sloot, 'Do Privacy and Data Protection Rules Apply to Legal Persons and Should They?' (n 60) 37.

[97] It does, however, provide definitions for certain specific sub-categories of 'sensitive data', notably: genetic data; biometric data; and data concerning health (Art 4(10)–(12)). See Paul Ohm, 'Sensitive Information' (2014) 88 S Cal L Rev 1125, 1132 et seq.

[98] Genetic and biometric data are two notable additions to the list in Directive 95/46. In 2007, WP29 had already highlighted the potential intrusiveness of such data, explaining that 'because of their unique link to a specific individual, biometric data may be used to identify the individual'. Article 29 Working Party, 'Opinion on Personal Data' (n 54) 8.

[99] *Lindqvist* [2003] Court of Justice of the European Union C-101/01 [83] para 51.

consent; (e) processing relates to personal data which are manifestly made public by the data subject; (j) processing is necessary for archiving purposes in the public interest, scientific or historical research purposes, or statistical purposes in accordance with Article 89(1). In that last case, the GDPR further requires suitable and specific measures are taken to safeguard the fundamental rights and the interests of the data subject. Article 10 sets out an even stricter regime for the processing of 'personal data relating to criminal convictions and offences [...]', which can only be processed 'under the control of official authority or when the processing is authorised by Union or Member State law providing for appropriate safeguards for the rights and freedoms of data subjects'. The additional protection granted to 'sensitive data' also constitutes one of the primary overlaps between the GDPR and the right to privacy in the Charter (Art 7) and the ECHR (Art 8). The latter gives effect to basic data protection principles, at the very least, with regard to sensitive data.[100]

Some Flexibility—With more and more data being captured and interconnected, one might argue that virtually all personal data could be qualified as 'sensitive' in one way or another.[101] Sensitive data may more or less easily be inferred from otherwise quite ordinary personal data.[102] It is no secret, for example, that social networks can infer political affiliation or sexual preferences from seemingly innocuous data such as page-likes.[103] Photographs also often expose much of the data categories listed above. Arguments for a more teleological interpretation of 'sensitive data'—looking at the controller's intentions—have been unsuccessful.[104] Nonetheless, the GDPR does seem to recognize these worries to a certain extent, by foreseeing some flexibility in interpreting the scope of these 'special categories of personal data'. Recital 51 explains that '[t]he processing of photographs should not systematically be considered to be processing of special categories of personal data as they are covered by the definition of biometric data only when processed through a specific technical means allowing the unique identification or authentication of a natural person'. With regard to pictures on Facebook, for example, this

[100] Peter Hustinx, 'Data Protection in the European Union' (2005) 2 Privacy & Informatie 62, 63 62; Paul De Hert and Serge Gutwirth, 'Data Protection in the Case Law of Strasbourg and Luxemburg: Con stitutionalisation in Action' in Serge Gutwirth and others (eds), *Reinventing Data Protection?* (Springer Science 2009) 27.

[101] WP29 also defends a broad interpretation of sensitive data and in particular 'health data', which would also include, for example, data on consumption of alcohol or drugs. See: Article 29 Working Party, 'Working Document on the Processing of Personal Data Relating to Health in Electronic Health Records (EHR)' (2007) WP 131 7 <http://ec.europa.eu/justice/article-29/documentation> accessed 1 June 2019.

[102] De Hert and Papakonstantinou (n 70) 133. The authors explain that 'by processing meal preferences or surnames of passengers one may incur information as to their religion, nationality or health, and therefore derive what is, in effect, sensitive data'. Also see: Paul Bernal, *Internet Privacy Rights: Rights to Protect Autonomy* (CUP 2014) 34.

[103] Michal Kosinski, David Stillwell, and Thore Graepel, 'Private Traits and Attributes Are Predictable from Digital Records of Human Behavior' (2013) 110 Proceedings of the National Academy of Sciences 5802.

[104] Kindt (n 57) 228.

essentially means that as long as Facebook does not convert those pictures into *biometric* data (eg through facial recognition software),[105] they should not be considered sensitive data under Article 9. Yet, the recital is silent about the fact that that same picture might still reveal other listed categories of data (race, sexual or political preferences, religious beliefs, etc).

Some guidance may be found in a WP29 letter to the Director of DG Connect on mHealth Apps.[106] In the Annex to the letter, WP29 recommends separating 'raw data' from whatever inferences are made on the basis of that data. For example, the data collected by a pedometer do not constitute health data when considered in isolation. It is only when combined with other data and/or used in a way to derive health aspects (eg calories burned in a running App), that one can talk about 'health data'. This seems to suggest one should look at data as having different layers, some of which may be sensitive, some not. How to operationalize data subject rights against this backdrop will be looked into later.[107]

VIGNETTES—The uncertainty about the exact scope of sensitive data is quite problematic in the ISS context. Indeed, data science enables deriving quite intrusive knowledge about seemingly innocuous data. In connection to the Uber vignette, it is worth referring to a 2012 blogpost the company has meanwhile removed from its website.[108] In this post, they revealed how their dataset of rides reveals one-night-stands (which they projected on the maps of a selection of US cities).[109] Does the location data constitute sensitive data in itself? Equally problematic is the Apple Siri vignette, where sensitive data may be revealed by a friend of the device-owner, who has not given explicit consent. Too strict an interpretation of the notion of sensitive data would also seem to render illegal Google's activities as a search engine (ie undoubtedly having large amounts of 'sensitive data' in its indexes).[110]

[105] Article 4(14) defines biometric data as 'personal data resulting from specific technical processing relating to the physical, physiological or behavioural characteristics of a natural person, which allow or confirm the unique identification of that natural person, such as facial images or dactyloscopic data'. In other words, the qualification of 'biometric data' depends on a technical process data has to go through first.

[106] Article 29 Working Party to Paul Timmers (DG Connect), 'Letter to the European Commission, DG CONNECT on MHealth' (5 February 2015) <http://ec.europa.eu/justice/article-29/documentation>.

[107] eg can one layer be unlawfully processed and 'erased' without the other?

[108] Bradley Voytek, 'Uberdata: The Ride of Glory' (*Uber Blog*, 26 March 2012) <http://blog.uber.com/2012/03/26/uberdata-the-ride-of-glory/> accessed 21 March 2018 via web.archive.org; Derrick Harris, 'The One-Night Stand, Quantified and Visualized by Uber' (26 March 2012) <https://gigaom.com/2012/03/26/uber-one-night-stands/> accessed 1 June 2019.

[109] The method for identifying one-night-stands in their data may not be the most scientific one, but appears to at least give a strong indication: '[A]nyone who took a ride between 10pm and 4am on a Friday or Saturday night, and then took a second ride from within 1/10th of a mile of the previous nights' drop-off point 4–6 hours later (enough for a quick night's sleep) [has engaged in a one-night stand]'.

[110] This last scenario is at the core of a CJEU case not yet decided at the time of writing. However, Advocate General Szpunar did already state that the general prohibition to process personal data *does* apply to search engines, *but* only 'by means of an *ex post facto* verification, on the basis of a de-referencing request by the data subject'. In his opinion, 'an ex ante systematic control is neither possible nor desirable'. AG Opinion in: *GC and Others* Court of Justice of the European Union C-136/17 [49; 56].

Existing case-law and doctrine suggest that, a priori, 'sensitive data' should be interpreted broadly (and thus casting the nets of the protective regime widely),[111] with some level of flexibility when assessing individual cases (allowing certain data which is, *stricto sensu*, 'sensitive data' to slip through the net).[112] Conversely, not appearing in the list does not automatically imply that data should not benefit from similar additional safeguards.[113] Depending on the circumstances, certain categories of data (eg location data or web browsing behaviour) will require thorough protection in light of other provisions in the Regulation (notably 'data quality requirements'). In conclusion, for all the criticism that a specific list of what constitutes 'sensitive data' received,[114] the categories have largely remained unchanged for several decades. This suggests both that the list is quite indicative of potentially risky data processing,[115] as well as that it offers sufficient flexibility to stand the test of time. A more cynical view would be that the list simply survived because it has never been strictly applied across the board, but only in extreme situations.

Ratio Legis—As mentioned before, the main reason for Article 9's existence, is that (the processing of) certain categories of personal data are considered particularly intrusive[116] and/or present great(er) risks to individuals (for example, the likelihood of unfair discrimination).[117] Sensitive data—or 'special categories of personal data'—was already recognized to present higher risks to the individual in Convention 108.[118] In 1972 Jon Bing explained 'sensitivity denotes the closeness of

[111] See the extensive literature and caselaw overview in: Kindt (n 57) 128 et seq.

[112] eg Pictures revealing the ethnicity of individuals. On the relativity of sensitive data lists, see: Spiros Simitis, 'Revisiting Sensitive Data' 3ff <https://www.coe.int/t/dghl/standardsetting/dataprotection/Reports/Report_Simitis_1999.pdf> accessed 1 June 2019 et seq.

[113] Already in 1978, it was acknowledged that no list of categories could ever be complete, nor that there are objective standards of 'sensitivity'. See: Norman Lindop, *Report of the Committee on Data Protection, Chairman: Norman Lindop* (HMSO 1978) 153–54.

[114] See, for example: Karen McCullagh, 'The Social, Cultural, Epistemological and Technical Basis of the Concept of "Private Data"' (PhD Thesis, University of Manchester—Faculty of Humanities 2011) 187 <https://www.escholar.manchester.ac.uk/api/datastream?publicationPid=uk-ac-man-scw:157750&datastreamId=FULL-TEXT.PDF> accessed 3 March 2016; Antoinette Rouvroy, '"Of Data and Men": Fundamental Rights and Freedoms in a World of Big Data' (Council of Europe 2016) T-PD-BUR(2015)09REV 26–29<www.coe.int/t/dghl/standardsetting/DataProtection/TPD_documents/T-PD-BUR(2015)09REV_Big%20Data%20report_A%20%20Rouvroy_Final_EN.pdf> accessed 1 February 2016; Lokke Moerel and Corien Prins, 'Privacy for the Homo Digitalis: Proposal for a New Regulatory Framework for Data Protection in the Light of Big Data and the Internet of Things' <http://papers.ssrn.com/abstract=2784123> accessed 13 July 2016 56 et seq.

[115] Or at least, what society considers as such.

[116] Indeed, processing any of these 'special categories of personal data' will most likely constitute an interference with the general right to privacy (Art 8 ECHR; 9 Charter).

[117] This also becomes evident when reading the UN Guidelines for the Regulation of Computerized Data Files, Adopted by General Assembly resolution 45/95 of 14 December 1990. Cited in: Karen McCullagh, 'Data Sensitivity: Resolving the Conundrum1' *British & Irish Law, Education and Technology Association Annual Conference, Hertfordshire* (2007) 2 <http://bileta.ac.uk/content/files/conference%20papers/2007/Data%20Sensitivity%20-%20resolving%20the%20conundrum.pdf> accessed 22 February 2016.

[118] At the national level, Sweden and the German Länder Hesse already made explicit references to 'sensitive data' in their data protection frameworks in the 1970s. At the supranational level, the OECD privacy guidelines almost included such a reference too. But, in the end, the Group of Experts inter alia considered 'it is probably not possible to identify a set of data which are universally regarded as being

the person to the information; or the degree of privacy of the information'.[119] The level of sensitivity, the author continues, depends on a variety of factors, such as the 'quantity of information'; the addressee(s), purpose(s) of collection, time, and context.[120] Others claimed that '[t]he sensitivity risk depends on the situation in which the information is used, not on the information itself'.[121] Indeed, De Hert and Gutwirth explain that 'all data can be abused, including the more ordinary ones'.[122] However, the authors explain that sensitive data 'belongs to the core of a person's private life' and that it is 'exactly this kind of information that individuals generally do not wish to disclose to others'.[123] The Council of Europe also recognized that some information—ie 'relating to the intimate private life of personas or information which might lead to unfair discrimination'—presents particular risks and should therefore 'not be recorded or, if recorded, should not be disseminated'.[124] According to Simitis, the explicit reference to sensitive data in data protection law serves the purpose of an alarm device, signalling standard rules may not be sufficient and inciting additional reflection on the intended processing.[125] In the same vein, Ohm explains that 'sensitive data can provide a rule of thumb for a more nuanced approach that takes all relevant circumstances into account'.[126]

In sum, Article 9 (and 10) GDPR lists a number of data categories considered to be sensitive data. Processing is prohibited, unless any of the situations in Art 9(2) applies. To be clear, controllers will still have to comply with all other GDPR requirements (notably lawfulness requirement in Art 6(1)).[127] Pursuant to recital 51, and the GDPR's risk-based approach more broadly, it appears that the sensitivity of data is not a binary, but can vary depending on the moment of assessment.[128]

sensitive'. OECD, 'The OECD Privacy Framework' (OECD 2013) 45 <www.oecd.org/sti/ieconomy/oecd_privacy_framework.pdf> accessed 9 May 2014.

[119] Jon Bing, 'Classification of Personal Information, with Respect to the Sensitivity Aspect', *The First International Oslo Symposium on Data Banks and Society, Presented by Klaus Lenk e.a.* (Universitetsforlaget 1972) 100.

[120] Similarly, see: Simitis (n 112) 5.

[121] Hondius (n 77) 120–21; similarly, see: Simitis (n 112) 5–6. This argument is also echoed in Nissenbaum's work, where sensitivity generally depends on context. Helen Nissenbaum, *Privacy in Context: Technology, Policy, and the Integrity of Social Life* (Stanford UP 2009).; Ohm (n 97) 1144 et seq; van Hoboken and Zuiderveen Borgesius (n 53) 206. In this regard, the last article explains that 'while a person's name is usually public information, it becomes sensitive when associated with a system of psychiatric treatment records'.

[122] The authors continue: 'the basic idea of data protection is to offer protection to all personal data (and a stronger protection to some types of sensitive data)'. De Hert and Gutwirth (n 100) 25.

[123] ibid 4. Some information, of course, is less easily concealed (eg race or gender).

[124] Explanatory Report to: Council of Europe—Committee of Ministers, 'Resolution (73) 22 on the Protection of the Privacy of Individuals vis-à-vis Electronic Data Banks in the Private Sector' para 1 <https://rm.coe.int/CoERMPublicCommonSearchServices/DisplayDCTMContent?documentId=0900001680502830>.

[125] Simitis (n 112) 8.

[126] Ohm (n 97); van Hoboken and Zuiderveen Borgesius (n 53) 205.

[127] Article 9(2) lists *exemptions*, not 'grounds for lawful processing'.

[128] See similarly: van Hoboken and Zuiderveen Borgesius (n 53) 206–07. Malgieri and Comandé propose a more formalized model for calculating the 'degree of sensitivity' of health data. See: Gianclaudio

The list in Article 9 constitutes a more straightforward trigger for the protective regime—ie data-categories inherently presenting a higher likelihood of riskiness/intrusiveness to individuals—rather than looking at the context and/or intentions of data controllers.[129] Despite its drawbacks,[130] such a list of 'sensitive data' has the key benefit of raising a red flag and forcing deeper reflection on the processing of such data. This is particularly relevant in light of exercising data subject rights. Given the stricter rules applicable to sensitive data, the right to erasure will generally be more readily applicable to such data. Another advantage of the sensitive data category for data subjects is that it serves as one of the most clearly delineated provisions in the framework. As such, it makes it easier to determine the controller's liability for non-compliance.

3.1.3 Fifty Shades of Data

Considerable uncertainty still exists as to the actual meaning and extent of 'personal data' as a concept, frustrating the invokability of the right to erasure. This may not come as a surprise in a society where every aspect of an individual's life can be expressed in 'data'. Privacy policies of ISS demonstrate the substantial amount of (categories of) data collected, but also the many different ways in which data can be categorized in the first place. Google's privacy policy, for example, makes a *summa divisio* between on the one hand 'information you give us', and on the other hand 'information we get from your use of our services'.[131] The first category is understood to refer, inter alia to name, photo(s), contact, and credit card information, whereas the first category contains device, log, and location information. The company further explains that it only treats this information as 'personal information' to the extent they associate it with a Google account.[132] Of course, the extent of personal data Google processes is much broader than this main distinction suggests.[133] Facebook's list of personal data collected also illustrates the difficulty in

Malgieri and Giovanni Comandé, 'Sensitive-by-Distance: Quasi-Health Data in the Algorithmic Era' (2017) 26 Information & Communications Technology Law 229.

[129] On the (issues with) teleological and context-dependent interpretations, see: McCullagh (n 117) 11–13; Rebecca Wong, 'Data Protection Online: Alternative Approaches to Sensitive Data?' (2007) 2 Journal of International Commercial Law and Technology 9, 12 et seq.

[130] In light of the above, a list of sensitive data may seem quite mechanical and both over- *and* under-inclusive. Ohm (n 97) 1146.

[131] See: https://www.google.com/intl/en/policies/privacy/?fg=1#infocollect accessed 22 March 2018. For a critical assessment of the rhetoric Google uses in its privacy policy (specifically in the context of its education apps) and how it conceals its business model, see: Maria Lindh and Jan Nolin, 'Information We Collect: Surveillance and Privacy in the Implementation of Google Apps for Education' [2016] 16(4) European Educational Research Journal 644.

[132] Seemingly ignoring the (much wider) definition of personal data.

[133] For example: web-browsing behaviour of people without a Google account; personal data contained on indexed webpages; data provided by others; etc. Not to mention all of the information Google derives or infers from this 'raw' information.

categorizing. It contains data-categories defined by who provides them,[134] the context they are used in,[135] or what they relate to[136,137] Academics in different fields have also attempted to devise a structure, taxonomy, or categorization for (personal) data.[138] As early as the 1970s Bing suggested an ambitious 'classification of personal information', mainly differentiating on the basis of sensitivity.[139] Similar attempts have been made from the perspective of popular science;[140] surveillance studies;[141] computer science;[142] and lobbyists.[143]

Clearly, not all (personal) data are equal. Certain categories of data (implicitly or explicitly) benefit from more or less protection.[144] Many legal texts specify or differentiate between particular kinds of personal data because of the heightened risk to the rights, interests, or freedoms of individuals or society at large. The 'riskiness' associated with specific kinds of data often depends on their very nature, but can also stem from the context or the way in which they are processed.[145] The ePrivacy

[134] eg 'Things you do and information you provide'; 'Things others do and information they provide'; 'Information from third-party partners'.

[135] eg 'Information about payments'.

[136] eg 'Your networks and connections'; 'Device information'.

[137] https://www.facebook.com/full_data_use_policy accessed 17 February 2016.

[138] On a higher level, there is also a whole field researching the 'philosophy of information' in general. See, in particular: Luciano Floridi, *Information: A Very Short Introduction* (OUP 2010). Or more applied: Lisa Gitelman, *'Raw Data' Is an Oxymoron* (MIT Press 2013); Rob Kitchin, *The Data Revolution: Big Data, Open Data, Data Infrastructures & Their Consequences* (Sage Publishing 2014).

[139] Bing (n 119).

[140] Schneier, for example, distinguishes six categories of information collected in a social networking environment: 'service data'; 'disclosed data'; 'entrusted data'; 'incidental data'; 'behavioral data'; 'derived data'. Bruce Schneier, *Data and Goliath: The Hidden Battles to Capture Your Data and Control Your World* (New York: W W Norton, 2015), ch 14 'Give People Rights to Their Data'.

[141] See, for example, the very elaborate attempt by Marx in: Gary T Marx, 'Personal Information as Influences on Attitudes towards Surveillance' in Richard Victor Ericson and Kevin D Haggerty (eds), *The New Politics of Surveillance and Visibility* (University of Toronto Press 2006). But also Roger Clarke's work on Dataveillance: www.rogerclarke.com/DV/ accessed 1 June 2019.

[142] See for instance: Rein Turn, 'Classification of Personal Information for Privacy Protection Purposes', *Proceedings of the June 7–10, 1976, National Computer Conference and Exposition* (ACM 1976) <http://doi.acm.org/10.1145/1499799.1499846> accessed 1 June 2019.

[143] Martin Abrams, 'The Origins of Personal Data and Its Implications for Governance' *OECD Expert Roundtable Discussion Protecting Privacy in a Data-Driven Economy: Taking Stock of Current Thinking* (2014) <http://informationaccountability.org/wp-content/uploads/Data-Origins-Abrams.pdf>. The author distinguishes between provided, observed, derived, and inferred data. Digital rights activist Joe McNamee also identified a category of data he calls 'bastard data': Joe McNamee, 'ENDitorial: Is "Privacy" Still Relevant in a World of Bastard Data?' (*EDRi*, 9 March 2016) <https://edri.org/enditorial-is-privacy-still-relevant-in-a-world-of-bastard-data/> accessed 1 June 2019.

[144] Meg L Ambrose, 'It's About Time: Privacy, Information Life Cycles, and the Right to Be Forgotten' (2013) 16 Stanford Technology Law Review 398. The author also recognizes the dynamic nature of information: '[d]ifferent information has different value and that value changes as time passes'.

[145] For example, banking and financial legislations often specify extra protections for processing specific data, such as data relate do assessing a person's creditworthiness or the publicity to be given to administrative penalties. See: Article 21(1) in Directive 2014/17/EU of the European Parliament and of the Council of 4 February 2014 on credit agreements for consumers relating to residential immovable property and amending Directives 2008/48/EC and 2013/36/EU and Regulation (EU) No 1093/2010; Articles 68–69 in Directive 2013/36/EU of the European Parliament and of the Council of 26 June 2013 on access to the activity of credit institutions and the prudential supervision of credit institutions and investment firms, amending Directive 2002/87/EC and repealing Directives 2006/48/EC and 2006/49/EC.

Directive notably confers additional protection to location and traffic data in the context of electronic communication services.[146] The GDPR too, refers to different kinds of personal data, each with specific characteristics. To the extent it determines the applicability of the GDPR overall, assessing whether or not data constitutes 'personal data' is only the first step in evaluating the applicability of the right to erasure in particular. The actual applicability and operationalization of a right to erasure will strongly depend on the category or type of personal data it targets. Untangling today's 'data-jumble' becomes all the more important in light of the 'datafication of everything' and the incredibly wide definition of 'personal data'. With this in mind, it is worth briefly looking at the different categories of data that are mentioned throughout the data protection framework. After this brief detour, an alternative approach to categorizing data will be proposed. One that is not fool-proof, but helps frame the assessment from the perspective of exercising data subject rights.

(a) *Pseudonymous and Anonymous Data*

As mentioned before, the GDPR is a data-centric piece of legislation, focusing first-and-foremost on personal data.[147] If data is not *personal* data, the GDPR does not apply. Anonymizing personal data—ie irreversibly removing the link with an identified/identifiable individual[148]—therefore liberates data from the GDPR's regulatory strains.[149] As such, anonymization is often used as a preferable alternative to erasing data altogether. In WP29's words, '[a]nonymisation may be a good strategy to keep the benefits and to mitigate the risks [of 'open data']'.[150] Importantly however, the act of 'anonymising data' itself, also constitutes processing, subject to the GDPR.[151] According to WP29, anonymizing personal data can generally be considered 'compatible with the original purposes of processing', if done in a reliable manner.[152]

[146] Eleni Kosta, *Consent in European Data Protection Law* (Martinus Nijhoff 2013) 324 et seq.

[147] For the purposes here, the concepts 'de-identification' and 'anonymization' will be used interchangeably. In the technical community, however, they are not synonymous ('anonymous data' is sometimes qualified as a sub-category of 'de-identified data'). See for example: ISO/TS. (2008). Health Informatics—Pseudonymisation ISO/TS 25237:2008; Garfinkel, S. L. (2015). De-Identification of Personally Identifiable Information. DRAFT NISTIR 8053 US Department of Commerce.

[148] For a more rigorous definition of 'anonymity' and related concepts, see: Andreas Pfitzmann and Marit Hansen, 'A Terminology for Talking about Privacy by Data Minimization: Anonymity, Unlinkability, Undetectability, Unobservability, Pseudonymity, and Identity Management' <https://dud.inf.tu-dresden.de/literatur/Anon_Terminology_v0.34.pdf> accessed 1 June 2019.

[149] See in this regard also: Article 29 Working Party, 'Opinion 1/2008 on Data Protection Issues Related to Search Engines' (2008) WP 20 <http://ec.europa.eu/justice/article-29/documentation> accessed 1 June 2019.

[150] Article 29 Working Party, 'Opinion 05/2014 on Anonymisation Techniques' (Article 29 Working Party 2014) WP 05/2014 5 <http://ec.europa.eu/justice/article-29/documentation> accessed 1 June 2019.

[151] See: Hon, Millard, and Walden (n 91) 214; Article 29 Working Party, 'Opinion 05/2014 on Anonymisation Techniques' (n 150) 7.

[152] Article 29 Working Party, 'Opinion 05/2014 on Anonymisation Techniques' (n 150) 7.

Anonymity in the GDPR—As a reaction to the disparity of interpretations between Member States on the meaning of anonymity,[153] the GDPR now explicitly includes a definition of the concept in its preamble. Recital 26 defines anonymous information as 'information which does not relate to an identified or identifiable natural person or data rendered anonymous in such a way that the data subject is not or no longer identifiable'. Quite redundantly—though providing added legal certainty—the recital adds that 'the principles of data protection should therefore not apply to anonymous information'.[154] Taking a step back, one might argue that anonymous information can be described as data that lacks one or more of the key characteristics of 'personal data'. With this in mind, one could argue—as some have done—that proper anonymization amounts to erasure.[155] Or, put differently, a right to erasure might be accommodated by anonymizing the respective data.

The GDPR incorporated WP29's position when stating that anonymization of personal data entails making it irreversibly impossible to identify the data subject, having regard to *all the means likely reasonably to be used*.[156] This test does not only depend on the relevant context and circumstances of each individual case,[157] its outcome can also change over time.[158] In order to assess whether or not a dataset is truly anonymous, one will reasonably have to take into account the risk of re-identification over time.[159] When the controller has no a priori means of

[153] European Commission, "Impact Assessment Accompanying the Proposals for General Data Protection Regulation and Directive on Data Protection in Police and Judicial Matters," Commission Staff working Paper (Brussels: European Commission, January 25, 2012) Annex 2, 15–16. Douwe Korff and Ian Brown, 'Comparative Study on Different Approaches to New Privacy Challenges, in Particular in the Light of Technological Developments' (European Commission—DG Justice 2010) Final Report 28. Some Member States have issues their own guidelines on 'anonymization'. See for example: Information Commissioner's Office, 'Anonymisation: Managing Data Protection Risk Code of Practice' <http://eprints.soton.ac.uk/345821/> accessed 1 June 2019; Marion Oswald, 'Data Anonymisation and Managing Risk—The ICO's New Code' (2012) 13 Privacy & Data Protection 3.

[154] A similar provision (though lacking the 'definition') could be found in Directive 95/46 (recital 26).

[155] *Dr Xaver X**** v **** AG* [2018] Datenschutz behörde (Austrian DPA) DSB-D123.270/0009-DSB/2018; Michèle Finck, 'Tweet' (*@finck_m*, 13 February 2019) <https://twitter.com/finck_m/status/1095593826436202496?s=11> accessed 14 February 2019; Brighter AI, 'Anonymized Data Is Not Subject to Privacy Regulations' (*Medium*, 19 February 2019) <https://medium.com/generate-vision/anonymized-data-is-not-subject-to-privacy-regulations-9e4667856261> accessed 25 February 2019.

[156] Recital 26 (both in the GDPR and Directive 95/46 before that). Also see: Article 29 Working Party, 'Opinion on Personal Data' (n 54) 15; Article 29 Working Party, 'Opinion 05/2014 on Anonymisation Techniques' (n 150) 5ff; Pagona Tsormpatzoudi, 'Eksistenz D7.4 Intermediate Report for D7.5' (CiTiP 2015) Deliverable D7.4 14 <http://eksistenz.eu/>.

[157] Important factors to take into account in this regard are: Who will the 'anonymized' dataset be shared with? How will it be processed? What other data will/might it be combined with? What are the means that a likely attacker would have?

See also: Article 29 Working Party, 'Opinion 05/2014 on Anonymisation Techniques' (n 150) 10.

[158] Particularly in the long run, Narayanan et al. explain there is no technical basis for believing de-identification techniques will be effective. Arvind Narayanan, Joanna Huey, and Edward W Felten, 'A Precautionary Approach to Big Data Privacy' 2 <http://randomwalker.info/publications/precautionary.pdf> accessed 1 June 2019. Similarly, Barocas and Nissenbaum explain '[a]s data sets become increasingly linked, anonymity is largely impossible to guarantee in the future'. Julia Lane and others, *Privacy, Big Data, and the Public Good: Frameworks for Engagement* (CUP 2014) 2.

[159] eg due to the development of ICTs and/or likelihood of identification through future combining with other databases. Article 29 Working Party, 'Opinion 05/2014 on Anonymisation Techniques' (n 150) 8–9. Also see: Korff, 'New Challenges to Data Protection Study-Working Paper No. 2' (n 33) 48.

distinguishing between anonymous and personal data in a mixed dataset, it will need to treat the entire set as personal data.[160]

In short, the GDPR seems to thread carefully between the binary nature of anonymity, while still maintaining some level of flexibility by only requiring to take into account 'all the means *likely reasonably* to be used for identification by the controller and third parties'.[161,162] This seems to be in line with the general idea of personal data to fall on a continuum. Identifiability is a versatile concept, inter alia subject to the context and circumstances of processing over time.[163]

Before moving on, three important issues related to 'anonymisation' are worth highlighting. First of all, adequately anonymizing personal data will often render the data much less useful, or even useless. When the controller's business-model is based on data processing, anonymization might therefore not be economically feasible. Secondly, rendering personal data truly anonymous becomes increasingly hard in light of today's information deluge.[164] Similarly, the AG in *Breyer* also recognized the danger of considering certain information anonymous today (eg dynamic IP addresses), which may soon become re-identifiable with new technology in the future.[165] Thirdly, as explained by Gürses, anonymization can be used counterintuitively to disempower data subjects. Anonymization may prevent

[160] WP29 gives the example of internet access providers who can generally not know what IP address does and does not allow identification. Article 29 Working Party, 'Opinion on Personal Data' (n 54) 16–17.

[161] Recital 26, emphasis added.

[162] In reality, accidental re-identification might always be possible. See: Korff, 'New Challenges to Data Protection Study-Working Paper No. 2' (n 33) 49; Article 29 Working Party, 'Opinion on Personal Data' (n 54) 20.

[163] Hon, Millard, and Walden (n 91) 224–25 On page 219, the authors argue that to 'a cloud provider storing encrypted data with no key and no means "reasonably likely" to be used for decryption, [that] data may be considered anonymous'; Antoinette Rouvroy, '"Of Data and Men": Fundamental Rights and Freedoms in a World of Big Data' (Council of Europe 2016) T-PD-BUR(2015)09REV 21 <www.coe.int/t/dghl/standardsetting/DataProtection/TPD_documents/T-PD-BUR(2015)09REV_Big%20Data%20report_A%20%20Rouvroy_Final_EN.pdf> accessed 1 June 2019; Sophie Stalla-Bourdillon and Alison Knight, 'Anonymous Data v. Personal Data—A False Debate: An EU Perspective on Anonymization, Pseudonymization and Personal Data' (2017) 34 Wisconsin International Law Journal 284.

[164] A vast body of literature—from law to computer sciences—exists on the shortfalls of many anonymization techniques. In the context of the EU data protection framework, see inter alia: Article 29 Working Party, 'Opinion 05/2014 on Anonymisation Techniques' (n 150); Korff and Brown, 'Comparative Study on Different Approaches to New Privacy Challenges, in Particular in the Light of Technological Developments' (n 153); Hon, Millard, and Walden (n 91) 214–15; Rouvroy, '"Of Data and Men". Fundamental Rights and Freedoms in a World of Big Data' (n 114) 21. A more general and/or US perspective can be found in: Ohm (n 97); Narayanan and Shmatikov (n 80); Paul M Schwartz and Daniel J Solove, 'PII Problem: Privacy and a New Concept of Personally Identifiable Information, The' (2011) 86 New York University Law Review 1814; Solon Barocas and Helen Nissenbaum, 'Big Data's End Run around Anonymity and Consent' in Julia Lane and others (eds), *Privacy, Big Data, and the Public Good: Frameworks for Engagement* (CUP 2014); Arvind Narayanan and Edward W Felten, 'No Silver Bullet: De-Identification Still Doesn't Work' [2014] White Paper <http://randomwalker.info/publications/no-silver-bullet-de-identification.pdf> accessed 1 June 2019; Yves-Alexandre de Montjoye and others, 'Unique in the Shopping Mall: On the Reidentifiability of Credit Card Metadata' (2015) 347 Science 536.

[165] AG Opinion in: *Patrick Breyer v Bundesrepublik Deutschland* (n 78) para 75 et seq. The same reasoning also explains the burgeoning field of research on 'post-quantum cryptography'.

individuals 'from understanding, scrutinising, and questioning the ways in which data sets are used to organise and affect their access to resources and connections to a networked world'.[166] Indeed, as will appear later (Part III), some controllers argue they cannot accommodate data subject rights because they allegedly have no way of reidentifying the data subject, effectively disempowering data individuals.[167]

PSEUDONYMITY—Finally, it is worth briefly reflecting on 'pseudonymity', a concept that is often conflated with anonymity in practice.[168] Contrary to anonymous data, pseudonymous data still falls within the GDPR's scope of application.[169] In 2007, WP29 described pseudonomyzation as 'the process of disguising identities'.[170] The technique is generally used to maintain the possibility of singling out individuals.[171]

The implications of this 'new category of personal data' have fluctuated throughout the GDPR's legislative process.[172] In line with WP29's interpretation,[173] the GDPR's final version primarily approaches pseudonymization[174] as a data security measure[175] and a concretization of the 'data protection by default and design' principle in Article 25. Pseudonomysation is seen as an organizational and/or technical measure that reduces risks for data subjects and helps controllers/processors to meet their data protection obligations.[176] Some have argued that different types of pseudonymization—ie retraceable/reversible v irreversible—may result in

[166] Seda Gürses, 'The Spectre of Anonymity' in Renée Turner (ed), *Sniff, Scrape, Crawl… {on Privacy, Surveillance and our Shadowy Data-Double}* (Mute Publishing Ltd 2012) 3; 5; Seda Gürses, 'Can You Engineer Privacy?' (2014) 57 Commun ACM 20, 4–5.

[167] Specifically, Apple denies access requests with regard to Siri voice data it collects and stores for up to two years, because they say they do not have the tools in place to re-connect such voice data to the user. Even if this argumentation can be contested significantly, it does raise a considerable hurdle to data subject empowerment. See notably: Michael Veale, Reuben Binns, and Jef Ausloos, 'When Data Protection by Design and Data Subject Rights Clash' (2018) 8 International Data Privacy Law 4.

[168] Article 29 Working Party, 'Opinion 05/2014 on Anonymisation Techniques' (n 150) 21.

[169] Frederik J Zuiderveen Borgesius, 'Singling out People without Knowing Their Names—Behavioural Targeting, Pseudonymous Data, and the New Data Protection Regulation' 32 Computer Law & Security Review 256.

[170] Also explaining that the mere removal of an identifier such as a name, will not render data 'non-personal'. Article 29 Working Party, 'Opinion on Personal Data' (n 54) 14; 18.

[171] Which is also why the practice of many online advertisers of merely using assigned numbers to distinguish users/consumers from one another, does not imply they are not processing personal data.

[172] For an account of the relevant changes, see: Frederik J Zuiderveen Borgesius, 'Personal Data Processing for Behavioural Targeting: Which Legal Basis?' [2015] International Data Privacy Law ipv011, 10–12.

[173] Article 29 Working Party, 'Opinion on Personal Data' (n 54) 20; Article 29 Working Party, 'Opinion 05/2014 on Anonymisation Techniques' (n 150) 20–23.

[174] Defined in Article 4(3)(b) as 'the processing of personal data in such a way that the data can no longer be attributed to a specific data subject without the use of additional information, as long as such additional information is kept separately and subject to technical and organisational measures to ensure non-attribution to an identified or identifiable person'.

[175] Articles 6(4)(e), 32(1)(a). Tsormpatzoudi (n 157) 16; Zuiderveen Borgesius, 'Singling out People without Knowing Their Names—Behavioural Targeting, Pseudonymous Data, and the New Data Protection Regulation' (n 169) 12.

[176] Recitals 23a; 61; 125.

a more flexible application of data protection rules.[177] Indeed, according to WP29, processing key-coded data may not be considered as 'processing of personal data', when being done by third parties within a specific scheme where 're-identification is explicitly excluded and appropriate technical measures have been taken in this respect'.[178] Others have explained that when used for more than one purpose, the added protection pseudonyms offer rapidly erodes (regardless of the form of the pseudonym).[179] In sum, pseudonymization should not be characterized as a tool for exempting (even partially) controllers from the GDPR's scope of application, but rather as a valid compliance measure to accommodate several data protection rights and obligations.[180] In light of this, pseudonymizing data might impact the applicability and operationalization of the right to erasure (eg in the balancing act, cf Part II).[181]

b) (Online) Identifiers

Whereas Directive 95/46 only implicitly made reference to the term 'identifier',[182] the term is now ingrained in the GDPR.[183] The definition of personal data (Art 4(1)) specifies that the identifiability of a person may occur 'in particular by reference to an identifier such as a name, an identification number, location data, online identifier'. Recital 30 goes on to cite several examples of 'identifiers by association', ie 'online identifiers provided by [individuals'] devices, applications, tools and protocols, such as Internet Protocol addresses, cookie identifiers or other identifiers such as Radio Frequency Identification tags'. In doing so, the Regulation makes explicit that generally, identifiers are a type of personal data sufficient in itself to identify individuals. In the words of WP29, '[i]dentification is normally achieved through particular pieces of information which we may call "identifiers" and which hold a particularly privileged and close relationship with the particular individual'.[184] Of course, even though a person's name is to be considered an

[177] Hon, Millard and Walden (n 91) 215–16. Other more technically-oriented differentiations exist too. See, for example the explanation of person-; role-; relationship-; or transactional pseudonym in: Jan Camenisch, Simone Fischer-Hübner, and Kai Rannenberg (eds), *Privacy and Identity Management for Life* (Springer; Dordrecht 2011) 14–15.

[178] Article 29 Working Party, 'Opinion on Personal Data' (n 54) 19–20; Hon, Millard, and Walden (n 91) 216. The latter explaining such measures might include, for example, cryptographic or irreversible hashing.

[179] Ross Anderson, cited in: Korff, 'New Challenges to Data Protection Study-Working Paper No. 2' (n 33) 50.

[180] Recitals 23a and c.

[181] Under some circumstances, for example, pseudonomizing personal data may be deemed a more adequate alternative to accommodating an erasure request.

[182] Article 29 Working Party, 'Opinion on Personal Data' (n 54) 12. The only explicit reference to the term 'identifier' appears in the specific context of 'special categories of personal data' and national identification numbers (Art 8(7)).

[183] According to Blume, the explicit inclusion in the GDPR, resulted in the 'increase of the scope of personal data'. Peter Blume, 'Will It Be a Better World? The Proposed EU Data Protection Regulation' [2012] International Data Privacy Law 6 <http://idpl.oxfordjournals.org/content/early/2012/04/14/idpl.ips007> accessed 1 June 2019.

[184] Article 29 Working Party, 'Opinion on Personal Data' (n 54) 12.

identifier, such data might not always be sufficient in itself to identify a particular individual.[185] Information not included in the list in Article 4(1) can still be considered 'identifiers', if used to single someone out.[186] Pseudonymization often consists of replacing common identifiers (notably those included in Article 4(1)) with abstract numbers (eg through a hash function).[187] Removing an identifier from a data set can arguably be seen as a data protection by design measure. Yet, as illustrated by the Apple vignette (and as explained in Part III), it may effectively render it very hard to accommodate data subject rights with regard to the remaining personal data.[188]

c) Traffic, Location, and Electronic Communications Data

Four more data-types are worth highlighting, given their relevance in the context at hand: traffic, location, (electronic communications) content, and metadata. Neither of these data-types explicitly featured in Directive 95/46. It is only with the adoption of the so-called ePrivacy Directive (2002/58/EC) that traffic and location data were specifically introduced in the broader data protection and privacy protection framework.[189] Meanwhile, in January 2017, the European Commission published a proposal for an ePrivacy Regulation, which is expected to replace Directive 2002/58. The main aim of both Directive 2002/58 and the proposed Regulation is to protect persons' fundamental right to privacy (Art 7 Charter) in the electronic communication services sector. To the extent it regulates data processing operations, the ePrivacy framework is meant to complement the *lex generalis* of the general data protection framework.[190]

Importantly, in the newly proposed ePrivacy Regulation, the terms location and traffic data have been removed.[191] Two other types of data have been

[185] ibid 12–13.

[186] ibid 14.

[187] Article 29 Working Party, 'Opinion 05/2014 on Anonymisation Techniques' (n 150) 20–21.

[188] In this vignette, Apple collects voice data recorded when asking Siri a question. This data is stored together with calendar and address book, but Apple says it cuts the link with the user's individual device.

[189] The ePrivacy directive defines both data types within its own confined scope (Art 2(b)–(c)): 'traffic data' means any data processed for the purpose of the conveyance of a communication on an electronic communications network or for the billing thereof; 'location data' means any data processed in an electronic communications network, indicating the geographic position of the terminal equipment of a user of a publicly available electronic communications service. Articles 6 and 9 set out a specific regime with regard to information obligations and consent requirements for these two data types.

[190] For a more elaborate discussion of the genesis, scope, and implications of the ePrivacy Directive, see: Kosta (n 146) 261 et seq. Also see: Jos Dumortier and others, 'EPrivacy Directive: Assessment of Transposition, Effectiveness and Compatibility with Proposed Data Protection Regulation' (European Commission DG Communications Networks, Content & Technology 2015) Study SMART 2013/0071 <https://ec.europa.eu/digital-agenda/en/news/eprivacy-directive-assessment-transposition-effectiveness-and-compatibility-proposed-data>.

[191] For the justification, see inter alia: European Commission, 'Ex-Post REFIT Evaluation of the EPrivacy Directive 2002/58/EC Accompanying the Proposal for a Regulation of the European Parliament and the Council on the Protection of Privacy and Confidentiality in Relation to Electronic Communications and Repealing Directive 2002/58/EC (Regulation on Privacy and Electronic Communications)' (European Commission 2017) Commission Staff working document 104–06.

introduced: (electronic communications) content and metadata.[192] This distinction is more ambitious as it aims to categorize *all* data, rather than simply pinpoint two types in particular. Whereas the old category of traffic data will largely fall within the new definition of metadata. The old category of 'location data' can either be content or metadata.[193] As a matter of fact, 'location data' is still used throughout both the proposed ePrivacy Regulation as well as the GDPR, but mainly by way of example. In Article 4(1) GDPR for instance, it is referred to as a potential *identifier*.

The key rationale for the new *summa divisio* between electronic communications content and metadata is to put in place the strictest safeguards for 'content' (Art 6(3)), which is considered to be inherently more sensitive.[194] In contrast to metadata, it also seems that the storing and further processing of the *content* of communications is not as inherently necessary to deliver electronic communications services. Article 7 of the proposal further specifies the narrow conditions under which content and metadata can be retained.

Taking a step back from the ePrivacy rules, location and traffic data but also electronic communications content and metadata constitute personal data within the meaning of the GDPR. As mentioned before, location data is even mentioned as an 'identifier' in Article 4(1). In other words, it is presumed that location data in itself might enable the (in)direct identification of individuals.[195] Traffic data, electronic communications content, and metadata are much broader categories and are implied throughout the GDPR. What justifies specifically calling attention to these data-types here, is their high potential of intruding the normative underpinnings of data protection law.[196] Back in 2011, German politician Malte Spitz famously illustrated the extent of location tracking by his telecom provider.[197] Even though location data does not qualify as 'sensitive data' (Art 9 GDPR) *stricto sensu*, WP29 has clearly recognized its particular nature, requiring special protection.[198] Similarly,

[192] Electronic Communications *content* is defined (Art 4(3)(b)) as 'the content exchanged by means of electronic communications services, such as text, voice, videos, images, and sound'. Electronic communications *metadata* is defined (Art 4(3)(c)) as 'data processed in an electronic communications network for the purposes of transmitting, distributing or exchanging electronic communications content; including data used to trace and identify the source and destination of a communication, data on the location of the device generated in the context of providing electronic communications services, and the date, time, duration and the type of communication'.

[193] Recital 17 of the proposal explains that Location data that is generated other than in the context of providing electronic communications services should not be considered as metadata.

[194] See Explanatory Memorandum to the ePrivacy Regulation Proposal. The very point that content data would be more sensitive than metadata is a contentious one that will not be developed further here.

[195] de Montjoye and others (n 164).

[196] European Commission, 'Ex-Post REFIT Evaluation of the EPrivacy Directive 2002/58/EC Accompanying the Proposal for a Regulation of the European Parliament and the Council on the Protection of Privacy and Confidentiality in Relation to Electronic Communications and Repealing Directive 2002/58/EC (Regulation on Privacy and Electronic Communications)' (n 191) 39.

[197] Zeit Online, 'Verräterisches Handy' *Zeit Online* (February 2011) <http://www.zeit.de/datenschutz/malte-spitz-data-retention> accessed 1 June 2019; *The Dark Side of Data* (2012) <http://www.ted.com/playlists/130/the_dark_side_of_data> accessed 1 June 2019.

[198] Location data might, for example, reveal where an individual spends the night and/or is employed. Location data may also reveal 'sensitive data' which can be inferred from presence at political

traffic data and metadata constitutes a potentially very intrusive category of personal data, enabling the detailed mapping of an individual's communications.[199,200]

The CJEU's *Rijkeboer* ruling offers a useful illustration of the distinction between content and metadata, and how that may affect the exercise of data subject rights.[201] In this case, Mr Rijkeboer requested his local municipality to provide him with information on all third parties with whom his personal data had been shared and when exactly. The municipality only returned said information for the preceding year, as older 'metadata' had automatically been erased pursuant to a national law. In other words, while *content* (eg address, name, etc) was stored indefinitely, the associated *metadata*, ie whom it was shared with and when, was only stored for a year.[202] This made it effectively impossible for Mr Rijkeboer to verify the accuracy and/or request erasure of his personal data from third parties to whom his data was communicated more than a year before his request with the municipality.[203]

In sum, neither location and traffic data (ePrivacy Directive), nor electronic communications content and metadata (proposal for ePrivacy Regulation) are explicitly accorded additional safeguards in the GDPR. Yet, they offer a useful way to qualify the relevant data at hand when exercising data subject rights, and the balancing exercise that will often ensue (see Part II).

demonstrations or party headquarters, as well as from frequent of visits to hospitals, religious places, or certain locations revealing information about one's sex life. Article 29 Working Party, 'Opinion 13/2011 on Geolocation Services on Smart Mobile Devices' (Article 29 Working Party 2011) WP 185 7 <http://ec.europa.eu/justice/article-29/documentation> accessed 1 June 2019.

199 Article 29 Working Party, 'Opinion on the Use of Location Data with a View to Providing Value-Added Services' (European Commission 2005) Opinion WP 115 2 <http://ec.europa.eu/justice/article-29/documentation>.

200 The huge body of literature on the implications of traffic data usage can roughly be subdivided into two main parts, depending on the respective context: (a) law enforcement (eg Arkaitz Gamino Garcia and others, 'Mass Surveillance: Part 1—Risks and Opportunities Raised by the Current Generation of Network Services and Applications' (European Parliament Research Service 2014) Science and Technology Options Assessment (STOA) IP/G/STOA/FWC-2013-1/LOT 9/C5/SC1 <http://www.europarl.europa.eu/stoa/webdav/site/cms/shared/0_home/STOA%20Study%20Mass%20Surveillance%20Part%201.pdf> accessed 1 June 2019); (b) commercial and/or private actors (eg Claude Castelluccia, 'Behavioural Tracking on the Internet: A Technical Perspective' in Serge Gutwirth and others (eds), *European Data Protection: In Good Health?* (Springer 2012)).

201 *College van burgemeester en wethouders van Rotterdam v MEE Rijkeboer* (n 51). Oostveen explains that both the ECtHR and the CJEU 'distinguish between content and metadata, with interferences with content being of a more serious character'. See: Manon Oostveen, 'Protecting Individuals Against the Negative Impact of Big Data: The Potential and Limitations of the Privacy and Data Protection Law Approach' (PhD Thesis, University of Amsterdam 2018) 88.

202 Importantly, the CJEU does not use the words content and metadata, but 'basic data' and 'information on recipients or categories of recipient to whom those basic data are disclosed and on the content thereof and thus relates to the processing of the basic data' (paragraphs 42–43). For the purposes here, it appears that the distinction between content and metadata can be projected onto the one made by the Court.

203 Eventually, the Court ruled that the different retention times 'do not constitute a fair balance of the interest and obligation at issue, unless it can be shown that longer storage of that information would constitute an excessive burden on the controller'. *College van burgemeester en wethouders van Rotterdam v MEE Rijkeboer* (n 51) para 70.

3.1.4 Personal Data Equalizer

From the above, it is evident that the overall applicability of the GDPR hinges on whether or not data constitutes 'personal data'. Additional safeguards are put in place for the sub-category 'sensitive data'. On top of this, the GDPR refers to several other data types/categories for a variety of reasons and with different implications. In light of the confusing hotchpotch that ensues, it is worth taking a step back and look at what can be learned with regard to data subject rights and the right to erasure in particular.

When assessing the applicability of the right to erasure, a nuanced examination of the relevant personal data is required. After all, different types of personal data will have a different impact on the data subject and the balancing act generally accompanying an erasure request. The few data categories explicitly or implicitly featuring in the GDPR are useful indicators. Still, it will become clear in the following chapters that the applicability of the right to erasure cannot be reduced to a mere qualification of the underlying data in either one of these categories. Developing a comprehensive 'personal data taxonomy' for the purposes of assessing data subject rights (the right to erasure in particular) is an unrealistic exercise.[204] As made clear at the beginning of this section, there are simply too many ways in which one could differentiate between different categories.[205] Google's and Facebook's privacy policies demonstrate that personal data can be qualified on the basis of its origin, its form, and its function. But data can also be differentiated on the basis of its nature, sensitivity, or visibility/obscurity. On top of that, the previous pages made clear that data categories that are specifically defined in law, may overlap in practice (eg location data and sensitive data).[206]

Instead of trying to come up with a data taxonomy—or even a more modest list of specific data categories—this subsection proposes an alternative. Data is not static, especially in the context of ISS.[207] From the perspective of exercising one's data subject rights, it makes more sense to identify relevant variables on a case-by-case basis. These may inter alia relate to the data itself (eg accuracy, public interest, sensitivity, format), the source (eg voluntarily shared, inferred), the data subject (eg role in public life, child), time, and context.[208] Each of these 'variables' should be seen as non-binary continuums. By analogy, one could think of an audio equalizer, ubiquitous in 1980's stereo sound-systems. Every slider represents a variable,

[204] In 1978 it was already recognized that no 'list of categories of information could ever be complete'. Lindop (n 113) 153–54.

[205] See eg Kitchin (n 138).

[206] Based on extensive empirical research, McCullagh concludes that the data protection framework is mis-focused in attempting at classifying data. McCullagh (n 114) 188–89.

[207] See for example: Chris Elsden and others, 'Fitter, Happier, More Productive: What to Ask of a Data-Driven Life' (2016) 23 *Interactions* 46.

[208] For a comprehensive overview in the specific context of search engine delisting requests, see: Aleksandra Kuczerawy and Jef Ausloos, 'NoC Online Intermediaries Case Studies Series: European Union and Google Spain' (2015) Annex <http://ssrn.com/abstract=2567183> accessed 1 June 2019.

impacting—to a greater or lesser extent—what comes out of the speakers. Similarly to its audio-counterpart, the 'personal data equalizer', may come with certain pre-sets. For certain situations or 'data types', there will be pre-defined defaults. Depending on the circumstances, certain sliders will be hardwired (eg format of the data, controller), whereas others might still be tweakable (eg visibility/obscurity). Crucially, determining the configuration of parameters is only possible a posteriori, when evaluating the applicability of data subjects' rights in a particular case.[209] Taking this 'personal data equalizer' perspective also accentuates the ability to accommodate data subject rights, interests, or concerns in a more nuanced way, ie by tweaking certain parameters in light of all interests at stake. With this in mind, the personal data equalizer will be of particular importance in assessing the balancing of fundamental rights (Part II) and the effectiveness of the right to erasure (Part III).

Concluding, the above has amply made clear that it is increasingly hard to determine what does and does not constitute *personal* data. Some have even suggested to drop the distinction altogether and move from '*personal* data protection to data protection *tout court*'.[210] Though this might be a bridge too far, it is fair to say that a priori determining the potential implications of one type of personal data or another on an individual is not possible. Today's vast—and quickly expanding—data processing eco-system transforms seemingly trivial and/or anonymous data to personal data and vice versa.[211] Unsurprisingly, determining the reach of data protection rights (notably, the right to erasure) is a tough exercise in the abstract. Though helpful indicators, the personal data categories predefined by the legislator do not offer quick-and-easy answers either.[212] The idea behind the 'personal data equalizer' recognizes the messiness of data and the importance of looking at the particular circumstances of each individual case. It acknowledges the fluidity of 'personal data', depending on time and context.[213] Determining the (most important) parameters in light of the right to erasure, will occur in the following chapters (4–6 and 8).

[209] This approach is in line with substantive empirical research in: McCullagh (n 114). Also see: van Hoboken and Zuiderveen Borgesius (n 53) 206–07.

[210] Serge Gutwirth and Paul De Hert, 'Regulating Profiling in a Democratic Constitutional State' in Mireille Hildebrandt and Serge Gutwirth (eds), *Profiling the European Citizen: Cross-Disciplinary Perspectives* (Springer 2008) 289; David Wright and others, 'Privacy, Trust and Policy-Making: Challenges and Responses' (2009) 25 Computer Law & Security Review 69, 77; Mireille Hildebrandt, 'Who Is Profiling Who? Invisible Visibility' in Serge Gutwirth and others (eds), *Reinventing Data Protection?* (Springer 2009) 239–40 <www.springerlink.com/index/P7710R0760613778.pdf> accessed 1 June 2019.

[211] Hildebrandt, 'Who Is Profiling Who?' (n 210) 239–40. An important, but under-referenced in legal scholarship, body of research demonstrates the ephemerality of information online. Many factors (eg changing file formats, link rot, etc) contribute to the fading of digital information. One study in 2006 claimed that only 15 per cent of information lasts for over a year. For a comprehensive overview, see: Ambrose, 'It's About Time' (n 144) 372.

[212] McCullagh (n 114) particularly 'Chapter 4: Conceptual (In)adequacy'.

[213] In this regard, also see: Ambrose, 'It's About Time' (n 144).

3.2 Processing

Article 3—Definitions

(3) 'processing' means any operation or set of operations which is performed upon personal data or sets of personal data, whether or not by automated means, such as collection, recording, organization, structuring, storage, adaptation or alteration, retrieval, consultation, use, disclosure by transmission, dissemination or otherwise making available, alignment or combination, restriction, erasure or destruction.

The second component determining the material scope of application of the GDPR overall is much less complex than the first one. Almost identical to Directive 95/46,[214] the GDPR defines *processing* of personal data as *any operation* performed upon that data. In defining the concept, the GDPR provides a non-exhaustive list of examples to clarify what such operations might entail. The legislator clearly ignored—at least for determining the material scope of application—the distinction between collection and further use of information. This is consistent with the normative underpinnings of data protection—ie not merely safeguarding against potential harm ensuing from the use of data—and reconfirms the position of data protection legislators since at least the 1970s.[215]

Technological neutrality is another crucial rationale behind the extensive definition of 'processing'. As explained in the GDPR (Recital 13), data protection dependent on the techniques used would create serious risks of circumvention. The intensity or frequency of operations is not relevant either. Especially today, even the smallest data processing operation might rapidly bring about a more or less huge impact on the data subject.[216] Whether or not a certain operation is *intended* to include the processing of personal data is irrelevant.[217] The absence of an intent-requirement is particularly obvious in light of data protection's rationale, and when considering the data subject's perspective. After all, substantial legal loopholes would emerge if data protection law would not cover *all* processing operations. Both the fundamental right to data protection and the GDPR follow personal data from cradle to grave. Indeed, the very acts of erasing, encrypting, or anonymizing personal data also constitute 'processing' operations, covered by the GDPR.

[214] Were added in the GDPR's definition: 'sets of data', and 'structuring'. The term blocking in the Directive 95/46 was replaced by the term restriction.

[215] Hondius (n 180) 86–87; 107 et seq; Council of Europe—Committee of Ministers (n 105) Explanatory Report, N17.

[216] See for example: *Lindqvist* (n 99); *Google Spain* (n 23).

[217] Emphasized by the CJEU in its landmark *Google Spain* Case. The Court rejected the search engine's argument that its operations cannot 'be regarded as processing of the data which appear on third parties' web pages displayed in the list of search results, given that search engines process all the information available on the internet without effecting a selection between personal data and other information'. *Google Spain* (n 23) paras 23; 28–31.

In sum, *processing* in the context of data protection law is a concept covering every act one can perform on personal data. The reason why it is useful to briefly elaborate on this concept is that it will play an important role throughout the rest of this book. Processing, in the end, is only an umbrella term for a wide variety of operations. Determining the level of responsibility of 'controllers' depends on a clear demarcation of these operations in a given case. Each of these processing operations individually will need to comply with the requirements as set out in the GDPR (eg lawfulness and purpose specification).[218] Non-compliance, as will appear in the next chapter, might trigger the applicability of data subject rights such as the right to erasure.

Section 4. Personal Scope

The third important piece to determine the applicability of data protection law, and hence the right to erasure, relates to the GDPR's *personal* scope of application. In light of data subject rights in particular, the personal scope determination can be subdivided into three main questions: (a) who can invoke the right; (b) vis-à-vis whom can one invoke the right; (c) whose right/interests/freedoms are affected and/or should be taken into account when invoking the right? In data protection law vocabulary, these three questions relate to the concepts of (a) data subject; (b) controller and processor; (c) third parties.

4.1 The Data Subject

The data subject is the main actor whom the data protection framework aims to protect. It is the entity the GDPR endows with specific rights (Chapter III GDPR) and as such, occupies a central role in this book. The GDPR does not provide a clear-cut definition of this—quite self-explanatory—concept. Instead, it is implicitly defined together with the concept of personal data discussed before. Put simply, a data subject is the natural person to whom personal data relates. The link between certain data and an individual is exactly what explains the normative underpinnings of the fundamental right to data protection (see Chapter 2). Because certain data relates to the data subject, he/she should have certain rights over that data as well as how it is used.[219]

Not all are protected equally. Certain categories of data subjects (implicitly or explicitly) benefit from more or less protection. Children are the only category of

[218] Korff, 'New Challenges to Data Protection Study-Working Paper No 2' (n 33) 58.
[219] Hondius (n 77) 100.

data subjects for whom the GDPR explicitly installs extra protections (Art 8).[220] As stated by the European Data Protection Supervisor, minors (or 'children') are generally considered 'as a specific category of individuals which deserve a particular, and reinforced, protection'.[221] Throughout the past two decades, the protection of children as a clear policy goal has gradually permeated EU primary law.[222] The GDPR aims to harmonize the wide array of different approaches to safeguarding children's data protection across Member-States.[223] Most notable in this regard, the Regulation sets the age for children's 'consent in relation to information society services' at 16 (which can be set lower, though not lower than 13, by Member-States).[224] Any data processing operation of a child below the age of 13 (potentially up to 16) will require parental consent.[225] More specific calls for increased protection for children can be found in provisions throughout the GDPR (eg with regard to the transparency principle;[226] legitimate ground;[227] and the right to erasure[228]).[229] Apart from children in particular, the Regulation also explains added safeguards might be needed for 'vulnerable individuals' more broadly

[220] Recital 38 states that '[c]hildren merit specific protection with regard to their personal data, as they may be less aware of the risks, consequences and safeguards concerned and their rights in relation to the processing of personal data'. Some have argued that the GDPR's special regime for children may be inappropriate. Peter Blume, 'The Data Subject' (2015) 1 European Data Protection Law Review 258, 261–62.

[221] European Data Protection Supervisor, 'Opinion of the EDPS on the Communication from the Commission—"European Strategy for a Better Internet for Children"' (2012) 3 <edps.europa.eu/EDPSWEB/webdav/site/mySite/shared/Documents/Consultation/Opinions/2012/12-07-17_Better_Iternet_Children_EN.pdf> accessed 1 June 2019.

[222] Lina Jasmontaite and Paul De Hert, 'The EU, Children under 13 Years, and Parental Consent: A Human Rights Analysis of a New, Age-Based Bright-Line for the Protection of Children on the Internet' (2015) 5 International Data Privacy Law 20, 22–23.

[223] On the discrepancies regarding the age for providing valid consent under data protection law prior to the GDPR, see notably: Terri Dowty and Douwe Korff, 'Protecting the Virtual Child—The Law and Children's Consent to Sharing Personal Data' (ARCH 2009) <nuffieldfoundation.org/sites/default/files/Protecting%20the%20virtual%20child.pdf> accessed 1 June 2019.

[224] Article 8. For a comprehensive account of the provision on Article 8 in the GDPR, see: Jasmontaite and Hert (n 222). For an up-to-date overview of the respective ages in all Member-States, see: <http://medconfidential.org/wp-content/uploads/2013/03/Protecting-the-virtual-child.pdf> accessed 1 June 2019.

[225] This provision has generated quite a backlash for its—paradoxical—potential of negatively impacting children. Requiring parental consent for one of the most active user-groups on social media, for example, would disproportionately impact their freedom of expression and privacy rights. Jasmontaite and Hert (n 222) 29 et seq.

[226] Recital 58; Article 12.

[227] Article 6(1)(f).

[228] Recital 65. Article 17 originally contained an explicit reference to children's data in the European Commission's proposal for a GDPR. It was later removed by the European Parliament, reintroduced by the Council and removed again in the final compromise text. Currently, the provision implicitly accords a dedicated right to erasure to personal data collected in the context of ISS offered directly to children (Art 17(1)(f), referring to Art 8(1)).

[229] For a more detailed account on applying data protection principles to children (pre-GDPR), see: Article 29 Working Party, 'Working Document 1/2008 on the Protection of Children's Personal Data' (Article 29 Working Party 2008) WP 147 <http://ec.europa.eu/justice/article-29/documentation> accessed 1 June 2019.

(Recital 75).[230] It will become clear in the following chapters that the specific characteristics of an individual might impact the application of a right to erasure and/or the balancing exercise that ensues.[231]

It may not come as a surprise that the beneficiary of data subject rights can only be a *natural* person.[232] As a matter of fact, the GDPR is permeated with references to the protection of *natural* persons (notably in its title) and explicitly excludes its applicability to *legal* persons (Recital 14).[233] Still, the question of granting data protection rights to *legal* persons has been raised occasionally, not in the least because some Member-States provide for such protection.[234] These Member-State level protections were—at least in part—the result of Convention 108 which, contrary to the GDPR, explicitly left open the possibility of including legal persons into national data protection legislation.[235] Information relating to legal persons can still enter the scope of EU data protection law when it (indirectly) relates to natural persons.[236] In practice, legal persons might still enjoy some level of data protection if they are lumped together with natural persons in a data controller's compliance strategy.[237] Importantly, such passive *de facto* protection does not enable *legal* persons to invoke their own data subject rights (eg to object or to erase).

[230] Though not specifically mentioned in the Regulation itself, Blume (non-exhaustively) lists several categories of individuals for whom added data protection safeguards might be appropriate: the elderly; people with a mental deficiency; and illiterates. Blume, 'The Data Subject' (n 220) 262–63.

[231] In its landmark *Google Spain* Ruling (C-131/12), the CJEU put forward a qualitative criterion for assessing the legitimacy of processing under Article 7(f) Directive 95/46: 'the role played by the data subject in public life' (paragraph 81). See also: Blume, 'The Data Subject' (n 220); Eva Lievens and Carl Vander Maelen, 'A Child's Right to Be Forgotten: Letting Go of the Past and Embracing the Future?' [2019] Latin American Law Review 61.

[232] Before the GDPR's adoption, this was confirmed *a contrario* by the ePrivacy Directive (Art 1(2)), which states: 'The provisions of this Directive particularise and complement Directive 95/46/EC for the purposes mentioned in paragraph 1. Moreover, they provide for protection of the legitimate interests of subscribers who are legal persons.'

[233] 'This Regulation does not cover the processing of personal data which concerns legal persons and in particular undertakings established as legal persons.'

[234] Douwe Korff, 'Study on the Protection of the Rights and Interests of Legal Persons with Regard to the Processing of Personal Data Relating to Such Persons' (European Commission 2000) Study ETD/97/B5-9500/78 <http://ec.europa.eu/justice/data-protection/document/studies/files/20000202_rights_interests_legal_en.pdf> accessed 1 June 2019; van der Sloot, 'Do Privacy and Data Protection Rules Apply to Legal Persons and Should They?' (n 60).

[235] Article 3(2)(b)). González Fuster, *The Emergence of Personal Data Protection as a Fundamental Right of the EU* (n 52) 136–37.

[236] As mentioned before (subsection 3.1.1 Personal Data), this might be the case for example with regard to the owner of an SME or a business's email traffic. See also: *Volker und Markus Schecke GbR and Hartmut Eifert v Land Hessen* (n 96) paras 52–54; *Salvatore Manni* [2017] Court of Justice of the European Union C-398/15. Article 29 Working Party, 'Opinion on Personal Data' (n 54) 23–24; van der Sloot, 'Do Privacy and Data Protection Rules Apply to Legal Persons and Should They?' (n 60) 37.

[237] From a controller's perspective, it might often make more economic sense to comply with data protection law with regard to all of the information it processes. As WP29 explains: '[i]n fact, it may be easier for the controller to apply the data protection rules to all sorts of information in his files than to try to sort out what refers to natural and what to legal persons'. Article 29 Working Party, 'Opinion on Personal Data' (n 54) 17.

The GDPR did introduce the possibility for an authority or organization (ie legal persons) to exercise rights in lieu of actual data subjects (Art 80).[238] The CJEU has also allowed companies to successfully invoke their customers' data protection rights to make their case.[239] Whether or not 'representative claims' can be made for multiple data subjects in so-called 'collective action' proceedings, remains debated.[240]

In short, the data subject is the natural person to whom personal data relates. By virtue of this fact, the data subject has certain rights over the use of his/her data. These rights—and the broader protection regime in the GDPR as a whole—naturally emanate from the normative underpinnings as set out in Chapter 2. Even though every data subject can invoke the right to erasure, the outcome might vary depending on specific characteristics of that individual.

4.2 Who to Ask for Erasure?

Article 3—Definitions

(5) 'controller' means the natural or legal person, public authority, agency or any other body which alone or jointly with others determines the purposes and means of the processing of personal data; […]

The controller is the main actor whose activities data protection law aims to regulate. Whereas the data subject is first-and-foremost a holder of data protection *rights*, the controller primarily holds data protection *obligations*. The controller is responsible for a given data processing operation. Identifying the controller is vital to ensure the protection of individuals' fundamental rights and freedoms (see Rationale).[241] According to Article 5(2) GDPR the controller needs to ensure (and be able to demonstrate) compliance with the so-called data quality principles and data protection law more broadly. This particularly includes that data is processed lawfully, fairly, and in a transparent manner.[242] In light of this, data subjects can in

[238] The provision's second paragraph specifies that they might even do so 'independently of a data subject's mandate'.

[239] ie in copyright enforcement cases: *Promusicae v Telefónica* [2008] Court of Justice of the European Union C-275/06; *Scarlet Extended v Sabam* [2011] Court of Justice of the European Union C-70/10; *SABAM v Netlog* [2012] Court of Justice of the European Union C-360/10. Cited in: van der Sloot, 'Do Privacy and Data Protection Rules Apply to Legal Persons and Should They?' (n 60) 39.

[240] eg because of different legal traditions in different jurisdictions. See: Maja Brkan, 'Data Protection and European Private International Law: Observing a Bull in a China Shop' (2015) 5 International Data Privacy Law 257, 263–64; van der Sloot, 'Do Privacy and Data Protection Rules Apply to Legal Persons and Should They?' (n 60) 37.

[241] See also Recital 62 GDPR and Article 29 Working Party, 'Opinion 1/2010 on the Concepts of "Controller" and "Processor"' (Article 29 Working Party 2010) WP 169 <http://ec.europa.eu/justice/article-29/documentation> accessed 1 June 2019.

[242] As a result, WP29 explains 'all provisions setting conditions for lawful processing are essentially addressed to the controller, even if this is not always clearly expressed'. ibid 4.

principle always approach the controller when exercising their rights under the GDPR. The *processor* is the entity that 'processes personal data on behalf of the controller'.

This subsection is aimed at briefly delineating the controller and processor concepts and the distribution of responsibilities in light of exercising the right to erasure. This necessarily includes a short detour highlighting the added layers of complexity regarding personal scope determination in today's information society.

4.2.1 Controller and Processor

a) The Controller

Article 3—Definitions

> (5) 'controller' means the natural or legal person, public authority, agency or any other body which alone or jointly with others determines the purposes and means of the processing of personal data; [. . .]

Apparent from the GDPR's definition, the key factor for identifying a controller, is to establish who determines the purpose and means of a given processing operation. In other words, the controller is the one deciding on the 'why' and the 'how' of certain processing activities.[243] In case of doubt, the answer to who determines the *purpose* will be decisive.[244] With regard to the 'how' question, it is sufficient only to look at who determines the 'essential means' (ie *what* data will be processed exactly, what will be the retention period, who will get access, etc).[245] In other words, decision power over merely technical and/or organizational means, may well be outsourced to a *processor*. The CJEU has also repeatedly supported a wide definition of controllers, 'in order to meet the objective of effective and complete protection pursued by [data protection law] and in the light of the decisive role of the controller'.[246] As explained by WP29, and later confirmed by AG's Bot and Mengozzi,[247] the controller concept is a functional one, 'intended to allocate responsibilities where the factual influence is, and thus based on a factual rather than a formal analysis'.[248] This also means that the 'inability to fulfil directly all the

[243] Directive 95/46 deliberately departed from the concept 'controller of the file' in Convention 108: '[t]he concept of 'controller' was thus no longer used for a static object ('the file') but related to activities reflecting the life cycle of information from its collection to its destruction'. ibid 3; 13.

[244] ibid 14–15; Korff, 'New Challenges to Data Protection Study-Working Paper No 2' (n 33) 60–61.

[245] Article 29 Working Party, 'Opinion 1/2010 on the Concepts of "Controller" and "Processor" ' (n 241) 14.

[246] See case law references in AG Opinion in: *Tietosuojavaltuutettu v Jehovan todistajat—uskonnollinen yhdyskunta* [2018] Court of Justice of the European Union C-25/17 [63].

[247] Opinion AG Bot in: *Unabhängiges Landeszentrum für Datenschutz Schleswig-Holstein v Wirtschaftsakademie Schleswig-Holstein GmbH* [2018] Court of Justice of the European Union C-210/16 [46; 62]; Opinion AG Mengozzi in: *Tietosuojavaltuutettu v Jehovan todistajat—uskonnollinen yhdyskunta* (n 246) paras 68–73.

[248] Article 29 Working Party, 'Opinion 1/2010 on the Concepts of "Controller" and "Processor" ' (n 241) 1; 8–9.

obligations of a controller, such as right of access, does not exclude the possibility of being a controller'.[249] Indeed, a (co-)controller does not even have to be able to access the personal data itself.[250] Complementing, but under no circumstances overriding, this assessment of *de facto* control are elements such as: reasonable expectations of data subjects and/or contractual designation of who is the controller for a specific processing operation.[251] In sum, the dynamic nature of the controller concept (both in scope and meaning), requires a case-by-case analysis, taking into account the circumstances at hand. This dynamic nature should be understood in conjunction with the flexibility in interpreting the extent of the controller's obligations.

b) The Processor

Article 3—Definitions

(6) 'processor' means a natural or legal person, public authority, agency or any other body which processes personal data on behalf of the controller.

Today, the processing of personal data generally involves many different entities, each with different roles. Part of identifying the controller will therefore consist of distinguishing it from the so-called processor. Despite the criticism the controller-processor dichotomy in Directive 95/46 received, it was maintained in the GDPR.[252] Essentially, the processor is an agent of the controller.[253] It is a legally separate entity to whom a controller can delegate/outsource part (or even the entirety) of the actual processing operations. The very existence of a processor is contingent on a controller's decision.[254] After all, Art 29 GDPR specifies that the processor 'shall not process [*personal data*] except on instructions from the controller'. Importantly, the GDPR explains that the controller is required only to use processors providing sufficient guarantees to comply with the Regulation.[255] The lawfulness of a processor's operations directly derives from

[249] ibid 22; Opinion AG Mengozzi in: *Tietosuojavaltuutettu v Jehovan todistajat—uskonnollinen yhdyskunta* (n 246) para 71.

[250] In the *Wirtschaftsakademie* case, it was ruled that administrators of Facebook fan pages can be considered co-controllers, jointly responsible with Facebook, even if they only get anonymized statistics about their demographics. *Wirtschaftsakademie* (n 247) para 38.

[251] Article 29 Working Party, 'Opinion 1/2010 on the Concepts of "Controller" and "Processor"' (n 241) 8–9.

[252] Some of the main criticisms raised with regard to the distinction in Directive 95/46 have been accommodated. Colette Cuijpers, Nadezhda Purtova, and Eleni Kosta, 'Data Protection Reform and the Internet: The Draft Data Protection Regulation' in Andrej Savin and Jan Trzaskowski (eds), *Research Handbook on EU Internet Law* (Edward Elgar Publishing 2014) 6–7. Patrick Van Eecke and Maarten Truyens, 'Privacy and Social Networks' (2010) 26 Computer Law & Security Review 535. For an extensive analysis, see: Brendan Van Alsenoy, *Data Protection Law in the EU: Roles, Responsibilities and Liability* (Intersentia 2019) 612ff.

[253] Korff, 'New Challenges to Data Protection Study-Working Paper No 2' (n 33) 61.

[254] Article 29 Working Party, 'Opinion 1/2010 on the Concepts of "Controller" and "Processor"' (n 241) 24–25.

[255] Recital 81, Article 28.

the mandate it receives from the controller.[256] Article 28 GDPR requires such mandate to be put down in a contract (or other legal act) and further stipulates the processor's obligations.

c) A Complex Relationship

Even though the concepts of 'controller' and 'processor' may seem straightforward in the abstract, they are often the source of quite some uncertainty in practice. Indeed, the controller-processor dichotomy is severely challenged in today's information society, as comprehensively demonstrated by Van Alsenoy in the specific contexts of e-Govenment identity management, online social networks, cloud computing, and search engines.[257] A proper discussion of this complex relationship would vastly go beyond the scope of this book. This section will briefly highlight/reflect on some key issues of the 'controller-processor' conceptual framework in light of the right to erasure's applicability. Part III will pick up this discussion to the extent the concepts frustrate the effectiveness of the right to erasure.

The vertical nature of the controller-processor relationship does not necessarily imply the processor is subordinate and/or entirely constrained in its activities. In practice, processors may have a more or less substantial decisional freedom over the means of processing.[258] When the processor's decisions extend to the *essential* means of the processing and/or the defining of (additional) purposes, processor status is lost. At what stage such an overspill occurs exactly, constitutes a much-debated grey zone. A useful indicator may be to assess whether the alleged processor serves only the controller(s)'s interests and nothing but the controller(s)'s interests.[259] When a processor disregards the controller's instructions, it shall be considered a controller in its own right.[260] The most important element to remember is that while the controller makes the strategic decisions on why personal data is processed in the first place, the processor has a more operational role.

According to Van Alsenoy, distinguishing processor from controller has implications on three levels: allocating responsibility and liability; determining applicable law; and compliance with substantive provisions.[261] It is particularly the first and last of these which will be relevant in light of exercising the right to erasure. Put simply, non-compliance with a substantive provision—by the controller *or* the

[256] Article 29 Working Party, 'Opinion 1/2010 on the Concepts of "Controller" and "Processor"' (n 241) 25.

[257] Van Alsenoy (n 252).

[258] '... delegation may still imply a certain degree of discretion about how to best serve the controller's interests, allowing the processor to choose the most suitable technical and organizational mean's. Article 29 Working Party, 'Opinion 1/2010 on the Concepts of "Controller" and "Processor"' (n 241) 14; 25.

[259] ibid 25.

[260] Brendan Van Alsenoy, 'Allocating Responsibility among Controllers, Processors, and "Everything in Between": The Definition of Actors and Roles in Directive 95/46/EC' (2012) 28 Computer Law & Security Review 25, 32.

[261] Van Alsenoy, 'Allocating Responsibility among Controllers, Processors, and "Everything in Between"' (n 260).

processor[262]—will trigger responsibility and liability. The (joint) controller(s) will be the one(s) responsible to accommodate data subject rights, even if it was the processor who did not comply with substantive provisions (and even given the fact that the data physically resides with the processor).[263]

The GDPR seems to imply that—depending on the circumstances—erasure requests can also be directed towards the processor(s). Article 28(3)(e) dictates that processors may need to assist the controller in accommodating data subject rights, notably by adopting 'appropriate technical and organisational measures, insofar as this is possible'. This could be interpreted as allowing a data subject to invoke his/her right to erasure vis-à-vis processors as well. Whereas they are not the ones responsible to effectively accommodate the data subject's rights, processors are liable to *assist* controllers in doing so. Hence, from a data subject's perspective, separating processors from (joint) controllers will not be fundamental to exercise the right to erasure. The right can be invoked vis-à-vis both controller and/or processor(s), the latter having to forward the request to the former. From a compliance perspective, separating the two entities will of course be more important.

4.2.2 Muddy Waters

The previous pages delineated (the interaction between) the concepts of 'controller' and 'processor' as set out in the EU data protection framework. Having a clear understanding on how to identify these two key actors is fundamental in light of accommodating the right to erasure. But, as already hinted at before, the controller-processor binary has been criticized for being surpassed by the reality of today's data processing landscape.[264] The definitions of both concepts seem over-simplistic in light of the exponential complexification of the 'personal data ecosystem', even when only looking at ISS providers.[265] Personal data is processed by countless entities, in an infinite number of constellations. Against this backdrop, data subjects are often left guessing vis-à-vis whom they need to address their rights (to erasure). Moreover, even if the data subject identifies a 'controller', the latter may simply pass on (or even ignore) the request, claiming not to be responsible *in casu*.[266] In order to (a) avoid situations in which the data subject would be left unable to effectively identify the relevant controller *and* (b) prevent

262 In principle, the processor is required to observe all relevant aspects of data protection law based, inter alia, on the contract concluded with the controller (Art 26). ibid 29.

263 This point illustrates the difference between *operational* and *legal* control under data protection law. The status of 'controller' follows from *legal* control, largely irrespective of the *operational* control (actual ability to manage the data). ibid 33.

264 Recognized and (partly) addressed by the WP29 in: Article 29 Working Party, 'Opinion 1/2010 on the Concepts of "Controller" and "Processor"' (n 241).

265 For a discussion on this complexity in the context of social networks, see: Van Eecke and Truyens (n 252) 537–38; Van Alsenoy (n 252).

266 For example, the alleged controller might argue not to fall within the GDPR's (territorial, material, or personal) scope of application, or might claim that it bears no responsibility with regard to the specific processing operation or personal data that the data subject is concerned about.

controllers from evading responsibility, this sub-section briefly elaborates on the key complexities relevant in light of the right to erasure. Three key questions are focused on:

- How to identify the relevant controller to approach with one's right to erasure in a context where many different entities process (the same) personal data?
- How can the right to erasure be invoked vis-à-vis entities that may not even be aware of the fact they process (personal) data?
- Can the right to erasure be invoked vis-à-vis entities that fall under the intermediary liability exemptions in the eCommerce Directive?

a) Multiplication of Actors

It is a truism to state that today's data processing landscape has reached unprecedented levels of complexity. The exponential increase of entities processing (the same) personal data in the online realm has rendered the allocation of responsibilities under data protection law a staggering challenge. Particularly from the perspective of exercising data subject rights, there is a particular need to untangle this disarray of actors.

The status of 'controller' primarily follows the purpose of the processing. Discerning who determines the purpose of a specific data processing operation, reveals who will be responsible for that operation, ie the controller. In line with the functional approach set forward by WP29, such determination should be based on factual circumstances,[267] and may vary over time,[268] and across activities.[269] The heterogeneity of entities processing personal data and ensuing complexity calls for a granular approach to the identification of controllers.[270] Particularly in light of exercising data subject rights, a necessary first step will be to determine what specific processing operation(s) one takes issue with exactly.

For example, the apparently simple action of uploading a picture onto an online social network (OSN) entails more than meets the eye. In fact, this activity can be dissected into several processing operations, each with different controllers. These may include, inter alia:

- The purpose for the initial act of uploading the picture itself (eg sharing with friends) will be determined by the uploader him/herself.

[267] WP29 explains that 'a person or entity who decides eg on how long data shall be stored or who shall have access to the data processed is acting as a "controller" concerning this part of the use of data'. Article 29 Working Party, 'Opinion 1/2010 on the Concepts of "Controller" and "Processor" ' (n 241) 15.

[268] For example, a contractor (ie processor) might increase its 'influence on the purpose and carry out the processing (also) for its own benefit, for example by using personal data received with a view to generate added-value services' and, as a result, become '*a controller (or possibly a joint controller)*'. ibid 14.

[269] Van Alsenoy (n 252) 68 et seq.

[270] Article 29 Working Party, 'Opinion 1/2010 on the Concepts of "Controller" and "Processor" ' (n 241) 18. Such a granular approach was also confirmed by the CJEU in *Google Spain* (n 23) para 35.

- The OSN will determine a whole set of elements independently as well, such as:
  - when and how that picture will appear on other people's timeline or feeds;
  - use of the picture for commercial purposes;
  - use of the picture for security purposes (eg fraud detection);
  - use for the detection of illegal content (eg based on copyright, terrorism, child pornography);
- Depending on the (available) privacy settings, connections, OSN users in general or even the public at large may have access to the picture too and potentially use it for their own purposes;
- (third-party) application providers installed by anyone having access to the picture might process the picture for their own purposes;
- Academic institutions may collaborate with the OSN in order to conduct research on uploaded material.

This non-exhaustive list briefly illustrates the potential complexity underlying a seemingly innocuous data processing activity.[271] As will be shown later on, different data subject rights will accommodate different goals. The right to object is fundamentally linked to a specific processing operation and will therefore require the data subject to identify which operation to target. The right to erasure focuses on the personal data itself, seemingly superseding the need to single out a specific processing operation. An inherent characteristic of the online environment, however, is that (personal) data is constantly being duplicated. Every entity processing the picture in the above example necessarily copies that data. Consequently, erasure of data in one place, does not necessarily entail erasure in another. In order to exercise one's right to erasure, it might thus still be necessary to specifically identify the relevant controller(s) for a specific processing operation. Chapter 4 will look more closely at Article 17(2) GDPR, which requires controllers who need to erase personal data to inform other controllers of that erasure.

Even a granular assessment might still result in associating multiple actors to just one purpose and/or processing operation. Indeed, WP29 explicitly acknowledges the possibility of such 'pluralistic control' and the fact that it may take a variety of forms and degrees.[272] In terms of the GDPR, there are roughly three categories of constellations relevant here: (a) controller-processor; (b) individual controller(s); (c) joint controllership. With regard to the first one, it is rather straightforward who data subjects should approach with their rights (ie the controller). With regard to

[271] A more thorough mapping exercise of the different actors processing personal data in a social networking environment can be found in: Brendan Van Alsenoy, 'Rights and Obligations of Actors in Social Networking Sites' (KU Leuven—CiTiP 2014) Deliverable D.6.2 <https://lirias.kuleuven.be/handle/123456789/453689> accessed 1 June 2019.

[272] Van Alsenoy, 'Allocating Responsibility among Controllers, Processors, and "Everything in Between"' (n 260) 32.

the latter two situations (ie a several individual controllers or co-controllership), some further explanation is warranted.

Autonomous Controllers—By definition, individual controllers separately and independently define their processing purposes. They are therefore each responsible to accommodate data subject rights individually with regard to their individual processing operations. This point is well-illustrated by the notorious *Google Spain* case. In this case, the CJEU clearly separated the processing activities (and purposes) of Google' search engine, from that of the websites that it refers to and that may (not) process personal data for their own purposes.[273] Each entity can be approached individually by the data subject. Other situations may be murkier. A case in point is the Facebook/Cambridge Analytica scandal, where a third-party app was able (through Facebook's API) to process the personal data of millions of users.[274] Who is the controller to whom individuals can target their rights? Whereas data subjects can surely approach the third-party app (eg to request access or erase personal data), it has been argued Facebook has a fiduciary duty to receive and accommodate these rights as well. Even if these data subject requests relate to operations that are not *stricto sensu* under the Facebook's own control.[275]

Another example can be found in the internet of things or smart home setting.[276] Apple's Siri may be the central node through which individuals communicate with baby monitors, toasters, and lighting. Each of these devices may share personal data (eg about the use or information captured via built-in cameras or microphones) with other entities. In such a complex environment, where every entity is a controller in their own right, the central node—ie Apple—can be held responsible for taking reasonable steps to make sure data subject rights (eg access, object, erasure) are properly accommodated. This is also exactly what Article 17(2) GDPR purports to do, ensuring the right to erasure trickles down to other controllers down the processing chain (see Chapter 4). Of course, the ability to approach Apple, does not prevent data subjects from going to the controllers behind their other smart home devices in parallel.

As a sidenote, it is also worth mentioning how the GDPR determines liability in case processing operations result in actual damage.[277] Following Article 82(4) GDPR, each controller responsible for any damage is jointly liable with any other

[273] *Google Spain* (n 23) para 83. As a matter of fact, a newspaper website may not even directly mention a name, while still being referred to on the basis of a name-search on Google.

[274] Emma Graham-Harrison and Carole Cadwalladr, 'Revealed: 50 Million Facebook Profiles Harvested for Cambridge Analytica in Major Data Breach' (*the Guardian*, 17 March 2018) <http://www.theguardian.com/news/2018/mar/17/cambridge-analytica-facebook-influence-us-election> accessed 19 March 2018.

[275] Van Alsenoy (n 252) 458–60.

[276] See for example: Jatinder Singh and others, 'Big Ideas Paper: Policy-Driven Middleware for a Legally-Compliant Internet of Things' *Proceedings of the 17th International Middleware Conference* (ACM 2016) 2 <http://doi.acm.org/10.1145/2988336.2988349> accessed 1 June 2019.

[277] This book is not about liability for damages, but rather about the possibility for exercising data subject rights (regardless of there being any damages).

controller (or processor) 'involved in the same processing'.[278] In other words, even if they are not co-controllers jointly determining purpose and means, controllers can still be held liable for the entire damage if they are involved in the same processing operations and are at least partly responsible for the damage incurred.

JOINT CONTROLLERS—Article 26 of the GDPR clarifies the concept of *joint controllers*: '[w]here two or more controllers jointly determine the purposes and means of the processing of personal data, they are joint controllers [. . .]'.[279,280] The article further requires such joint controllers to delineate, in a transparent manner, their respective responsibilities in light of complying with the GDPR. Importantly, data subjects can exercise their rights (to erasure) vis-à-vis any of the joint controllers, regardless of the arrangement (of respective roles and responsibilities) between these controllers (Art 26(2)). In other words, even though 'joint controllership' might have considerable ramifications as to GDPR compliance and allocation of responsibilities,[281] from the perspective of a data subject exercising his/her rights it is less relevant.

Getting back to the example, OSN and third-party application providers cannot, as a general matter, be considered joint controllers.[282] Even though such application providers are usually constrained by legal and technical measures imposed by the OSN provider, their very goal is generally to offer separate services (ie separate processing purposes). As mentioned before, however, the OSN still has a fiduciary duty, or 'platform responsibility' to accommodate data subject rights, even regarding third-party apps that have access to the personal data.[283] With regard to fan-pages created on Facebook (eg for a sportsclub, band, or bar), the CJEU decided that the administrators of those fan pages *can* be considered joint controllers together with Facebook.[284] In the same case, the CJEU also explained that

[278] Brendan Van Alsenoy, 'Liability under EU Data Protection Law: From Directive 95/46 to the General Data Protection Regulation' (2017) 7 JIPITEC 284 <http://www.jipitec.eu/issues/jipitec-7-3-2016/4506>.

[279] The concept of 'joint controllership' only first made appearance during the legislative process of Directive 95/46 (inserted by the European Parliament) Article 29 Working Party, 'Opinion 1/2010 on the Concepts of "Controller" and "Processor" ' (n 241) 17–18.

[280] Olsen and Mahler distinguish four 'degrees of collaboration': (a) single controller; (b) collaborating single controllers; (c) partly joint controllers; (d) full scope joint controllers. Thomas Olsen and Tobias Mahler, 'Identity Management and Data Protection Law: Risk, Responsibility and Compliance in "Circles of Trust"—Part II' (2007) 23 Computer Law & Security Review 415. The model is discussed in detail by Van Alsenoy in: Van Alsenoy (n 252) 76ff According to Van Alsenoy, 'the more generic the specified purpose' by a service provider, the less likely there will be joint controllership (but rather a controller-processor relationship or a collaboration among 'single controllers'). Van Alsenoy, 'Allocating Responsibility among Controllers, Processors, and "Everything in Between" ' (n 260) 37–38.

[281] Van Alsenoy, 'Allocating Responsibility among Controllers, Processors, and "Everything in Between" ' (n 260); Korff, 'New Challenges to Data Protection Study-Working Paper No 2' (n 33) 61. The latter author highlighting issues arising from joint controllership between entities located in different jurisdictions.

[282] This is not to say the social network bears some level of responsibility to ensure third party application providers comply with data protection requirements. For an extensive analysis, see: Van Alsenoy (n 252) 395ff.

[283] Van Alsenoy(n 252) 358–60380–82.

[284] *Wirtschaftsakademie* (n 247).

mere Facebook users cannot be considered 'a controller jointly responsible for the processing of personal data by that network'.[285] Similarly, the CJEU also ruled that websites embedding 'social share' buttons (eg 'like' or 'share' functions) can be considered joint controllers with the OSN, though only with regard to those specific operations it effectively co-decided the purposes and means for.[286]

The previous paragraph demonstrates that very often, joint controllership manifests itself in asymmetric relationships. Asymmetry between controllers sharing purpose and means, renders more complex the identification of which (joint) controller is competent and liable for accommodating data subject rights.[287] WP29 has been quite ambiguous on whether or not to consider uploader and OSN in the example mentioned above, as joint controllers or not.[288] Commentators have suggested a pragmatic approach, where the different entities involved, ie OSN and users, 'share the burdens of compliance in light of their respective roles'.[289] Such an interpretation seems somewhat in line with the GDPR's Article 24, which states that controllers shall ensure compliance, taking into account the 'nature, scope, context and purposes of the processing as well as the risks of varying likelihood and severity for the rights and freedoms of natural persons'. Similarly, it is worth referring to the *Google Spain* case again, where the CJEU declared that each controller must ensure that its processing meets legal requirements 'within the framework of its responsibilities, powers and capabilities'.[290] More recently, the CJEU explained that

> joint responsibility does not necessarily imply equal responsibility of the various operators involved in the processing of personal data. On the contrary, those operators may be involved at different stages of that processing of personal data and to different degrees, so that the level of responsibility of each of them must be assessed with regard to all the relevant circumstances of the particular case.[291]

[285] ibid 38.

[286] 29 July 2019: *Fashion ID* Court of Justice of the European Union C-40/17.

[287] Article 29 Working Party, 'Opinion 1/2010 on the Concepts of "Controller" and "Processor"' (n 241) 21–22.

[288] Even WP29's Opinion on the specific topic of social networking remains remarkably silent on this question. Article 29 Working Party, 'Opinion 5/2009 on Online Social Networking' (Article 29 Working Party 2009) WP 136 <http://ec.europa.eu/justice/article-29/documentation> accessed 1 June 2019; Van Alsenoy (n 252) 395ff. Article 29 Working Party, 'Opinion 1/2010 on the Concepts of "Controller" and "Processor"' (n 241) 17–24. Noteworthy in Opinion 1/2010 is Example 12, which is located in the sub-section discussing joint controllership. The example unambiguously states social network service providers are controllers with regard to the personal data uploaded by its users. It goes on to state that social network users themselves, may also be considered controllers vis-à-vis personal data they upload concerning third parties (for as long as no exemptions apply). On page 24, WP29 further explains that joint liability might arise when 'clear and equally effective allocation of obligations and responsibilities has not been established by the parties involved or does not clearly stem from factual circumstances'.

[289] Van Alsenoy (n 252) 455; Natali Helberger and Joris van Hoboken, 'Little Brother Is Tagging You—Legal and Policy Implications of Amateur Data Controllers' (2010) 4 Computer Law International 101.

[290] *Google Spain* (n 23) para 83.

[291] *Wirtschaftsakademie* (n 247) para 43.

As will appear in Chapters 7 and 8, from a practical perspective, the accommodation of data subject rights in complex environments (eg with OSNs and individual users), will be a matter of degree as well. In sum, the question of who can be approached with data subject rights requires a 'substantive and functional' assessment of the factual circumstances at hand.[292]

Eventually, the question of joint controllership largely remains theoretical from the perspective of a data subject wanting to exercise his/her right to erasure. Whether or not the uploader and OSN are considered joint controllers, the data subject will be able to invoke his/her rights vis-à-vis both of them. Either way, the successfulness of such a claim will depend on the applicability of exemptions (notably, the household and freedom of expression exemptions). When the uploader is considered to benefit from the household exemption, the right to erasure can only be invoked vis-à-vis the OSN, regardless of the joint controllership status.[293] Freedom of expression interests can be invoked as a counter-argument by both the uploader and the social network. So, in practice, the data subject may only legally be able to ask the OSN provider to erase the picture uploaded by another user who benefits from the household exemption. Whether or not that OSN provider has the obligation to then erase that picture is a different question, which will be discussed in the following chapters (notably Chapter 7).

In conclusion, the plurality of actors processing personal data should not hinder the effective exercise of data subject rights. Identifying the relevant controller responsible for accommodating one's right to erasure requires a granular, substantive, and functional approach.[294] A data subject will carefully need to determine which processing operation(s) he/she takes issue with and then identify who is the relevant controller. A granular approach will also facilitate distinguishing between controller and processor (one entity can even be both at the same time with regard to different processing operations).[295] Still, it has been argued above that data subjects might also approach processors with erasure requests, even though the controller is the one who is ultimately responsible to accommodate such claims.[296] Even when the complexity of a processing chain causes the data subject to invoke the right to erasure vis-à-vis the wrong controller, the latter could still be

[292] Article 29 Working Party, 'Opinion 1/2010 on the Concepts of "Controller" and "Processor"' (n 241) 18.

[293] As will be explained later on, the household exemption liberates natural persons from being subject to the GDPR's strict regulatory framework. It does not constitute a *defense* or counter-argument that can be used to fight the exercise of data subject's rights.

[294] Article 29 Working Party, 'Opinion 1/2010 on the Concepts of "Controller" and "Processor"' (n 241) 18.

[295] ibid 25.

[296] Depending on the circumstances, the processor might be more approachable and have an obligation to 'assist the controller by appropriate technical and organisational measures [...] to respond to requests for exercising the data subject's rights' (Art 26(2)(e)).

required to forward the request (Arts 17(2) and 19).[297] Importantly, the granular approach—dissecting processing operations—does not prevent a group of processing operations to have an overarching/joint purpose (and/or means), defined by *one* (or joint) controller(s).[298] In sum, from the perspective of exercising data subject rights, untangling the exact roles and responsibilities within today's complex data processing landscape should not be overstated. Data subjects will be able to exercise their right to erasure vis-à-vis joint or individual controllers equally, even if the eventual responsibility to accommodate the right will vary.[299] Though the right can also be invoked vis-à-vis the processor, it will only be enforceable against the controller(s).

b) The Automation Fallacy

The sheer scale at which information society service providers operate, is only possible through intense reliance on information and communication technologies. Modern-day online services such as search engines, social networks, and eCommerce platforms would simply not be (technically, economically, etc) viable if they would be managing their databases manually. Powerful algorithms have become necessary instruments to automate most aspects under the information society's 'hood'. Even though these points may seem self-evident, they are worth reiterating in light of assessing the GDPR's (personal) scope of application.

An often-recurring line of arguments for escaping the GDPR's scope, primarily relies on this growing automation. Three consecutive arguments are generally invoked and can be summarized as: (a) no knowledge; (b) no intent; (c) no humans. Firstly, ISS providers processing vast amounts of data often argue that—due to size and scale of their operations—they have no knowledge of what does (not) constitute personal data.[300] Secondly, even if they acknowledge they *are* processing personal data, ISS providers often argue they have no intention of doing so.[301] Thirdly, even if ISS providers intentionally process personal data, they sometimes argue—similarly to intelligence agencies—that it is only 'computers' looking at the data.[302] Convincing as these arguments may appear to some, they are irrelevant for determining the GDPR's personal scope of application. Three key reasons can

[297] These two provisions require controllers to communicate erasure requests to potential recipients of the personal data. Given the specific link of these provisions to the right to erasure, they will further be discussed in Chapter 4.

[298] Article 29 Working Party, 'Opinion 1/2010 on the Concepts of "Controller" and "Processor"' (n 241) 20.

[299] *Wirtschaftsakademie* (n 247) para 43; Opinion AG Bobek in: *Fashion ID* (n 286) para 108.

[300] See notably the Opinion of AG Jääskinen in *Google Spain*, paras 81–84. Also see: W Kuan Hon, Christopher Millard, and Ian Walden, 'Who Is Responsible for "Personal Data" in Cloud Computing?—The Cloud of Unknowing, Part 2' (2012) 2 International Data Privacy Law 3; Kevin Bankston and Amie Stepanovich, 'When Robot Eyes Are Watching You: The Law & Policy of Automated Communications Surveillance' (2014).

[301] See notably the arguments made by Google in: *Google Spain* (n 23) para 22.

[302] Bankston and Stepanovich (n 300).

be identified: (a) knowledge, intent, or 'human eyes' are no requirements for determining the personal scope; (b) yielding to this argumentation would generate a gaping hole in data protection; and (c) the reasoning ignores the rationale of the fundamental right to data protection.

KNOWLEDGE/INTENT ARE NO REQUIREMENTS—Similarly to the maxim 'ignorance of the law is no defence',[303] ignorance of one's data processing activities does not exempt one from responsibility. The scope of application of the GDPR does not hinge upon knowledge or intent and especially does not require 'human eyes' to see the personal data.[304] To the contrary, data protection law applies first and foremost to the *automated* processing of personal data (Art 2 GDPR).[305] Stricter rules are even in place with regard to '*automated individual decision-making, including profiling*' (Art 22). As made clear before, determining the purpose and means for a processing operation is sufficient to acquire the status of controller. Whether or not the controller had the knowledge or intention to process *personal* data is irrelevant.[306] The scope determination is based on *factual* circumstances. Modern-day information gatekeepers such as social media and search engines do not—at least in some respects (eg the timeline, search results)—process personal data *because* it is personal data. It only happens to be part of the much broader stream of data passing through their network/platform/services. Even an entity with no access to the *actual* personal data itself (but only statistics for example), can still be considered a controller if it (co-)determines purpose and means of the underlying processing.[307]

NON-ARGUMENT—Even if the GDPR would contain a knowledge and/or intent requirement, such information gatekeepers generally would not be able to benefit from it anyway. The entire modus operandi / business model of many ISS providers is to aid people in sifting through, and making sense of, the vast information-expanses online.[308] In light of this, it is hard for such entities to claim they have no knowledge of the fact that—at least part of—the information they process contains personal data. Even more absurd is the claim there would be no intent, as their added value generally derives from analysing, organizing, and directing (flows of) information.[309] Aside from these 'information gatekeepers', a considerable portion

[303] '[R]egardless of whether or not you actually knew, or were conscious, of the legal consequences of your actions you may be held legally accountable for them'. In: Uta Kohl, 'The Rule of Law, Jurisdiction and the Internet' (2004) 12 International Journal of Law and Information Technology 365, 367 et seq.

[304] See similarly: AG Opinion in: *Tietosuojavaltuutettu v Jehovan todistajat—uskonnollinen yhdyskunta* (n 246) para 71.

[305] Indeed, as was made clear in Chapter 2, it is exactly the automated nature of data processing which was part of the main impetus to install data protection laws in the first place.

[306] Also see: Kindt (n 57) 268.

[307] *Wirtschaftsakademie* (n 247) para 38.

[308] Google's mission statement famously reads: 'to organize the world's information and make it universally accessible and useful'. https://www.google.com/about/

[309] On the basis of the content, (potential) source and/or destination of that information (all of which may include personal data). This is not to say that there is a discernible trend of ISS providers trying to minimize the capturing, storing and/or processing of personal data (all of which are increasingly seen

of ISS providers factually process personal data, but without determining purposes (or means). This is the case, for example for many cloud computing service providers, who maintain a certain level of passivity with regard to the data they process.[310] Under these circumstances, the ISS provider might rather be considered a processor, still falling within the GDPR's scope of application.

Gap in Protection—Secondly, requiring knowledge or intent in order to be considered a controller subject to data protection law, would generate a huge gap in the protection of individuals. The data deluge trends described in the Introduction (Chapter 1), emphasized the rise to power and growing impact ISS providers have on individuals' daily lives.[311] Exempting them from data protection rules because most of their operations occur on an automated basis—something that enabled their exponential growth in the first place—would leave unregulated an expanding set of *de facto* data processing operations. In the same vein, one should reject the argument that processing generally occurs without a priori knowledge about the 'personal' nature of data or the intention to process said data. Whatever entity deciding on the purpose and means of a processing operation—even if only tangentially covering *personal* data—will be responsible for that operation. If not, data subjects would essentially have no opportunity to exercise their data protection rights with regard to that processing operation.[312]

Ignores the Rationale of Data Protection—The postulation that no 'human eyes' but only 'computers' look at personal data underlies much of the 'nothing to hide' rhetoric.[313] Indeed, at first sight privacy seems to be most viscerally affected when another human sees personal data.[314] But, as was amply made clear in Chapter 2, the GDPR safeguards much more than just 'privacy'. It is aimed to protect the fundamental right to data protection *in particular*. This right—encapsulating values such as individual autonomy and informational self-determination—is affected regardless of whether data is processed by humans or machines, intentionally/knowingly or not. Automated processing, due to its sheer scale, even has a much bigger impact on these normative values and further

as potential liabilities tipping the cost-benefit analysis). Elizabeth Dwoskin, 'What's Driving Silicon Valley to Become "Radicalized"' *Washington Post* (24 May 2016) <https://www.washingtonpost.com/news/the-switch/wp/2016/05/24/what-is-driving-silicon-valley-to-become-radicalized/> accessed 1 June 2019.

310 Hon, Millard, and Walden (n 300).

311 See for example: Frank Pasquale, *The Black Box Society: The Secret Algorithms That Control Money and Information* (Harvard UP 2014) 8.

312 In the same vein, see: *Google Spain* (n 23) para 34.

313 Many people's first reaction to surveillance practices (whether by the government or corporations) is that they do not care much as they do not have anything to hide from a computer algorithm. Daniel Solove, '"I've Got Nothing to Hide" and Other Misunderstandings of Privacy' (2007) 44 The San Diego Law Review 745.

314 Though of course, the general right to privacy protects people from much more than just peeping Tom's. Arguably, non-human/automated data processing is in fact much more intrusive due it vast scope, speed, and accuracy. Bankston and Stepanovich (n 300) 35 et seq.

exacerbates power asymmetries.[315] The following quote by Rushkoff, writing in the wake of the Facebook/Cambridge Analytica scandal, is illustrative:

> Neither Facebook nor the marketers buying your data particularly care about what you do with your clothes off, whom you're cheating with or any other sordid details you may find embarrassing. That's the great fiction of social media: That you matter as a person. You don't. The platform cares only about your metadata, from which they can construct a psychological profile and then manipulate your behavior.[316]

Data protection law is not just about safeguarding what people would traditionally experience as invasions of their privacy, such as the publication of embarrassing pictures or being spied upon. Its main role is to safeguard against the negative externalities of mass-scale automated data processing. That is also why the GDPR (Art 22)—and Directive 95/46 (Art 15) before that—specifically protects data subjects from entirely automated decision-making (eg by granting a right to obtain human intervention). Absence of knowledge, intent, or 'human eyes' does not reduce the potential impact on other normative values the GDPR is instrumental to either (ie non-discrimination or freedom of expression and access to information). Especially when considering how automated processing increasingly affects (physical and virtual) environments and as a result the rights, freedoms, and interests of data subjects within those environments. In another illustrative quote Solove compares the position of individuals vis-à-vis mass-scale data processing, to Joseph K. in Kafka's *The Trial*. A metaphor that has become even more salient today:

> [I]ndividuals are pawns, not knowing what is happening, having no say or ability to exercise meaningful control over the process. This lack of control allows the trial to completely take over Joseph K.'s life. The Trial captures the sense of helplessness, frustration, and vulnerability one experiences when a large bureaucratic organization has control over a vast dossier of details about one's life. At any time, something could happen to Joseph K.; decisions are made based on his data, and Joseph K. has no say, no knowledge, and no ability to fight back. He is completely at the mercy of the bureaucratic process.[317]

One more quote worth mentioning dates back to nearly half a century ago. It raises an important issue that only fairly recently seems to be gaining traction

[315] Bankston and Stepanovich (n 300).

[316] Douglas Rushkoff, 'How Facebook Exploited Us All' (*latimes.com*) <http://www.latimes.com/opinion/op-ed/la-oe-rushkoff-leaving-facebook-20180325-story.html> accessed 28 March 2018.

[317] Daniel Solove, *The Digital Person: Technology and Privacy in the Information Age* (New York UP 2004) 38.

again:[318] ie the risks in overrelying on (the objectiveness and/or fairness of) automated data processing:

> This connexion [sic] which may be established between different items of information concerning a given individual, may be used as the basis for passing judgment on him, a secret judgement from which there can be no appeal and which, because it is based on a computer, is thought to be objective and infallible. But in fact the information used may be inexact, or out of date or of no real significance, with the result that the final conclusion amounts to a 'scientific sophism'.[319]

THE *GOOGLE SPAIN* RULING—The CJEU's Ruling in *Google Spain* demonstrates the inaptness of the 'no knowledge; no intent; no humans' argument when assessing the data protection framework's scope of application. In this case, Google argued that it could not be considered a data controller vis-à-vis its indexing activities, as it would do so indiscriminately (of whether or not data is personal or not).[320] Its role would only be accessory to the actual publication of content on the source web-pages.[321] The Advocate General further built on this argument, claiming that in order to be qualified 'controller', one needs to process personal data at least 'with some intention which relates to their processing as *personal* data'.[322] Even though search engines know—as a statistical fact—that some portion of the information they will crawl, analyse, and index contains personal data, they would not be 'aware of what kind of personal data [it] is processing and why'.[323]

[318] eg: Kate Crawford, 'The Hidden Biases in Big Data' (*Harvard Business Review*, 1 April 2013) <http://blogs.hbr.org/2013/04/the-hidden-biases-in-big-data/> accessed 1 June 2019; Cathy O'Neil, *Weapons of Math Destruction: How Big Data Increases Inequality and Threatens Democracy* (Penguin 2017); John Cheney-Lippold, *We Are Data: Algorithms and the Making of Our Digital Selves* (New York UP 2017); Virginia Eubanks, *Automating Inequality: How High-Tech Tools Profile, Police, and Punish the Poor* (St Martin's Press 2018).

[319] International Commission of Jurists, 'The Protection of Privacy' (1972) XXIV International Social Science Journal 428–29. Similarly, see: Explanatory Report to: Council of Europe—Committee of Ministers (n 105) para 3.

[320] Brendan Van Alsenoy, Aleksandra Kuczerawy, and Jef Ausloos, 'Search Engines after "Google Spain": Internet@Liberty or Privacy@Peril?' (2013) 14<http://papers.ssrn.com/abstract=2321494> accessed 1 June 2019. A summary of the main arguments during the hearing can be found at: Jef Ausloos, 'Google v Spain at the Court of Justice of the EU' (*Tech, Policy & Society*, 5 March 2013) <https://jefausloos.wordpress.com/2013/03/05/google-v-spain-at-the-european-court-of-justice/> accessed 28 March 2018.

[321] Ignoring the granular approach to personal scope determination explained in the previous sub section.

[322] Advocate General Opinion in: *Google Spain SL, Google Inc v Agencia Española de Protección de Datos (AEPD)*, Mario Costeja González, InfoCuria, 82 (Court of Justice of the EU 2014). Emphasis added. This reasoning does not seem far off from an Italian Supreme Court ruling, where it was considered that a video hosting platform can only be qualified as a 'controller' from the moment it gains knowledge about the nature of a certain piece of user generated content. Corte di Cassazione, sez III Penale, sentenza 17 dicembre 2013—deposit ail 3 febbraio 2014, sentenza n 5107/14, at paragraph 7.2. Cited and extensively commented on, in: Van Alsenoy (n 252) 412–13.

[323] Advocate General Opinion in: *Google Spain* (n 24) paras 82–84. Also see: Van Alsenoy, Kuczerawy, and Ausloos (n 320) 13–19.

The CJEU eventually ruled that search engines *are* to be considered controllers, inter alia for the (automatic) indexing of third-party content and subsequent making available to users 'according to a particular order of preference'.[324] The fact that a search engine does not make an a priori distinction between personal and non-personal data is irrelevant.[325] In the case at hand, it was exactly the search engine's activity of linking a name to a result that affected the plaintiff the most. Search engines are undeniably the primary responsible for this specific activity. After all, linking search terms to results is their *raison d'être*. Not considering search engines to be controllers—subject to data protection law—would therefore go against the 'effective and complete protection of data subjects'.[326]

In conclusion, it is clear that the European data protection framework does not—neither in letter or spirit—require knowledge, intent, or humans for being qualified a controller. Automated processing of personal data—even if done regardless of the fact it is personal data—undeniably falls within the GDPR's *material* scope of application. As a result, whoever determines the purpose and means for that processing operation (eg designs and manages the algorithms) will be the controller. If not, such *de facto* processing of personal data will end up in a legal vacuum, leaving data subjects unprotected and without recourse. Moreover, it would go against the normative underpinnings of the fundamental right to data protection. Self-proclaimed 'information-agnostic' ISS providers have an ever-increasing impact on individuals and society at large. Exempting them from regulation on how (personal) data can be used would go against the very rationale of the fundamental right to data protection and many other values society holds dear.

c) *Intermediary Liability v Data Protection*

So-called 'internet intermediaries' are an important category of actors in the information society. Put simply, intermediaries enable or facilitate the flow of information, without entirely being responsible for (the creation or content of) that information. Directive 2000/31 (eCommerce Directive) lists three types of such intermediaries and exempts them from liability for the information they transmit or host: mere conduit (Art 12); caching (Art 13); and hosting (Art 14) service providers. A discussion on the actual scope and implications of these exemptions would go beyond the ambit of this book.[327] Suffice to say that the intermediaries in Arts 12–14 eCommerce Directive are, under certain conditions, not liable for infringing content passing through their metaphorical hands (eg copyright infringing material or child pornography). When either a caching or hosting

[324] *Google Spain* (n 24) para 41.
[325] ibid para 28.
[326] ibid para 34.
[327] For a relevant (and referenced) overview in light of the issues discussed here, see: Kuczerawy and Ausloos (n 208).

provider gains knowledge about the (infringing nature of the) content it stores, the intermediary loses its exemption.[328]

Given their increasingly powerful role as central nodes in the information society, they constitute an appealing target to approach with data subject rights. As demonstrated by ECtHR[329] and CJEU[330] case law, approaching an internet access provider or hosting platform with erasure requests will often seem more easy and/or effective than going after individual entities. Yet, it might seem contradictory to allow data subjects to exercise their right to erasure vis-à-vis intermediaries which are otherwise exempted from liability over the content they host or transfer. On top of that, Article 1(5)(b) eCommerce Directive provides that the Directive (ie intermediary liability exemptions) does not apply to questions relating to the data protection framework. Article 2(3) GDPR[331] on the other hand, explains the Regulation shall be 'without prejudice to the application' of the eCommerce Directive. Hence the question remains, can an individual invoke his/her right to erasure vis-à-vis an intermediary such as a hosting provider, for information uploaded/created by a third party?

Whenever personal data passes through them, intermediaries do, as a matter of fact, process personal data. Transmitting or hosting personal data both constitute processing operations within the meaning of Article 3(3) GDPR. Hence, the operations of internet intermediaries fall within the *material* scope of application of data protection law when performed on *personal data*. Next, one needs to assess whether these 'intermediaries' are to be considered *controllers* falling within the GDPR's *personal* scope of application. As explained before, assessing whether an entity processing personal data is in fact the controller, one needs to ascertain who determines the purpose and means for that specific processing operation. Intermediaries as described in the eCommerce Directive are, by definition, passive vis-à-vis the information they facilitate/enable access to.[332] Put differently, they only process information *on behalf of* their users. Any other operation they might perform on information for their own purposes will be outside

[328] Not benefiting from one of the exemptions does not automatically and/or necessarily result in the liability of the intermediary. This will still depend on a case-by-case analysis under Member-State law.

[329] *Delfi AS v Estonia (Grand Chamber Hearing)* [2015] European Court of Human Rights 64569/09; *Case of Magyar Tartalomszolgtatk Egyeslete and Index.hu ZRT v Hungary* [2016] European Court of Human Rights 22947/13.

[330] *Google Spain* (n 23); *Scarlet Extended v Sabam* (n 239); *SABAM v Netlog* (n 239).

[331] And Recital 21.

[332] Indeed, the exemption regime in the eCommerce Directive is primarily predicated on the passiveness or neutrality of intermediaries vis-à-vis the respective third-party content/activities. In the CJEU's words, an intermediary's conduct is merely 'technical, automatic and passive, pointing to a lack of knowledge or control of the data which it stores'. See: Court of Justice of the European Union, Joined Cases C-236/08 to C-238/08, 23 March 2010 (*Google France and Google v Louis Vuitton Malletier ao*), paragraphs 113–14. The CJEU also addressed the issue of neutrality of hosting service providers in the *L'Oréal eBay* Case, where it ruled that Art 14 of the Directive applies to hosting providers if they don't play an active role that would allow them to have knowledge or control of the stored data. Court of Justice of the European Union, Case C-324/09, 12 July 2011 (L'Oréal v eBay), paragraphs 112–16.

their capacity as 'intermediary'. As a result, for any processing performed purely as 'intermediary' (mere conduit, caching, hosting), benefitting from the exemptions under the eCommerce Directive, they can at most be considered processors under the GDPR. The initiative for the processing operation will be taken by the users of these intermediaries. In light of the granular approach (see multiplication of actors), for any other processing operation these intermediaries perform *on their own behalf* they will be considered controller.[333] With regard to these additional activities, intermediaries will also not be able to benefit from the liability exemptions in Arts12–14 eCommerce Directive.[334] Certainly today, it seems that many 'intermediary' ISS providers offer multiple 'value-added' operations, for which they do bear responsibility under data protection law (eg ranking content or performing image recognition).[335]

Further debunking the alleged contradiction between the eCommerce Directive and the GDPR is the distinction between liability and responsibility (see Chapter 2). Articles 12–14 eCommerce Directive exempt actors (ie intermediaries) from *liability* with regard to the content or activities of third parties. The GDPR sets out a regime for *responsibility* for one's own activities. This responsibility follows from the nature of information they process and the potential impact it might have on individuals and/or society (see Chapter 2).[336] Failure to comply with any of the provisions in the GDPR may result in liability. Data subjects may claim damages from the controller or processor, *unless* it can be proven that the controller (or processor) is *not* responsible for those damages.[337] As pointedly summarized by van Alsenoy: '[a]n absence of liability for mere distribution or storage does not however, imply an absence of responsibility with regard to other operations performed on that content'.[338]

Finally, it is worth referring to Erdos, who takes a more pragmatic, actor-centric point of view, ie trying to categorize entities rather than individual activities per se. In short, his 'synthetic interpretation' aims to align the GDPR responsibility regime with the eCommerce directive's liability exemptions, in light of human/fundamental rights.[339] Erdos looks at 'intermediary publishers' in particular, which

[333] The need for a granular approach is further confirmed in the GDPR, for example in Article 89(4), which states that the legitimacy of processing of personal data in pursuit of one purpose (ie archiving in the public interest, scientific or historical research, or statistical purposes) does not extend to processing of that same personal data for any other purposes.

[334] See notably: Article 29 Working Party, 'Opinion 1/2010 on the Concepts of "Controller" and "Processor"' (n 931), Example 16 and 1.

[335] Article 29 Working Party, 'Opinion 1/2008 on Data Protection Issues Related to Search Engines' (n 41) 14.

[336] *Google Spain* (n 24) para 80. One can also draw a parallel with environmental protection and the responsibility of certain actors in the petrochemical industry for example, who bear some responsibilities when transporting precious or dangerous materials.

[337] Article 82 *juncto* Recital 146. See also: Van Alsenoy (n 252) 509.

[338] Van Alsenoy, 'Liability under EU Data Protection Law' (n 278) 284.

[339] David Erdos, 'Delimiting the Ambit of Responsibility of Intermediary Publishers for Third Party Rights in European Data Protection: Towards a Synthetic Interpretation of the EU Acquis' (University

he defines as 'any online actor which is not immediately responsible for directly initiating an initial publication of data but which performs publication-related processing directly linked to this act of the "original publisher"'.[340] In reconciling the different regimes, Erdos puts forward a general underlying principle, implying the more autonomous the control over processing, the stronger the responsibilities under the GDPR and weaker the liability shields under the eCommerce Directive.[341] Three categories of 'intermediary publishers' can be identified along this continuum: processor hosts,[342] controller hosts,[343] and independent intermediaries[344].[345] When determining the level of responsibility and duties in a given case, the 'resource capacity' of these actors should be considered as well. Though Erdos' model is certainly quite valuable in determining the ambit of responsibility on intermediaries' shoulders, its importance is more nuanced when taking the data subject's perspective wishing to exercise *ex post* empowerment rights. All three categories of 'intermediary publishers' can in principle be targeted with a right to erasure/object. The 'processor-host' may not be *responsible* to accommodate the right itself, but as mentioned before, it still has a duty of care to pass on the request to the relevant entity (or at least inform data subjects about this).[346]

In sum, the interaction between intermediary liability exemptions in the eCommerce Directive and the responsibility regime under the GDPR, can be untangled by taking a functional and granular approach. Dissecting the complex operations of today's ISS providers has become necessary to separate their intermediary functions from others. Such distinction can inter alia be made by looking at what operations the ISS provider determines the purpose and means for. With regard to these operations, the provider will be considered a controller. With regard to traditional intermediary functions (e.g. the specific act of hosting information), however, the entity cannot be considered a controller. Hence, ISS providers will not be required to accommodate data subject rights with regard to its purely

of Cambridge, Faculty of Law 2017) Legal Studies Research Paper 31/2017 <https://papers.ssrn.com/abstract=2993154> accessed 1 June 2019.

340 ibid 4.

341 ibid 21 et seq.

342 Encompassing those which fall within the 'host' intermediary shield and outside the definition of 'controller' under data protection. For example: website/blog hosting.

343 Covering those who fall within the 'host' intermediary shield and also within the 'controller' definition under data protection. For example: video-sharing websites such as YouTube.

344 Comprising those who fall within the 'controller' definition under data protection and outside 'host' intermediary shield. For example: search engines or rating websites.

345 Erdos, 'Delimiting the Ambit of Responsibility of Intermediary Publishers for Third Party Rights in European Data Protection' (n 339) 21 et seq.

346 Erdos does rightly point out that imposing too much responsibility on these processor-hosts, could disproportionately impact freedom of expression and information, as well as the privacy interests of the original publishers (eg when required to keep track of the identity and contact details of original publishers). ibid 22–23. On the interaction with information freedoms and balancing more generally, see Chapter 6.

'intermediary' activities. The more involved they become in further processing (personal) data, however, the more they enter the realm of data protection law. Data subject rights can be invoked vis-à-vis all processing operations performed on ISS providers' own behalf. The functional/granular approach, prescribing the dissection of ISS providers' activities will also be relevant with regard to giving effect to data subject rights in a proportionate manner (see Parts II and III).[347]

4.3 Third Parties and Recipients

Article 4—Definitions

(9) 'recipient' means a natural or legal person, public authority, agency or another body, to which the personal data are disclosed whether a third party or not [...];

(10) 'third party' means a natural or legal person, public authority, agency or body other than the data subject, controller, processor and persons who, under the direct authority of the controller or processor, are authorised to process personal data;

Third Parties—Two final categories of entities referred to throughout the GDPR, are relevant to the matter discussed here: 'recipients' and 'third parties'.[348] The importance of both concepts in the data protection framework overall is fairly marginal and not much has been written (or litigated) on the matter. Put simply, the vaguely defined concept of 'third parties' refers to any person who does not already fall within one of the other categories mentioned before (ie data subject, controller, or processor) and are authorized, 'under the direct authority of the controller' to process personal data. Following the CJEU, it seems the concept should be interpreted broadly (also overlapping with 'third party' notions in other legal frameworks).[349] WP29 explains the concept is not that dissimilar as the one often used in civil law, 'where third party is usually a subject which is not part of an entity or of an agreement'.[350] Given the fact that such a 'third party' is legally different from the controller, disclosing information to them will

[347] Indeed, *Google Spain* illustrates that mere delisting (ie cutting the link between a specific name and search result), will suffice to accommodate a data subject right, without necessitating a full erasure from the search engine's indexes.

[348] When compared to Directive 95/46, the concept seems to have decreased in importance (notably, by not being included anymore in several provisions relating to data subject rights).

[349] *Salvatore Manni* (n 236).

[350] Article 29 Working Party, 'Opinion 1/2010 on the Concepts of "Controller" and "Processor"' (n 931) 31. The WP goes on to say that, under data protection law, 'third parties' should be 'interpreted as referring to any subject who has no specific legitimacy or authorization—which could stem, for example, from its role as controller, processor, or their employee—in processing personal data'.

always require a specific legal basis.[351] Van Alsenoy explains third parties should be understood as a residual category, 'referring to any party which is not part of the "inner circle" of a particular data processing'.[352] Importantly, 'third parties' do not cover employees or branches of the controller/processor (under direct authority of their headquarters), but would cover persons working for separate organizations in the same corporate group for example. Compared to Directive 95/46, the concept of third parties seems to have diminished in importance. For the purposes here, perhaps the most important appearance of the notion is in Article 6(1)f, which explicitly recognizes interests of third parties can enter the legitimate interests test for rendering processing lawful (see amply Chapter 5). Finally, it should be pointed out that upon receiving personal data, 'third parties' become controllers in their own right, liable to comply with the GDPR requirements.[353]

RECIPIENTS—The category of recipients as defined in Art 4(9) GDPR, should be understood in its natural language meaning, as any entity to whom the personal data is disclosed.[354] Recipients are said to constitute a broader concept than that of 'third parties', as it also includes persons within the processor or controller (eg an employee or division).[355] Sharing personal data with recipients does not necessarily require a separate lawful ground (eg when the recipient is an employee), but doing so with third parties always does. Processors will always be deemed recipients, but not third parties.[356] Having said all that, third parties should not be seen as a subset of recipients, but the two categories should rather be represented as a Venn-diagram. Indeed, it would appear that 'third parties' as mentioned in Article 6(1)f GDPR, do not necessarily cover persons/entities having *received* personal data (yet).[357] This is especially apparent when comparing with the provision's predecessor (Art 7(f) Directive 95/46), which talked about 'third parties *to whom the data are disclosed*'.[358] The main purpose of this category appears to be for transparency, accountability, and enabling data subject empowerment.[359] The term is used in connection with the information obligations of the controller (Arts13–14; 19; 30) and the data subject's right of access (Art 15).

[351] European Union Agency for Fundamental Rights (FRA) and Council of Europe, *Handbook on European Non-Discrimination Law* (Publications Office of the European Union 2011)55.

[352] Van Alsenoy (n 252) 130.

[353] ie the lawfulness of their processing cannot be derived from the one covering the initial controller's processing.

[354] Disclosure, here, should also be interpreted very broadly, irrespective of medium or modalities. See: Van Alsenoy (n 252) 132–33.

[355] European Union Agency for Fundamental Rights (FRA) and Council of Europe (n 351) 55.

[356] Van Alsenoy (n 252) 134–35.

[357] Article 6(1f) will be extensively analysed in Chapter 4.

[358] Highlighted words have been removed in the GDPR.

[359] Van Alsenoy (n 252) 134–35.

4.4 Interim Conclusion

The personal scope of EU data protection law is challenged by the complex tangle of entities processing personal data. In order for the right to erasure to have any meaningful role in safeguarding data protection law's normative underpinnings, it is crucial to have a clear understanding of the relevant entities.[360] If anything, this section has made quite clear that in order to identify those responsible for accommodating data subject rights in the ISS context, a granular and functional approach is required. Without such an approach—ie lumping different processing operations and/or personal data together—it will generally be hard to identify one entity responsible for accommodating data subjects' rights. As will appear later-on (Part II-III), a non-granular approach also unnecessarily thwarts a balanced and/or effective implementation of the right to erasure. WP29 and several AGs have also confirmed that a non-functional or too rigid approach would result in a serious lacuna in the protection of personal data.[361] In sum, dissecting the processing activities of relevant entities will be necessary to identify who is responsible for accommodating the right to erasure with regard to that specific personal data set.

Section 5. Derogations and Exemptions

GDPR Exemptions—Sometimes the processing of personal data may escape the regulatory cloak of the GDPR, in full or in part. Exemptions and derogations are a necessary corollary of the GDPR's incredibly broad scope of application. To use a nautical metaphor, a large fishing-net requires flexibility and wide holes (to prevent over-capturing and the trawler from sinking). In light of its rationale, data protection law requires a very large net, preventing unforeseen nefarious or problematic processing operations from evading its reach. Derogations/exemptions constitute the 'holes' in the GDPR's net, compensating potential over-inclusiveness. Without any such exemptions virtually nothing in today's information society would escape the GDPR's scope and its regulatory burden. The interpretative flexibility constitutes the necessary elasticity of the GDPR's net, in order to prevent it from sinking under its own weight altogether. This flexibility essentially implies that the obligations/responsibility imposed by the GDPR need to be interpreted in light of 'the nature, scope, context and purposes of processing

[360] Also recognized in Recital 79 GDPR.

[361] Article 29 Working Party, 'Opinion 1/2010 on the Concepts of "Controller" and "Processor"' (n 931) 9; Opinion AG Bot in: *Wirtschaftsakademie* (n 247) paras 46; 62; Opinion AG Mengozzi in: *Tietosuojavaltuutettu v Jehovan todistajat—uskonnollinen yhdyskunta* (n 246) paras 71–73.

as well as the risks of varying likelihood and severity for the rights and freedoms of natural persons' (Art 24(1)).[362]

Exemptions effectively absolve the beneficiary from having to comply with one or more provisions altogether. Derogations on the other hand, aim to alleviate certain obligations. Both should be construed narrowly, and 'apply only in so far as is strictly necessary'.[363] Roughly two layers of derogations and exemptions can be discerned in the GDPR. On the one hand, there are general ones, exonerating entities and/or processing operations from multiple provisions at the same time or even from the GDPR altogether. On the other hand, there are specific derogations and exemptions that are only relevant with regard to one particular provision (often to be found in the second or third paragraphs).[364] Whereas the 'provision-specific' derogations/exemptions to the right to erasure will be analysed in the following chapter (4), this section will only expound the first level of derogations/exemptions. Given their general nature, they will, inter alia, impact the ability to invoke data protection rights too. More specifically, a data subject might not be able to invoke the right to erasure or object vis-à-vis an entity that benefits from a derogation or exemption. Even though the GDPR does list a number of general exemptions (notably in Article 2(2)), only a few are relevant with regard to the focus of this book, ie power asymmetries between individuals and information society service providers.[365] In the same vein, Article 23 will also not be further discussed.[366] The provision lists a number of situations in which EU or Member-State law *may* restrict the scope of data subject rights, though nine out of ten relate to situations

[362] In its *Google Spain* ruling, the CJEU also explained that controllers must ensure the processing meets the requirements laid down in law, 'within the framework of [their] responsibilities, powers and capabilities'. *Google Spain* (n 23) para 83.

[363] Frequently confirmed by the CJEU. See notably: *Rīgas satiksme* [2017] Court of Justice of the European Union C-13/16 para 30; *ietosuojavaltuutettu v Satakunnan Markkinapörssi & Satamedia* [2008] Court of Justice of the European Union C-73/07 para 56; *Volker und Markus Schecke GbR and Hartmut Eifert v Land Hessen* (n 96) para 86; *IPI v Englebert* [2013] Court of Justice of the European Union C-473/12 [39]; *František Ryneš v Úřad pro ochranu osobních údajů* (n 78) para 28; *Maximillian Schrems v Data Protection Commissioner* [2015] Court of Justice of the European Union C-362/14 para 92; AG Opinion in: *Tietosuojavaltuutettu v Jehovan todistajat—uskonnollinen yhdyskunta* (n 246) para 29.

[364] eg Article 17(3) on the right to erasure; Article 22(2) on automated individual decision-making. It should be said that these 'provision-specific' exemptions are generally based on more general exemptions (see notably Article 17(3)(a) and (c); Article 21(6)).

[365] Will therefore not be further discussed: the exemptions concerning data processing in the context of activities (b) relating to common foreign and security policy of the Member-States; and (d) relating to the prevention, investigation, detection, or prosecution of criminal offences, the execution of criminal penalties, including the safeguarding against and the prevention of threats to public security (Art 2(2) GDPR).

[366] For a detailed criticism of Article 23, see: Amberhawk, 'Council's Exceptions from the Data Protection Regulation Degrade the Privacy Protection below Directive 95/46/EC' (*Hawktalk*, 3 August 2015) <http://amberhawk.typepad.com/amberhawk/2015/08/councils-exceptions-from-the-data-protection-regulation-degrade-the-privacy-protection-below-directive-9546ec.html> accessed 1 June 2019. The CJEU has also explored this provision's predecessor (Art 13 Directive 95/46) in: *Bara* [2015] Court of Justice of the European Union C-201/14.

not directly dealt with here.[367] A proper analysis requires looking at Member-State laws, which would distract too much from the main goal pursued in this book.[368]

Four derogations/exemptions in particular have a more or less significant role in light of this book: personal data is processed (a) in the course of an activity falling outside the scope of EU law;[369] (b) by a natural person in the course of a purely personal or household activity;[370] (c) for journalistic, academic, artistic, or literary expression purposes;[371] or (d) for archiving purposes in the public interest, scientific or historical research purposes, or statistical purposes.[372] These four situations—abridged to 'outside the scope of EU law', 'household exemption', 'freedom of expression', and 'public interest or research purposes'—will briefly be elucidated in the following pages. It should be said that the exemptions/derogations discussed here, should not be confused with the interests involved in balancing acts (which will elaborately be analysed in Part II). Exemptions and derogations essentially are situations where the legislator already predefines what side the balance should tip over to.[373]

5.1 Outside the Scope of EU Law

Article 2—Material Scope

(2) This Regulation does not apply to the processing of personal data: (a) in the course of an activity which falls outside the scope of Union law.

The GDPR—and data subject rights with it—does not apply to the processing of personal data related to activities which fall outside the scope of EU law.[374] This exemption can be considered a catch-all, or umbrella-, exemption for a variety of activities such as those related to national security or common foreign and security policy (Recital 16).[375] Despite its open-ended nature, the exemption needs to be

[367] eg national security; defence; public security; prevention, investigation, detection, or prosecution of criminal offences; etc.

[368] For a critical appraisal of the inclusion of these restrictions in the GDPR, see: Lynskey, *The Foundations of EU Data Protection Law* (n 60) 20–23.

[369] Article 2(2)(a) GDPR.

[370] Article 2(2)(c) GDPR.

[371] Article 85 GDPR.

[372] Article 89 GDPR.

[373] See M Jozwiak, 'Balancing the Rights to Data Protection and Freedom of Expression and Information by the Court of Justice of the European Union: The Vulnerability of Rights in an Online Context' (2016) 23 Maastricht Journal of European and Comparative Law (MJ) 404, 415–16.

[374] Article 2(2)(A) *juncto* Recital 16

[375] Previously, Article 3(2) Directive 95/46 specified these activities 'falling outside the scope of Community law', included processing operations concerning public security, defence, State security (including the economic well-being of the State when the processing operation relates to State security matters), and the activities of the State in areas of criminal law. The CJEU explicitly stated that this exemption only applied to activities of 'State or of State authorities' and not those of individuals. *Lindqvist* (n 99) 43. Cited in: David Erdos, 'Confused? Analysing the Scope of Freedom of Speech Protection

interpreted narrowly. As emphasized in two 2003 CJEU rulings, a liberal interpretation of this exemption would be conducive of legal uncertainty and go against data protection law's objective.[376] As such, there seems to be no inherent reason for the 'outside the scope of Union law' exemption to still be included in the GDPR aside from the formal fact that the EU cannot legislate *ultra vires*.[377]

Aside from its vague and limited relevance, the 'outside the scope of Union law' exemption is also only marginally relevant in light of this book. After all, the scope of this research is limited to power asymmetries over personal data between individuals and economic operators online, ie ISS providers. The data processing activities of these entities plainly fall within the scope of EU law overall. Still, there is an argument to be made that—in this specific (online commercial) context—that the line between inside or outside EU law is increasingly hard to draw. Indeed, over the past decade, multiple scandals have illustrated private/commercial entities (particularly ISS providers) are often co-opted by public bodies (eg intelligence agencies) to share user-data.[378] Without wanting to discard the incredible importance of this trend, it is an issue that extends beyond the scope of this contribution and will thus not be discussed in detail here. Having said that, ISS providers' (in)voluntary collaboration with public authorities may play a role in assessing and weighing their (economic) interests against those of data subjects invoking their data protection rights (see Chapter 6).

5.2 Household Exemption

Article 2—Material Scope

(2) This Regulation does not apply to the processing of personal data: . . . (c) by a natural person in the course of a purely personal or household activity.

Definition—Following the so-called household exemption, natural persons are *not* subject to data protection law when they process personal data *in the course of a purely personal or household activity*. Examples include 'correspondence and the holding of addresses, or social networking and online activity undertaken within the context of such activities'.[379] The exemption can be considered an

Vis-à-Vis European Data Protection' (Oxford University 2012) 48/2012 6<http://papers.ssrn.com/abstract=2119187> accessed 1 June 2019.

[376] *Österreichischer Rundfunk and others* (n 51) para 39ff. Going entirely against the Advocate General (Tizzano) Opinion; *Lindqvist* (n 99) 40 et seq.

[377] Korff, 'New Challenges to Data Protection Study-Working Paper No 2' (n 33) 4. See also: Lynskey, *The Foundations of EU Data Protection Law* (n 60) 18 et seq.

[378] Korff, 'New Challenges to Data Protection Study-Working Paper No 2' (n 33) 3. Writing in 2010, the author refers to the SWIFT, PNR and data retention controversies.

[379] Recital 18, GDPR.

'all-or-nothing' provision, meaning that its applicability results in the beneficiary not being subject to any data protection rule whatsoever. Data subject rights such as the right to erasure cannot be invoked vis-à-vis someone benefitting from the household exemption. Conversely, if an individual's processing operations do not qualify under the household exemption, he/she will a priori be subject to the full range of data protection law.[380]

Rationale—The reason for having a household exemption is quite self-evident. It would be unreasonable to submit an individual to the full regulatory weight of data protection law for data processing activities carried out in a purely personal capacity. Indeed, since at least the drafting of the OECD Guidelines as well as Directive 95/46, it was assumed that such processing only generates very small—to non-existent—threats to others.[381] Not having the exemption in place would also result in potentially disproportionate interference in the fundamental rights and freedoms of the person who is processing personal data in such a private capacity.[382] Whereas the rationale has remained virtually the same throughout the previous decades, the exemption's relevance has increased tremendously. Not in the least due to the 'datafication' of everything and the emergence of so-called 'web 2.0' or 'read-write' services.[383] Virtually every individual in today's information society processes vast amounts of (personal) data in the course of their daily lives. Additionally, data protection authorities report that a growing number of queries and complaints they receive relates to the publication of personal data by other individuals.[384]

Not only has this evolution rendered the household exemption increasingly relevant, it has most certainly made defining and interpreting its scope more complex. A narrow interpretation might fail to exempt individual processing of personal data with no impact on the data protection or privacy interests of the data subject, whereas a flexible interpretation might be over-inclusive, exempting

[380] Brendan Van Alsenoy, 'The Evolving Role of the Individual Under EU Data Protection Law' (KU Leuven—CiTiP 2015) Working Paper 23 5<http://papers.ssrn.com/abstract=2641680> accessed 1 June 2019.

[381] Van Eecke and Truyens (n 252) 540; Van Alsenoy, 'The Evolving Role of the Individual Under EU Data Protection Law' (n 380) 8.

[382] This was already implicit in the pioneering French data protection Act of 1978, which specifically included an exemption for 'non-automated or mechanised processing of personal data', the use of which exclusively takes place within the context of one's (right to a) private life. Article 45, Loi 78-17 du 6 janvier 1978 relative à l'informatique, aux fichiers et aux libertés. Also see: ACM Nugter, *Transborder Flow of Personal Data within the EC: A Comparative Analysis of the Privacy Statutes of the Federal Republic of Germany, France, the United Kingdom and The Netherlands and Their Impact on the Private Sector* (Kluwer Law and Taxation Publ 1990) 82; André Holleaux, 'La Loi Du 6 Janvier 1978 Sur Informatique et Les Libertés — II —' (1978) 31 La Revue administrative, 165. Cited in: Van Alsenoy, 'The Evolving Role of the Individual Under EU Data Protection Law' (n 380) 7.

[383] Korff, 'New Challenges to Data Protection Study-Working Paper No 2' (n 33) 5 et seq; Van Alsenoy, 'The Evolving Role of the Individual Under EU Data Protection Law' (n 380) 4.

[384] Article 29 Working Party, 'Annex 2: Proposals for Amendments Regarding Exemption for Personal or Household Activities' 1 <http://ec.europa.eu/justice/article-29/documentation> accessed 1 June 2019.

processing operations clearly impacting data subjects.[385] Though a crucial—and so far unresolved—conversation to have,[386] a critical analysis of the household exemption in EU data protection law falls outside the scope of this book. In light of its focus on the relationship between data subjects and ISS providers, the household exemption will only be relevant tangentially.[387] Hence, this section will be limited to a description of how the exemption is currently interpreted and applied.

CRITERIA—As succinct as its predecessor in Directive 95/46, Article 2(2)(c) GDPR restricts the applicability of the exemption to *natural* persons processing personal data in a *purely personal or household activity*. Recital 18 further clarifies that, in order to qualify as a 'purely personal or household activity', the processing operation cannot have a 'connection to a professional or commercial activity'.[388] The CJEU has provided additional guidance in at least two landmark rulings. In *Lindqvist*, the household exemption was hinged onto two criteria: (a) the relevant activities need to be carried out in the course of the individual's private or family life; and (b) the data cannot be made available to an indefinite number of people.[389] The language of the former seems to refer to the general right to privacy in Article 7 Charter and Article 8 ECHR.[390] Indeed, it confirms the role of the GDPR as a fair balancing framework, safeguarding *all* fundamental rights and freedoms, and not just the right to data protection of the data subject (see Chapter 2). The second *Lindqvist* criterion, however, has raised quite some eyebrows, as it would exclude almost any processing of information by individuals in an online context.[391]

385 Korff and Brown (n 153) 23; Van Alsenoy, 'The Evolving Role of the Individual Under EU Data Protection Law' (n 380) 4–6.

386 See, for example: Rebecca Wong and Joseph Savirimuthu, 'All or Nothing: This is the Question? The Application of Article 3(2) Data Protection Directive 95/46/EC to the Internet', 25 J Marshall J Computer & Info L 2008 241–66; Brendan Van Alsenoy, Joris/Ballet, and Aleksandra Kuczerawy, 'Social Networks and Web 2.0: Are Users also Bound by Data Protection Regulations?', Identity in the Information Society (IDIS) 2009 75–76 and Natali Helberger and Joris van Hoboken, 'Little Brother Is Tagging You—Legal and Policy Implications of Amateur Data Controllers', Computer Law Review International (Cri) 2010, Vol 4 104 et seq. Cited in: Van Alsenoy, 'The Evolving Role of the Individual Under EU Data Protection Law' (n 380) 5. Also: Zuzanna Warso, 'There's More to It than Data Protection—Fundamental Rights, Privacy and the Personal/Household Exemption in the Digital Age' (2013) 29 Computer Law & Security Review 491.

387 ISS providers, after all, by definition can not rely on the exemption for the processing operations they are controllers for.

388 Something that was mentioned in Directive 95/46, but was introduced by the EC in its GDPR proposal and persisted throughout the stormy legislative process.

389 *Lindqvist* (n 99) paras 46–48. A year before, AG Tizzano had already explained in his Opinion (para 34) that the household exemption could especially not apply to activities when they involve 'loading personal data on a home page accessible by anyone, anywhere in the world, through a specific link on a site well-known to the public (and therefore easy to find with a search engine) ...'. Also see: Van Alsenoy, 'The Evolving Role of the Individual Under EU Data Protection Law' (n 380) 9.

390 Similarly to the provision in the 1978 French data protection act, which exempted processing activities occurring within the realm of one's right to private life.

391 Flora J Garcia, 'Bodil Lindqvist: A Swedish Churchgoer's Violation of the European Union's Data Protection Directive Should Be a Warning to U.S. Legislators' Fordham Intell Prop Media & Ent LJ 15 no 4 (Summer 2005): 1205–44 particularly the references on pp.1229–30; Warso, 'There's More to It than Data Protection—Fundamental Rights, Privacy and the Personal/Household Exemption in the Digital Age' (n 386).

This 'restricted-access' was later nuanced—though not explicitly overturned—by WP29[392] and in Recital 18 GDPR.[393]

More than a decade after *Lindqvist*, the CJEU was asked to interpret the household exemption again. In the *Ryneš* Case, the Court ruled that video surveillance of one's front door, exclusively operated by the private individual living in that respective house, does not benefit from the household exemption to the extent it also monitors public space (ie a public pathway and the entrance to the house opposite). Arriving at this conclusion, the CJEU emphasized the exemption needs to be interpreted narrowly because: (a) the primary objective of data protection law is to ensure a 'high level of protection of the fundamental rights and freedoms of natural persons';[394] (b) 'derogations and limitations in relation to the protection of personal data must apply only in so far as is strictly necessary';[395] and (c) the provision's explicit reference to '*purely* personal or household activities'.[396] In sum, currently the household exemption needs to be interpreted *narrowly*, with guiding—though not determinative—questions including:

- Is the processing carried out within the context of *purely* personal or household activities?
- Does the processing have a connection to commercial or professional activities?
- Does the relevant processing activity occur within the context of one's private and family life, protected under Article 7 Charter and Article 8 ECHR?
- Is the personal data made available to an indefinite number of people?
- Is a high level of data protection ensured/maintained?

[392] WP29 explained that the 'making available to an indefinite number of people' criterion is an important, though *not determinative* factor to consider. Article 29 Working Party, 'Opinion on Online Social Networking' (n 288) 6; Article 29 Working Party, 'Annex 2: Proposals for Amendments Regarding Exemption for Personal or Household Activities' (n 384) 9; Warso (n 386) 496; Van Alsenoy, 'The Evolving Role of the Individual Under EU Data Protection Law' (n 380) 22. It is also important to emphasize that *not* making available, or only making available to a limited number of people, does not automatically render the exemption applicable. *Digital Rights Ireland Ltd* [2014] Court of Justice of the European Union Joined Cases C-293/12 and C-594/12 invalidating the Data Retention Directive (2006/24/EC para 34. Referred to in: AG Jääskinen Opinion in *František Ryneš v Úřad pro ochranu osobních údajů* (n 78) para 59.

[393] Explicitly referring to social networking and online activities undertaken within the context of personal or household activities. This addition was clearly based on the WP29's Opinion on Social Networking, which states: 'A high number of contacts could be an indication that the household exception does not apply.' In: Article 29 Working Party, 'Opinion on Online Social Networking' (n 288) 6.

[394] See paragraph 27.

[395] Paragraphs 28–29.

[396] The Court's reasoning very much followed that of AG Jääskinen's Opinion (paragraph 53), which appears to equate the term *purely* to the term *exclusively*. Also see: Van Alsenoy, 'The Evolving Role of the Individual Under EU Data Protection Law' (n 380) 11; Lorna Woods, 'Big Brother's Little Brother? The Scope of the "Household Exception" to EU Data Protection Law' (EU Law Analysis, 10 July 2014) <http://eulawanalysis.blogspot.co.uk/2014/07/big-brothers-little-brother-scope-of.html> accessed 1 June 2019.

Narrow or Flexible—The narrow interpretation of the household exemption—supported by both the law in the books as well as the CJEU's case law—has been criticized for neglecting practical reality.[397] A narrow construction results in many individuals falling outside the exemption's scope, even though their data processing activities may be benign, small-scale, and low-risk. As explained by Van Alsenoy, data protection law is geared towards organizations, not individuals.[398] With no a priori differentiation between (eg small/large) controllers or goals, the same regulatory scheme is applied to all, potentially leading to excessively burdensome and even unrealistic situations.[399] Moreover, most of the conflicts arising from data processing activities by natural persons are better dealt with through other (national) legal frameworks anyway (ie libel or harassment laws, general tort law, intellectual property law, anti-discrimination rules, etc).[400] Article 57(1)f GDPR would also allow data subjects to approach their national DPA, even though the relevant processing operation is exempted).[401]

In light of the above, Van Alsenoy advocates for the household exemption to apply to 'all activities which may reasonably be construed as taking place in the course of an individual's private or family life'.[402] Warso muses about whether or not a narrow interpretation of the household exemption might in fact pass muster with the ECHR (Art 7).[403] Erdos, points out the undesirable and unrealistic consequences of too narrow a construction in the context of 'individual publications' (eg user-generated content, including personal data of others).[404] He proposes a well-developed 'tripartite approach', aimed at resolving conflicts with the freedom

[397] Van Eecke and Truyens (n 252) 539–40; Norberto Andrade, 'Oblivion: The Right to Be Different from Oneself—Reproposing the Right to Be Forgotten' (2012) 13 Revista de Internet, Derecho Y Política 127–28; Van Alsenoy, 'The Evolving Role of the Individual Under EU Data Protection Law' (n 380).

[398] This is apparent, the author clarifies, from both the language and substance of data protection law's provisions. Van Alsenoy, 'The Evolving Role of the Individual Under EU Data Protection Law' (n 380) 13 et seq.

[399] Particularly with regard to *ex ante* measures in the 'Data Protection Matrix' (see Chapter 2). See also: Warso (n 386) 495; Van Alsenoy, 'The Evolving Role of the Individual Under EU Data Protection Law' (n 380) 14–15.

[400] Not to mention the vast array of non-legal/judiciary routes available to solve inter-personal conflicts. Such inter-personal conflicts involve the unwanted publication of personal data. See also: David Erdos, 'Filling Defamation's "Gaps": Data Protection and the Right to Reputation' (OUP 2013) 69/2013 <http://papers.ssrn.com/abstract=2283284> accessed 1 June 2019.

[401] This very open-ended provision (similarly to Article 28(4) Directive 95/46) requires DPA's to 'handle complaints lodged by a data subject ...'. See: Van Alsenoy, 'The Evolving Role of the Individual Under EU Data Protection Law' (n 380) 33.

[402] ie what would be covered by Article 8 Charter or Article 7 ECHR. Substantiating this, the author refers to the first criterion promulgated by the *Lindqvist* Court. ibid 34.

[403] Warso (n 386) 495.

[404] David Erdos, 'Beyond "Having a Domestic"? Regulatory Interpretation of European Data Protection Law and Individual Publication' Computer Law & Security Review <http://www.sciencedirect.com/science/article/pii/S0267364917300730> accessed 1 June 2019.

of expression and limited capabilities (to comply with the entire GDPR) of individuals.[405]

During the first half of the GDPR's legislative process, WP29 seemed to call for a more flexible approach to the household exemption as well.[406] Eventually though, WP29 reversed course, favouring 'a limited and carefully balanced household exemption applying to 'purely' household activities'.[407] Ultimately, the household exemption provision that was finally adopted as part of the GDPR, largely sustained the status quo. This approach can be justified by the 'all-or-nothing' nature of the household exemption. Any provision exempting someone from an entire legal framework—particularly when said framework safeguards fundamental rights—should be interpreted very strictly. Having said that, Recital 18 does subtly hint at a slightly less narrow scope (compared to the exemption in Directive 95/46) by removing the word *exclusively*.[408] Erdos has also pointed out that DPAs do not all interpret the exemption very narrowly either.[409] Regardless, it should be reiterated that failure to fall within the exemption's scope, does not necessarily render illegitimate the relevant processing operation by a natural person.[410] The respective individual might well have a legitimate ground for processing and/or benefit from another (partial) exemption.[411]

Even though an important issue, this book will not devote much more attention to data protection conflicts exclusively between natural persons, because of: (a) its focus on the relationship between individuals and ISS providers, justified by; (b) the rationale of data protection law to counter power asymmetries; and (c) the fact that both from a substantive and normative perspective, other (non-)legal avenues are better suited to tackle most inter-personal conflicts arising from data

[405] This approach can be summarized as (a) the household exemption should cover individual publications which do not pose serious *prima facie* risks; (b) individual publications should be covered by the freedom of expression derogations in Article 85(2); and (c) problematic individual publications should only be made subject to data protection's core substantive and supervisory provisions.

[406] Article 29 Working Party, 'Annex 2: Proposals for Amendments Regarding Exemption for Personal or Household Activities' (n 384). Van Alsenoy summarizes the five criteria listed by WP29 for guiding the assessment as: publicity; data subjects involved; scale and frequency; concerted action; and adverse impact. Van Alsenoy, 'The Evolving Role of the Individual Under EU Data Protection Law' (n 380) 17–19.

[407] Article 29 Working Party, 'Appendix: Core Topics in View of the Trilogue' (2015) 3 <http://ec.europa.eu/justice/article-29/documentation> accessed 1 June 2019; Article 29 Working Party, 'Opinion 01/2015 on Privacy and Data Protection Issues Relating to the Utilisation of Drones' (2015) Opinion WP 231 9 <http://ec.europa.eu/justice/article-29/documentation> accessed 1 April 2018.

[408] In the original Commission proposal, Recital 15 still read 'This Regulation should not apply to processing of personal data by a natural person, which are *exclusively* personal or domestic . . .'.

[409] Erdos, 'Beyond "Having a Domestic?"' (n 404).

[410] Notably confirmed by the CJEU (and Advocate General Jääskinen) in *Ryneš, František Ryneš v Úřad pro ochranu osobních údajů* (n 78) para 34; AG Opinion at paragraphs 44; 63 et seq. Also see: Van Alsenoy, 'The Evolving Role of the Individual Under EU Data Protection Law' (n 380) 11.

[411] WP29 also acknowledged that natural persons who do not benefit from the household exemption, might still only be subject to a 'relatively lite' version of rules, 'depending on scale and nature'. Article 29 Working Party, 'Annex 2: Proposals for Amendments Regarding Exemption for Personal or Household Activities' (n 384) 4–5.

processing. Moreover, the fact that a social network user benefits from the household exemption for example, does not—in itself—prevent a data subject to invoke his/her right to erasure vis-à-vis the network for data uploaded by that user.[412] Indeed, the granular and functional approach to the GDPR's scope determination, implies that data subject rights might still be available (vis-à-vis the same personal data) with regard to some actors but not others.

5.3 Freedom of Expression and Information

The third derogation/exemption to data protection law discussed here already brings us to the edge of the murky waters to be analysed in Part II. Indeed, the relationship between the fundamental rights to data protection and freedom of expression/information—epitomized by the right to erasure—is a complex one. It is also an interaction that increasingly presents itself to data protection authorities, who are receiving a growing number of complaints concerning the publication of individuals' personal data.[413] Recital 153 GDPR recognizes the importance of reconciling data protection rules with freedom of expression/information, especially in the 'audio-visual field and in news archives and press libraries'.[414]

As mentioned in the previous chapter already, the GDPR actively pursues a fair balance between all fundamental rights and freedoms. When it comes to the right to freedom of expression/information, such fair balance is achieved in two ways. Either, the balance is to be found by the actors involved in a particular situation, or the legislator predefines what side the balance should tip over to. The former is by definition context-dependent and will be analysed in Part II (eg the *Google Spain* or delisting scenario). The latter takes shape in exemptions or derogations, which will be discussed in this Part. Freedom of expression/information derogations and exemptions can relate both to swathes of GDPR provisions as specified in Member-State law (pursuant to Art 85, to be discussed here),[415] or to specific provisions (eg Art 17(3)(a), to be discussed in Chapter 4).

Article 85 GDPR specifies the need for freedom of expression and information derogations. It lays out instructions to Member-States so as to align the right to freedom of expression and information (Art 11 Charter) with the right to the

[412] Recital 18 GDPR; Korff and Brown (n 153) 23–24. As will be explained later on, the household exemption liberates natural persons from being subject to the GDPR's strict regulatory framework. It does not constitute a *defense* or counter-argument that can be used to fight the exercise of data subject's rights.

[413] Article 29 Working Party, 'Annex 2: Proposals for Amendments Regarding Exemption for Personal or Household Activities' (n 384) 1–2.

[414] Chapter 6 will look at the right to erasure in the context of news archives in particular.

[415] Technically, Article 23(1)(i) also empowers Member-States to restrict the application of some GDPR provisions in order to safeguard freedom of expression/information.

protection of personal data (Art 8 Charter). Put differently, it essentially outsources the effective balancing between fundamental Charter rights, to national legislators. The provision has two substantive paragraphs.[416] Article 85(1) remains very broad, merely mandating Member-States to reconcile the two rights, including (but not limited to) 'processing carried out for journalistic purposes or the purpose of academic artistic or literary expression'[417] (JAAL). Article 85(2) is more specific and requires Member-States to at least provide for exemptions and derogations for JAAL purposes, 'if they are necessary to reconcile the right to the protection of personal data with the freedom of expression and information'.[418] In delegating this difficult task to the Member-States, the GDPR sustains the wide divergence in national provisions that emerged from Directive 95/46's implementation.[419] It also prevents the CJEU from providing much substantial interpretative guidance at the EU level.[420] Further signalling the fact there is still no pan-European agreement in this matter is the fact that a specific clarification on what should be understood as 'journalistic activities' was removed from the final version of the GDPR.[421]

[416] The third and final paragraph only stipulates that Member-States should notify the commission of their relevant national laws on the matter.

[417] Interestingly, academic expression was only added at the final stage, with the General Approach of the Council. Before the GDPR, 'scholarly research' was traditionally left outside this exemption regime. Erdos, 'Confused?' (n 375) 24–27.

[418] The paragraph lists these exemptions/derogations can relate to almost all of the provisions of the GDPR: Chapter II (principles), Chapter III (rights of the data subject), Chapter IV (controller and processor), Chapter V (transfer of personal data to third countries or international organizations), Chapter VI (independent supervisory authorities), Chapter VII (cooperation and consistency), and Chapter IX (specific data processing situations). The ones excluded are: Chapter I (General provisions); Chapter VIII (Remedies, liability and penalties); and Chapter X (Delegated acts and implementing acts). This is important, as it implies that derogations installed under Article 85 cannot take away ability for adequate redress. Also see: Article 29 Working Party, 'Recommendation 1/97 Data Protection Law and the Media' (1997) Recommendation 1/97 8 <http://ec.europa.eu/justice/article-29/documentation> accessed 1 June 2019.

[419] Douwe Korff, 'EC Study on Implementation of Data Protection Directive: Comparative Summary of National Laws' (2002) 127 <https://ssrn.com/abstract=1287667>; Korff, 'New Challenges to Data Protection Study-Working Paper No 2' (n 33) 10–21; Annex 2 in: European Commission, 'Commission Staff Working Paper: Impact Assessment Accompanying the Proposals for General Data Protection Regulation and Directive on Data Protection in Police and Judicial Matters' (n 153) 12 et seq; David Erdos, 'From the Scylla of Restriction to the Charybdis of Licence? Exploring the Scope of the "Special Purposes" Freedom of Expression Shield in European Data Protection' (2015) 52 Common Market Law Review 119; and notably, the comprehensive empirical research in: David Erdos, 'European Union Data Protection Law and Media Expression: Fundamentally Off Balance' (2016) 65 International and Comparative Law Quarterly 139. In this last publication, Erdos explains—based on extensive comparative research—that there is a total lack of even minimal harmonization or consensus across Europe in the area of media exemptions.

[420] Francesca Bignami, 'The Case for Tolerant Constitutional Patriotism: The Right of Privacy before the European Courts' (2008) 41 Cornell International Law Journal 211, 213–14. As referred to in: Warso (n 386) 494. According to the authors, the fact that both the CJEU and the GDPR are still delegating these issues to national courts, is emblematic of the European constitutional order still being 'too thin to settle many of the heated conflicts among rights-holders that emerge routinely at national level'.

[421] Recital 153 (then still 121), contained a specification at the end that 'Member States should classify activities as "journalistic" for the purpose of the exemptions and derogations to be laid down under this Regulation if the object of these activities is the disclosure to the public of information,

This strong diversity[422]—fostered by differing legal cultures and approaches to freedom of expression—makes it impossible to define the exact scope and criteria of the JAAL exemption at a European level.

Interpreting the Derogation—Both the CJEU[423] and the GDPR[424] do aim to give at least some guidance on how to interpret JAAL derogations, notably by prescribing freedom of expression—and related concepts such as journalism—should be interpreted broadly.[425] It is worth highlighting Article 85 refers to JAAL *purposes* and not *actors*, so that in principle anyone can benefit from the exemption.[426] The GDPR legislator also removed the requirement (in Directive 95/46)[427] that processing needs to occur *solely* for journalistic purposes, though ambiguously maintaining that term in Recital 153.[428] Activities may be considered 'journalistic' the CJEU explained in its *Satamedia* Ruling, 'if their object is the disclosure to the public of information, opinions or ideas'.[429] Jozwiak interprets the CJEU (and ECtHR) case law as connecting 'journalistic expression' with a contribution to the public debate.[430]

opinions or ideas, irrespective of the medium which is used to transmit them. They should not be limited to media undertakings and may be undertaken for profit-making or for non-profit making purposes.'

422 Supported by the European Data Protection Supervisor: European Data Protection Supervisor, 'Opinion of the European Data Protection Supervisor (EDPS) on the Data Protection Reform Package' 46 <www.edps.europa.eu/EDPSWEB/webdav/site/mySite/shared/Documents/Consultation/Opinions/2012/12-03-07_EDPS_Reform_package_EN.pdf> accessed 1 June 2019.

423 *Satamedia* (n 363) para 56.

424 Recital 153, repeating the CJEU's dictum in *Satamedia* almost verbatim.

425 This broad interpretation, contrasting with the narrow construction of the household exemption, is justified by the fact that freedom of expression/information derogations do not exempt the beneficiary from the GDPR altogether. Moreover, it actively invites to consider freedom of expression/information as a countervailing interest. See in this regard: Woods, 'Big Brother's Little Brother?' (n 396), who contrasts the CJEU's *Satamedia* and Ryneš cases. See also: Erdos, 'Confused?' (n 375) 9.

426 *Satamedia* (n 363); *Buivids* [2019] Court of Justice of the European Union C 345/17 [52]; Erdos, 'Beyond "Having a Domestic"?' (n 404) 15.

427 Article 9 Directive 95/46 read: 'Member States shall provide for exemptions or derogations from the provisions of this Chapter, Chapter IV and Chapter VI for the processing of personal data carried out solely for journalistic purposes or the purpose of artistic or literary expression only if they are necessary to reconcile the right to privacy with the rules governing freedom of expression.'

428 It is both curious and ambiguous that the legislator has not simply dropped the word 'solely' altogether. Something which was advocated, inter alia, by the EDPS: European Data Protection Supervisor, 'Opinion of the European Data Protection Supervisor (EDPS) on the Data Protection Reform Package' (n 422) para 286.

429 *Satamedia* (n 363) para 61. In her Opinion (para 128), Advocate-General Kokott had already noted that '[t]he processing of personal data serves journalistic purposes within the meaning of Article 9 of Directive 95/46 within the meaning of that provision when it aims to *communicate information and ideas on matters of public interest*' (emphasis added). See also: *Buivids* (n 426) para 53.

430 Jozwiak (n 373) 412; *Satakunnan Markkinapörssi Oy et Satamedia Oy v Finland* [2017] European Court of Human Rights 931/13 [175]. In a 2019 case, for example, the CJEU explained that when determining the applicability of the derogation, the referring court 'may, in particular, take into consideration the fact that, according to Mr Buivids, the video in question was published on an internet site to draw to the attention of society alleged police'.

Having said that, neither the nature of the potential beneficiary (legal or natural person), the presence/absence of a profit-making purpose, nor the medium of communication are determinative criteria in themselves.[431] Despite this apparent 'broadness', Erdos notes that DPAs and courts across the EU (including the CJEU) have interpreted the exemption so as to exclude 'commercial speech', as well as publications that pursue more than just 'journalistic purposes'.[432] He also observed courts generally distinguish between information dissemination to the public communally (eg a newspaper), versus through a database designed to enable public access and use, but on a discrete basis (eg a search engine), only granting a JAAL exemption to the former.[433] The CJEU in particular, also made very clear that one entity's ability to rely on a JAAL exemption (ie a newspaper website), does not imply other entities down the publication chain (ie search engines) are automatically exempted as well.[434] The little interpretative guidance that exists for what should be understood as 'journalistic processing' is entirely absent as to the terms 'academic, artistic, or literary expression'. These last three purposes allegedly have to be interpreted far more narrowly than the concept of 'artistic or literary creation within intellectual property law'.[435]

It is clear the European legislator's main concern in Article 85 is to safeguard 'expressive purposes which, in principle, have a particularly strong social value'.[436] This focus on *expressive* (JAAL) purposes, seems to push to the background the right to *receive* information (also covered by Art 11 Charter), which may equally be affected by the GDPR. Still, information freedoms are recognized explicitly as an exemption to the right to erasure (Art 17(3)(a) and implicitly as a countervailing interest in the legitimate interests ground (Art 6(1)(f) and the right to object

[431] *Satamedia* (n 363) paras 58–60.

[432] Erdos, 'Confused?' (n 375) 13–14; Erdos, 'From the Scylla of Restriction to the Charybdis of Licence?' (n 419) 138. The author explains that rating websites (for teachers, lawyers, doctors, etc) or street mapping services, for example, are generally excluded as well.

[433] Erdos, 'Confused?' (n 375) 19; Erdos, 'From the Scylla of Restriction to the Charybdis of Licence?' (n 419) 138. In the latter publication (page 146), the author explains that for this reason 'European law is clear that street mapping services, general search engines and databases [...] should not be shielded'. At least one Member-State Court (ie *Google t X* [2017] Gerechtshof Den Haag ECLI:NL:GHDHA:2017:1360, Rechtspraak.nl [5.8–5.9.]) ruled that general search engines cannot categorically be excluded from falling within the 'journalism derogation'. In an UK case—still ongoing at the time of writing—Google's argument that it could benefit from the journalistic exemption, was met with strong opposition from the ICO. See: Gareth Corfield, 'Info Commissioner Tears into Google's "Call Us Journalists" Trial Defence' (*The Register*, 8 March 2018) <https://www.theregister.co.uk/2018/03/08/ico_declares_war_google/> accessed 10 March 2018.

[434] *Google Spain* (n 23) para 85. '[T]he processing by the publisher of a web page [...] may, in some circumstances, be carried out 'solely for journalistic purposes' and thus benefit [...] from derogations [...], whereas that does not appear to be so in the case of the processing carried out by the operator of a search engine'.

[435] Erdos, 'Confused?' (n 375) 32; Erdos, 'From the Scylla of Restriction to the Charybdis of Licence?' (n 419) 131.

[436] Erdos, 'Beyond "Having a Domestic"?' (n 404) 16.

(Art 21(1)). Nonetheless, the GDPR remains quite abstract and vague, essentially leaving it up to controllers,[437] courts, and DPAs to fill in the blanks in particular circumstances. In an attempt to bring at least some level of uniformity and legal certainty, Erdos proposes concrete derogations for what he calls 'intermediary publishers',[438] and that 'private individuals processing for their own expressive purposes (but outside both the household exemption and the special expressive purposes derogation) should only be subject to a minimum of substantive and supervisory data protection requirements'.[439]

Finally, it is worth reiterating that JAAL derogations should only be adopted to the extent they are *necessary* to reconcile the right to data protection with the right to freedom of expression.[440] Evidently inspired by fundamental rights theory, this may seem quite one-sided from a freedom of expression perspective.[441] However, one should remember that this provision concerns the putting in place of *derogations*, effectively exonerating beneficiaries from regulatory requirements. Given the potential impact on the fundamental rights of data subjects, it is crucial that any derogation (or exemption) is formulated rigorously. Once it becomes law, an inconsiderate derogation/exemption might quickly result in a massive loophole in data subjects' protection. A narrow formulation of a JAAL derogation however, does not prevent a broad interpretation of the concept of 'journalism' or 'academic, artistic or literary expression'.[442] Moreover, the right to freedom of expression and information does not solely hinge on Member-State laws pursuant to Article 85, but features throughout the GDPR.[443] Indeed, looking at the GDPR as a whole, freedom of expression and information is actively safeguarded. The framework pursues a middle ground (ie 'fair balance'), between all fundamental rights and freedoms in the context of data processing. Whereas the GDPR in general does not prioritize one fundamental right over the other, its exemptions and derogations do.[444] Put differently, Article 85

[437] As long as they are not challenged (eg by data subjects or a DPA), controllers are effectively free to interpret the GDPR's provisions as they see fit. This might cause issues (eg regarding balancing acts) which will be discussed later.

[438] See above (intermediary liability v data protection). Erdos, 'Delimiting the Ambit of Responsibility of Intermediary Publishers for Third Party Rights in European Data Protection' (n 1029).

[439] ibid 21–22.

[440] Article 85(2)

[441] Indeed, it would arguably not hold up as an adequate balancing solution in light of ECtHR case law. Korff, 'New Challenges to Data Protection Study-Working Paper No 2' (n 33) 12–13.

[442] *Satamedia* (n 363) paras 54; 56; *Satakunnan Markkinapörssi Oy et Satamedia Oy v Finland* (n 430) para 20.

[443] After all, as explained in Chapter 2, the GDPR constitutes a fair balancing framework in the context of personal data being processed.

[444] As explained by Jozwiak, 'Balancing two fundamental rights is, in theory, something essentially different to limiting one fundamental right in order to protect some other interest. The latter process implicitly assumes the priority of the invoked fundamental right, infringement of which can be only allowed in exceptional, narrowly constructed cases.' Jozwiak (n 373) 415–16.

derogations are in fact situations where the fair balance tips in favour of freedom of expression/information by default.

5.4 Archiving Purposes in the Public Interest, Scientific or Historical Research Purposes, or Statistical Purposes

The last derogation/exemption to data protection law that has a potentially far-reaching impact on data subjects' ability to invoke their rights (to erasure) vis-à-vis ISS providers, has as its focal point Article 89 GDPR (but features throughout the GDPR). Situated in the same chapter ('specific processing situations')[445] as the JAAL provision (Art 85), this provision provides for 'safeguards and derogations relating to processing for archiving purposes in the public interest, scientific or historical research purposes or statistical purposes' (ASHRS).[446] Despite a narrower version of this provision already present in Directive 95/46 (albeit in a scattered manner),[447] there is barely any interpretative guidance on the matter.[448]

Following Recital 159, scientific research 'should be interpreted in a broad manner including for example technological development and demonstration, fundamental research, applied research and privately funded research. [...] Scientific research purposes should also include studies conducted in the public interest in the area of public health.' Recital 158 clarifies the meaning of 'archiving in the public interest', calling in particular for legal obligations for the preservation of information in the public interest. Most of such (Member-State) laws already in place do indeed govern (access to) archives and generally already have safeguards in place.[449] Statistical purposes are defined in Recital 162 as 'any operation of collection and the processing of personal data necessary for statistical surveys or for the production of statistical results'. According to WP29, statistical purposes

[445] The other provisions in this chapter are not relevant for the purposes of this book.

[446] Recital 157 illustrates why it is important to have such derogations/exemptions.

[447] Indeed, the potential conflict between scientific/research and the protection of individuals' privacy and personal integrity has been the subject of debate for quite a while already. In 1976, a symposium in Sweden was aimed at tackling exactly this thorny relationship between 'science and personal integrity'. See: Tore Dalenius, Anders Klevmarken, and Statens råd för samhällsforskning (Sweden) (eds), *Proceedings of a Symposium on Personal Integrity and the Need for Data in the Social Sciences, Held at Hässelby Slott, Stockholm March 15–17, 1976 and Sponsored by the Swedish Council for Social Science Research* (Swedish Council for Social Science Research [Statens råd för samhällsforskning]: [Humanistisk-samhällsvetenskapliga forskningsrådet], distr 1976).

[448] On the inability to predict how exactly the new exemption will be interpreted in the future, see: Gabe Maldoff, 'How GDPR Changes the Rules for Research' (*IAPP*, 19 April 2016) <https://iapp.org/news/a/how-gdpr-changes-the-rules-for-research/> accessed 1 June 2019.

[449] Article 29 Working Party, 'Opinion 03/2013 on Purpose Limitation' (Article 29 Working Party 2013) WP 03/2013 28–33 <http://ec.europa.eu/justice/article-29/documentation> accessed 1 June 2019. By way of example, WP29 lists 'national archives, archives on recent history of particular interest (such as archives evidencing oppressive regimes), and court files kept by the judiciary'.

should be understood widely and can pursue both commercial purposes or public interests.[450]

Article 89(1) requires that processing for ASHRS purposes be subject to appropriate safeguards, in accordance with the Regulation.[451] At least with regard to 'scientific research purposes', the GDPR prescribes a broad interpretation.[452] Some have suggested it is implied there may be a requirement for the research to be published, or otherwise made available.[453] Archiving purposes in the public interest can only be done by 'public or private bodies […] which, pursuant to Union or Member State law, have a legal obligation to acquire, preserve, appraise, arrange, describe, communicate, promote, disseminate and provide access to records of enduring value for general public interest'.[454] Statistical purposes are constrained to those processing operations that are *necessary* for statistical surveys or the production of statistical results and the result of which constitutes not personal but aggregate data.[455] It is important to emphasize that any processing for ASHRS purposes still needs a lawful ground pursuant to Article 6(1).[456] In all cases, the derogation requires technical and organizational measures that support the data minimization principle, ie through pseudonymization and anonymization. WP29 also suggests a 'functional separation' to be put in place whenever possible, lists a number of techniques to ensure effective anonymization/pseudonymization and generally recommends a risk-based approach.[457] Further safeguards may be specified in 'professional codes of conduct and/or further guidance released by the competent data protection authorities'.[458,459]

450 For commercial purposes, WP29 gives the example of 'analytical tools of websites or big data applications aimed at market research', and public interests are illustrated with the example of 'statistical information produced from data collected by hospitals to determine the number of people injured as a result of road accidents'.

451 The relevance of this provision is regularly highlighted because of research institutions carelessly publishing findings that enable the identification of individuals, often with the excuse that the data were public already. See notably: Woodrow Hartzog, 'There Is No Such Thing as "Public" Data' [2016] *Slate* <http://www.slate.com/articles/technology/future_tense/2016/05/okcupid_s_data_leak_shows there_s_no_such_thing_as_public_data.html> accessed 1 June 2019.

452 Recital 159 lists the following examples, in light of Article 179(1) TFEU: 'technological development and demonstration, fundamental research, applied research and privately funded research […] studies conducted in the public interest in the area of public health'.

453 Making it harder to invoke this exemption in a corporate context for 'product improvement, or 'marketing purposes' for example. Maldoff (n 448).

454 Recital 158.

455 Recital 162–63.

456 Recital 33 explains how consent can be relied upon even if it may be hard to fully identify the exact research purposes in advance.

457 Article 29 Working Party, 'Opinion 03/2013 on Purpose Limitation' (Article 29 Working Party 2013) WP 03/2013 30–32 <http://ec.europa.eu/justice/article-29/documentation> accessed 1 June 2019.

458 ibid 28.

459 Examples of self-regulatory efforts in this sphere can be found here: Jules Polonetsky and Dennis D Hirsch, 'The Emerging Ethical Standards for Studying Corporate Data' (*Recode*, 14 June 2016)

Subject to these safeguards, Article 89(2)–(3) enables Member-States to install derogations/exemptions to certain data subject rights. When personal data is processed for scientific or historical research purposes or statistical purposes, the derogations/exemptions can relate to Articles 15 (right of access), 16 (right to rectification), 18 (right to restriction of processing), and 21 (right to object). When processed for archiving purposes in the public interest, this list is complemented with Articles 19 (notification obligation regarding rectification or erasure of personal data or restriction of processing) and 20 (right to data portability). Importantly, the derogations/exemptions can only extend in so far these rights 'are likely to render impossible or seriously impair the achievement of the specific purposes, and such derogations are necessary for the fulfilment of those purposes'.

Looking beyond Article 89, it is worth highlighting that processing for ASHRS purposes is by default deemed compatible with the purposes for which the data was initially collected and can therefore also be further stored (Art 5(1)(b), (e) (*j*) Recital 50).[460] It can also be exempted from the prohibition for processing sensitive data (Art 9(2)(j).[461] Similarly, processing for these purposes may also be exempted from the information obligation in Article 14[462] when providing that information 'proves impossible or would involve a disproportionate effort', or if it 'is likely to render impossible or seriously impair the achievement of the objectives of that processing'.[463] Article 21(6) importantly leaves an opportunity to data subjects to invoke the right to object, overriding potential national exemptions, vis-à-vis processing for scientific or historical research purposes or statistical purposes.[464] With regard to the right to erasure, the GDPR does not leave it up to Member-States to decide (on how) to implement exemptions for these processing purposes (Art 17(3)(d)). In this particular case the processing for ASHRS purposes should rather be seen as a potential defence, than an exemption. Regardless of these specific exemptions, such special processing operations are still subject to the GDPR overall.[465] Controllers should still implement

<https://www.recode.net/2016/6/14/11923286/facebook-emotional-contagion-controversy-data-research-review-policy-ethics> accessed 2 April 2018.

[460] Having said that, WP29 also clarifies that this does not entail a general authorization to further process personal data for these purposes. 'Just like in any other case of further use, all relevant circumstances and factors must be taken into account when deciding what safeguards, if any, can be considered appropriate and sufficient.' Article 29 Working Party, 'Opinion 03/2013 on Purpose Limitation' (n 457) 28.

[461] See also Recitals 52–53.

[462] Information to be provided where personal data have not been obtained from the data subject.

[463] See also Recital 62.

[464] *Unless* the processing is necessary for the performance of a task carried out for reasons of public interest (Art 21(6)). For it to be a 'task carried out in the public interest', the processing should have a basis in EU or Member-State law (Recital 45).

[465] Recitals 156–62.

safeguards (eg adjusted procedures for accommodating data subject rights) and pursue the proportionality and necessity principles.[466] Finally, any derogations/ exemptions will exclusive cover the processing for ASHRS purposes (Art 89(4)).

Section 6. Conclusion—Wide Scope, Flexible Application

The GDPR protects fundamental rights and freedoms of natural persons and in particular their right to the protection of personal data (see Chapter 2). In order to do so—especially in the context of today's information society—the regulatory framework requires a broad scope combined with a functional, granular interpretation. Without such an approach, the GDPR would fail to effectively protect individuals in situations where their fundamental freedoms and rights are factually impacted. This chapter delineated the scope of the GDPR from the perspective of exercising the right to erasure in an information society services context.

BROAD SCOPE—The framework's material scope may be the most evident example of the GDPR's broad scope of application, potentially capturing every information processing operation in an ISS context. Such a broad scope ensures (some level of) technological neutrality, and is aimed at preventing legal loopholes so as to guarantee an effective and complete protection of data subjects.[467] This last motivation also underlies the broad interpretation of the controller concept, so that for every processing operation, there will be an entity responsible (and approachable with data subject rights).[468] It also explains why the exemptions—particularly the ones exonerating entities from the GDPR overall—are to be interpreted narrowly.[469] Indeed, the applicability of data protection law should be the default,[470] with exemptions and derogations only applied exceptionally.[471]

FUNCTIONAL APPROACH—The GDPR's incredibly broad scope of application is to be combined with a functional approach, looking at the particular facts and

[466] Recital 156.

[467] See in this regard: Lynskey, *The Foundations of EU Data Protection Law* (n 60) 149; *Peter Nowak v Data Protection Commissioner* (n 51) paras 46; 49.

[468] In this regard, it is worth referring to WP29 and AGs Mengozzi and Bot, all of which have emphasized that 'inability to fulfil directly all the obligations of a controller, such as right of access, does not exclude the possibility of being a controller'. Article 29 Working Party, 'Opinion 1/2010 on the Concepts of "Controller" and "Processor"' (n 241) 22; Opinion AG Bot in: *Wirtschaftsakademie* (n 247) para 62; Opinion AG Mengozzi in: *Tietosuojavaltuutettu v Jehovan todistajat—uskonnollinen yhdyskunta* (n 246) paras 71; 73. See also: David Lindsay, 'The "Right to Be Forgotten" by Search Engines under Data Privacy Law: A Legal Analysis of the Costeja Ruling' (2014) 6 Journal of Media Law 159, 167.

[469] Explaining why the CJEU (and its Advocate Generals) have interpreted the household exemption more narrowly than the JAAL exemption. Woods, 'Big Brother's Little Brother?' (n 396).

[470] De Hert and Gutwirth (n 164) 30. Referring to CJEU case law in: *Österreichischer Rundfunk and others* (n 55); *Lindqvist* (n 99). Also see: Korff, 'New Challenges to Data Protection Study-Working Paper No 2' (n 33) 43.

[471] See, inter alia: *Satamedia* (n 363) para 56.

circumstances of a case, rather than conducting a mere formal analysis. Such a functional approach is relevant when determining the framework's territorial scope of application for example. It is also quite useful in identifying the controller, particularly in light of the multiplication of actors (159–65) and the automation fallacy (165–70).[472] This was confirmed by the CJEU in *Wirtschaftsakademie*: 'the level of responsibility of each of them must be assessed with regard to all the relevant circumstances of the particular case'.[473]

Granular Interpretation—Information society services exemplify the progressive complexification of the information processing ecosystem. In order to effectively and proportionately exercise one's right to erasure in this context, it is necessary to adopt a granular approach. Such an approach is critical in untangling the intricate ways in which personal data is processed jointly, consecutively or separately by different entities, for different or similar purposes. Indeed, the field where a granular interpretation is most recommended concerns the GDPR's *personal* scope of application.

Flexible Application—Not all situations that are captured by the GDPR are equal and deserve the same regulatory burden. Two elements minimize undesirable consequences of the framework's broad scope of application: (a) derogations/exemptions aimed at preventing over-inclusion (176–93); and (b) a flexible interpretation of the GDPR's actual substantive provisions (see Chapters 4; 5; 7; and 8). The proportionality principle does not enter the assessment of the GDPR's scope of application,[474] but *is* quite important in interpreting the framework's regulatory burden.[475] As will become apparent in Chapter 4, the flexibility of substantive data protection rules is apparent throughout the GDPR (eg Art 24) and was already repeatedly emphasized by both the WP29[476] and

[472] AG Opinion in: *Tietosuojavaltuutettu v Jehovan todistajat—uskonnollinen yhdyskunta* (n 246) para 73.

[473] *Wirtschaftsakademie* (n 247) para 43.

[474] Despite several scholars arguing that the data protection framework's wide scope of application leads to disproportionate results. See, inter alia: Hon, Millard, and Walden (n 91) 224; Svantesson, 'A "Layered Approach" to the Extraterritoriality of Data Privacy Laws' (n 735); Erdos, 'From the Scylla of Restriction to the Charybdis of Licence?' (n 419) 146; references in: Lynskey, *The Foundations of EU Data Protection Law* (n 60) 10.

[475] In this vein, also see: Article 29 Working Party, 'Opinion on Personal Data' (n 54) 5–6; Van Alsenoy, Kuczerawy, and Ausloos (n 320) 67–68; *Lindqvist* (n 99) 88.

[476] For example, in 2007 WP29 explained that 'flexibility is embedded in the text to provide an appropriate legal response to the circumstances at stake'. (Article 29 Working Party, 'Opinion on Personal Data' (n 54) 4–6.) In 2010, it explained that 'not being able to directly fulfil all controller's obligations (ensuring information, right of access, etc) does not exclude being a controller.' (Article 29 Working Party, 'Opinion 1/2010 on the Concepts of "Controller" and "Processor"' (n 241) 22.) In 2013, WP29 acknowledged that smaller entities (eg SMEs or even individuals) that fall within the GDPR's scope of application, may be subject to a relatively 'lite' version of rules. (Article 29 Working Party, 'Annex 2: Proposals for Amendments Regarding Exemption for Personal or Household Activities' (n 384) 4–5.). In 2014, WP29 explained that 'the need for some flexibility also comes from the very nature of the right to the protection of personal data and the right to privacy. Indeed, these two rights, along with most (but not all) other fundamental rights, are considered relative, or qualified, human rights. These types of rights must always be interpreted in context.' (Article 29 Working Party, 'Opinion 06/

CJEU.[477,478] Put briefly, it means that a controller's obligations might indeed be lighter or more onerous, depending on the context at hand.[479] To hold otherwise would preclude both the adaptability and longevity of EU data protection law.[480]

The Right to Erasure—From what preceded, it is clear that there are not many a priori obstacles to the applicability of the right to erasure. This is absolutely necessary in order for the right to erasure—and data subject empowerment more broadly—to meaningfully contribute to data protection's objectives in an information society services context. It ensures that the right can apply with regard to unanticipated contexts and/or data. The functional approach and granular interpretation of the GDPR's scope of application are critical to an effective and proportionate application of the right to erasure, providing specific answers to (a) exactly what data/processing operation is targeted; (b) who is/are responsible for what processing operations performed on that data; and (c) do these operations fall within EU law in the first place.

2014 on the Notion of Legitimate Interests of the Data Controller under Article 7 of Directive 95/46/EC' (n 105) 11–12.). Also in 2014, WP29 explained that the core data protection principles are inherently scalable, dependent on the nature and scope of processing (Article 29 Working Party, 'Statement on the Role of a Risk-Based Approach in Data Protection Legal Frameworks' (2014) WP 218 3 <http://ec.europa.eu/justice/article-29/documentation>).

477 *Lindqvist* (n 99) para 83; *College van burgemeester en wethouders van Rotterdam v MEE Rijkeboer* (n 51) paras 56; 59; *Volker und Markus Schecke GbR and Hartmut Eifert v Land Hessen* (n 96) as explained in; Van Alsenoy, Kuczerawy, and Ausloos (n 320) 29; *Google Spain* (n 23); *František Ryneš v Úřad pro ochranu osobních údajů* (n 78) para 34; AG Opinion in: *Rīgas satiksme* (n 363) para 98; AG Opinion in: *Tietosuojavaltuutettu v Jehovan todistajat—uskonnollinen yhdyskunta* (n 246) para 61.

478 Even the 1978 French Data Protection Act already included a provision foreseeing some level of flexibility in determining data protection obligations: '*Pour les catégories les plus courantes de traitements à caractère public ou prive, qui ne comportent manifestement pas d'atteinte à la vie privée ou aux libertés, la commission nationale de l'informatique et des libertés établit et publie des normes simplifiées inspirées des caractéristiques mentionnées à l'article 19.*'

479 See also: Erdos, 'Delimiting the Ambit of Responsibility of Intermediary Publishers for Third Party Rights in European Data Protection' (n 339) 30.

480 Van Alsenoy, Kuczerawy, and Ausloos (n 320) 44. Indeed, without flexibility, '"application absolutism" might result in discrediting the original idea too, which was in itself very important and legitimate'. AG Opinion in: *Rīgas satiksme* (n 363) para 96.

4
Conditions of the Right to Erasure

Section 1. Introduction

Article 17—Right to Erasure ('Right to Be Forgotten')

1. The data subject shall have the right to obtain from the controller the erasure of personal data concerning him or her without undue delay and the controller shall have the obligation to erase personal data without undue delay where one of the following grounds applies:
   (a) the personal data are no longer necessary in relation to the purposes for which they were collected or otherwise processed;
   (b) the data subject withdraws consent on which the processing is based according to point (a) of Article 6(1), or point (a) of Article 9(2), and where there is no other legal ground for the processing;
   (c) the data subject objects to the processing pursuant to Article 21(1) and there are no overriding legitimate grounds for the processing, or the data subject objects to the processing pursuant to Article 21(2);
   (d) the personal data have been unlawfully processed;
   (e) the personal data have to be erased for compliance with a legal obligation in Union or Member State law to which the controller is subject;
   (f) the personal data have been collected in relation to the offer of information society services referred to in Article 8(1).
2. Where the controller has made the personal data public and is obliged pursuant to paragraph 1 to erase the personal data, the controller, taking account of available technology and the cost of implementation, shall take reasonable steps, including technical measures, to inform controllers which are processing the personal data that the data subject has requested the erasure by such controllers of any links to, or copy or replication of, those personal data.
3. Paragraphs 1 and 2 shall not apply to the extent that processing is necessary:
   (a) for exercising the right of freedom of expression and information;
   (b) for compliance with a legal obligation which requires processing by Union or Member State law to which the controller is subject or for the performance of a task carried out in the public interest or in the exercise of official authority vested in the controller;
   (c) for reasons of public interest in the area of public health in accordance with points (h) and (i) of Article 9(2) as well as Article 9(3);

The Right to Erasure in EU Data Protection Law. First Edition. Jef Ausloos. Oxford University Press (2020). © Jef Ausloos
DOI: 10.1093/oso/9780198847977.001.0001

(d) for archiving purposes in the public interest, scientific or historical research purposes or statistical purposes in accordance with Article 89(1) in so far as the right referred to in paragraph 1 is likely to render impossible or seriously impair the achievement of the objectives of that processing; or
(e) for the establishment, exercise or defence of legal claims.

The first chapter suggested that the right to erasure seems to constitute data protection law's empowerment tool *par excéllence*. Indeed, the right is fundamentally aimed at giving data subjects control over their personal data. Still, when studying the right to erasure, it is important to remain aware of its origins, as laid out in Chapter 2. Rather than being framed as a right, erasure was originally framed as an *obligation* on controllers' shoulders.[1] Even given the strong appearance of being a fully-fledged data subject right, Article 17 still contains the remnants of this ancestry. Most notably, its opening sentence is phrased as somewhat of a hybrid between a right and an obligation:

> '[t]he data subject shall have the right to ... and the controller shall have the obligation to erase'.

In doing so, the provision aims to capitalize on the benefits of both types of regulatory measures. On the one hand, erasure of personal data is framed as a *duty*, part of proper data management (see 'protective data protection measures', Chapter 2). On the other hand, as becomes apparent when reading Article 17, the right to erasure is primarily aimed at empowering data subjects in situations where certain obligations have not been adequately observed by controllers. It is deemed necessary to explicitly enable data subjects to invoke a right to erasure, counter-balancing the strong incentives to maximize processing in a data-hungry ecosystem. This is all the more evident when considering the fact that Article 17 is located in Chapter 8 on the rights of the data subject. Yet, it will appear throughout this chapter that the right has not managed to shake off its pedigree as an obligation. Indeed, the most appropriate way to look at Article 17 is as a central node within the GDPR where key rights and obligations meet.

The opening paragraph of Article 17 also specifies the right to erasure should be accommodated *without undue delay*. Even if no specific timespan is foreseen in the provision itself, a systemic reading dictates a limit of one month. Indeed, Article 12(3) and Recital 59 require controllers to respond to data subject requests (access, rectification, erasure, object) 'without undue delay and at the latest within one month'. This period may, exceptionally, be extended with another two months when the controller can establish such extension is necessary in light of

[1] Similar to other data subject rights. See notably: Article 29 Working Party, 'Opinion 1/2010 on the Concepts of "Controller" and "Processor"' (n 931) 4.

the complexity of number of requests. Further practical modalities of the right to erasure will be described in Part III.

As was made evident in Chapter 3, the overall scope of application of the GDPR is very broad. In light of this, there seem to be little a priori thresholds for the invokability of data subject rights. Taking a closer look—particularly at the right to erasure—it appears that questions relating to who exactly to approach (ie personal scope) and with regard to what specific personal data (ie material scope) are particularly tough to answer in practice. Yet, these are necessary steps to take before one can determine whether the conditions for invoking Article 17 itself are met. In other words, whereas the previous chapter investigated the applicability of the GDPR in general,[2] this chapter will investigate the applicability of the right to erasure in particular.

Article 17 GDPR on the right to erasure ('right to be forgotten') has a three-part structure.[3] The first paragraph sets out six situations in which the right can be invoked (right-to-erasure 'triggers'); the second paragraph defines an obligation on controllers in case the personal data at stake has been made public (right to be forgotten 2.0); and the third paragraph frames five exceptions to the applicability of the right to erasure (exemptions). Each of these paragraphs will be thoroughly examined in the following pages, which are arranged in the same three-part structure.

Section 2. When Can the Right to Erasure Be Invoked?

Article 17(1) sets out six non-cumulative grounds for invoking the right to erasure. As will become clear throughout the following pages, each of the preconditions for invoking the right to erasure—also referred to here as 'right-to-erasure triggers'—is intrinsically linked to other key provisions in the GDPR. In light thereof, this section is aimed at untangling the complex web of interactions and clearly delineating under what circumstances the right to erasure can (not) be invoked. Importantly, this chapter is limited to looking at the specific provisions in the GDPR only. In other words, this section will only expound the invokability of the right to erasure from a data protection law perspective. How potential conflicts arising from the applicability of the right to erasure should be resolved and how the right should be made workable in practice will be discussed in Parts II and III of this book.

[2] Albeit, focusing on situations and issues that are relevant in light of the right to erasure.

[3] The number of paragraphs within Article 17 has varied considerably in the different drafts throughout the GDPR's legislative process (see Chapter 2). At some stage, the provision contained ten paragraphs, many of which even including further sub-paragraphs (see Chapter 2).

2.1 Purpose Expiration

Article 17(1)

> The data subject shall have the right to [...] erasure [...] where (a) the personal data are no longer necessary in relation to the purposes for which they were collected or otherwise processed

Overview—The first right-to-erasure trigger can be traced back to three data quality principles in Article 5(1): (a) purpose limitation, (c) data minimization, and (e) storage limitation. For the purposes here, they are jointly referred to as 'purpose expiration'. Personal data can only be processed for specified, explicit, and legitimate purposes and it cannot be further processed in a manner that is incompatible with those purposes (Art 5(1)(b) GDPR).[4] This so-called 'purpose limitation principle' consists of two building blocks: the purpose specification principle and the use limitation (or compatible use) principle. Explicitly specifying legitimate purposes for which personal data will be processed, enables holding controllers accountable throughout the chain of data processing.[5] It is a sine qua non for the processing to have a lawful ground (Art 6 GDPR).[6] When personal data is not 'adequate, relevant or necessary'[7] (anymore) to achieving those purposes, the personal data needs to be erased (or anonymized).[8] In order to ensure effectiveness of the purpose limitation and storage limitation principles, the GDPR also recommends time limits to be established for erasure (Recital 39).[9] When, however, the controller can demonstrate the personal data is still 'adequate, relevant and necessary' for different—but compatible—purposes, the data should not be erased. Regardless, Article 17(1)a grants data subjects a *right* to request erasure when they believe the personal data are no longer necessary in relation to the purposes

[4] The purpose limitation principle also features in the Charter (Art 8(2)). The very legitimacy of a data processing operation will depend on the purpose of the processing. European Union Agency for Fundamental Rights (FRA) and Council of Europe, *Handbook on European Non-Discrimination Law* (Publications Office of the European Union 2011)70.

[5] Indeed, as specified by WP29, 'the principle of purpose limitation inhibits "mission creep"'. Article 29 Working Party, 'Opinion 03/2013 on Purpose Limitation' (Article 29 Working Party 2013) WP 03/2013 4<http://ec.europa.eu/justice/article-29/documentation> accessed 1 June 2019.

[6] Indeed, without a clear idea about what purpose personal data will be processed for, it is impossible to obtain valid data subject consent or rely on any of the other lawful grounds in Article 6 GDPR. See also: Bart Custers and others (eds), *Discrimination and Privacy in the Information Society—Data Mining and Profiling in Large Databases* (Springer Berlin Heidelberg 2013) 347.

[7] Data minimization principle in Article 5(1)(c).

[8] See Article 5(1)(e), specifying the 'storage limitation' principle. This principle has a long tradition in case law already. See notably: Lee A Bygrave, 'Data Protection Pursuant to the Right to Privacy in Human Rights Treaties' (1998) 6 International Journal of Law and Information Technology 247, 276. Similarly, Article 7 of the proposed ePrivacy Regulation lays down a storage limitation principle with regard to electronic communications data.

[9] In a draft GDPR proposal that was leaked on 10 November 2011 (on file with the author), it was said that such an obligation to establish time limits for erasure under Article 5, constitutes 'an essential element for the right to be forgotten'.

for which they were collected. When the controller disagrees, a conflict arises requiring a careful case-specific analysis that might escalate to an adjudicatory body such as a data protection authority or a court.[10]

2.1.1 Requirements

Explicit, Specified, and Legitimate—Purposes need to be explicitly specified and legitimate. This means that the purposes, apart from being in accordance with the law,[11] need to be clearly and unambiguously defined so as to enable the implementation of data protection safeguards.[12] In other words, the controller will need to sufficiently delineate the scope of its processing operations making it possible to determine whether or not (a) these specified boundaries are exceeded and/or (b) said purposes have been achieved.[13] Explicitly laying down the purpose(s) therefore forces the controller to properly consider its processing plans from a data protection perspective and enables assessing its actual operations over time.[14] Explicitly specified legitimate purposes further compel controllers to (implicitly) determine an end-point in the respective personal data's life-cycle where possible.[15] The legitimacy of a specified purpose extends beyond having a lawful ground pursuant to Article 6(1), and requires compliance with the GDPR as a whole 'as well as other applicable laws such as employment law, contract law, consumer protection law, and so on'.[16] Whether or not a given purpose meets the requirement of being legitimate, specific, and explicit will strongly depend on the context of a specific situation (notably reasonable expectations of the data subject). Purposes such as 'improvement of the service' or 'offering of personalised advertising' for example, have been qualified as insufficient.[17] For the purposes here, a useful rule of thumb might be to assess whether the specified purpose could, in fact, ever 'expire'.

[10] See notably below (this sub-section, and Chapters 5–8).

[11] To be interpreted in the broadest sense, also including for example 'customs, codes of conduct, codes of ethics, contractual arrangements'. Article 29 Working Party, 'Opinion 03/2013 on Purpose Limitation' (Article 29 Working Party 2013) WP 03/2013 19–20 <http://ec.europa.eu/justice/article-29/documentation> accessed 1 June 2019.

[12] ibid 12 et seq.

[13] WP29 explains that 'it must be detailed enough to determine what kind of processing is and is not included within the specified purpose, and to allow that compliance with the law can be assessed and data protection safeguards applied'. ibid 15. Recital 54 GDPR illustrates the importance of a granular approach (ie clearly delineating and distinguishing purposes) and preventing mission creep: '[P]rocessing of data concerning health for reasons of public interest should not result in personal data being processed for other purposes by third parties such as employers or insurance and banking companies'.

[14] Mireille Hildebrandt, 'The Dawn of a Critical Transparency Right for the Profiling Era' *Digital Enlightenment Yearbook 2012* (IOS Press 2012) 51 <https://works.bepress.com/mireille_hildebrandt/40> accessed 1 June 2019.

[15] As such, the purpose limitation principle aligns with the idea of 'expiry dates' that was inter alia alluded to in: Viktor Mayer-Schönberger, *Delete: The Virtue of Forgetting in the Digital Age* (1st edn, Princeton UP 2009) ch VI: Reintroducing Forgetting.

[16] Article 29 Working Party, 'Opinion 03/2013 on Purpose Limitation' (n 11) 19–20.

[17] According to WP29, they are 'too broadly defined to offer an appropriate framework to judge the legitimacy of the purpose', Article 29 Working Party, 'Opinion 1/2008 on Data Protection Issues Related to Search Engines' (2008) WP 20 <http://ec.europa.eu/justice/article-29/documentation> accessed 1 June 201916.

Adequate, Relevant, and Necessary—A second crucial piece of the puzzle is whether the respective personal data is (still) 'adequate, relevant and necessary' to achieve the 'explicit, specified and legitimate' purpose(s).[18] This so-called data minimization principle further directs controllers on how to delimit their processing activities, specifically qualifying the relationship between personal data and the purposes for which they are processed. Importantly, the adequacy, relevance, and necessary nature dynamically change over time.[19] Nonetheless, at every point on the processing timeline, all three requirements need to be fulfilled cumulatively. The moment personal data is not adequate, relevant, or necessary to achieve the purposes anymore, the controller will need to erase them. Given the interpretative flexibility of these concepts, determining their invalidity may be debatable in practice. Article 17(1)(a) explicitly grants data subjects the ability to contend their personal data is not adequate, relevant and/or necessary (anymore), forcing the controller to (re)consider its own position, and potentially lead to erasure. When the controller disagrees with the data subject's claims, the data subject will have to take the initiative to escalate his/her case before a court or data protection authority.

2.1.2 Compatible Use

Particularly in the context of information society service (ISS) providers—and today's information society more generally—cynics argue the purpose limitation principle has become obsolete.[20] After all, the information processing ecosystem has become so complex, making it virtually impossible to anticipate every potential way in which a particular set of personal data may be used.[21] Indeed, the very point of many so-called 'Big Data' operations, advocates would claim, is to uncover unanticipated information in—or uses for—(personal) data.[22] Recognizing this, the EU legislator provided for some leeway, allowing personal data to be used for new purposes as long as they are *compatible* with the originally specified purposes.[23] If such is the case, there will be no obligation (or right) to erase.[24]

[18] Article 5(1)(c).

[19] See notably *Google Spain SL, Google Inc v Agencia Española de Protección de Datos (AEPD), Mario Costeja González* [2014] Court of Justice of the European Union C-131/12 §94.

[20] See, inter alia: Bert-Jaap Koops, 'The Trouble with European Data Protection Law' (2014) 4 International Data Privacy Law 250, 252; Lokke Moerel and Corien Prins, 'On the Death of Purpose Limitation' (*IAPP*, 2 June 2015) <https://privacyassociation.org/news/a/on-the-death-of-purpose-limitation/> accessed 1 June 2019; Custers and others (n 6) 347.

[21] Matthias Leese, 'The New Profiling: Algorithms, Black Boxes, and the Failure Of Anti-Discriminatory Safeguards in the European Union' (2014) 45 Security Dialogue 504.

[22] Viktor Mayer-Schönberger and Kenneth Cukier, *Big Data: A Revolution That Will Transform How We Live, Work and Think* (Houghton Mifflin Harcourt 2013).

[23] Article 6(4). This situation should be distinguished from a controller specifying a new purpose (even if compatible with the original) for processing altogether, in which case the controller will also need to obtain a new lawful ground under Article 6(1).

[24] Obviously, the other right to erasure triggers remain available.

Compatibility of purposes can only be determined on a case-by-case basis and requires a substantive assessment of particularly the following factors: the (textual and substantial) link between initial and new purposes; context of initial collection and data subjects' reasonable expectations; the nature of the personal data and impact of further processing on data subjects; and any (additional) safeguards implemented by the controller.[25] The legislator also installed a strong presumption of compatibility when personal data is further processed for archiving purposes in the public interest, scientific or historical research purposes or statistical (ASHRS) purposes,[26] even when they are performed in a commercial setting (eg 'analytical tools of websites or big data applications aimed at market research').[27] In light of this, and for as long as the requirements under Article 89(1) are met, one may argue that Facebook's infamous 'emotional contagion' experiments could qualify as 'further processing for scientific research purposes'.[28] Importantly, Facebook would have to properly inform the affected data subjects and make sure they can invoke their rights vis-à-vis this processing operation. Given the 'intertwinedness' of both the scientific and commercial aspects of said data processing, it may be hard to identify the moment at which the compatibility presumption does not apply anymore in practice.[29]

Compatibility in Practice—In practice, compatible further use of personal data will often be a sizeable obstacle to a data subject's right to erasure. After all, a priori it is the controller alone who will determine the compatibility of purposes, leaving it up to the data subject to challenge that decision.[30] Doing so will be particularly difficult for the average individual who lacks the resources (legal, financial, knowledge, and/or time) to properly determine incompatibility. Furthermore, the

[25] These criteria were established by WP29—in an attempt to harmonize different approaches in the member states—and have subsequently been put into law in Article 6(4) GDPR. Article 29 Working Party, 'Opinion 03/2013 on Purpose Limitation' (n 5) 10; 23 et seq; European Union Agency for Fundamental Rights (FRA) and Council of Europe (n 4) 70–71. Also see Recital 50 GDPR.

[26] ie Archiving purposes in the public interest, scientific or historical research purposes, or statistical purposes in accordance with Article 89(1). The presumption of compatibility hinges on the controller putting in place appropriate safeguards including technical and organizational measures in light of the data minimization principle. See Chapter 3. Also see Article 29 Working Party, 'Opinion 03/2013 on Purpose Limitation' (n 5) 32 et seq.

[27] ibid 29.

[28] After all, this study was done in collaboration with academics in a scientific context. Adam DI Kramer, Jamie E Guillory, and Jeffrey T Hancock, 'Experimental Evidence of Massive-Scale Emotional Contagion through Social Networks' (2014) 111 Proceedings of the National Academy of Sciences 8788.

[29] For example, when the social network manipulates emotions for identifying sentiment in the context of elections, or when used to maximize time-spent on the platform, or to increase click-through-rates for advertisements. Some have raised that the regulatory uncertainty ensuing form this may well lead to the perverse result of companies conducting these (scientific research) experiments entirely behind closed doors. See: Jules Polonetsky and Dennis D Hirsch, 'The Emerging Ethical Standards for Studying Corporate Data' (*Recode*, 14 June 2016) <https://www.recode.net/2016/6/14/11923286/facebook-emotional-contagion-controversy-data-research-review-policy-ethics> accessed 2 April 2018.

[30] Paul De Hert and Vagelis Papakonstantinou, 'The Proposed Data Protection Regulation Replacing Directive 95/46/EC: A Sound System for the Protection of Individuals' (2012) 28 Computer Law & Security Review 135.

black-box way in which most ISS controllers operate today also renders it quasi-impossible to obtain a comprehensive picture of their data processing activities.[31] Moreover, the still vague and potentially broad scope of the ASHRS presumption dilutes data subjects' chances of establishing incompatibility even further. For example, a general search engine operator can a priori further process user data in order to optimize its search algorithms, though not for the development of entirely new services (unless it obtains a separate lawful ground for such new processing).[32] It is also worth pointing out, finally, that the GDPR explicitly states that even 'incompatible' further processing is allowed when the data subject has given consent.[33] In any case, the controller should still ensure compliance with the other GDPR requirements (notably information requirements) and offer data subjects the ability to withdraw consent.

In sum, this first right-to-erasure trigger might be quite hard for data subjects to invoke in the reality of information society services. The complex and multifaceted nature of processing operations will make it hard to establish a purpose is, in fact, 'expired'. Especially against the backdrop of a predominant 'big data' mentality, according to which further processing will always be justified, even just for research purposes. Having said that, there will be five more right-to-erasure triggers that might still be applicable in these circumstances. Indeed, withdrawal of consent might be the most straightforward one. If (further) processing is based on a lawful ground other than consent, the last four triggers also still remain available. What is important, however, if the first trigger is to have any practical relevance, is that controllers define their processing purposes as granularly as possible.

2.1.3 Granularity as the Sine Qua Non

The purpose limitation principle constitutes the core of the right to erasure's first envisaged scenario of application.[34] When the respective personal data are no longer necessary to achieve the initially specified purposes, the data subject has a right to erasure (just as much as the controller has an obligation to erase).[35] The basic idea of such 'purpose expiration' is not new[36] and is implied in other GDPR

[31] Custers and others (n 6) 347.

[32] Article 29 Working Party, 'Opinion 1/2008 on Data Protection Issues Related to Search Engines' (n 17) 19–20.

[33] Opening sentences of Recital 50 and Article 6(4).

[34] Article 5(1)(b). Albeit read together with the data minimization (Art 5(1)(c) and storage limitation (Art 5((1)(e)) principles.

[35] As explained by WP29, the controller cannot further process the personal data for a new and disconnected purpose simply 'by using one of the legal grounds in Article 7 to legitimise the processing'. Article 29 Working Party, 'Opinion 03/2013 on Purpose Limitation' (n 5) 36.

[36] In a 1969 article it was already explained that—in the context of computer data processing—'the desirability of preserving different types of recorded personal information should be re-evaluated continuously in light of privacy considerations'. Arthur R Miller, 'Personal Privacy in the Computer Age: The Challenge of a New Technology in an Information-Oriented Society' (1969) 67 Michigan Law Review 1089. The pioneering French and German data protection laws (see Chapter 2) also included similar ideas of 'erasure upon purpose expiration' already. See notably: ACM Nugter, *Transborder Flow of Personal Data within the EC: A Comparative Analysis of the Privacy Statutes of the Federal Republic*

provisions too.[37] In 2008, WP29 also elaborated on appropriate retention periods for user data in the context of search engines.[38] Indeed, especially with the GDPR in place now, it will be critical for controllers to put in place an adequate data management policy 'with a section on retention and destruction supported by retention schedules, which may be in different levels of granularity'.[39]

The specific reference to the purpose limitation principle in Article 17 highlights the importance of granularity in the application of data protection law. Indeed, a purpose which is not specific enough (ie granularly defined *ex ante*, and distinguished from other purposes), may never appear to expire in practice.[40] In order not to deprive this first 'right to erasure scenario' from its very substance, leaving data subjects without recourse under Article 17(1)a, controllers will have to be very precise in defining their purposes.[41] Embracing granularity in specifying purposes also greatly benefits controllers themselves, as it draws functional separations between different processing operations. In other words, explicitly specifying purposes in a very detailed manner could serve as a containment strategy, with some purposes being more, and others less, prone (or immune) to being targeted with data subject rights. This means that in practice, a data subject might have to resort to the right to object (Art 21) or to restriction of processing (Art 18) rather than the right to erasure (because not *all* purposes have expired).

In conclusion, for Article 17(1)(a) to have any practical relevance, a granular approach to purpose limitation is key. Granularity both with regard to the focus of

of Germany, France, the United Kingdom and The Netherlands and Their Impact on the Private Sector (Kluwer Law and Taxation Publ 1990) 62; 92.

[37] eg Article 5(1)(e) implying personal data should at the very least be anonymized after purpose expiration. Importantly, anonymizing personal data constitutes 'processing of personal data' as well, though is generally considered to be 'compatible with the original purposes for as long as the process reliably produces anonymized information. Article 29 Working Party, 'Opinion 05/2014 on Anonymisation Techniques' (Article 29 Working Party 2014) WP 05/2014 7 <http://ec.europa.eu/justice/article-29/documentation> accessed 1 June 2019.

[38] Article 29 Working Party, 'Opinion 1/2008 on Data Protection Issues Related to Search Engines' (n 17) 19–20. Since the 2010s there is certainly a noticeable trend of companies to define their retention policies more concretely (which is not to say they cannot still be problematic). For example Facebook (Brendan Van Alsenoy and others, 'From Social Media Service to Advertising Network—A Critical Analysis of Facebook's Revised Policies and Terms' (KU Leuven & VUB 2015) 1.3 <www.law.kuleuven.be/icri/en/news/item/icri-cir-advises-belgian-privacy-commission-in-facebook-investigation>) and Apple (Michael Veale, Reuben Binns, and Jef Ausloos, 'When Data Protection by Design and Data Subject Rights Clash' International Data Privacy Law <https://academic.oup.com/idpl/advance-article/doi/10.1093/idpl/ipy002/4960902> accessed 5 April 2018).

[39] Rosemary Jay, *Data Protection: Law and Practice* (Sweet & Maxwell 2012) 283. See notably also Articles 13(2)(a); 14(2)(a); 25(2); and 30(1)(f).

[40] Granularity in specifying the purpose for processing is also implied in the fairness principle underlying the GDPR as a whole. See: Damian Clifford and Jef Ausloos, 'Data Protection and the Role of Fairness' (2018) 37 Yearbook of European Law 130; European Group on Ethics in Science and New Technologies (n 33) 45.

[41] See European Data Protection Board, 'Draft Guidelines 2/2019 on the Processing of Personal Data under Article 6(1)(b) GDPR in the Context of the Provision of Online Services to Data Subject' (EDPB 2019) 10 <https://edpb.europa.eu/sites/edpb/files/consultation/edpb_draft_guidelines-art_6-1-b-final_public_consultation_version_en.pdf> accessed 19 April 2019.

the processing operation as well as time. Though not necessarily illegitimate, purposes that are phrased so vaguely that they may never expire should be looked at with great suspicion.

2.2 Withdrawal of Consent

Article 17(1)

> The data subject shall have the right to […] erasure […] where: (b) the data subject withdraws consent on which the processing is based according to point (a) of Article 6(1), or point (a) of Article 9(2), and where there is no other legal ground for the processing.

Overview—The second right-to-erasure trigger essentially gives data subjects the ability to demand removal of their personal data upon withdrawing their consent for data processing. It emphasizes that data subject consent (Art 6(1)(a)) should be understood as a continued licence to process personal data. A licence that can be revoked at any time.

Consent as a Lawful Ground—Article 6(1) GDPR lists six bases—so-called lawful grounds—under which data processing operations can be rendered lawful (also see Section 2.4). Data subject consent constitutes the first such lawful ground[42] and may well be the most debated one in academic scholarship.[43] Put very briefly, controllers may process personal data for one or more purposes if the data subject has consented, ie provides a 'freely given, specific, informed and unambiguous indication of [his/her] wishes by which he or she, by a statement or by a clear affirmative action, signifies agreement to the processing of personal data relating to him

[42] Consent also constitutes the first of ten situations under which the GDPR allows the processing of 'special categories of personal data' or sensitive data (Art 9(2)(a)).

[43] See, most importantly: Eleni Kosta, *Consent in European Data Protection Law* (Martinus Nijhoff 2013) 46. But also: Paul Bernal, 'Collaborative Consent: Harnessing the Strengths of the Internet for Consent in the Online Environment' (2010) 24 International Review of Law, Computers & Technology 287; Liam Curren and Jane Kaye, 'Revoking Consent: A "Blind Spot" in Data Protection Law?' (2010) 26 Computer Law & Security Review 273;; Article 29 Working Party, 'Opinion 15/2011 on the Definition of Consent' (Article 29 Working Party 2011) WP187 <http://ec.europa.eu/justice/article-29/documentation>; Serge Gutwirth, 'Short Statement about the Role of Consent in the European Data Protection Directive' <http://works.bepress.com/serge_gutwirth/80/>; Fred H Cate and Viktor Mayer-Schönberger, 'Notice and Consent in a World of Big Data' (2013) 3 International Data Privacy Law 67; Solon Barocas and Helen Nissenbaum, 'Big Data's End Run around Anonymity and Consent' in Julia Lane and others (eds), *Privacy, Big Data, and the Public Good: Frameworks for Engagement* (CUP 2014); Bart Custers, Simone van der Hof, and Bart Schermer, 'Privacy Expectations of Social Media Users: The Role of Informed Consent in Privacy Policies' (2014) 6 Policy & Internet 268; Alessandro Mantelero, 'The Future of Consumer Data Protection in the E.U. Re-Thinking the "Notice and Consent" Paradigm in the New Era of Predictive Analytics' (2014) 30 Computer Law & Security Review 643; Cesare Bartolini and Lawrence Siry, 'The Right to Be Forgotten in the Light of the Consent of the Data Subject' [2016] Computer Law & Security Review <http://www.sciencedirect.com/science/article/pii/S026736491630019X> accessed 1 June 2019.

or her'.[44] Recital 32 explicitly excludes the validity of consent obtained through an opt-out scheme (ie derived from 'silence, pre-ticked boxes or inactivity').[45] Further conditions for obtaining valid consent are set out in Article 7 (inter alia placing the burden of proof with the controller)[46] and Article 8 (setting out specific requirements for obtaining children's consent in relation to information society services). It is important to look at consent as a continued engagement, rather than a one-off approval of certain processing operations. All requirements for consent should be met throughout the entire processing cycle.[47] So, consent should not be seen as a data subject 'surrendering' (even partially) control over their personal data.[48] On the contrary, just like the right to erasure, data subject consent is a prototypical example of an empowerment measure in data protection law.[49]

Withdrawal of Consent—Article 7(3) GDPR explicitly grants data subjects the right to withdraw their consent at any time and in an easy manner.[50] Indeed, the very validity of consent as a lawful ground for processing personal data depends on the data subject's ability to 'withdraw consent without detriment' (Recital 42).[51] WP29 has explained that withdrawing consent should be equally as easy as it was to provide consent in the first place (ie through same interface and same action such as (un)ticking a box for example).[52] Importantly, such withdrawal shall not work retroactively, ie it does not retroactively render past processing operations

[44] Article 4(11) GDPR.

[45] De Hert and Papakonstantinou (n 30) 135–36; AG Opinion in: *Planet49* Court of Justice of the European Union C-673/17.

[46] Also see Recital 42 which explains that consent cannot be considered as freely given 'if the data subject has no genuine or free choice or is unable to refuse or withdraw consent without detriment'.

[47] See in this regard: Ian Kerr, Valerie Steeves, and Carole Lucock (eds), *Lessons from the Identity Trail Anonymity, Privacy, and Identity in a Networked Society* (OUP 2009) 14 <http://site.ebrary.com/id/10476908> accessed 1 June 2019. The authors argue that consent in data protection law differs from contractual consent. The latter is expressed in an instant (ie once parties have reached consensus, the contract is in place and obligations become fixed), whereas in the data protection context, consent is an ongoing engagement.

[48] Bartolini and Siry (n 43) 221–22.

[49] Illustrated by the fact that the concept only gained particular importance after the landmark 1983 German Census Case, introducing the concept of *informational self-determination*. See: Brendan Van Alsenoy, Eleni Kosta, and Jos Dumortier, 'Privacy Notices versus Informational Self-Determination: Minding the Gap' (2013) 28 International Review of Law, Computers & Technology 185, 4.

[50] Very much following the recommendations made by WP29 in its 2011 Opinion on Consent (Article 29 Working Party, 'Opinion on Consent' (n 43)). Under Directive 95/46 things were not as clear, withdrawal of consent only explicitly being granted with regard to traffic and location data in Articles 6(3) and 9(1) of the ePrivacy Directive. Some argued that a right to the withdrawal of consent was implied in Directive 95/45 all along, though did not correspond with an automatic obligation/right to erasure (Alfred Büllesbach, Yves Poullet, and C Prins (eds), *Concise European IT Law* (Kluwer Law International 2006) 36; Article 29 Working Party, 'Opinion on Consent' (n 43); Jef Ausloos, 'The "Right to Be Forgotten"—Worth Remembering?' (2012) 28 Computer Law & Security Review 150; Kosta (n 43) 251, while others were more sceptical about such an implied right of withdrawal (Curren and Kaye (n 43); Bartolini and Siry (n 43)).

[51] This requirement emphasizes the nature of consent as a continuing data protection safeguard, rather than a singular once-and-for-all surrender of control over one's personal data.

[52] Article 29 Working Party, 'Guidelines on Consent under Regulation 2016/679' (2018) WP 259 21–23 <http://ec.europa.eu/justice/article-29/documentation>.

unlawful.[53] Withdrawal of consent does however ipso facto remove the lawful ground for said processing operation(s) henceforward. Unless the controller can rely on another lawful ground for further processing—be it for the same or different purposes—it will have an obligation (and the data subject will have a right) to erase the relevant personal data under Article 17(1)(b). Put briefly, this provision includes two cumulative conditions: (a) consent must be withdrawn *and* (b) the further processing (for the same or a subset of purposes) cannot be based on another lawful ground than consent.

WITHDRAWAL OF CONSENT V UNLAWFUL PROCESSING—Requesting the erasure of personal data on the basis of withdrawal of consent under Article 17(1)(b), presupposes that the processing operations were validly based on consent in the first place. In other words, if any of the requirements (see Arts 4(11); 6(1a); 7–8; 9(2(a)) are *not* met, consent cannot constitute the processing's lawful ground and the data subject would have nothing to revoke. Unless the controller can rely on another lawful ground, the processing operations will be unlawful *ab initio* and the data subject may request erasure under Article 17(1)(d) (see below). It is important to mention in this regard, that if a controller can rely on another lawful ground for the same processing purposes, requesting consent can be considered misleading and unfair.[54] Having said that, WP29 did recognize that controllers could switch or 'fall back' on a different lawful ground when there is a substantial change in circumstances.[55]

CONSENT ISSUES—Particularly in the ISS context, one may be sceptical about the practical use of Article 17(1)(b). The likelihood of a data subject ever revoking consent and request their personal data to be erased is arguably quite slim in reality. First of all, despite (or because of) being asked to consent to personal data processing on a regular basis, individuals have developed some level of notice fatigue[56] and general indifference—or even ignorance—about the existence and breadth of the processing involved.[57] Secondly, a significant body of research suggests that individuals are very unlikely to withdraw consent anyhow.[58] The potential benefit of withdrawal will often be quite abstract, distant, and uncertain when compared to the immediate loss of the use of a service for example.[59] It is fair to say that this cognitive dissonance is further exploited by many ISS providers,

[53] Kosta (n 43) 252.

[54] Article 29 Working Party, 'Opinion on Consent' (n 43) 13.

[55] eg When a new law is adopted that dictates certain processing operations (Art 6(1)(c)). ibid.

[56] Van Alsenoy, Kosta, and Dumortier (n 49) 5–6.

[57] See, for example: Bart W Schermer, 'The Limits of Privacy in Automated Profiling and Data Mining' (2011) 27 Computer Law & Security Review 49; Barocas and Nissenbaum (n 43); James Grimmelmann, 'An Offer You Can't Understand' (*Jotwell: The Journal of Things We Like (Lots)*, 15 May 2015) <http://cyber.jotwell.com/an-offer-you-cant-understand/> accessed 1 June 2019; Bart Custers, 'Click Here to Consent Forever: Expiry Dates for Informed Consent' (2016) 3(1) Big Data & Society, 1.

[58] Kerr, Steeves, and Lucock (n 47) 17–18.

[59] Ausloos, 'The "Right to Be Forgotten"—Worth Remembering?' (n 50) 144.

primarily through user experience (UX) design.[60] In what has been dubbed the 'autonomy trap',[61] individuals are left with the illusion of choice, subtly but strongly being disincentivized to not give or revoke consent,[62] while simultaneously being nudged to (perpetuate their) consent.[63] The current status quo in the ISS context of either having to consent or simply not use the service at all has also been referred to as 'mandatory volunteerism'.[64] Article 7(4) GDPR was specifically introduced to prevent such situations where access to a service depends on consenting to unnecessary processing of personal data.[65] Chapter 6 will analyse to what extent such take-it-or-leave-it choices are in fact legitimate in light of the Charter.

Effectiveness of Withdrawing Consent—Even when—despite all the odds—a data subject is determined enough to withdraw his/her consent *and* knows how to do so, there is another important caveat preventing such withdrawal from resulting in actual erasure. When data subjects withdraw their consent, particularly in the context of ISS, there is a considerable chance the controller(s) will continue processing the same personal data on the basis of another lawful ground (but for a limited subset of purposes) and/or argue not to be capable of actually erasing the personal data itself.[66] Indeed, the same personal data can be processed for different purposes, each with different lawful grounds. One of the most likely grounds that could still be relied upon despite the data subject's withdrawal of consent is the legitimate interests ground in Article 6(1)(f).[67] This provision permits

[60] See, for example, the pioneering work (in offline context) of: Jon D Hanson and Douglas A Kysar, 'Taking Behavioralism Seriously: The Problem of Market Manipulation' (1999) 74 NYUL Rev 630; Jon D Hanson and Douglas A Kysar, 'Taking Behavioralism Seriously: Some Evidence of Market Manipulation' [1999] Harvard Law Review 1420. And more recently, specifically covering online entities: Kerr, Steeves, and Lucock (n 47) 20; Rob Heyman and Niels Van Dijk, 'Who Can Afford Users as Targets? Interfaces, Transparency and the Commodification of Relations in Online Social Networks' (iMinds—SMIT—VUB 2013) Research Report <http://emsoc.be/wp-content/uploads/2013/11/D322-SMIT-and-LSTS.pdf> accessed 19 December 2013; Natali Helberger, 'Form Matters: Informing Consumers Effectively' (University of Amsterdam) 2013–10 8 et seq <http://papers.ssrn.com/abstract=2354988> accessed 1 June 2019; Ryan Calo, 'Digital Market Manipulation' (2014) 82 Geo Wash L Rev 995.

[61] Mireille Hildebrandt, 'Who Is Profiling Who? Invisible Visibility' in Serge Gutwirth and others (eds), *Reinventing Data Protection?* (Springer 2009) <www.springerlink.com/index/P7710R0760613778.pdf> accessed 1 June 2019242.

[62] eg exploiting lock-in and network effects

[63] eg providing immediate rewards and rendering cumbersome the process of withdrawing consent.

[64] Gary T Marx, 'Soft Surveillance: The Growth of Mandatory Volunteerism in Collecting Personal Information—"Hey Buddy Can You Spare a DNA?"' in Torin Monahan (ed), *Surveillance and Security: Technological Politics and Power in Everyday Life* (Routledge 2006). Also see: Kerr, Steeves, and Lucock (n 47) 9; Custers (n 1227) 3–4.

[65] Incorporating WP29's guidelines, which specified inter alia that 'data subjects should be free to choose which purpose they accept, rather than having to consent to a bundle of processing purposes'. Article 29 Working Party, 'Guidelines on Consent under Regulation 2016/679' (n 52) 11. Later confirmed by AG Opinion in: *Planet49* (n 45).

[66] For example, because the data has been anonymized, absorbed in a group profile or because their technical infrastructure is not designed in a way that enables granular erasure. See following two paragraphs.

[67] In theory, it is not allowed to 'fall back' on this ground to render lawful processing operations that were initially rendered lawful on the basis of consent. However, it is possible that only some purposes

the processing of personal data when the 'legitimate interests pursued by the controller or by a third party' outweigh the 'interests or fundamental rights and freedoms of the data subject'. Given the vagueness of this provision, it will often be difficult for the data subject to effectively challenge the controller's position in this regard. As a result, revoking consent with the purpose of having personal data erased, might often culminate in a *de facto* balancing act (see Part II).

GROUP PROFILES—An interesting illustration of the potential complexities involved in withdrawing consent (and requesting erasure) can be drawn from the Facebook vignette (see Chapter 1). Personal data is often used to generate 'group profiles', construed from large volumes of personal data, but transcending their individualized nature. For example, based on a large number of individuals' data, researchers may develop of psychometric prototypes.[68] Once personal data is sucked up into the construction of such a 'group profile', withdrawing consent will not affect that group profile. After all, such group profiles in isolation are not personal data anymore and therefore fall outside the scope of data protection law.[69] Only when they are reapplied to individuals, will the GDPR kick in again. As explained by WP29, the right to erasure applies 'to both the "input personal data" (the personal data used to create the profile) and the "output data" (the profile itself or "score" assigned to the person)'.[70] In short, withdrawal of consent (or erasure) is not available vis-à-vis the group profile itself but is available with regard to the links between the group profile and you. That being said, such 'group profiles' and/or how they are used, might still be problematic for many different reasons that require political[71] and/or legal[72] intervention (eg to prevent discrimination).

In sum, the second situation where the right to erasure can be invoked is upon withdrawal of consent. This second trigger illustrates the dynamic and longitudinal nature of consent as a lawful ground for processing.[73] If it is to have any meaning in the practical reality of ISS providers, data subjects should be enabled to granularly

are based on consent, while others rely on the legitimate interests ground. As mentioned before, a change in circumstances might also justify falling back on a different lawful ground.

[68] Carole Cadwalladr, '"I Made Steve Bannon's Psychological Warfare Tool": Meet the Data War Whistleblower' *The Guardian* (18 March 2018) <http://www.theguardian.com/news/2018/mar/17/data-war-whistleblower-christopher-wylie-faceook-nix-bannon-trump> accessed 29 March 2018.

[69] *A contrario*, see: Veale, Binns, and Edwards (n 38).

[70] Article 29 Working Party, 'Guidelines on Automated Individual Decision-Making and Profiling for the Purposes of Regulation 2016/679' (Article 29 Working Party 2018) Guidelines WP 251 17–18 <http://ec.europa.eu/justice/article-29/documentation>.

[71] Hildebrandt, 'Who Is Profiling Who?' (n 61).

[72] Wim Schreurs and others, 'Cogitas, Ergo Sum. The Role of Data Protection Law and Non-Discrimination Law in Group Profiling in the Private Sector' in Mireille Hildebrandt and Serge Gutwirth (eds), *Profiling the European Citizen: Cross-Disciplinary Perspectives* (Springer 2008).

[73] See in this regard: Luke Hutton and Tristan Henderson, 'Beyond the EULA: Improving Consent for Data Mining' [2017] arXiv:1701.07999 [cs] <http://arxiv.org/abs/1701.07999> accessed 1 June 2019. See also: Andreas Geiger, "Die Einwilligung in Die Verarbeitung von Persönlichen Daten Als Ausübung Des Rechts Auf Informationelle Selbstbestimmung," Neue Zeitschrift Für Verwaltungsrecht 8, no 1 (1989): 35–37 cited in: Bartolini and Siry (n 43) 222.

and easily withdraw such consent.[74] While the law (notably the new Art 7 GDPR) is quite clear on this, it remains to be seen how this will be dealt with by controllers whose business-model is based on data-extraction (eg in light of behavioural advertisement)[75] or whose technical infrastructure does not enable granular erasure (eg Apple Siri vignette).[76]

2.3 Right to Object

Article 17(1)

> The data subject shall have the right to […] erasure […] where: (c) the data subject objects to the processing pursuant to Article 21(1) and there are no overriding legitimate grounds for the processing, or the data subject objects to the processing pursuant to Article 21(2).

Overview—The third situation in which Article 17(1) grants data subjects a right to erasure, is upon a successful exercise of the right to object under Article 21(1)–(2). As explained before, Article 21 empowers data subjects to object to specific processing operations performed on their personal data. In other words, whereas the right to object focuses on processing operations (and the underlying purposes), the right to erasure focuses on the personal data itself. What this means in practice is that a successful right to object, may stop one or two specific processing operations, but not others. In circumstances where there is a continued lawful ground for further processing the same personal data, the right to erasure will effectively not be available after the right to object has been invoked.[77]

[74] For an illustration in the social networking context, see: Article 29 Working Party, 'Opinion on Consent' (n 43) 19. See also: AG Opinion in: *Planet49* (n 45).

[75] This may effectively result in a balancing act involving the controller's economic freedoms protected under the Charter (see Chapter 6).

[76] In this vignette it appears that Apple effectively fails to accommodate granular access and erasure rights because, so it argues, it cannot individually find back the respective personal data as its database is not organized in such a manner. Even if one is to withdraw consent in such a context, actual erasure will therefore not automatically ensue. A similar situation applies with regard to some of Facebook's custom audiences data, see notably: Paul-Olivier Dehaye, 'Written Evidence to House of Commons DMCS Committee' (March 2018) <http://data.parliament.uk/writtenevidence/committeeevidence.svc/evidencedocument/digital-culture-media-and-sport-committee/fake-news/written/80117.html#_ftn3> accessed 29 March 2018.

[77] A literal reading of Article 17(1)(c) may suggest the right to erasure is available even if the right to object only related to part of the processing of the respective personal data. Such an interpretation might further be corroborated when reading the second right to erasure trigger. This second trigger specifies that the right to erasure will not be available upon withdrawal of consent when there is another lawful ground justifying further processing. The third trigger conspicuously lacks such specification, suggesting *a contrario* that erasure will be available upon the right to object, even if there is still a remaining lawful ground. That being said, a systemic interpretation dictates that the right to erasure will not be available when the right to object only pertains to part of the processing purposes of personal data.

Right to Object Scope—The GDPR limits the right to object's applicability to processing activities which are based on either one of the last two lawful grounds in Article 6(1). In other words, the right to object can only be invoked when the processing is necessary for:

> (e) the performance of a task carried out in the public interest or in the exercise of official authority vested in the controller'; or (f) 'the purposes of the legitimate interests pursued by the controller or by a third party, except where such interests are overridden by the interests or fundamental rights and freedoms of the data subject which require protection of personal data, in particular where the data subject is a child.

In light of this book focus on ISS providers, the last one is most relevant. Interestingly, Article 21(1)–(2) specifically emphasizes the right to object is available to *profiling* based on any of these lawful grounds as well. This may seem quite redundant as profiling also constitutes *processing* of personal data, though it might usefully stress the availability of the right to object in more complex situations such as group profiles.

Right to Object Requirements—Successfully exercising the right to object requires a motivation—ie data subjects need to give 'grounds relating to their particular situation'. The controller can always defend itself—and thus decline to accommodate the right to object—when demonstrating 'compelling legitimate grounds for the processing which override the interests, rights and freedoms of the data subject or for the establishment, exercise or defence of legal claims' (Article 21(1)). The balancing act in Article 21(1) is stricter but also more flexible for controllers than the one in Article 6(1)(f). It is stricter because, contrary to Article 6(1)f the grounds for continuing to process personal data need to be *compelling*.[78] It is more flexible because in Article 21(1), the controller can invoke *any* compelling ground to block the right to object[79] (and not just the 'legitimate interests pursued by the controller and/or third parties' as in Article 6(1)(f)).[80] Of course, these grounds should still override the interests, rights, or freedoms of the data subject involved. For the period between invoking the right to object and determining the outcome of the actual balance, the controller may have to restrict its processing of the personal data at stake (Art 18(1)(d)).[81] Importantly, data subjects

[78] Article 29 Working Party, 'Guidelines on Automated Individual Decision-Making and Profiling for the Purposes of Regulation 2016/679' (n 70) 18–19.

[79] eg technical difficulties in accommodating the right to object.

[80] Jef Ausloos, 'Balancing in the GDPR: Legitimate Interests v. Right to Object' (*CITIP blog*, 28 February 2017) <https://www.law.kuleuven.be/citip/blog/balancing-in-the-gdpr-legitimate-interests-v-right-to-object/> accessed 1 June 2019.

[81] Restriction of processing means that 'personal data shall, with the exception of storage, only be processed with the data subject's consent or for the establishment, exercise or defence of legal claims or for the protection of the rights of another natural or legal person or for reasons of important public interest of the Union or of a Member State'. Article 18(2).

do not need to motivate their right to object with regard to processing operations for direct marketing purposes (Art 21(2)). Neither can controllers demonstrate counter-veiling interests in order to continue processing for direct marketing purposes nonetheless.

Right to Object Modalities—The threshold for invoking the right to object has been lowered (in comparison to Directive 95/46), not requiring the data subject to present *compelling* grounds anymore. Moreover, the burden of proof is clearly put on the controller's shoulders, who needs to demonstrate further processing is still legitimate (see Recital 69). Put differently, the intention of the GDPR's right to object is to make it easy and low-effort to invoke the right to object. This is further substantiated by another novelty in the GDPR, which is that, in the context of ISS providers, data subjects can now exercise their right to object through automated means 'using technical specifications' (Art 21(5)).[82] Exercising the right to object through such technical means, however, will not suffice—in and on itself—to subsequently invoke one's right to erasure as well. Neither will a successful exercise of the right to object to personal data processing for 'scientific or historical research purposes or statistical purposes pursuant to Article 89(1)' trigger the applicability of the right to erasure.[83] The latter can only be based on a valid exercise of the right to object under Article 21(1), ie substantiated and not overridden by 'legitimate grounds for processing', or Article 21(2), ie when personal data is specifically being processed for direct marketing purposes.

Right to Object v Right to Erasure—As mentioned before, the rights to erasure (Art 17) and to object (Art 21) have a different scope, one focusing on personal data, the other on specific processing operations. This distinction is crucial in a modern-day ISS context, where the same personal data is often processed for an incalculable number of purposes. The right to object only prevents further processing for one or more delineated purposes, whereas the right to erasure prevents processing of any kind as the data can no longer be stored by the controller. This being said, it is true that a successful exercise of the right to object will increase the likelihood of the right to erase to be successful as well (not in the least because of Art 17(1)(c)). Still, neither right can be considered a subset of the other.[84] Both rights can be invoked and applied independently from one another, without affecting each other. A data subject may successfully object to the processing of his/her personal data in the context of so-called group profiles for example. Whereas this would likely result in severing the link between the profile and the data subject,

[82] eg by using technical tools to block the tracking of one's web browsing behaviour. In 2013 already, WP29 emphasized that for the right to object to serve its purpose, '[i]t is ... essential that reasonable infrastructure (such as, for example, a 'Robinson list' or other mail preference service) be created and maintained so that this right can be effectively exercised'. Article 29 Working Party, 'Opinion 03/2013 on Purpose Limitation' (n 5) 35.

[83] Article 21(6) does grant data subjects the right to object under such circumstances, 'unless the processing is necessary for the performance of a task carried out for reasons of public interest'.

[84] Contrary to the claim of Bartolini and Siry (n 43) 225.

it does *not* result in a right to have the group profile itself erased. Similarly, in the Google vignette, what is in fact at stake is a right to object. The data subject has the ability to object to the specific processing operation of linking name to a certain webpage. This should be clearly differentiated from the removal of either the name or webpage from the search engine's indexes altogether.

BALANCING—From a practical point of view, exercising the right to object—whether or not with the intention of subsequently invoking the right to erase—will generally result in a de facto balancing act. The GDPR, after all, grants controllers a straightforward ability to refuse either accommodating the right to object itself (Art 21(1)), or erasure ensuing from a successful right to object (Art 17(1)(c)), by demonstrating their own compelling legitimate interests override those of the data subject. Determining the relative importance of all interests at stake can only be done on a case-by-case basis.[85] When balancing, WP29 specifies that controllers should consider 'the importance of the profiling to their particular objective' and 'the impact of the profiling on the data subject's interest, rights and freedoms [which] should be limited to the minimum necessary to meet the objective'.[86] Particularly in complex data processing ecosystems and/or in light of vaguely defined processing purposes—both of which are quite pervasive in the ISS context—controllers may often try to counter the right to object. What ensues is a weighing exercise, clearly inspired by Article 6(1)(f) and framed in the controller's terms.[87] Both at the time of initiating data processing operations based on Article 6(1)(f), as well as at the time the right to object is invoked, it will be the controller who determines whether the balance of interests, rights, and freedoms tips to its benefit. When the data subject disagrees with the controller's 'balancing act', he/she will have to take the initiative to escalate the case (eg to the data protection authority or court).

In sum, when a data subject successfully[88] invokes his/her right to object pursuant to Article 21(1)-(2), and the personal data is not processed for other

[85] Lee A Bygrave, *Data Protection Law: Approaching Its Rationale, Logic and Limits* (Kluwer 2002) 160.

[86] Article 29 Working Party, 'Guidelines on Automated Individual Decision-Making and Profiling for the Purposes of Regulation 2016/679' (n 70) 18–19.

[87] The so-called legitimate interests balancing act under Article 6(1)(f) GDPR will amply be discussed in Chapter 5.

[88] It is interesting to note that during the negotiations it was proposed to add the word 'successfully' to Article 17(1)(c). Even if this was not retained in the final version, it would appear absurd to conclude the right to erasure can also be invoked on the basis of Art 17(1)(c) if the right to object was not successful. The period in between invoking the right to object, and its evaluation (ie result of the balancing act), is covered by Article 18(1)(d). In short, upon invoking the right to object (and before its validity is confirmed/denied), the data subject can request the processing is *restricted*. The respective amendment and motivation can be found in: Committee on Civil Liberties, Justice and Home Affairs (Rapporteur Albrecht JP), 'Draft Report on the Proposal for a Regulation of the European Parliament and of the Council on the Protection of Individual with Regard to the Processing of Personal Data and on the Free Movement of Such Data (General Data Protection Regulation). Amendments (4) 1189–1492' (European Parliament (Committee on Civil Liberties, Justice and Home Affairs) 2013) 2012/0011(COD).

purposes than those objected to, he/she can request the data to be erased as well (Art 17(1)(c)).

2.4 Unlawful Processing

Article 17(1)

The data subject shall have the right to […] erasure […] where: (d) the personal data have been unlawfully processed.

The fourth situation in which data subjects have a right to erasure (and controllers an obligation to erase) is when the relevant personal data 'have been unlawfully processed'. This may seem quite evident *in abstracto*, as personal data should not be unlawfully processed in the first place. Yet when looked at more closely, several questions arise in relation to this fourth trigger for invoking the right to erasure. Firstly, it may not be straightforward to determine *in concreto* what exactly constitutes unlawful processing. Secondly, should personal data be erased when only part of the ways in which it is processed is unlawful?

2.4.1 Defining 'Unlawfulness'

Within the confines of EU data protection law, lawfulness constitutes the first so-called 'data quality' principle. Similarly to Directive 95/46 (Art 6(1)(a), the GDPR (Art 5(1)(a) requires personal data to be processed lawfully.[89] The GDPR also seems to have clarified the meaning and scope of this lawfulness requirement, which should be distinguished from other principles such as fairness and legitimacy (of purposes). Fairness constitutes a dynamic safeguard—changing over time—compelling controllers to take account of the interests and reasonable expectations of data subjects. It is connected to concepts such as reasonableness, proportionality, and transparency in their broadest meaning.[90] Legitimacy is a term generally used in conjunction with the purposes for processing and implies being 'in accordance with the law in the broadest sense'.[91]

Lawfulness, as used in the GDPR, specifically refers to having a lawful ground for processing under Article 6(1). In the context of Directive 95/46 still, the term *lawfulness* was used in a broad(er) meaning, implying general compliance with

[89] In Directive 95/46, personal data had to be processed 'fairly and lawfully', whereas in the GDPR, personal data shall be processed 'lawfully, fairly and in a transparent manner'.

[90] Bygrave (n 85) 58 et seq; Büllesbach, Poullet and Prins (50) 44; Clifford and Ausloos (n 40).

[91] Article 29 Working Party, 'Opinion 03/2013 on Purpose Limitation' (n 5) 19–20. The WP29 lists several examples, including all forms of written and common law, constitutional principles, jurisprudence, customs, codes of conduct/ethics, and so on. See also Chapter 5. Also see: Paolo Balboni and others, 'Legitimate Interest of the Data Controller New Data Protection Paradigm: Legitimacy Grounded on Appropriate Protection' (2013) 3 International Data Privacy Law 254.

the (key) provisions of data protection law.[92] Now, the GDPR has exclusively connected 'lawfulness' to one of the grounds in Article 6(1). The title of this provision changed significantly from 'criteria for making data processing *legitimate*' in the Directive (Art 7) to 'lawfulness of processing' in the Regulation.[93] The new provision's opening sentence now also explicitly reads '[p]rocessing shall be lawful only if ... '. Further evidence of the narrower construction of the term *lawfulness* in the GDPR can be found in the legislative history of Article 82 on the 'Right to compensation and liability', which initially started with '[a]ny person who has suffered damage as a result of an unlawful processing operation ...'[94] but, after several iterations, now starts with '[a]ny person who has suffered (...) damage as a result of an infringement of the Regulation ... '. This change signals that 'lawfulness' within the data protection framework is no longer to be interpreted broadly (more corresponding with concepts such as 'legality' or compliance with the Regulation overall). The legislator's intention of exclusively referring to Article 6 when requiring data processing to be *lawful*, is further illustrated in the recitals (notably 40ff)[95] and satellite provisions such as Article 8 on processing of children's information in an ISS context.[96] The CJEU's case law in *Breyer*[97] and *ASNEF*[98] also suggests lawfulness within the context of data protection law, refers specifically to one of the grounds in Article 6(1) GDPR (Art 7 Directive 95/46).

The way in which to interpret the meaning of *lawfulness* as used in the GDPR bears strong relevance from the perspective of the right to erasure. Within Directive 95/46, a right to erasure was still granted when the relevant processing operation did 'not comply with the provisions of this Directive' (Art 12(b)). This phrasing was copied almost verbatim in the EC's 2012 GDPR proposal,[99] but later criticized

[92] Compliance with data quality principles was also seen as a requirement for data processing operations to be considered lawful. De Hert and Papakonstantinou (n 30) 135. 'The principle of lawfulness provides that processing may only be undertaken upon a specific legal basis (ground) *and within the existing legal framework*.' Büllesbach, Poullet and Prins (n 50) 43–44. [emphasis added.] As appears from much scholarship and policy documents prior to 2016, lawfulness is also often used interchangeably with legitimacy of legality. See, for example: European Commission, "Impact Assessment Accompanying the Proposals for General Data Protection Regulation and Directive on Data Protection in Police and Judicial Matters," Commission Staff working Paper (Brussels: European Commission, January 25, 2012) Annex 2 26.

[93] Evident in at least the English, French, Dutch, and German language versions.

[94] Article 77 in: European Commission, 'Proposal for a Regulation of the European Parliament and of The Council on the Protection of Individuals with Regard to the Processing of Personal Data and on the Free Movement of Such Data (General Data Protection Regulation)' (25 January 2012) COM(2012) 11 final.

[95] Though arguably, some confusion may arise from the legislator's inconsistent wording, referring to the grounds in Article 6 as legitimate basis or legal basis. Also see Recital 69.

[96] This provision adds another lawfulness requirement in situations where ISS are directly offered to a child under 16-years-old (in which case parental consent is required).

[97] *Patrick Breyer v Bundesrepublik Deutschland* [2016] Court of Justice of the European Union C-582/14 [31–49] para 57.

[98] *Joined ASNEF and FECEMD Cases* [2011] Court of Justice of the European Union Joined Cases C-468/10 and C-469/10 [42] paras 30; 32.

[99] Granting a right to erasure when 'the processing of the data does not comply with this Regulation for other reasons'. Article 17(1)(d), European Commission, 'GDPR Proposal' (n 94).

for being too far-reaching.[100] Indeed, it would seem absurd that non-compliance with a minor obligation in the GDPR[101] would already be sufficient in itself to invoke a right to erasure. Especially considering the fact that Article 17(1)(c) is phrased in the past tense (ie 'personal data *have been* unlawfully processed'). A wide interpretation of 'lawfulness' would imply that even if the processing currently fully complies with the GDPR, the slightest transgression in the past would already be sufficient to request full erasure now. In short, it seems to have been the GDPR-legislator's clear intention to limit the invokability of the right to erasure for 'unlawful processing' to situations in which the controller cannot rely on any of the grounds listed in Article 6. Recital 65, finally, explains that despite the right to erasure being applicable, 'further retention of the personal data should be lawful' if one of the requirements in Article 17(3) is met. As will appear below (Section 4 When Can the Right to Erasure Not Be Invoked?) these 'exceptions' each correspond or can easily be qualified under one of the lawful grounds in Article 6(1).

2.4.2 Different Types of (Un)Lawfulness

Even though Article 6 lists six non-hierarchical lawful grounds, only three of them are especially relevant here.[102] The bulk of personal data processing operations by ISS providers will have to rely on either (a) consent; (b) necessity for the performance of a contract; or (f) necessity for the legitimate interests of the controller or third parties, without being overridden by the interests, rights, or freedoms of the data subject.[103] If a lawful ground is considered invalid, the processing operation can be deemed unlawful from the start and the data subject can request personal data to be erased based on Article 17(1)(d). How to determine when these grounds are invalid, will briefly be elucidated in the following pages.

[100] Committee on Civil Liberties, Justice and Home Affairs (Rapporteur Albrecht JP), 'Draft Report on the Proposal for a Regulation of the European Parliament and of the Council on the Protection of Individual with Regard to the Processing of Personal Data and on the Free Movement of Such Data (General Data Protection Regulation). Amendments (4) 1189–1492' (n 88) notably amendment 1401. It should be said that this phrasing has survived the amendments to some extent and still appears in Recital 65 GDPR. This recital essentially says that the right to erasure is available when the processing of personal data does not comply with the Regulation. A literal reading would lead to absurd consequences.

[101] eg partially incomplete records of processing pursuant to Article 30.

[102] For a concise overview of all six, see: Article 29 Working Party, 'Opinion 06/2014 on the Notion of Legitimate Interests of the Data Controller under Article 7 of Directive 95/46/EC' (European Commission 2014) Opinion WP 217 47 <http://ec.europa.eu/justice/article-29/documentation> accessed 1 June 2019 16–24.

[103] This is not only dictated by common sense (the remaining grounds relate to processing that is necessary for (c) compliance with a legal obligation; (d) protecting the data subject's vital interests; (e) performing a task in the public interest), but has also been confirmed—at least with regard to search engine providers—by WP29 (Article 29 Working Party, 'Opinion 1/2008 on Data Protection Issues Related to Search Engines' (n 41) 15 et seq). Van Eecke et al. claim that social network operators can generally only rely on the first two, and exceptionally on the last ground for lawful processing. In: Van Eecke and Truyens (n 942) 542.

a) Consent

When a controller relies on consent as a lawful ground for processing (Art 6(1)(a), the right to erasure can be triggered when said consent appears invalid. Put differently, whenever the requirements for consent under the GDPR are not fully met, the data subject may invoke the right to erasure. Accordingly, this right to erasure 'trigger' should be distinguished from the one under Article 17(1)(b) (see subsection 2.2 Withdrawal of Consent), which presupposes consent was lawfully obtained in the first place.

The validity of consent as a lawful ground needs to be assessed in light of its definition, ie 'any freely given, specific, informed and unambiguous indication of the data subject's wishes by which he or she, by a statement or by a clear affirmative action, signifies agreement to the processing of personal data relating to him or her' (Art 4(11)(*j*) Recital 32).[104] Contrary to Directive 95/46 before it, the GDPR includes a specific provision on the 'Conditions for consent' (Art 7): (a) putting the burden of proof (for establishing validity) with the controller; (b) requiring consent for data processing to be clearly distinguished, intelligible, easily accessible, and in clear and plain language; (c) explicitly granting a right to withdraw consent; and (d) contextualizing the concept of 'freely given consent'.[105,106]

In light of Article 7 GDPR, the right to erasure may be triggered when the *controller* cannot establish that the relied-upon consent is a freely given, specific, informed affirmative action indicating the data subject's wishes. Similarly, the right to erasure may be unlocked when the controller only solicited one combined consent for both its privacy policy *and* the general terms and conditions for example. When a controller does not grant the data subject an opportunity to withdraw, consent will equally be invalid and not constitute a lawful ground for processing. This means that whether or not the controller offers an opportunity to withdraw one's consent, the data subject will always have an opportunity to request the personal data to be erased.

[104] Contextualizing these requirements, one could say that 'a clear/unambiguous affirmative action' prevents so-called opt-out systems; 'freely-given' requires that true choice be available (ie is it possible not to consent without disproportionate repercussions); 'specific' requires granularity; and 'informed' requires levelling information asymmetries. See AG Opinion in: *Planet49* (n 43). For a thorough analysis of consent's basic requirements, see notably: Article 29 Working Party, 'Opinion on Consent' (n 43); Eleni Kosta, *Consent in European Data Protection Law* (Martinus Nijhoff 2013) 46.; Article 29 Working Party, 'Guidelines on Consent under Regulation 2016/679' (n 52).

[105] In its 2011 Opinion on Consent, WP29 repeatedly emphasized the need for granularity. Article 29 Working Party, 'Opinion on Consent' (n 43). A few years later, WP29 also explained that the 'freely given' requirement is doubtful at best, when there are no real alternative services available. Article 29 Working Party, 'Opinion 06/2014 on the Notion of Legitimate Interests of the Data Controller under Article 7 of Directive 95/46/EC' (n 102) 47.

[106] Article 8 further specifies requirements for valid consent to personal data processing in relation to information society services directly offered to children. This notably includes a requirement to obtain parental consent for under 16-year-olds (unless provided otherwise by Member-State law) and a 'reasonable efforts' obligation to verify age.

The requirements for obtaining valid consent highlight the link between Article 5 (data quality) and Article 6 (lawfulness). Indeed, *informed* and *specific* consent should be interpreted in conjunction with the transparency and purpose limitation principles.[107] The specified purpose will be a yardstick to verify whether the original consent extends to further (compatible) processing or not.[108] The fairness principle constitutes the lens through which all consent requirements should be evaluated.

The problems with informed consent as a lawful ground for personal data processing—particularly in an ISS context—are manifold. Summarizing the vast body of literature on these issues, Custers identifies four categories:

> (1) people do not read privacy policies; (2) if they do read them, they do not understand them; (3) if people read and understand them, they often lack enough background knowledge to make an informed decision; (4) if people read them, understand them and can make an informed decision, they are not always offered the choice that reflects their preferences.[109]

With this in mind, it seems quite naive to assume clicking the omnipresent 'I Agree' button under ISS providers' privacy policies actually constitutes valid consent. Indeed, the vast body of empirical evidence supporting Custers's first two claims[110] seriously calls into question whether consent is truly 'informed'. In light of the latter two, individuals are also often put before a take-it-or-leave-it choice, ie being required to consent to their personal data being processed in order to be able to make use of the service.[111] Combine this with the general power asymmetry between controller and data subject and it is not hard to also question whether consent is truly 'freely given'.[112] This is also one of the key arguments in four pending cases brought against Facebook, Instagram, WhatsApp, and Google.[113]

[107] See, inter alia: Custers and others (n 6) 347.

[108] As explained by the Advocate General in *Volker und Markus Schecke GbR and Hartmut Eifert v Land Hessen* [2010] Court of Justice of the European Union Joined Cases C-92/09 and C-93/09 para 79. Consenting to a publication of some kind may happen 'is not the same as giving "unambiguous" consent to a particular kind of detailed publication'. For more, see: Frederik Zuiderveen Borgesius, 'Improving Privacy Protection in the Area of Behavioural Targeting' (PhD Thesis, University of Amsterdam 2014) 165ff<http://hdl.handle.net/11245/1.434236>8.

[109] Custers (n 57) 2.

[110] See, for example, the many references in: Van Alsenoy, Kosta, and Dumortier (n 385) 5–6; Kosta (n 43) 217; Custers (n 1227) 2 et seq.

[111] See notably the example of external applications in a social networking context in: Article 29 Working Party, 'Opinion on Consent' (n 43) 19.

[112] Kosta (n 43) 256. See also the illustrative example of a 'market-leading social networking and photo-sharing site' in: Article 29 Working Party, 'Opinion 03/2013 on Purpose Limitation' (n 5) 60–61. WP29 explains that when such an ISS provider expands its processing purposes and derives data subject consent when they do not object within a period of 30 days after receiving the updated privacy policy, consent is unlikely to be valid in light of the power imbalance, lack of alternatives, specific context, and circumstances.

[113] All full complaints, filed in four different jurisdictions, can be found on: https://noyb.eu.

The uncertainty as to consent being truly informed and freely given in the ISS context, suggests that the 'right to erasure door' is always open with regard to consent-based personal data processing operations. From a practical perspective, however, such an assumption may be too unnuanced. Indeed, even when consent is deemed invalid, controllers may still refuse erasure when the respective personal data is also processed for other purposes with separate lawful grounds (eg legitimate interests). Also, the controller's information obligation (Arts12–14)—typically conveyed through its privacy policy—is separate from the requirement for consent to be informed. In other words, consent may well be 'informed', without the data subject having gone in full through the privacy policy. Indeed, the minimum amount of information required for consent to be valid is—similarly to the other consent-criteria—context-dependent and should be determined in light of the fairness principle.[114] With this in mind, an ISS controller may well obtain valid consent through an appropriately designed box-ticking module or another technical procedure.[115]

In conclusion, it is important to emphasize once more that obtaining data subject consent does not constitute a *carte blanche* for any type of processing.[116] Indeed, data subject consent should be embedded in the data protection framework's values and principles, instead of being reduced to the bureaucratic procedural justification it has often degraded into today.[117] Explicitly opening up the right to erasure in cases of invalid consent in the GDPR may certainly incentivize controllers to consider it more seriously as a lawful ground. After all, not fully meeting each requirement cumulatively may result in an obligation for them to erase all the data. The vagueness and context-dependent nature of consent-requirements however, make it hard to establish they have not been fulfilled appropriately.[118] In light of the right to erasure, the discussion on the validity of consent may seem quite in vain. After all, the data subject will be able to invoke his/her right to erasure either way: through withdrawal in case of valid consent and through unlawfulness when

[114] Kosta (n 43) 219; Article 29 Working Party, 'Guidelines on Consent under Regulation 2016/679' (n 52) 12 et seq.

[115] Recital 32. This recital does stress that a request for consent 'must be clear, concise and not unnecessarily disruptive to the use of the service for which it is provided'.

[116] See inter alia: Gutwirth, 'Short Statement about the Role of Consent in the European Data Protection Directive' (n 43).

[117] As explained by Brownsword, consent in data protection law functions as 'a "procedural" rather than as a "substantive" ' justification'. See: Roger Brownsword, 'Consent in Data Protection Law: Privacy, Fair Processing and Confidentiality' in Serge Gutwirth and others (eds), *Reinventing Data Protection?* (Springer Netherlands 2009) 88–89 <http://link.springer.com/10.1007/978-1-4020-9498-9> accessed 1 June 2019. Van Alsenoy, Kosta, and Dumortier (n 385) 4–5; Kosta (n 43) 218. The last author explains that '[r]eliance merely on the consent of the data subject for the processing of his personal data definitely does not ensure the protection of the individual [e]specially in [...] the online world'. Referred to by Brownsword as the 'fallacy of sufficiency' in Brownsword, Roger, 'The Cult of Consent: Fixation and Fallacy' (2004) 15 King's Law Journal 224 as referred to in: ibid 218.

[118] Even despite the reversal of burden of proof. Controllers will presumably always claim that they met all requirements adequately, leaving it up to the data subject to establish the reverse.

consent is invalid. Controllers wishing to continue processing personal data (for the same or new purposes) may therefore move away from consent as (the sole) lawful ground for processing and rely more heavily on other grounds in Article 6(1), notably the last one (legitimate interests).

b) Contract

DEFINITION—The lawful ground in Article 6(1)(b), essentially covers two scenarios: processing is necessary (a) for the performance of a contract to which the data subject is a party; or (b) to take steps at the request of the data subject *prior* to entering into a contract. A typical example of the former in an ISS context would be the processing of credit card details in order to charge individuals for a product or service. An example of the latter would be the processing of address information for delivering a price offer for a certain product or service at the request of the data subject.

REQUIREMENTS—Firstly and most importantly, a processing operation needs to be objectively necessary in order to either perform the contract or make the requested pre-contractual arrangements.[119] Any processing operation going beyond the purely necessary will therefore *not* be able to rely on this ground. It is also important to distinguish between (a) processing operations necessary for performing (or preparing) the contract; (b) processing operations that may become necessary in case a problem arises; and (c) processing operations that may be agreed upon in the contract itself.[120] Only the first hypothesis (a) is covered by Article 6(1)(b). The second hypothesis (b) may arise when, for example, a conflict arises due to non-compliance and a mediation procedure is initiated.[121] The third hypothesis (c) concerns situations where, for example, a contract for ordering products online contains a provision that address and credit card details will be used for tailored suggestions and/or for market segmentation purposes, these cannot rely on Article 6(1)(b) as a lawful ground. After all, they are not *necessary* for executing the contract.[122] Similarly, pre-contractual processing operations—even if initiated by the data subject—could also extend beyond the strictly necessary (eg detailed background checks in the context of obtaining health insurance or credit).[123] In sum, to be able to rely on Article 6(1)(b) for as a lawful ground, 'there needs to be a direct

[119] European Data Protection Board, 'Draft Guidelines 2/2019 on the Processing of Personal Data under Article 6(1)(b) GDPR in the Context of the Provision of Online Services to Data Subject' (n 41) 8–10.

[120] Article 29 Working Party, 'Opinion 06/2014 on the Notion of Legitimate Interests of the Data Controller under Article 7 of Directive 95/46/EC' (n 102) 16–18.

[121] In such circumstances, Article 6(1)(f) might be the relevant lawful ground.

[122] WP29 lists grey areas that are generally considered to go beyond what is necessary to perform a contract: employee internet tracking; customer tracking and profiling for fraud prevention purposes. Article 29 Working Party, 'Opinion 06/2014 on the Notion of Legitimate Interests of the Data Controller under Article 7 of Directive 95/46/EC' (n 102) 17.

[123] ibid 18.

and objective link between the processing of the data and the purpose of the execution of the contract'.[124]

RIGHT TO ERASURE—The right to erasure may be triggered whenever one of the requirements of Article 6(1)(b) are not met and there is no other lawful ground to fall back on (Art 17(1)(d)). In order to assess non-compliance with this provision (resulting in unlawfulness), it will firstly be important to clearly identify the rationale of the contract itself.[125] Subsequently, the rationale will have to be put next to the purposes for personal data processing which the controller needs to specify pursuant to Articles 5(1)(b); 13–14. This could be visualized through a Venn-diagram. To the extent both the contract's rationale and the specified purposes overlap, processing is lawful under Article 6(1)(b) and the right to erasure is not triggered. When, however, the controller has specified multiple purposes and/or the purpose(s) is/are broader than the contract's rationale, Article 6(1)(b) cannot be relied upon. Put differently, every processing operation that falls outside the overlapping field in the Venn-diagram and cannot rely on another lawful ground in Article 6(1), will be unlawful and open up the possibility for the right to erasure to be invoked.

INCOMPATIBLE BUSINESS MODELS—A complicated and unresolved issue relates to whether exchanging personal data in return for 'free services' could fall under Article 6(1)(b).[126] This is particularly relevant for ISS providers whose business model relies on behavioural advertisement (eg Facebook or Google).[127] In my opinion, such processing cannot rely on the second lawful ground as it is not strictly necessary for the provision of the service provided to the data subject. This also appears from both WP29[128] and

[124] Article 29 Working Party, 'Guidelines on Consent under Regulation 2016/679' (n 52) 8; European Data Protection Board, 'Draft Guidelines 2/2019 on the Processing of Personal Data under Article 6(1)(b) GDPR in the Context of the Provision of Online Services to Data Subject' (n 41).

[125] Article 29 Working Party, 'Opinion 06/2014 on the Notion of Legitimate Interests of the Data Controller under Article 7 of Directive 95/46/EC' (n 102) 17.

[126] For an analysis of the issues involved regarding the provision of personal data in return for 'free' services, see: Damian Clifford, Inge Graef, and Peggy Valcke, 'Pre-Formulated Declarations of Data Subject Consent—Citizen-Consumer Empowerment and the Alignment of Data, Consumer and Competition Law Protections' (KU Leuven 2018) CiTiP Working Paper 33/2017 <https://papers.ssrn.com/abstract=3126706> accessed 18 April 2018.

[127] After having asked Facebook about the lawful ground for processing my personal data for behavioral advertisement, the company explained that '*[f]or processing the signals we have collected on the Facebook Company Products to serve personalised advertisements to you, we rely upon Article 6(1)(b) of the General Data Protection Regulation ("GDPR")*'. Facebook Support to Jef Ausloos, 'Data Policy Questions #178930139475103' (15 June 2018) 178930139475103.

[128] Article 29 Working Party, 'Opinion 03/2013 on Purpose Limitation' (n 5) 46; Article 29 Working Party, 'Opinion 06/2014 on the Notion of Legitimate Interests of the Data Controller under Article 7 of Directive 95/46/EC' (n 102) 16; 47. In the former Opinion, WP29 expressly states that 'when an organisation specifically wants to analyse or predict the personal preferences, behaviour and attitudes of individual customers, which will subsequently inform "measures or decisions" that are taken with regard to those customers [...] free, specific, informed and unambiguous "opt-in" consent would almost always be required, otherwise further use cannot be considered compatible. Importantly, such consent should be required, for example, for tracking and profiling for purposes of direct marketing, behavioural advertisement, data-brokering, location-based advertising or tracking-based digital market research.' In

EDPS[129] guidance; if the contract can technically be performed without the respective data processing, it cannot be covered by Article 6(1)(b), even if the controller specifies this in contractual clauses nonetheless.[130] As explained by WP29 in 2014:

> The provision must be interpreted strictly and does not cover situations where the processing is not genuinely necessary for the performance of a contract, but rather unilaterally imposed on the data subject by the controller. Also the fact that some data processing is covered by a contract does not automatically mean that the processing is necessary for its performance. For example, Article 7(b) [currently Article 6(1)b GDPR] is not a suitable legal ground for building a profile of the user's tastes and lifestyle choices based on his click-stream on a website and the items purchased. This is because the data controller has not been contracted to carry out profiling, but rather to deliver particular goods and services, for example. Even if these processing activities are specifically mentioned in the small print of the contract, this fact alone does not make them 'necessary' for the performance of the contract.[131]

More recently even, the European Data Protection Board (replacing WP29 after the GDPR entered into force in May 2018) even dedicated an entire set of guidelines on the 'processing of personal data under Article 6(1)(b) GDPR in the context of the provision of online services to data subject', in which it explained that

> [i]n some cases, a controller may wish to bundle several separate services or elements of a service with different fundamental purposes, features or rationale into one contract. This may create a 'take it or leave it' situation for data subjects who may only be interested in one of the services. As a matter of data protection law, controllers need to take into account that the processing activities foreseen must have an appropriate legal basis. Where the contract consists of several separate services or elements of a service that can in fact reasonably be performed independently of one another, the question arises to which extent Article 6(1)(b) can serve as a legal basis. In line with the fairness principle, *the applicability of*

the latter Opinion, WP29 only mentions consent (Art 6(1)(a)) and legitimate interests (Art 6(1)(f)) as lawful grounds in the context of 'free' on-line services.

[129] European Data Protection Supervisor, 'Opinion on the Proposal for a Directive on Certain Aspects Concerning Contracts for the Supply of Digital Content' (EDPS 2017) Opinion 4/2017 14 <https://edps.europa.eu/sites/edp/files/publication/17-03-14_opinion_digital_content_en_0.pdf> accessed 1 June 2019.

[130] See also example 6 in: Article 29 Working Party, 'Guidelines on Consent under Regulation 2016/679' (n 52) 9.

[131] Article 29 Working Party, 'Opinion 06/2014 on the Notion of Legitimate Interests of the Data Controller under Article 7 of Directive 95/46/EC' (n 102) 16–17.

> *Article 6(1)(b) should be assessed in the context of each of those services separately,* looking at what is objectively necessary to perform each of the individual services which the data subject has actively requested or signed up for. This assessment may reveal that *certain processing activities are not necessary for the individual services requested by the data subject, but rather necessary for the controller's wider business model. In that case, Article 6(1)(b) will not be a legal basis* for those activities. However, other legal bases may be available for that processing, such as Article 6(1)(a) or (f), provided that the relevant criteria are met. Therefore, the assessment of the applicability of Article 6(1)(b) does not affect the legality of the contract or the bundling of services as such.[132]

This is not to say, of course, that the ISS controller has a legitimate interest in having a viable business model. But, economic advantageousness should not be equated to necessity for the performance of a contract, especially when that contract is unilaterally defined by the ISS provider.[133] Said processing will have to rely on a different lawful ground. An *a contrario* argument—ie claiming that data processing for economically supporting the business-model *can* rely on Article 6(1)(b)—would effectively imply putting a price tag on personal data and making it an exchangeable 'commodity', 'price', or 'counter-performance'. Such reasoning would conflict not just with the rationale of the GDPR, but would also undermine the fundamental right to data protection (Art 8 Charter) and individual autonomy more broadly.[134]

c) Legitimate Interests

Definition—The final lawful ground relevant in the context of this book is generally referred to as the 'legitimate interests' ground (Art 6(1)(f)). According to this provision, processing personal data shall be lawful when 'necessary for the purposes of the legitimate interests pursued by the controller or by a third party, except where such interests are overridden by the interests or fundamental rights and freedoms of the data subject which require protection of personal data, in particular where the data subject is a child'. The provision constitutes the default balancing act in the data protection framework. Because of its importance to the central theme of this book overall—ie applying the right to erasure in an ISS context—Article 6(1)(f) will be examined extensively in Chapter 5. At this stage, only its relevance in light of Article 17(1)(d) will be covered.

132 European Data Protection Board, 'Draft Guidelines 2/2019 on the Processing of Personal Data under Article 6(1)(b) GDPR in the Context of the Provision of Online Services to Data Subject' (n 41) 10. Emphasis added.

133 ibid 5.

134 For an extensive analysis of the issues involved with 'paying for apps with data', see: Katherine J Strandburg, 'Free Fall: The Online Market's Consumer Preference Disconnect' [2013] University of Chicago Legal Forum 79, 130 et seq.

Requirements—As with the two lawful grounds discussed before, data subjects will be able to invoke their right to erasure when the controller does not meet all the requirements for Article 6(1)(f) (and cannot rely on another lawful ground either). These requirements include, cumulatively: (a) necessity for the purpose of the (b) legitimate interests pursued by the controller or a third party; and (c) no overriding interests or fundamental rights and freedoms of the data subject.[135] Either one of these elements not being met may trigger the applicability of the right to erasure on the basis of Article 17(1)(d).

Legitimate Interests—First of all, the processing needs to serve a legitimate interest.[136] Importantly, such legitimate interest(s) can either be pursued by the controller or any third party. In the *Google Spain* case, for example—ie a search engine linking a person's name to a webpage—this provision can refer to the interests of the search engine operator, the websites referred to, search engine users and the public at large. Each of these actors can further be subdivided into a multitude of entities with an inconceivable number of interests.[137] The remarkable width of this provision—at least from a 'personal scope of application' perspective[138]—makes this specific requirement almost superfluous in practice. After all, the processing of personal data will virtually always serve some(one's) interests. It must be said though, that WP29 specified interests should 'actually be pursued' and cannot be 'too vague or speculative'.[139] Importantly, the interests also need to be *legitimate*, which links back to the purpose limitation principle (Art 5(1)(b)) and requires purposes for processing to comply with the law in its broadest interpretation.[140] Compliance with this first requirement, therefore, should be assessed in light of Article 5(1) (particularly (a)[141] and (b)[142]).

Necessity—Secondly, the processing should be *necessary* for the purpose of pursuing the controller's or third party's legitimate interest. This stipulation qualifies and curbs the previous one, requiring an inextricable link between the

135 See similarly: AG Opinion in: *Rīgas satiksme* [2017] Court of Justice of the European Union C-13/16 [95] para 62.

136 A representative list of examples is put forward by WP29: Article 29 Working Party, 'Opinion 06/2014 on the Notion of Legitimate Interests of the Data Controller under Article 7 of Directive 95/46/EC' (n 102) 24–25.

137 Explicitly—but not exhaustively—recognized in the GDPR are: fraud prevention; direct marketing; intra-company data transfers; computer and network security (Recitals 47–49).

138 While Directive 95/46 was still slightly more constrained—referring to controllers and *third parties to whom the data have been disclosed* (Art 7(f))—the GDPR seems to have removed any boundaries by referring to *third parties* in general.

139 Article 29 Working Party, 'Opinion 06/2014 on the Notion of Legitimate Interests of the Data Controller under Article 7 of Directive 95/46/EC' (n 102) 24; AG Opinion in: *Rīgas satiksme* (n 135) para 57.

140 Also including, for example, customs and codes of conduct/ethics. For more, see above and: Article 29 Working Party, 'Opinion 03/2013 on Purpose Limitation' (n 338) 19–20; Article 29 Working Party, 'Opinion 06/2014 on the Notion of Legitimate Interests of the Data Controller under Article 7 of Directive 95/46/EC' (n 102) 25; Büllesbach, Poullet and Prins (n 50) 49.

141 Notably the fairness and transparency principles. See: Büllesbach, Poullet, and Prins (n 50) 44; 49.

142 See notably above, subsection 2.1. Also see: Balboni and others (n 91) 253–54.

processing operation(s) and the legitimate interests pursued. It implies a qualitative assessment of whether the controller's and/or third party's interests cannot be achieved without the relevant processing, or indeed through 'less intrusive processing'.[143] For example, while 'service improvements' may constitute a genuine and legitimate interest, it will generally not be necessary to process *personal* data in order to pursue it.[144] An advertising-based business model may constitute a legitimate interest to process personal data, but processing should still be necessary and proportionate.[145]

Overriding Interests—The last component in Article 6(1)f requires the legitimate interests of the controller and/or third parties *not* to be overridden by the 'interests or fundamental rights and freedoms of the data subject'. It is this requirement that turns the last lawful ground into a de facto balancing act. Any attempt at listing potential interests, rights, or freedoms of the data subject would be in vain. According to WP29, such a list would even be larger than that of the controller(s) or third parties on the other side of the scale.[146] Necessarily, therefore, how the scale will tip in any given situation inherently requires a case-by-case analysis.[147] It is safe to say at this stage already, that the more proactive a controller is in furthering data protection—notably having due regard of the accountability principle—the more likely its interests will not be overridden.[148] The more processing operations expand in width (eg cross-combining) and in depth (eg more detailed), the higher the likelihood the scale will tip in the data subject's favour.[149] Elements such as

143 ibid 253. Also see Chapter 5.

144 Specifically in the context of search engines, WP29 further elaborated on the 'necessity' for processing *personal* data for the purposes of achieving legitimate interests such as, for example: system security, fraud prevention, accounting, and personalized advertising. Article 29 Working Party, 'Opinion 1/2008 on Data Protection Issues Related to Search Engines' (n 17) 17–18.

145 Monitoring behaviour and combining data from multiple sources in order to treat the data subject differently, for example, was said not to be lawful under the legitimate interests provision by the Dutch DPA. College Bescherming Persoonsgegevens, 'Investigation into the Combining of Personal Data by Google—Report of Definitive Findings' (Dutch Data Protection Authority 2013) z2013-00194 54 <https://cbpweb.nl/sites/default/files/downloads/mijn_privacy/en_rap_2013-google-privacypolicy.pdf> 88.

146 Article 29 Working Party, 'Opinion 06/2014 on the Notion of Legitimate Interests of the Data Controller under Article 7 of Directive 95/46/EC' (n 102) 20.

147 The following chapter will thoroughly investigate how to go about this case-by-case balancing exercise.

148 See eg: Balboni and others (n 91) 252; Article 29 Working Party, 'Opinion 06/2014 on the Notion of Legitimate Interests of the Data Controller under Article 7 of Directive 95/46/EC' (n 102) 24; 43–44 emphasizing the need for interests to be sufficiently articulated.

149 See for example the regulatory upheaval following the (change in) practices of tech giants such as Google (notably the company's move to combine personal data across their services. College Bescherming Persoonsgegevens (n 145); CNIL, 'CNIL Review of Google's New Privacy Policy: Incomplete Information and Uncontrolled Combination of Data across Services' (16 October 2012) <www.cnil.fr/english/news-and-events/news/article/googles-new-privacy-policy-incomplete-information-and-uncontrolled-combination-of-data-across-ser/> accessed 1 June 2019; Article 29 Working Party, 'Letter Addressed to Google' (16 October 2012) <http://ec.europa.eu/justice/article-29/documentation> accessed 1 June 2019; Article 29 Working Party to Larry Page, 'Google Privacy Policy' (23 September 2014) <http://ec.europa.eu/justice/article-29/documentation>) and Facebook (notably the company's tracking practices. Statement, 'Common Statement by the Contact Group of the Data Protection Authorities of The Netherlands, France, Spain, Hamburg and

reasonable expectations and the trivial or compelling nature of interests involved will also play a decisive role.[150]

RIGHT-TO-ERASURE TRIGGER—In short, the right to erasure will be triggered when the controller and/or third parties (a) have no legitimate interest in processing personal data; and/or (b) the processing is not necessary to achieve their legitimate interest(s); and/or (c) those interests are overridden by the interests, fundamental rights, or freedoms of the data subject. Particularly the last two requirements are very context-dependent and result in a de facto balancing act. In many situations such a balancing act will be straightforward to make, as one or more of the criteria are clearly not met (eg the processing operations are manifestly disproportionate and/or the underlying interests illegal). Other cases may be less straightforward and necessitate a careful assessment to be made. In any case, relying on Article 6(1)(f) as a lawful ground implies a strong(er) responsibility for controllers to proactively comply with data protection obligations and accommodate data subject rights. As a result, the right to erasure will be hard or impossible to invoke in only a small subset of situations where data processing is based on Article 6(1)(f) (ie in cases where there is a wish to continue processing despite contrary wishes of the data subject). In light of the complexity of these particular situations, Chapter 5 will provide more clarity on how exactly to go about this Article 6(1)(f) balancing act.

2.4.3 Article 5 Principles

THEORY V REALITY—As explained before, Article 17(1)(d) only triggers the right to erasure when the respective processing operation(s) cannot rely on a lawful ground under Article 6(1) (anymore). In other words, non-compliance with one or more of the principles in Article 5 does not in itself trigger the applicability of the right to erasure under Article 17(1)(d), even though the processing itself will still be illegal. Theoretically, an operation may have a lawful ground, while still breaching one or more of the Article 5 principles. For example, a processing operation rendered lawful by the data subject's consent can still run afoul of the data minimization principle (Art 5(1)(c)) or the integrity and confidentiality requirements (Art 5(1)(f)). In reality however—especially in the context of ISS—a violation of one or

Belgium' (4 December 2015) <www.privacycommission.be/sites/privacycommission/files/documents/Common%20Statement%20Facebook%20-%20final%20-withOUT%20signatures.pdf> accessed 1 June 2019). Van Alsenoy explains that '[w]hile a "general purpose" search engine might be able to avail itself of article 7(f) [Directive 95/46, now Art 6(1)(f) GDPR] to engage in the indiscriminate collection of data on the web, a search engine dedicated to people searches using facial recognition arguably can't. Such service providers may reasonably be expected to verify compliance with all data protection requirements prior to making the service available to the public at large.' In: Brendan Van Alsenoy, 'The Evolving Role of the Individual Under EU Data Protection Law' (KU Leuven—CiTiP 2015) Working Paper 31 <http://papers.ssrn.com/abstract=2641680> accessed 1 June 2019.

[150] Recital 47; Article 29 Working Party, 'Opinion 06/2014 on the Notion of Legitimate Interests of the Data Controller under Article 7 of Directive 95/46/EC' (n 102) 26.

more principles under Article 5 will often lead to a lack of lawfulness under Article 6. Non-compliance with Article 5, therefore, can indirectly trigger the invokability of the right to erasure.

ARTICLE 5 PRINCIPLES—In light of the above, it makes sense to briefly elucidate how non-compliance with either one of the Article 5 principles may relate to (the lack of) either one of the three lawful grounds discussed before.

- *Article 5(1)a* lays down the requirements of lawfulness, fairness, and transparency. As mentioned before (see section 2.4.1), the first requirement refers to compliance with Article 6 in general. One may interpret this as Article 6 being a subset of Article 5, occurring sequentially later—if not also situated lower hierarchically.[151] Non-compliance with the fairness principle, if it can be established, will render it very unlikely that the processing can still rely on a lawful ground, particularly Article 6(1)(f) (legitimate interests). Fairness, after all, constitutes the lens through which one needs to assess and apply the lawful grounds in Article 6.[152] Similarly, non-compliance with the transparency principle will render it very hard to still claim a lawful ground. Inadequate transparency may result in consent not to be 'informed' or failure to set reasonable expectations leading to an imbalance under Article 6(1)f. Yet, the vagueness and elasticity of fairness and transparency render it quite hard to demonstrate them being breached in practice (apart from manifest violations).
- Apart from the general, overarching principles in Article 5(1)(a), the purpose limitation principle in *Article 5(1)(b)* arguably holds the most direct link with Article 6. By definition, lawful grounds relate to a specific processing purpose. In other words, no lawful ground can be relied upon for processing operations that have no (adequately) specified purpose. Consent (Art 6(1)(a)) needs to be specific, Article 6(1)(b) explicitly connects the processing to the specific purpose of performing/preparing a contract, and Article 6(1)(f) also requires processing to be constrained to what is 'necessary for the purposes of the legitimate interests'. Failure to provide for a (sufficiently) specific, explicit and legitimate purpose[153] will therefore render it near-to-impossible for a processing operation to still be lawful. Failure to comply with the use limitation

[151] Such a reading could also be deduced from CJEU caselaw, explaining 'all processing of personal data must comply, first, with the principles relating to data quality set out in Article 6 of the directive and, second, with one of the criteria for making data processing legitimate listed in Article 7'. *Österreichischer Rundfunk and others* [2003] Court of Justice of the European Union Joined Cases C-465/00, C-138/01 and C-139/01 [68] para 65.

[152] It should be said that processing could be considered fair a priori, but appear unfair at a later stage, upon the data subject invoking his/her right to erasure/object. Invoking data subject rights effectively triggers an *ex post*, more contextualized and individualized balancing act. This will amply be discussed in the following Chapter (5). Also see: Clifford and Ausloos (n 40) 34.

[153] Explained in more detail in subsection 2.1. The difference between legitimate *purpose* and legitimate *interests* will be discussed in Chapter 5.

principle (ie 'compatible use'), in turn, will also result in a lack of lawfulness.[154] At least, in theory. In reality, the interpretative leeway of both Articles 5 and 6 may result in a controller claiming lawfulness under Article 6(1)(f), while not having explicitly specified the purpose for processing.

- The other Article 5 principles—ie data minimization, accuracy, storage limitation, integrity, and confidentiality—less obviously relate to the lawful grounds in Article 6. However, non-compliance with either one of them will generally correspond with the lack—or disappearance—of lawfulness. This is particularly the case where Article 6(1)(f) is relied upon, requiring the controller to take a proactive role in making sure all data protection principles and obligations are adequately complied with in order to ensure a balanced outcome. When consent is purported to be the lawful ground, non-compliance with the data minimization principle (ie 'over-processing') and storage limitation (ie exceeding the agreed-upon duration of processing) will be the most evident signals that the lawful ground is not valid (anymore). Non-compliance with the accuracy and storage limitation principles will be main indicators for unlawfulness when Article 6(1)(b) is relied upon.

RELEVANCE—The distinction between non-compliance with any of the principles in Article 5 and unlawfulness under Article 6 may seem quite academic/theoretical. Indeed, in practice both provisions ought to be read conjunctively.[155] A processing operation will have to adhere to both provisions in order to be considered legal, ie in compliance with data protection law overall. Yet, from the perspective of the right to erasure's invokability, the distinction remains important. Article 17(1)(d), after all, is only triggered when the respective processing operation lacks a lawful ground (irrespective of compliance with Article 5). In order to substantiate one's request to have personal data erased, it is important therefore to use Article 6 as the main point of reference. The principles in Article 5 will generally constitute important elements/arguments to demonstrate the lack/presence of a lawful ground, as was made clear in this subsection. Having said that, non-compliance with any of the Article 5 principles will often result in the right to erasure to be applicable in one way or another. Directly in case of violating the compatible use requirement (ie subset of the purpose limitation principle) or storage limitation principle on the basis of Article 17(1)(a) or indirectly via the right to object (Art 17(1)(c)).

[154] As explained before, non-compatible further use of personal data should be treated as a new processing operation which—according to WP29—cannot be rendered lawful by simply relying on a new lawful ground. Article 29 Working Party, 'Opinion 03/2013 on Purpose Limitation' (n 5) 36. Article 6(4), however, specifies that such 'incompatible' further use may still be lawful when based on data subject consent (or on an EU or Member-State law which constitutes a necessary and proportionate measure in a democratic society to safeguard the objectives referred to in Article 23(1)).

[155] De Hert and Papakonstantinou (n 30) 135; Gutwirth, 'Short Statement about the Role of Consent in the European Data Protection Directive' (n 43).

2.4.4 Conflating the Right to Object with the Right to Erasure

The requirement for having a lawful ground is inherently connected to a specific processing operation. The data subject consents to, or the controller claims necessity of a specific processing operation to achieve a specific purpose. With this in mind, the legislator seems to confound the right to object and the right to erasure. As mentioned amply before (subsection 2.3 and also Chapter 2), the key distinction between both rights is that the right to erasure focuses on *data*, whereas the right to object focuses on *processing operations*. In light of the multiple ways in which the same personal data is processed (for different purposes and/or by different entities), unlawfulness of any one of these operations does not necessarily imply unlawfulness of the others. Applying the right to erasure when only one specific processing operation is deemed unlawful may seem disproportionate as it would prevent that same personal data from being lawfully processed for other purposes and/or by other entities.

- Example 1: Take the Google vignette for example. When entering a high-profile politician's name, a search engine lists links to articles on a well-reported fraud case involving the individual. Such a case would generally be considered to be lawful under Article 6(1)(f).
- Example 1bis: Imagine now that the search engine builds upon knowledge accumulated through the connection it makes between search terms and results for advertisement purposes. In other words, the politician could be sent personalized advertisements on reputation managers, legal aid, etc. The lawfulness for such processing operations is questionable. If indeed such processing is deemed unlawful under Article 6(1)(f) or the politician objects to such processing, does this also give him the right to have the link erased between his name and the newspaper articles. ie should the unlawfulness of one processing operation lead to the applicability of the right to erasure to all processing operations involving that data and hence also affecting lawful uses?
- Example 2: Alice uploads pictures of a recent city trip to Amsterdam in a shared folder on Google Photos or Apple Photo Stream. Considered to be a processor with regard to the storage of those pictures (Alice being the controller), Google/Apple also offers value-added services. These rely on analysing the pictures in order to, for example, recognize faces or categorize them according to their setting (eg mountains, city, beach). Necessarily, the facial recognition algorithms will identify people appearing in the background of pictures taken in public spaces. For example, in the background of Alice's family picture, Google/Apple may identify Bob exiting an establishment in Amsterdam's red-light district. Does this constitute an unlawful processing operation? And if so, can Bob request that picture to be erased altogether?
- Example 2bis: Consider now that Google/Apple develop an algorithm—used only internally—which analyses people appearing in pictures in order to

determine ethnic diversity on their platform. Strong claims can be made that such processing operation is unlawful, even if the uploader consented to it (as the processing also involves sensitive personal data of others). Does the unlawfulness of this one particular processing operation imply that any individual appearing on the picture can request the erasure altogether?

These examples illustrate that, specific real-life cases can be tough to resolve. Expecting data to be erased entirely, when only one specific processing operation lacks a lawful ground would seem disproportionate. A more nuanced—maybe even teleological—approach would be to only enable the right to erasure when *all* processing operations (if there are more than one) in a given context are unlawful. Or, to only grant the right to erasure when the primary processing operation is unlawful (the linking between name and link in Example 1 and the hosting of the picture in Example 2). In other situations, the right to object or blocking may be more appropriate (see Part III).

2.5 Legal Obligation

Article 17(1)

The data subject shall have the right to [. . .] erasure [. . .] where: (e) the personal data have to be erased for compliance with a legal obligation in Union or Member State law to which the controller is subject.

Data subjects will have a right to erasure—and controllers will have an obligation to erase—when such erasure is required in order to comply with a legal obligation in EU or Member-State law to which the controller is subject. This fifth trigger for the invokability of Article 17 can be broken down into three components: (a) necessity; (b) a legal obligation; (c) to which the controller is subject.

NECESSITY—Even though Article 17(1)(e) does not explicitly use the word, clearly it implies some level of necessity or urgency. Indeed, the right to erasure is only triggered when 'personal data *have to* be erased for compliance with a legal obligation'.[156] In other words, the legal obligation cannot by complied with, without the controller erasing the personal data. Necessity can ensue from erasure being either implied or directly ordered by the legal obligation itself. As such, 'necessity' in Article 17(1)(e) could be considered a softer counterpart to Article 6(1)(c), which renders lawful processing which 'is necessary for compliance with a legal obligation to which the controller is subject'. The slight deviation between both provisions illustrates the GDPR's defensive position towards personal data

[156] Emphasis added.

processing. Either 'processing' *or* 'erasure' of personal data can be considered *necessary* to comply with a legal obligation. When a legal obligation is relied upon to render processing operations lawful, the language and subsequent paragraphs in Article 6[157] as well as other GDPR provisions (notably the accountability principle in Article 5(2)) suggest stricter scrutiny of what is necessary (than when a legal obligation is relied upon for requesting erasure).

Legal Obligation—In order for Article 17(1)(e) to apply, the erasure of personal data will have to be necessary to comply with a legal obligation. Contrary to Article 6,[158] the GDPR remains quite vague on what such a legal obligation should look like, implying a broader interpretation.[159] One can think, for example, of Article 6(1) in the ePrivacy Directive,[160] Article 33 in the Regulation on the statute and funding of European political parties and European political foundations,[161] Article 14(6) of the IMI Regulation,[162] or Article 4(4) in the Council Directive on control of the acquisition and possession of weapons.[163,164] This fifth right to erasure trigger appears quite redundant at first sight; it seems evident that a controller should erase personal data when a legal provision obliges it to do so. Still, Article 17(1)e does provide some added value, besides stating the obvious. In some

[157] Article 6(2)–(3) specifying modalities for lawfulness in light of necessity for compliance with a legal obligation.

[158] Article 6(1)(c)(*j*) (2)–(3). It is not unlikely that the same provision rendering lawful a processing operation under Article 6(1)(c) also includes the trigger for Article 17(1)(e) (eg by defining strict storage periods).

[159] Any attempt at listing them would be in vain. Suffice to say that such legal provisions defining—or implying—an obligation to erase personal data are scattered throughout EU and Member State legislations.

[160] 'Traffic data relating to subscribers and users processed and stored by the provider of a public communications network or publicly available electronic communications service must be erased or made anonymous when it is no longer needed for the purpose of the transmission of a communication . . . '.

[161] Specifically paragraph 4: 'The Member States and independent bodies or experts authorised to audit accounts shall use the personal data they receive only in order to exercise control over the financing of European political parties and European political foundations. They shall erase those personal data in accordance with applicable national law after transmission pursuant to Article 28.' Regulation (EU, Euratom) No 1141/2014 of the European Parliament and of the Council of 22 October 2014 on the statute and funding of European political parties and European political foundations.

[162] Article 14 deals with Retention of personal data and its sixth paragraph specifies that '[t]he Commission shall ensure by technical means the blocking and deletion of personal data and their retrieval in accordance with paragraph 3'. Regulation (EU) No 1024/2012 of the European Parliament and of the Council of 25 October 2012 on administrative cooperation through the Internal Market Information System and repealing Commission Decision 2008/49/EC ('the IMI Regulation') Text with EEA relevance 2012 (OJ L).

[163] '[. . .] Member States shall ensure that the personal data are deleted from the data-filing systems upon expiry of the periods specified in the second and third subparagraphs. [. . .]' Council Directive of 18 June 1991 on control of the acquisition and possession of weapons (91/477/EEC).

[164] In Belgian law, one can refer to Article 13 of the environmental protection law, for example (25 APRIL 2014—Wetboek van inspectie, preventie, vaststelling en bestraffing van milieumisdrijven, en milieuaansprakelijkheid). This provision permits video recording devices for investigative—ie monitoring/discovering infringements—purposes, but clearly delineates the boundaries for which it can be used, especially when personal data is involved. Criminal clean slate laws also constitute informative examples. See for example Articles 619 *et seq 16 december 1808—Wetboek van strafvordering (Boek II, Titel VII)*. See in the same vein also: André Holleaux, 'La Loi Du 6 Janvier 1978 Sur l'informatique et Les Libertés-I' (1978) 31 la Revue administrative 38–39.

cases, a controller could bypass a duty to erase personal data (ensuing from a legal obligation outside the GDPR) by invoking lawfulness of further processing under the GDPR. Article 17(1)e explicitly provides data subjects the ammunition to request erasure of their personal data nonetheless.

To which the Controller Is Subject—Finally, Article 17(1)(e) requires the relevant legal obligation (ordering or implying erasure) to be applicable to the controller. This may seem quite evident in the abstract but could raise questions in practice. What about expungement laws for criminal records for example? Even though not directly subject to such laws, should search engines, publishers, or social network users, remove such information as well (when asked by the data subject)? The provision is not entirely clear on this. As a result, it may turn a request for erasure into a procedural dispute where the controller evades any discussion on the substance by arguing not to be subject to the relevant legal obligation *stricto sensu*.

In sum, the fifth right to erasure trigger may seem the most straightforward one of all six. After all, it presents itself as a clear and objective binary, ie if a legal obligation requires erasure, the data subject can request such erasure. But, beneath this apparent simplicity may lie tremendous complexity and/or ambiguity. Article 17(1)(e) simply outsources the nitty-gritty of determining when personal data should be erased to external legal frameworks. The relevant provisions in those other legal frameworks may raise a lot of interpretative questions as well.

2.6 Children's Personal Data Online

Article 17(1)

> The data subject shall have the right to [...] erasure [...] where: (f) the personal data have been collected in relation to the offer of information society services referred to in Article 8(1).[165]

The sixth and last right to erasure trigger is aimed at protecting children in an ISS context. It grants data subjects a right to erasure with regard to personal data that was collected 'in relation to the offer of information society services directly to a child' and relying on consent as a lawful ground (Arts 8(1) 17(1)(f)(*j*)). Whether or not the data subject has entered adulthood already when invoking the right to

[165] Article 8(1) reads: 'Where point (a) of Article 6(1) applies *[ie consent]*, in relation to the offer of information society services directly to a child, the processing of the personal data of a child shall be lawful where the child is at least 16 years old. Where the child is below the age of 16 years, such processing shall be lawful only if and to the extent that consent is given or authorised by the holder of parental responsibility over the child. Member States may provide by law for a lower age for those purposes provided that such lower age is not below 13 years.'

erasure is irrelevant. What matters is that the respective personal data was collected at the time the data subject was a child (in the context of ISS directly aimed at children and based on consent as a lawful ground).

The desire for an added layer of protection for children—particularly in today's information society—has been infused throughout the GDPR.[166] Recital 38 explains children 'merit specific protection with regard to their personal data, as they may be less aware of the risks, consequences and safeguards concerned and their rights in relation to the processing of personal data'. It is generally deemed that in a free and liberal society, individuals should not be pursued forever by personal data shared or captured in their formative years.[167] From that perspective, a strong(er) right to erasure for children's personal data does make sense.[168] The Commission's initial proposal of Article 17 already highlighted the need for extra protection for children, be it in an awkward manner.[169] Originally, Article 17(1) referred to children in its opening sentence and listed only five situations prompting a right to erasure. The Commission's 2012 proposal accorded a right to erasure '*especially in relation to personal data which are made available by the data subject while he or she was a child*'. Criticized for being of no practical effect and diluting the content of the right to erasure as a whole,[170] this specification was removed in the 2013 Parliament's compromise text.[171] The general approach of the Council reintroduced a reference to children, granting a right to erasure 'especially in relation to personal data which are collected when the data subject was a child'.[172] It also

166 Eva Lievens and Valerie Verdoodt, 'Looking for Needles in a Haystack: Key Issues Affecting Children's Rights in the General Data Protection Regulation' (2018) 34 Computer Law & Security Review 269.

167 Valerie Verdoodt, Damian Clifford, and Eva Lievens, 'Toying with Children's Emotions, the New Game in Town? The Legality of Advergames in the EU' (2016) 32 Computer Law & Security Review 599; Milda Macenaite, 'From Universal towards Child-Specific Protection of the Right to Privacy Online: Dilemmas in the EU General Data Protection Regulation' (2017) 19 New Media & Society 765; Lievens and Verdoodt (n 166); High Level Expert Group on Artificial Intelligence, 'Policy and Investment Recommendations for Trustworthy AI' (European Commission 2019) 14.

168 It is worth mentioning at least one author who has criticized a stronger protection of children's personal data (in particular a stronger right to erasure). See: Peter Blume, 'The Data Subject' (2015) 1 European Data Protection Law Review 262.

169 See in this regard: Cécile de Terwangne, *The Right to Be Forgotten and the Informational Autonomy in the Digital Environment* (Publications Office 2013) 4ff<http://dx.publications.europa.eu/10.2788/54562> accessed 1 June 20198; Eva Lievens and Carl Vander Maelen, 'A Child's Right to Be Forgotten: Letting Go of the Past and Embracing the Future?' [2019] Latin American Law Review 61.

170 The text suggests different degrees of the right to erasure's applicability, whereas it should apply to children as to any other individual, for as long as the requirements are met. Xawery Konarski and others, 'Reforming the Data Protection Package (Study Drafted for EP Committee on Internal Market and Consumer Protection)' (EP Committee on Internal Market and Consumer Protection 2012) IP/A/IMCO/ST/2012-02 60–61 <http://www.europarl.europa.eu/document/activities/cont/201209/20120928ATT52488/20120928ATT52488EN.pdf>.

171 Committee on Civil Liberties, Justice and Home Affairs (Rapporteur Albrecht JP), 'Draft Report on the Proposal for a Regulation of the European Parliament and of the Council on the Protection of Individual with Regard to the Processing of Personal Data and on the Free Movement of Such Data (General Data Protection Regulation). Amendments (4) 1189–1492' (n 88) amendments 1388 et seq.

172 When compared with the Commission's original proposal, this specification is wider, also covering personal data not made available by the data subject him or herself. Yet it still gives rise to the

introduced the text of current Article 17(1)(f), but as an entire second paragraph. In the end, the finally adopted version of Article 17 did away with any reference to children in the introductory sentence and converted the proposed second paragraph into a sixth trigger under Article 17(1) for readability purposes.[173]

On the face of it, this last right-to-erasure trigger seems redundant. After all, the provision only covers a very specific set of situations, fulfilling three cumulative requirements: (a) personal data of a child;[174] (b) processing operations that rely on consent[175] as a lawful ground; and (c) only for processing in relation to information society services directly offered to the child. Article 17(1)(b) already accords a right to erasure in situations where personal data are being processed on the basis of consent, ie through the withdrawal of such consent (whether or not the data subject was a child at the time of collection and not limited to processing in relation to ISS only). Having said that, it does remove doubt by making clear that the right to erasure is available to data subjects, 'notwithstanding the fact that he or she is no longer a child' (Recital 65). Furthermore, one might also argue that this last right-to-erasure trigger is stronger than the second one on withdrawal of consent. The latter explicitly recognizes controllers' ability to 'fall back' on another lawful ground for further processing. *A contrario*, the absence of such specification regarding the last trigger on children's right to erasure suggests a stricter take where data cannot be further processed on the basis of another ground.

In light of the above, the only added value of Article 17(1)(f)[176] seems to relate to a small subset of processing operations. The provision arguably clarifies those situations where consent for the processing of a child's personal data in relation to an ISS directly offered to the child is given or authorized by the holder of parental responsibility over that child. In this specific set of situations,[177] the data subject—ie the child—may not be qualified to withdraw consent. Once the data subject 'reaches the age of digital consent', he/she can withdraw the consent given by the holder of parental responsibility.[178]

In conclusion, the practical relevance of Article 17(1)(f) hinges upon how Article 8(1)—a fiercely debated provision in itself[179]—will be interpreted and

same criticism as the one to the initial proposal (ie being of no practical effect and potentially diluting the right overall).

[173] Council of the European Union, 'Presidency De-Briefing on the Outcome of the Data Protection Trilogue on 16/17 September 2015 and Preparation for Trilogue (Chapter III)' (2015) 12733/1/15 5 <http://www.statewatch.org/news/2015/oct/eu-council-dp-reg-Chap-III-12733-re01-15.pdf> accessed 1 June 2019.

[174] See Chapter 3, subsection 4.1.

[175] ie Article 6(1)(a).

[176] Apart from its symbolical, political value.

[177] Covering all children below the age of 16 (or lower depending on diverging Member-State laws which can reduce the age to 13 at most).

[178] Article 29 Working Party, 'Guidelines on Consent under Regulation 2016/679' (n 52) 27.

[179] Blume, 'The Data Subject' (n 168); Macenaite (n 167); Milda Macenaite and Eleni Kosta, 'Consent for Processing Children's Personal Data in the EU: Following in US Footsteps?' (2017) 26 Information & Communications Technology Law 146; Lievens and Verdoodt (n 166).

implemented. From the perspective of the right to erasure, its importance only seems marginal. Whenever processing of personal data in the context of ISS is rendered lawful on the basis of consent, the data subject will have a right of withdrawal and ensuing right to erasure. If such consent was obtained at the time the data subject was a child, it can be argued that the controller cannot fall back on another lawful ground (contrary to 'plain' consent withdrawal in Article 17(1)(b). For the narrow subset of cases where the data subject has not consented him/herself because he/she was still a child at the time of collection, Article 17(1)(f) makes clear the data subject can still request the personal data to be erased.

2.7 Interim Conclusion on the Right to Erasure Triggers

Article 17(1) lists six situations in which a data subject may request his/her personal data to be erased. These 'right to erasure triggers' are deeply rooted into the data protection framework and touch upon many key provisions and principles in the GDPR. Indeed, it has appeared that analysing Article 17(1) in isolation is not possible. The provision's strong interconnectedness also puts into perspective its main added value. As illustrated throughout this section, all six right-to-erasure triggers are somewhat implied in the data protection framework already. Each trigger largely corresponds to an (implicit) obligation to erase the personal data in the first place. The fourth (unlawful processing) and fifth (compliance with a legal obligation) may be the most evident examples of this. Though it also seems evident that when the purpose expires, consent is withdrawn or the right to object has been successfully invoked, the controller has an obligation to erase the personal data if it cannot rely on a(nother) lawful ground for further processing. Regardless of the data subject having to invoke his/her right to have that personal data erased. Article 17(1)'s main added value therefore, might seem primarily symbolic.

Yet, the reality of information society services does give some practical relevance to Article 17(1). Explicitly granting a right to erasure in situations where personal data should have been erased in the first place comprises an important empowerment function.[180] This empowerment aim—further emphasized by the fact harm is not a requirement for invoking the right to erasure—is particularly important in the context of ISS providers, with complex data processing ecosystems and vast power asymmetries. Personal data may not be proactively erased for a wide variety of reasons, ranging from ignorance or lack of (economic) incentives,

[180] Fuster astutely explains data subject rights constitute mirrors 'that data subjects can, when they wish, place in front of data controllers so the latter are forced to examine their own compliance (or lack of) with data protection obligations. Responsibility for such compliance had always fallen on their shoulders, irrespective of whether somebody was looking, or whether somebody complains.' Gloria González Fuster, 'Beyond the GDPR, Above the GDPR' (*Internet Policy Review*, 30 November 2015) <http://policyreview.info/articles/news/beyond-gdpr-above-gdpr/385> accessed 1 June 2019.

to concerns with regard to integrity of systems or impact on third parties' interests. Not erasing personal data—whether deliberately or not—is a decision made exclusively by the controller(s) before anything else (see Chapter 2). Article 17(1) provides data subjects with the ammunition to contest such decisions and hold controllers accountable.

From a practical perspective, questions remain with regard to when exactly the right to erasure is triggered in the context of ISS. Without a rigorous commitment to granularity, it seems questionable purposes can ever expire (*first trigger*). Not to mention the difficulty data subjects may have establishing such expiration. The *second* and *third triggers* (consent withdrawal and right to object) also have considerable loopholes built-in, making it potentially easy for controllers to ignore erasure requests (and difficult for data subjects to retort). Whether or not a specific processing operation is in fact (un)lawful will oftentimes be difficult to determine (*fourth trigger*), as is clearly illustrated by the high volume of scholarship on lawful grounds for processing personal data (notably (a) consent and (f) legitimate interests). Fending off erasure requests based on the *fifth trigger* (legal obligation), may also be fairly easy, either by contesting the necessity, denying the controller is subject to the obligation, or by relying on a(nother) lawful ground for further processing personal data.[181] The practical relevance of the *sixth* and last right-to-erasure *trigger* finally, is considerably curbed by its limited scope.

In short, apart from the straightforward cases (eg clearly illegal processing of personal data), the applicability and extent of the right to erasure triggers will always be debatable.[182] Data subjects will generally rely on more than one of these triggers to make their case. The stickiest counter-argument will generally boil down to the claim there is still a lawful ground for further processing. As a matter of fact, regardless of what arguments the controller uses against erasure requests, it will at the very least still need a lawful ground to continue processing the personal data. Depending on the strength of the controller's lawful ground, the further processing of personal data might be reduced or shifted to different processing operations and/or purposes (and/or involving different entities).

To all intents and purposes, only three lawful grounds are relevant in the ISS context: (a) consent, (b) necessity for the performance of a contract, and (f) legitimate interests. The former two will generally not constitute realistic defences against erasure claims. Necessity for the performance of a contract only renders lawful a very narrow set of processing operations. It also seems nonsensical to solicit a data subject's consent for further processing, when that same person has already expressed his/her desire to have the data erased. As a result, the only lawful

[181] Not to mention that the legal obligation referred to can come with its own legal uncertainties.

[182] Not in the least due to vague phrasing (driven by the need for some level of technological neutrality) and the complexity of the data processing ecosystem (ie multiple actors and purposes for processing the same personal data).

ground that controllers might realistically rely upon to fend off erasure requests is the one relating to legitimate interests (Art 6(1)(f)).[183] The de facto balancing act that will ensue—and all the issues it entails—will be thoroughly investigated in Part II of this book.

Section 3. Extending the Right to Erasure

Article 17(2)

> Where the controller has made the personal data public and is obliged pursuant to paragraph 1 to erase the personal data, the controller, taking account of available technology and the cost of implementation, shall take reasonable steps, including technical measures, to inform controllers which are processing the personal data that the data subject has requested the erasure by such controllers of any links to, or copy or replication of, those personal data.

3.1 Right to be Forgotten 2.0?

If it was still worth maintaining the terminology 'right to be forgotten' in the GDPR,[184] paragraph 2 of Article 17 is probably the reason why. In short, this provision requires controllers who made personal data public to communicate successful erasure requests to all controllers processing that same personal data. In doing so, the provision goes beyond a 'right to erasure' *stricto sensu*, justifying the legislator's use of different, but complementing language. While the first paragraph is constrained to the erasure of a specific set of data by a specific actor, the second paragraph is much wider, aiming to have personal data removed across the board. The former can be seen as an obligation to achieve a result and the latter constitutes an obligation of means.

Rationale—It is not hard to imagine the rationale behind Article 17(2). In general, once personal data is made public on the Internet, it will amply be replicated and linked to. Indeed, the very fact of personal data being multiplied and cross-referenced will oftentimes be the reason for invoking the right to erasure in the first place. An extensive 2016 study uncovered that only 10 per cent of ISS providers confirm *not* to share personal data with third parties for commercial reasons.[185]

183 Leaving a minimum of interpretive leeway to justify further processing benefitting the controller(s) and/or third parties.

184 The terminology is used notably in Recitals 65–66 and the title of Article 17, albeit between parentheses and quotation marks.

185 Fifty popular 'online platforms' were investigated. Jamila Venturini and others, *Terms of Service and Human Rights: An Analysis of Online Platform Contracts* (Revan 2016) 74 <http://

In such circumstances, only removing personal data at the source will typically not bring relief to data subjects. Hence, Recital 66 explains, in order to 'strengthen the right to be forgotten in the online environment, the right to erasure should also be extended'. Importantly, the 'right to be forgotten' is not about stopping people from knowing, but rather stopping from disseminating.[186]

From earlier drafts of the GDPR, it becomes clear the legislator had a particular set of actors in mind, ie 'any publicly available communication service which allows or facilitates the search of or access to this personal data'.[187] This quite clearly seems to refer to ISS providers such as search engines[188] and social media. Still, throughout the legislative process, the provision has become more generic. In the European Commission's official proposal from 2012, paragraph 2 referred to *third parties who 'are' processing the personal data* but also made the initial controller *responsible* for any authorized third party publication.[189] After the European Parliament's first reading, this language had been changed to an obligation to take reasonable steps to have data erased by third parties as well.[190] Only after the Council's general approach in 2015 did the provision get its current shape, requiring all 'controllers which are processing such personal data to erase any links to, or copies or replications of those personal data'.[191] The move from 'third parties' to 'controllers' refines the scope to a more clearly delineated notion. Another explanation for adopting the term 'controller' only so late in the legislative process might simply be the result of the CJEU's *Google Spain* Ruling, which made it clear that search engines can be considered controllers as well.[192]

internet-governance.fgv.br/sites/internet-governance.fgv.br/files/publicacoes/terms_of_services_06_12_2016.pdf> accessed 1 June 2019.

[186] de Terwangne (n 169) 2; 9–10.

[187] Paragraph 2 of Article 15 on the right to erasure and the right to be forgotten in a leaked draft of the GDPR. European Commission, 'Leaked Proposal for a General Data Protection Regulation' (on file with the author).

[188] In the same leaked draft, Recital 47 even explicitly stated the second paragraph was aimed at 'replications in websites and search engines'.

[189] The exact language was: 'Where the controller referred to in paragraph 1 has made the personal data public, it shall take all reasonable steps, including technical measures, in relation to data for the publication of which the controller is responsible, to inform third parties which are processing such data, that a data subject requests them to erase any links to, or copy or replication of that personal data. Where the controller has authorised a third party publication of personal data, the controller shall be considered responsible for that publication.'

[190] Exact text: 'Where the controller referred to in paragraph 1 has made the personal data public without a justification based on Article 6(1), it shall take all reasonable steps, to have the data erased, including by third parties, without prejudice to Article 77. The controller shall inform the data subject, where possible, of the action taken by the relevant third parties.'

[191] Recital 66.

[192] The paragraph only started referring to 'controllers' (rather than 'publicly available communication services that allowing or facilitating search of data' or 'third parties') after the CJEU issued its ruling in *Google Spain*. *Google Spain* (n 19); Council of the European Union—Working Group on Information Exchange and Data Protection (DAPIX), 'Note to the Working Group on Information Exchange and Data Proection (DAPIX) on the Proposal for a General Data Protection Regulation—The Right to Be Forgotten and the Google Judgment' (2014) 11289/14 <http://register.consilium.europa.eu/doc/srv?l=EN&f=ST%2011289%202014%20INIT>.

OLD WINE, NEW BARRELS—Article 17's second paragraph is clearly rooted in the historic understanding of the 'right to be forgotten' (see the traditional *droit a l'oubli* cases referred to in Chapter 2). These cases concern the publication of information, potentially inflicting harm on the individual. They are not about compliance with data protection law *stricto sensu* (but instead are generally based on the right to privacy, defamation, or tort law) and are aimed at scrapping all publications of that information as well as preventing further publications. In light of this, courts have been reticent in granting such a right. Even though clearly inspired by this pre-existing 'right'—seeking to prevent further publicity of erased personal data—Article 17(2) also differs from the traditional *droit a l'oubli*. On the one hand the new provision is broader, not having the same de facto requirements (notably harm, journalistic content, and relating to criminal facts)[193]. On the other hand, Article 17(2) is narrower because it is still embedded in data protection law, meaning that the right to erasure itself needs to be applicable in the first place (which may not be the case with regard to journalistic content in light of the exceptions in Articles 85 and 17(3) GDPR).

FROM RIGHT TO OBLIGATION TO SOMEWHERE IN-BETWEEN—Article 17's second paragraph has evolved significantly throughout the legislative process. In one of the earliest drafts that was leaked, it gave data subjects who had successfully invoked erasure on the basis of the first paragraph, the right to request erasure of any reference to that data from 'publicly available communication service which allows or facilitates the search of or access to this data'.[194] In a draft that was leaked not even a month later, the language had already been changed to '[w]here the controller referred to in paragraph 1 has made the data public, it shall in particular ensure the erasure of any public Internet link to, copy of, or replication of the personal data … '.[195] This change significantly shifted the burden from data subjects' (who no longer have to proactively invoke their right) onto controllers' shoulders. Only after the Council's General Approach in 2015, was this changed again to somewhat of a middle ground. The burden is still on the initial controller, but only when the data subject has requested the erasure by other controllers (of links or copies of his/her data).[196]

[193] As explained in Chapter 2. The *droit a l'oubli* is a jurisprudential construct and the criteria for applying it may vary.

[194] Leaked draft from 10 November 2011. On file with the author.

[195] European Commission, 'Leaked Proposal for a General Data Protection Regulation' (n 684).

[196] At least two potential reasons for this change can be drawn from the Council negotiations. Firstly, several Member-States had raised a potential conflict with the intermediary liability exemptions and prohibition for general monitoring obligations in the eCommerce Directive 2000/31 (Articles 12–15). Secondly, concerns were raised that too much of a proactive obligation on controllers' shoulders could have a 'chilling effect' on freedom of expression. See notably: Council of the European Union, 'Note to the Working Party on Information Exchange of Data Protection. Council Revised Version of the Proposal for a Regulation of the European Parliament and of the Council on the Protection of Individuals with Regard to the Processing of Personal Data and on the Free Movement of Such Data (General Data Protection Regulation)' (n 192) nn 143–45.

ARTICLE 17(2) V ARTICLE 19—One may also wonder what the added value is of Article 17(2) when put next to Article 19 GDPR. This last provision explicitly requires controllers to 'communicate any [...] erasure of personal data [...] carried out in accordance with Article [...] 17(1) [...] to each recipient to whom the personal data have been disclosed, unless this proves impossible or involves disproportionate effort'. This obligation has a long tradition within data protection legislation. The pioneering French Data Protection Act (1978)[197] and subsequent national acts such as the Dutch one in 1987[198] contained similar provisions. Later, Article 12(c) in Directive 95/46 granted data subjects a right to obtain from the controller 'notification to third parties to whom the data have been disclosed of any [...] erasure'. It may not come as a surprise, therefore, that Article 17(2) was almost removed altogether after the European Parliament's first reading.[199] When data is published, it was reasoned, the original controller should only be obliged to inform 'third parties which it can reasonably expect to be further processing the data'. A situation arguably covered by Article 19 already. Indeed, Article 19 is broader than Article 17(2) to the extent that it also covers non-published personal data.

In light of the above, a cynic might say the main reason why Article 17(2) is only symbolic, a remnant justifying the 'right to be forgotten' terminology. Yet, from a more optimistic perspective, one can still see some added value in this provision. Indeed, the key difference between Article 17(2) and Article 19 (and hence also the *raison d'être* of the former) relates to their scope of application. Whereas the latter only concerns the 'recipients to whom the personal data have been disclosed', the former covers situations where the controller has made the respective personal data public and extends to *any* controller processing that same personal data. Not only those it has shared the personal data with. Without Article 17(2) therefore, a shrewd controller who has published personal data on the Internet might argue the obligation to inform all recipients under Article 19 would be disproportionate.[200]

[197] Article 38, Loi 78-17 du 6 janvier 1978 relative à l'informatique, aux fichiers et aux libertés 1978; André Holleaux, 'La Loi Du 6 Janvier 1978 Sur Informatique et Les Libertés — II —' (1978) 31 La Revue administrative 160, 164. '*Si une information a été transmise à un tiers, [...] son annulation doit être notifiée à ce tiers*'.

[198] Nugter (n 36) 158–59. The Dutch data protection Act required the communication of erasure requests to third parties to whom the controller *knowingly disclosed* 'data concerned within a period of a year preceding the request'.

[199] See the Committee on Legal Affairs as well as the Committee on Industry, Research and Energy in: Committee on Civil Liberties, Justice and Home Affairs (Rapporteur Albrecht JP), 'Report on the Proposal for a Regulation of the European Parliament and of the Council on the Protection of Individuals with Regard to the Processing of Personal Data and on the Free Movement of Such Data (General Data Protection Regulation)' (European Parliament (Committee on Civil Liberties, Justice and Home Affairs) 2013) A7-0402/2013 300–01; 565. See also: Amendment 1414 (Sarah Ludford): Committee on Civil Liberties, Justice and Home Affairs (Rapporteur Albrecht JP), 'Draft Report on the Proposal for a Regulation of the European Parliament and of the Council on the Protection of Individual with Regard to the Processing of Personal Data and on the Free Movement of Such Data (General Data Protection Regulation). Amendments (4) 1189–1492' (n 88).

[200] Hans Graux, Jef Ausloos, and Peggy Valcke, 'The Right to Be Forgotten in the Internet Era' in Jorge Pérez, Enrique Badía, and Rosa María Sáinz Peña (eds), *The Debate on Privacy and Security over the*

Article 17(2) installs a higher responsibility for when personal data has been made public. How far precisely this responsibility should go, and what exactly should be understood as 'making public', merits some closer attention.

3.2 Criteria and Obligations

3.2.1 Making Personal Data Public

Two main requirements are put forward in order for Article 17's second paragraph to become applicable.[201] Firstly, the respective controller will need to be obliged to erase personal data pursuant to the article's first paragraph. This has been amply discussed in the previous pages already and will not be further developed here. Secondly, the controller will need to 'have made the personal data public'. Despite—or maybe *because* of—the apparent straightforwardness of this requirement, the GDPR offers no guidance as to its exact scope or meaning.

Looking for guidance on how to interpret 'making public' within the GDPR, two provisions are tangentially relevant. Article 9(2)(e) permits the processing of so-called 'sensitive data' 'which are manifestly made public by the data subject'. But apart from suggesting there are different degrees of 'making public', this provision offers little assistance on how to interpret 'making public'. Article 70(1)—setting out the tasks of the European Data Protection Board (EDPB)—seems to be more useful. The EDPB's fourth task is to 'issue guidelines, recommendations, and best practices on procedures for erasing links, copies or replications of personal data from publicly available communication services as referred to in Article 17(2)'. Does the legislator imply that Article 17(2) only (or primarily) applies to 'publicly available electronic communications services' as defined in Directive 2002/21/EC?[202] It seems that this phrasing is a remnant of the initial scope of Article 17(2), and was not properly aligned after that provision's scope was widened to first

Network: Regulation and Markets, vol 36 (Ariel 2012) <publicpolicy.telefonica.com/blogs/wp-content/uploads/2011/01/net_privacy.pdf> accessed 18 April 2013.

[201] During the legislative process, some argued (unsuccessfully) for an implicit third requirement according to which Article 17(2) would *not* apply when the data subject made the personal data public him/herself, or instructed the controller to do so. Opinion of the Committee on the Internal Market and Consumer Protection, Committee on Civil Liberties, Justice and Home Affairs (Rapporteur Albrecht JP), 'Report on the Proposal for a Regulation of the European Parliament and of the Council on the Protection of Individuals with Regard to the Processing of Personal Data and on the Free Movement of Such Data (General Data Protection Regulation)' (n 199) 467. Also see the Explanatory Statement to the EP's legislative resolution at page 201.

[202] Directive 2002/21/EC of the European Parliament and of the Council of 7 March 2002 on a common regulatory framework for electronic communications networks and services (Framework Directive) *j.* Directive 2002/58/EC of the European Parliament and of the Council of 12 July 2002 concerning the processing of personal data and the protection of privacy in the electronic communications sector (ePrivacy Directive).

'third parties' and eventually to 'controllers'. If one were to interpret Article 17(2) as still only referring to 'publicly available communications services', this would significantly reduce its (already limited) practical relevance. That is, if the legislator uses this terminology in reference to 'electronic communications service', defined very narrowly in Framework Directive 2002/21.[203] In light of the rationale behind Article 17(2) GDPR, and especially its terminological metamorphoses, it can safely be assumed that Article 70(1)(d) only refers to one specific set of 'secondary controllers' that might especially require guidance.

LINDQVIST—Given the lack of a definition or interpretative guidelines within the GDPR, the terminology 'have made the personal data public' should in principle be understood in its natural language meaning. Such an approach still offers little legal certainty. Looking beyond the GDPR, two CJEU cases seem to provide some assistance: *Lindqvist* (C-101/01) and *Satamedia* (C-73/07). In the former, the CJEU articulated as a threshold for the household exemption, the 'making available to an indefinite number of people' (see Chapter 3).[204] At first glance, this criterion seems *mutadis mutandis* useful to assess what constitutes 'making public' under Article 17(2) as well. Yet, one may wonder whether making personal data available to a defined number of people is excluded from qualifying under Article 17(2). Sharing personal data on a members-only forum, for example, could arguably still qualify as 'making available to the public' as used in Article 17(2). Hence, the 'indefinite number of people' criterion from *Lindqvist* seems to be a good 'positive' criterion. When it is fulfilled, the 'making available to the public' in Article 17(2) will automatically be triggered as well. However, when the *Lindqvist* criterion is *not* met, this does not necessarily result in the inapplicability of Article 17(2).

SATAMEDIA—The *Satamedia* case involved a text-messaging service allowing people to receive information about the incomes of Finnish citizens that had been published by the national tax authorities.[205] In other words, *Satamedia* built a business-model (ie on-demand tax and revenue records of fellow citizens) around personal data that was 'made public' already. This case is interesting in light of Article 17(2) GDPR, because it raises the question of whether further sharing of publicly available personal data still constitutes 'making data public'? Does each consecutive 'making public' of personal data result in the application of Article 17(2). Would *Satamedia*—the text-messaging service—be subject to Article 17(2),

[203] Article 2(c), Directive 2002/21: 'a service normally provided for remuneration which consists wholly or mainly in the conveyance of signals on electronic communications networks, including telecommunications services and transmission services in networks used for broadcasting, but exclude services providing, or exercising editorial control over, content transmitted using electronic communications networks and services; it does not include information society services, as defined in Article 1 of Directive 98/34/EC, which do not consist wholly or mainly in the conveyance of signals on electronic communications networks'.

[204] Notably paras 47–48.

[205] *ietosuojavaltuutettu v Satakunnan Markkinapörssi & Satamedia* [2008] Court of Justice of the European Union C-73/07 paras 25–29.

despite the fact that the personal data was made public already? Would a search engine, for that matter, be subject to Article 17(2)? It seems fair to argue that information can only be 'made public' once,[206] even if that 'publication' remains obscure (due to for example its nature or findability). To all intents and purposes, it is only through subsequent processing by secondary entities that information effectively becomes 'public'.[207] In *Satamedia*, the CJEU also emphasized that exonerating processing of *published* personal data from data protection law, would largely deprive the law from its effect.[208] In light of all this, one may equally argue that every '*re*-publication' of personal data should still be subject to Article 17(2).

Something that can be drawn from *Satamedia* (and was also implied in the *Google Spain*[209] and *Manni*[210] cases), is that 'making public' also covers information that is only made accessible upon request. In other words, 'making information public' is not confined to stereotypical situations where someone puts information on a website for everyone to see. It also covers situations where personal data is only accessible when specifically asked for (eg via a general-purpose search engine, a text messaging service or a local chamber of commerce's website). That is, when essentially anyone could get access to that information (if they search/pay for it).

In short, Article 17(2)'s scope of application is still frustratingly unclear. Even though criteria such as 'indefinite number of people', 'first publication', 'restricted access', 'broader context', or a 'permission to publish'[211] may certainly be useful indicators, they do not appear conclusive. Indeed, what about the situation of a social network, where one could say it is the data subject who 'makes his/her personal data public', but the service provider certainly has a role in it as well.[212] Another case in point is the Facebook/Cambridge Analytica saga, where personal data was obtained through an app (not just from users who downloaded the app, but also their friends) and subsequently shared with a 'political consultancy' firm.[213]

[206] Especially when considering that the obligation under Article 17(2) extends to *all controllers* processing that personal data. This implies that all these controllers have obtained the personal data through the making public by the original controller.

[207] See *Google Spain* (n 19).

[208] *Satamedia* (n 205) para 48.

[209] *Google Spain* (n 19).

[210] *Salvatore Manni* [2017] Court of Justice of the European Union C-398/15.

[211] In the Explanatory Statement accompanying the Draft European Parliament Legislative Resolution, it was concluded that '[w]here the individual has agreed to a publication of his or her data, however, a "right to be forgotten" is neither legitimate nor realistic'. Committee on Civil Liberties, Justice and Home Affairs (Rapporteur Albrecht JP), 'Report on the Proposal for a Regulation of the European Parliament and of the Council on the Protection of Individuals with Regard to the Processing of Personal Data and on the Free Movement of Such Data (General Data Protection Regulation)' (n 199) 201.

Explanatory statement by the EP, adjoining its amendments to the GDPR proposal (2013.11.21_European_Parliament_final_LIBE_report_draft_Legislative_resolution).

[212] de Terwangne (n 169) 10–11.

[213] Emma Graham-Harrison and Carole Cadwalladr, 'Revealed: 50 Million Facebook Profiles Harvested for Cambridge Analytica in Major Data Breach' (*the Guardian*, 17 March 2018) <http://www.theguardian.com/news/2018/mar/17/cambridge-analytica-facebook-influence-us-election> accessed 19 March 2018.

Facebook essentially is a controller who makes available personal data of its users to third party app developers. The latter only gain access when users actually download said apps. Who, in this case, is 'making public' the personal data: the data subject, Facebook, or both? Despite the jury still being out, one should not overstate the importance of these questions either. Given its central position in the ecosystem, Facebook can certainly be held responsible to communicate data subject requests to the entities it has allowed access to. Even controllers that have shared personal data with a limited set of others and or subject to requirements, Article 19 will generally still be applicable. Save for some subtle differences, both provisions result in the same obligation on the controller's shoulders.

3.2.2 Obligation of Means

When Article 17(2)'s two cumulative criteria are met, the controller will have to inform other controllers who are processing that same personal data about the erasure request. Importantly, this obligation to inform is not absolute.[214] Controllers will only need to take *reasonable steps* to inform, which may include technical measures. Moreover, the obligation will need to be assessed 'taking into account available technology and the cost of implementation'. In short, Article 17(2) constitutes an obligation of means (in contrast to Article 17(1) which puts down an obligation of result).[215] As explained by Zanfir, such an obligation of means or 'obligation of best efforts' is assessed in light of 'the efforts a reasonable person of the same kind would have made in similar circumstances'.[216] What this means, essentially, is that the initial controller who has published personal data, is not automatically liable if it has failed to inform another controller about the initial erasure request.[217]

In this regard, Article17(2) is similar to the obligation in Article 19 which can be ignored when proved 'impossible to achieve' or 'requires disproportionate effort'. Contrary to Article 19, however, Article 17(2) covers situations where the controller does not necessarily know all entities that (might) have accessed the published personal data (proposals to constrain the duty to communicate under Article 17(2) to known controllers only[218] did not make it to the final

[214] Contrary to earlier drafts, which were considered over-burdensome. Bartolini and Siry (n 43) 228.

[215] European Data Protection Supervisor, 'Opinion of the European Data Protection Supervisor (EDPS) on the Data Protection Reform Package' paras 146–47.<www.edps.europa.eu/EDPSWEB/webdav/site/mySite/shared/Documents/Consultation/Opinions/2012/12-03-07_EDPS_Reform_package_EN.pdf> accessed 1 June 2019.

[216] Gabriela Zanfir, 'Tracing the Right to Be Forgotten in the Short History of Data Protection Law: The "New Clothes" of an Old Right' in Serge Gutwirth, Ronald Leenes, and Paul de Hert (eds), *Reforming European Data Protection Law* (Springer Netherlands 2015) 236 <http://link.springer.com/chapter/10.1007/978-94-017-9385-8_8> accessed 1 June 2019. Referring to: International Institute for the Unification of Private Law (n 505) Article 5.1.4. The author summarizes: 'if the debtor was obliged to fulfil an *obligation de résultat*, it falls on the obligée only to prove that the result owed was not achieved. If the debtor however was only obliged to fulfill an *obligation de moyens*, the obligée has to prove that the debtor *a été défaillant dans l'emploi des moyens* (has failed in the use of best efforts).'

[217] Zanfir (n 216) 237.

[218] Council of the European Union, 'Note to the Working Party on Information Exchange of Data Protection. Council Revised Version of the Proposal for a Regulation of the European Parliament and of

version).[219] This key difference has an important impact on how the controller will have to give effect to its obligation to inform others about the erasure request. From the CJEU's *Rijkeboer* Ruling, it appears that under some circumstances, it might be considered a disproportionate effort for controllers to maintain a record of all recipients of personal data.[220] But this seems to be a consideration more applicable to Article 19 than to Article 17(2), which not only covers recipients but any other controller processing the same personal data.

Requiring the installation of a technical system, simply to monitor everyone who had access to the published data might be considered disproportionate, especially in light of others' fundamental rights and freedoms (privacy, freedom of expression and information). That being said, such infrastructure may already be in place, for example on closed platforms such as a social network, where the platform operator effectively monitors who accesses what. In any case, it is clear that given the potential breadth of the duty in Article 17(2), the legislator primarily thought of this obligation in terms of technology. The provision explicitly refers to *technical measures*. An obvious example would be exclusion codes (eg robots.txt) in websites' code to prevent indexing (on the basis of certain keywords) from search engines. Others have suggested adding 'sticky policies' (eg including retention period and terms of use) to the respective personal data.[221] A less obvious example, but one that might potentially have considerable practical impact, is for digital assistants to perform Article 17(2)'s duty. Services such as Apple's Siri present themselves as our new personal assistants, and could play a central role in making sure our data protection rights are effectively enforced down the processing chain (not in the least in a smart home environment, with potentially hundreds of interacting sensors, devices and services having access to personal data).[222,223]

the Council on the Protection of Individuals with Regard to the Processing of Personal Data and on the Free Movement of Such Data (General Data Protection Regulation)' (n 192) n 146.

[219] European Data Protection Supervisor, 'Opinion of the European Data Protection Supervisor (EDPS) on the Data Protection Reform Package' (n 215) 24–25; Article 29 Working Party, 'Opinion 01/2012 on the Data Protection Reform Proposals' (Article 29 Working Party 2012) WP 191 13–14 <http://ec.europa.eu/justice/article-29/documentation> accessed 1 June 2019.

[220] 'If, for example, the relevant recipients are numerous or there is a high frequency of disclosure to a more restricted number of recipients, the obligation to keep the information on the recipients or categories of recipient of personal data and on the content of the data disclosed for such a long period could represent an excessive burden on the controller.' *College van burgemeester en wethouders van Rotterdam v MEE Rijkeboer* [2009] Court of Justice of the European Union C-553/07 paras 59; 64.

[221] Maryline Boizard, 'Le Droit Au Respect de La Vie Privée, Un Instrument Effectif Du Droit à l'oubli?' (2015) 1 Montesquieu Law Review 145.

[222] Most of these devices (eg lightbulbs, toaster) will often not even have an interface that would enable data subjects to easily exercise their rights directly in the first place. See in this regard: Meg Leta Jones, 'Privacy without Screens & the Internet of Other People's Things' (2014) 51 Idaho Law Review 639, 647.

[223] For an interdisciplinary perspective on the complex ecosystem and hints at how to tackle data protection issues through 'middleware', see: Jatinder Singh and others, 'Big Ideas Paper: Policy-Driven Middleware for a Legally-Compliant Internet of Things' *Proceedings of the 17th International Middleware Conference* (ACM 2016) 2 <http://doi.acm.org/10.1145/2988336.2988349> accessed 1 June 2019.

Streisand—A careful reading lays bare two more important issues in Article 17's second paragraph. First of all, the provision sets out an obligation to inform other controllers that the 'data subject has requested the erasure by such controllers of any links to, or copy or replication of, those personal data'. The way in which this should be read is that the data subject should explicitly ask for the initial controller to communicate the erasure request under Article 17(2). Put differently, the controller should not proactively communicate erasure requests regarding published data. This follows from the legislative history of Article 17(2), which was triggered automatically in the Commission's proposal and after the Parliament's first reading, but changed into its current language after the Council's general approach. Indeed, it is not unlikely that a data subject might *not* want the initial controller to communicate his/her erasure request regarding published personal data. Under certain circumstances, the obligation in Article 17(2) could have a perverse effect that the data subject might wish to avoid. Widely communicating the fact that published personal data is erased, may paradoxically draw more attention to that data, leading to the so-called Streisand effect.[224] Data subjects may therefore wish the controller whom they have successfully asked to erase personal data, not to take any further action under Article 17(2).[225]

The second element that requires some further thought is the fact that Article 17(2) only requires controllers to *communicate* that the data subject wishes to have his/her personal data erased by those other controllers. An obligation which in no way guarantees that personal data will effectively be erased down the chain (also neutralizing 'censorship concerns'). This also appears from comparing the different versions of Article 17(2), with both the Commission and the Parliament requiring at least in part, that the 'publishing' controller is responsible for erasure by other entities as well. This was changed in the Council's general approach in 2015, to a 'mere' obligation to inform other controllers. Each of these other controllers (having replicated or linked to the erased personal data) will need to comply with the GDPR in their own right. This means that they may well have a lawful ground for processing the personal data, despite the personal data being erased at the source.[226] The legislator clearly intended to emphasize this by explicitly using

[224] 'Streisand Effect', *Wikipedia* (2018) <https://en.wikipedia.org/w/index.php?title=Streisand_effect&oldid=835810997> accessed 12 April 2018.

[225] Similarly, WP29 also suggested that when accommodating the right to be delisted, search engines should as a general rule *not* notify the respective website operators. Article 29 Working Party, 'Guidelines on the Implementation of the Court of Justice of the European Union Judgment on "*Google Spain and Inc v Agencia Española de Protección de Datos (AEPD) and Mario Costeja González*" C-131/12' (n 19); Julia Powles, 'The Case That Won't Be Forgotten' (2015) 47 Loy U Chi LJ 583, 598. The last author explains how Google's practice of notifying webmasters about delisted URLs 'seems to have been calculated to frustrate, confuse, disempower, and antagonize the recipients of those notifications, when there are far better, clearer, and more respectful ways to both inform publishers and protect data subject privacy'.

[226] In this regard, it is also worth referring to the justification for the EP's amendment to the GDPR, deleting Article 17(2) altogether: '[I]f a publication of personal data took place based on legal grounds, as referred to in Article 6(1) of this Regulation, a "right to be forgotten" is neither realistic nor legitimate.

the term *controllers* instead of 'third parties', 'processors', or even 'recipients', all of which suggest a closer tie with the original controller.[227] That being said, the legitimacy of processing of these other controllers might hinge (to a bigger or lesser extent) on the initial publication. This is the case with regard to search engines, for example, where results can be expected to change after webpages are erased or anonymized.

CONCLUSION—In conclusion, Article 17(2) could be seen as an attempt at translating the *droit a l'oubli* into data protection law (in the context of the information society). Though well-intentioned, the practical relevance of Article 17(2) remains to be proven.[228] Indeed, the meaning of its requirements—notably 'making public'—as well as the ensuing obligations—ie 'communicating the erasure request to other controllers'—is far from clear-cut. At best, the provision results in signalling to controllers that the data subject expressed a wish to have his/her personal data erased. Something that may in turn affect the further processing by those controllers. At worst, the provision could be ineffective (eg due to technical complexities involved in implementing it) or even counterproductive (eg Streisand effect resulting from broadcasting the data subject's wish for erasure). It will therefore be important (a) for the data subject to be able to oppose to certain ways of implementations of Article 17(2); and (b) for all stakeholders, that clear guidelines and best practices (eg tailored to specific industries and/or contexts) are issued by the EDPB pursuant to Article 70(1)d.

Section 4. When Can the Right to Erasure Not Be Invoked?

Article 17(3) explicitly foresees five situations in which the right to erasure does not apply, despite it being triggered pursuant to the first paragraph.[229] Summarized, these 'exemptions' relate to (a) freedom of expression and information; (b) legal obligation or public interest; (c) public health; (d) archiving and research; and (e) legal claims. These specific exclusions complement

[...] This does not imply that third parties can further process published personal data if there is no legal ground for them to do so.' Justification to the EP's amendments 35 and 147 (ie to Recital 54 and Art 17(2)) in: Committee on Civil Liberties, Justice and Home Affairs (Rapporteur Albrecht JP), 'Report on the Proposal for a Regulation of the European Parliament and of the Council on the Protection of Individuals with Regard to the Processing of Personal Data and on the Free Movement of Such Data (General Data Protection Regulation)' (n 199).

[227] Earlier drafts still referred to 'third parties'.

[228] In this regard, it is worth mentioning both WP29 and the EDPS have raised question marks as to the practicability of this provision. Article 29 Working Party, 'Opinion 01/2012 on the Data Protection Reform Proposals' (n 17) 13–14; European Data Protection Supervisor, 'Opinion of the European Data Protection Supervisor (EDPS) on the Data Protection Reform Package' (n 215) 24–25. Also see: Bartolini and Siry (n 43) 229 et seq.

[229] Also see Recital 65 *in fine*.

the more general derogations and exemptions to the GDPR overall (see Chapter 3).[230]

The main rationale behind Article 17(3) is to safeguard conflicting rights, interests and/or norms. Indeed, as has been discussed in Chapter 1, accommodating a right to erasure will virtually always result in a conflict of interests. This almost intrinsic conflict resulting from invoking the right to erasure is a consequence of the right's own force. It is one of the most far-reaching data protection empowerment measures, because when successfully invoked Article 17(1) effectively results in the eradication of the respective data. In light of the complexity of the information processing landscape (particularly in the ISS context), such eradication could have a considerable and wide-reaching impact. Foreseeing all these conflicts is impossible and very often the outcome will depend on a careful balancing act in light of the concrete situation of each individual case (see notably Chapter 5). There are some situations, however, in which the legislator already pre-determined that the data subject's right to erasure can *not* prevail.[231] These are the situations set out in Article 17(3).

Before going through each one of the Article 17(3) exemptions, it is worth referring to a quasi-exemption located in Article 11(2) GDPR. According to this provision, the right to erasure (nor Arts 15–20) cannot be invoked against controller that can demonstrate not to be in a position to identify the data subject. In such circumstances, the data subject can still have their personal data erased if they provide additional information enabling their identification.[232] Still, it seems the controller has the final word. Following Article 12(2) *in fine*, the controller still has an opportunity to refuse accommodating erasure requests (and any other Arts 15–22 rights) if it can demonstrate not being in a position to (re-)identify, even after being provided with additional information by the data subject. It is fair to say that the burden of proof on controllers' shoulders would be considerable here.[233]

[230] At the time the GDPR was proposed, the EDPS criticized Article 17(3) for creating confusion as it would only duplicate the 'system of exemptions, restrictions and specific rules already foreseen in the proposed Regulation'. European Data Protection Supervisor, 'Opinion of the European Data Protection Supervisor (EDPS) on the Data Protection Reform Package' (n 215) 25. Similar criticism was also uttered in a European Parliament study on the original GDPR proposal. See: Konarski and others (n 170) 61.

[231] With this in mind, one can look at the exemptions in Article 17(3) as clarifying the boundaries of the GDPR and its interactions with external legal frameworks. See: Clifford and Ausloos (n 40) 25.

[232] Something which may be more difficult than one might expect in certain contexts (eg cloud computing, or some actors in the online advertisement industry that work on the basis of hashes or other information not normally in the possession of the data subject him/herself). See in this regard: Veale, Binns, and Ausloos, 'When Data Protection by Design and Data Subject Rights Clash' (n 38) 12.

[233] ibid 12–13; Chris Norval and others, 'Reclaiming Data: Overcoming App Identification Barriers for Exercising Data Protection Rights' [2018] arXiv:1809.05369 [cs] <http://arxiv.org/abs/1809.05369> accessed 20 September 2018; Coline Boniface and others, 'Security Analysis of Subject Access Request Procedures How to Authenticate Data Subjects Safely When They Request for Their Data' (2019) <https://hal.inria.fr/hal-02072302/document> accessed 4 April 2019.

4.1 To the Extent Processing Is Necessary for . . .

Article 17(3)'s opening sentence qualifies the right to erasure exemptions, only granting them *to the extent* further processing of the respective personal data is *necessary* in light of any of the subsequent situations. Even though this language may seem evident at first, it does raise some important questions when looked at more carefully. When exactly will the processing of personal data be *necessary* in light of any of the situations foreseen in Article 17(3)? Is a balancing act implied? Are all processing operations that bear even the slightest link with the exemptions covered?

The lack of a definition within the GDPR requires looking elsewhere. Following a natural language interpretation, the term necessity can be understood as 'not possible (in the same way) without . . . '. This would imply, with regard to the first exemption for instance, that from the moment personal data has some 'publicness' (eg shared on a social network, published on a blog, news website, or forum), no erasure requests can be made whatsoever. Erasure requests—even with regard to a small portion of data—will necessarily result in not being able to exercise the freedom of information/expression right in exactly the same manner. The example also highlights another complication, ie whether the necessity test only relates to the controller itself (the speaker in the example), or whether the exemptions cover *any* person who may be affected by the situations prescribed in Article 7(3)(a)–(e)? These are all crucial questions for the right to erasure's *locus standi*.

ECtHR as Source of Inspiration for Interpreting Necessity—The first question that needs tackling is how 'necessity' is to be defined and/or interpreted within the context of Article 17(3). One of the first sources of inspiration that springs to mind is ECtHR case law. The European Court has a rich history in defining and demarcating the criterion of 'necessity', primarily in relation to assessing whether a given interference with certain rights is 'necessary in a democratic society'.[234] In this context, necessity incorporates a balancing exercise, permitting interferences that 'correspond to a pressing social need' and are 'proportionate to the legitimate aim pursued'.[235] It will also be important that the reasons justifying

[234] Bygrave (n 8) 273; references in: Article 29 Working Party, 'Opinion 01/2014 on the Application of Necessity and Proportionality Concepts and Data Protection within the Law Enforcement Sector' (2014) Opinion WP 211 7 et seq <http://ec.europa.eu/justice/article-29/documentation> accessed 1 June 2019.

[235] *Leander v Sweden* [1987] European Court of Human Rights 9248/81 [58]. For caselaw on the necessity of interferences with the right to family and private life under Article 8 ECHR, see notably, in the context of surveillance: *Roman Zakharov v Russia* [2015] European Court of Human Rights 47143/06 [232 et seq] and the references made within.; economic interest of the country: *Hatton and Others v the United Kingdom* [2003] European Court of Human Rights 36022/97 inter alia paragraph 121 et seq; protection of children: *Elsholz v Germany* [2000] European Court of Human Rights 25735/94 [48–53]. See also: European Data Protection Supervisor, 'Case Law Overview 1 December 2014– 31 December 2015' (EDPS 2016) Working document 39 et seq <https://secure.edps.europa.eu/EDPSWEB/webdav/site/mySite/shared/Documents/EDPS/MembersMission/Members/Documents/16-03-15_Case_Law_Overview_2015_EN.pdf> accessed 1 June 2019. Bygrave (n 8) 273.

interference are relevant and sufficient.[236] With regard to personal data in particular, the more intimate or sensitive the data are, the stricter the necessity test will generally be.[237]

It is surely tempting to apply this notion of necessity under ECtHR case law *mutadis mutandis* to define/interpret the *necessity* of interferences with the data protection right to erasure in Article 17(3). Yet, it is important to separate the meaning of the necessity concept in the GDPR from how it is interpreted by the ECtHR.[238] The CJEU has emphasized that 'necessity' in EU data protection law (specifically Article 7e Directive 95/46) is aimed at precisely delimiting 'situations in which the processing of personal data is lawful'.[239] The CJEU further explains that necessity in Directive 95/46 'is a concept which has its own independent meaning in Community law and must be interpreted in a manner which fully reflects the objective of that directive'.[240] Hence, the meaning of 'necessity' within Art.17(3) should be derived from the GDPR itself.

Necessity in Article 6(1) GDPR—Even though not defined as such, the concept of necessity appears several times throughout the GDPR. For the purposes of interpreting the Article 17(3) exemptions, Articles 5–6 are particularly relevant. As mentioned before, Article 6(1) renders lawful the processing of personal data when *necessary* in five specific 'scenarios'.[241] While not identical, the conditions described in Article 6(1)(b)–(f) and Article 17(3) were written with the same intention: to define circumstances under which the processing of personal data can be considered lawful, independently from the data subject's wishes. As such, the exemptions in Article 17(3) correspond with a presumption of lawfulness under Article 6.[242] Clarifying the meaning of necessity under Article 6(1)(b)–(f),[243]

[236] Article 29 Working Party, 'Opinion 01/2014 on the Application of Necessity and Proportionality Concepts and Data Protection within the Law Enforcement Sector' (n 1404) 7 et seq.

[237] Bygrave (n 8) 273–74.

[238] Not in the least because it is not used in the context of limiting a human right per se. See also: European Data Protection Supervisor, 'Developing a "Toolkit" for Assessing the Necessity of Measures That Interfere with Fundamental Rights. Background Paper' 4 <https://secure.edps.europa.eu/EDPSWEB/webdav/site/mySite/shared/Documents/Consultation/Papers/16-06-16_Necessity_paper_for_consultation_EN.pdf> accessed 1 June 2019.

[239] *Huber v Germany* [2008] Court of Justice of the European Union C-524/06 para 52.

[240] ibid. Which is not to say, of course, that ECtHR case law may provide helpful guidance. Article 29 Working Party, 'Opinion 06/2014 on the Notion of Legitimate Interests of the Data Controller under Article 7 of Directive 95/46/EC' (n 102) 11 referring to the Judgment of the European Court of Human Rights in 'Silver & Others v United Kingdom (25 March 1983), para 97, discussing the term "necessary in a democratic society": "the adjective "necessary" is not synonymous with "indispensable", neither has it the flexibility of such expressions as "admissible", "ordinary", "useful", "reasonable" or "desirable" . . . ".

[241] Article 29 Working Party, 'Opinion 06/2014 on the Notion of Legitimate Interests of the Data Controller under Article 7 of Directive 95/46/EC' (n 102) 13. The sixth situation is consent, which does not explicitly require necessity in Article 6(1)(a). But, when read together with Article 7(4), it is clear that 'necessity' also affects the evaluation of valid consent. See also: Article 9(2)(b)–(c); (f)–(j). In these cases, a more stringent necessity test applies (Bygrave (n 8) 343).

[242] See notably Recital 65: '[T]he further retention of the personal data should be lawful where it is necessary, for . . . '.

[243] Then still Article 7(b)–(f) Directive 95/46.

WP29 declared *a direct and objective link* between the processing and the purposes is required.[244] This ties back to the natural language interpretation of necessity: is one (im)possible without the other? Elsewhere, WP29/EDPB advised against an 'unduly broad interpretation' of necessity (within Article 6(f)), suggesting a least intrusive means test.[245] In sum, necessity here can be understood as requiring an objective, direct link between the processing purpose and the exemption, complemented with a least intrusive means test.

Necessity in Article 5 GDPR—Evaluating necessity in any of the scenarios in Article 6(1)—or article 17(3) for that matter—hinges upon the concrete purpose of the respective processing operation. Put differently, the purpose limitation principle (in conjunction with the data minimization and storage limitation principles)[246] is the yardstick for determining necessity in the GDPR.[247] The exemptions in Article 17(3) can be seen as a list of categories of purposes that are presumed legitimate and superseding data subjects' interests in having data erased. The link between Articles 5(2) and 17(3) also implies that it will be up to the controller to demonstrate the necessity of the processing operations. In other words, the right to erasure is only non-applicable in situations where further processing is *demonstrably* necessary for any of the purposes in Article 17(3).[248]

No Balancing—Does the phrase 'to the extent necessary' introduce a balancing act into Article 17(3)? This is a particularly pressing question in light of the first exemption on the right to freedom of expression and information as it would impose a considerable task on the controller's shoulders. In my view Article 17(3)—despite appearances—does not prescribe a balancing act in its opening sentence. *Firstly*, one needs to distinguish *exemptions* from *balancing acts*. The latter comprises an open-ended measuring and weighing of all interests at stake, leading to a proportionate outcome. Exemptions can still require a substantive assessment of a particular case, but are aimed at determining the applicability of a rule. Balancing acts assume applicability and are rather a determination of degree.

[244] Even though WP29 only declared this in relation to the second lawful ground (necessary for the performance of a contract), this guidance can easily be transposed to the other grounds as well. Article 29 Working Party, 'Opinion 8/2014 on the on Recent Developments on the Internet of Things' (2014) Opinion WP 223 15<http://ec.europa.eu/justice/article-29/documentation> accessed 1 June 2019.

[245] 'As in other cases, this means that it should be considered whether other less invasive means are available to serve the same end.' Article 29 Working Party, 'Opinion 06/2014 on the Notion of Legitimate Interests of the Data Controller under Article 7 of Directive 95/46/EC' (n 102) 29; 55; European Data Protection Board, 'Opinion 5/2019 on the Interplay between the EPrivacy Directive and the GDPR, in Particular Regarding the Competence, Tasks and Powers of Data Protection Authorities' (EDPB 2019) Opinion 5/2019 7 <https://edpb.europa.eu/sites/edpb/files/files/file1/201905_edpb_opinion_eprivacydir_gdpr_interplay_en_0.pdf> accessed 22 March 2019.

[246] When elucidating the concept of 'kept no longer than necessary' in the context of the 'Internet of Things', WP29 emphasized the need for granularity. Article 29 Working Party, 'Opinion 8/2014 on the on Recent Developments on the Internet of Things' (n 244) 17.

[247] See, for example: Article 29 Working Party, 'Opinion 06/2014 on the Notion of Legitimate Interests of the Data Controller under Article 7 of Directive 95/46/EC' (n 102) 17.

[248] See in this regard also Article 12(2) and (4).

Secondly, the lack of a balancing exercise becomes more apparent when comparing Article 17(3) with other provisions. Articles 6(1)(f)[249] and 23(1),[250] for example, include specific references to the need for a balancing act in conjunction with assessing necessity.[251] The lack of such specification in Article 17(3)'s opening sentence, *a contrario*, suggests no balancing exercise is required.[252] *Thirdly*, instead of a balancing act, the legislator defined specific scenarios in which it considered that other rights and/or interests supersede those of the data subject by default.

If Article 17(3) does not prescribe a balancing act, one may wonder, could it render the right to erasure inapplicable in evidently disproportionate situations that fall *stricto sensu* within one of the exemptions? Arguably, the answer to this question is yes. It is important to note though, that processing operations still need to comply with Arts 5–6 regardless. In other words, even though data subjects cannot invoke the right to erasure *in casu*, their rights will still be safeguarded. For example, the right to erasure may not be applicable in the context of the press publishing intimate details about a politician's life (pursuant to Art 17(3)(a). But, this does not automatically render such publication lawful under Article 6 and compliant with the principles in Article 5.[253] Moreover, as will appear later, most of the exemptions in Article 17(3) provide for some nuance, parrying a blunt yes-or-no test. Finally, it should also be pointed out that many other legal (and non-legal) tools are available to data subjects who are left incapable of invoking Article 17 (notably claims under defamation law, tort law, intellectual property law, criminal liability, etc).

Necessity Implies Granularity—To sum up in the EDPS' words, 'necessity in data protection law is a facts-based concept, rather than an abstract legal notion—necessity is a consequence of the factual details of a processing operation, considered in the light of the circumstances surrounding the adoption of the measure and the concrete purpose it aims to achieve'.[254] With this in mind, 'to the extent necessary' in Article 17(3) is to be assessed in light of the actual purpose(s)

[249] 'For the controller's legitimate interest to prevail, the data processing must be "necessary" and "proportionate"...'. Article 29 Working Party, 'Opinion 06/2014 on the Notion of Legitimate Interests of the Data Controller under Article 7 of Directive 95/46/EC' (n 102) 34 et seq.

[250] Article 23(1) explains that restrictions (inter alia to the right to erasure) in Member-State law need to be both necessary *and* proportionate.

[251] Lee Bygrave and Dag Wiese Schartum, 'Consent, Proportionality and Collective Power' in Serge Gutwirth and others (eds), *Reinventing Data Protection?* (Springer Netherlands 2009) 165 <http://link.springer.com/10.1007/978-1-4020-9498-9> accessed 1 June 2019.

[252] As will appear later (Chapter 5), pseudo-balancing exercises can implicitly be found in several specific exemptions in Article 17(3).

[253] According to WP29 such processing would indeed be unlawful pursuant to Article 6(1)(f). See notably: Article 29 Working Party, 'Opinion 06/2014 on the Notion of Legitimate Interests of the Data Controller under Article 7 of Directive 95/46/EC' (n 102) 34.

[254] European Data Protection Supervisor, 'Developing a "toolkit" for Assessing the Necessity of Measures That Interfere with Fundamental Rights. Background Paper' (n 238) 8. See European Data Protection Board, 'Draft Guidelines 2/2019 on the Processing of Personal Data under Article 6(1)(b) GDPR in the Context of the Provision of Online Services to Data Subject' (n 41) 7.

of the processing operation. To the extent this purpose corresponds with one of the scenarios in Article 17(3), the right to erasure cannot be invoked. Importantly, the right to erasure is only inapplicable with regard to those specific processing operations. Hence, when only a subset of processing operations is exempted pursuant to Article 17(3), it is in fact more appropriate to speak about a right to object rather than a right to erasure. After all, only a subset of *processing* operations is targeted, while the personal data itself remains intact. As such, the use of 'to the extent that' in Article 17(3) emphasizes the need for granularity.[255]

CONCLUSION—The 'necessity test' in Article 17(3) incorporates a facts-based assessment of the link between purposes and processing, in combination with a least-intrusive means test. Importantly, it does not require a full-blown fair balancing test, ie weighing the proportionate merit of the purpose(s) versus the data subject's interests. Even if this renders the right to erasure inapplicable in a large number of situations, data subjects are still protected by (quasi-)balancing acts in Articles 5–6, providing for a stricter necessity test. Thus, every processing operation needs to pass a necessity test anyway. A broad interpretation of Article 17(3) does not exonerate an unscrupulous app developer from having to comply with the lawfulness, purpose limitation, data minimization and storage limitation principles for example. Violating Articles 5–6 will generally result in the applicability of the right to erasure by virtue of Article 17(1), leading to a catch-22 situation when at the same time the processing would be exempted under Article 17(3). In these situations, data subjects might still find solace in the right to restriction of processing (Art 18) or the right to object (Art 21).

4.2 Freedom of Expression and Information

Article 17(3)

Paragraphs 1 and 2 shall not apply to the extent that processing is necessary: (a) for exercising the right of freedom of expression and information

RATIONALE—The right to erasure cannot be invoked to the extent the processing is necessary for exercising the right of freedom of expression and information. This first exemption is aimed at neutralizing what is probably the most oft-recurring criticism to the right to erasure. Removing information published online, regardless of it being personal data or not, has always raised legitimate concerns. Article 17 GDPR was feared to put in place an opportunity to 'censor the Internet'. In light of these fears, the legislator installed a considerably wide exemption for processing operations that are necessary to exercise the right to freedom of expression and

255 Further evidence of the need for granularity when assessing necessity in the GDPR, can be found in: Article 29 Working Party, 'Opinion 8/2014 on the on Recent Developments on the Internet of Things' (n 244) 17.

information (Art 17(3)(a)). Even though there is no hierarchy between the exemptions, being the first one still clearly signals the legislator's intention of preventing the right to erasure to be (ab)used in order to hamper freedom of expression and information rights.[256]

No Balancing Exercise—On the face of it, the exemption seems quite evident and maybe even redundant. Of course a fundamental right (ie Art 11 Charter) trumps a 'micro-right' in secondary EU legislation (ie Art 17(1)–(2) GDPR). As a result, and despite appearances, Article 17(3)(a) does *not* in itself install a balancing act. Only when the inapplicability of the right to erasure (pursuant to Article 17(3)(a) would elicit an interference with the fundamental right to data protection in Article 8 Charter, will there be a substantive balancing act with the right to freedom of expression and information in Article 11 Charter. As mentioned earlier, Article 6(1)(f) is how balancing acts are translated into the GDPR specifically (this will amply be developed in the following Chapter as well). Conflicts between the GDPR as a whole and freedom of expression are mitigated through Article 85 GDPR.[257] It is interesting, therefore, that Article 17(3)(a) does not refer to Article 85 GDPR. All the more so, given the fact that earlier drafts of Article 17 still contained such an explicit reference.[258] The deliberate removal of a link with Article 85 further suggests no balancing act is required when interpreting the exemption's applicability.[259] It also emphasizes that the exemption should be interpreted broadly, not limited (or even focused) on 'journalistic purposes or the purpose of academic artistic or literary expression'. Finally, the removal of any reference to Article 85 also signals that the legislator wished to avoid legal pluralism across Member-States regarding the first right to erasure exemption.[260]

[256] All the more when considering that in one of the earlier leaked drafts (of 10 November 2011, on file with the author) had the ASHRS exemption (currently fourth) first.

[257] Which requires Member-States to 'reconcile the right to the protection of personal data pursuant to this Regulation with the right to freedom of expression and information', with an emphasis on processing for 'journalistic, purposes and the purposes of academic, artistic or literary expression' (see Chapter 3). Also see Recital 153. Whereas Article 85 requires Member-States to reconcile the GDPR in general with information freedoms, Article 23(1)(i) *enables* them to install certain restrictions on data subject rights, when necessary and proportionate to safeguard 'the rights and freedoms of others'.

[258] See for example: Committee on Civil Liberties, Justice and Home Affairs (Rapporteur Albrecht JP), 'Draft Report on the Proposal for a Regulation of the European Parliament and of the Council on the Protection of Individual with Regard to the Processing of Personal Data and on the Free Movement of Such Data (General Data Protection Regulation)' (European Parliament (Committee on Civil Liberties, Justice and Home Affairs) 2012) 2012/0011(COD) Amendment 148 (n 88).

[259] The absence of a balancing act, as well as the exemption's open-endedness, broad scope, and overall brevity are made more conspicuous when compared with the other four exemptions. Indeed, from a systemic reading of all five exemptions in Article 17(3), it appears neither one of them prescribes a balancing act.

[260] The tremendous diversity in how all the Member-States regulate and adjudicate the interaction between freedom of expression and data protection has extensively been documented by Erdos. See notably: David Erdos, 'From the Scylla of Restriction to the Charybdis of Licence? Exploring the Scope of the "Special Purposes" Freedom of Expression Shield in European Data Protection' (2015) 52 Common Market Law Review 127.

Criteria/Conditions—It is hard to distil any concrete criteria from the first exemption to the right to erasure. Given the novelty of Article 17, no interpretative guidance can be found on this specific exemption either. In the end, the exemption in Article 17(3)a boils down to what exactly is covered by the 'right to freedom of expression and information'. Even though no specific reference is made, it is fair to assume the EU legislator intended to refer to the right proclaimed in Article 11 of the Charter.[261] A definition of the meaning and scope of this provision would go beyond the ambit of this book, and particularly this sub-section.[262] What follows is a dramatically shortened summary of the key elements of Article 11 Charter, relevant to Article 17(3) GDPR.

Article 11 Charter—Article 11(1) Charter declares '[e]veryone has the right to freedom of expression. This right shall include freedom to hold opinions and to receive and impart information and ideas without interference by public authority and regardless of frontiers.' Pursuant to Article 52(3) of the Charter, the content of Article 11 can be equated to Article 10 of the ECHR.[263] The right extends to any kind of expression, content, disseminated or accessed by any individual group or type of media.[264] Indeed, Article 11 also applies to 'the means of transmission or reception' of information, 'since any restriction imposed on the means necessarily interferes with the right to receive and impart information'.[265] A rich body of case law has identified different categories of 'expression', each of which may benefit from a different degree of protection by Article 11 Charter (10 ECHR).[266] In sum, and for the sake of conciseness, it can simply be stated that the fundamental right to freedom of expression and information has a very broad scope.[267]

261 And, pursuant to Article 52(3) Charter, also Article 10 ECHR.

262 See short summary and references of (some of) the theories underlying the right to freedom of expression in: Joris van Hoboken, 'Search Engine Freedom: On the Implications of the Right to Freedom Expression for the Legal Governance of Web Search Engines' (PhD Thesis, University of Amsterdam 2012) 51 et seq <http://dare.uva.nl/document/357527> accessed 1 June 2019; Lorna Woods, 'Freedom of Expression and Information' in Steve Peers and others (eds), *The EU Charter of Fundamental Rights: A Commentary* (Hart 2014) <https://www.bloomsburycollections.com/book/the-eu-charter-of-fundamental-rights-a-commentary/>.

263 Woods, 'Freedom of Expression and Information' (n 262) para 11.23.

264 ibid paras 11.25 et seq.

265 *Neij and Sunde Kolmisoppi v Sweden (Pirate Bay Case)* [2013] European Court of Human Rights 40397/12.

266 eg: political speech, artistic speech, and commercial speech, the latter typically attracting a lower level of protection. See notably the references in: Woods, 'Freedom of Expression and Information' (n 262) paras 11.28; 11.59; Brendan Van Alsenoy, Aleksandra Kuczerawy, and Jef Ausloos, 'Search Engines after "Google Spain": Internet@Liberty or Privacy@Peril?' (2013) 47<http://papers.ssrn.com/abstract=2321494> accessed 1 June 2019. The only content-based restrictions that have explicitly been permitted concern the 'dissemination of ideas promoting the Nazi ideology, denying the holocaust and inciting to hatred and racial discrimination.' See: Monica Macovei, 'Freedom of Expression: A Guide to the Implementation of Article 10 of the European Convention on Human Rights' [2004] Human Rights Handbooks 7 <http://www.supremecourt.ge/files/upload-file/pdf/article10eng.pdf> accessed 1 June 2019. Also see: Paolo Lobba, 'Holocaust Denial before the European Court of Human Rights: Evolution of an Exceptional Regime' (2015) 26 European Journal of International Law 237.

267 Woods, 'Freedom of Expression and Information' (n 262) para 11.33.

In light of freedom of expression and information's broad scope, it seems Article 17(3)a exempts a tremendous number of situations from the right to erasure's applicability. Any situation where personal data has some level of 'publicness' would in fact trigger the right to freedom of expression and information (of the 'speaker' and/or 'receiver'), even if minimally. Interpreted as such, Article 17(1) would not be applicable with regard to posts on social networks, newspaper articles, search engine results and any other information publicly available online.[268] This interpretation would, *ad absurdum*, render Article 17's second paragraph—aimed at situations 'where the controller has made the personal data public'—entirely in vain. Is there anything that prevents such a mechanical interpretation of the exemption?

To the Extent Necessary for Exercising Article 11 Charter—Picture two large circles, one capturing all situations covered by the fundamental right to freedom of expression, the other covering all 'processing of personal data'. Where the two overlap, the right to erasure cannot be invoked. Without further requirements or specifications, this overlapping zone is immense, as was explained before. In order to prevent undesirable overreach of the exemption, both circles should be pulled apart in order to reduce the overlap. The tool used for doing so can be found in the opening sentence of Article 17(3), described in the previous section: 'to the extent necessary'.[269] Instead of a balancing act, Article 17(3)(a) requires an evaluation of the inextricability of the link between on one hand the processing operation and on the other hand exercising the right to freedom of expression and information. This includes a dynamic (ie time-sensitive) evaluation of the 'expression'; 'communication', or 'information' purported to be covered by Article 11 Charter.

Assessing the inextricability—ie the necessary link—between 'processing of personal data' and 'freedom of expression and information', constitutes the core of determining Article 17(3)a's applicability. This is the case, for example, when the identity of the data subject constitutes the main focus of a newspaper article.[270] Article 5 (data quality principles) and Article 6 (lawfulness) offer some guidance on how to go about the necessity assessment. Both of these provisions are '*ex ante* protective measures' (see 'data protection matrix', Chapter 2), and as a result will already have to be complied with before the right to erasure can even be considered. Pursuant to Article 5(1)(b)–(c), the processing operation can only extend to what is necessary to achieve the purposes. Article 6(1)(b)–(f) further emphasizes the need for such an inextricable connection between the processing and the specific purpose(s) of the controller. In light of this, any processing operation for

[268] Erdos makes a similar argument with regard to the general derogation in Article 85. See: Erdos, 'From the Scylla of Restriction to the Charybdis of Licence?' (n 260) 148–49.

[269] See also: M Boulanger and others, 'La Protection Des Données à Caractère Personnel En Droit Communautaire: Deuxième Partie' [1997] Journal des Tribunaux—Droit Européen 145, 149.

[270] This was ruled to be the case in an Irish ruling, concerning a politician who had been called a homophobe. See: *Savage v Data Protection Commissioner* [2016] Circuit Court 2015/02589.

the purposes of exercising one's freedom of expression and/or information, will already have undergone the 'necessity'-test.[271] At least in theory. As an *ex post* empowerment tool, the right to erasure enables data subjects to force controllers to actively re-assess the required necessity at this moment in time.[272] If such necessity is (still) present, the controller will be able to continue processing the respective personal data, regardless of Article 17(3)(a). With this in mind, Article 17(3)(a) is primarily a flagpole, highlighting particular attention to be given to freedom of expression and information when determining the applicability of the right to erasure.

A 2016 case before the Belgian supreme court (*Cour de Cassation*) offers a great illustration of the time-sensitivity of the necessity-test in Articles 5–6 and 17(3).[273] The facts concerned the digitization and making available online of a decades old newspaper article. Whereas the value of this article was not contested at the time of the original publication, the mentioning of a full name was not deemed necessary to achieve the journalistic (ie subset of freedom of expression) purposes at the time the respective individual brought his case.

LEAST INTRUSIVE MEANS—It was highlighted in the previous section that the necessity requirement in Article 17(3)'s opening sentence also implies a least intrusive means test. In other words, can the right to freedom of expression and information also be achieved *without* negating data subjects their right to erasure? Looking at the specifics of individual situations, this might often be the case. Take the Belgian *Cour de Cassation* case, for example. The same purpose underlying the freedom of expression and information was deemed to be achieved without mentioning the specific name of the data subject.

GRANULARITY—Importantly, Article 17(3)(a) only exempts *to the extent* processing is necessary for exercising the right to freedom of expression and information. This choice of words highlights the need for granularity in assessing the reach and implementation of the exemption. Take for example, the underlying facts in the *Google Spain* case: ie the digitization and making online available of a fore closure announcement in a local Spanish newspaper. Arguably, the exemption in Article 17(3)(a) would extend to the mention of the person's name in the archived article (rendering the right to erasure inapplicable to anonymize the article at the source). Including that name in the newspaper's online search-index—or even external search engines—is a separate processing operation that may or may not benefit from the exemption. Arguably the indexation of the person's name to be

[271] Article 29 Working Party, 'Opinion 06/2014 on the Notion of Legitimate Interests of the Data Controller under Article 7 of Directive 95/46/EC' (n 102) 28.

[272] See in this regard also: *Salvatore Manni* (n 210) para 63.

[273] Despite the relevance of the facts, it should be said that this particular case did not rely on data protection law. Jef Ausloos, 'Vergetelheids-zaken voor de Hoven van Cassatie te België en Frankrijk—Contradictoir of Complementair? (noot onder Hof van cassatie 29 april 2016, nr C.15.0052.F' [2017] Computerrecht: Tijdschrift voor Informatica, Telecommunicatie en Recht 31.

used as a search term for referring to the article is not absolutely critical (ie 'necessary') to achieve the original freedom of expression and information interests. And even *if* name-based searchers are considered necessary, perhaps this also depends on the type of search engine at stake (specialized, intra-website, general-purpose, etc). 'To the extent' can also refer to granularity in implementing the right's exemption. Depending on what one considers the core value of the foreclosure announcement, the exemption may only extend to the inclusion of the article in the archive, but not, for example, to raising access-restrictions or pseudonymization. In sum, it is important to clearly separate the different relevant processing activities at hand (eg digitization, publishing on own website, making available to all visitors, making searchable on the basis of personal data, allowing access to external search engines, etc) and assess the necessity of each of these activities separately.

In isolation, Article 17(3)(a) does not install an obligation to balance the fundamental right to freedom of expression and information against the data subject's interests. Of course, the processing operation will still need a lawful ground under Article 6(1) GDPR, regardless of the (in)applicability of Article 17. In the context of ISS, and particularly when processing occurs for freedom of expression and information purposes, the most likely such ground will be the last one on legitimate interests (Art 6(1)(f)). Here, a catch-22 situation may emerge, where processing may be unlawful pursuant to Article 6(1)(f)—because overridden by the interests or fundamental rights and freedoms of the data subject—but the right to erasure is inapplicable because the processing is necessary *stricto sensu* for exercising freedom of expression and information. It would not appear that such situations would effectively occur in practice. If it can be established that processing is unlawful, it should not take place to begin with. If the processing of personal data serves a freedom of expression and information related purpose, it is also likely to be covered by the derogation regime in Article 85. As a result, the practical relevance of Article 17(3)(a) is easily be overstated.

In sum, several lessons can be drawn from the exemption in Article 17(3)(a). *Firstly*, it emphasizes the importance of the fundamental right to freedom of expression and information as well as the impact data protection—and the right to erasure in particular—may have on it. *Secondly*, it re-emphasizes the need for granularity in evaluating processing operations. As was amply made clear in the previous sections/chapters, one needs to clearly distinguish between processing operations in order to assess the rights and obligations emanating from the GDPR. In order to benefit from the exemption in Article 17(3)(a), the controller will need to demonstrate the extent to which further processing is necessary in order to exercise the right to freedom of expression and information (something the controller will have to be able to do anyway, pursuant to Article 5(2)). *Thirdly*, the broadness and vagueness of the exemption may potentially leave data subjects without a right to erasure in situations where they are disproportionately impacted by others' speech nonetheless. The data subject will then have to take a more difficult route to find relief either within the GDPR (eg Arts 5–6, or one of the rights in Arts 18 or 21) or beyond (eg defamation law, tort law, general right to privacy, intellectual property rights). Arguably, these non-GDPR provisions are more tailored to deal with individuals wishing to delete (or decrease the visibility of) information that has some public-facing nature.[274] In other words, from a practical perspective, Article 17(3)(a) in no way prevents those exercising the right to freedom of expression and/or information from having to remove personal data. *Fourthly*, the exemption significantly curbs the relevance of Article 17's second paragraph. Arguably, any situation where personal data is 'made public' (ie the focus of Art 17(2)) automatically also involves freedom of expression and/or information rights, a priori exempting the applicability of Article 17(1)–(2). The only situations where Article 17(2) would still apply, seem to be where (a) the (compatible) purposes do not encompass 'exercising the right to freedom of expression and information'; or (b) processing the published personal data appears not to be necessary (anymore) to achieve freedom of expression and information purposes.

Concluding, it is clear what the intention behind the first exemption to the right to erasure is: preventing abuse of the right to erasure in order to silence or restrict access to legitimate expression. A politician, for example, should not have the possibility to use Article 17 to censor the press. Still, this gut-feeling—or intuition—one may have with regard to the rationale of the freedom of expression exemption in Article 17(3)(a) does not emerge from a legalistic reading of the provision. To the contrary. It is far from clear whether situations with a clear moral standard in favour of removing personal data—eg the full name of a rape-victim on a revenge porn website—are still covered by the exemption or not, making it harder for grieved individuals to find relief. Of course, it is worth reiterating once more that Article 17(3)(a) only prevents the right to erasure from being applied. The individual will still be protected by the GDPR as a whole, by Article 7 and 8 in the Charter and other legal frameworks aimed at preventing abusive speech. So, even though Article 17(3)(a) does not in itself pursue a balanced outcome, the GDPR and the Charter still aim to safeguard such balance in the end.

4.3 Legal Obligation, Task Carried Out in Public Interest or Official Authority

Article 17(3)

Paragraphs 1 and 2 shall not apply to the extent that processing is necessary: […]

(b) for compliance with a legal obligation which requires processing by Union or

[274] And conversely, data protection rules are ill-suited to deal with these types of situations, rather being of a procedural nature with a focus on data management geared towards organizations. See: Van Alsenoy, 'The Evolving Role of the Individual Under EU Data Protection Law' (n 149) 13 et seq.

> Member State law to which the controller is subject or for the performance of a task carried out in the public interest or in the exercise of official authority vested in the controller.

The second exemption to the right to erasure bundles three related situations. Data subjects cannot invoke their right to erasure when further processing is necessary: (a) in order to comply with a legal obligation to which the controller is subject; (b) for the performance of a task carried out in the public interest; or (c) in exercising official authority vested in the controller. What becomes apparent right away is that this second exemption is much more specific than the first one. Each of the three situations described in Article 17(3)(b) is also almost entirely identical to the lawful grounds in Article 6(1)c and e. These provisions render lawful processing necessary for (c) 'compliance with a legal obligation to which the controller is subject', and (e) 'for the performance of a task carried out in the public interest or in the exercise of official authority vested in the controller'. As such, one could regard Article 6(1)(c) and (e) and Article 17(3)(b) as two sides of the same coin. Determining the applicability of the exemption will correspond to (re-) assessing the applicability of the lawful ground.

COMPLIANCE WITH A LEGAL OBLIGATION—The first situation foreseen in Article 17(3)(b) corresponds to the third lawful ground in Article 6(1), which in turn is a continuation of Article 7(c) Directive 95/46. Data protection authorities have always prescribed a strict interpretation of this provision. It must genuinely concern an obligation put down in a law (no contractual agreements or self-regulatory documents for example)[275] and the controller must have no other choice than to comply.[276] Examples range from processing operations in the context of HR management (eg reporting employees' salary data to social security and tax authorities) to duties of financial institutions to report suspicious behaviour to competent authorities for anti-money-laundering purposes.[277] On top of replicating the text in Article 6(1)(c), Article 17(3)(b) adds 'a legal obligation *which requires processing by Union or Member State law*'. This suggests an even stricter interpretation than the one in Article 6. The processing of personal data must be

[275] WP29 further specifies that the respective law needs to 'fulfil all relevant conditions to make the obligation valid and binding, and must also comply with data protection law, including the requirement of necessity, proportionality and purpose limitation'. In: Article 29 Working Party, 'Opinion 06/2014 on the Notion of Legitimate Interests of the Data Controller under Article 7 of Directive 95/46/EC' (n 102) 19.

[276] Christopher Kuner, *European Data Protection Law: Corporate Compliance and Regulation* (OUP 2007) para 5.28. WP29 explains that 'if— without a clear and specific legal obligation to do so—an Internet service provider decides to monitor its users in an effort to combat illegal downloading, Article 7(c) will not be an appropriate legal ground for this purpose'. Article 29 Working Party, 'Opinion 06/2014 on the Notion of Legitimate Interests of the Data Controller under Article 7 of Directive 95/46/EC' (n 102) 19.

[277] Boulanger and others (n 269) 147; Article 29 Working Party, 'Opinion 06/2014 on the Notion of Legitimate Interests of the Data Controller under Article 7 of Directive 95/46/EC' (n 102) 19.

explicitly required in the respective rule and cannot merely be implied.[278] The reference to EU or Member-State legislation also re-emphasizes that compliance with foreign legal obligations cannot in itself justify an exemption to the right to erasure on the basis of Article 17(3)(b).

Public Interest Tasks and Official Authority /1—The second part of Article 17(3)(c) is identical to the lawful ground in Article 6(1)(d) (and Article 7(e) in Directive 95/46). Any processing necessary for the performance of a task carried out in the public interest *or* exercise of official authority vested in the controller is exempted from the right to erasure. Not much interpretative guidance exists on this fourth lawful ground (let alone as an exemption to the right to erasure).[279] At the time Directive 95/46 was adopted, the provision was said to specifically target processing operations in the public sector, ie in the context of traditionally governmental tasks.[280] As a lawful ground, the provision needs to be interpreted restrictively, but still in light of the proportionality principle.[281] The first half ('public interest') may refer to situations where a controller accidentally notices illegal behaviour and communicates it to the authorities, whereas the second half (public authority vested in the controller) may refer to organizations such as a bar association or a chamber of medical professionals processing members' data.[282] WP29 explained that such 'public interest tasks' or 'official authority' should typically stem from 'statutory laws or other legal regulations'.[283] Recitals 10, and 50–52 in the GDPR seem to implicitly confirm this, suggesting the lawful ground may be specified in (sector-specific) EU or Member-State laws. It must be said though, that Article 23(1)(e) permits further 'general public interest' derogations, inter alia with regard to the right to erasure, but *only* on the basis an EU or Member-State law.[284] The absence of such an explicit law-requirement in Article 17(3)(b) *in fine*,

[278] On the other hand, it must also be said that during the legislative process, an important specification was removed from this particular exemption. The EC's Committee on Industry, Research, and Energy successfully requested the removal of 'Member State laws shall meet an objective of public interest, respect the essence of the right to the protection of personal data and be proportionate to the legitimate aim pursued.' See: Opinion of the Committee on Industry, Research and Energy for the LIBE Committee on Civil Liberties, Justice and Home Affairs (Rapporteur Albrecht JP), 'Report on the Proposal for a Regulation of the European Parliament and of the Council on the Protection of Individuals with Regard to the Processing of Personal Data and on the Free Movement of Such Data (General Data Protection Regulation)' (n 199) pt Amendment 165.

[279] A very useful clarification, specifically looking at the use of this lawful ground in the public sector though, can be found in: Dirk De Bot, *Gegevensverwerking in de publieke sector: een verkennend onderzoek van de relatie tussen privacy-, gegevensbeschermings-, administratief en grondwettelijk recht aan de hand van de uitwisseling van gegevens tussen besturen* (Politieia 2015) 264 et seq.

[280] Boulanger and others (n 269) 147–48.

[281] Kuner, *European Data Protection Law* (n 276) para 5.28; Article 29 Working Party, 'Opinion 06/2014 on the Notion of Legitimate Interests of the Data Controller under Article 7 of Directive 95/46/EC' (n 102) 22.

[282] Article 29 Working Party, 'Opinion 06/2014 on the Notion of Legitimate Interests of the Data Controller under Article 7 of Directive 95/46/EC' (n 102) 21.

[283] ibid 22. The idea being that in a democracy, what is in the 'public interest' should be determined by the people, ie politicians who then translate it into law. De Bot (n 279) 269–70.

[284] EU or Member-State laws may further restrict the applicability of inter alia the right to erasure 'when such a restriction respects the essence of the fundamental rights and freedoms and is a necessary

at the very least leaves room for interpretation as to the necessity for a legal ground dictating public interest or official authority processing.[285]

Public Interest Tasks and Official Authority /2—Despite some interpretative guidance on Article 6(1)(d) GDPR,[286] important questions remain unanswered as to Article 17(3)(b) in the ISS context, particularly given (a) increased government outsourcing to the private sector and (b) the difficulty of identifying and distinguishing 'government' activities in a fast-moving environment with whole new industries emerging and/or transforming. WP29 listed 'epidemiological studies' and 'research' as examples of private sector data processing activities that may be covered by the lawful ground in Article 6(1)(d) GDPR. Would this also include public-private-partnerships such as the one between the UK's National Health Service and Google's DeepMind to research kidney injuries for example?[287] One may also wonder to what extent 'sharing-economy' platforms, search engines, and social networks fulfil—at least in part—'public interest tasks'. Such an argument would most likely not hold up as a lawful ground to justify data processing by ISS providers under Article 6(1). But, does this also mean it could not be used as a (first line of) defence against erasure requests.[288]

In public law, the concept of 'public interest' itself is generally considered to be too vague. In the abstract, the concept is so broad that it can also cover potentially bad or undesirable activities. For this reason, it is generally deemed that in order to rely on this ground, 'public interest' should be made more tangible in a concrete legal document applicable to one's situation.[289] From the perspective of data protection law in the ISS context particularly, it is also worth highlighting that relying on 'public interest' as such will never be specific enough to comply with the purposes limitation requirement in Article 5(1)(b). This does not necessarily imply the same level of specification is necessary when relying on the exemption in Article 17(3)(b), but it does put things in perspective. Finally, it should be stressed that

and proportionate measure in a democratic society to safeguard: [. . .] (e) other important objectives of general public interest of the Union or of a Member State, in particular an important economic or financial interest of the Union or of a Member State, including monetary, budgetary and taxation a matters, public health and social security'.

[285] It has even been argued that this exemption potentially lowers the protection afforded to data subjects below the level of Directive 95/46. Amberhawk, 'Council's Exceptions from the Data Protection Regulation Degrade the Privacy Protection below Directive 95/46/EC' 6 (*Hawktalk*, 3 August 2015) <http://amberhawk.typepad.com/amberhawk/2015/08/councils-exceptions-from-the-data-protection-regulation-degrade-the-privacy-protection-below-directive-9546ec.html> accessed 1 June 2019.

[286] Or at least its predecessor Article 7(e) Directive 95/46

[287] Julia Powles, 'DeepMind's Data Deals Raise Some Serious Questions' *Financial Times* (4 December 2016) <https://www.ft.com/content/ddd1478e-b70d-11e6-961e-a1acd97f622d> accessed 1 June 2019; Julia Powles and Hal Hodson, 'Google DeepMind and Healthcare in an Age of Algorithms' (2017) 7 Health and Technology 351.

[288] Even under Directive 95/46, with no explicit Article 17(3) equivalent, the CJEU acknowledged that the public interest is a factor when assessing erasure of personal data in the context of search engines, albeit tied to the freedom of expression and information. See notably *Google Spain* (n 19) para 81.

[289] De Bot (n 279) 269.

the GDPR (both in the lawful ground in Article 6(1)(e) and right to erasure exemption in Article 17(3)b) only covers *tasks carried out* in the public interest. This implies that the respective processing operation's *raison d'être* is to serve the public interest (rather than it being tangential or ad hoc). This last observation makes Article 17(3)(b) very unlikely to exempt ISS providers from an obligation to erase.

In conclusion, the potentially broad scope of Article 17(3)(b)'s exemption requires a strict interpretation. This holds particularly true with regard to the second sub-exemption on 'tasks carried out in the public interest',[290] the first one (legal obligation) and the third one (official authority vested in the controller) leaving much less room for interpretation. In each individual case, the respective public interest(s) and/or official authority should clearly be identified.[291] Furthermore the reference to a *task* carried out in the public interest, also implies a predefined assignment, rather than mere hypothetical estimations. The specification 'to the extent necessary' in Article 17(3)'s opening sentence further enables narrowing down this second exemption. It implies that even if applicable, the exemption only exonerates one particular activity. This results in a de facto transformation of the right to erasure in the right to object: the data are not entirely erased, but cannot be processed for other purposes than the one(s) strictly corresponding to what is specified in the exemption. Indeed, the right to object (Art 21) explicitly applies to processing operations based on Article 6(1)(e). So even if one would come to the conclusion in an individual case that the controller benefits from the exemption in Article 17(3)(b), the data subject will still have a valid right to object pursuant to Article 21(1).

4.4 Public Interest in the Area of Public Health

Article 17(3)

> Paragraphs 1 and 2 shall not apply to the extent that processing is necessary: […]
> (c) for reasons of public interest in the area of public health in accordance with points (h) and (i) of Article 9(2) as well as Article 9(3).

The right to erasure cannot be invoked to the extent processing of the respective personal data is necessary 'for reasons of public interest in the area of public health

[290] Further guidance on what 'public interest' means exactly, can be drawn from the European Commission's efforts to come to a common understanding of the concept of 'services of general economic interest'. In a 2003 Green Paper, the Commission identified several characteristics: 'universal service, continuity, quality of service, affordability, as well as user and consumer protection'. European Commission, 'Green Paper on Services of General Interest' (2003) COM(2003) 270 final 15 et seq <http://eur-lex.europa.eu/legal-content/EN/TXT/PDF/?uri=CELEX:52003DC0270&from=EN> accessed 1 June 2019.

[291] Cullen International, *A Business Guide to Changes in European Data Protection Legislation* (Kluwer Law International(IS), Kluwer Law International 1999) 49; Article 29 Working Party, 'Opinion 06/2014 on the Notion of Legitimate Interests of the Data Controller under Article 7 of Directive 95/46/EC' (n 102) 22.

in accordance with points (h) and (i) of Article 9(2) as well as Article 9(3)'.[292] This seems to be logical when considering that data processing may contribute significantly to public health objectives.[293] Article 17(3)'s *third* exemption comprises three main criteria: (a) sensitive data; (b) public interest in the area of public health; and (c) protective safeguards.

SENSITIVE DATA—By explicitly requiring the processing to be in accordance with (certain paragraphs in) Article 9, the exemption automatically restricts itself to so-called sensitive data only (see Chapter 3). In other words, pursuant to Article 17(3)(c), the right to erasure will only be inapplicable with regard to *sensitive* data. This exemption highlights, once again, the paradoxical nature of this type of personal data, benefitting from extra protection (eg processing is prohibited by default in Art 9), while also restricting the extent of protection (eg inapplicability of right to erasure).[294]

PUBLIC INTEREST IN THE AREA OF PUBLIC HEALTH—Of course the right to erasure is not inapplicable with regard to all sensitive data under any circumstances. Article 17(3)c only exempts situations where such sensitive data is used for the purpose of public interest in the area of public health. The first part of this requirement is reminiscent of the right to erasure's second exemption. Processing of personal data 'for important objectives of general public interest' are permitted, even irrespectively of the compatibility with the original purpose (Recital 50 GDPR). One such objective of public interest could be considered the

[292] Article 9(2) permitting the processing of sensitive data when '(h) processing is necessary for the purposes of preventive or occupational medicine, for the assessment of the working capacity of the employee, medical diagnosis, the provision of health or social care or treatment or the management of health or social care systems and services on the basis of Union or Member State law or pursuant to contract with a health professional and subject to the conditions and safeguards referred to in paragraph 3; (i) processing is necessary for reasons of public interest in the area of public health, such as protecting against serious cross-border threats to health or ensuring high standards of quality and safety of health care and of medicinal products or medical devices, on the basis of Union or Member State law which provides for suitable and specific measures to safeguard the rights and freedoms of the data subject, in particular professional secrecy'; and Article 9(3) proclaiming that the '[p]ersonal data referred to in paragraph 1 may be processed for the purposes referred to in point (h) of paragraph 2 when those data are processed by or under the responsibility of a professional subject to the obligation of professional secrecy under Union or Member State law or rules established by national competent bodies or by another person also subject to an obligation of secrecy under Union or Member State law or rules established by national competent bodies'.

[293] Recital 53, for example, states that so-called sensitive data 'which merit higher protection should be processed for health-related purposes only where necessary to achieve those purposes for the benefit of natural persons and society as a whole'. During the legislative process, it was also said inter alia that '[i]t is in the vital interests of the data subject to keep a complete record of their health in order to deliver the most appropriate care and treatments during the course of their life'. See: Justification to Amendment 491 in: Committee on Civil Liberties, Justice and Home Affairs (Rapporteur Albrecht JP), 'Draft Report on the Proposal for a Regulation of the European Parliament and of the Council on the Protection of Individual with Regard to the Processing of Personal Data and on the Free Movement of Such Data (General Data Protection Regulation). Amendments (4) 1189–1492' (n 88). See also: Concetta Tania Di Iorio and Fabrizio Carinci, 'Privacy and Health Care Information Systems: Where Is the Balance?' in Carlisle George, Diane Whitehouse, and Penny Duquenoy (eds), *eHealth: Legal, Ethical and Governance Challenges* (Springer 2012) 87.

[294] See, for example, Recital 53.

area of public health.[295] The exemption in Article 17(3)(c) covers those situations where 'public interest' and 'public health' processing overlap. Accordingly, the exemption does not prevent the right to erasure from being invoked in the context of individual healthcare relationships between a doctor and a patient. This is not to say that personal data collected in such an individual doctor-patient relationship can enter the scope of the exemption when that data is further pooled with other data in the context of medical research for example. Still, in order to benefit from the exemption, such processing still needs to comply with the third requirement.

SAFEGUARDS—The last requirement that curbs the scope of the exemption in Article 17(3)(c) concerns safeguards (Art 9(3)).[296] Only when certain minimum safeguards are met, can the right to erasure be blocked 'for reasons of public interest in the area of public health'. Most importantly is that the respective processing operation(s) need to occur either 'pursuant to a contract with a health professional'[297] or 'on the basis of Union or Member State law'.[298] This can also be deduced from Recital 54 which explains that processing of 'data concerning health for reasons of public interest should not result in personal data being processed for other purposes by third parties such as employers or insurance and banking companies'.

In other words, it would seem hard for a non-healthcare professional (organization) to invoke Article 17(3)(c) to fend off a right to erasure request. It would seem similarly hard to do so when the processing of 'sensitive' personal data is not based on a specific legal rule with an objective of public interest in the area of public health. Still, a lot depends on how strict the 'legal rule' requirement will be interpreted in practice. Do the provisions in Article 9(2h–i) require a legal rule specifically permitting the processing of personal data for a particular purpose (eg early stage lung-cancer discovery)? Or is it sufficient if a legal rule lays down a general mission of pursuing public health objectives? Some indirect guidance can be found in WP29's opinion on legitimate interests. Here, WP29 suggests that controllers that are official authorities themselves do not necessarily require

[295] Recital 54 refers to Regulation (EC) No 1338/2008 of the European Parliament and of the Council of 16 December 2008 on Community statistics on public health and health and safety at work (OJ L 354, 31.12.2008, p 70) and defines 'public health' as 'all elements related to health, namely health status, including morbidity and disability, the determinants having an effect on that health status, health care needs, resources allocated to health care, the provision of, and universal access to, health care as well as health care expenditure and financing, and the causes of mortality'.

[296] Also already recognized by scholars prior to the adoption of the GDPR. Di Iorio and Carinci (n 293) 87.

[297] ie '[P]rocessed by or under the responsibility of a professional subject to the obligation of professional secrecy under Union or Member State law or rules established by national competent bodies or by another person also subject to an obligation of secrecy under Union or Member State law or rules established by national competent bodies'.

[298] Some nuances exist depending on whether the respective processing operation relies on Article 9(2)(h) or (i), such as the need for 'suitable and specific measures to safeguard the rights and freedoms of the data subject, in particular professional secrecy'.

a legal obligation to process the data.[299] Where the controller is a private sector entity, or the processing implies an important invasion of privacy, 'the legal basis should be specific and precise enough in framing the end of data processing that may be allowed'.[300]

In light of the above, it seems that this third exemption is of limited relevance in the context of most ISS, particularly those that are emblematic of the power asymmetries that are focused on in this book. Still, tangential questions remain as to the exemption's applicability to app developers specialized in health or fitness (eg tracking sleep, eating, or work-out patterns). Even though part of their activities (eg statistics, research) may arguably be of some value to public interest in the field of public health, their operations will generally not be based on a EU or Member-State law. Things would change, when such an app is developed by an official healthcare provider or another institution decreed by law to pursue objectives of 'public interest in the area of public health. Constraints in adequate resources (financially, technically, knowhow, etc) will often cause such actors or institutions to outsource to, or partner with, third party ISS providers. In some situations, this would translate to straightforward controller-processor relationships (eg a doctor using online storage platforms or email services).

More complicated are situations where official institutions pursuing objectives of 'public interest in the area of public health' effectively partner with ISS providers to perform big data analyses for example. This is exactly what happened in the UK in 2015. The country's NHS entered a data-sharing agreement with the Google-owned artificial intelligence company DeepMind.[301] The deal involved 'developing Streams, a mobile app, to integrate data and co-ordinate push alerts concerning acute kidney injury'.[302] Experts are unclear whether the deal is consistent with data protection law, let alone the broader implications it has on market power dynamics. In the context of the specific exemption in Article 17(3)c, one could argue that DeepMind is exempted to the extent it processes as a *joint* controller with the NHS. In light of granularity, any activity that is not co-determined by the NHS for the purpose of public interest in the area of public health', would not be covered. To the extent DeepMind determines purposes autonomously and/or does not foresee sufficient safeguards for securing and silo-ing the respective personal data, it cannot invoke the exemption. Importantly, this assessment only applies to the right to erasure exemption and not to the compliance of said processing with the GDPR overall.

[299] Article 29 Working Party, 'Opinion 06/2014 on the Notion of Legitimate Interests of the Data Controller under Article 7 of Directive 95/46/EC' (n 102) 21.leg

[300] ibid 22.

[301] 'The agreement gives DeepMind access to a wide range of healthcare data on the 1.6 million patients who pass through three London hospitals run by the Royal Free NHS Trust [...]'. Hal Hodson, 'Google Knows Your Ills' (2016) 230 New Scientist 22. Julia Powles, "Google DeepMind and Healthcare in An Age of Algorithms" (2016) forthcoming in Journal of Health and Technology.

[302] Powles (n 301).

4.5 Public Interest Archiving, Scientific and Historical Research, or Statistical Purposes

Article 17(3)

Paragraphs 1 and 2 shall not apply to the extent that processing is necessary: [...] (d) for archiving purposes in the public interest, scientific or historical research purposes or statistical purposes in accordance with Article 89(1) in so far as the right referred to in paragraph 1 is likely to render impossible or seriously impair the achievement of the objectives of that processing.

The fourth exemption to the right to erasure can be considered the flipside to the storage limitation principle in Article 5(1)(e), which foresees derogations for when personal data is 'processed solely for archiving purposes in the public interest, scientific or historical research purposes, or statistical purposes' (ASHRS). It also reiterates and fine-tunes a more general derogation in the GDPR overall. Article 89(2) (discussed in Chapter 3) permits Member-States to render inapplicable specific *ex post* empowerment measures in Arts 15–16 and 18–21 of the GDPR (eg right of access, right to restriction of processing) when personal data are processed for 'archiving purposes in the public interest, scientific or historical research purposes or statistical purposes'. The conspicuous absence of any reference to Article 17 in Article 89(2) suggests the GDPR does not want to leave it up Member-States to decide whether or not to introduce exemptions to the right to erasure in this context.[303] Incorporating the exemption into Article 17 itself—rendering it applicable in the same way across the EU—recognizes the potency of the right to erasure and the potentially far-reaching consequences it may have on any of the purposes specified in Article 89. Indeed, contrary to other *ex post* empowerment tools,[304] the right to erasure is irreversible. This may prove particularly problematic when pursuing archiving purposes in the public interest, scientific or historical research purposes, or statistical purposes.

The exemption in Article 17(3)(d) does make explicit reference to Article 89(1). This provision requires any processing for ASHRS purposes to be subject to appropriate safeguards, notably by ensuring 'technical and organisational measures are in place in particular in order to ensure respect for the principle of

[303] It must be said though, that some confusion arises when comparing the list of data subject rights mentioned in Article 89 with those mentioned in Recital 156. Whereas the right to erasure is not featured in Article 89, the recital does state that 'Member States should be authorised to provide, under specific conditions and subject to appropriate safeguards for data subjects, specifications and derogations with regard to the [...] rights to rectification, to erasure, to be forgotten, [...]'. This seems to suggest that Member-States still have some leeway in interpreting the exemption of the right to erasure in this context.

[304] The right to object, for example, can still be invoked—even despite potential national exemptions in light of Article 89—whenever the respective processing of personal data for scientific or historical research purposes or statistical purposes is not necessary for the performance of a task carried out for reasons of public interest (Art 21(6)).

data minimisation' (eg pseudonymization). The need for such safeguards stems from the privileged position ASHRS processing often gets in the GDPR.[305] Even if somewhat redundant, the explicit reference to these safeguards in Article 17(3)(d) emphasizes their importance. The right to erasure can only be negated if further processing is necessary for ASHRS purposes *and* adequate safeguards can be ensured.

The last words of Article 17(3)(d), further curb the scope of the exemption. Only when the right to erasure would likely *render impossible* or at least *seriously impair* the achievement of ASHRS purposes will the right to erasure *not* be invokable. In doing so, this second half of the sentence merges requirements already present in Article 17(3)'s opening sentence and Article 89(1) and (4). It effectively emphasizes the importance of the granularity principle, constraining the exemption to apply only with regard to processing for any of the protected purposes.

In sum, the right to erasure cannot be invoked whenever further processing is vital to achieving ASHRS purposes and such processing is subject to appropriate safeguards. The ambiguity revolving the scope and meaning of what exactly is covered by 'archiving purposes in the public interest, scientific or historical research purposes or statistical purposes' has already been discussed in Chapter 3.

4.6 Legal Claims

The fifth and last exemption to the right to erasure specifically, relates to the 'establishment, exercise or defence of legal claims'.[306] This exemption could arguably be qualified as the narrowest one, specifically aimed at preventing potential loss of evidence in legal actions. The exemption can be seen as the flipside of the data subject's right to restriction of processing in Article 18(1)(c). Following this provision, it is possible to prevent controllers from erasing personal data but only store it passively (ie not process it for any other purpose), when that data is still 'required by the data subject for the establishment, exercise or defence of legal claims'. Essentially this means that data subjects can ask Apple *not* to erase their Siri voice data despite company policies, because it contains audio on an attempted murder in the background.

In light of Article 17(3)'s opening sentence, it is of course important to note once again that the exemption will only extend in so far it is *necessary*. This implies that

[305] eg also as a derogatory regime to the general prohibition of processing 'sensitive data' (Art 9(2)(j) and Recitals 52–53).

[306] At the time of writing, at least one national case was found where a right to erasure request was successfully blocked based on this exemption: *X v het college van burgemeester en wethouders van de gemeente Bladel* [2019] Rechtbank Oost-Brabant SHE 18/2806.

all *other* processing operations—not necessary for the establishment, exercise, or defence of legal claims—will not be covered by the exemption and should cease. Of course, in practice, a risk of abuse still exists. ISS providers may well claim that all (personal) data they collect or generally have access to, is necessary for potential future legal action. Such an intelligence services ethos of 'collect-it-all' is, in fact, already pursued by the likes of Facebook to defend why it needs to track the browsing habits of *all* internet users (even those without a Facebook account), in order to ensure the security of their platform.[307] Similarly, it is unclear whether a video hosting platform, for example, may rely on this exemption when an individual uploads (copyright) infringing material and wants to erase any personal data enabling his/her identification. This second hypothesis raises the question of whether the exemption can also be invoked by entities that are not themselves 'establishing, exercising, or defending' a legal claim. These examples illustrate that a seemingly narrow exemption could potentially encompass the majority of personal data processed by ISS providers.

Based on a systemic interpretation of this exemption, as well as considering the alternative, it is fair to say that this last exemption only applies when erasure would effectively obstruct the preparation of a concrete legal claim. Indeed, any exemption or derogation to data protection rights should be interpreted strictly. Moreover, even if not addressed directly by WP29, its guidance does suggest a narrow interpretation as well; ie only when a concrete legal claim is actually being prepared,[308] not simply when further storage *might* be useful in the future.[309,310] Such an interpretation would also seem to correspond to the CJEU's *Sabam* cases (where installing a general filtering mechanism for intellectual property enforcement purposes was inter alia not deemed to be fairly balanced against data protection rights of those monitored).[311]

[307] See inter alia: Samuel Gibbs, 'Facebook "Tracks All Visitors, Breaching EU Law"' *The Guardian* (31 March 2015) <www.theguardian.com/technology/2015/mar/31/facebook-tracks-all-visitors-breaching-eu-law-report> accessed 1 June 2019; Hannah Kuchler, 'Facebook Blocks Belgian Users after Privacy Ruling over Cookies' *Financial Times* (3 December 2015) <https://www.ft.com/content/9c9bf084-994f-11e5-95c7-d47aa298f769> accessed 1 June 2019. An overview of relevant news-articles, as well as the report giving rise to court proceedings in Belgium, can be found at: http://www.law.kuleuven.be/citip/en/news/item/icri-cir-advises-belgian-privacy-commission-in-facebook-investigation

[308] Article 29 Working Party, 'Opinion 06/2014 on the Notion of Legitimate Interests of the Data Controller under Article 7 of Directive 95/46/EC' (n 102) 61.

[309] In its SWIFT Opinion, WP29 explained that the company could not legitimize data transfers on the basis of its infrastructure being critical in the global financial industry. Article 29 Working Party, 'Opinion 10/2006 on the Processing of Personal Data by the Society for Worldwide Interbank Financial Telecommunication (SWIFT)' (Article 29 Working Party 2006) Opinion WP 128 24–25 <http://ec.europa.eu/justice/article-29/documentation> accessed 1 June 2019.

[310] WP29 explained that after 'the processing activity ends, proof of consent should be kept no longer then strictly necessary for compliance with a legal obligation or for the establishment, exercise or defence of legal claims, in accordance with Article 17(3)(b) and (3)(e)'. Article 29 Working Party, 'Guidelines on Consent under Regulation 2016/679' (n 52) 20.

[311] *Scarlet Extended v Sabam* [2011] Court of Justice of the European Union C-70/10; *SABAM v Netlog* [2012] Court of Justice of the European Union C-360/10.

4.7 Interim Conclusion on the Right to Erasure Exemptions

The right to erasure can be denied to data subjects on at least two levels. The first level relates to broader exemptions and derogations to the GDPR overall (see Chapter 3). Personal data being processed in the course of a purely household activity (Art 2(2)(c)) will not be targetable by the right to erasure. Article 23 also permits Member-States to install specific restrictions to the right to erasure in their national laws as well.[312] These may be flat-out exemptions or more nuanced derogation regimes such as replacing erasure with pseudonymization or access-restrictions. The second level relates to exemptions specific to the right to erasure itself, ie the five situations set out in Article 17(3) and analysed in this section:

(a) Freedom of expression and information;
(b) Legal obligation, task carried out in the public interest or exercise of official authority;
(c) Public interest in the area of public health;
(d) Public interest archiving, scientific or historical research, or statistical purposes;
(e) Establishment, exercise, or defence of legal claims.

The main added value of these exemptions is that they safeguard broader interests than just that of the controller. This is important, as the assessment of whether or not to accommodate an erasure request will firstly fall on the shoulders of the controller. This assessment will often result in a de facto balancing act (see Chapter 5) and it may be problematic to rely on controllers to defend interests, rights and freedoms that are not its own. With the exemptions in Article 17(3), the legislator pre-empts such issue by defining what side the balance should tip over to by default.

It is fair to say that the exemptions leave quite some room for interpretation. Not in the least because neither of them can be assessed in isolation. In fact, most of them require assessments that supersede the GDPR as a whole. Either by referring to other legal frameworks (b)–(c) or requiring a functional fundamental rights assessment (a). Whereas the scope and meaning of some underlying notions have been more developed (eg (a)) than others (eg (d)), the practical operation and reach of these exemptions remains one big question mark at the moment.[313] Disjointed, vague, and somewhat superfluous, Article 17(3) is a classic example of the EU legislator's intense compromise-seeking. At best, the provision will

[312] On the problematic interaction between Article 23 and Article 17(3), see notably: de Terwangne (n 169) 23–24.

[313] When first announced, the EDPS even recommended deleting the paragraph altogether. See: European Data Protection Supervisor, 'Opinion of the European Data Protection Supervisor (EDPS) on the Data Protection Reform Package' (n 215) n 149.

safeguard important values and interests in case of data protection overreach. At worst, it might undermine any effectiveness of the right to erasure in practice. Undoubtedly an emerging body of case-law, EDPB guidance, and self-regulatory efforts will help clarify the boundaries of these exemptions.

As a starting point, the least that can be said is that, as a general rule, all five right to erasure exemptions are subject to a narrow and strict interpretation. They largely mirror the grounds for lawful processing in Article 6(1). Both provisions define specific situations in which (further) processing of personal data can be deemed lawful by default. Indeed, the exemptions in Article 17(3) all concern situations where the data subject's interests are overridden by stronger interests, rights and/or freedoms at the other side of the balance. It is this default *against* the data subject which further justifies a narrow interpretation. Most exemptions also hinge on extra safeguards being put in place to ensure the data subject is still somewhat protected. Furthermore, the opening sentence of Article 17(3) implies a granular approach. This means that only the specific processing operation(s) qualifying under any of the listed situations are in fact exempted.

Section 5. Conclusion

Summary—The right to erasure in Article 17 GDPR is composed of three main parts: (a) triggers; (b) extensions; and (c) exemptions. Six right-to-erasure triggers are described in Article 17(1), each of which refer implicitly or explicitly to other provisions. The same observation can be made with regard to the right to erasure exemptions in Article 17(3). Neither the triggers nor the exemptions can be assessed in isolation but will require a broader assessment (sometimes even reaching beyond the GDPR). The second paragraph comprises what one could call a 'right to be forgotten 2.0'. It essentially puts in place an obligation of means on controllers who have made personal data public, to communicate successful erasure requests to all other controllers processing that same personal data (see Table 4.1).

Looking at the practical operation of the right to erasure—ie when assessing a concrete case— it makes sense to first look at Article 17's last paragraph on the exemptions. After all, when either one of them applies, the right to erasure cannot be invoked and there will be no point in evaluating the triggers. Apart from this pragmatic suggestion, it is also worth briefly highlighting the key modalities for exercising/accommodating the right to erasure as specified by the GDPR. First of all, controllers should facilitate the exercise of the right to erasure (Art 12(2)). This can be done electronically, through clear and unequivocal dashboards for instance (Rec 59). The right to erasure should also be accommodated (or at least responded to) *without undue delay* and in any event within one month of the request (Arts 17(1), 12(3), Rec 59). Exercising the right to erasure shall be free of

Table 4.1 Summary overview Article 17

1. Right to erasure applies when:	**2. Right to be forgotten 2.0**	**3. Right to erasure does not apply:**
(a) Purpose expiration	*When controller made personal data public*	*To the extent processing is necessary for:*
(b) Consent withdrawal		*(a) Freedom of expression and information*
(c) Right to object	⇩	*(b) Legal obligation or task in public interest / official authority*
(d) Unlawful processing		*(c) Public interest in area of public health*
(e) Legal obligation	*Obligation of means to communicate request to all other controllers*	*(d) Archiving, scientific/historical research or statistical purposes*
(f) Minors' withdrawal of consent in ISS context		*(e) Legal claims*

charge (Art 12(5), Rec 59).[314] The controller may also require the data subject to provide additional information in order to prove his/her identity (Arts 11, 12(2)).

Having now thoroughly analysed Article 17, does the provision contribute to the empowerment goal underlying the right to data protection in Article 8 Charter (see Chapter 2)? In other words, does it put an effective tool in the hands of data subjects to control their personal data in the face of powerful ISS providers processing that data? It appears that Article 17's main contribution is how it reemphasizes, clarifies, and centralizes key data protection components from a data subject's perspective.[315] It *reemphasizes* how many existing data protection elements already imply a right (and obligation) to erasure. It *clarifies* by unambiguously specifying how other provisions may (not) result in erasure. And it *centralizes*, as it effectively constitutes a central node in the GDPR drawing together the key provisions that are relevant in light of *ex post* empowerment, as suggested in the table below (see Table 4.2). In light of this, the provision offers a great starting point for data subjects interested in reclaiming control over their personal data.

Apart from clarifying the nature of Article 17 as a 'hub' for other provisions aimed at protecting or empowering data subjects, this chapter also enabled the identification of some key requirements for making the right to erasure effective. Firstly, it appears that granularity is essential for the right to erasure to have any practical

[314] Unless requests are manifestly unfounded or excessive, in particular because of their repetitive character, in which case the controller may charge a reasonable fee, taking into account the administrative costs for accommodating the erasure.

[315] As opposed to from the perspective of controllers.

Table 4.2 Cross-references for right-to-erasure triggers

Right-to-erasure triggers Article 17(1)	Cross-references	
	Articles	Recitals
(a) Purpose expiration	5(1)(b), (c), and e; 6(4); 13(2)(a); 14(2)(a)	*39; 50*
(b) Consent withdrawal	*4(11); 6(1)*(a)*; 7; 8; 9(2)a*	*32; 42*
(c) Right to object	*21*	*69; 70*
(d) Unlawful processing	*4(11); 5(1)*(a)*; 6(1); 7; 8; 9*	*32; 65; 69*
(e) Legal obligation	*6(1)(c)*	*10; 45*
(f) Minors' withdrawal of consent in ISS context	*7; 8*	*38*

relevance in the ISS context. Previous chapters amply illustrated how in this environment personal data is processed for many different purposes, by different actors at the same time. In order to assess the applicability of the right to erasure, it will be critical to clearly differentiate between these operations. The legitimate claim for a public library to maintain newspaper archives, for example, does not exempt people search engines from the right to erasure. Uber's use of personal data to manipulate driver (or rider) behaviour may be targeted with erasure requests, but this should be separated from other activities such as connecting drivers to riders or billing purposes, for example. Essentially, such granular approach will often mean that the right to object (to particular processing operations but not to other) will be more adequate then outright erasure (see Part III). Secondly, an effective right to erasure requires transparency. Transparency is not just an absolute requirement for ensuring *fairness* throughout the GDPR overall, it is an absolute sine qua non in order for the right to have any practical relevance.[316] Without proper knowledge about what personal data is processed and/or for what purposes, *ex post* empowerment measures are empty promises. The right of access (Art 15) can play a particularly important role in forcing proper transparency, which can then result in the effective exercise of other data subject rights.[317]

Product of vigorous compromise-seeking, Article 17 remains somewhat problematic. It is the ugly offspring of a *marriage de raison* between proponents and opponents of data subject empowerment, freedom of expression, big data promises, and many more. Yet, ugly ducklings can grow out to become elegant swans.

[316] See in the same vein: Article 29 Working Party, 'Opinion on Consent' (n 43) 9; Van Alsenoy, Kosta and Dumortier (n 49) 8; Directorate General of Human Rights and Rule of Law, 'Guidelines on the Protection of Individuals with Regard to the Processing of Personal Data in a World of Big Data' (Council of Europe 2017) T-PD(2017)01 1.

[317] Jef Ausloos and Pierre Dewitte, 'Shattering One-Way Mirrors—Data Subject Access Rights in Practice' (2018) 8 International Data Privacy Law 4.

Ensuring such a future for the right to erasure will require resolving some complex issues. Depending on the particular circumstances at hand, Article 17 will direct data subjects to other provisions for the substantial assessment. Eventually, these assessments will often result *not* in a binary erasure/preservation, but a plethora of more nuanced in-between solutions. In sum therefore, the right to erasure is not about erasure per se but rather constitutes the switchboard for redirecting data subjects in search of *ex post* empowerment to the relevant provisions. As appeared throughout this Chapter, this process will very often result in a balancing act. Given the complexity of data processing in the ISS context, such balancing needs closer attention.

PART II

BALANCING AND DATA PROTECTION

5
Balancing in the GDPR

Section 1. Introduction

> *D'une manière générale, pondérer les intérêts désigne plutôt le but à poursuivre lors de l'analyse d'un conflit de libertés que la démarche à suivre pour y arriver.*[1]

As will appear in more detail below, the right to erasure virtually always results in a balancing act. Indeed, safeguarding the fundamental rights to privacy (Art 7 Charter) and data protection (Art 8 Charter) will generally require the balancing of competing values.[2] This book would therefore not be complete without dedicating attention to this crucial legal exercise. The goal of this Part is not to define balancing acts in general, but rather untangle the complexities surrounding balancing in an EU data protection context. Indeed, the intricacies of balancing acts merit PhDs in themselves.[3] With this in mind, the present part is divided into three chapters. This Chapter 5 will position balancing acts in data protection law. Chapter 6 will ground that abstract chapter by looking more closely at three discrete balancing scenarios that are most prevalent in the context of the right to erasure in the information society (ie privacy and data protection versus economic freedoms, information freedoms, and research or security interests). Chapter 7 will then highlight and analyse some of the key issues emerging from data protection balancing in the ISS context.

[1] Yves Poullet and Thierry Léonard, 'Les libertés comme fondement de la protection des données nominatives' in François Rigaux, *La vie privée: une liberté parmi les autres?* (Larcier 1992) 251.

[2] See David H Flaherty, *Protecting Privacy in Surveillance Societies: The Federal Republic of Germany, Sweden, France, Canada, and the United States* (University of North Carolina Press 1989) 9.

[3] Readers interested in such work, either focusing on balancing per se or more specifically in an information society services context, may wish to consult the following works: Sébastien Van Drooghenbroeck, *La proportionnalité dans le droit de la Convention européenne des droits de l'Homme: prendre l'idée simple au sérieux* (FUSL 2001) 624ff; Pieter-Augustijn Van Malleghem, 'Proportionality and the Erosion of Formalism' (PhD Thesis, KU Leuven—Faculty of Law 2016); Stijn Smet, *Resolving Conflicts Between Human Rights: The Judge's Dilemma* (CRC Press 2018); and more applied in an information society context: CJ Angelopoulos, 'European Intermediary Liability in Copyright: A Tort-Based Analysis' (PhD Thesis, University of Amsterdam 2016) <http://dare.uva.nl/record/1/527223> accessed 1 June 2019; Aleksandra Kuczerawy, *Intermediary Liability and Freedom of Expression in the EU: From Concepts to Safeguards* (Intersentia 2018).

The Right to Erasure in EU Data Protection Law. First Edition. Jef Ausloos. Oxford University Press (2020). © Jef Ausloos
DOI: 10.1093/oso/9780198847977.001.0001

Section 2. Balancing—From the Charter to the GDPR

Balancing constitutes a notorious legal exercise. Lauded for its apparent simplicity and context-awareness, it is also criticized for being volatile and producing legal uncertainty. From a legal perspective, balancing acts appear at many different levels. With regard to the highest normative level—ie fundamental human rights—it is more common to talk about the proportionality principle (subsection 2.2). In the context of data protection law in particular, balancing seems to be more common parlance (subsection 2.3).

2.1 Introductory Remarks

Balancing acts pervade law. They operate at several levels —hierarchical, jurisdictional, subject-specific—and interact in different ways. For the purposes here, it is useful therefore to briefly highlight these interactions as they relate to the GDPR and the right to erasure in particular. Perhaps the most evident distinction that can be made is a hierarchical one between balancing fundamental rights in the Charter versus balancing acts within (or between) secondary frameworks such as the GDPR. Both will be discussed in more depth in the following pages.

Whether talking about balancing acts at the level of the Charter or secondary frameworks, they remain open-ended legal instruments, requiring further interpretative guidance. As astutely observed by Angelopoulos:

> on its own, balancing as a legal principle is too vague to offer sufficient guarantees of rationality, objectivity, transparency and legal theoretical coherence. If no other tools are provided to help flesh it out, intuition, obscure reasoning and subjectivity will inevitably be left to fill the gaps.[4]

In order to further elucidate balancing acts as precipitated by the right to erasure, a distinction can be made between the substantive and procedural dimensions to balancing. Following the 'balancing' metaphor, the latter concerns the construction/mechanics of the balance itself, whereas the former relates to the actual content in each of the scales.[5] Determining the content of the scales—ie substantive balancing—is impossible in the abstract as it inherently relates to specific situations and the corresponding rights and interests that are engaged.[6] In order to lift the veil to some extent, the following Chapter (6) will look more closely at three of the most

[4] Angelopoulos (n 3) 284.

[5] See Van Drooghenbroeck (n 3) 169 et seq. The author explains that procedural requirements for balancing focus on the way in which one achieves a 'just equilibrium' (ie decisional procedure), rather than the content of said equilibrium.

[6] See generally: Angelopoulos (n 3) 74 et seq.

oft-recurring balancing scenarios in the ISS context (ie economic freedoms, information freedoms, and research or security interests). The vagueness and difficulty of balancing's substantive dimension increases the importance for the procedural component to be particularly well-defined.[7] All the more in situations characterized by strong power asymmetries where one party controls the de facto operation of 'the balance' (such as often the case in the ISS environment).

SOME SCEPTICISM—The procedural dimension of balancing is not free from some vigorous criticism, especially at the level of fundamental human rights conflicts, but also within data protection law itself. De Schutter and Tulkens, for example, argue that 'balancing may be closer to a slogan than to a methodology',[8] while Van Drooghenbroek explains '*[d]e sa méthode, le juge européen parle peu. Peut-être est-ce tout simplement parce qu'il n'en a en réalité aucune*'.[9] Indeed, even a properly defined procedural framework will not prevent the fact that, identifying, assessing, and balancing the 'weight' in each scale, constitutes an inherently subjective if not absurd exercise when talking about 'rights' and 'freedoms'.

COUNTERING SCEPTICS—Despite the important issues generally associated with balancing, it undeniably remains a crucial legal tool to resolve conflicts between different rights, freedoms, and interests. Indeed, perhaps its most valuable hallmark relates to its flexibility, in turn ensuring the effectiveness—ie actual, meaningful, and sustainable application—of the relevant provisions.[10] Such flexibility is all the more important with regard to vague, open norms in an environment characterized by complexity and rapid change. Much of the tension between flexibility and legal certainty can be alleviated through structural procedural safeguards. Rather than sacrificing one in favour of the other, Van Drooghenbroeck argues to aim for a *concordance pratique* between the two, an unachievable and unstable 'ideal' state that should inform fair balancing.[11] As a response to sceptics arguing inter alia, that the inherent vagueness of fair balancing leads to arbitrary outcomes and legal uncertainty,[12] it is also worth referring to Angelopoulos who

[7] See in this regard also: Van Drooghenbroeck (n 3) 307–08.

[8] Olivier De Schutter and Françoise Tulkens, 'Rights in Conflict: The European Court of Human Rights as a Pragmatic Institution' (Université Catholique de Louvain 2007) Working Paper 22.

[9] 'The European judge talks little about his methods. Perhaps this is simply due to the fact that he effectively does not have one' [translation by the author]. Van Drooghenbroeck (n 3) 278.

[10] Also recognized in: *ietosuojavaltuutettu v Satakunnan Markkinapörssi & Satamedia* [2008] Court of Justice of the European Union C-73/07 paras 143–44.

[11] Both, after all, are crucial components in ensuring the effective protection of rights and freedoms. Van Drooghenbroeck (n 3) 19; 24–25. The concept can be traced back Konrad Hesse's work on German constitutional law, see: Stijn Smet, 'Resolving Conflicts between Human Rights: A Legal Theoretical Analysis in the Context of the ECHR' (PhD Thesis, Ghent University 2014) 124 et seq.

[12] See notably: De Schutter and Tulkens (n 8) 22 et seq; Bart van Der Sloot, 'The Practical and Theoretical Problems with "Balancing": Delfi, Coty and the Redundancy of the Human Rights Framework' (2016) 23 Maastricht Journal of European and Comparative Law (MJ) 439; Bart van der Sloot, 'Editorial' (2017) 3 European Data Protection Law Review 1; and the references to Habermas in Angelopoulos (n 3) 73–74. The first author also asserts that balancing of fundamental rights and freedoms is nonsensical by nature.

explains that the notion of fair balance should be approached 'not as a myth applied by the courts to obfuscate their subjective assessments or as a scientific method capable of providing definitive answers, but as a metaphor for the exercise of a detailed dissection, comparison and ordering of the available options with a view of identifying the optimal outcome: a call for rational discourse'.[13] EU data protection law, as will appear amply throughout this and Chapter 6, purports to provide a procedural framework, ordering a rational methodology for resolving conflicts of rights, freedoms and interests in the context of data processing. Before looking at balancing in data protection law specifically, it is worth briefly recalling the operation of fair balancing at the level of fundamental human rights.

2.2 Balancing Fundamental Rights

Balancing as Preferred Tool for Resolving Conflicts Between Fundamental Rights—Fundamental rights and freedoms—notably those relating to the respect for private life (Art 7) and protection of personal data (Art 8)—are inherently relational, ie they need to be assessed 'in relation to other rights'.[14] Indeed, the full enjoyment of these freedoms will almost always be in tension with other fundamental rights, freedoms, and/or the public interest more broadly. It is crucial therefore, to have a closer look at how to deal with these tensions. The law can only take you so far and does not have the purpose nor ambition to foresee every potential conflict. Especially with regard to fundamental rights and freedoms, which represent very high-level and abstract values, interpretation is required in order to apply them in specific situations.[15] Yet, even with the strictest interpretation frameworks in place, such 'translation' will never be fully objective.

Fair Balancing—Fair balancing constitutes the dominant and preferred mechanism to resolve conflicts between fundamental rights and freedoms in the Charter.[16] As evidenced by CJEU (as well as ECtHR) case law, fair balancing is naturally vague and flexible.[17] The very point of fair balancing is that it cannot be

[13] Angelopoulos (n 3) 85.

[14] Serge Gutwirth, 'De Toepassing van Het Finaliteitsbeginsel van de Privacywet van 8 December 1992 Tot Bescherming van de Persoonlijke Levenssfeer Ten Opzichte van de Verwerking van Persoonsgegevens' [The Application of the Purpose Specification Principle in the Belgian Data Protection Act of 8 December 1992] (1993) 1993 Tijdschrift voor Privaatrecht—TPR 1417–18; *Volker und Markus Schecke GbR and Hartmut Eifert v Land Hessen* [2010] Court of Justice of the European Union Joined Cases C-92/09 and C-93/09 para 48; AG Opinion in: *Salvatore Manni* [2017] Court of Justice of the European Union C-398/15 para 47.

[15] Van Drooghenbroeck (n 3) 213–14.

[16] And the ECHR, for that matter. Angelopoulos (n 3) 77–78 and references on p 73 to: Stephen Gardbaum, 'Limiting Constitutional Rights' (2007) 54(4) UCLA Law Review 789; J Bomhoff, Balancing Constitutional Rights: The Origins and Meanings of Postwar Legal Discourse (CUP 2013) 6. Also confirmed in: *Sky Österreich* [2013] Court of Justice of the European Union C-283/11.

[17] For a critique and more generally on the tension between flexibility and legal certainty, see: Van Drooghenbroeck (n 3).

defined at an abstract theoretical level as its application is defined by the particular context in which it is applied. This amorphous nature is a by-product of the absence of a hierarchy between fundamental rights and freedoms in the Charter (at least from Article 6 onwards).[18] Indeed, whether one fundamental right or freedom overrides another cannot be determined in absolute terms but only on a case-by-case basis.[19] The normative equality of fundamental rights and freedoms necessitates a context-dependent assessment of the relationship and interaction between the relevant rights and freedoms in the specific circumstances of each case.[20]

Searching for Guidance—On a general level, it seems the most useful guidance on fair balancing of fundamental rights and freedoms would relate to the formal components that dictate its practical operation. The primary source for such guidance within the Charter itself can be found in Article 52(1), which clarifies the extent to which rights and freedoms can be limited:

> Any limitation on the exercise of the rights and freedoms recognised by this Charter must be provided for by law and respect the essence of those rights and freedoms. Subject to the principle of proportionality, limitations may be made only if they are necessary and genuinely meet objectives of general interest recognised by the Union or the need to protect the rights and freedoms of others.

From this provision, four main requirements can be extracted: limitations must (a) be provided for by law; (b) respect the essence of the affected right or freedom; (c) respect the proportionality principle; and (d) be necessary and genuinely meet objectives of general interest recognized by the EU, or the need to protect the rights and freedoms of others.[21] Peers and Prechal categorize these requirements into a 'a

[18] For an elaborate discussion on the (non-)derogable nature of the Charter's first five provisions see: Steve Peers and others (eds), *The EU Charter of Fundamental Rights: A Commentary* (Hart 2014) 3–119 <https://www.bloomsburycollections.com/book/the-eu-charter-of-fundamental-rights-a-commentary/>. Brkan also explains how *absolute* rights (eg prohibition of forced labour, torture, etc) cannot be interfered with whatsoever, because their scope corresponds entirely with their 'essence' (see Art 52(1)). Maja Brkan, 'The Concept of Essence of Fundamental Rights in the EU Legal Order: Peeling the Onion to Its Core' (2018) 14 European Constitutional Law Review 332, 358 et seq.

[19] Angelopoulos (n 3) 76–78.

[20] See in this regard also: Gutwirth, 'De Toepassing van Het Finaliteitsbeginsel van de Privacywet' (n 14) 1434–35; Article 29 Working Party, 'Opinion 06/2014 on the Notion of Legitimate Interests of the Data Controller under Article 7 of Directive 95/46/EC' (European Commission 2014) Opinion WP 217 11 <http://ec.europa.eu/justice/article-29/documentation> accessed 1 June 2019; Angelopoulos (n 3) 76. At least one author, has suggested an implied hierarchy between fundamental rights, 'which should be helpful for privacy and data protection in an internet environment for the [. . .] the difference in the standard of review, the balancing between rights, efficient use of resources and the extraterritorial application'. Hielke Hijmans, *The European Union as Guardian of Internet Privacy: The Story of Art 16 TFEU* (Springer International Publishing 06) 217 et seq.

[21] Others have structured these differently. For example, the EDPS and Fuster González consider necessity to be part of the third criterion—European Data Protection Supervisor, 'Developing a "Toolkit" for Assessing the Necessity of Measures That Interfere with Fundamental Rights. Background Paper' 4 <https://secure.edps.europa.eu/EDPSWEB/webdav/site/mySite/shared/Documents/Consultation/Papers/16-06-16_Necessity_paper_for_consultation_EN.pdf> accessed 1 June 2019; Gloria González Fuster, 'Curtailing a Right in Flux: Restrictions of the Right to Personal Data Protection' in Artemi

procedural rule' (limitations on rights 'must be provided for by law'), a rule on the justifications for limiting rights ('objectives of general interest recognised by the Union or the need to protect the rights and freedoms of others'), and a number of interlinked rules on the balancing test to be applied as between rights and limitations (the obligation to 'respect the essence of' the rights; the 'principle of proportionality'; and the requirement of necessity).[22]

Peers and Prechal's first two requirements can be deemed fulfilled with regard to data subject rights in the GDPR (which are provided by law and pursue, at the very least, the protection of the data subject's rights and freedoms).[23] This leaves only the third category of conditions. Even though they can be phrased as binary questions, the answer will generally not be. The question of respecting the *essence* of a Charter provision is a case in point, with not much clarity on its contours.[24] The 'essence' is composed of the core elements of the respective fundamental right or freedom, without which the right/freedom cannot be exercised.[25] With regard to the right to data protection at least, it can be inferred from CJEU case law that the essence *is* interfered with whenever measures affecting the fundamental right comprise no safeguards whatsoever aimed at mitigating said interference.[26] Indeed, the essence of a fundamental right can be considered affected when 'the limitation goes so far that it empties the right of its core elements and thus prevents the exercise of the right'.[27] Only when the essence of the fundamental right or freedom is

Rallo Lombarte and Rosario García Mahamut (eds), *Hacia un nuevo derecho europeo de protección de datos = Towards a New European Data Protection Regime* (Tirant lo Blanch 2015).

[22] Steve Peers and Sasha Prechal, 'Scope and Interpretation of Rights and Principles' in Steve Peers, Tamara Hervey, Jeff Kenner, and Angela Ward (eds), *The EU Charter of Fundamental Rights: A Commentary* (Hart 2014) para 52.35 et seq.

[23] See the three-part test for assessing limitations to several ECHR rights (eg to freedom of expression, Article 10; right to private life, Article 8): measures must be 'prescribed by law', 'have a legitimate aim', and 'be proportionate'. Pursuant to Article 52(3), the rich body of case law of the ECtHR may also serve as guidance when assessing and balancing Charter provisions.

[24] See also Chapter 6 Balancing Scenarios, for an exploration of the essence of information freedoms (Art 11) and economic freedoms (Arts 16–17) in the Charter.

[25] *Maximillian Schrems v Data Protection Commissioner* [2015] Court of Justice of the European Union C-362/14 para 95; European Data Protection Supervisor, 'Assessing the Necessity of Measures That Limit the Fundamental Right to the Protection of Personal Data: A Toolkit' (EDPS 2017) Footnote 8 <https://edps.europa.eu/sites/edp/files/publication/17-04-11_necessity_toolkit_en_0.pdf> accessed 1 June 2019.

[26] More specifically, this can be gathered from the *Digital Rights Ireland* Case in which the CJEU struck down the so-called Data Retention Directive. The Court did confirm that Directive did not 'adversely affect the essence of the fundamental right to the protection of personal data enshrined in Article 8 of the Charter, because Article 7 of Directive 2006/24 provides, in relation to data protection and data security, that, without prejudice to the provisions adopted pursuant to Directives 95/46 and 2002/58, certain principles of data protection and data security must be respected by providers of publicly available electronic communications services or of public communications networks'. *Digital Rights Ireland Ltd* [2014] Court of Justice of the European Union Joined Cases C-293/12 and C-594/12 invalidating the Data Retention Directive (2006/24/EC) para 40.

[27] European Data Protection Supervisor, 'Assessing the Necessity of Measures That Limit the Fundamental Right to the Protection of Personal Data: A Toolkit' (n 25) Footnote 8. See more generally: Brkan (n 18).

not adversely affected, will it become necessary to engage the proportionality principle. This 'proportionality principle' constitutes the legal manifestation of what is often also referred to as 'balancing'.

PROPORTIONALITY PRINCIPLE—The proportionality principle lays down a three-pronged test, requiring any limitation to a fundamental human right/freedom to be (a) suitable; (b) necessary; and (c) proportionate *stricto sensu*.[28] The former two—also referred to as the 'effectiveness' and 'least intrusive means' tests—are generally not contested by the ECtHR in its case law,[29] assuming Member-States are in a better position to make such decisions with regard to their actions.[30] Hence, it is the third and last step that constitutes the heart of the proportionality assessment, requiring an actual balancing act between opposing rights, freedoms, and interests.[31] In other words, within its more constricted legal meaning, 'balancing' refers to the specific third sub-test of the proportionality principle.

FAIR BALANCING—Alexy famously, but perhaps not very helpfully, summarized the third proportionality requirement as 'the greater the degree of non-satisfaction of or detriment to one principle, the greater the importance of satisfying the other'.[32] Indeed, the balancing—or proportionality *stricto sensu*—test is undoubtedly the most elusive, complex and subjective component in assessing the proportionality of an interference with fundamental rights. It requires an interpretative exercise, identifying (a) what interests are relevant in a given situation,[33] and (b) some type of a common denominator between the different rights at stake to enable the actual weighing. In sum, it appears that fair balancing of fundamental human rights inherently requires a case-by-case approach.

CASUISTIC APPROACH TO FAIR BALANCING—The growing importance of fair balancing in resolving conflicts (between rights, freedoms, interests) can be explained by the complexification of such conflicts, and the corresponding move from approaching fundamental human rights and freedoms as 'principles' rather

[28] For fairly recent, extensive overviews of the proportionality principle in EU law, see for example: Tor-Inge Harbo, *The Function of Proportionality Analysis in European Law* (Brill Nijhoff 2015); Van Malleghem (n 3); Takis Tridimas, *The General Principles of EU Law* (New Edition, 3rd edn, OUP 2018).

[29] As mentioned before, pursuant Article 52(3), ECtHR case law can inform the interpretation of Charter provisions.

[30] Van Drooghenbroeck (n 3) 174–96. Articles 218–19, the same author also explains that absence of necessity does not automatically lead to the overall outcome being considered disproportionate, but will still significantly affect the balancing act in the proportionality *stricto sensu* test. The first two tests in the proportionality analysis are also referred to as rationality-based means-end tests (they assess the objectively verifiable link between means and end). The proportionality *stricto sensu* test, on the other hand, is a reasonability assessment, weighing different values against each other and evaluating what constitutes an excessive burden. See: Harbo (n 28) pt 1 and pp 198 et seq.

[31] See references in: Angelopoulos (n 3) 73.

[32] Robert Alexy, *A Theory of Constitutional Rights* (OUP 2002) 102 as referred to in; Angelopoulos (n 3) 73.

[33] Van Drooghenbroeck stresses the importance of having a proper method for identifying these interests, proposing four 'axes' that need to be taken into account: structural, personal, temporal, and probabilistic. Van Drooghenbroeck (n 3) 236.

than 'rules'.[34] The 'rules' approach implies legal provisions are seen as binary syllogisms, fixing the conditions for their applicability, while the 'principles' approach sees them as more relative, with variable weight depending on the circumstances at hand. A 'principles-perspective' therefore allows for a more nuanced, context-dependent approach to resolving conflicts. The flexibility allowed by fair balancing allows for an opportunity to challenge the application of an 'abstract' norm, and have one's case assessed *in particular*. Neither the judiciary nor the legislator can anticipate a priori every potential conflict and norms need to be interpreted *in concreto*, without which they would quickly lose their effectiveness.[35] The infinite diversity of potential conflicts, with many values dynamically changing and interacting over time, actively necessitates a case-by-case approach. As amply illustrated further down in this chapter and Chapter 6, this is especially true with regard to conflicts between fundamental rights and freedoms emerging from personal data processing.

Defending Context-Dependent Fair Balancing—It must be said, however, that the openness and flexibility of context-dependant balancing may lead to some level of legal uncertainty. Still, I tend to follow Van Drooghenbroeck's preference for the flexible logic of principles, with their inherent contextual rationality and implied case-by-case based approach, over the rigid rule-based approach that would be necessary to ensure absolute legal certainty. The 'principles' approach aligns diversity rather than forcibly reducing it; allows a broader debate while still providing a concrete decision; and recognizes the dynamic nature of norms over time. Put briefly, they adapt to reality rather than requiring reality to adapt to them, eventually leading to a more effective application of the law.[36] Importantly, the above should not be read as advocating *against* legal certainty itself. Neither legal certainty, nor the flexible and casuistic nature of balancing acts should be entirely sacrificed in favour of the other. Both can be pursued simultaneously with a robust framework of procedural safeguards.[37] The GDPR constitutes such a framework, specifically with regard to conflicts in the context of personal data processing.

[34] See: ibid 624–29; referring to: Robert Alexy, *Theorie der Grundrechte* (Suhrkamp 1986) 582.

[35] Van Drooghenbroeck (n 3) 213–14. It has also been confirmed by both the ECtHR (*Gaskin v the United Kingdom* [1989] European Court of Human Rights 10454/83 [49]) and the CJEU (*Salvatore Manni* (n 14)) that any measure impacting fundamental human rights, should always have a failsafe built-in, that allows for an *in casu* determination in specific cases.

[36] Van Drooghenbroeck (n 3) 641–52. See also: François Ost and Michel van de Kerchove, *Entre la lettre et l'esprit: les directives d'interprétation en droit* (Bruylant 1989) 323.

[37] Note the fact that this sentence uses the word *pursued* instead of *achieved*. The pursuit of both legal certainty and flexibility offered by fair balancing, is dubbed '*concordance pratique*'. The concept hinges on (a) methodological legal certainty; and (b) a transitory jurisprudential right. Methodological legal certainty comprises *formal* requirements (ie foreseeablility, guarantees against abuse, and a formal obligation to put in place proportionality in internal decision-making processes) and *material* requirements (ie suitability, necessity, balancing). A transitory jurisprudential right ('*droit transitoire jurisprudentiel*') consists of identifying and pursuing a common denominator, among individual cases over time. Van Drooghenbroeck (n 3) 706 et seq.

Safeguards Ensuring Fair Balancing—Proper consideration of the specificities in each individual case should not come at the cost of sacrificing legal certainty or the rule of law. To prevent this, Van Drooghenbroeck lists several requirements that ought to be included in any framework of procedural safeguards. Formal requirements include predictability (ie can the outcome be reasonably expected), availability of appeal and guarantees against abuse, and have the substantial elements of the fair balance be *motivated* (ie demonstrably reflected upon).[38] As will appear later, the GDPR includes all of these elements, at least in theory. Finally, apart from having a strong procedural/formal framework in place, legal certainty will also increase as the number of individual fair balancing cases increases.[39] A critical mass of *in concreto* decisions may allow the identification of a normative median that can be re-applied to future cases.[40] This last 'safeguard' is also relevant in the context of balancing acts under the GDPR.

CJEU Case Law on Balancing Charter Rights—Since the Charter entered into force in 2009, a progressively growing body of case law involving conflicts between fundamental rights and freedoms shines some light on how fair balancing might operate in practice. For example, on several occasions the CJEU has had the opportunity to assess how legislators (at the EU[41] and Member-State[42] level) have failed/succeeded to adequately consider fair balancing of fundamental rights in secondary frameworks. Similar to the ECtHR, the CJEU also seems to consider unlimited restrictions on fundamental rights or freedoms—even if provided by law and with a limited scope—unlikely to comply with the proportionality principle.[43] Where things get particularly murky however, is with regard to conflicts materializing in interpersonal/private relationships. In this context, the CJEU has primarily limited itself to clarifying how to balance rather than making the final call, which is generally left for Member-State courts to decide.[44]

[38] ibid 728.

[39] Not unlike the logic of big data, where the size of the dataset impacts the reliability of patterns and correlations that are identified.

[40] See *droit transitoire jurisprudentiel* in footnote 1512. While asserting durability/continuity—and thus legal certainty—such a principle would still be subject to change, whenever it turns out a posteriori, that there is a clear mismatch (ie clear inaptness to deal with) between the norm(s) and the reality/facts it purports to regulate.

[41] eg *Digital Rights Ireland Ltd* (n 26) invalidating the data retention directive; *Maximillian Schrems v Data Protection Commissioner* [2015] Court of Justice of the EU C-362/14, Curia invalidating of the so-called Safe Harbour agreement; *Opinion 1/15 of the Court on PNR Agreement between Canada and the EU* (Court of Justice of the European Union) declaring incompatible the PNR agreement.

[42] For example see the Manni case, which concerned an Italian law dictating visibility of commercial registers. *Salvatore Manni* (n 14).

[43] Steve Peers and Sasha Prechal, 'Scope and Interpretation of Rights and Principles' in Steve Peers, Tamara Hervey, Jeff Kenner, and Angela Ward (eds), *The EU Charter of Fundamental Rights: A Commentary* (Hart, 2014) para 52.85. By way of illustration, the authors refer to 'a complete ban on a marketing strategy (*ASNEF*), a complete exclusion of an economic sector from the application of an equality right (*Test-Achats*), or a complete invasion of privacy (*Volker* and *Scarlet Extended*)'.

[44] See for example *Lindqvist* [2003] Court of Justice of the European Union C-101/01 [83]; *Satamedia* (n 10); *Google Spain SL, Google Inc v Agencia Española de Protección de Datos (AEPD), Mario Costeja González* [2014] Court of Justice of the European Union C-131/12. Quite ironically, the applicant in the *Google Spain* case was denied a new right to be delisted in 2015 by the Spanish

Horizontal Effect—Looking at it from a distance, the right to erasure in the ISS context does often seem to bring about a conflict between fundamental rights and freedoms of private entities (see notably the balancing scenarios examined in Chapter 6). Indeed, as sketched out in the Introduction to this book, globalization, privatization of public functions, and the centralization of power in corporate hands challenge the status quo of a State-centric approach to fundamental/human rights protection.[45] The enjoyment of fundamental rights is increasingly dependent on and affected by private entities. Yet, the question of horizontal application of fundamental rights—ie directly in a relationship between two private actors—is a contentious one.[46] Indeed, Article 51(1), which lays down the Charter's scope, conspicuously leaves out private parties and together with Art 51(2) emphasizes the limits of the Union's competencies.[47] Put briefly, it is generally not possible for individuals to directly hold another private entity liable for violating *or* safeguarding their Charter (or ECHR) rights.[48]

Direct Horizontal Effect—The State is the primary addressee to identify and uphold a fair balance between fundamental human rights.[49] In reality, however, it seems direct horizontal effect cannot be entirely excluded either (eg national laws may install de facto direct horizontality).[50] Tridimas explains direct

DPA, because meanwhile he had entered the public limelight due to his role in the *Google Spain* case. See: Miquel Peguera, 'No More Right-to-Be-Forgotten for Mr. Costeja, Says Spanish Data Protection Authority' (*Center for Internet and Society (CIS) at Stanford University*, 3 October 2015) <https://cyberlaw.stanford.edu/blog/2015/10/no-more-right-be-forgotten-mr-costeja-says-spanish-data-protection-authority> accessed 1 June 2019.

[45] Eleni Frantziou, 'The Horizontal Effect of the Charter of Fundamental Rights of the EU: Rediscovering the Reasons for Horizontality' (2015) 21 European Law Journal 674–75.

[46] Unsurprisingly, the CJEU's current president is quite ambiguous about it as well. See for example: Koen Lenaerts and José Antonio Gutiérrez-Fons, 'The Place of the Charter in the EU Constitutional Edifice' in Steve Peers and others (eds), *The EU Charter of Fundamental Rights: A Commentary*, vols 1559–94 (Hart 2014) para 55.52 et seq <https://www.bloomsburycollections.com/book/the-eu-charter-of-fundamental-rights-a-commentary/>; Frantziou (n 343). This last author also explains the reason why the CJEU has so far failed to address the actual issue of horizontality head-on is because of the fact that most cases coming before it are very context-dependent requests for preliminary rulings (p 672). See also: Angelopoulos (n 3) 72 et seq; the many contributions in Part III: Horizontal Direct Effect, in: Ulf Bernitz, Xavier Groussot, and Felix Schulyok (eds), *General Principles of EU Law and European Private Law* (Kluwer Law International 2013).

[47] Juliane Kokott and Christoph Sobotta, 'The Charter of Fundamental Rights of the European Union after Lisbon' (2010) Working Paper 14 <http://cadmus.eui.eu//handle/1814/15208> accessed 1 June 2019.

[48] AG Trstenjak Opinion in: *Dominguez v Centre informatique du Centre Ouest Atlantique (CICOA)* [2012] Court of Justice of the European Union C-282/10 [84]. The AG deduced this *a contrario* from Article 51(1), explaining 'it is not absolutely essential for fundamental rights to be directly binding on private individuals in order to guarantee reasonable protection'.

[49] François Rigaux, *La vie privée: une liberté parmi les autres?* (Larcier 1992) 47.

[50] Reality is a bit more nuanced indeed, though elaborating on this would fall outside the scope of this book. Suffice to say that both the ECtHR and CJEU have been ambiguous regarding horizontal effect and interpretation also differs depending on what fundamental right or freedom is at stake. Where relevant, these elements will be discussed in Chapter 6 on balancing scenarios (notably with regard to information freedoms).

horizontality will 'depend on the right invoked, the circumstances of the case, and the relationship between the parties' and is even explicitly addressed in some Charter provisions (eg Art 24(2)).[51,52] Some level of direct horizontality also seems to be implied in the CJEU's case law. Indeed, a closer look suggests the Luxembourg Court is not entirely unsympathetic to the idea of burdening powerful players with some level of responsibility for observing fundamental rights of their users. At least in the *Telekabel*[53] and *Google Spain*[54] cases, the CJEU required addressees of take-down injunctions/requests to observe and ensure adequate protection of the fundamental right of Internet users to freedom of information.[55] To quote Tridimas again, 'the most important question is not, perhaps, determining the addressee of a fundamental right but ascertaining whether it has a clear and precise minimum normative content which may be said to have been breached in the circumstances of the case',[56] which also explains the focus of Chapter 6 (ie delineating economic and information freedoms in the Charter in relation to the rights to data protection and privacy). Indeed, the direct horizontality question is rendered less acute when considering the fact that fundamental human rights should inform decision-making and conflict resolution, regardless of it being done by a public or private entity.[57] Which brings us to the *indirect* horizontal effect of Charter rights.

Indirect Horizontal Effect—Charter rights and freedoms can have indirect horizontal effect, meaning inter alia that they inform and indeed constrain the behaviour of private actors in horizontal relations.[58] The reading and application of laws governing private relations such as the GDPR for example, should be done in conformity with the Charter.[59,60] Indeed, the outcome of applying GDPR provisions in a given situation cannot result in a violation of a Charter right, something

[51] Stating: 'In all actions relating to children, whether taken by public authorities or private institutions, the child's best interests must be a primary consideration.'

[52] Takis Tridimas, 'Fundamental Rights, General Principles of EU Law, and the Charter' (2014) 16 Cambridge Yearbook of European Legal Studies 361, 390.

[53] *UPC Telekabel* [2014] Court of Justice of the European Union C-314/12 [55]; Angelopoulos (n 3) 72.

[54] *Google Spain* (n 44) para 81.

[55] Such outsourcing of balancing acts raises important questions in itself, which will be addressed in Chapter 7.

[56] Tridimas (n 28) 390.

[57] See notably: *Google Spain* (n 44) para 74.

[58] According to Tridimas, the absence of any explicit rejection of direct horizontality by the Court—even though it had the chance on numerous occasions—'may be seen as an endorsement [. . .] of the argument that, in appropriate circumstances, the Charter, as the general principles of law, may produce at least indirect horizontality'. Tridimas (n 28) 392. See also: Hielke Hijmans, *The European Union as Guardian of Internet Privacy: The Story of Art 16 TFEU* (Springer 2016) 36 et seq.

[59] This implies that indirect horizontal effect of fundamental rights effectively requires a legal 'vehicle' to exist. Without any legal framework regulating a specific issue between private actors, there is nothing to be 'interpreted in conformity with'.

[60] Angela Ward, 'Field of Application (Article 51)' in Steve Peers and others (eds), *The EU Charter of Fundamental Rights: A Commentary* (Hart 2014) para 51.47 <https://www.bloomsburycollections.com/book/the-eu-charter-of-fundamental-rights-a-commentary/>; *UPC Telekabel* (n 53) para 55; *Maximillian Schrems v Data Protection Commissioner* (n 25) para 38; *Salvatore Manni* (n 14) para 39.

which may not always be as evident as it seems keeping in mind the GDPR's expansive scope of application. This also explains and justifies why fair balancing is imbued throughout the GDPR, aimed at preventing tunnel-vision, and forcing a broader perspective in applying the framework.[61] In the event the outcome of complying with GDPR provisions would still violate a fundamental right/freedom, the entity liable would be the state (through proxy of a judge or the legislator).[62] Particularly prevalent in the ISS context, is the impact on fundamental rights/freedoms of third parties, ie those not involved in (or even unaware of) the respective decision-making. As illustrated by the *Google Spain* ruling, even though the ISS *should* take into account the information freedoms of Internet users in general, those users are not offered any guarantees or actionable rights against the platform (this question will be discussed in depth in the following Chapter 6).

From the Fundamental Right to Data Protection to the GDPR—The question of horizontal effect of the fundamental right to data protection (Art 8) in the Charter is rendered convoluted by the fact that it is the only provision under Title II of the Charter with an explicitly dedicated secondary framework operationalizing it (following the explicit mandate to legislate in Art 16 TFEU).[63] As such, it is easy to confuse the rationale and functioning of Article 8 Charter with the GDPR.[64] Indeed, the existence of the GDPR may give the appearance of a *de facto* direct horizontal effect of the fundamental right to data protection. Yet, it is important to maintain the distinction between Art 8 Charter and the GDPR. Even if Article 16 TFEU—requiring the adoption of rules on the protection of personal data—forms the legal basis for adopting the GDPR, the rationale of the GDPR extends beyond safeguarding the fundamental right to data protection alone. It is aimed at protecting *all* fundamental rights and freedoms of natural persons whenever their personal data is being processed, 'and *in particular* their right to the protection of personal data' (Art 1 GDPR).[65] Whereas Article 8 of the Charter ensures the protection of individuals' digital persona and how it is being treated, the GDPR defines a (legal) infrastructure for processing personal data respectful of the rights, freedoms, and interests of all stakeholders involved, including broader societal considerations.

[61] One can identify all of the requirements identified by Peers and Prechal in Article 52 Charter, in the GDPR as well. See also: Damian Clifford and Jef Ausloos, 'Data Protection and the Role of Fairness' (2018) 37 Yearbook of European Law 130.

[62] Being the actor that failed to safeguard that right or freedom in the face of these issues.

[63] Only with regard to Article 8, the CJEU has a precise framework for resolving conflicts and 'it does not have a similar [secondary] framework in respect of other fundamental rights and public interests, where the competences are exercised by the Member States'. See: Hielke Hijmans, *The European Union as Guardian of Internet Privacy : The Story of Art 16 TFEU*. Law, Governance and Technology Series 31. (Springer.2016) 222.

[64] Illustrated by: Hielke Hijmans, 'The European Union as a Constitutional Guardian of Internet Privacy and Data Protection' (PhD Thesis, University of Amsterdam 2016) <http://dare.uva.nl/document/2/169421> accessed 1 June 2019. See criticism in: Clifford and Ausloos (n 61).

[65] See also Recital 4.

The distinction between the right to data protection (Article 8 Charter) and the GDPR has also been explained in Chapter 2. Whereas the former pursues an architecture of control for data subjects, the latter pursues a fair balancing infrastructure in the data processing ecosystem. This is important to re-emphasize here as it clarifies the operation of fair balancing in this context. As mentioned before, balancing fundamental rights is a quintessentially open-ended instrument and, on its own, 'is too vague to offer sufficient guarantees of rationality, objectivity, transparency and legal theoretical coherence'.[66] The GDPR fleshes out fair balancing specifically in the context of data processing. It is a framework that provides necessary tools and actively enables to weigh conflicting interests involved on the basis of the facts in each individual case.[67]

2.3 Balancing in the GDPR

FAIR BALANCING AS THE GDPR's MISSION—Data processing operations can affect any and all of the fundamental rights and freedoms as laid down in the Charter. The expanding 'datafication of everything' increases the occurrence and magnifies this potential impact. In light of this, the GDPR is a secondary framework aimed at safeguarding all (often conflicting) fundamental rights and freedoms. In doing so, the GDPR operationalizes fair balancing of conflicting rights, freedoms, and interests that involve the processing of personal data. As such, one could say the framework as a whole is at least partly a manifestation of Article 52(1) Charter, providing a legal infrastructure[68] that actively pursues a fair balance in light of the Charter, striving for the protection of *all* fundamental rights and freedoms.[69] Indeed, the GDPR needs to be interpreted and applied 'so as to allow a fair balance to be struck between the various fundamental rights protected by the EU legal order'.[70] In sum, not only do balancing acts within the GDPR need to be informed by the Charter

[66] Angelopoulos (n 3) 284.

[67] See in this regard: *Bonnier Audio AB* [2012] Court of Justice of the European Union C-461/10 [58–60]; Orla Lynskey, *The Foundations of EU Data Protection Law* (OUP 2016) 158.

[68] Constituting a piece of legislation, the GDPR already fulfils the first condition in Article 52(1), though it should be said that the 'prescribed by law' requirement comes with certain quality checks: '[i]n particular, it must be clear and accessible, and the persons subject to it must be able to foresee the circumstances in which it will apply'. In: Steve Peers and Sasha Prechal, 'Scope and Interpretation of Rights and Principles' in Steve Peers and others (eds), *The EU Charter of Fundamental Rights: A Commentary* (Hart 2014) paras 52.40–52.42 <https://www.bloomsburycollections.com/book/the-eu-charter-of-fundamental-rights-a-commentary/>.

[69] Of course, every piece of legislation that might impact a fundamental right and/or freedom in the Charter should be in accordance with Article 52(1) Charter. What makes the GDPR so special is (a) its direct link with a fundamental freedom (Art 8); and (b) it's heightened impact on Charter rights/freedoms due to its expansive scope.

[70] AG Opinion in: *Rīgas satiksme* [2017] Court of Justice of the European Union C-13/16 paras 97–99. Referring to: *Promusicae v Telefónica* [2008] Court of Justice of the European Union C-275/06 para 68. See also: AG Opinion in: *Salvatore Manni* (n 14) para 44.

(and the ECHR),[71] the framework as a whole in fact pursues the fair balancing of fundamental rights and freedoms in situations where these are affected by the processing of personal data.

ARTICLE 52(1) CHARTER MANIFESTED IN THE GDPR—As mentioned before, the GDPR aims to protect *in particular* the right to the protection of personal data (Art 1 GDPR).[72] Any limitation to that right specifically will be scrutinized by the framework. As such, it provides a more detailed materialization of Article 52(1) Charter,[73] specifically for limitations to the right to the protection of personal data. The 'prescribed by law' or 'legality' requirement can be found throughout the GDPR, but most notably in Article 6(1), which lays down the requirements for rendering data processing lawful. Rather than laying down a permissive regime, only listing data processing operations that are *not* permitted, the GDPR provides an exhaustive list of situations in which personal data is allowed to be processed. For two of these (Art 6(1)(c) and (e)),[74] the GDPR relies on external legal provisions to render lawful the processing of personal data (requirements for such laws are laid down in Art 6(2)–(3)). The four remaining lawful grounds strictly define the legal boundaries within which personal data can be processed, in light of Article 8 Charter. The second Article 52(1) requirement—justifications for limiting rights—is also spread across the GDPR, but most importantly stems from the very rationale of the framework overall, ie to protect natural persons' fundamental rights and freedoms and in particular their right to the protection of personal data (Art 1(2) GDPR). For limitations to the right to data protection itself, the GDPR generally foresees clear justifications such as public interest (eg Art 6(1)(e), Art 89(1)) or other fundamental rights and freedoms (eg Art 23(1)(i), Art 85). Thirdly, a range of interlinked provisions ensures a fair balance between rights, freedoms, and interests throughout the GDPR. This is most notably the case with regard to so-called data quality principles in Article 5(1), but can also be found in the operation of the rights to erasure (Art 17) and to object (Art 21) for example, as well as principle of accountability in Arts 5(2) (*j*), 24.[75] Put briefly, as a whole the GDPR can be seen as reflecting and further detailing fair balancing of fundamental rights/freedoms as described in Art 52(1) Charter. As laying down the infrastructure—the skeleton or framework if you will—for

[71] European Data Protection Supervisor, 'Developing a "Toolkit" for Assessing the Necessity of Measures That Interfere with Fundamental Rights. Background Paper' (n 21) 5.

[72] This also follows from the GDPR's legislative basis being Article 16 TFEU.

[73] And its three requirements as identified by Peers and Prechal.

[74] Rendering lawful processing only when necessary for compliance with a legal obligation, or the performance of a task carried out in the public interest or in the exercise of official authority vested in the controller.

[75] Gellert explains Article 5(1)(c) (data minimization) contains a strict proportionality test and the other paragraphs contain further balancing safeguards (eg accuracy, purpose, and storage limitation). Raphaël Gellert, 'Discussion—On Risk, Balancing, and Data Protection: A Response to van Der Sloot' (2017) 3 European Data Protection Law Review 180, 182–83.

ensuring that the processing of personal data occurs within a fair, ie balanced and equitable, way.[76]

Moving away from the Charter and looking at the GDPR in particular, two key distinctions can be made between the many 'fair balancing' mutations appearing throughout: *ex ante* versus *ex post* balancing; and internal vetsus externalized balancing. Many provisions in Chapters II (Principles); III (Rights of the Data Subject); and IV (Controller and Processor) in the GDPR can be located in the following Table 5.1.

Table 5.1 Examples of Balancing Acts in the GDPR

	Ex Ante	Ex Post
Internal	Art 5: Principles relating to processing of personal data Art 6(1): Lawfulness of Processing (a) consent; (b) contract; (d) vital interests; (f) legitimate interests Art 9 (+10): Processing of special categories of personal data Art 25: Data protection by design and by default Art 12: Transparent information [. . .]	Art 15(3): Right of Access Art 17: Right to Erasure ('Right to be Forgotten') Art 21: Right to Object
External	Art 6(1)©: compliance with a legal obligation, and (1)e: task carried out in the public interest. Art 23: Restrictions	Art 17(1)(e): legal obligation as a right to erasure trigger, and (3)(b)–(c): legal obligation, public interest, or public health as right to erasure exemptions

BALANCING ACTS TABLE—The above table lists some of the most important examples of balancing provisions in the GDPR. Similarly to the 'Data Protection Matrix' described in Chapter 2 (see Table 2.1: Data Protection Matrix), the distinction between *ex ante* and *ex post* balancing is based on whether it occurs before or after the processing has initiated. Whereas the former installs safeguards *preventing* unfair data processing, the latter *remedies* imbalances resulting from data processing operations. Given its importance with regard to data subject rights to erasure and to object, this *ex ante* v *ex post* divide will further be detailed in the following section. The distinction between internal and external balancing refers to the GDPR either providing respective balancing tools internally, or whether it refers to an outside source for doing the actual balancing.[77] An example

[76] For a more thorough examination of the fairness concept and its pivotal role in the GDPR, see: Clifford and Ausloos (n 61).

[77] It is worth referring to Burket's distinction between *implied* and *explicit* balancing mechanisms: 'Implied analysis occurs when the specific data protection regulation allowing or prohibiting

of the latter can be found in Article 6(1)(c), which renders lawful processing if 'necessary for compliance with a legal obligation', which may be the case pursuant to Article 79 Directive 2007/64/EC (payment services),[78] permitting 'the processing of personal data by payment systems and payment service providers when this is necessary to safeguard the prevention, investigation and detection of payment fraud'. In this case, the legislator of a different legal document has predetermined the balance should tip in favour of data processing under these specific circumstances.

FAIRNESS—Finally, it is worth highlighting that fair balancing in the GDPR operates at two levels: (a) as part of specific provisions; and (b) as a fundamental principle underlying the framework as a whole.[79] The first level may well be the most straightforward one and comprises all of the provisions in the Balancing Acts Table (see *Table 5.1*: *Examples of Balancing Acts in the* GDPR). The second level is arguably vaguer and more arcane. It can basically be traced back to the general EU law principle of proportionality and Article 52(1) Charter, constraining limitations to Article 8 on the protection of personal data (see paragraph 29).[80] It is translated into the GDPR as the fairness principle in Article 5(1)(a).[81] This principle feeds into all other data protection provisions, which need to be interpreted and applied so as to ensure *fair* processing. With this in mind, strict compliance with all of the 'explicit statutory requirements' under the GDPR does not necessarily guarantee a fair balance, and hence compliance with the GDPR overall. Indeed, as observed by Gutwirth, the dynamic and interactive nature of data processing necessitates flexible criteria and a context-dependent analysis taking into account potentially conflicting freedoms as well as the public interest.[82] In sum, therefore, fairness in the GDPR

information handling already contains a process of analysis and balance. Explicit analysis occurs when a particular handling of data is not regulated by a law and its implied mechanism for balancing conflicting interests.' Herbert Burkert, 'Institutions of Data Protection—An Attempt at a Functional Explanation of European National Data Protection Laws' (1981) 3 Computer/LJ 173.

[78] Of the European Parliament and of the Council of 13 November 2007 on payment services in the internal market amending Directives 97/7/EC, 2002/65/EC, 2005/60/EC and 2006/48/EC and repealing Directive 97/5/EC.

[79] See in this regard also Kuner, who makes this distinction specifically with regard to the proportionality principle. Christopher Kuner, 'Proportionality in European Data Protection Law And Its Importance for Data Processing by Companies' (2008) 7 Privacy & Security Law Report 1615, 2–3.

[80] Even though Article 8 Charter should be conceptually separated from the GDPR, it should be said that in reality, falling within the scope of one will generally also trigger the applicability of the other. As such, they complete each other.

[81] Lee Bygrave and Dag Wiese Schartum, 'Consent, Proportionality and Collective Power' in Serge Gutwirth and others (eds), *Reinventing Data Protection?* (Springer Netherlands 2009) 162–63 <http://link.springer.com/10.1007/978-1-4020-9498-9> accessed 1 June 2019.

[82] Gutwirth, 'De Toepassing van Het Finaliteitsbeginsel van de Privacywet' (n 14) 1418. Also see: Burkert (n 77) 173 et seq; Poullet and Léonard (n 1) 240.

implies personal data must not be processed in a way which unreasonably infringes the fundamental rights and freedoms of data subjects and in particular, their right to the protection of personal data.[83]

Fair Balancing and Power Asymmetries—Fair balancing in data protection law is not just about resolving conflicts between different rights and interests, but also about preventing and countering (the detrimental effects caused by) information and power asymmetries. Writing in 1993, Gutwirth already highlighted that data subject-controller relations were de facto quite vertical and unidirectional. The role of fair balancing in data protection law therefore only became more important, as power asymmetries dramatically grew even larger. Indeed, as further stressed by Gutwirth, it is the task of data protection law to advance the position of individual citizens (ie data subjects) in increasingly *im*balanced relationships with controllers.[84]

Interim Conclusion—In sum, Article 8 Charter on the protection of personal data, exclusively defends a fundamental freedom with control and individual autonomy as its underlying rationale (see Chapter 2). It does not in itself seek a balance, but rather defines the minimum requirements for this fundamental freedom. The GDPR on the other hand, actively pursues the protection of *all* fundamental rights and freedoms (as affected by the processing of personal data), and *in particular* Article 8 Charter. In light of this mission, this secondary framework is pervaded by *ex ante* and *ex post* 'micro-fair balances' to arrive at outcomes safeguarding all Charter provisions. In doing so, the GDPR also aims to increase legal certainty in situations where different rights, freedoms, and interests collide as a result from data processing. With this mind, the GDPR can be seen as a fair balancing instrument reflecting and operationalizing Article 52(1) Charter in the context of personal data processing.

Section 3. *Ex Ante* and *Ex Post* Balancing in the GDPR

3.1 From *Ex Ante* to *Ex Post* Balancing and Back Again

Timing of Fair Balancing in GDPR—As a whole, the GDPR aims to achieve a fair balance throughout personal data processing's lifecycle (see Convention

[83] See: *Maximillian Schrems v Data Protection Commissioner* (n 25) para 42; *Bavarian Lager* [2010] Court of Justice of the European Union C-28/08 P [115]; *Lindqvist* (n 262) para 90; *Satamedia* (n 10) para 56; *Volker und Markus Schecke GbR and Hartmut Eifert v Land Hessen* (n 14) para 88; *Joined ASNEF and FECEMD Cases* [2011] Court of Justice of the European Union Joined Cases C-468/10 and C-469/10 [42] para 43; *Michael Schwarz v Stadt Bochum* [2013] Court of Justice of the European Union C-291/12 para 33; *Coty Germany v Stadtsparkasse Magdeburg* [2015] Court of Justice of the European Union C-580/13 [34–35]; *Google Spain* (n 44) para 81.

[84] Gutwirth, 'De Toepassing van Het Finaliteitsbeginsel van de Privacywet' (n 14) 1425–27.

108+).[85] This appears most evidently from the fairness principle in Article 5(1)(a), but also for example through provisions on accountability (Arts 5(2) and 24) and data protection by design and by default (Art 25). The dynamic nature of fair balances also becomes clear from fundamental and human rights case law involving the rights to privacy and data protection.[86] Looking at ECtHR case law in particular, it appears that the lapse of time can be used both as an argument *for*[87] as well as *against*[88] a 'right to be forgotten'. Within data protection law, *time* effectively occupies two roles. Firstly, as one factor among many in the fair balance.[89] Secondly as a scale upon which all other factors are projected, ie as a variable of each element involved in performing the required fair balance. It is this second role which is the most important and underlies the logic of *ex ante* v *ex post* balancing in the GDPR.

Balancing acts in the GDPR may operate either *ex ante*—notably in the case of the legitimate interests ground (Art 6(1)(f) and data protection impact assessments (Art 35)—or *ex post*—notably following the exercise of a data subject right such as the right to erasure (Art 17) or to object (Art 21). As will appear throughout the rest of this chapter, there is an important interaction between *ex ante* and *ex post* balancing acts. One cannot be described without the other. Indeed, notwithstanding the fact that naturally, *ex ante* and *ex post* balancing occur sequentially, they may in reality form a loop, one feeding back into the other.[90] The circular nature ensures fairness by allowing to challenge and reassess the balances in light of changed/particular circumstances.[91] In short, such a joint reading is necessary in order to look at the GDPR as a 'fair balancing' instrument. While this may still sound abstract at this stage, the following pages should make clear how this loop operates.

[85] Article 5(1) states that '[d]ata processing shall be proportionate in relation to the legitimate purpose pursued and *reflect at all stages of the processing a fair balance* between all interests concerned, whether public or private, and the rights and freedoms at stake' (emphasis added).

[86] Paulan Korenhof and others, 'Timing the Right to Be Forgotten: A Study into "Time" as a Factor in Deciding About Retention or Erasure of Data' in Serge Gutwirth, Ronald Leenes, and Paul De Hert (eds), *Reforming European Data Protection Law*, Vol 20 (First, Springer 2015) <www.springer.com/law/international/book/978-94-017-9384-1> accessed 1 June 2019.

[87] *Österreichischer Rundfunk v Austria* [2006] European Court of Human Rights 35841/02 [68].

[88] *Éditions Plon v France* [2004] European Court of Human Rights 58148/00 [53]. In this case, the heirs of former French President François Mitterrand had opposed the publication of a book by the ex-President's private doctor. The ECtHR ruled, however, that 'the more time that elapsed, the more the public interest in discussion of the history of President Mitterrand's two terms of office prevailed over the requirements of protecting the President's rights with regard to medical confidentiality'.

[89] eg in the *Digital Rights Ireland* Case, the Advocate General argued that the data retention directive (2006/24) did not respect the principle of proportionality, in requiring data retention for up to two years. Although the Directive's ultimate objective is perfectly legitimate, the AG claimed, there is no justification for extending the data retention period anything beyond one year.

[90] See in this regard also: *Google Spain* (n 44) para 75.

[91] A generalized balance made *ex ante* cannot foresee all and in light of the 'fairness' principle, requires an ability to be challenged *ex post*. See similarly: Van Drooghenbroeck (n 3) 212–15.

Inspired by this circular nature (and the book's overall focus on the right to erasure), the present chapter will first discuss *ex post* balancing before looking at *ex ante* balancing. This is also justified by the very focus of this book overall, dissecting the right to erasure and *ex post* empowerment measures in the GDPR. With this in mind, it makes sense to take the position of an average data subject who wishes to have his/her personal data erased (or certain processing operations stopped).

3.2 *Ex Post* Balancing: Rights to Object and Erasure

Ex post balancing in the GDPR refers to measures which trigger a balancing act to be made with regard to an already ongoing processing operation. The two most important such provisions are the right to erasure (Article 17) and the right to object (Article 21).[92] Both data subject rights are key empowerment tools that force a *re*-balancing act of processing operations at hand. As explained before (and will further be elaborated on in subsection 3.3 on *ex ante* balancing), each and every processing operation will already need to reflect a fair balance *ab initio* (in light of Arts 5–6). With that in mind, the rights to object and to erasure challenge the alleged *ex ante* balance in an individual case. The rights to erasure and to object 'balance' in different ways. The latter internalizes the balancing, whereas the former outsources it. This will be made clearer in the following subsections.

3.2.1 Right to Object—*Ex Post* Balancing Par Excéllence?

Article 21(1)

> The data subject shall have the right to object, on grounds relating to his or her particular situation, at any time to processing of personal data concerning him or her which is based on point (e) or (f) of Article 6(1), including profiling based on those provisions. The controller shall no longer process the personal data unless the controller demonstrates compelling legitimate grounds for the processing which override the interests, rights and freedoms of the data subject or for the establishment, exercise or defence of legal claims.

Definition—The right to object offers data subjects an opportunity to oppose the further processing of their personal data for specific purposes. It is a clear application of fair balancing, with a much stronger focus on the specific context in an individual situation than the *ex ante* balancing in Article 6(1)(f).[93] Even though processing may be 'lawful' under Article 6(1)(e)–(f) GDPR, the right to object still offers a context-dependant and individualized re-assessment. This can be derived

[92] A noteworthy third one, but with a considerably narrower scope is the right not to be subject to automated decision-making (Art 22).

[93] See also: Clifford and Ausloos (n 61).

both from the use of the broader term 'grounds' (as opposed to interests as contained in Article 6(1)(e)–(f))[94] and the words 'relating to his or her particular situation' (as opposed to a more generic situation in Article 6(1)(f)).[95]

REQUIREMENTS—The right to object is available whenever personal data is processed on the basis of either one of the last two grounds for lawful processing in Article 6(1) ((e) public interest or official authority; (f) legitimate interests). Data subjects do have to motivate their request, referring to 'grounds relating to their particular situation'. Controllers may refuse to accommodate the right to object if they can demonstrate 'compelling legitimate grounds for the processing which override the interests, rights and freedoms of the data subject *or* for the establishment, exercise or defence of legal claims'.[96] When the respective processing operation serves direct marketing purposes, there are no requirements (and the right object will therefore always be available and enforceable). The meaning and scope of 'compelling legitimate grounds' remains elusive and can by definition only be evaluated in relation to the impact on the data subject. According to WP29, that impact should be limited to a minimum necessary to meet the respective objective which should in turn be critical for the controller.[97]

BALANCING THROUGH THE RIGHT TO OBJECT—As becomes clear from the previous paragraph, the practical operation of the right to object effectively results in a balancing act. It puts the data subject's grounds relating to his/her particular situation' as well as his/her interests, rights, and freedoms more broadly in one scale, and 'compelling legitimate grounds for processing' in the other scale. The active verb is '*override*', which also suggests the balance tips in favour of the data subject by default.[98] A conclusion which seems to be in line with both the (control) rationale of the fundamental right to data protection, *and* the mission of the GDPR to achieve a fair balance in situations characterized by great power asymmetries.[99] It is also because of these rationales (both of Art 8 Charter and the GDPR) that uncertainty stemming from inconsistencies between Recital 69 and the right to object in Article 21(1) should be interpreted in favour of the data subject.[100]

[94] The language used implies that the term 'grounds' here can be understood as broader than 'interests' (ie given the fact that the data subject grounds to object appear to include; context, interests rights, and freedoms).

[95] See in this regard also: *Google Spain* (n 44) paras 75–76.

[96] Put differently, the GDPR has reversed the burden of proof, which now rests with the controller rather than the data subject. See: Article 29 Working Party, 'Guidelines on Automated Individual Decision-Making and Profiling for the Purposes of Regulation 2016/679' (Article 29 Working Party 2018) Guidelines WP 251 25 <http://ec.europa.eu/justice/article-29/documentation>.

[97] ibid.

[98] Further evidenced by Recital 69, which clearly puts the burden of proof with the controller.

[99] Gutwirth, 'De Toepassing van Het Finaliteitsbeginsel van de Privacywet' (n 14). Moreover, it should also be kept in mind that the GDPR—even if having fair balancing as its rationale—still grants special attention to Article 8 Charter in particular (Art 1(2)).

[100] As explained in the previous Chapter (4), Recital 69 conflicts with Art 21(1) on three occasions, referring to (a) the controller's own legitimate interests only; (b) 'interests' instead of 'grounds', the former being narrower; and (c) data subjects' fundamental rights and freedoms. See also: Jef Ausloos,

Illustration—The CJEU's *Google Spain* ruling offers a useful illustration of the right to object's practical operation and how *ex ante* and *ex post* balancing interact. As a general purpose internet search engine, Google by definition processes personal data whenever they index a webpage containing such data, as well as in their (automated) decisions what to show on the basis of a search term that constitutes personal data (eg a natural person's name, telephone number, or username). Essentially, the *Google Spain* ruling suggests that such processing of personal data can be presumed legitimate *ex ante* under Article 6(1)(f) GDPR (at the time Article 7(f) Directive 95/46/EC).[101] Naturally, in the context of general purpose internet search engines such balancing act under Article 6(1)(f) GDPR will be conducted on a more abstract, less individualized level (see below). Indeed, the CJEU explains search engines must ensure their processing operations meet the requirements of data protection law 'within the framework of their responsibilities, powers and capabilities'.[102] The right to object assumes (and in a way subsumes) the lawfulness of the conditions in Article 6 GDPR (and hence the fair balancing test in (Article 6(1)(e)–(f) GDPR) but then offers a right to object based on broader considerations in order to better contextualize the individual fair balancing assessment.

Contextualized Re-Balancing—In light of the above, one could define the right to object as the extension and specification of the Articles 6(1)(e) and (f) GDPR balancing acts. The right to object is an *ex post* empowerment measure that explicitly imposes a re-balancing exercise for an existing processing operation. As such, data subject rights complement Articles 6(1)(e) and (f) GDPR by effectively enabling ways to question the balance defined by the controller. This is because, from a practical perspective, and taking into account the scale at which they operate, most ISS controllers will construct their balancing under Article 6(1)(f) GDPR a priori on the basis of the median context and the average individual. In contrast, *ex post* empowerment tools such as the rights to erasure and especially the right to object are aimed at enabling data subjects to question this initial balancing act in light of their particular circumstances.[103]

Difference with Right to Erasure—It is now possible to highlight yet another difference between the rights to object and to erasure, most of which have already been alluded to in previous chapters. Both provisions trigger—and subsequently manage—balancing acts in different ways. As illustrated by the previous paragraphs, and contrary to the right to erasure, the right to object internalizes the

'Balancing in the GDPR: Legitimate Interests v. Right to Object', *CITIP Blog* 28 February 2017, https://www.law.kuleuven.be/citip/blog/balancing-in-the-gdpr-legitimate-interests-v-right-to-object/.

[101] *Google Spain* (n 44) paras 73–74.

[102] ibid para 83.

[103] See in this line also: *Google Spain* InfoCuria (n 44) para 82; *Salvatore Manni* (n 14) paras 46–47.

actual balancing act. The right is self-sufficient, ie it provides all of the tools necessary to do the balancing. The right to erasure on the other hand, essentially defers to other provisions to do the actual balancing.

3.2.2 Right to Erasure—Balancing Shell

Invoking the right to erasure will virtually always trigger a balancing act. Indeed, erasure implies data is still being processed (even if only passively stored), which in turn implies someone has an interest in that processing, or at the very least would be affected by an obligation to erase said data. In contrast with the right to object however, the right to erasure (Art 17) outsources balancing acts. It operates as a 'shell', with both right-to-erasure triggers (Art 17(1)) and exemptions (Art 17(3)) referring to other provisions for operationalizing the actual balancing. Put differently, Article 17 groups together or 'clusters' balancing provisions in the GDPR. Some triggers (Art 17(1)) or exemptions (Art 17(3)) even outsource such balancing to different legal frameworks (see Table 5.1: Examples of Balancing Acts in the GDPR). The goal of this subsection is to untangle how exactly this balance outsourcing operates. The conclusion will be that the two *de facto* most important balancing acts (ie the ones that are less straightforward to decide) are the internal *ex ante* 'legitimate interests' balancing act in Article 6(1)(f) (to be discussed later), and the *ex post* right to object balancing act in Article 21(1).

Logic of Applying Article 17—Determining whether a data subject can invoke the right to erasure under Article 17 can roughly be divided into three steps (see Chapter 4). The chronological order of these steps is informed by how each one informs the next one (see Figure 5.1). While it may initially appear counter-intuitive (ie starting with the last paragraph of Art 17), it is the most logical sequence to follow in order to minimize unnecessary legal analyses:

- *Firstly*, do any of the exemptions in Article 17(3) apply? If the answer is yes, there will be no need for further assessment.
- Secondly, if none of the exemptions apply, on the basis of what lawful ground(s) in Article 6(1) is the relevant personal data being processed? This second step will determine what right to erasure triggers will be available to the data subject (see below).
- Thirdly, does any of the relevant triggers (Art 17(1)) apply? If yes, the controller will effectively have to erase personal data. That is, unless the controller can demonstrate a lawful ground for further processing that personal data (eg for a different or narrower set of purposes).

Exemptions—A quick glance at the list of exemptions in Article 17(3) already reveals that they all relate to a specific (processing) interest and/or purpose. In that regard, they could arguably even be seen as variations on the lawful ground

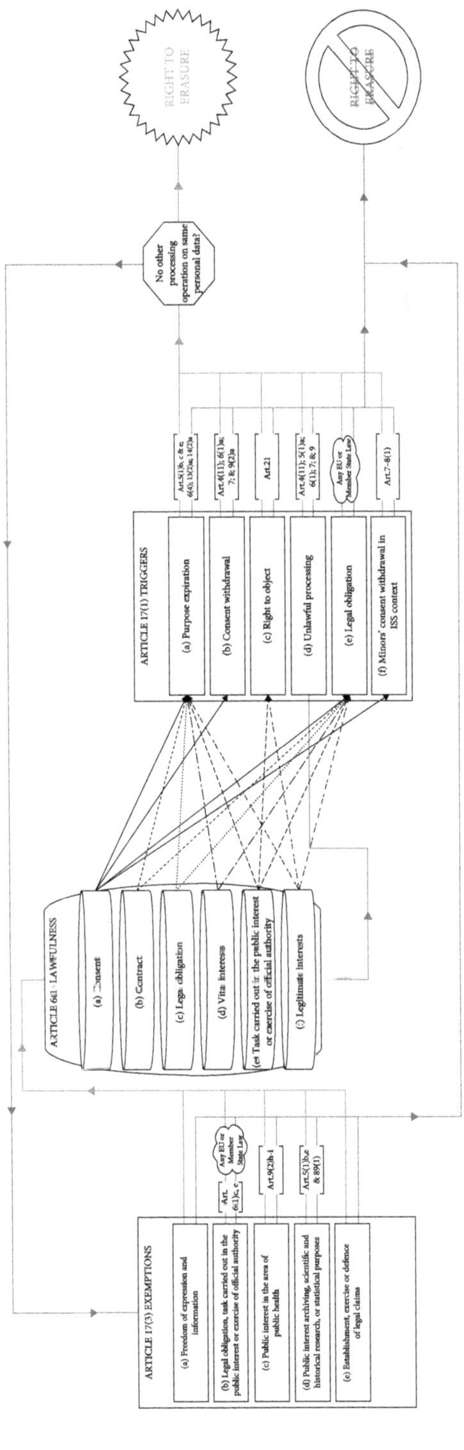

Figure 5.1 Flowchart for determining applicability of the right to erasure

in Article 6(1)(f). Whenever processing is necessary in light of any of the exemptions, the legislator determined that the data subject's right in having the data erased is overridden by default. In doing so, the exemptions effectively safeguard broader (societal, public) interests in processing operations that controllers may have less of an incentive to defend against erasure. It is also no surprise therefore, that two exemptions—b (compliance with a legal obligation or task carried out in the public interest) and c (public interest in area of health)—clearly correspond to the lawful grounds in Articles 6(1)(c), (e) and 9(2)(h)–(i). Exemptions a (freedom of expression and information) and d (archiving purposes in the public interest, scientific or historical research, or statistical purposes) clearly represent broader interests as well.[104] Interests that controllers cannot simply be counted on to defend in a potential balancing act. With this in mind, the exemptions constitute an important first step in ensuring an appropriate use of the right to erasure (and conversely, prevent abuse). When any of them is applicable, the right to erasure is off the table.

Exemptions in Practice—All exemptions in Article 17(3) are phrased as binary questions, the answer to which can only be found through other provisions (in/outside the GDPR). Turning to the reality of ISS providers however, it was made clear before already that the applicability of any of the exemptions in Article 17(3) will generally be debatable, still leaving open the right to erasure's door. The binary nature of the exemptions in theory (processing is either *necessary* or not) conceal the fact that in practice a complicated qualitative assessment may be required. Moreover, personal data will rarely be processed in pursuit of one interest and/or purpose only. It is important to reiterate therefore, that the exemptions will only safeguard the processing for the specific purposes and/or interests they define. Any processing outside of that will not be exempted and may still be targeted with data subject rights. In these circumstances, as will also appear in the following chapters, it may be more appropriate to talk about the right to object rather than the right to erasure. After all, the data will not be *erased*, but the way in which it may further be processed will effectively be constrained to the situations defined in Article17(3).

Lawful Ground—The second step in determining the right to erasure's applicability in a concrete case requires identifying the relevant lawful ground that is relied upon for processing the targeted personal data. This is important because the lawful ground will inform what triggers can be invoked or not. For intelligibility purposes, Table 5.2 clarifies the relationship between lawful ground (Art 6(1)) and right-to-erasure triggers (Art 17(1)). Importantly, the fourth (unlawful processing) and fifth (legal obligation) triggers will always be

[104] Further emphasized by the exemption regimes specified in Articles 85 and 89.

Table 5.2 Relation between lawful grounds (Art 6(1)) and right to erasure triggers (Art 17(1))

Lawful Ground in Art 6(1)	Relation	Right-to-Erasure Triggers Art 17(1)
(a) Consent	When consent is relied on as lawful ground, the most relevant right-to-erasure trigger will be **b**, ie withdrawing consent. When consent was given in the context of ISS while the data subject was a child, the last trigger **f** could also be used. Theoretically, triggers **a** (purpose expiration), **e** (legal obligation), and **d** (unlawful processing) will also be applicable. Given the difficulty of demonstrating expiration of purposes or unlawfulness in practice, it seems much more straightforward to simply rely on the less ambiguous withdrawal of consent to obtain erasure.	a purpose expiration b consent withdrawal d unlawful processing e legal obligation f consent withdrawal in context of ISS offered to children
(b) Contract	When necessity for the performance of a contract is relied on as lawful ground for processing, the most relevant trigger to rely on will be **a** purpose expiration (which will generally occur at the latest upon rescinding the contract). Trigger **d** may also be relevant when the lawful ground is not valid (anymore). To the extent this ground overlaps with the first lawful ground on consent, trigger **b** might also be of some relevance. Finally, it cannot be excluded that an external legal obligation imposes erasure, even when processing is still necessary for the performance of a contract (so trigger **e** remains open).	a purpose expiration b consent withdrawal d unlawful processing e legal obligation
(c) Legal Obligation *(d) Vital Interests*	These two lawful grounds are largely outside the control of any of the parties involved. The most relevant triggers therefore will be **a** (purpose expiration) and **e** (legal obligation). As always, trigger **d** remains available in those situations where the lawful ground is incorrectly relied upon in the first place.	a purpose expiration d unlawful processing e legal obligation
(e) Task in Public Interest	Compared to the previous two, this lawful ground leaves more room for interpretation as to the scope of processing operations that it may cover. So, on top of triggers **a** (purpose expiration), **e** (legal obligation), and **d** (unlawful processing), data subjects will also be able to request erasure on the basis of trigger **c**, following a right to object.	a purpose expiration c right to object d unlawful processing e legal obligation

(*Continiued*)

Table 5.2 Continued

Lawful Ground in Art 6(1)	Relation	Right-to-Erasure Triggers Art 17(1)
(f) Legitimate Interests	Contrary to the previous three, the last lawful ground leaves considerable freedom to controllers to define their interests and purposes. Particularly triggers **a** (purpose expiration), **c** (right to object), and **d** (unlawful processing) will be relevant, though **e** (legal obligation) remains open as well.	a purpose expiration c right to object d unlawful processing e legal obligation

relevant. The former because it directly concerns the actual validity of the lawful grounds in the first place. The latter because it depends on existing and future EU or Member-State laws dictating erasure for an unpredictable number of different reasons.

Right-to-Erasure Triggers—In sum, the second step identifies what right-to-erasure triggers may be relevant to the data subject in his/her particular case. The third and final step will then be to evaluate whether or not the relevant trigger(s) is/are applicable.[105]

Trigger 1: Purpose Expiration—The first right-to-erasure trigger relates to the expiration of the processing purpose(s). Assuming the purpose is valid in the first place (see Article 5(1)), there are roughly two scenarios imaginable. Either the purpose is defined in such a way that the (non-)expiration is obvious from the outset, or it is framed more ambiguously and/or without clear limits. In the first situation, the applicability of the trigger is straightforward. The second situation will require a substantive assessment in light the purpose limitation (Art 5(1)(b)), data minimization (Art 5(1)(c)) and storage limitation (Art 5(1)(e)) principles. These last principles generally require somewhat of a balancing act in themselves. The minimum amount of personal data and time necessary for achieving a processing purpose will have to be assessed in relation to potential impact on data subjects. From a practical perspective therefore, it seems this first trigger is only realistic when the purpose and/or retention period are clearly delineated and expiration is evident. Especially so in the ISS context, characterized by extremely asymmetric relationships between controller(s) and data subjects.

Trigger 2: Withdrawal of Consent—The second trigger may well be the most straightforward and useful one in the ISS context. Whenever personal data is processed on the basis of consent (Art 6(1)(a)), which will often be the case in

[105] For a more elaborate overview of the triggers and exemptions of the right to erasure in Article 17 GDPR, see Chapter 4.

the ISS context, the data subject can simply exercise the right to erasure by withdrawing his/her consent. After all, Article 7(3) explicitly grants data subjects the right to withdraw their consent unconditionally and at any time. Two important caveats severely limit the practical relevance of this second trigger. Firstly, withdrawing consent to the processing of personal data will often effectively result in the inability to further use the respective service. Despite efforts to prevent this (eg Article 7(4)), practical reality suggests granular erasure/objection in the context of ISS providers, will often result in de facto inability to (fully) enjoy the respective service.[106] Secondly, withdrawal of consent will not result in erasure when the controller can fall back on another lawful ground for further processing (for a subset of purposes). Especially in the ISS context, the only realistic lawful ground for doing so will be the last one on legitimate interests,[107] effectively leading to a balancing act.

Trigger 3: Right to Object—The third right to erasure trigger directly depends on the invokability of the right to object in Article 21. As mentioned before, the right to object only relates to specific processing operations (rather than the underlying data). It may only lead to a right to erasure when no other processing operations exist than the one(s) objected to. Importantly, the right to object—as well as the corresponding trigger in Article 17(1)(c)—install a balancing exercise that bears striking resemblance to the one in Article 6(1)(f)(see Section 0).[108] Indeed, as explained before, the right to object foresees a context-dependant and individualized re-assessment of fair balances in light of Article 6(1)(f).[109]

Trigger 4: Unlawful Processing—The fourth right to erasure trigger (unlawful processing) directly links back to the grounds in Article 6(1). This trigger will be successful when the processing of personal data appears unlawful (ie without a lawful ground under Article 6(1)) *ab initio*. If this is the case, the personal data should never have been processed in the first place and therefore be erased instantly. As mentioned before, ISS providers will generally only be able to rely on either the first (consent), second (necessary for performance of a contract), or last (legitimate interests) grounds. The second ground is so restrictive—only permitting a narrow set of processing operations[110]—that it will not be very relevant in

[106] For more, see Chapter 6; balancing scenario on commercial interests.

[107] To be complete, any other lawful ground remains theoretically available as well. However, if consent is the lawful ground relied upon for the contested processing operation, it is unlikely that same operation can also still be rendered lawful under any other lawful ground apart from the last one on legitimate interests. If that would be the case, the controller would presumably have relied on them from the start already.

[108] See also: *Google Spain* (n 44) para 75 et seq.

[109] ibid paras 75–76; Jef Ausloos, 'The Interaction between the Rights to Object and to Erasure in the GDPR' (*CITIP blog*, 25 August 2016) <https://www.law.kuleuven.be/citip/blog/gdpr-update-the-interaction-between-the-right-to-object-and-the-right-to-erasure/> accessed 1 June 2019; Ausloos, 'Balancing in the GDPR' (n 100).

[110] European Data Protection Board, 'Draft Guidelines 2/2019 on the Processing of Personal Data under Article 6(1)(b) GDPR in the Context of the Provision of Online Services to Data Subject' (EDPB

situations where a data subject clearly expressed the desire to have personal data erased. The validity of the first ground will have to be assessed in light of Articles 4(11) and 7. But even if the validity of consent as a lawful ground is uncertain, data subjects will always have the ability to withdraw their consent and obtain erasure much more easily like that (Art 17(1)(b)). This leaves the last lawful ground (Art 6(1)(f)), the validity of which inherently depends on a balancing act.

Trigger 5: Legal Obligation—The fifth right to erasure trigger (legal obligation) is quite straightforward, referring to objective EU or Member-State laws which include obligations to erase the personal data. Of course, it may well be possible that these legal obligations to erase personal data include ambiguities or balancing acts themselves.

Trigger 6: Consent Withdrawal in the Context of ISS Used by Children—The sixth right to erasure trigger (minors' consent in ISS context) has a very narrow scope and directly ties back to the second (consent withdrawal) trigger. Its main added value as opposed to the second trigger is that it offers minors (that meanwhile became adults), the ability to withdraw the consent given by their parents or legal guardians.

Ubiquity of Balancing in Right to Erasure Triggers—As summarized and demonstrated in the previous paragraphs, most right-to-erasure triggers will effectively result in a balancing act to be made. This becomes even clearer when taking a step back from the minutiae of Article 17 in particular (see Chapter 4). Indeed, whenever a controller will be confronted with a right-to-erasure request that it wishes to reject, it will at the very least need a lawful ground to continue processing that personal data despite the data subject's request. In the context of ISS providers, as amply highlighted before, the only relevant/realistic grounds will be (a) consent, (b) necessity for a contract, and (f) legitimate interests. Relying on the first of these would be nonsensical after the data subject clearly expressed a desire for his/her personal data to be erased. The second has a particularly narrow scope (see Chapter 4), and hinges on a potentially difficult assessment of what is in fact *necessary* to perform the respective contract. The last one offers most flexibility and will generally make most sense for ISS providers *after* an erasure request has been submitted.

Interim Conclusion—Concluding, to all intents and purposes, the balancing act in Article 6(1)(f) will be virtually impossible to avoid by ISS controllers, especially after the right to erasure has been invoked. Depending on the circumstances, such a balancing act may be very straightforward (eg in manifest cases) but it may also be ignored or not adequately observed (eg when the controller has strong conflicting incentives). With this in mind, the following subsection is aimed at shedding light on how exactly the GDPR prescribes Article 6(1)(f)'s balancing exercise

2019) 10 <https://edpb.europa.eu/sites/edpb/files/consultation/edpb_draft_guidelines-art_6-1-b-final_public_consultation_version_en.pdf> accessed 19 April 2019.

to be performed in theory. It will do so, not from the perspective of an *ex ante* protective measure, but from the perspective of the right to erasure as an exemplary *ex post* empowerment measure. In other words, it will focus in particular on how the validity of a presumed balance under Article 6(1)(f) may (not) be challenged. This analysis prepares the reader for Chapter 6 which will examine three discrete balancing scenarios.

3.3 *Ex Ante* Balancing: Legitimate Interests

The previous section (and chapter) made clear that Article 17 does not install a system of strict liability for erasing personal data but will oftentimes require a de facto balancing act. This is because there are many options for contesting the right to erasure's applicability in a given situation.[111] Balancing acts emanating from the right to erasure may be externalized to different legal frameworks (eg erasure dictated by a legal obligation pursuant to Art 17(1)(e)[112] but generally refer to other GDPR provisions. Regardless, any opposition to the right to erasure, implies a desire to further process the relevant personal data, and therefore a context-dependent assessment in light of the fairness principle (Art 5(1)(a)) and a lawful ground for further processing (Art 6(1)). Even though initiated by the data subject, the actual balancing act will *prima facie* be made by the controller. In the ISS context, Article 6(1)(f) on legitimate interests will generally (or realistically) be the only available lawful ground to further process personal data *after* a right to erasure has been invoked.[113] It is crucial therefore, to properly comprehend the *modus operandi* of Article 6(1)(f) balancing in order to understand balancing as triggered by Article 17.

3.3.1 Importance of the Legitimate Interests Ground

Positioning Article 6(1)(f)—Before delving into the mechanics of Article 6(1)(f), it is important to briefly expand on its role as key balancing act in the GDPR.

[111] The fact that in a given case, the right's application is not contested, does not mean there is no balancing act. The balance may either be very clearly in favour of the data subject and/or the controller may simply not wish to bother contesting the right to erasure in the first place.

[112] Even if, within the GDPR, these provisions are phrased as binaries (ie an external legal provision dictates processing (Art 6(1)(c), Art 17(3)(b), *or* erasure (Art 17(1(e)), they still conceal a balancing act. That external legal source, after all, is the product of legislative deliberation, pre-defining a balance and/or putting down the conditions for deciding on such a balance in concrete situations.

[113] As explained before, the other lawful grounds are unrealistic in those circumstances. Consent (Art 6(1)(a)) can be withdrawn and the contract (Art 6(1)(b)) can be rescinded. If processing is necessary for compliance with a legal obligation (Art 6(1)(c)), the right to erasure would not be applicable in the first place (see Art 17(3)(b)). Finally, the narrow set of purposes that fit within Article 6(1)(d)–(e) (necessity for protecting data subject's vital interest, performance of a task carried out in the public interest, or in the exercise of official authority) are not generally associated with the primary activities of ISS providers.

As made clear before, balancing pervades the data protection framework in many different mutations and layers. It does so inter alia via the ample use of concepts such as 'proportionality',[114] 'appropriateness', and particularly through the pivotal fairness requirement in Article 5(1)(a) which arguably constitutes the overarching principle in this regard.[115] Indeed, as explained above, fair balancing constitutes the very rationale of the GDPR. With this in mind, the legitimate interests ground in Article 6(1)(f) is the most important operational provision for internal *ex ante* balancing.[116] 'Internal' as it provides a self-sustained infrastructure for balancing within the confines of the GDPR.[117] '*Ex ante*' as the infrastructure it defines, constitutes the mould within which future processing needs to be construed. 'Operational' as it lays down a concrete infrastructure for *ex ante* balancing acts (contrary to the fairness principle in Art 5(1)(a), for example, which remains much more abstract).

The balancing act put forward in Article 6(1)(f) transcends merely being one lawful ground among others. The preceding four grounds (*necessary* for (b) performance of a contract, (c) compliance with a legal obligation, (d) protect the data subject's vital interests, (e) tasks carried out in the public interest), can be seen as variations on a theme. They are simply situations where the interests, fundamental rights, and freedoms of the data subject are overridden by default (which is not to say the balance can still tip the other way depending on the specifics of a given case).[118] The same can be said with regard to the first lawful ground on consent, which installs a presumption of fair balance.[119] This is particularly true in light of the new Article 7, inter alia putting forward the unconditional ability to withdraw one's consent as well as guarding against all-or-nothing clauses. Put differently, the seemingly binary logic of the first five lawful grounds merely hides the fact that they are also essentially balancing acts. The main difference is that said balance has been pre-set by the legislator.[120] In sum, whereas the first five lawful grounds contain

[114] For example: *Lindqvist* (n 44) para 87.

[115] Clifford and Ausloos (n 61).

[116] See Table 1: Examples of Balancing Acts in the GDPR.

[117] Contrary to provisions outsourcing balancing to different legal frameworks (eg Art 23 on the ability to adopt legal measures restricting data subject rights).

[118] See in this regard, Article 29 Working Party, 'Opinion 06/2014 on the Notion of Legitimate Interests of the Data Controller under Article 7 of Directive 95/46/EC' (n 20) 9. WP29 explains that when processing relies on any of the first five grounds, 'it is considered as a priori legitimate [...]. There is in other words a presumption that the balance between the different rights and interests at stake—including those of the controller and the data subject—is satisfied—assuming, of course, that all other provisions of data protection law are complied with'. Similarly, but more extremely arguing the redundancy of other lawful grounds altogether, see: Lokke Moerel and Corien Prins, 'Privacy for the Homo Digitalis: Proposal for a New Regulatory Framework for Data Protection in the Light of Big Data and the Internet of Things' 13 <http://papers.ssrn.com/abstract=2784123> accessed1 June 2019.

[119] See in this regard: Serge Gutwirth, 'Short Statement about the Role of Consent in the European Data Protection Directive' <http://works.bepress.com/serge_gutwirth/80/>; Moerel and Prins (n 118) 74.

[120] This ties back to the discussion on how syllogisms are essentially balancing acts in disguise. See: Van Drooghenbroeck (n 3) 288–90.

implied balancing acts for specified situations, the last lawful ground comprises an *explicit* balancing act for residual cases.[121] To put it more visually, the legitimate interests ground is the large circle enveloping the other five lawful grounds.

The practical relevance of this consideration is that the lawfulness of any processing operation under Article 6(1), will effectively be subject to Article 6(1)(f)'s balancing act.[122] Indeed, the legitimate interests test constitutes the most evident manifestation of the fairness principle (Art 5(1)(a)) in the shape of a lawful ground. With this in mind, Article 6(1)(f) will inform—not determine—the validity of the other lawful grounds. Put differently, it can be used as a proxy for evaluating the validity of any of the lawful grounds, even in situations where Article 6(1)(f) can *stricto sensu* not be relied upon as a lawful ground.[123] Indeed, whenever there is a clear imbalance between controllers, third parties, and the data subject (to the detriment of the latter) as specified by Article 6(1)(f), it will virtually be impossible for the processing operation to be lawful under any Article 6(1) ground. Such a conclusion may be particularly valuable to controllers looking for legal certainty,[124] in light of the difficulty for delineating and determining the applicability of the other lawful grounds.[125]

Another reason explaining the pivotal nature of Article 6(1)(f)'s balancing act, relates to the fact that it effectively enables to introduce fundamental rights/freedoms balancing in horizontal relationships (ie between controller and data subject).[126] Such fundamental rights/freedoms are captured by the notion of 'legitimate *interests*',[127] and will often be the only viable counterbalances when the other

[121] This *summa divisio* between implied and explicit balancing acts in data protection law is also put forward by: Burkert (n 77) 173. See also: Raphaël Gellert, 'We Have Always Managed Risks in Data Protection Law' (2016) 2 European Data Protection Law Review 481, 485.

[122] See Moerel and Prins (n 118) 47 et seq.

[123] According to WP29, any processing falling within the definition in Article 22(1) ('decision based solely on automated processing, including profiling, which produces legal effects concerning him or her or similarly significantly affects him or her'), cannot rely on Article 6(1)(f) as lawful ground. This does not prevent however, that the general structure provided by the legitimate interests ground—and underlying all other lawful grounds—can be used to evaluate the lawfulness. See: Article 29 Working Party, 'Guidelines on Automated Individual Decision-Making and Profiling for the Purposes of Regulation 2016/679' (n 96) 21.

[124] This may also explain why in a 2017 survey of 223 companies asking about their GDPR readiness about a year before its entry into force, about a third anticipated making more use of the legitimate interests ground under the GDPR than they were doing under Directive 95/46. Admittedly, several of them may consider so inappropriately (eg assuming the ground should do simply because processing is useful to enhance their business). See: Wim Nauwelaerts, 'Practitioner's Corner—GDPR—The Perfect Privacy Storm: You Can Run from the Regulator, but You Cannot Hide from the Consumer' (2017) 3 European Data Protection Law Review 251, 253.

[125] Article 29 Working Party, 'Opinion 06/2014 on the Notion of Legitimate Interests of the Data Controller under Article 7 of Directive 95/46/EC' (n 20) 35–36.

[126] Gutwirth explains data protection law grants controllers the ability/power to make a unilateral decision to process personal data (*not own*), and as such interfere in the enjoyment of fundamental/human rights of data subjects (who have to tolerate this in so far said interference is not disproportionate). In: Gutwirth, 'De Toepassing van Het Finaliteitsbeginsel van de Privacywet' (n 14) 1454.

[127] This allowed the CJEU in its *Google Spain* Ruling to essentially consider the fundamental freedom of expression and information, without explicitly mentioning it.

side of the balance already contains another fundamental right/freedom, ie the data subject's right to the protection of private life in Article 7 Charter or personal data in Article 8 Charter. Of course, such de facto balancing of fundamental rights/freedoms does not supplant or equate to a fully-fledged balancing of Charter provisions. It rather constitutes a *prima facie* balancing outsourced to private entities (ie controllers) in a specific context. The fact that such important legal exercise is done by a private entity,[128] which is also actively interested in the outcome of the balance, does raise important questions which will be dealt with in Chapter 7.

One final element to stress is that the balancing act in Article 6(1)(f) is *not* concerned about—and is therefore not an appropriate tool to tackle—broader societal interests that may be affected by the processing operations at stake.[129] Even though the provision explicitly incorporates the interests of 'third parties' into the balancing act, it does so only to the extent the processing takes place in function of those interests. In other words, it does not seem to consider how third parties may be (negatively) affected by processing operations outside of their grasp. Moreover 'third parties' still implies a collection of individuals, negating the potential broader interests that cannot easily be ascribed to individuals in particular. Yet, increasingly so, ISS providers have a considerable impact on broader societal values transcending specific individuals (eg media pluralism, equality). The legitimate interests ground should not be seen as the designated legal tool to ensure data processing operates in pursuit of those values in general. These are rather safeguarded by other provisions in (and outside) the GDPR such as Article 25 on data protection by design and by default, or Article 35 on data protection impact assessments, and most prominently the fairness principle in Article 5(1)(a). Having said that, the legitimate interests ground in Article 6(1)(f) and data subject rights to erasure (Art 17) and to object (Art 21), may still indirectly protect broader societal interests to the extent they affect the individual controller-data subject relationship.

3.3.2 Structure of Article 6(1)(f) Legitimate Interests Balancing

> **Article 6—Lawfulness of processing**
>
> 1. Processing shall be lawful only if and to the extent that […] (f) processing is necessary for the purposes of the legitimate interests pursued by the controller or by a third party, except where such interests are overridden by the interests or fundamental rights and freedoms of the data subject which require protection of personal data, in particular where the data subject is a child.

As explained before, balancing is ubiquitous throughout the data protection framework. To the extent that all lawful grounds in Article 6(1) can be traced back

[128] See in this vein: Burkert (n 77) 174.

[129] eg when group profiles are generated on the basis of individuals' social media usage, which in turn are used to customize news reporting to a wider audience.

to the basic template as laid down in Article 6(1)(f), the legitimate interests balancing paradigm underlies virtually all processing operations. This is not to say that balancing does not appear in different shapes and forms elsewhere in the GDPR. Article 6(1)(f) is simply the most prominent *and* structured *ex ante* balancing measure. Because data subject rights to erasure and object actively question said balance—ie effectively trigger a re-assessment of the balance as defined by the controller—a better understanding of how exactly such balance is established in the first place is imperative. This section will therefore set out the constitutive elements of the balancing exercise under Article 6(1)(f).

Deliberate Open-Endedness—Article 6(1)(f) is phrased in a deliberately vague and open-ended manner in order to foist a case-by-case evaluation.[130] Rather than simply providing for a mere compliance checklist, it lays down an abstract blueprint for doing context-dependent balancing.[131] Prescriptive lists fail to give sufficient flexibility in assessing situations *in concreto*.[132] The open-ended nature of the legitimate interests ground in Art 6(1)f was also confirmed in the *Breyer* Ruling,[133] where the CJEU indicated that narrow constructions and/or criteria categorically limiting the ground's width are not allowed.[134] The Advocate General had already explained that Article 7(f) Directive 95/46 (now Art 6(1)f GDPR) inherently requires a case-by-case analysis on which not much guidance can be given in the abstract.[135] This was indirectly confirmed in the *Manni* case, where it was ruled that even in situations where the default balance strongly weighs against the data subject, it should still be possible to reverse that balance under very particular circumstances.[136]

Basic Structure—The balancing act defined in Article 6(1)f GDPR differentiates between three different entities: the controller, third parties and the data subject. Each of these actors may have relevant interests that will need to be accounted

[130] For the link with the proportionality principle's case-based approach, see subsection 2.2.

[131] Something which also led to quite some divergence in how the provision has been implemented and interpreted in the different Member States under Directive 95/46. Federico Ferretti, 'Data Protection and the Legitimate Interest of Data Controllers: Much Ado about Nothing or the Winter of Rights?' (2014) 51 Common Market Law Review 856–57.

[132] ibid 865. Referring to European Data Protection Supervisor, 'Additional EDPS Comments on the Data Protection Reform Package' (Brussels, 15 March 2013).

[133] *Patrick Breyer v Bundesrepublik Deutschland* [2016] Court of Justice of the European Union C-582/14 para 58 et seq.

[134] This also seems to correspond to the stance taken by the ECtHR with regard to human rights balancing. See for example: *KU v Finland* [2009] European Court of Human Rights 2872/02 [48–49]; Evangelia Psychogiopoulou, 'The European Court of Human Rights, Privacy and Data Protection in the Digital Era' in Maja Brkan and Evangelia Psychogiopoulou, *Courts, Privacy and Data Protection in the Digital Environment* (Edward Elgar 2017) 36.

[135] AG Opinion in: *Patrick Breyer v Bundesrepublik Deutschland* (n 133) paras 102–03. Responding to Mr Breyer's claim that storing dynamic IP addresses is not 'necessary to protect the proper functioning of Internet services against possible attacks', the AG does 'not think that a categorical answer can be given in relation to that problem, whose solution, on the contrary, must be preceded, in each particular case, by a balancing of the interests of the website owner and the rights and interests of users'.

[136] *Salvatore Manni* (n 14) para 60.

for. As will appear throughout the rest of this chapter, Article 6(1)f is not a straightforward weighing of one element against another, but incorporates many different factors each of which may be difficult to identify and quantify.[137] Still, the provision groups together the legitimate interests of the controller *and* third parties on one side of the scale, against the interests or fundamental rights and freedoms of the data subject on the other. As the balancing act will a priori exclusively be performed by the controller (exceptionally in dialogue with the data subject), in practice third party interests will generally only enter the equation to the extent they correspond with (or relate to) the controller's interests.[138]

NECESSITY—Similarly to the four preceding lawful grounds, Article 6(1)(f) hinges upon a 'necessity' test. According to the CJEU, necessity in this context 'has its own independent meaning in [Union] law and must be interpreted in a manner which fully reflects the objective of [the Regulation]'.[139] Put briefly, necessity in Article 6(1) can be understood as there being an inextricable link between the *purpose* and the *processing operation(s)*.[140] This means that the purpose cannot effectively be achieved without the respective processing operation, though rendering the processing more effective might still be covered as well.[141] *A contrario*, operations that are merely 'useful' or 'facilitating' cannot be considered to be 'necessary' within the meaning of Article 6(1).[142] Necessity, the EDPS explains, 'is a facts-based concept, rather than a merely abstract legal notion, and that the concept must be considered in the light of the specific circumstances surrounding the case'.[143]

NECESSITY AND GRANULARITY—Even though these observations may seem obvious, they are worth reemphasizing in light of granularity and the rights to erasure and to object. Only a granular approach to purpose limitation will enable discerning *necessary* from trivial processing operations. Oftentimes—particularly in the ISS context—the purposes initially defined by the controller will be broad and vague, rendering almost impossible the necessity test and effectively opening the

[137] Article 29 Working Party, 'Opinion 06/2014 on the Notion of Legitimate Interests of the Data Controller under Article 7 of Directive 95/46/EC' (n 20).

[138] On the confusing term of third parties, see Chapter 3.

[139] *Huber v Germany* [2008] Court of Justice of the European Union C-524/06 para 52. See above: Exemptions to the Right to Erasure.

[140] WP29 explains the necessity test requires considering whether 'less invasive means are available to serve the same end' Article 29 Working Party, 'Opinion 06/2014 on the Notion of Legitimate Interests of the Data Controller under Article 7 of Directive 95/46/EC' (n 20) 29.

[141] *Huber v Germany* (n 139) para 62 et seq. At least in the context of Article 6(1)(e) (task carried out in the public interest or in the exercise of official authority). More specifically, the respective processing in this case concerned the centralization of the register for foreign nationals so as to render more effective the application of the legislation on rights of residence.

[142] Referring to ECtHR case law, WP29 explains that 'necessity' is neither synonymous with the narrower 'indispensable', nor with the more flexible 'admissible', 'reasonable', or 'desirable'. Article 29 Working Party, 'Opinion 06/2014 on the Notion of Legitimate Interests of the Data Controller under Article 7 of Directive 95/46/EC' (n 20) 11.

[143] European Data Protection Supervisor, 'Assessing the Necessity of Measures That Limit the Fundamental Right to the Protection of Personal Data: A Toolkit' (n 25) 8.

door to 'over-processing'.[144] Data subject rights, and the right to erasure and to object in particular, aim to put data subjects in a position to challenge those purposes, to define them more granularly in light of their particular situation and hence separate the wheat from the chaff, rendering the overall processing operation(s) more lean.

NECESSITY V LEGITIMACY—Finally, it is important to conceptually separate necessity from legitimacy. The latter is used to qualify interests and purposes (see next section) and chronologically precedes the necessity test, which relates to the personal data to be used. Indeed, necessity evaluates the link between processing and purposes, independently from their legitimacy. The distinction is also exemplified in the two-part test of the purpose limitation principle: (a) the legitimacy of the purpose as laid down by the controller or law in name of a freedom or interest; and (b) the necessity to process the respective personal data to achieve said purpose (see data minimization (Art 6(1)c)).[145] In the case of direct marketing, for example, the key question relates to the *legitimacy* (and associated balancing of interests), rather than necessity of the relevant data processing to achieve the purpose.[146]

3.3.3 Legitimate Interests v Legitimate Purposes

RELATED BUT DIFFERENT CONCEPTS—Article 6(1)(f) refers to 'the purposes of the legitimate interests pursued by the controller or by a third party'. Key in this excerpt is the concept of *interests*, which needs to be separated from *purposes*. According to WP29 *purposes* refer to the specific reasons why personal data are processed (ie the aim or intention), whereas *interests* relate to the broader stake or benefit in the processing (to the controller or third parties).[147] Health and safety of a nuclear power plant's staff, for example, is an *interest*, whereas using biometric data for access-control to the premises would constitute processing *purposes*. The distinction is further made clear in an example provided by Moerel and Prins:[148] imagine a smartphone app that monitors several data streams (eg location, phone calls), in order to accurately predict the likelihood of catching the flu. The authors posit that people's appreciation of such an app would differ significantly when provided by a private company as opposed to the World Health Organization for instance. The reason for this, they explain, is connected to the underlying *interests* at stake. Whereas the purposes for processing are identical, the private company processes

[144] Despite such practices being criticized by WP29: Article 29 Working Party, 'Opinion 03/2013 on Purpose Limitation' (Article 29 Working Party 2013) WP 03/2013 15–16 <http://ec.europa.eu/justice/article-29/documentation> accessed 1 June 2019. This is also the reason why some have advocated for shifting the focus of data protection from specified purposes to legitimate interests, especially in the context of 'big data' and 'internet of things'. See notably: Moerel and Prins (n 118).

[145] Poullet and Léonard (n 1) 258–60.

[146] ibid 263–64.

[147] Article 29 Working Party, 'Opinion 06/2014 on the Notion of Legitimate Interests of the Data Controller under Article 7 of Directive 95/46/EC' (n 20) 24.

[148] Moerel and Prins (n 118).

personal data for commercial interests, and the WHO pursues public interests (ie public health). The authors use this example to argue for abandoning the purpose limitation principle and embrace 'the legitimate interests principle as the main and only test for all the various phases of the life cycle of personal data'.[149] Especially in a big data age, Moerel and Prins claim, purposes are much more fickle, changing over time, and therefore argued to be less well-suited for effective legal analyses.

Difficult to Separate in Practice—The *interest(s)* related to personal data processing constitute(s) the overarching added-value of that operation (to the controller and/or third parties). The *purpose(s)* of processing personal data are the actual goals or incentives for a given processing operation. In practice, the interests and purposes may be hard—or even impossible—to separate from one another. As explained by Van Alsenoy 'interest' and 'purpose' often go hand in hand: '[i]f a party involved in the processing of personal also has an interest in the outcome of the processing, he or she will typically also be involved in deciding the [purpose] of processing'.[150]

Interests for Persons, Purposes for Processing Operations—A useful conceptualization to better understand the difference between interests and purposes can be made on the basis of their object. Interests relate to a person or entity, whereas purposes relate to a specific processing operation. This is evident from a systemic reading of the data protection framework, which always refers to interests in relation to persons and purposes in relation to processing operations.[151] This differentiation is relevant with regard to Article 6(1)(f), as it emphasizes that what matters in (re-)balancing acts is (the interests of) actual persons, rather than processing operations (with specified purposes) in the abstract.

Goal of the Distinction—The purpose of processing is used to determine the identity of the controller, the extent of its obligations, and the object of several data subject rights. This pivotal role of purpose limitation in the GDPR[152] also explains the importance of granularity, ie to specify the extent and object of data protection obligations and rights. The primary role of *interests* on the other hand, is mostly confined to balancing acts in the GDPR. This also justifies the—arguably deliberate—broadness and vagueness of the term, aiming to capture the many different elements that may influence fair balancing under the GDPR. The only constraining factor, according to WP29, is that interests need to be 'real and present'—ie actually pursued and not speculative—in order to be validly considered

[149] ibid 2.

[150] 'This is logical,' the author continues, 'seeing as the pursuit of an interest will involve the use of functionalities (ie instruments which yield certain outputs) that actually advance the interests of the actor concerned' Van Alsenoy Brendan Van Alsenoy, *Data Protection Law in the EU: Roles, Responsibilities and Liability* (Intersentia 2019) 561; also see 500 et seq where the author looks at the particular use-case of cloud computing.

[151] Javier Aparicio Salom, '"A Third Party to Whom Data Are Disclosed": A Third Group among Those Processing Data' (2014) 4 International Data Privacy Law 177, 181.

[152] Contrary to what Moerel and Prins advocate for.

in the balancing act.[153] In sum, purposes define the scope of the data protection assessment, whereas interests enable assessing the outcome of the assessment.[154]

CONFLATING INTERESTS AND PURPOSES IN THE ISS CONTEXT—Conflating purposes and interests is particularly prevalent (and easy) in the context of online platforms (eg search engines, video-hosting platforms, social networks), which partially explains the slew of criticism of alleged data protection overreach here. Users of such platforms will pursue their own interests (eg finding an adequate employee, entertainment, or maintaining social relationships) to which the platform is largely indifferent. Indeed, the platform is pursuing its own—first and foremost commercial—interests, often even apathetic to the fact that the respective information constitutes *personal* data in the first place.[155] Yet, the *purposes* of the underlying processing operations will generally be in pursuit of both the interests of the controller as well as those of its users (eg finding all relevant information on the basis of a name-search; publishing a video; sharing a family memory). As was explained before (Chapter 3), whomever determines the *purpose(s)* will be the (joint) controller, regardless of what interests are served. Interests, on the other hand, are the key component (rather than purposes) in performing the balancing act in Article 6(1)(f). In practice, confusion may arise from the fact that in these situations it is often the interest of the platform *user* that is most apparent/pronounced in a given scenario (eg naming and shaming someone in an uploaded video), whereas the interests of the platform itself in the processing are more inconspicuous and abstract.[156] Yet, identifying who needs to do the balancing is based on who determines the *purposes* of the respective processing operation. The interests involved only become relevant at the stage of actually performing the balancing exercise.

ILLUSTRATING THE RELEVANCE OF THE DISTINCTION—The vignettes from Chapter 1 offer a useful template for exploring the distinction between interests and purposes. Uber is clearly the controller with regard to the processing of personal data of riders and drivers. It determines the purposes and means for connecting one with the other. Even if Uber unilaterally determines purpose and means, the processing does not just serve its interests, but also those of riders and drivers using the service. When, however, Uber starts applying advanced psychometrics on drivers, the constellation of interests changes (presumably both Uber and riders will have an interest in said processing, while drivers' interests, rights, and freedoms are affected). When Uber starts using information on the remaining battery on riders'

[153] Article 29 Working Party, 'Opinion 06/2014 on the Notion of Legitimate Interests of the Data Controller under Article 7 of Directive 95/46/EC' (n 20) 24.

[154] See similarly: Burkert (n 77) 174–75.

[155] Which, as amply discussed in Chapter 3 (automation fallacy) of course does not exempt them from being subject to data protection law.

[156] See also: Van Alsenoy (n 150) 544. 'Even if the provider of a search engine has no personal interest in the content or outcome of a specific search query (other than providing the most relevant search results), it still determines the finality of the processing required to deliver the search engine service.'

smartphones in order to set prices,[157] the constellation of interests changes as well (presumably such processing purposes would be in the interest of both Uber and drivers, but not in the interest of riders). In all of these scenarios, Uber is the controller, but a granular identification of the relevant purposes brings to light dramatically different arrangements of interests. The Facebook vignette offers another illustration of the important difference between interests and purposes. Cambridge Analytica (CA) infamously obtained access to millions of Facebook users through a particularly permissive API (ie third-party apps could access personal data of Facebook users who had installed the app as well as their friends' data). CA developed advanced psychological profiles on the basis of this data, which it then used to micro-target political ads to individuals through Facebook. In essence, CA was doing the exact same thing as what Facebook already does itself (with the same personal data). In both situations, the constellation of interests is roughly similar (ie commercial interests of Facebook and CA versus the interests, freedoms, and rights of Facebook users). Yet, in the vignette, CA determines purposes for processing itself as well, becoming an independent controller too.

SUMMARY—In sum, what should be highlighted in terms of this book is that the data subject rights to erasure and to object primarily target *purposes* of processing operations. Once invoked, the ensuing balancing exercise hinges on the *interests* involved. In light of all of the above, the suggestion by Moerel and Prins—shifting data protection law's focus from purposes to interests—is therefore quite trifling, especially when looked at from the perspective of the rights to erasure/object. The authors propose it as a grand new scheme for preserving data protection law's relevance in the big data age, where specific purposes cannot always be defined *ex ante*, but interests can. Yet, the authors do not seem to recognize that both concepts fulfil different (though admittedly interacting) objectives: *purposes* to identify the controller, and *interests* to assess the balance. From the perspective of *ex post* empowerment measures, it does not matter that an exact (sub-)purpose only materializes (implicitly or explicitly) at a later stage. The rights to object and to erasure are only relevant in relation to specific processing purposes (without which they would have no object). Put yet differently, purposes circumscribe the aim of the rights to erasure and object, whereas interests determine the ensuing balance.

3.3.4 Legitimate Interests Balancing in Operation

In 2014, WP29 defined a methodology for approaching the balancing act in Article 6(1)(f).[158] The following pages will describe and build on this methodology, giving

[157] Amit Chowdhry, 'Uber: Users Are More Likely To Pay Surge Pricing If Their Phone Battery Is Low' (*Forbes*, 25 May 2016) <https://www.forbes.com/sites/amitchowdhry/2016/05/25/uber-low-battery/> accessed 20 April 2018.

[158] Article 29 Working Party, 'Opinion 06/2014 on the Notion of Legitimate Interests of the Data Controller under Article 7 of Directive 95/46/EC' (n 20). Early 2019, it was announced that the EDPB would update this 2014 Opinion by the end of 2020. European Data Protection Board, 'Work Program

structure to balancing exercises emanating from the right to erasure. Put briefly, four steps can be identified: (a) determining the controller and third parties' legitimate interests; (b) determining the impact on the data subject; (c) determining the provisional balance; and (d) assess additional safeguards to prevent any undue impact on the data subjects.[159] It can be observed at this stage already that the balancing act only concerns itself with the specific relationship between data subject and controller.[160] In light of their size and user-base, ISS providers will generally define the balancing act vis-à-vis the 'average' data subject (as they see it). Where said balance is inadequate, *ex post* empowerment tools effectively enable data subjects to challenge that balance in their specific situation.

a) *Step One: Controller and Third Parties*

CONTROLLERS V THIRD PARTIES—The first step of Article 6(1)f's balancing exercise will be identifying the legitimate interests pursued by the controller and third parties. The inclusion of third-party interests seems welcome, as it appears to recognize—and actively engage with—the complexity of the 'data processing ecosystem', where many different actors and interests collide.[161] Still, the intended meaning and extent of third parties in this provision remains unclear. Article 4(10) defines third parties quite narrowly, only including those who, 'under the direct authority of the controller or processor, are authorised to process personal data'. Following this definition, the concept would not cover publishers or search engine users in delisting cases for example (as they are neither under the direct authority of, nor 'authorised' by, the search engine). WP29 seems to ignore the definition in Article 4(10), interpreting the term more liberally (and arguably, more sensibly) in the context of legitimate interests balancing, including any individual whose legitimate interests may be furthered by the processing (eg in the context of whistle-blowing or journalism for example).[162] Van Alsenoy explains that 'third parties' refer to 'any party which is not part of the "inner circle" of a particular

2019-2020' <https://edpb.europa.eu/sites/edpb/files/files/file1/edpb-2019-02-12plen-2.1edpb_work_program_en.pdf> accessed 14 February 2019.

[159] Article 29 Working Party, 'Opinion 06/2014 on the Notion of Legitimate Interests of the Data Controller under Article 7 of Directive 95/46/EC' (n 20) 33.

[160] As mentioned before, unless their interests overlap with those of the controller, third parties will generally not be considered in the initial balancing act pursuant to Article 6(1)(f). The following Chapter (6) will elaborate extensively on this issue in light of third parties' information freedoms under Article 11 Charter.

[161] Interestingly, the European Commission's original proposal for a GDPR in 2012 had removed any reference to third parties, but the concept was reintroduced after the first reading in the European Parliament. A notable difference with its predecessor (Art 7(f) Directive 95/46), is that Article 6(1)(f) GDPR is no longer limited to third parties *to whom the data have been disclosed.*

[162] Article 29 Working Party, 'Opinion 06/2014 on the Notion of Legitimate Interests of the Data Controller under Article 7 of Directive 95/46/EC' (n 20) 27–28; 57–59. At several occasions throughout this opinion, WP29 refers to the example of the broader interest (of employees or the public) in publishing the salaries of top management in high-profile companies.

data processing'.[163] Despite this interpretation, involving a potentially wide array of entities with even more interests, the impact of 'third party interests' on the balance may remain quite constrained in practice. To all intents and purposes, the scope of third parties' legitimate interests in the context of Article 6(1)f will depend on the controller's interests and purposes. As third parties are not involved in the actual defining of the balance, their interests will generally only be incorporated to the extent they serve the controller's cause. After all, it is the controller who will define the initial balance and it will also be the controller alone who will defend that balance when challenged by the data subject. Third parties have no actionable right to insert themselves in this balancing act. This will become particularly apparent in the information freedoms balancing scenario in Chapter 6.

LEGITIMACY—The interests pursued by the controller (and third parties) are what actually underlies the specified purposes for processing. Whereas an interest is the broader stake (eg security, commercial), the purposes for processing are the precise aims or intentions of the processing operations themselves (eg IP-address monitoring for preventing DDOS-attacks, placing cookies for managing one's shopping cart). Importantly, the first step in Article 6(1)(f) will be to determine whether the *interest* is *legitimate*. If not, there will be no need to perform the balancing exercise in the first place and the processing operation can be considered unlawful altogether. The meaning of this legitimacy requirement can be traced onto that of the purpose limitation principle in Article 5(1)(a) (see Chapter 4). In short, the interests should be acceptable under the law; sufficiently clearly articulated; and be real and present.[164] For example, as highlighted by Advocate General Bobek in *Rīgas Satiksme*, the CJEU has already held that transparency[165] or the protection of the property, health and family life[166] are legitimate interests. The notion of legitimate interests is elastic enough to accommodate other kinds of considerations. There is no doubt in my mind that the interest of a third party in obtaining the personal information of a person who damaged their property in order to sue that person for damages can be qualified as a legitimate interest.[167]

The weight of third parties' legitimate interests and likelihood of them being used in the balancing act, will also be influenced by the fact of them being explicitly defined in other legal frameworks.[168] Finally, it should be stressed that the

[163] Van Alsenoy (n 150) 129–30. Such a broader 'natural language' understanding of third parties also follows from the concept's use in the *Google Spain* Ruling for example, where it is used to refer to original publishers.

[164] Article 29 Working Party, 'Opinion 06/2014 on the Notion of Legitimate Interests of the Data Controller under Article 7 of Directive 95/46/EC' (n 20) 24–25; Article 29 Working Party, 'Opinion 03/2013 on Purpose Limitation' (n 144) 19–20.

[165] *Volker und Markus Schecke GbR and Hartmut Eifert v Land Hessen* (n 14) para 77.

[166] *František Ryneš v Úřad pro ochranu osobních údajů* [2014] Court of Justice of the European Union C-212/13 para 34.

[167] AG Opinion in: *Rīgas satiksme* (n 70) para 65.

[168] eg laws regulating the publicity of certain data in companies registers so as to ensure legal certainty in commercial transactions. See: AG Opinion in: *Salvatore Manni* (n 14) para 61.

legitimacy of the controller's (and/or third parties') interests can evolve over time, something which is of particular significance in light of the right to erasure.[169]

Hierarchy of Interests—Once the legitimacy of the interests has been determined, it is possible to assess their merit. In its 2014 Opinion, the WP29 provides for an implicit hierarchy of interests which, albeit not being absolute, still constitutes useful guidance.[170] Highest on the list are those interests that are exercises of a fundamental right (either in the Charter or the ECHR). Secondly, the processing may pursue public interests, or interests of the wider community. Indeed, compelling interests that are not exclusively to the benefit of the controller, and are acknowledged/expected in the community, will have more weight in the balancing exercise (eg combating fraud, health research).[171] Thirdly, WP29 mentions 'other legitimate interests', primarily referring to situations where it is not entirely clear whether any of the other lawful grounds apply (notably (b) contract, (c) legal obligation, or (e) public task). Assessing the respective legitimate interest(s) should also take into account the potential detriment to the controller, third parties, or the broader community in case the processing operation would not or no longer take place.[172] The weight of any legitimate interest will finally also be affected by the 'legal and cultural/societal recognition of the legitimacy of the interest'. This may be apparent, for example, in the case of guidance issued by regulatory agencies or other authoritative bodies.[173]

Margin of Appreciation—Related to this last point, it is fair to say that the outcome of balancing acts will generally be influenced by the social context in which they are performed. Indeed, on multiple occasions, the CJEU has stressed that it will be upon national courts and authorities to interpret, implement, and apply data protection rules in light of national sensibilities. This is particularly relevant in situations where different important interests, fundamental rights, and/or freedoms are at stake and may need to be reconciled.[174] In *Lindqvist*, the CJEU determined 'it is, rather, at the stage of the application at national level of the legislation implementing Directive 95/46 in individual cases that a balance must be found between the rights and interests involved'.[175] The CJEU similarly deferred balancing acts to the Member-State level when requiring an evaluation, for example, of the merits of publishing salaries of public body employees;[176] the extent of the

[169] Article 29 Working Party, 'Opinion 03/2013 on Purpose Limitation' (n 144) 20.

[170] Article 29 Working Party, 'Opinion 06/2014 on the Notion of Legitimate Interests of the Data Controller under Article 7 of Directive 95/46/EC' (n 20) 34 et seq.

[171] This seems particularly relevant in the context of ISS providers such as search engines and social networks, where there are certain expectations as to the interests of specific processing operations. ibid 35.

[172] ibid 36.

[173] ibid.

[174] Ferretti (n 131) 860.

[175] *Lindqvist* (n 44) para 85.

[176] *Österreichischer Rundfunk and others* [2003] Court of Justice of the European Union Joined Cases C-465/00, C-138/01 and C-139/01 [68] para 88.

journalistic exemption;[177] access to records of working times;[178] and the sharing of personal data to facilitate an insurance claim.[179,180] Importantly, such flexibility cannot go as far as a Member State actually prescribing 'for certain categories of personal data, the result of the balancing of the opposing rights and interests, without allowing a different result by virtue of the particular circumstances of an individual case'.[181] In other words, balancing acts can be defined a posteriori on a case-by-case level, but not a priori, in a categorical manner.[182]

NECESSITY—Finally, it should be reiterated that the relevant processing operation(s) should be *necessary* in light of the legitimate interests pursued by the controller (and third parties).[183] This necessity-test should prevent excessive data processing and needs to be assessed considering Article 5 principles.[184] It is a facts-based concept, meaning that it needs to be evaluated on a case-by-case basis, taking into account the concrete purpose and circumstances of the intended processing operation(s).[185] This means, inter alia that the interests need to be 'real and present' and not merely speculative.[186] WP29 suggests the necessity requirement in Art 6(1)f should be read together with a limited proportionality test as well, which may be guided by 'specific legislation, case law, jurisprudence, guidelines, as well as codes of conduct and other formal or less formal standards'.[187] The CJEU has further articulated key facets of the necessity requirement in the legitimate interests test. Notably, at several occasions the Court has pushed for an expansive interpretation of necessity in Article 7 Directive 95/46 (now Art 6(1) GDPR).[188] Still, in

[177] *Satamedia* (n 10) para 62.

[178] *Worten* [2013] Court of Justice of the European Union C-342/12 [22] para 43.

[179] *Rīgas satiksme* (n 70).

[180] Also see: Lynskey, *The Foundations of EU Data Protection Law* (n 67) 144 et seq. Most of these deferrals to the Member States can also be explained by the fact that they often include a freedom of expression and information element (conflicts with which the data protection framework explicitly defers).

[181] AG Opinion in: *Rīgas satiksme* (n 70) para 68. Referring to: *Joined ASNEF and FECEMD Cases* (n 83) para 47; *Patrick Breyer v Bundesrepublik Deutschland* (n 133) para 62. This is not to say of course, national legislation may specify and guide how balances should be struck, especially when multiple rights and frameworks are at stake. See notably the CJEU's case-law in *Bonnier Audio AB* (n 67); *Promusicae v Telefónica* (n 70) on data protection v intellectual property enforcement, reported in: Lynskey, *The Foundations of EU Data Protection Law* (n 67) 158–61.

[182] See notably: *Patrick Breyer v Bundesrepublik Deutschland* (n 133) paras 62–63.

[183] See above, subsection 3.3.2 Structure of Article 6(1)(f) Legitimate Interests Balancing.

[184] Article 29 Working Party, 'Opinion 06/2014 on the Notion of Legitimate Interests of the Data Controller under Article 7 of Directive 95/46/EC' (n 20) 11.

[185] European Data Protection Supervisor, 'Developing a "Toolkit" for Assessing the Necessity of Measures That Interfere with Fundamental Rights. Background Paper' (n 21) 8.

[186] Moerel and Prins (n 118) 50.

[187] Article 29 Working Party, 'Opinion 06/2014 on the Notion of Legitimate Interests of the Data Controller under Article 7 of Directive 95/46/EC' (n 20) 34–35. See similarly: Bygrave and Wiese Schartum (n 81) 165.

[188] See, for example: *Huber v Germany* (n 139) para 62; *Worten* (n 178) para 37; Lynskey, *The Foundations of EU Data Protection Law* (n 67) 32. In these cases, the CJEU explained necessity (within the meaning of Art 7(e) Directive 9546, now Art 6(1)(e) GDPR) could be present when the processing 'contributes to the more effective application of the legislation'.

Bavarian Lager it was made clear that the necessity of a processing operation needs to be *demonstrated*, failure to which will render a balance impossible (see 'accountability' principle in the GDPR).[189] And in *Huber*, the CJEU linked the necessity requirement to data minimization.[190]

In sum, the first step in Article 6(1)(f)'s balancing test can be subdivided into several criteria. *Firstly*, all relevant entities—ie the controller(s) and third parties—will need to be identified, along with their interest(s) in the respective processing operation. In practice, this 'mapping exercise' may be severely crippled by the fact that it is a priori exclusively performed by the controller. *Secondly*, all the identified interests will need to be demonstrably legitimate. Similarly to processing purposes, the legitimacy of interests is to be interpreted very broadly and can evolve over time (which will be particularly important with regard to the right to erasure). *Thirdly*, an implied hierarchy of legitimate interests can be inferred from the work of WP29 (now EDPB) and CJEU case law. Considerable flexibility is left for the importance and legitimacy of interests to be assessed in light of local sensibilities in individual cases. *Fourthly*, the necessity of processing to achieve the legitimate interests will need to be established. Following WP29 and the CJEU, this last requirement installs a facts-based least intrusive means test. This will be particularly relevant in asymmetrical relationships (eg large-scale ISS controllers) and upon invoking the rights to erasure or to object (which trigger a re-assessment of these requirements in a specific case).

b) Step Two: Impact on the Data Subject

Once established what processing operations are necessary to achieve the legitimate interests of the controller (and third parties), the next step will be to assess their impact on data subjects. This impact should be expressed in terms of the effects on data subjects' interests or fundamental rights and/or freedoms which require the protection of personal data. Only after evaluating the impact will it be possible to determine what side the balance tips over to.

IDENTIFICATION—Firstly, one will need to identify the interests or fundamental rights and freedoms requiring protection of personal data that are at stake in the relevant processing scenario. Compared to the other side of the balance, this side is much broader, capturing virtually any way in which the data subject may be affected, even covering illegitimate interests.[191] Indeed, even though the (il)legitimate character of the interests involved may affect the eventual outcome of the balancing exercise, illegitimacy does not exclude individuals from data protection

[189] *Bavarian Lager* (n 1570) para 78.

[190] *Huber v Germany* (n 139) para 66. Even though the Court was talking about necessity in the context of a public task carried out in the public interest (ie Art 7(e) of Directive 95/46, Art 6(1)(e) GDPR), its verdict applies *mutadis mutandis* to necessity in the context of Article 6(1)(f) GDPR.

[191] Article 29 Working Party, 'Opinion 06/2014 on the Notion of Legitimate Interests of the Data Controller under Article 7 of Directive 95/46/EC' (n 20) 29–30.

per se.[192] This may be relevant in the context of right-to-erasure triggered balancing exercises with regard to illegal behaviour for example (fraud,[193] illegal possession of weapons,[194] paedophilic activities[195]).[196] An important—though logical—restriction on what interests, fundamental rights, or freedoms can be invoked is that their enjoyment needs to *require* the protection of personal data. As made clear before, this is not limited to the scope of Article 8 Charter, but can relate to any of the other fundamental rights and freedoms in the Charter, notably the right to private and family life (Art 7); freedom of thought, conscience, and religion (Art 10); freedom of expression and information (Art 11); equality (Art 20); and non-discrimination (Art 21).[197]

IMPACT—After the relevant interests, fundamental rights, and freedoms have been identified, the impact of the respective data processing operation(s) needs to be evaluated.[198] This evaluation should consider both negative and positive, actual and potential repercussions (not just 'harm') of the data processing. WP29 provides four categories of criteria that guide the impact assessment.[199] *Firstly*, the nature of the personal data itself must be considered (eg sensitive, old).[200] This is also where the data equaliser (see Chapter 3) comes into play, dynamically qualifying the nature of personal data throughout time. *Secondly*, the way in which the data are processed should be considered (eg published, cross-combined).[201,202] The use

[192] ibid 30.

[193] See for example a 2016 delisting case before the French Court de Cassation, brought by two brothers with regard to an administrative sanction: *Dokhan v Les Echos* [2016] Cour de Cassation (France) 15-17.729.

[194] Frederik Zuiderveen Borgesius, 'Het "Right to Be Forgotten" en Bijzondere Persoonsgegevens' (2016) 126 Computerrecht; Lucien Wopereis, 'David vs Googliath: Het Recht Om Vergeten Te Worden' (*Advocatie*, 18 January 2017) <http://www.advocatie.nl/david-vs-googliath-het-recht-om-vergeten-te-worden> accessed 1 June 2019; *X v Google Netherlands and Google Inc* [2017] Hoge Raad der Nederlanden 15/03380.

[195] Martin Untersinger, 'Le Conseil d'Etat face au casse-tête du "droit à l'oubli"' *Le Monde.fr* (2 February 2017) <http://www.lemonde.fr/pixels/article/2017/02/02/le-conseil-d-etat-face-au-casse-tete-du-droit-a-l-oubli_5073709_4408996.html> accessed 1 June 2019; *X v Google* [2017] Rechtbank Overijssel C/08/192336 / HA RK 16-147.

[196] The ECtHR also confirmed that '[t]he fact that he was the subject of criminal proceedings, albeit for a very serious offence, cannot deprive him entirely of the protection of Article 8 of the Convention'. *Axel Springer SE and RTL Television GmbH v Germany* [2017] European Court of Human Rights 51405/12 [47]. This, in contrast to what the ECtHR stated in an earlier ruling: 'Article 8 cannot be relied on in order to complain of a loss of reputation which is the foreseeable consequence of one's own actions such as, for example, the commission of a criminal offence' *Axel Springer AG v Germany* [2012] European Court of Human Rights 39954/08 [83].

[197] See Recitals 2 and 4 GDPR.

[198] This evaluation is different from the risk analysis in Article 35 GDPR, which is not to say that the risk analysis and balancing exercise can interact in individual cases.

[199] Bygrave also offers a list of criteria to determine the impact of processing on data subjects: Lee A Bygrave, *Data Protection Law: Approaching Its Rationale, Logic and Limits* (Kluwer 2002) 160.

[200] See Chapter 3. Also see: Article 29 Working Party, 'Opinion 06/2014 on the Notion of Legitimate Interests of the Data Controller under Article 7 of Directive 95/46/EC' (n 20) 38–39.

[201] ibid 25–26.

[202] ibid 39–40. More recently, WP29 also emphasized that in the context of profiling, the comprehensiveness and level of detail of the profile(s) plays an important role. See: Article 29 Working Party, 'Guidelines on Automated Individual Decision-Making and Profiling for the Purposes of Regulation 2016/679' (n 96) 21.

of personal data to make predictions—customary in the ISS context and big data environment more generally—may have an intrusive impact on an individual's right to privacy and personal autonomy.[203] *Thirdly*, WP29 instructs to look at the data subject's reasonable expectations which may be affected by the controller's status, the nature of the relationship and/or the applicable legal or contractual obligations (eg therapist, social network provider).[204] *Fourthly*, the status or nature of both the controller (eg SME, research organization) and the data subject (eg politician, crime victim) will play important roles in determining the impact.[205] These elements will be particularly relevant in the ISS context where asymmetric relationships proliferate. So, the status of the data subject will be relevant both in itself (eg public figure, child), but also in relation to the controller (ie defining the bargaining power, for example with regard to vulnerable persons versus a global ISS provider). Noteworthy in this regard is that the legislator mentions a specific type of data subjects that inherently suffer a higher impact, ie children. In sum, one might qualify the first two steps (*data* and *processing*) as relating to the *material* scope, and the last two steps (*reasonable expectations and status of actors*) as relating to the *personal* scope of application.

Case Law—The CJEU has had the opportunity to clarify this second step at several occasions, not in the least by shedding light on what exactly constitutes an 'impact' on fundamental rights and freedoms. Such an impact, as the Court often reiterated, does not hinge on the processed information being sensitive or the individuals being inconvenienced in any way.[206] The nature,[207] sensitivity, and degree of publicity of personal data will of course still influence the degree of the impact in a particular case.[208] As made clear in *ASNEF*, such factors should be evaluated in light of individual circumstances, on a case-by-case basis.[209] For instance, 'the

[203] Importantly, processing operations covered by Article 22(1)—ie decisions based solely on automated processing, including profiling, which produce legal effects concerning the data subject or similarly affect him or her—cannot rely on Article 6(1)(f) as a lawful ground. See: Article 29 Working Party, 'Guidelines on Automated Individual Decision-Making and Profiling for the Purposes of Regulation 2016/679' (n 96) 21.

[204] See also: Moerel and Prins (n 118) 50. Nauwelaerts even interprets legitimate interests as 'mostly an expectation test that requires companies to consider whether individuals can reasonably expect their data to be collected'. In: Nauwelaerts (n 124) 253.

[205] See Recital 47 and Article 29 Working Party, 'Opinion 06/2014 on the Notion of Legitimate Interests of the Data Controller under Article 7 of Directive 95/46/EC' (n 20) 40–41.

[206] *Österreichischer Rundfunk and others* (n 176) para 75; *Digital Rights Ireland Ltd* (n 301) para 33; as referred to in: European Data Protection Supervisor, 'Developing a "Toolkit" for Assessing the Necessity of Measures That Interfere with Fundamental Rights. Background Paper' (n 21) 10; *Michael Schwarz v Stadt Bochum* (n 83) paras 24–26.

[207] Biometric data, for example, may intensify the impact as it can unequivocally link back to an individual. European Data Protection Supervisor, 'Developing a "Toolkit" for Assessing the Necessity of Measures That Interfere with Fundamental Rights. Background Paper' (n 21) 10; referring to: Article 29 Working Party, 'Opinion 3/2012 on Developments in Biometric Technologies' (Article 29 Working Party 2012) Opinion WP 193 <http://ec.europa.eu/justice/article-29/documentation> accessed 1 June 2019.

[208] See notably case law references in: *Rīgas satiksme* (n 70) paras 31–33 as well as the case law references in the AG Opinion paras 67–69.

[209] *Joined ASNEF and FECEMD Cases* (n 83) para 40.

seriousness of the infringement of the data subject's fundamental rights resulting from that processing can vary depending on whether or not the data in question already appear in public sources'.[210] The relevance of the controller's status (eg market power or position down the information dissemination chain) as well as the way in which personal data is processed in determining the impact on data subjects, was highlighted in *Google Spain*.[211] The CJEU explained that a search engine's processing—ie linking a person's name to a list of results—is liable to constitute a more significant interference with data subjects' fundamental rights and freedoms than the original publication referred to.[212] The age of the data subject may also influence the outcome of the balancing act.[213]

c) *Step Three: Initial Balance*

Once the impact on the data subject's interests, fundamental rights, and freedoms is established, it can effectively be weighed against the legitimate interests of the controller (and third parties). Indeed, the goal of Article 6(1)(f) is not to prevent any (negative) impact on the data subject whatsoever, but rather avoid a *disproportionate* impact.[214] This assessment of the *relation* between both scales of the balance is the core of the balancing act and inherently depends on the specificity with which both sides are defined. The GDPR does not give an a priori preference to either side.[215] Yet, the *de facto* information and power asymmetries in the ISS context (see Chapter 2), do imply the balance should be interpreted in favour of data subjects by default.[216]

Determining what side the balance should tip over to is an impossible assessment to make in the abstract.[217] It is also not the goal of the data protection framework

[210] ibid paras 44–46.

[211] Article 29 Working Party, 'Opinion 03/2013 on Purpose Limitation' (n 144) 46; *Google Spain* (n 44); Lynskey, *The Foundations of EU Data Protection Law* (n 67) 148.

[212] *Google Spain* (n 44) paras 86–87; Lynskey, *The Foundations of EU Data Protection Law* (n 67) 148.

[213] *Rīgas satiksme* (n 70) paras 31–33. This also appears from the wording of Art 6(1)(f) itself, which emphasizes the rights and freedoms of children in particular. Google has also recognized that the acceptance rate for delisting requests coming from minors is twice as much as the average. Theo Bertram and others, 'Three Years of the Right to Be Forgotten' (Google 2018) 7 <https://drive.google.com/file/d/1H4MKNwf5MgeztG7OnJRnl3ym3gIT3HUK/view>.

[214] Article 29 Working Party, 'Opinion 06/2014 on the Notion of Legitimate Interests of the Data Controller under Article 7 of Directive 95/46/EC' (n 20) 41. See similarly: European Data Protection Supervisor, 'Developing a "Toolkit" for Assessing the Necessity of Measures That Interfere with Fundamental Rights. Background Paper' (n 21) 14.

[215] It must be said though that to rely on Article 6(1)(f), the controller will need to have demonstrated compliance with Article 5 already as well as establish the legitimacy of its interests and the necessity of the corresponding processing operations.

[216] Article 29 Working Party, 'Opinion 06/2014 on the Notion of Legitimate Interests of the Data Controller under Article 7 of Directive 95/46/EC' (n 20) 25–26; 30. Also implied in: Moerel and Prins (n 118) 4. And illustrated by the WP29's Opinion in SWIFT: Article 29 Working Party, 'Opinion 10/2006 on the Processing of Personal Data by the Society for Worldwide Interbank Financial Telecommunication (SWIFT)' (Article 29 Working Party 2006) Opinion WP 128 18–19 <http://ec.europa.eu/justice/article-29/documentation> accessed 1 June 2019.

[217] For example, as explained by Woods, the CJEU's *Satamedia* ruling illustrates that 'it is not possible to give automatic priority to freedom of expression over data protection and privacy. Even fundamental rights do not have automatic priority over other societal interests'. See: Lorna Woods, 'Freedom of

(and nor should it be).[218] While Article 6(1)f provides the definition, guidance for making the actual assessment in individual cases can be found in specific legislation, case law, jurisprudence, and soft-law instruments such as industry guidelines or codes of conduct.[219] This follows from the intrinsically context-dependent nature of each individual situation. Balancing should not be an abstract or hypothetical exercise, WP29 explains, but 'consider the effect of actual processing on particular individuals'.[220] An EU company may well have a (strong) legitimate interest in complying with a request to share user data of dissidents with an oppressive regime in a third country, but in light of the potentially huge impact on the data subject, such processing can still be considered disproportionate overall.[221] Similarly, in its 2006 SWIFT Opinion, WP29 explicitly declared that while a company may have a legitimate interest in complying with subpoenas under US law, this is not sufficient to supersede the considerable impact on data subjects of data processing in a 'hidden, systematic, massive and long term manner'.[222] As a final illustration, the processing of biometric data may have an increased impact on data subjects, but still be considered lawful under Art 6(1)(f) if used in light of narrow and strong interests (eg fraud prevention[223] or access-control in high security environments).[224,225]

Expression and Information' in Steve Peers and others (eds), *The EU Charter of Fundamental Rights: A Commentary* (Hart 2014) 330<https://www.bloomsburycollections.com/book/the-eu-charter-of-fundamental-rights-a-commentary/>. See also: Article 29 Working Party, 'Opinion 06/2014 on the Notion of Legitimate Interests of the Data Controller under Article 7 of Directive 95/46/EC' (n 20) 51–52; Lynskey, *The Foundations of EU Data Protection Law* (n 67) 158. As mentioned before, the CJEU also emphasized that the legitimate interests ground does not tolerate categorical and generalized exclusions, and inherently requires 'opposing rights and interests at issue to be balanced against each other in a particular case'. *Joined ASNEF and FECEMD Cases* (n 83) para 48.

[218] WP29 explains Article 6(1)(f) is aimed at flexibility while also preventing misuse (Article 29 Working Party, 'Opinion 06/2014 on the Notion of Legitimate Interests of the Data Controller under Article 7 of Directive 95/46/EC' (n 20) 50). Though currently the provision may realize the former, it is less successful in achieving the latter.

[219] ibid 57. It should be said that Recital 47 GDPR does give some further pointers on how to perform the legitimate interests test, eg: 'a relevant and appropriate relationship between the data subject and the controller'; 'reasonably expectations'; 'time and context'.

[220] ibid 56; *Joined ASNEF and FECEMD Cases* (n 83) para 40.

[221] See Example 22 in: Article 29 Working Party, 'Opinion 06/2014 on the Notion of Legitimate Interests of the Data Controller under Article 7 of Directive 95/46/EC' (n 20) 66–67.

[222] ibid 26; Article 29 Working Party, 'Opinion 10/2006 on the Processing of Personal Data by the Society for Worldwide Interbank Financial Telecommunication (SWIFT)' (n 216) 18–19. Also see the case law on mass surveillance by both the CJEU (eg *Digital Rights Ireland Ltd* (n 301); *Maximillian Schrems v Data Protection Commissioner* (n 7); *Tele2 Sverige AB* [2016] Court of Justice of the European Union C-203/15.) and ECtHR (eg *Roman Zakharov v Russia* [2015] European Court of Human Rights 47143/06 [232ff]; *Szabó and Vissy v Hungary* [2016] European Court of Human Rights 37138/14).

[223] *Michael Schwarz v Stadt Bochum* (n 83).

[224] Article 29 Working Party, 'Opinion 3/2012 on Developments in Biometric Technologies' (n 207) 13.

[225] Even if, under the GDPR, processing biometric data cannot rely exclusively on legitimate interests in Article 6(1)(f) as lawful ground (as it qualifies as a special category of personal data in Art 9), said processing will at the very least still need to respect the basic balancing paradigm laid down (see subsection 3.3.1).

EX POST BALANCE—Even though this section focuses on *ex ante* balancing in Article 6(1)(f), it does make sense to re-emphasize the circular nature of balancing in the GDPR here. As mentioned before (see subsections 3.1–3.2), the data subject rights to erasure and to object will effectively introduce a stress-test of the balancing act under Art 6(1)(f). In other words, they require a re-assessment of the alleged balance the controller relied upon to process the personal data in the first place. Unsurprisingly, this *re*assessment will be tougher than the one performed at the start of the processing operation. Firstly, because it will need to duly take into account the details of the specific case (something which will generally not be done *ex ante* in the ISS context). Secondly, the (further) processing needs to be proportionate even though it is evidently against the will of the data subject who has exercised his/her rights. This last point suggests that further processing will only be proportional in exceptional situations. Put differently, to override the interests, fundamental rights, and freedoms of the data subject (exercising the right to erasure as an important manifestation of one's Charter rights), the controller or third parties' legitimate interests will need to be significant (see hierarchy of interests).[226] Merely exerting the right to erasure will generally tilt the balance significantly in the data subject's favour. Which is not to say, of course, that there will be no need to evaluate the actual impact of the processing on the data subject. Indeed, an erasure request with regard to trivial data which is used for a very specific and narrow purpose and in light of a valuable legitimate interest (eg access-security of a critical infrastructure network), may still fail. Higher thresholds also apply, for example, with regard to public figures requesting erasure of published information because despite the potentially high impact on them as data subjects, the corresponding legitimate interests of controllers and third parties will often be important as well (see Chapter 6).

d) Step Four: Fine-tuning

EX ANTE—The final step in the Article 6(1)(f) assessment relates to fine-tuning the balance. This last phase is described by WP29 as an opportunity for the controller to have an initially 'negative' balance tip over in its favour nonetheless and/or make it generally more sustainable. The way in which to do this, WP29 explains, is to install additional safeguards offering added layers of data protection so 'that data subjects' interests or fundamental rights or freedoms are less likely to be interfered with'.[227] Among the most important and relevant suggestions are: strict expiration dates; aggregating data where possible; extensive anonymization techniques; increased transparency; explicit and unconditional opportunities to opt-out;

[226] It should be reiterated that this balancing exercise only becomes relevant after it has been established that none of the exemptions in Article 17(3) apply (safeguarding broader societal interests in the further processing of personal data).

[227] Article 29 Working Party, 'Opinion 06/2014 on the Notion of Legitimate Interests of the Data Controller under Article 7 of Directive 95/46/EC' (n 20) 28; 31; 41–43.

technical and organizational measures to ensure functional separation and prevent so-called 'purpose creep'. For example, a general-purpose search engine that processes large quantities of (personal) data (a priori everything publicly available on the internet), may benefit from the lawful ground in Article 6(1)(f) under the condition that it installs safeguards such as: making diligent efforts to prevent abusive publications of sensitive data showing up in search results; and offering easy and effective opportunities to challenge the balance (ie delisting requests) to data subjects.

The predominant ISS business-model—ie offering 'free services' in return for large-scale data processing used for advertisement purposes but also feeding directly back into the offered services—raises quite some challenges in light of Article 6(1)(f). Indeed, commercial interests alone (especially in light of the scale at which many ISS providers process personal data) will generally not be able to trump the interests or fundamental rights and freedoms of data subjects that are affected by the respective processing operations (see more elaborately Chapter 6).[228] With this in mind, the last fine-tuning step also constitutes a final opportunity for ISS providers to rely on Article 6(1)(f) as a lawful ground nonetheless. Relevant safeguards in this context would be the presence of genuine alternatives (eg using the service without tracking for advertisement purposes);[229] silo-ing datasets; offering effective ways to have specific data removed without hampering quality of service;[230] direct access to data in a portable, user-friendly and machine-readable format; making additional efforts on being transparent about data practices combined with effective choice and control opportunities.[231] In light of the CJEU's *Digital Rights Ireland* ruling, one may also consider defining different retention periods for different categories of personal data (ie granularity).[232]

EX POST—Again, it is useful to look at this step from the perspective of balancing's circular nature in the GDPR. Exercising data subject rights effectively force 're-doing' the initial balancing act, albeit in a more individualized fashion (applied to the specific data subject and context). While the initial balance as defined by the

[228] ibid 25–26.

[229] Article 29 Working Party, 'Opinion 02/2010 on Online Behavioural Advertising' (Article 29 Working Party 2010) WP 171 <http://ec.europa.eu/justice/article-29/documentation> accessed 1 June 2019.

[230] In its SWIFT Opinion, for example, WP29 emphasized the need for additional safeguards when relying on Article 6(1)(f) GDPR (then Art 7(f) Directive 95/46) and in particular the availability of a right to object. Article 29 Working Party, 'Opinion 10/2006 on the Processing of Personal Data by the Society for Worldwide Interbank Financial Telecommunication (SWIFT)' (n 216) 18–19.

[231] Article 29 Working Party, 'Opinion 06/2014 on the Notion of Legitimate Interests of the Data Controller under Article 7 of Directive 95/46/EC' (n 20) 47.

[232] Even though this ruling concerned data retention for law enforcement purposes specifically, this particular element can easily be transposed to the context at hand. *Digital Rights Ireland Ltd* (n 26) paras 63–64. Cited in: European Data Protection Supervisor, 'Developing a "Toolkit" for Assessing the Necessity of Measures That Interfere with Fundamental Rights. Background Paper' (n 21) 17–18. Too much granularity, as will appear later, may also backfire though, as it could render even more complex how data is managed.

controller may have seemed to be adequate, this very fact can be challenged by the data subject. This is all the more relevant in the ISS context where Article 6(1)(f) balancing exercises will generally be made on the basis of the median user and context. When a right to erasure or to object leads to a case-specific balancing act, the mere fact of having exercised that right will weigh heavily in the data subject's favour. The fine-tuning step facilitates finding a compromise or at least may prevent the controller from having to cease its processing operations altogether. It enables, for example, mitigating the impact on data subject by diligently pseudonymizing personal data or installing access restrictions[233]. In the context of open data initiatives for example, personal data could be rendered non-machine-readable, or robots.txt could be incorporated into published material so that it is not searchable via third party search engines. It may be useful here, to think in terms of the 'data equaliser' (see Chapter 3), tweaking several sliders (eg publicity, accuracy) in order to fine-tune the outcome of the balancing act depending on the particular circumstances at hand.

Section 4. Summary and Conclusion

Balancing constitutes a crucial legal tool to resolve conflicts between rights, freedoms, and interests. Guidance for doing so in the context of fundamental rights/freedoms is consigned to remain abstract and high-level. Indeed, when done at the Charter level, balancing is bare-bones, ie only involving core components. It only contains the primary colours of society's normative palette. Secondary legislation steps in to lay down the infrastructures ensuring balances in specific contexts. This is no different for the GDPR, which has balancing at the core of its rationale. The framework is designed to resolve conflicts between different rights, freedoms, and/or interests, specifically in the context of data processing.[234] As such, it should clearly be separated from the rationale of the fundamental right to data protection (Art 8 Charter), which is to safeguard individual control and informational self-determination. This distinction makes it possible to see how the GDPR can equally be used to safeguard other fundamental rights/freedoms than the one in Article 8 Charter, which in turn can also be safeguarded by other legal frameworks. Article 8 Charter and the GDPR are surely very closely connected, but they pursue different goals and their relationship is by no means exclusive.

Balancing in the GDPR—The GDPR pursues fair balances whenever personal data is processed. It does so in a variety of ways: internally or externally; *ex*

[233] See for example: Paolo Balboni and others, 'Legitimate Interest of the Data Controller New Data Protection Paradigm: Legitimacy Grounded on Appropriate Protection' (2013) 3 International Data Privacy Law para 61.

[234] Notably see Recital 4 GDPR. *Joined ASNEF and FECEMD Cases* (n 83) para 43; *Promusicae v Telefónica* (n 70) para 68. Also see: Balboni and others (n 233).

ante or *ex post*. The first division is based on whether the respective provision lays down the elements for doing balancing itself, or whether it (implicitly or explicitly) relies on / refers to external balancing provisions. The second division relates to the moment in time the balance initiates; before or after processing has started. This distinction enables a better understanding of the interaction between lawful grounds for processing in Article 6(1), and data subject rights (to erasure and to object in Articles 17 and 21). The latter effectively trigger a re-assessment of the *ex ante* balance, but then individualized to the specific circumstances of the data subject(s). Hence, and as explained in more detail in the following three paragraphs, one could look at this process as circular, with Article 6(1)(f) balancing as beginning and end.[235]

Article 6(1)f Legitimate Interests Balancing—Article 6(1)(f) constitutes the pivotal balancing provision in the GDPR. It explicitly defines the terms for the proportionate processing of personal data. In short, it puts the legitimate interests of controllers *and* third parties up against the interests, fundamental freedoms, and rights of data subjects. The interests need to be *legitimate*, and the respective processing operations need to be *necessary* and *proportionate* in relation to the impact they may have on the data subject. The outcome of an article 6(1)(f) assessment is inherently context-dependent[236] as well as variable according to time (the balance can shift either way depending on changing factors) and space (interpretative flexibility in function of the locale or Member State). The personal data equalizer (see Chapter 3) constitutes a valuable conceptual tool for construing and fine-tuning this balancing in practice.

Relation to Right to Erasure—A priori, balancing in Article 6(1)(f) will exclusively and unilaterally be defined by the controller. Controllers, after all, are the entities taking the initiative to process personal data in the first place (ie determining the purpose and means). This modus operandi is also exactly what makes the legitimate interests provision (and Article 6 more broadly) an *ex ante* protective measure (see Chapter 2, Table 2.1). With this in mind, one could define the rights to erasure and to object as the flipside of Article 6(1)(f) balancing acts. These rights are *ex post* empowerment measures that impose a re-balancing act for an already ongoing processing operation, at the initiative (and at least in theory, on the terms) of data subjects. They increase controllers' burden of establishing the existence of a balance, requiring stronger arguments tailored to data subjects' particular situation. As such, data subject rights complement Article 6(1)(f), by effectively enabling ways to question the balance defined by the controller. This 'threat' will

[235] Summary of the logic behind this circular nature: Lawfulness of processing needs to subscribe at the very least to the baseline balance in Article 6(1)(f); this balance can be challenged by data subjects through the rights to erasure (Art 17) or to object (Art 21); to continue processing despite data subject's challenge, the controller will still need to have a (reinforced) balance under Article 6(1)(f).

[236] *Rīgas satiksme* (n 70) para 31 A.

ideally induce controllers to put in place an infrastructure that takes into account the dynamic nature of such balances (see Step Four: Fine-tuning).

IN ABSTRACTO V *IN CONCRETO* BALANCING—Given the fact that Article 6(1)(f) balances underpin *all* processing operations (as argued in Section 3.3.1), an effective opportunity for contestation is certainly valuable. All the more so considering the way in which fair balances are defined in the 'real-world' ISS context. Indeed, from a practical perspective, and taking into account the scale at which they operate, most ISS providers will unilaterally construct their balancing under Article 6(1)(f) a priori on the basis of the median context and the average individual. *Ex post* empowerment tools such as the rights to erasure and to object are aimed at effectively enabling data subjects to challenge this initial balancing act in light of their particular circumstances.[237] This is important as an ISS controller's tolerance for errors will generally be higher than that of an individual data subject.[238] In case the controller contests such right and/or wishes to continue processing the personal data, it will still need a lawful ground under Article 6(1). As explained earlier in this chapter, the legitimate interests balance as defined in Article 6(1)(f) underlies all others and can therefore be used as bare minimum test for rendering lawful further processing.

PROCEDURE/THIRD PARTIES—From a procedural point of view, the balance under Article 6(1)f initially established by the controller may be challenged by data subjects, data protection authorities, and ultimately, courts. WP29 even suggests the initial balance may be challenged by 'other stakeholders', eg to whom the personal data may be disclosed, or entities that otherwise benefit from the processing taking place.[239] It is unlikely however, that third parties will challenge the lawfulness of processing in practice. More realistically they will want to contest challenges to the balance (eg they will want to protest against data subjects invoking their right to erasure or right to object). Paradoxically, involving third parties into the (re-)assessment of the balance under Article 6(1)(f) would potentially constitute an unlawful processing operation in itself.[240] This is a particularly pressing issue with regard to *published* personal data in the public interest, more on which later

[237] See in this line also: *Google Spain* (n 44) InfoCuria para 82; *Salvatore Manni* (n 14) paras 46–47. The logic of having a more generic, standardized balance as the default, but with an explicit opportunity to challenge also aligns with the proportionality principle in human rights law. See in this regard: Van Drooghenbroeck (n 3) 212–15.

[238] See in this regard also: Bygrave (n 199) 161 et seq.

[239] '[. . .] it can be considered that the public disclosure is done primarily not in the interest of the controller who publishes the data, but rather, in the interest of other stakeholders, such as employees or journalists, or the general public, to whom the data are disclosed'. Article 29 Working Party, 'Opinion 06/2014 on the Notion of Legitimate Interests of the Data Controller under Article 7 of Directive 95/46/EC' (n 20) 14; 27.

[240] See David Erdos, 'Communicating Responsibilities: The Spanish DPA Targets Google's Notification Practices When Delisting Personal Information' (*Inforrm's Blog*, 21 March 2017) <https://inforrm.wordpress.com/2017/03/21/communicating-responsibilities-the-spanish-dpa-targets-googles-notification-practices-when-delisting-personal-information-david-erdos/> accessed 1 June 2019.

(Chapter 6). A more generous interpretation of 'third parties' could also involve entities that might want to challenge the *ex ante* balance themselves (independently from the data subject him/herself). This may be the case, for example, with regard to children or mentally disabled people whose interests and rights are defended by legal guardians.[241] One may also think of collectives (eg gym customers, employees) jointly contesting a balance that does not necessarily affect all of them in the same manner (eg HIV testing) or civil society organizations acting akin to a data protection authority. Overall, and regardless of 'what side the third parties are on', involving them into the mix seems primarily aimed at increasing accountability and transparency (notably Arts 5(2) and 12).[242] With this in mind, the least that can be expected from controllers—particularly large-scale ISS providers—is to be as clear and detailed as possible in their internal decision-making procedures on balancing.[243] This should be furthered by the emphasis on accountability and higher fines in the GDPR (Arts 5(2) and 83(5)).

Conclusion—In theory, Article 6(1)f constitutes an increasingly relevant safeguard countering information/power asymmetries in an ever-expanding data-hungry processing eco-system.[244] WP29 also emphasized time and again that this lawful ground should not be seen as an easy subterfuge or 'get-out-of-jail card' to ensure lawful processing, but as a thorough and durable ground.[245] Practice, however, suggests this lawful ground *is* often used as a catch-all, when none of the other grounds are workable. Indeed, it is fair to say that Article 6(1)f's core features also constitute its main problems. Flexibility translates into vagueness and legal uncertainty. Efficiency translates into centralization and abuse of power. These are considerable pitfalls that may weaken data subjects' position and significantly undermine data protection's aims more broadly.[246] Yet such is the paradox of balancing. It necessarily needs to be open-ended and malleable to fit the infinitely wide array of scenarios falling within the GDPR's scope, each with unique constellations of values which are constantly changing over time.[247] Most valuable

241 See the notorious Italian *Google Video* or *Vividown* case, where an association brought action against Google for a video in which a person suffering from down syndrome was abused by three fellow students. See: *Google Video* [2013] Corte di Cassazione, sez III Penale sentenza n. 5107/14; EDRi, 'Italian Supreme Court: Google's Youtube Is Just a Hosting Provider' (*EDRi*, 12 February 2014) <http://edri.org/italian-supreme-court-search-engines-just-hosting-providers/> accessed 1 June 2019.

242 Article 29 Working Party, 'Opinion 06/2014 on the Notion of Legitimate Interests of the Data Controller under Article 7 of Directive 95/46/EC' (n 20) 43–44, 54.

243 A concrete example is provided by the Open Letter, calling for Google to be more open and transparent about the way in which it deals with delisting requests. Ellen Goodman, 'Open Letter to Google From 80 Internet Scholars: Release RTBF Compliance Data' (*Medium*, 14 May 2015) <https://medium.com/@ellgood/open-letter-to-google-from-80-internet-scholars-release-rtbf-compliance-data-cbfc6d59f1bd> accessed 1 June 2019.

244 Article 29 Working Party, 'Opinion 06/2014 on the Notion of Legitimate Interests of the Data Controller under Article 7 of Directive 95/46/EC' (n 20) 25–26; 30.

245 eg explaining that it 'should thus not be considered as "the weakest link" or an open door to legitimize all data processing activities which do not fall under any of the other legal grounds'. See: ibid 10.

246 ibid 5.

247 For a similar argument in the context of human rights, see: Van Drooghenbroeck (n 3) 641–52.

therefore, is to clearly define the procedural elements, ie the structure of balancing analysis. To put it in Angelopoulos's words: 'the real value of the listing of factors by the courts [. . .] lies not in the identified factors themselves, but in the ensuing analysis'.[248] WP29 seems to have put its hopes on a burgeoning body of case law and sector-specific hard/soft law rules for further guiding balancing exercises in practice.[249] Looking back at how balances have been interpreted across Member States in the past two decades[250] does not paint a very promising picture as to a homogeneous approach in the future. In an attempt at levelling the playing field to some extent, the following two chapters are aimed at clarifying core issues related to GDPR balancing in the ISS context: Chapter 6 will do a deep-dive into three oft-recurring balancing scenarios, and Chapter 7 will explore remaining criticism.

[248] She continues: 'This realisation moves us closer to a real understanding of how to approach the notion of "fair balance": not as a myth applied by the courts to obfuscate their subjective assessments or as a scientific method capable of providing definitive answers, but as a metaphor for the exercise of a detailed dissection, comparison and ordering of the available options with a view of identifying the optimal outcome: a call for rational discourse.' Angelopoulos (n 3) 85.

[249] Article 29 Working Party, 'Opinion 06/2014 on the Notion of Legitimate Interests of the Data Controller under Article 7 of Directive 95/46/EC' (n 20) 57. Also see Article 40(2)(b) GDPR: 'Associations and other bodies representing categories of controllers or processors may prepare codes of conduct, or amend or extend such codes, for the purpose of specifying the application of this Regulation, such as with regard to: the legitimate interests pursued by controllers in specific contexts.'

[250] Douwe Korff, 'Data Protection Laws in the EU: The Difficulties in Meeting the Challenges Posed by Global Social and Technical Developments' (2010) Working Paper No.2. Comparative Study on Different Approaches to New Privacy Challenges, in Particular in the Light of Technological Developments, European Commission - DG Justice. <http://ssrn.com/abstract=1638949> accessed 1 June 2019; Annex 2 in: European Commission, 'Commission Staff Working Paper: Impact Assessment Accompanying the Proposals for General Data Protection Regulation and Directive on Data Protection in Police and Judicial Matters' Brussels, Commission Staff working Paper SEC(2012) 72 final. European Commission. January 25, 2012. Specifically on the great disparities regarding balancing freedom of expression interests, see: David Erdos, 'European Union Data Protection Law and Media Expression: Fundamentally Off Balance' (2016) 65 International and Comparative Law Quarterly 139.

6

Balancing Scenarios

Section 1. Introduction

Invoking the right to erasure or the right to object forces a (re-)balancing act under the GDPR (see Chapter 5). In other words, the rights to erasure and to object effectively 'stress test' the initial balance as defined by the controller. Exercising *ex post* empowerment rights such as the right to erasure and to object will put substantial weight in the data subject's scale, tipping the balance in his/her favour by default. Further processing of personal data against the clear will of the data subject can be presumed *unfair* by default. That is, unless a strong(er) counter-weight cancels out that default. This is the case, for example, with regard to the lawful grounds in Article 6(1)(b)–(e), where the legislator clearly delineates situations in which personal data can continue to be processed regardless of the data subject's will. With regard to the legitimate interests lawful ground (Art 6(1)(f), controllers will have a particularly strong burden of proof to demonstrate the interests in further processing still override the data subject's wish against it. The reason why is that ignoring data subject rights to erasure or to object implicates the control rationale of the fundamental right to data protection (Art 8 Charter). In other words, the balancing act as triggered by *ex post* empowerment measures directly affects the enjoyment of a fundamental right. Hence, any refusal to accommodate the rights to erasure and/or to object will have to be justified by a provision in the Charter as well (be it a specific right or freedom, or a legislative measure in light of Art 52(1)).[1]

This reasoning is also confirmed by the CJEU in *Google Spain*, recognizing inter alia that the rights to object and to erasure (in Arts 14 and 12 Directive 95/46) implement the requirements laid down in Article 8 Charter.[2] Indeed, data protection provisions that regulate 'processing of personal data liable to infringe fundamental freedoms [. . .] must necessarily be interpreted in the light of fundamental rights'.[3] Hence, when invoking these data subject rights in the 'delisting' context, Articles 7–8 Charter will override the other interests at stake by default (ie economic and information access).[4] The ball is left in the controller's court to reverse this default,

[1] The exemptions to the right to erasure, and the GDPR more broadly (see Chapters 3 and 4) constitute important such limitations already.

[2] *Google Spain SL, Google Inc v Agencia Española de Protección de Datos (AEPD), Mario Costeja González* [2014] Court of Justice of the European Union C-131/12 para 69.

[3] ibid para 68. Referring to: *Connolly v Commission* [2001] Court of Justice of the European Union C-274/99 P [37]; *Österreichischer Rundfunk and others* [2003] Court of Justice of the European Union Joined Cases C-465/00, C-138/01, and C-139/01 [68] para 65.

[4] *Google Spain* (n 2) paras 81; 97.

The Right to Erasure in EU Data Protection Law. First Edition. Jef Ausloos. Oxford University Press (2020). © Jef Ausloos
DOI: 10.1093/oso/9780198847977.001.0001

by arguing that *in casu*, these other interests outweigh the data subject's nonetheless. In doing so, the controller will have to establish that the respective interests are actively pursued, real, and present.[5]

In sum, invoking a valid right to erasure and/or to object (see Chapter 4) will tilt the balance in favour of data subjects by default. This default is a priori not affected by the perhaps seemingly trivial nature of such requests. The very rationale of the fundamental right to data protection (Art 8) consists of ensuring autonomy, informational self-determination, and *control* over one's personal data (see Chapter 2). By virtue of this rationale, exercising a data subject right (as circumscribed in the GDPR) should a priori not be constrained, regardless of the motivation for exercising the right. Put differently, as long as its minimum requirements are met, exercising a data subject right cannot be categorically discarded because of allegedly being a *de minimis* claim. The very ability of exercising these rights is what lies at the core of the fundamental right to data protection (Art 8). That being said, the GDPR is aimed at making sure such aim is achieved in a fair and proportionate manner (and does so by laying down some conditions and restrictions to the right).

Building on Chapter 5, the question this chapter hopes to answer further is how exactly to go about '*ex post* (re-balancing exercises' triggered by the rights to erasure or to object in the information society services (ISS) environment. Three discrete scenarios are identified, each representing particularly widespread conflicts in the ISS context. This approach should not be understood as negating the fact that practical reality is much more intricate.[6] Rather, untangling these complex situations into 'archetypal' balancing scenarios is aimed at teasing out the main legal issues more concretely.

- Commercial interests: primarily pursued by the controller;
- Information freedoms: primarily pursued by third parties;
- Research and security interests: pursued by both controller and third parties.

This selection of balancing scenarios can be justified because (a) of their prevalence in the ISS context; (b) they each enable separating the perspectives of the different key actors; (c) they are strong counter-interests according to the GDPR itself (notably in light of Arts 85 and 89); and (d) are representative of most conflicts making their way to the CJEU. It should be emphasized that this selection in no way purports to be exhaustive. There are several other important interests that might weigh against the data subject. One can think for example of the right to

[5] Article 29 Working Party, 'Opinion 06/2014 on the Notion of Legitimate Interests of the Data Controller under Article 7 of Directive 95/46/EC' (European Commission 2014) Opinion WP 217 24 <http://ec.europa.eu/justice/article-29/documentation> accessed 1 June 2019.

[6] See notably: Seda es and Joris Van Hoboken, 'Privacy after the Agile Turn' in Jules Polonetsky, Omer Tene, and Evan Selinger (eds), *Cambridge Handbook of Consumer Privacy* (CUP 2017) <https://osf.io/preprints/socarxiv/9gy73> accessed 1 June 2019.

an effective remedy;[7] accountability and transparency of government subsidies;[8] national/public security;[9] but also non-discrimination; other people's privacy,[10] and so on.

Finally, it should be re-emphasized that a balance implies at least two sides. Up until now, this book has primarily focused on the data subject. Yet, when it comes to balancing, data subjects' position (including their interests, rights, and freedoms at stake) should be assessed *in relation to* the other side(s) of the balance. This is what is implied by the proportionality principle and further justifies the structure of this chapter. The balancing scenarios examined here are shaped around powerful interests that generally weigh against the data subject. This side of the balance is often much more complex as it involves more entities (including controllers and third parties) and covers a much more heterogeneous set of interests. Be that as it may, in the ISS context several clusters of interests can be identified, each circling an important Charter provision or societal value. Having distilled three balancing scenarios from these clusters enables bringing some clarity in this quagmire. Moreover, the selection of balancing scenarios is further guided by the three typical constellations of actors in the ISS context: processing in the interest of (i) primarily controller alone (commercial interests); (ii) primarily third parties (information freedom interests); or (iii) a mix of both controller and third parties (research/security interests).

Section 2. Balancing Scenarios

2.1 Commercial Interests

> We use the information we collect from all of our services to provide, maintain, protect and improve them, to develop new ones and to protect Google and our users. We also use this information to offer you tailored content—like giving you more relevant search results and ads.[11]

[7] *Coty Germany v Stadtsparkasse Magdeburg* [2015] Court of Justice of the European Union C-580/13 [33].

[8] *Volker und Markus Schecke GbR and Hartmut Eifert v Land Hessen* [2010] Court of Justice of the European Union Joined Cases C-92/09 and C-93/09.

[9] *Digital Rights Ireland Ltd* [2014] Court of Justice of the European Union Joined Cases C-293/12 and C-594/12 invalidating the Data Retention Directive (2006/24/EC); *U v Stadt Karlsruhe* [2014] Court of Justice of the European Union C-101/13.

[10] For example, when one person in a group picture wants it erased and the others do not. Another interesting example is provided by Van Hoboken, who explains that intervening in the search rankings of a search engine may affect other people's right to private life (Art 7 Charter, Art 8 ECHR) as the relationship between most search engines and their users today is often very private and personalized. See: Joris Van Hoboken, *Search Engine Freedom: On the Implications of the Right to Freedom Expression for the Legal Governance of Web Search Engines* (First edn, Kluwer Law International 2012) 68–74.

[11] https://www.google.com/policies/privacy/ accessed March 2017.

2.1.1 Relevance with Regard to the Right to Erasure

Personal data processing in the ISS context is primarily driven by commercial interests. This is apparent from a quick glance at the most popular such services as well as more generally considering the predominant business-model in the *information* society.[12] Against this background, virtually every conflict of interests triggered by the right to erasure will involve the controller's commercial interests in one way or another. Still quite broad and vague in the abstract, this subsection will analyse more concretely the meaning and scope of 'commercial interests' in light of right to erasure triggered re-balancing acts in the ISS context. As a working definition, commercial interests in this book can be understood as interests of the ISS controller that directly relate to its own profit-seeking objective.

The extent to which personal data processing contributes to the controllers' commercial interests differs greatly. In the context of ISS, data processing will generally be at the very core of a company's identity/*raison d'être*. In other words, both the services they offer as well as the underlying business incentives will be predicated on the processing of (personal) data. In other words, virtually all ISS—particularly those investigated in this book—inherently depend on (personal) data processing in order to 'stay in business'. This is manifestly the case for consumer-oriented companies such as search engines and social networks for example, but also for any other company built around 'big data', 'artificial intelligence', or 'machine learning'.

As mentioned before, a qualitative difference exists between the initial (*ex ante*) balancing act to render processing lawful in the first place, and the re-balancing (*ex post*) act as a result of invoking the right to erasure/object. The breadth of interests that can be relied upon with regard to the former is significantly larger than the latter. Indeed, only those interests that can directly be traced back to the Charter *may* constitute valid weights in *ex post* re-balancing exercises (see beginning of this chapter). This also follows from the fact that commercial (or economic) interests as such are generally deemed subordinate to the rights to privacy or data protection.[13] A crucial question will therefore be to what extent commercial interests are covered by the Charter. Key reference point in this regard will of course be Article 16 on the freedom to conduct a business. Other Charter rights might more or less directly be relevant as well, such as the right to (intellectual) property in Article 17.[14]

[12] The incessant urge to extract value from (personal) data is gradually also permeating traditional industries. For more, see Chapter 1.

[13] Serge Gutwirth, 'De Toepassing van Het Finaliteitsbeginsel van de Privacywet van 8 December 1992 Tot Bescherming van de Persoonlijke Levenssfeer Ten Opzichte van de Verwerking van Persoonsgegevens' [The Application of the Purpose Specification Principle in the Belgian Data Protection Act of 8 December 1992] (1993) 1993 Tijdschrift voor Privaatrecht—TPR 1431; Hielke Hijmans, *The European Union as Guardian of Internet Privacy: The Story of Art 16 TFEU* (Springer 2016) 258; *Google Spain* (n 2).

[14] Pursuant to Article 52(3) Charter, the corresponding ECHR provision (Art 1 of the First Protocol to the ECHR) may also be informative.

2.1.2 Article 16 Charter—Freedom to Conduct a Business

Broad Interpretation—Similarly to the right to data protection in Article 8 of the Charter, the freedom to conduct a business in Article 16 is a fairly young fundamental right. The right is said to constitutionally endorse a commitment to a certain political economical model, with an emphasis on the performative component of economic freedom, ie safeguarding the very ability for individuals to be entrepreneurial.[15] The freedom to conduct a business, explains the CJEU, 'covers the freedom to exercise an economic or commercial activity, the freedom of contract and free competition' and 'must be viewed in relation to its social function'.[16] The broad interpretation given to this freedom was confirmed in a 2017 ruling where the CJEU controversially declared that (under certain conditions) '[a]n employer's wish to project an image of neutrality towards customers' is also covered by Article 16, effectively legitimizing head-scarf prohibitions on the work floor.[17]

Limitations to Article 16—Any obstacles hampering this freedom should—in line with Article 52 of the Charter—be provided for by law, respect the essence of the freedom, be proportionate (ie suitable, necessary, and proportionate *stricto sensu*) and genuinely meet objectives of general interest recognized by the EU or the need to protect the rights and freedoms of others. The right to erasure/object will often constitute an interference with the ISS provider's freedom to conduct a business. Particularly so, when that provider's main source of revenue consists of drawing value from personal data. The question then becomes, whether it constitutes a justified interference. Clearly, the right to erasure/object is provided by law (ie Arts 17 and 21 GDPR) and 'genuinely meets the objective to protect the rights and freedoms' of the data subject (at the very least the ability to control (the use of) one's personal data as protected by Article 8 Charter). The core questions regarding this first balancing scenario therefore revolve around the last two steps of the proportionality assessment (ie necessary and balanced) and what constitutes the *essence* of the freedom to conduct a business. These are questions of degree, requiring yet again a functional approach, looking at the particularities in each individual case. Both are strongly interconnected and will be explored jointly in the following pages.

15 Michele Everson and Gonçalves Rui Correia, 'Freedom to Conduct a Business' in Steve Peers and others (eds), *The EU Charter of Fundamental Rights: A Commentary* (Hart 2014) 438 et seq <https://www.bloomsburycollections.com/book/the-eu-charter-of-fundamental-rights-a-commentary/>. Oliver explains 'the freedom to conduct a business is rooted in the Constitutions of a number of Member States, including Germany, Ireland and Italy'. Peter Oliver, 'What Purpose Does Article 16 of the Charter Serve?' in Ulf Bernitz, Xavier Groussot, and Felix Schulyok (eds), *General Principles of EU Law and European Private Law* (First, Kluwer Law International 2013) 282.

16 See case law referred to in: *Spain and Finland v Parliament and Council* [2004] Court of Justice of the European Union C-184/02 [51–52]; *Sky Österreich* [2013] Court of Justice of the European Union C-283/11 paras 42; 45; *Pillbox 38 (UK) v Secretary of State for Health* [2016] Court of Justice of the European Union C-477/14 [157].

17 *G4S Secure Solutions* [2017] Court of Justice of the European Union C-157/15 [38; 42].

Right to Erasure and Article 16 Charter—In practice, the balancing act that is triggered by the right to erasure or to object will require a granular dissection of the activities/data that are targeted. Subsequently, for each single activity or piece of data, it will need to be assessed whether stopping or erasing it will effectively impact the *essence* of the ISS provider's freedom to conduct its business. Even though some case law and scholarly interpretation on the freedom to conduct a business has emerged in the last few years, it is still hard to ascertain what exactly does (not) constitute an interference with the *essence* of this freedom.

CJEU on the Essence of Article 16—The essence of Article 16 has been described as 'a general principle of economic autonomy that unfolds within the prescribed contours of the legal-economic institutions of the European Economic Constitution'.[18] For the purposes here, a few useful elements can be derived from the CJEU's case law. First of all, the Court repeatedly suggested a high threshold, permitting a wide array of potential limitations, even ones that have 'substantial adverse consequences'.[19] A limitation is considered to affect the essence of Article 16 when there are no viable alternatives and the business is effectively deprived of its freedom to contract.[20] The CJEU also explained that with limitations that only affect a clearly defined area of business, the essence of the freedom remains intact.[21] Indeed, a legal prohibition to advertise, for example, does not prevent 'economic operators from manufacturing and marketing electronic cigarettes and refill containers'.[22] Similarly, requiring an internet access provider to password-protect its users' internet connections in light of protecting intellectual property rights, has been considered *not* to damage the essence of Article 16, 'in so far as the measure is limited to marginally adjusting one of the technical options open to the provider in exercising its activity'.[23]

Right to Erasure v *Essence* of Article 16—What can be learned from the above in terms of how the right to erasure/object may affect the (essence) of the freedom to conduct a business? *In casu*, the (continued) processing in pursuit of economic interests affects the right to data protection (Art 8 Charter). Hence, the core question can essentially be reduced to: does the right to erasure/object make it effectively impossible for the economic operator to conduct its business? This immediately puts the spotlight on companies that have (personal) data at the heart

[18] Everson and Rui Correia (n 15) 441.

[19] *AffishBV v Rijksdienst voor de Keuring van Vee en Vlees* [1997] Court of Justice of the European Union C-183/95 [17]; *R v MAFF ex parte Fedesa* [1990] Court of Justice of the European Union C-331/88 [42]; *Nycomed Danmark ApS v European Medicines Agency (EMA)* [2011] General Court of the European Union T-52/09 [89]; *Pillbox 38 (UK) v Secretary of State for Health* (n 16) para 158.

[20] See notably *Parkwood Leisure Ltd* [2013] Court of Justice of the European Union C-426/11 [30–35]; Steve Peers and Sasha Prechal, 'Scope and Interpretation of Rights and Principles' in Steve Peers and others (eds), *The EU Charter of Fundamental Rights: A Commentary* (Hart 2014) paras 52.75.

[21] *Land Rheinland-Pfalz* [2012] Court of Justice of the European Union C-544/10 [56–58]. *In casu* the alleged 'limitation' concerned rules regarding the labelling and advertising of alcoholic beverages.

[22] *Pillbox 38 (UK) v Secretary of State for Health* (n 16) paras 161–62.

[23] *McFadden* [2016] Court of Justice of the European Union C-484/14 [92].

of their business model, potentially implicating any ISS provider whose primary revenue stream comes from behavioural advertising or profiling more broadly. Stripping these entities from the possibility to draw value from (users') personal data, one may argue, affects the *essence* of their economic freedom as their survival depends on it. However, this last claim can also be contested, for example, by the fact that there are many alternative advertisement/profiling models that do not (as heavily) rely on the processing of personal data.[24] Some business models may rely even more fundamentally on the processing of personal data as (part of) the core of the service they deliver (eg rating websites, people search engines, social networks, 'smart assistants', etc). Some of the practices of these economic operators may however cut deeper into the essence of the fundamental right to data protection than vice versa, effectively rendering (part of) the business model itself in conflict with Article 8 Charter.[25] Indeed, Article 16 does not safeguard economic freedom with regard to business models or practices that are essentially illegal. This might arguably be the case when rights to erasure/object are refused with regard to processing not necessary to deliver the service requested (in breach of the GDPR).

Technical Considerations—Commercial interests may also be negatively affected to the extent the actual operation of accommodating the rights to erasure/object is disproportionately difficult. This may particularly be the case when, from a technical perspective, erasure requires significant resources. Effectively *erasing* data may be near-to-impossible because data is stored in different locations, it may be hard to identify and locate *specific* sets of data, it could corrupt databases, it may require physically destroying the storage device as merely overwriting is not irrevocable, and so on.[26] These issues are only exacerbated with the rise of artificial intelligence and machine learning, but also—quite paradoxically—increased efforts to install data protection by design measures. This last point appears from responses to data subject access requests directed at Apple's Siri and a range of entities active at the back end of the advertisement industry.[27,28] These actors say not to be able

[24] This requires more of a legal-economical analysis that goes beyond the scope of this book. On this topic, see: Frederik Zuiderveen Borgesius, 'Improving Privacy Protection in the Area of Behavioural Targeting' (PhD Thesis, University of Amsterdam 2014) 165ff<http://hdl.handle.net/11245/1.434236>.

[25] David Erdos, 'Confused? Analysing the Scope of Freedom of Speech Protection Vis-à-Vis European Data Protection' (Oxford University 2012) 48/2012 10–14<http://papers.ssrn.com/abstract=2119187> accessed 1 June 2019; David Erdos, 'From the Scylla of Restriction to the Charybdis of Licence? Exploring the Scope of the "Special Purposes" Freedom of Expression Shield in European Data Protection' (2015) 52 Common Market Law Review 132 et seq.

[26] See Peter Druschel, Michael Backes, and Rodica Tirtea, 'The Right to Be Forgotten—Between Expectations and Practice' (ENISA 2012) 8ff <https://www.enisa.europa.eu/activities/identity-and-trust/library/deliverables/the-right-to-be-forgotten/> accessed 1 June 2019.

[27] Such as data management platforms, exchanges, aggregators, etc. See notably: Luma Partners, 'Display LumaScape'.

[28] See notably: Jef Ausloos and Pierre Dewitte, 'Shattering One-Way Mirrors—Data Subject Access Rights in Practice' (2018) 8 International Data Privacy Law 4; Michael Veale, Reuben Binns, and Jef Ausloos, 'When Data Protection by Design and Data Subject Rights Clash' International Data Privacy Law <https://academic.oup.com/idpl/advance-article/doi/10.1093/idpl/ipy002/4960902> accessed 5 April 2018; Jef Ausloos, 'Paul-Olivier Dehaye and the Raiders of the Lost Data' (*CITIP blog*, 10 April

to accommodate data subject rights because, they claim, it is impossible to trace back the respective personal data. Intelligence services, on the other hand, claim they can and do indeed effectively *erase* personal data.[29] Regardless of the veracity of these claims,[30] they illustrate that the right to erasure/object brings to the surface a (growing) disparity between the *legal* and *technical* definition of what constitutes 'data erasure'. Important for the purposes of this section is whether such technical difficulties may amount to an interference with the *essence* of ISS controllers' freedom to conduct a business. The CJEU's *Telekabel* ruling—concerning an injunction to block access to a copyright-infringing website—is informative in this regard:

> [S]uch an injunction does not seem to infringe the very substance of the freedom of an internet service provider such as that at issue in the main proceedings to conduct a business.
> First, an injunction such as that at issue in the main proceedings leaves its addressee to determine the specific measures to be taken in order to achieve the result sought, with the result that he can choose to put in place measures which are best adapted to the resources and abilities available to him and which are compatible with the other obligations and challenges which he will encounter in the exercise of his activity.
> Secondly, such an injunction allows its addressee to avoid liability by proving that he has taken all reasonable measures. That possibility of exoneration clearly has the effect that the addressee of the injunction will not be required to make unbearable sacrifices, which seems justified in particular in the light of the fact that he is not the author of the infringement of the fundamental right of intellectual property which has led to the adoption of the injunction.[31]

Technical Difficulties Are Not Sufficient—Even though not involving the fundamental right to data protection per se, the facts in *Telekabel* and the respective balance (ie Article 17(2) Charter v Article 16 and 11 Charter) are sufficiently similar so that the above statement is relevant *mutadis mutandis* to the right

2018) <www.law.kuleuven.be/citip/blog/paul-olivier-dehaye-and-the-raiders-of-the-lost-data> accessed 23 April 2018.

[29] European Union Agency for Fundamental Rights (FRA), 'Surveillance by Intelligence Services: Fundamental Rights Safeguards and Remedies in the EU. Volume I: Member States' Legal Frameworks' (Fundamental Rights Agency 2015) <http://fra.europa.eu/en/publication/2015/surveillance-intelligence-services>; European Union Agency for Fundamental Rights (FRA), 'Surveillance by Intelligence Services: Fundamental Rights Safeguards and Remedies in the EU Volume II: Field Perspectives and Legal Update' (2017) <http://fra.europa.eu/en/publication/2017/surveillance-intelligence-socio-lega>.

[30] Something which is particularly hard to demonstrate without full access to the technical infrastructure of these actors.

[31] *UPC Telekabel* [2014] Court of Justice of the European Union C-314/12 [55]; paras 51–53.

to erasure as well. Indeed, it is about enforcing an *ex post* control measure on an individualized basis,[32] requiring a demonstrable but reasonable effort. Given the interpretative flexibility left to controllers on how to effectuate the right to erasure in practice, it does not seem that technical difficulties in implementing the right to erasure will infringe the essence of the freedom to conduct a business. The balance tips in data subjects' favour even more when considering that non(-effective) erasure will also entails risks with regard to hacking and surveillance practices (the mere potentiality of which already affects data subjects' rights and interests).[33] Indeed, the very existence (and expansion) of a corporate surveillance infrastructure creates risks and problems to much more than just the right to data protection alone. When there is no method to accommodate the right to erasure/object in any way whatsoever, the controller's technical infrastructure is simply not in compliance with data protection law (and Art 8 Charter). The freedom to conduct a business does not extend to the ability to put in place illegal technical infrastructure.

Targeted Erasure—Assuming that the ISS provider's data processing operations comply with the GDPR in general, another defence against erasure requests may be derived from the CJEU's *Sabam* cases. In both of these cases, the Court ruled against broad-sweep injunctions against internet access providers (*Scarlet*)[34] or social networks (*Netlog*)[35] in order to protect copyright. These injunctions concerned filtering software, applied as a preventive measure to all customers for an unlimited period. The service providers' economic interests were an important, though not exclusive, justification against the general injunctions. One might similarly expect that too vaguely defined or far-reaching request to erasure/object under the GDPR could equally be opposed on the basis of the arguments developed the *Sabam* cases. Yet, it is unlikely such arguments would succeed without involving additional fundamental rights (eg the privacy and/or information freedoms of ISS users). In sum, the key take-away is that in order to improve the viability of one's right to erasure/object, it is recommended to make it as specific and targeted as possible. This may be easier said than done in practice when the relevant personal data easily propagates. Specific versus broad-sweep requests are two ends of a sliding scale. How much leeway the right to erasure/object has on this scale will depend on the context, and on interpretations by courts and regulators. The Belgian Privacy Commission, for example, has already suggested delisting requests can be validly expanded to searches on the basis of the data subject's name plus any other search term.[36]

[32] Separating it, for example, from other intellectual property cases where the emphasis was on *ex ante* measures such as general filtering mechanisms. Notably: *Scarlet Extended v Sabam* [2011] Court of Justice of the European Union C-70/10 paras 48–49.

[33] See Veale, Binns, and Ausloos, 'When Data Protection by Design and Data Subject Rights Clash' (n 28) 9–10.

[34] *Scarlet Extended v Sabam* (n 32).

[35] *SABAM v Netlog* [2012] Court of Justice of the European Union C-360/10.

[36] Belgian Privacy Commission, 'Advies 75/2017 Ingevolge Een Klacht Gericht Tegen Een Zoekmotor Betreffende de Modaliteiten Voor de Uitvoering En de Geografische Reikwijdte van Een

EX ANTE V EX POST—At this stage, it is worth reiterating the distinction between *ex ante* protective measures and *ex post* empowerment measures (see Chapter 2). *Ex ante* protective measures arguably interfere more severely with the freedom to conduct a business, as they install general constraints. Big Data evangelists may well argue that the purpose limitation principle interferes with (the essence of) their freedoms. *Ex post* empowerment measures such as the right to erasure and object, on the other hand do not install a priori prohibitions, and only apply in individual cases.[37] The existence of these rights, and their occasional exercise, therefore, does not seem to interfere with the essence of ISS providers' freedom to conduct their business per se. Yet, considering the level of granularity with which they can be invoked, the opposite could be argued as well. To what extent can data subjects target only those processing activities that actually make the ISS provider (controller) money, while still continuing to use the service? For example, do data subjects have the right to use a social networking service, without being profiled for any commercial purposes whatsoever? This could undermine or even sabotage ISS providers' very business model (eg objecting to personal data being used for fraud prevention).[38] This conundrum is reminiscent of the circular or reiterative nature of balancing in the GDPR (see Chapter 5). Expansive processing by ISS providers (including commercial profiling for example) may be 'balanced' and lawful pursuant to Article 6(1) *ex ante*.[39] Yet such *ex ante* balance can be targeted with the right to erasure/object instigating a new *ex post* balancing act in light of the specifics of the individual case. It is this *ex post* balancing act which is very unlikely to tip in favour of the controller.

ERODING DATA-PROFITS—How far can data subjects go in requesting certain personal data and/or processing operations to be deleted/halted, while still being capable of using the service? At the very least, the GDPR gives data subjects an unconditional right to object to their personal data being used for direct marketing

Verwijdering van URL's Uit de Zoekresultaten (CO- A-2017-088)' (2017) Advies 75/2017 <https://www.privacycommission.be/sites/privacycommission/files/documents/advies_75_2017.pdf> accessed 17 April 2018.

[37] Even when exercised through collective action mechanisms, they are still exercised with regard to particular relationships, processing activities and/or data.

[38] See, in this regard, Facebook's arguments in the case brought against the company by the Belgian DPA (ie claiming wide-scale tracking was necessary in order to ensure security). Belgian Privacy Commission, 'Own-Initiative Recommendation Relating to 1) Facebook, 2) Internet and/or Facebook Users as Well as 3) Users and Providers of Facebook Services, Particularly Plug-Ins' (2015) Recommendation no. 04/2015 20 <https://www.gegevensbeschermingsautoriteit.be/sites/privacycommission/files/documents/recommendation_04_2015_0.pdf> accessed 1 June 2019; Günes Acar, 'Preserving Privacy in Belgium' (*COSIC*, 26 October 2015) <https://www.esat.kuleuven.be/cosic/preserving-privacy-in-belgium/> accessed 1 June 2019.

[39] Commercial profiling will generally only be lawful under Article 6(1)(a), ie consent by the data subject. Yet, consent is not necessarily required in each case: Article 29 Working Party, 'Opinion 06/2014 on the Notion of Legitimate Interests of the Data Controller under Article 7 of Directive 95/46/EC' (n 5) 46–47; Indra Spiecker genannt Döhmann and others, 'The Regulation of Commercial Profiling—A Comparative Analysis' (2016) 2 European Data Protection Law Review 535, 547 et seq.

purposes, *including profiling* to the extent it is related to that direct marketing (Art 21(2) *j* recital 70).[40] Of course, ISS providers may process personal data for other purposes in pursuit of economic interests. The controller may draw value from the (processing of) personal data directly or indirectly. In the first case (eg data-brokering, market analysis) consent will almost always be the only valid lawful ground,[41] entitling data subjects to withdraw consent (and hence request erasure, Art 17(1)(b)) at any time. This effectively empowers data subjects to continue using the service, without any other processing operations than those that are *necessary* for providing the requested service (ie the performance of the contract, Art 7(4)). In the second case (eg ratings on an ecommerce platform, web-analytics, generalist search engine results), other lawful grounds—and Article 6(1)(f) in particular—may be more appropriate. Even though this eliminates the ability to withdraw consent, in these situations the controller's interest is arguably even weaker as the actual revenue stream is not challenged per se. Indeed, when the processing of *personal* data is only tangentially benefitting Article 16 Charter interests (either because the 'personal' character is irrelevant, or because it does not directly contribute to the controller's revenue stream), and there are no other interests at play, the balance will tip in data subjects' favour. This also appears from the CJEU's *Google Spain* Ruling, that indicated mere delisting on the basis of a person's name does not challenge the economic interests of operating a search engine.[42]

The above analysis reaffirms that the current take-it-or-leave-it deal offered by many ISS providers cannot be justified by their economic freedoms under the Charter. Article 16 Charter only extends to business models that are legitimate in the first place.[43] Individuals should be free to use services without any excess data processing not inherently necessary to the specific purpose for which those individuals use the service (eg profiling or being tracked across the internet).[44] This ties back to the need for a granular approach, dissecting all the different processing operations taking place and assessing their legitimacy individually.[45] If this approach

[40] Article 29 Working Party, 'Opinion 06/2014 on the Notion of Legitimate Interests of the Data Controller under Article 7 of Directive 95/46/EC' (n 5) 46–47.

[41] Article 29 Working Party, Article 29 Working Party, 'Opinion 03/2013 on Purpose Limitation' (Article 29 Working Party 2013) WP 03/2013 46 <http://ec.europa.eu/justice/article-29/documentation> accessed 1 June 2019.

[42] *Google Spain* (n 2).

[43] Article 16 Charter cannot be relied on to defend gambling directed at children, hazardous waste dumping, illegitimate data processing, even if it would mean the end of the respective business.

[44] A 2016 study confirmed the pervasiveness of the surveillance infrastructure created by ISS providers (eg with two thirds of investigated online platforms explicitly acknowledging they track users outside their platforms and 80 per cent allowing for third-party tracking). See: Jamila Venturini and others, *Terms of Service and Human Rights: An Analysis of Online Platform Contracts* (Revan 2016) 67ff<http://internet-governance.fgv.br/sites/internet-governance.fgv.br/files/publicacoes/terms_of_services_06_12_2016.pdf> accessed 1 June 2019.

[45] Article 29 Working Party, 'Opinion 15/2011 on the Definition of Consent' (Article 29 Working Party 2011) WP187 19<http://ec.europa.eu/justice/article-29/documentation>; Serge Gutwirth, 'Short Statement about the Role of Consent in the European Data Protection Directive' <http://works.bepress.com/serge_gutwirth/80/>.

makes the service less/not profitable, the problem is the business model itself.[46] A case in point is the 2018 decision of the French *Conseil d'État*, confirming that advertisement cookies cannot be considered 'strictly necessary for the delivery of a service', even if the economic viability of a website depends on it.[47] Similarly, UK regulators have come down hard on the legality of Facebook's business model[48] and that of many actors within the AdTech and Real-Time-Bidding sector.[49] The Uber and Facebook vignettes illustrate the need for drawing a line between economic freedoms and the interests, rights, and freedoms of data subjects. Applying advanced data processing specifically aimed at sidestepping individuals' rationality and free choice in the name of economic freedom cannot override data subjects' right to data protection.[50]

In sum, it is virtually impossible to consider the right to erasure/object to affect the essence of the freedom to conduct a business, because it is both constrained in breadth[51] and depth.[52,53] If the essence is not affected, it is still necessary to look at whether invoking the right to erasure/object is in fact proportionate. The suitability/effectiveness test will depend on the data subject's goals. The necessity or least intrusive means test may require some fine-tuning of the actual operationalization of the right (see 'Fifty Shades of Erasure' in Chapter 7 and Chapter 8). The proportionality *stricto sensu* test will be the most debatable. Yet, in light of what was said before, I would suggest that in the context of invoking the

[46] See more generally in this regard: Arvind Narayanan, 'When the Business Model *is* the Privacy Violation' (*Freedom to Tinker*, 12 April 2018) <https://freedom-to-tinker.com/2018/04/12/when-the-business-model-is-the-privacy-violation/> accessed 16 April 2018. The EDPS quite vividly explains '[t]here might well be a market for personal data, just like there is, tragically, a market for live human organs, but that does not mean that we can or should give that market the blessing of legislation. One cannot monetise and subject a fundamental right to a simple commercial transaction, even if it is the individual concerned by the data who is a party to the transaction.' European Data Protection Supervisor, 'Opinion on the Proposal for a Directive on Certain Aspects Concerning Contracts for the Supply of Digital Content' (EDPS 2017) Opinion 4/2017 7 <https://edps.europa.eu/sites/edp/files/publication/17-03-14_opinion_digital_content_en_0.pdf> accessed 1 June 2019.

[47] Etienne Wery, 'Les cookies peuvent coûter très cher ...' (*Droit & Technologies*, 18 June 2018) <https://www.droit-technologie.org/actualites/cookies-peuvent-couter-cher-tres-cher/> accessed 31 July 2018; *Editions Croque Futur v CNIL* [2018] Conseil d'État 412589.

[48] Digital, Culture, Media, and Sport Committee, 'Disinformation and "Fake News": Final Report' (House of Commons 2019) 8 40 et seq.

[49] Information Commissioner's Office, 'Update Report into AdTech and Real Time Bidding' (ICO 2019) <https://ico.org.uk/media/about-the-ico/documents/2615156/adtech-real-time-bidding-report-201906.pdf> accessed 20 June 2019.

[50] This is not to say that some level of emotional/psychological manipulation (subject to adequate safeguards) may be deemed legitimate in order to prevent violence for example. Rosalind W Picard, *Affective Computing* (MIT Press 2000) 123–24.

[51] ie it cannot be exercised on a generalized basis but is subject to requirements. It is also to be invoked on an individual (data subject) basis.

[52] ie it does not essentially make impossible the enjoyment of the freedom to conduct a business.

[53] These are the core elements for the essence test according to CJEU president Lenaerts, based, inter alia on the Schrems Ruling (*Maximillian Schrems v Data Protection Commissioner* [2015] Court of Justice of the European Union C-362/14 paras 93–94). Koen Lenaerts, 'Opening Address: Limit to Limitations: The Essence of Fundamental Rights in the EU' (Conference—The Essence of Fundamtenal Rights in EU Law, Leuven, Belgium, 17 May 2018).

right to erasure/object vis-à-vis powerful ISS providers the balance tips in favour of the data subject *by default*. Indeed, all three branches of the EU—legislative,[54] executive,[55] and judicial[56]—point in the direction that data subjects should be able to continue using services, without their personal data being processed for anything else than they explicitly want.[57] Yet, this logical conclusion seems to be fundamentally at odds with ISS providers' predominant business model today; ie the tacit bargain people can use 'free' services in return for being profiled (eg to get tailored commercial, social, or search recommendations). In theory, individuals should have the ability to continue using such services while remaining free to granularly object to certain processing operations and/or have specific data erased. The fact that these services did not design their infrastructure so as to easily accommodate such requests does not constitute an excuse. This radical disconnect, will not be resolved overnight but requires substantial efforts and a shift in mindset that will further be explored in the following chapters. What can be concluded at this stage is that it will be incredibly rare to have commercial interests alone override data subject rights in *ex post* balancing acts resulting from the right to erasure/object.

2.1.3 Article 17 Charter—Right to Property

Intellectual Property v Data Protection—Article 17 in the Charter protects the right to (intellectual) property. Even though the CJEU generally mentions this provision in the same breath as Article 16,[58] this fundamental right can still be invoked in isolation in order to fend off rights to erasure/object. Particularly in the ISS context, the most common occurrence of a clash between the fundamental right to data protection and Article 17 concerns *intellectual* property (IP). More specifically, conflicts that have been brought before the CJEU already, generally relate to (internet) service providers being asked to share the data of users

[54] European Commission, 'Commission Staff Working Paper: Impact Assessment Accompanying the Proposals for General Data Protection Regulation and Directive on Data Protection in Police and Judicial Matters' (European Commission 2012) Commission Staff working Paper SEC (2012) 129 Annex 7.

[55] Article 29 Working Party, 'Opinion 03/2013 on Purpose Limitation' (n 41) 46; European Data Protection Supervisor, 'Preliminary EDPS Opinion on the Review of the EPrivacy Directive (2002/58/EC)' (EDPS 2016) Opinion 5/2016 14–16 <https://edps.europa.eu/sites/edp/files/publication/16-07-22_opinion_eprivacy_en.pdf> accessed 1 June 2019; European Data Protection Supervisor, 'Opinion on the Proposal for a Directive on Certain Aspects Concerning Contracts for the Supply of Digital Content' (n 46) 7 et seq; European Data Protection Board, 'Draft Guidelines 2/2019 on the Processing of Personal Data under Article 6(1)(b) GDPR in the Context of the Provision of Online Services to Data Subject' (EDPB 2019) 10 <https://edpb.europa.eu/sites/edpb/files/consultation/edpb_draft_guidelines-art_6-1-b-final_public_consultation_version_en.pdf> accessed 19 April 2019.

[56] Ample CJEU case law since *Google Spain* (n 2).

[57] '*Dans le secteur privé, "le service attendu de l'entreprise collectrice des données est à la fois la justification et la limite de l'usage des renseignements" concluait déjà le rapport Tricot*.' In: Yves Poullet and Thierry Léonard, 'Les libertés comme fondement de la protection des données nominatives' in François Rigaux, *La vie privée: une liberté parmi les autres?* (Larcier 1992) 244.

[58] Ferdinand Wollenschläger, 'Right to Property' in Steve Peers and others (eds), *The EU Charter of Fundamental Rights: A Commentary* (Hart 2014) 467–68 <https://www.bloomsburycollections.com/book/the-eu-charter-of-fundamental-rights-a-commentary/>.

suspected of IP infringement with rights holders.[59] Another type of conflict—that has not yet reached the CJEU—concerns ISS providers refusing to (fully) accommodate data subject access requests as this might implicate sharing trade secrets and proprietary software (protected by intellectual property).[60] Considerable as they are, these conflicts seem to be of limited relevance with regard to right to erasure induced *ex post* balancing. Indeed, the former relates to an *ex ante* measure, determining whether a certain processing operation—ie sharing personal data with IPR holders—*will be* fair and lawful.[61] The latter type of conflict does relate to *ex post* empowerment measures, but will only be triggered when some type of transparency is requested—whether through the right of access or the right to data portability—something which is not necessarily required to exercise the right to erasure per se.[62]

CJEU Case-Law—In order to determine how the fundamental right to (intellectual) property may (not) block the right to erasure, a brief synopsis of the relevant CJEU case law is warranted. In *L'Oreal* the Court explicitly stated that 'in order to ensure that there is a right to an effective remedy against persons who have used an online service to infringe intellectual property rights, the operator of an online marketplace may be ordered to take measures to make it easier to identify its customer-sellers'.[63] Four years later, the CJEU similarly ruled that in light of 'a fair balance' between fundamental rights to data protection and (intellectual) property, banks may—under certain conditions—be ordered to communicate client data as well.[64] Yet, in order to safeguard that 'fair balance' between Arts 8 and 17 Charter when disclosing personal data, 'there must be clear evidence of an infringement, the information disclosed must be regarded as facilitating the investigation, and the reasons for the measure must outweigh the nuisance or other harm which the measure may entail for the person affected by it or for some other conflicting interest'.[65] Indeed, both *Sabam* cases

[59] eg *Promusicae v Telefónica* [2008] Court of Justice of the European Union C-275/06; *Scarlet Extended v Sabam* (n 32); *SABAM v Netlog* (n 35).

[60] Gianclaudio Malgieri, 'Trade Secrets v Personal Data: A Possible Solution for Balancing Rights' (2016) 6 International Data Privacy Law 102.

[61] This may stem from an external legal obligation, such as in the context of copyright enforcement rules. See the (case law references in): Christina Angelopoulos, 'European Intermediary Liability in Copyright: A Tort-Based Analysis' (PhD Thesis, University of Amsterdam 2016) <http://dare.uva.nl/record/1/527223> accessed 1 June 2019 68–70.

[62] See in this regard also Recital 63 in the GDPR.

[63] The Court continued to say that 'although it is certainly necessary to respect the protection of personal data, the fact remains that when the infringer is operating in the course of trade and not in a private matter, that person must be clearly identifiable'. *L'Oreal v eBay* [2011] Court of Justice of the European Union C-324/09 [142].

[64] Specifically, the CJEU declared invalid national legal provisions that enable banking institutions to invoke banking secrecy 'in order to refuse to provide, pursuant to Article 8(1)(c) of [Directive 2004/48], information concerning the name and address of an account holder'. *Coty Germany v Stadtsparkasse Magdeburg* (n 7) para 43. For more background, see: Stéphanie De Smedt, 'Data Protection May Have to Yield in IP Infringement Cases (Case C-580/13, Coty Germany)' (2015) 1 European Data Protection Law Review 316.

[65] Orla Lynskey, *The Foundations of EU Data Protection Law* (OUP 2016) 157–58.

(*Scarlet*[66] and *Netlog*[67]) made clear that a general filtering system would not respect such a fair balance. In sum, the CJEU's case law regarding IP and data protection conflicts gives particular importance to fair balancing.[68] With that in mind, the only conclusions that can be drawn are that generalized, unconditional denials of either right are no-go's; the mere potentiality of an IPR breach will not be sufficient to impinge on the right to data protection; and each case needs to be evaluated on its own merits.

Intellectual Property v Right to Erasure—Zooming into the right to erasure (and thus *ex post* balancing) in particular, one may wonder now, how the right to intellectual property may be used as a counter-interest. For example, Article 17 Charter might be invoked against erasure requests that would effectively 'remove traces' of data subjects' IP infringements (eg asking internet access providers to erase IP-logs; asking a video-hosting or e-commerce platform to remove contact details). Unless there is an ongoing investigation—in which case Article 17(3)(e) would block an erasure request anyway already—it will not be possible for the right to (intellectual) property to block erasure requests in these situations. After all, this would effectively amount to a generalized retention obligation, which in itself has been ruled invalid in the CJEU's *Digital Rights Ireland* ruling.[69] Even in the context of IPR enforcement specifically,[70] all relevant CJEU case law suggests that the potentiality of an IP infringement will not be sufficient to breach the fundamental right to data protection.[71]

Right to Erasure v Trade Secrets—The right to (intellectual) property may also obstruct the right to erasure from being applied in a granular manner. In order to exercise the right to erasure/object granularly—ie only targeting specific (categories of) personal data—data subjects will generally need to gain access to all data, and how exactly it is processed, first. To the extent full compliance with such access requests may legitimately be blocked by the controller (eg in order to safeguard trade secrets and/or IP rights in the underlying processing software), data subjects may not have a true understanding of the width and depth of

66 *Scarlet Extended v Sabam* (n 32) para 53.

67 *SABAM v Netlog* (n 35) para 51.

68 See also: *Promusicae v Telefónica* (n 59) paras 65–70; *LSG Order* [2009] Court of Justice of the European Union C-557/07; Angelopoulos (n 61). Whereas in the former case, the CJEU ruled that Member States are *not required* to put down in law an obligation to communicate personal data for ensuring effective protection of intellectual property rights, in the latter it ruled that Member States are not precluded from doing so either. For more, see: Lynskey, *The Foundations of EU Data Protection Law* (n 65) 158 et seq.

69 *Digital Rights Ireland Ltd* (n 9).

70 Directive 2004/48 (Recitals 2 and 15 and Article 8(3)(e) http://eur-lex.europa.eu/legal-content/EN/TXT/?qid=1491559133132&uri=CELEX:32004L0048. For more, see: Smedt (n 64).

71 Indeed, 'systematic processing of personal data in the name of copyright enforcement is incompatible with the protection of EU fundamental rights'. Federico Ferretti, 'Data Protection and the Legitimate Interest of Data Controllers: Much Ado about Nothing or the Winter of Rights?' (2014) 51 Common Market Law Review 861. Also see the AG Opinions in *Bonnier Audio AB* [2012] Court of Justice of the European Union C-461/10 [58–60]; *Rīgas satiksme* [2017] Court of Justice of the European Union C-13/16 para 46; Lynskey, *The Foundations of EU Data Protection Law* (n 65) 159.

personal data being processed, making it impossible to exercise the right to erasure in an informed manner. As illustrated in Max Schrems' battle against Facebook (see Chapter 1), the 'trade secrets and IP rights argument' is effectively used by ISS providers to justify only partial compliance with access requests.[72] Yet, several authors have argued that whenever data subject rights conflict with trade secrecy, the former should prevail.[73] Recital 63 GDPR does acknowledge access rights should not adversely affect 'trade secrets or intellectual property and in particular the copyright protecting the software,' but also mentions that such arguments cannot be (ab)used to refuse access altogether. It has been proposed that data be 'decontextualized', so as to protect Article 17 Charter interests while still accommodating data subject rights. In conclusion, trade secrets and IP rights should not prevent data subjects from exercising their right to erasure in a granular manner. Informing them about the specific categories of personal data being processed will already go a long way in facilitating granular erasure.

Copyright in Personal Data—One of the most evident illustrations of a potential clash between Articles 8 and 17 Charter relates to copyrighted works. Invoking the right to erasure against a photographer, writer, or film-director for personal data in their works would effectively bring about an important conflict.[74] Moreover, such conflicts will generally also involve the freedom of expression and information (Art 11 Charter) and the right to respect for private life (Art 7 Charter). Importantly, cases where processing of personal data is copyright protected, will generally also be considered 'artistic and/or literary expression', therefore (partially) exempted from data protection law altogether (see Art 85 GDPR). It is also exactly this 'artistic' or 'creative' aspect, generally implying some type of narrative/message associated with the personal data, that will make other legal frameworks much more appropriate to tackle the respective conflict (eg defamation, libel, or personality rights). Within the confines of this particular book, this conflict will also be of lesser importance as ISS providers generally do not own the copyright over the content including personal data.

Integrity of Intellectual Property—Another interesting potential conflict that may arise between the right to erasure and Article 17(2) Charter, relates to the integrity of the ISS providers' IP protected processing ecosystem. The underlying models/software for achieving processing purposes such as dynamically evaluating or predicting consumer behaviour are increasingly complex.[75] Fully accommodating a right to erasure could compromise the integrity of this technical infrastructure. The burden for proving that this is the case will be on the controller,

[72] Malgieri (n 60) 103.

[73] Caroline Colin and Yves Poullet, 'Du Consommateur et de Sa Protection Face à de Nouvelles Applications Des Technologies de l'information: Risques et Opportunités' (2010) 2010/3 DCCR 94, 117; Malgieri (n 60) 103.

[74] For an overview of case law in the US, UK, France, Germany, and Italy, see: Malgieri (n 60) 114.

[75] ibid 113–14.

who will still be subject to other data protection provisions such as data minimization, data protection by design/default and the accountability principle. In sum, even though the right to erasure may not be fully accommodated, the controller will have to demonstrate a genuine best effort in doing so. As mentioned before, designing one's data processing infrastructure in such a way that accommodating data subject rights is impracticable is not an argument to ignore them.

DATA OWNERSHIP—The right to erasure may also prompt a conflict between the fundamental right to data protection and the fundamental right to property itself (Art 17(1)). This is brought to the front by the '(personal) data ownership' debate. One that has been ongoing for two decades already.[76] If one takes the view that personal data can indeed be owned, this may effectively prevent a data subject from having it erased when that data is owned by someone else. Yet, based on the normative underpinnings of the fundamental right to data protection (see Chapter 2), it is this author's opinion that personal data cannot be 'owned', not even by data subjects themselves. It would also go entirely against the very rationale of the right to erasure that 'legal ownership' may simply block it.[77] Having said that, ownership may still be possible indirectly. For example, (personal) data can represent a financial value which in turn can be owned and traded.[78] Also, the database in which personal data resides may itself be protected by the *sui generis* database right. It does not seem clear, however, how such *sui generis* right could block a right to erasure (though it might conceivably be invoked to counterargue the right of access (Art 15) or the right to data portability (Art 20)). The same can be said for the physical medium on which the ISS provider stores the personal data.

DESTRUCTION (OR OTHER KINDS OF PHYSICAL VIOLATIONS) OF PHYSICAL PROPERTY—A final potential conflict that the right to erasure may provoke relates to the protection of physical property. Indeed, from a technical/practical perspective, *erasing* data from a storage device is not a sinecure.[79] Physically destroying the device is generally said to be (one of) the only method(s) guaranteeing actual

[76] Pamela Samuelson, 'Privacy As Intellectual Property?' (2000) 52 Stanford Law Review 1125; Lawrence Lessig, *Code: And Other Laws of Cyberspace* (Basic Books 1999); Paul M Schwartz, 'Property, Privacy, and Personal Data' (2004) 117 Harvard Law Review 2056; Nadezhda Purtova, *Property Rights in Personal Data: A European Perspective*, vol 24 (Kluwer Law International 2012) 44; Nadezhda Purtova, 'The Illusion of Personal Data as No One's Property' (2015) 7 Law, Innovation and Technology 83.

[77] Indeed, according legal ownership over personal data may reduce effective protection as it would render that data a tradable commodity. See similarly: European Data Protection Supervisor, 'Opinion on the Proposal for a Directive on Certain Aspects Concerning Contracts for the Supply of Digital Content' (n 46) 3.

[78] For a discussion and overview of CJEU case law regarding the ownership of 'immaterial positions' such as economic value, company shares, and so on, see: Wollenschläger (n 58) 472. This is a complex issue with many different legal implications that will not be tackled here. See, for example, the work from scholars such as Martha Poon, Inge Graef, and Ariel Ezrachi.

[79] Druschel, Backes, and Tirtea (n 26); Information Commissioner's Office (ICO), 'Deleting Your Data from Computers, Laptops and Other Devices' <https://ico.org.uk/for-the-public/online/deleting-your-data/> accessed 1 June 2019.

erasure. It goes without saying that such an approach is unworkable in the context of ISS providers where all (personal) data is stored in large server farms across the world. Requiring physical destruction in these situations would undoubtedly be disproportionate in light of Article 17 Charter.[80] Where that leaves the meaning of 'erasure' in practical terms is unclear. Indeed, the current status quo is that data subjects simply have to trust controllers that data is effectively 'erased' (for more on the operationalization of the right to erasure, see Part III).

CONCLUSION—In conclusion, the right to (intellectual) property may exceptionally tip the (re-)balancing act as triggered by the right to erasure, against the data subject. The IP rights over the processing infrastructure could justify access restrictions which in turn might prevent effective and/or granular erasure. The same rights might also thwart erasure when (full) compliance would affect their integrity. When accommodating the right to erasure would affect someone's physical property, the balance may also tip in favour of the controller. Personal data (processing) incorporated in some form of artistic expression—covered by copyright—will generally be more adequately addressed through other legal avenues and likely be exempted from data subject rights anyway (see Arts 23 and 85). Having said all that, the right to (intellectual) property cannot be used to justify blanket, generalized refusals to accommodate all erasure requests (regardless of the facts and/or granularity). The impact on Article 17 Charter will have to be actual (ie not potential) and substantial. In light of the accountability (Arts 5(2) and 24) and data protection by design and by default principles (Art 25), data processing infrastructure that is not (sufficiently) designed with data subject rights compliance in mind, will not be able to rely on the arguments derived from Article 17 charter to fend off erasure requests.

2.1.4 Interim Conclusion

Overall, it seems rather hard for commercial interests alone to trump data subjects' interests, rights, or freedoms in *ex post* balancing. Even if they can fairly easily render lawful processing operations *ex ante* on a generalized basis, their weight in particularized *ex post* situations will be significantly lower. This also appears from the general drafting of the GDPR, which took a rigorous 'fundamental human rights' approach, implying that 'data protection automatically trumped other interests and could not be traded-off for economic benefits'.[81] Indeed, even if the GDPR still incorporates internal market objectives, these have certainly moved to the

[80] Wollenschläger (n 58) 485–86.

[81] Ferretti (n 71) 852. Referring to: *Österreichischer Rundfunk and others* (n 3). Case C-465/00, *Rechnungshof v Österreichischer Rundfunk and others* [2002] ECR I-4989. See also Heisenberg, *Negotiating Privacy* (Lynne Rienner 2005), Chs 1, 2, 3; Mayer-Schonberger 'Generational Development of Data Protection in Europe' in Agre and Rotenberg (eds), *Technology and Privacy: The New Landscape* (MIT Press 1997) 219–41; Simitis 'From the Market to the Polis: The EU Directive on the Protection of Personal Data' 80 Iowa Law Review (1995), 445–69.

background when compared to Directive 95/46. The new legislative basis for the GDPR in Article 16 TFEU implies a stronger focus on the protection of fundamental rights and freedoms, and in particular the right to data protection.[82]

The only situations where commercial interests (alone) may effectively block a right to erasure/object, will be when accommodating these rights would affect the *essence* of a fundamental right in the Charter[83] or at the very least not be proportionate *stricto sensu*. The two most relevant fundamental rights in the present context are the freedom to conduct a business (Art 16 Charter) and the right to (intellectual) property (Art 17 Charter). Both of these have repeatedly been declared not to be absolute rights, to be considered in relation to their social function.[84] All evidence suggests that, as a general rule, they are not self-sufficient to override individual freedoms in the Charter[85] such as the rights to privacy (Art 7), data protection (Art 8), or freedom of expression (Art 11).[86] Indeed, pursuant to Article 52(3)—which aligns Charter provisions with those in the ECHR—it would be difficult to claim economic objectives alone can constrain fundamental rights/freedoms representing essential values in a democratic society.[87] Only when, in light of Article 52(1), a specific legal provision ordains processing for commercial purposes and/or raises obstacles to invoke certain data subject rights, does it seem realistic that a controller can legitimately *not* accommodate the right to object/erase purely on the basis of commercial interests.[88] In conclusion, the freedoms granted to economic operators by Articles 16–17 Charter cannot legitimize undermining other fundamental rights or freedoms.

[82] See Damian Clifford, Inge Graef, and Peggy Valcke, 'Pre-Formulated Declarations of Data Subject Consent—Citizen-Consumer Empowerment and the Alignment of Data, Consumer and Competition Law Protections' (KU Leuven 2018) CiTiP Working Paper 33/2017 33<https://papers.ssrn.com/abstract=3126706> accessed 18 April 2018.

[83] And this would not entail undermining the essence of any other fundamental rights/freedoms.

[84] See, for example, the following cases, and the many references included within: *Land Rheinland-Pfalz* (n 21) para 54; *Herbert Schaible v Land Baden Wurttemberg* [2013] Court of Justice of the European Union C-101/12 [28]; *Sky Österreich* (n 16) para 45.

[85] See similarly: Peter Oliver, 'The Protection of Privacy in the Economic Sphere before the European Court of Justice' (2009) 46 Common Market Law Review 1443, 1481.

[86] Gutwirth, 'De Toepassing van Het Finaliteitsbeginsel van de Privacywet' (n 13) 1431. Hijmans calls the rights in Arts 16–17 Charter 'peripheral rights' that are always overridden by data protection rights. Hielke Hijmans, 'The European Union as a Constitutional Guardian of Internet Privacy and Data Protection' (PhD Thesis, University of Amsterdam 2016) 196, 216–17, 258<http://dare.uva.nl/document/2/169421> accessed 1 June 2019.

[87] Gutwirth, 'De Toepassing van Het Finaliteitsbeginsel van de Privacywet' (n 13) 1430–31; Orla Lynskey, 'Regulating "Platform Power"' (LSE 2017) Working Paper 1/2017 25–26<https://papers.ssrn.com/abstract=2921021> accessed 1 June 2019; Hijmans, 'The European Union as a Constitutional Guardian of Internet Privacy and Data Protection' (n 86) 258. Hijmans refers to Craig and De Búrca who explain that permitting economic objectives to limit the scope of fundamental rights, would go against ECHR jurisprudence. See: Paul P Craig and Gráinne De Búrca, *EU Law: Text, Cases, and Materials* (OUP 2011) n 221.

[88] This can be the case, for example, when the controller can invoke a legal obligation to process the personal data as a lawful ground (Art 6(1)(c) and/or as an exemption to the right to erasure (Art 17(3)(b)). Regardless, further processing in this context will be constrained to what the legal obligation requires only (again reiterating the importance of the need for a granular approach).

2.2 Information Freedoms

> You can delete your account any time. When you delete your account, we delete things you have posted, such as your photos and status updates. […] Keep in mind that information that others have shared about you is not part of your account and will not be deleted when you delete your account.[89]

IMPORTANCE OF INFORMATION FREEDOMS—Freedom of expression and information is of critical importance to personal development as well as the broader fabric of any democratic society.[90] As explained by the ECtHR:

> Freedom of expression constitutes one of the essential foundations of [a democratic society], one of the basic conditions for its progress and for the development of every man. Subject to paragraph 2 of Article 10 [of the ECHR], it is applicable not only to 'information' or 'ideas' that are favourably received or regarded as inoffensive or as a matter of indifference, but also to those that offend, shock or disturb; such are the demands of that pluralism, tolerance and broadmindedness without which there is no 'democratic society'.[91]

Information communication technology, the Internet in particular, has had an unprecedented impact on this fundamental freedom.[92] Whereas initially this impact was seen as largely positive (ie connecting the world), a more sobering image now appears with 'fake news', 'filter bubbles', and corporate information control.

CRITICAL CONFLICT—One of the most decried conflicts that the right to erasure/object may bring about in the ISS context involves information freedoms (the clearest manifestation of which is the fundamental right to freedom of expression and information in Art 11 Charter and Art 10 ECHR).[93] Indeed, erasing (personal) data that has some level of publicity, will necessarily affect (even if minimally) the rights of those who conveyed it as well as those who may want to access it. The conflict can occur at different levels. The emergence of 'Web 2.0',[94] has given rise to the exponential increase of individuals posting (personal) data on the internet, from the trivial and vile to the significant and benign. Even though these

[89] <https://www.facebook.com/full_data_use_policy> accessed April 2017.

[90] Lorna Woods, 'Freedom of Expression and Information' in Steve Peers and others (eds), *The EU Charter of Fundamental Rights: A Commentary* (Hart 2014) 320<https://www.bloomsburycollections.com/book/the-eu-charter-of-fundamental-rights-a-commentary/>.

[91] *Connolly v Commission* (n 3) para 39; *Satakunnan Markkinapörssi Oy et Satamedia Oy v Finland* [2017] European Court of Human Rights 931/13 para 78. And the case-law references within.

[92] See generally: La Rue (n 473); Wolfgang Benedek and Matthias C Kettemann, *Freedom of Expression and the Internet* (Council of Europe 2013).

[93] One can also think of the right of access to documents under Article 42 Charter.

[94] Or, as Tim Berners-Lee calls it: the 'read-write web'. John Naughton, *From Gutenberg to Zuckerberg: What You Really Need to Know about the Internet* (Quercus 2012) 228 et seq.

'individual publications' raise critical questions in light of data protection law,[95] they are not the focus area of this section or book, which instead focuses on a different dynamic, ie that between data subjects and (large) ISS providers.

Third Party Interest—When looking at from the perspective of ISS providers—and data subjects' right to erasure vis-á-vis these actors—the fundamental right to freedom of expression/information will predominantly relate to third parties. The individual publishers and potential audience are in effect 'third parties' to the relationship of rights and obligations between data subjects and ISS providers in their capacity as controller.[96] This second balancing scenario will look exactly at this curious situation where third parties' interests are of critical importance in finding a balance following erasure requests directed at ISS providers directly. In other words, how do these 'third-party interests' enter the relationship between data subject and controller (ISS provider) against the backdrop of *ex ante / ex post* balancing in the GDPR?

Right to Privacy—One final observation relates to the fact that balancing exercises involving information freedoms, will generally also involve data subjects' right to respect for private and family life, ie their right to privacy (Art 7 Charter and Art 8 ECHR).[97] This illustrates once again how Article 6(1)(f) effectively constitutes a proxy through which the GDPR incorporates the balancing of many fundamental rights in the context of personal data processing. While this section may lay bare some systematic issues in this regard, it is not aimed at providing a detailed analysis of the privacy versus freedom of expression debate. This is, after all, an age-old debate—albeit amplified by ICTs—that cannot be resolved in any comprehensive a priori manner (given legal, normative, cultural disparity).[98] Neither will this section devise a comprehensive/exhaustive hierarchy or taxonomy of criteria to do the balancing. Doing so risks reducing balancing acts to an algorithmic logic, assuming that simply looking at a set number of predefined parameters determines the outcome in all cases. That said, it cannot be denied of course that many

[95] Notably in light of the applicability of the household exemption and/or freedom of expression or 'special purposes' derogation. See notably: David Erdos, 'Beyond "Having a Domestic"? Regulatory Interpretation of European Data Protection Law and Individual Publication' Computer Law & Security Review <http://www.sciencedirect.com/science/article/pii/S0267364917300730> accessed 1 June 2019. Hijmans, 'The European Union as a Constitutional Guardian of Internet Privacy and Data Protection' (n 86) 204.

[96] This is not to say there are no rights and obligations in the relationship between data subjects and 'individual publishers' directly (see Chapter 3).

[97] Reminiscent of data protection's roots in the general right to privacy, and the CJEU's phrasing of the hybrid 'right to respect for private life with regard to the processing of personal data' (see Chapter 2). Even in its seminal *Google Spain* Case, the CJEU connected the 'right to be forgotten' to the 'right to privacy'. There are of course also situations where the right to privacy may not be engaged (eg when there is no expectation of privacy because the data are published in an official bulletin for example).

[98] Some have tried to come up with general frameworks for when one prevails over the other. Others criticize the idea of balancing altogether. See (the many references in): Bart van der Sloot, 'Do Privacy and Data Protection Rules Apply to Legal Persons and Should They? A Proposal for a Two-Tiered System' (2015) 31 Computer Law & Security Review 26, 27–28.

important factors and criteria *do* exist and frequently recur in case law.[99] Yet, what I want to stress here is that there is no a priori overarching structure, hierarchy, or selection procedure to these factors and criteria.[100] With these caveats in mind, this section modestly aims only to (a) illustrate the inherent context/facts-based nature of these conflicts;[101] (b) identify some broad stroke (categories of) criteria in case law; and (c) pinpoint issues ensuing from outsourcing the balancing exercise to private entities.

2.2.1 Relevance with Regard to the Right to Erasure

Exemptions and Derogations—Why, one may wonder, is it necessary to look at balances involving information freedoms in the context of the right to erasure under the GDPR? After all, as explained in Chapter 5, Article 17(3)(a) explicitly excludes the right to erasure from situations where the processing is necessary to exercise the right of freedom of expression and information. This broad and bold phrasing suggests a wide interpretation, exempting by default all situations involving freedom of expression and/or information. With this exemption, the legislator evidently wanted to appease critics, clearly signalling that the right to erasure cannot overstep information freedoms. On top of that, the GDPR requires (Art 85) and enables (Art 23(1)(i) derogations in light of information freedoms at the Member-State level, further eroding the (applicability of the) right to erasure and object in practice.

Right To Erasure Through the Backdoor—Having said that, it would be naïve to assume no conflict or balancing exercises exist in this context. Indeed, even when taking the view that Article 17(1) itself can never be invoked whenever the rights to freedom of expression and/or information are involved, data subjects may still achieve the same result via another route. As was made evident in Chapters 4 and 5, any of the right to erasure triggers ex-/implicitly refer to other provisions in the GDPR. Instead of relying on Article 17(1) directly, data subjects can still fall back on those original provisions (eg purpose expiration, withdrawal of consent, or right to object). When any of these apply, it will not be legal for controllers

[99] See for example (the references in): *Buivids* [2019] Court of Justice of the European Union C-345/17 paras 63–68.

[100] Trying to create some structure to factors and criteria does of course have some value in order to facilitate the balancing. Rather than doing so in the abstract (ie for *all* conflicts between privacy and freedom of expression for example), there might be more value in doing so for specific contexts. In earlier, co-authored work, I have done so for balancing acts in the delisting context in particular: Aleksandra Kuczerawy and Jef Ausloos, 'NoC Online Intermediaries Case Studies Series: European Union and Google Spain' (2015) <http://ssrn.com/abstract=2567183> accessed 1 June 2019 Annex.

[101] A clear illustration can already be found in the growing number of post-*Google Spain* delisting cases. See: Geert Van Calster and others, 'Not Just One, but Many "Rights to Be Forgotten". A Global Status Quo' (Foundation for European Progressive Studies 2016) <https://lirias.kuleuven.be/handle/123456789/559109> accessed 1 June 2019; Miquel Peguera, 'In the Aftermath of Google Spain: How the "Right to Be Forgotten" Is Being Shaped in Spain by Courts and the Data Protection Authority' (2015) 23 International Journal of Law and Information Technology 325.

to continue processing the personal data (unless they can rely on another lawful ground), effectively resulting in an obligation to erase the personal data nonetheless. So, even though personal data is processed in the context of exercising the right to freedom of expression and/or information—and the exemption in Art 17(3)(a) applies—a 'backdoor-right-to-erasure' still remains available to data subjects. Having said all that, it should of course be remembered that pursuant to Arts 23(1)(i) and 85, Member States can install *external* balancing provisions (either *ex ante* or *ex post*) that interfere with any or all of the right-to-erasure triggers.

2.2.2 Freedom of Expression, from Derogation to Balancing Factor

Freedom of Expression Throughout the GDPR—The GDPR is the only legal document at EU level that governs the interaction between Articles 8 and 11 in the Charter.[102] Freedom of expression features explicitly and implicitly throughout the GDPR. As discussed in previous chapters, it constitutes a potential derogation/restriction to the framework overall (Arts 23(1)(i) and 85) and an exemption to the right to erasure in particular (Art 17(3)(a)). Freedom of expression is also relevant in balancing provisions such as the 'legitimate interests' lawful ground (Art 6(1)(f)) and the right to object (Art 21). All these provisions require freedom of expression to be considered in determining the extent of data protection obligations and/or rights.[103]

Three Layers of Freedom of Expression Safeguards—A systematic approach in individual cases requires first to look at whether derogations under the national implementation of Article 85 (and Art 23(1)(i) if present) apply. These constitute external balancing acts that the legislator either pre-defines or provides the parameters for. If not, the next step will be to see if the exemption in Article 17(3)(a) applies (phrased more broadly). If this exemption does not apply either, but erasure of personal data might still affect information freedoms, Article 6(1)(f) constitutes the final safeguard in the GDPR, ensuring freedom of expression/information is not unduly affected. In theory, it is also possible to challenge any part of this process for not adequately safeguarding the fundamental right to freedom of expression and information, in light of permissible limitations (see Article 52 Charter). Importantly, even when the answer to either of the first two steps is affirmative, this does not absolve the processing operation from any balancing in light of information freedoms. Looking at the current implementations of Article 85's predecessor (Art 9 Directive 95/46), most Member States still require a lawful ground and even more still require compliance with the fairness principle (both of which constitute de facto balancing acts).[104]

102 Lynskey, *The Foundations of EU Data Protection Law* (n 65) 144.

103 Put differently, they operationalize Article 52(1) Charter.

104 David Erdos, 'European Union Data Protection Law and Media Expression: Fundamentally Off Balance' (2016) 65 International and Comparative Law Quarterly. Especially see Annex 1.

Three seminal CJEU cases illustrate these different layers of freedom of expression and information safeguards. In *Lindqvist*,[105] and *Satamedia*,[106] the controllers relied on freedom of expression derogations, which led the Court to delegate the actual fair balancing to the Member States (in light of their national law). In *Google Spain*,[107] on the other hand, the controller did not invoke the derogation (at least not with regard to its own processing activities) and the balancing therefore occurred at a different layer, ie internally through the legitimate interests ground, right to object, and to erasure.

Delegating Balancing—If the controller still needs to comply with Arts 5–6 GDPR (requiring de facto fair balancing) anyway, what is the added value of still having these exemptions and derogations? The main added value is that in those instances, the legislator pre-determined a presumption/default against the right to erasure/object (in favour of processing). Balancing under Article 6(1)(f) (and Art 21) is more open-ended[108] and does not pre-define a default pro/contra information freedoms. The net result, one might say, is that in these last situations—ie internal balancing via Articles 6(1)(f) and 21 GDPR—the burden of balancing is entirely passed onto the controller (albeit within the confines of the GDPR and subject to oversight by courts and data protection authorities). This also appears from CJEU case law, which delegated conflicts involving derogations to the Member States[109] and conflicts emanating from Article 6(1)(f) to the controller itself.[110] In conclusion, evaluating the role of information freedoms in Article 6(1)(f) following an erasure request is not concerned about the definition and scope of the exemptions and derogations (and the many issues associated with it),[111] but rather with their merits/weight in themselves.

2.2.3 Freedom to Impart Information

Scope—Article 11 Charter establishes everyone has a right to freedom of expression, which includes the freedom to hold opinions, impart information and ideas without interference and regardless of frontiers.[112] Pursuant to Article 52(3) Charter, the meaning and scope of the right to freedom of expression can be equated to Article 10 ECHR (and the rich body of case law that comes with it).[113]

[105] *Lindqvist* [2003] Court of Justice of the European Union C-101/01 [83].

[106] *Tietosuojavaltuutettu v Satakunnan Markkinapörssi & Satamedia* [2008] Court of Justice of the European Union C-73/07.

[107] *Google Spain* (n 2).

[108] Allowing for more information freedoms than just 'freedom of expression and information' (or even 'journalistic, academic, artistic and literary' expression) but also for example the right of access to documents (Art 42 Charter).

[109] Notably: *Lindqvist* (n 105); *Satamedia* (n 106). See also: Ferretti (n 71) 860; Lynskey, *The Foundations of EU Data Protection Law* (n 65) 144–45.

[110] *Google Spain* (n 2).

[111] Erdos, 'From the Scylla of Restriction to the Charybdis of Licence?' (n 25).

[112] See inter alia: *Connolly v Commission* (n 3) paras 39–40.

[113] Woods, 'Freedom of Expression and Information' (n 90) para 11.23.

As explained in previous chapters, the right protects any kind of expression and even extends to the medium used for exercising the right.[114] The right to freedom of expression constitutes first and foremost a negative obligation on the state, ie a 'duty to abstain', to 'not interfere'. Having said that, Article 11 Charter and 10 ECHR may also give rise to *positive* obligations, ie 'ensuring an effective enjoyment of the right'.[115] The distinction is relevant because it may affect the involvement required by public bodies to ensure freedom of expression is safeguarded (not unduly interfered with), for example in the context of the right to erasure/object.

Indirect Horizontal Effect—Positive obligations may play a more or less important role in horizontal relationships between private actors (eg data subject v controller and third parties).[116] Importantly however, the fundamental right to freedom of expression cannot be invoked against private actors directly.[117] The right to freedom of expression does have *indirect* horizontal effect, meaning inter alia that it informs the reading and application of laws governing private relations such as the GDPR for example.[118] So, even if the right may be actionable with regard to 'injunctions and bans, blocking and filtering as well as take-down notices, [...] [l]icensing and ownership requirements [...] distributed denial-of-service attacks, advertising rules limiting the products that may be advertised',[119] the entity liable would still be the State (through proxy of a judge or the legislator).[120] In other words, it is not possible to directly request a private entity to safeguard one's rights under Article 11 Charter (10 ECHR). Only to the extent it has trickled down into secondary legislation can freedom of expression play a more or less important role in horizontal relationships.[121] For the purposes here, what all of this essentially means is that the only way to still incorporate this fundamental right into internal GDPR balancing between private entities, is as an 'interest'.[122] Rights holders may still challenge the (lack of adequate) protection offered by public bodies.

[114] ibid para 11.25; *Neij and Sunde Kolmisoppi v Sweden (Pirate Bay Case)* [2013] European Court of Human Rights 40397/12.

[115] It should be said that this is still quite a vague and debated area, where neither courts nor scholars have been able to delineate the exact meaning or scope of positive obligations under Article 11 Charter and 10 ECHR. For more see: AR Mowbray, *The Development of Positive Obligations under the European Convention on Human Rights by the European Court of Human Rights* (Hart 2004); Woods, 'Freedom of Expression and Information' (n 90); Kuczerawy (n 1490).

[116] *Özgür Gündem v Turkey* [2000] European Court of Human Rights 23144/93 [43] and the cases referred to within; Woods, 'Freedom of Expression and Information' (n 90); Kuczerawy (n 1490).

[117] This point should slightly be nuanced in light of so-called *Drittwirkung* and the ECtHR's recognition of some level of horizontal applicability of human rights (eg ECtHR, *Fuentes Bobo v Spain*, 29.02.2000). For more, see Joris Van Hoboken, (n 10).

[118] *UPC Telekabel* (n 31) para 55; Van Hoboken, *Search Engine Freedom* (n 117) 70; Takis Tridimas, *The General Principles of EU Law* (New Edition, 3rd edn, OUP 2018) 390.

[119] Woods, 'Freedom of Expression and Information' (n 90) para 11.33.

[120] Being the actor failed to safeguard the right to freedom of expression in the face of these issues.

[121] Importantly, however, the CJEU did specify in its *Telekabel* Ruling that private entities may need to 'ensure compliance with the fundamental right of internet users to freedom of information' when implementing measures to comply with an injunction. *UPC Telekabel* (n 31) para 55.

[122] This might also explain why the CJEU did not refer to Article 11 directly in its *Google Spain* Ruling, even though it did recognize information freedoms as an important interest.

WHO: INFORMATION PROVIDERS—In light of its broad scope,[123] freedom of expression may cover different entities in the specific context of erasure requests vis-à-vis ISS providers. Most importantly, it covers the activity of whomever originally conveyed the contested personal data (eg blogger, social network user, journalist). This person's right also includes protection from interference with the medium used to convey that data, ie the ISS. The 'speaker' does not need to have deliberately picked a specific medium, in order to be protected from interference. For example, even though a blogger did not take initiative for certain content to be included in a search engine's index, a portal or social networking site, removal of said content from those services may still interfere with the blogger's freedom of expression. This example also hints at another consideration, which can be summarized as 'the chain of expression'. With the rise of 'Web 2.0', sharing, re-publication, and mashups have become ubiquitous. This means that the same content (including personal data) can be 'expressed' by many different persons. A re-tweet of a re-tweet of a re-tweet of a newspaper article arguably comprises the freedom of expression of everyone involved (albeit in different degrees), from the last re-tweeter to the author of the article.

WHO: ISS PROVIDERS—ISS providers themselves may also benefit from the right to freedom of expression. Indeed, as explained by Van Hoboken, Article 10 ECHR (and thus Art 11 Charter) covers search engines' result-pages as well as the process of crawling making those results possible in the first place.[124] *Mutadis mutandis*, the same can be said of other ISS providers performing similar activities, of which there seem to be many. The selection, ranking, and presentation of information by ISS providers—be it in the context of a video hosting platform, a social network or a search engine—is to be considered an editorial process, benefitting from protection under the right to freedom of expression, but also entailing duties and responsibilities.[125] Their right to freedom of expression can legitimately be interfered with in light of Article 52(1) Charter (and Art 10(2) ECHR). To the extent the GDPR constitutes such an interference, it also appears to comply with the requirements in those provisions.[126] According to Van Hoboken, the less an ISS provider considers 'professional standards with regard to quality and mode of communication', the less strong its right to freedom of expression is.[127]

[123] Woods, 'Freedom of Expression and Information' (n 90) para 11.33.

[124] In other words, the information provider's freedom of expression primarily covers the content, whereas the ISS provider's freedom of expression generally covers presentation (which is not to say the nature of the content may not influence the latter). Van Hoboken, *Search Engine Freedom* (n 117) 197.

[125] ibid 228.

[126] ie provided by law, respect the essence of the right to freedom of expression, proportional and necessary (see Art 52(1) Charter). These requirements clearly trace those in the ECHR (Art 10(2)): 'prescribed by law', 'legitimate aim', and 'necessary in a democratic society'.

[127] Factors such as 'reliability' and 'professional context' are drawn from ECtHR case law (eg *Open Door v Ireland*, HUDOC (European Court of Human Rights 1992)). Van Hoboken, *Search Engine Freedom* (n 117) 209; 229.

Information Provider v ISS Provider—Separating the freedom of expression of ISS providers (eg in ranking and presenting information) from that of the information providers brings to the surface an important issue. Information providers' right to freedom of expression with regard to their content being processed by ISS providers can at most be qualified as 'negative', ie they should be protected from undue interference. No 'positive' right to freedom of expression—ie to have their content included, presented, or ranked in a certain way by the ISS provider—exists. Indeed, such a claim would bring about a direct conflict between the information provider and the ISS provider's freedom of expression rights. It is not entirely unimaginable, however, that in light of their ever-expanding power—constituting the de facto modes of information dissemination and retrieval—certain ISS providers may have to consider the freedom of expression rights of information providers more proactively.[128] This constitutes a difficult balancing act between two fundamental rights to freedom of expression (not to mention other rights, freedoms, and interests involved) that reaches beyond the scope of this book.[129]

What Freedom of Expression to Consider—In sum, when confronted with right to erasure requests involving personal data created, shared, or otherwise made accessible by others, ISS providers will have to consider the freedom of expression interests of the information providers (including, for example, re-publication and mashups) as well as their own. The responsibility to do so only extends to what the GDPR (and Member State implementations) requires. Oversight by public bodies (notably DPAs, courts, and the legislator) should ensure the right to freedom of expression is not unduly interfered with in light of the Charter/ECHR.

Criteria—In the search for criteria to assess the balance, it is worth reiterating there is no 'harm-requirement'. The data subject does not need to be inconvenienced by the publication in any way, nor does the communicated data have to be of a 'sensitive character'.[130] The type of expression will play an important role in

[128] Particularly in light of the stranglehold some ISS providers have on traditional news and journalism outlets. See, in this regard: Emily Bell, 'Who Owns the News Consumer: Social Media Platforms or Publishers?' (Tow Center 2016) <https://www.cjr.org/tow_center/platforms_and_publishers_new_research_from_the_tow_center.php> accessed 1 June 2019.

[129] For some expansion, see: Van Hoboken, *Search Engine Freedom* (n 117) ch 8. Talking specifically about search engines, Van Hoboken explains on page 350 that 'it is impossible to argue that all information providers could have a legal claim to be in a dominant general purpose search engine index, or to receive favourable treatment by selection and ranking algorithms. […] The best possible outcome from the perspective of information providers is that they would have a claim to be treated fairly and that interferences by dominant search engines providers to effectively reach an online audience would need to be reasonable and justified.' Several years later now, and looking further ahead, one may contemplate how this claim to be 'treated fairly' should be interpreted and if it may require some 'right to be included' and/or other interferences with search engines' freedom to select, rank, and present. See also: Aleksandra Kuczerawy, 'Private Enforcement of Public Policy: Freedom of Expression in the Era of Online Gatekeeping' (PhD Thesis, KU Leuven—Faculty of Law 2018) <http://limo.libis.be>.

[130] *Österreichischer Rundfunk and others* (n 3) para 75.

considering the level of protection or interference permitted.[131] Even though any attempt at elaborating a comprehensive taxonomy of expression would be entirely in vain in the abstract, a rich body of case law did acknowledge some differences (in value) between certain specific types of expression (eg political speech, artistic speech, and commercial speech, the latter typically attracting a lower level of protection).[132] According to Lynskey, the CJEU seems to implicitly assume only expression in the 'public interest' benefits protection when the rights to privacy and data protection are at stake.[133] Following ECtHR case law, such expression is still to be interpreted broadly and extends beyond 'political speech' only for example.[134] Apart from the content itself, other factors will play a role in determining the weight of freedom of expression in the balancing act as well.[135] For example, the availability or absence of alternatives[136] may be important in the ISS context. Reliability and professional context in which the information is provided[137] may also result in more weight given to freedom of expression interests (eg in the context of niche ISS providers).

GDPR As a Safeguard Against Information Power—The right to erasure/object evidently may impact information providers' freedom of expression. But, it is important to nuance this impact when expression occurs in an ISS context. As made clear before, ISS providers are entirely free—ie have no positive obligations—to in-/exclude information as they see fit. Offering no guarantees for freedom of expression,[138] these platforms could even be considered as censors by

[131] See for a list of important factors in this regard: Kuczerawy and Ausloos (n 100) Annex 1. One example of a particularly impactful factor as repeatedly specified by the ECtHR relates to the format of the respective information (audio-visual, textual, etc). See (the many case law references in): *Mosley v United Kingdom* [2011] European Court of Human Rights 48009/08 [114 et seq].

[132] See notably the references in: Woods, 'Freedom of Expression and Information' (n 90) paras 11.28; 11.59; Brendan Van Alsenoy, Aleksandra Kuczerawy, and Jef Ausloos, 'Search Engines after "Google Spain": Internet@Liberty or Privacy@Peril?' (2013) 47<http://papers.ssrn.com/abstract=2321494> accessed 1 June 2019; Monica Macovei, 'Freedom of Expression: A Guide to the Implementation of Article 10 of the European Convention on Human Rights' [2004] Human Rights Handbooks 7 <http://www.supremecourt.ge/files/upload-file/pdf/article10eng.pdf> accessed 1 June 2019. ibid 7. Also see: Paolo Lobba, 'Holocaust Denial before the European Court of Human Rights: Evolution of an Exceptional Regime' (2015) 26 European Journal of International Law 237.

[133] Lynskey, *The Foundations of EU Data Protection Law* (n 65) 150. See also on the notion of public interest in ECtHR case law: *Satakunnan Markkinapörssi Oy et Satamedia Oy v Finland* (n 91) para 167 et seq.

[134] *Axel Springer SE and RTL Television GmbH v Germany* [2017] European Court of Human Rights 51405/12 [90]; *Von Hannover v Germany (No2)* [2012] European Court of Human Rights 40660/08 and 60641/08 [109]; Rebecca Moosavian, 'Deconstructing "Public Interest" in the Article 8 vs Article 10 Balancing Exercise' (2014) 6 Journal of Media Law 234, 245.

[135] In a 2017 ruling, the ECtHR summarized the key criteria for determining the necessity requirement in balancing acts between privacy and freedom of expression. See: *Satakunnan Markkinapörssi Oy et Satamedia Oy v Finland* (n 91) para 165 et seq.

[136] Acknowledged in: *Appleby and others v the United Kingdom* [2003] European Court of Human Rights 44306/98 [49]. See also: Woods, 'Freedom of Expression and Information' (n 90) para 11.32. Referring to *Neij and Sunde Kolmisoppi v Sweden (Pirate Bay Case)* (n 114).

[137] *Open Door v Ireland* (n 127) paras 71–77 and Concurring Opinion of Judge Morenilla; Van Hoboken, *Search Engine Freedom* (n 117) 209; *Case of Magyar Tartalomszolgtatk Egyeslete and Index.hu ZRT v Hungary* (n 242) para 77.

[138] See, for example: Venturini and others (n 44) 96.

nature.[139] Their information management practices (pre-selecting and ranking) are of course the exact reason they are so heavily relied upon. People similarly rely for example on newspapers, medical practitioners, and lawyers, to select and suggest relevant information or advice. One of the key distinguishing factors with powerful ISS providers however, is the scale at which they operate as well as their ubiquity and how they constitute central nodes where many communication channels converge. They increasingly constitute the de facto first step in information sharing and access, merging a previously much more dispersed landscape of media and information channels. Considering this trend, it becomes gradually more desirable to install certain 'information safeguards' which are grounded in norms, fundamental rights, and societal interests in general, rather than terms of service designed in light of ISS providers' private interests. The GDPR constitutes one such legal safeguard, protecting both freedom of expression, privacy, and data protection in the face of quasi-monopolistic information control.[140] Indeed, just as much as it protects the data subject, the right to erasure/object (and the GDPR more broadly) can also be used to protect information providers' freedom of expression, that might otherwise be at the mercy of ISS providers free to in/exclude information at their own behest. Put differently, the GDPR quite counterintuitively constitutes an important safeguard *for* freedom of expression whenever personal data is requested to be erased, as it explicitly incorporates the interests of those that might otherwise be ignored by powerful ISS providers.[141] Especially if the alternative is to surrender to ISS providers' unilateral information control, which already gave rise to a grey market of reputation managers manipulating information flows for those who can afford it. Rather than effectively limiting the erasure or delisting of personal data to the well-resourced, data subject rights install a template for balancing fundamental rights/freedoms based in law.

Checks and Balances—Having said that, much depends on how Member States will implement the freedom of expression derogations (in Arts 85, 23) and how judicial/administrative bodies will interpret and apply the GDPR. As the initial balance and freedom of expression consideration needs to be done by a private entity (ie the ISS provider, controller), the interests of any of the parties involved (eg information providers' freedom of expression or data subjects' right to private life) may be inappropriately affected. Current checks and balances, consisting of procedural provisions in the GDPR and the option of judicial/administrative oversight, might well be considered inadequate in practice/future. In contexts where

[139] 'Even if one accepts that there may not and should not be a legally correct way to select and rank references, it is possible that there are unethical as well as legally problematic ways of selecting and ranking search results.' Van Hoboken, *Search Engine Freedom* (n 117) 203.

[140] Next to, for example, competition and consumer protection law.

[141] That is, whenever the respective information falls within the scope of application of the GDPR. Arguably, freedom of expression rights holders could claim damages from ISS controllers under Article 82(1) GDPR for not sufficiently taking into account freedom of expression and information interests in its balancing acts.

imbalances seem to be endemic (eg because of ISS providers' scale and automation, the ease of abusing rights), regulatory intervention may be required. Considering the inherently case-dependent nature of almost all right to erasure cases, such intervention should primarily focus on installing *procedural safeguards*.[142]

2.2.4 Freedom to Receive Information

a) Who Is Responsible for What?

Who—The fundamental right to freedom of expression and information (Art 11 Charter) also entitles individuals to freely access and receive information. In the context of this book and its focus on ISS providers, the freedom to receive information may be a considerable factor in both *ex ante* and *ex post* GDPR balancing acts. Indeed, in situations where the right to erasure is directed at published information, this will often be the freedom affecting most individuals, as it may cover anyone potentially accessing the respective personal data. Moreover, the ISS provider itself might also invoke its own freedom to receive information (eg a search engine crawling the web or a sharing economy platform using contact details and a mapping service).[143] Once accessed, that entity or person of course becomes a controller, subject to GDPR requirements itself (and thus targetable with the right to erasure/object). A priori, the freedom to receive information constitutes a more or less strong legitimate interest for general purpose ISS providers to render lawful the initial processing under Article 6(1)(f).[144] For the purposes of this chapter, the most important manifestation of the freedom to receive information is as a third-party interest in the balancing act to be performed by the ISS provider-controller.

No Direct Horizontal Effect—In a position to control information flows, ISS providers have become hugely important in how people find, access, and consume information. By their very nature, these entities therefore have an impact on the freedom to receive information. Van Hoboken, for example, suggests 'that referencing information in search engines has become as necessary for end-users to inform themselves about matters of public concerns as the underlying stories themselves'.[145] As mentioned before, ISS users cannot invoke their freedoms under Article 10 ECHR or Article 11 Charter against providers directly (no direct horizontal effect). Public bodies however (be it administrative, judicial, or legislative authorities) can be held liable for ensuring due consideration of this fundamental freedom, particularly with regard to powerful ISS providers.[146] As such, these private entities may still incur some level of (indirect) responsibility to ensure freedom of access to information is safeguarded.[147] So, even though a priori,

142 Kuczerawy (n 1866).
143 Van Hoboken, *Search Engine Freedom* (n 117) 199–200.
144 See also Recital 47.
145 Van Hoboken, *Search Engine Freedom* (n 117) 198.
146 Palomo Sánchez and Others v Spain App no 28955/06 [GC (Judgment 12 September 2011) [60]. Referred to in: Woods, 'Freedom of Expression and Information' (n 90) 324.
147 See notably: Van Hoboken, *Search Engine Freedom* (n 117) 208–09.

neither primary law (ie Charter and ECHR), nor the GDPR gives an actionable/positive right to individuals against ISS providers for respecting their freedom of information in the face of the right to erasure/object, it cannot be excluded that such will be the case in the future (eg through Member-State laws).

Direct Horizontal Effect through Liability Provision—An interesting, though unexplored, avenue would be for rights holders to claim damages under Article 82(1) GDPR for not respecting their freedom of expression and information. After all, this provision grants '[a]ny person who has suffered material or non-material damage as a result of an infringement of this Regulation [. . .] the right to receive compensation from the controller or processor for the damage suffered'. It might be argued that such could be the case when an ISS controller does not sufficiently take into account freedom of expression and information interests in its balancing acts or when considering the exemption in Article 17(3)(a). Of course, this would require freedom of expression/information rights holders are informed about erasure requests, something which might raise a number of additional data protection challenges in its own right.[148] Aggregated information about takedowns and detailed takedown policies might solve this issue somewhat. Ultimately though, this type of 'direct horizontal effect' hinges on Courts' interpretation in individual cases. The mere potentiality of liability might force ISS providers to be more considerate of information freedoms when processing personal data.

ISS Provider Freedom—A crucial question relates to the fact that ISS providers—as people's go-to information selectors, rankers, and presenters—already erase, block, discriminate data on their own terms. What then, is the difference with legal requirements (such as in the GDPR) on how information flows are controlled? Van Hoboken does not seem to see much harm in the liberty of search engines (and the argument translates *mutadis mutandis* to other ISS providers as well) to freely control information flows. They do this in function of their users, who make a deliberate decision to use the ISS to access and receive information, *because* they select, rank, present, filter it in a certain way. In this line of reasoning, only external interferences with the ISS providers' freedom (eg through a legal requirement to erase certain information), that are not informed by users' interests, will impact their freedom to access information. To put it in his own words:

> The selection and ranking of results is at the basis of making search engines work for end-users. They will evaluate the quality of search engines in light of the information they are presented in return to their queries. Any ranking obligation

[148] See analysis of Article 17(2) in Chapter 4. At least in the delisting context, WP29 has advised against notifying by default website operators whose website is delisted. Article 29 Working Party, 'Guidelines on the Implementation of the Court of Justice of the European Union Judgment on "*Google Spain and Inc v Agencia Española de Protección de Datos (AEPD) and Mario Costeja González*" C-131/12' (n 2); Julia Powles, 'The Case That Won't Be Forgotten' (2015) 47 Loy U Chi LJ 598.

therefore, if not specifically informed by and enhancing the rights and interests of end-users, runs the risk of harming them in their interest to freely inform themselves.[149]

Freedom of Information v Freedom of Expression—ISS users' right to receive information may enter into conflict with the providers' fundamental freedoms (of expression and to conduct a business) in how they manage and control information flows. In the *Satiksme* Ruling, the CJEU confirmed that Article 6(1)(f) does not allow a controller to be forced to share certain personal data, even if third parties have a compelling interest in getting access to that information.[150] ISS providers' freedom to include, exclude, or prioritize information at their own behest, is often the very reason why most people rely on these service providers in the first place (ie to make such decisions for them in the face of information-overload).[151] This freedom, however, is constrained by—or rather channelled through—economic goals, most commonly by extracting value from data (eg commercial profiling), which in turn is influenced by end-users wishes (ie freedom of information). ISS providers' freedom to control their services has increasingly been criticized and challenged in light of the disproportionate impact on users' right of access to information.[152] This important issue—also referred to as 'corporate censorship'[153]—is not the focus of this book. Yet, it is important to flag as it highlights the fact that erasure or manipulation of information is to be situated in a broader context, requiring broader policy responses as well. The right to erasure itself is not necessarily a threat to ISS users' right to receive information, rather than providers' power over information flows in general. So, to react to Van Hoboken's point, I would express considerable reservations with regard to his claim that ISS providers' information control is a mere function of users' wishes.[154] Neither would I agree that the alleged trust or choice users would have in using one ISS over the other, will result in self-correction of the relevant actors.[155]

[149] Van Hoboken, (n 10).

[150] *Rīgas satiksme* (n 71). This case concerned an application with the national police for sharing personal details about the perpetrator of a traffic accident, exclusively for the purposes of starting civil proceedings. The police only shared limited information, insufficient to identify the respective individual. The AG had already compellingly explained that even though Article 6(1)(f) cannot be used to force information sharing in pursuit of third parties' interests (ie the damaged party's compensation), common sense dictates otherwise.

[151] Van Hoboken, *Search Engine Freedom* (n 117) 217.

[152] See for example: Tarleton Gillespie, 'Facebook Can't Moderate in Secret Any More' (*Data & Society: Points*, 24 May 2017) <https://points.datasociety.net/facebook-cant-moderate-in-secret-any-more-ca2dbcd9d2> accessed 1 June 2019.

[153] Rebecca MacKinnon, *Consent of the Networked: The Worldwide Struggle for Internet Freedom* (Basic Books 2012) ch 8.

[154] It is first and foremost aimed at maximizing economic gain, most often by extracting value from data. The easiest—or at least most frequently used in the ISS context—way for doing so is through commercial profiling and targeting.

[155] ie in light of the massive power asymmetries, explained in the first chapters, it seems naïve to assume that large ISS providers would, at their own initiative, pursue strong fundamental rights/freedoms protection, just to attract/maintain users.

GDPR Constrains ISS Freedom and Protects Information Freedoms—Put briefly, the more powerful an ISS is, the bigger the impact on individuals' freedom of information. In individual cases where personal data is requested to be erased, protecting freedom of information will solely be in the hands of the controller (ISS provider). The GDPR does curb this power and impact on information freedoms through its exemptions (notably in Art 17(3)) and derogations (notably Arts 23(1)(i) and 85), which lay down safeguards for third party interests that might otherwise not have a voice. So, a priori ISS providers are largely free to determine what (not) to include on their platform and/or how to direct information flows without any duty to proactively ensure freedom of expression/information. But, the GDPR does constrain this freedom by introducing third party interests in the balancing test (as well as through derogations to be found in Member-State legislation). The fact remains, however, that in an individual case, potentially affected third parties will not have a direct say in the determination (not) to erase personal data.[156] The controller may not adequately consider their interests in having access to that information and/or the derogations in national law might fail to adequately capture those interests *in casu*. This not unlikely scenario again ties back to the issue of ISS providers (too) powerful in information control and a failure of public bodies (be it administrative, judicial, or the legislative) to ensure information freedoms are adequately protected in society as a whole.[157]

Who is Responsible for Information Control?—In sum, any control over how information is accessed—whether by ISS providers independently, or through a legal obligation or injunction—will interfere with individuals' freedom of information under Article 11 Charter (and Article 10 ECHR). What is important is that such control and decisions should be informed by the interests of individuals affected.[158] When the trigger comes from the law (eg the GDPR), there can at least be a presumption that this will be the case (laws are a democratic product and need to be interpreted in light of primary law after all). It might be more problematic when done by ISS providers autonomously, eg through personalization and targeting designed in light of the provider's commercial objectives. It has been argued that any blocking/discriminating of information on grounds that are not selected by the user, undermine their freedom of information.[159] The lack of an actionable claim in this regard, raises the (normative) question of whether ISS providers have a duty/responsibility to reflect users' preferences in the first place. Currently, most important such actors—ie search engines, social networks, sharing economy, or ecommerce platforms—manage information flows (primarily) on the basis of

156 Except, perhaps, via the detour of claiming damages under Article 82 (see above: 411).
157 Where the majority of such freedoms are exercised through these private actors.
158 Van Hoboken, *Search Engine Freedom* (n 117) 208–09.
159 Jennifer A Chandler, 'A Right to Reach an Audience: An Approach to Intermediary Bias on the Internet Reclaiming the First Amendment: Constitutional Theories of Media Reform' (2006) 35 Hofstra Law Review 1095; as referred to in: Van Hoboken, *Search Engine Freedom* (n 117) 216–17.

personalization, engagement, and marketing, rather than quality, independence, and institutional legitimacy.[160] The shift to ISS providers as primary sources for information consumption, should go together with a reconfiguration of assumptions about professional guidelines and ethics of traditional media actors.[161] Without wanting to suggest ISS providers should be equated to high-quality news-media, it is important to have a thorough discussion on their responsibilities in society, in light of their power and user expectations.

b) How to Balance?

Criteria—In light of the above, I would claim powerful ISS providers have a responsibility to take into account third-party (information freedom) interests when considering erasure requests. Ideally this should be ordained and detailed in (Member-State) law pursuant to Articles 85 (and 23) GDPR. Private actors as they are, adequately considering third-party interests will depend (inter alia) on legal certainty and guidance available to ISS providers. The most practice-oriented type of guidance relevant here would be criteria for determining the significance of, and impact on, information freedoms. Public interest may be the pivotal criterion in this regard, to be found in CJEU and ECtHR case law dealing with relevant balancing exercises.[162] Some have even argued 'public interest' constitutes the only sine qua non for blocking an erasure request on the basis of information freedoms.[163] This of course shifts the question to what exactly constitutes information of public interest. Because, as the saying goes, not everything that is of interest to the public is in the public interest.

Public Interest—As observed by Lynskey, 'personal data protection shall prevail except where there is a "public interest" (as opposed to interest on behalf of the public) in the information'.[164] Elucidating what the CJEU may understand under 'the public', Erdos explains the concept 'must be understood as referencing a collective grouping along the lines of the "body politic" as opposed simply to an indefinite number of persons'.[165] According to the CJEU, whether personal data is 'in the public interest' will depend on 'the role played by the data subject

[160] The latter three being benchmarks for some more traditional (news) media. Van Hoboken, *Search Engine Freedom* (n 117) ch 8. Nicole Wong explains that the emergence of social networks and behavioural advertising in the mid-2000s has shuffled the pillars of search from 'comprehensiveness, relevance' and speed' to 'personalization, engagement, and speed'. Kara Swisher, Interview with Nicole Wong, 'Is It Time for a "Slow Food" Movement for the Internet?' (12 September 2018) <https://www.recode.net/2018/9/12/17848384/nicole-wong-cto-lawyer-google-twitter-kara-swisher-decode-podcast-full-transcript> accessed 13 September 2018.

[161] See for instance: Erin C Carroll, 'Making News: Balancing Newsworthiness and Privacy in the Age of Algorithms' (Georgetown University Law Center 2016) <https://papers.ssrn.com/abstract=2877335> accessed 1 June 2019.

[162] See for example: *Buivids* (n 99) paras 63–68.

[163] See Lynskey, *The Foundations of EU Data Protection Law* (n 65) 150. See also: Moosavian (n 134) 243.

[164] Lynskey, *The Foundations of EU Data Protection Law* (n 65) 150.

[165] Erdos, 'From the Scylla of Restriction to the Charybdis of Licence?' (n 25) 129; 151–52.

in public life'.[166] More recently, the ECtHR explained the concept captures information that may affect the well-being of citizens or the life of the community, are subject of controversy, concerns an important social issue, or involves issues that the public has an interest in being informed about.[167] This may stem from the nature of the information itself, as well as the context in which it appears.[168] Information solely aimed at satisfying individuals' curiosity as to others' private lives will not be 'in the public interest'. Dedicated legal frameworks can also establish that the publication of certain personal data in specific contexts, is in the public interest, albeit subject to oversight by national courts.[169] Indeed, it has been argued that the abstract language in the Charter and ECHR requires translation in light of political and social arguments and ultimately depends on the application by judges in concrete cases.[170] In light of the increased importance of information conflicts, authoritative guidance on the public interest criterion is critical.

Non-Legal Criteria—Apart from the extensive number of traditional legal sources (notably case law and scholarship), a lot of inspiration can be found in other fields as well.[171] Deontological codes for journalists,[172] or archaeology and library ethics[173] are clear examples of this. Perhaps more unusual, but definitely very relevant are Wikipedia's guidelines on biographies of living persons.[174] These guidelines are a bottom-up product of long discussions and correspond surprisingly well with some of the post-*Google Spain* (official) guidelines.[175] Born in the online environment, dynamic and often incredibly specific, these guidelines may offer a useful rule of thumb for ISS providers to decide individual cases.

The Internet as a Paradigm Shift—The Internet, and information (communication) technologies more generally have brought about a paradigm shift in

[166] *Google Spain* (n 2) para 81.

[167] *Satakunnan Markkinapörssi Oy et Satamedia Oy v Finland* (n 91) para 167 et seq. See also the numerous ECtHR case law references in: Leto Cariolou, 'The Developing Law of Privacy and the Limits to the Public Interest Defence: The Grand Chamber Judgment in Couderc and Hachette Filipacchi Associés v France' (2016) 8 Journal of Media Law 138, 147.

[168] *Satakunnan Markkinapörssi Oy et Satamedia Oy v Finland* (n 91) para 167 et seq.

[169] *Österreichischer Rundfunk and others* (n 3); *Satakunnan Markkinapörssi Oy et Satamedia Oy v Finland* (n 91) para 172 et seq.

[170] Moosavian (n 134) 242.

[171] For a nice sample of criteria drawn from legal and non-legal sources, see: Meg Leta Jones, 'Privacy without Screens & the Internet of Other People's Things' (2014) 51 Idaho Law Review ch 4.

[172] eg BBC Academy, 'Journalism Law/Privacy' (2013) <http://www.bbc.co.uk/academy/journalism/article/art20130702112133653> accessed 1 June 2019; Raad voor de Journalistiek, 'Journalistieke Code' <http://www.rvdj.be/sites/default/files/pdf/code-rvdj.pdf> accessed 26 May 2017. This may also involve content moderation guidelines: 'Community Standards and Participation Guidelines' *The Guardian* (7 May 2009) <https://www.theguardian.com/community-standards> accessed 22 May 2017.

[173] eg: Society of American Archivists, 'Core Values Statement and Code of Ethics' <http://www2.archivists.org/statements/saa-core-values-statement-and-code-of-ethics> accessed 26 May 2017.

[174] https://en.wikipedia.org/wiki/Wikipedia:Biographies_of_living_persons.

[175] Reuben Binns, 'How to Be Open about Being Closed' [2016] Limn <http://limn.it/how-to-be-open-about-being-closed/> accessed 1 June 2019.

the accessibility of information. This Copernican revolution becomes really apparent when reading the seminal 1978 Lindop report that played down the impact of publication of information:

> Many things are published in newspapers or broadcasts, but by no means everyone reads them, sees them, or hears them—or necessarily remembers them later even if he once knew them. The truth is that any piece of information about any data subject will at any given time be known only to a finite number of people. The number may be large or small, but (with very few exceptions) it will never be comprise the whole of the population of the United Kingdom. Moreover, as time passes the number will necessarily become smaller—by death and by forgetting—unless the information is circulated anew. In short, personal information is not just either 'public' or 'private': there is a wide range of possible knowledge among the public for any given item. [. . .] In theory, of course, much information which has once been published is accessible to anyone who is willing to spend enough time and trouble in retrieving it. The British Library newspaper library at Colindale, for example, has copies of all newspapers ever published in the United Kingdom. But the diligent researcher needs to do a good deal more than go to Colindale, for there is no subject index to the collection: he first needs to know where to look among some hundreds of thousands of filed newspapers. Unless he has a pretty accurate idea of the date and place of the original report, he is unlikely to be able to find what he wants. The same is true for many other public records.[176]

The quote is telling, and readers today immediately realize how these basic assumptions have completely shifted. In general, the increased accessibility of information can be regarded as a good thing for society.[177] Yet, the elimination of practical obscurity does come with undesirable side-effects, notably with regard to data protection and privacy interests. This also explains why *ex post* balancing as triggered by the right to erasure/object defaults in favour of the data subject.[178] Two specific contexts in which this shift has raised quite some issues already, relate to the online availability of public registers and journalistic archives. Laudable in the abstract, but potentially problematic in individual cases.

[176] Norman Lindop, *Report of the Committee on Data Protection, Chairman: Norman Lindop* (HMSO 1978) 270.

[177] Confirmed by the ECtHR in *Times v United Kingdom*: 'the Internet plays an important role in enhancing the public's access to news and facilitating the dissemination of information generally. The maintenance of Internet archives is a critical aspect of this role.' ECtHR 10 March 2009, *Times v United Kingdom*, §27.

[178] After all, the current status quo—ie ubiquitous information availability—results in *ex ante* balances to effectively tip in favour of processing personal data. See in this regard: Hijmans, *The EU as Guardian of Internet Privacy* (n 13) 232–33.

c) What about Public Registers?

LEGALLY ORDAINED PUBLICATION V DATA PROTECTION—The clash between information freedoms and the right to data protection particularly manifests itself in situations where specific legal frameworks or provisions regulate the publication of (personal) data.[179] This is, for example the case with laws translating the fundamental right of access to documents (Art 42 Charter) into national law.[180] Indeed, Article 86 GDPR explicitly recognizes the potential clash and affirms the need to reconcile public access to official documents with the right to the protection of personal data.[181] While being debated at the European Parliament, an amendment was even proposed, to explicitly exclude such situations in the opening sentence of the right to erasure (Art 17 GDPR).[182] Rightfully, this suggestion was not retained, as it is already implied in the second exemption to the right to erasure, ie compliance with a legal obligation or task carried out in the public interest (Art 17(3)(b)).

In the mid 2010s, a relevant case made its way to the CJEU from Italy. The *Manni* Ruling concerned an individual requesting a local chamber of commerce to remove personal data from the companies register.[183] The case lays bare the issue of (Member-State and EU level) legal frameworks regulating public registers that were often not drafted in light of the Internet and ISS providers massively facilitating access to those registers. These frameworks[184] serve clear and important

[179] Deirdre Curtin and Joana Mendes, 'Right of Access to Documents (Article 42)' in Steve Peers and others (eds), *The EU Charter of Fundamental Rights: A Commentary* (Hart 2014) 1103 <https://www.bloomsburycollections.com/book/the-eu-charter-of-fundamental-rights-a-commentary/>; Bilyana Petkova, 'Towards an Internal Hierarchy of Values in the EU Legal Order: Balancing the Freedom of Speech and Data Privacy' (2016) 23 Maastricht Journal of European and Comparative Law (MJ) 421, 432 et seq and the many quotes contained within.

[180] See generally: Christopher Docksey, 'Four Fundamental Rights: Finding the Balance' (2016) 6 International Data Privacy Law 195, 198; Maeve McDonagh, 'Balancing Disclosure of Information and the Right to Respect for Private We in Europe' (2012) 16 Journal of Internet Law; New York 3.

[181] In full, Article 86 states (emphasis added) 'Personal data in official documents held by a public authority or a public body or a private body for the performance of a task carried out in the public interest may be disclosed by the authority or body in accordance with Union or Member State law to which the public authority or body is subject in order to reconcile public access to official documents with the right to the protection of personal data pursuant to this Regulation.'

[182] Concretely, the amendment suggested the opening sentence would read: 'The data subject shall have the right to obtain from the controller the erasure of personal data relating to them and the abstention from further dissemination of such data, unless the data controller is a public authority or an entity commissioned by the authority or otherwise acting on the behalf of an authority for the performance of the commission....' The justification for this specification was: 'Authorities have a statutory obligation to maintain several registers, and the data in those registers cannot be erased by the request of the data subject.' See: Committee on Civil Liberties, Justice and Home Affairs (Rapporteur Albrecht JP), 'Draft Report on the Proposal for a Regulation of the European Parliament and of the Council on the Protection of Individual with Regard to the Processing of Personal Data and on the Free Movement of Such Data (General Data Protection Regulation). Amendments (4) 1189–1492' (n 616) Amendment 1386.

[183] Mr Manni—director of a building company—claimed that his business was suffering because 'it was apparent from the companies register that he had been the sole director and liquidator of Immobiliare e Finanziaria Salentina Srl ('Immobiliare Salentina'), which had been declared insolvent in 1992 and struck off the companies register, following liquidation proceedings, on 7 July 2005'. *Salvatore Manni* [2017] Court of Justice of the European Union C-398/15 paras 23–24.

[184] *In casu* Article 2(1)(d) and (j) Council Directive 68/151/EEC of 9 March 1968 on co-ordination of safeguards which, for the protection of the interests of members and others, are required by Member

goals—notably legal certainty in the internal market—and any processing involved will be lawful on the basis of Article 6(1)(f) and generally also Article 6(1)(c) (compliance with a legal obligation) and Article 6(1)(e) (relating to the exercise of official authority or the performance of a task carried out in the public interest).[185] This is also why the AG asserted that data protection law cannot be used to overrule other laws installing publicity, even if they do not include elements such as (conditional) anonymization or access-restrictions for example.[186] Official disclosure through public registers can only reach their general interest objective, the AG convincingly argues, if access to them is open to all and available indefinitely.[187]

No Categorical Exclusion of Data Protection—The CJEU eventually followed much of the AG's reasoning, but arrived at a slightly more nuanced conclusion. Overall, data subjects should not be able to have their personal data removed from company registers because (a) they only involve a limited number of personal data items; (b) natural persons participating in trade through a limited liability company are aware of their data being disclosed in light of safeguards to third parties; and (c) the need to protect the interests of third parties in relation to joint-stock companies and limited liability companies and to ensure legal certainty, fair trading, and thus the proper functioning of the internal market in principle take precedence.[188] Having said that, the CJEU did acknowledge that exceptionally, under very specific circumstances and after a sufficiently long period following the dissolution of the company, access may be restricted only 'to third parties who can demonstrate a specific interest in their consultation' on the basis of the right to object.[189] The mere claim that the data subject's current business is suffering (allegedly because of the availability of information through the company register) would not qualify in this regard. A similar conclusion would probably be reached under the GDPR as well. In light of Article 17(3)(a)–(b), the right to erasure itself would not be applicable,[190] but the right to object, however, remains available. Overall, the issue brought forward in this case may perhaps

States of companies within the meaning of the second paragraph of Article 58 of the Treaty, with a view to making such safeguards equivalent throughout the Community, OJ L 65, 14.3.1968, 8. Repealed and currently to be found in: Article 14 Directive (EU) 2017/1132 of the European Parliament and of the Council of 14 June 2017 relating to certain aspects of company law, OJ L 169, 30.6.2017, 46.

[185] *Salvatore Manni* (n 183) para 42.
[186] AG Opinion in: ibid 50 et seq.
[187] AG Opinion in: ibid 65–89.
[188] ibid 58–60.
[189] Whether or not to allow this, remains to be decided by the Member State. In light of this, it is worth referring to the Explanatory Memorandum of the Dutch Act implementing Directive 95/46, which distinguishes between public registers that are ordained by law (eg company register), and those that are factually public (eg phone book), suggesting that only the latter category can be targeted with a right to object. This specification, however, was made in the second half of the 1990s, before the massive adoption of the Internet and information ecosystem it precipitated. Memorie van Toelichting—Regels inzake de bescherming van persoonsgegevens (Wet bescherming persoonsgegevens) [25 892] 24 et seq.
[190] Also confirmed by AG Opinion in: *Salvatore Manni* (n 183) para 101.

rather stem from the out-of-datedness of the legal framework regulating companies registers (ie in light of Article 52(1) Charter and the current information landscape).

Publicity v Erasure Is No Binary—The *Manni* Ruling is reminiscent of the debate on freedom of information requests and the CJEU's *Bavarian Lager* case. Here, access to meeting-minutes held by the Commission was refused because they contained personal data and the requestor did not provide 'any express and legitimate justification or any convincing argument in order to demonstrate the necessity for those personal data to be transferred'.[191] Confirming the so-called 'renvoi theory', the CJEU essentially required freedom of information requests made under Regulation 1049/2001,[192] to comply in their entirety with the data protection framework (ie Regulation 45/2001).[193,194] This is important as it affirms that even though an erasure/object request may not be available, data subjects' interests will still be safeguarded through access-restrictions. Some read in this case the CJEU establishing data protection primacy over freedom of information laws.[195] A more interesting takeaway however, is that it establishes publicity of information should not be qualified as a binary.[196] It also highlights the need for more fine-grained policies and/or legislation on these matters articulating (how to make) the balance in different contexts, for different public institutions.[197] In one Italian case, for example, the DPA (*Garante*) ruled that a data subject could not have his personal data erased from a Baptism Register, but could request an

[191] *Bavarian Lager* [2010] Court of Justice of the European Union C-28/08 P [115] para 78.

[192] Regulation (EC) No 1049/2001 of the European Parliament and of the Council of 30 May 2001 regarding public access to European Parliament, Council, and Commission documents. This Regulation provides for a general right of access to EU documents (Art 2), exempting, inter alia, situations 'where disclosure would undermine the protection of [. . .] privacy and the integrity of the individual, in particular in accordance with Community legislation regarding the protection of personal data' (Art 4(1)(b)).

[193] Regulation (EC) No 45/2001 of the European Parliament and of the Council of 18 December 2000 on the protection of individuals with regard to the processing of personal data by the Community institutions and bodies and on the free movement of such data.

[194] Rather than the 'threshold-theory', which postulates 'that it should first be established that the privacy of the persons involved was affected, before the data protection rules would come into play'. See: European Data Protection Supervisor, 'Public Access to Documents Containing Personal Data after the Bavarian Lager Ruling' (EDPS 2011) <https://edps.europa.eu/data-protection/our-work/publications/papers/public-access-documents-and-data-protection_en> accessed 1 June 2019.

[195] Lynskey, *The Foundations of EU Data Protection Law* (n 65) 139 et seq, 143.

[196] A similar observation can be made when reading the *Rundfunk* Ruling, where the CJEU suggested to evaluate whether the objectives underlying the publication of certain public officials' salaries cannot be achieved equally effectively in a more limited way (ie sharing specific names only with monitoring bodies). *Österreichischer Rundfunk and others* (n 3) paras 84–88. See also: European Data Protection Supervisor, 'Developing a "Toolkit" for Assessing the Necessity of Measures That Interfere with Fundamental Rights. Background Paper' 15 <https://secure.edps.europa.eu/EDPSWEB/webdav/site/mySite/shared/Documents/Consultation/Papers/16-06-16_Necessity_paper_for_consultation_EN.pdf> accessed 1 June 2019. In the same vein, it is also worth referring to Article 10 GDPR, specifying that '[a]ny comprehensive register of criminal convictions shall be kept only under the control of official authority'.

[197] European Data Protection Supervisor, 'Public Access to Documents Containing Personal Data after the Bavarian Lager Ruling' (n 194); *Salvatore Manni* (n 183) para 60.

adequate representation of his current beliefs to be reflected in the Register nonetheless (ie by adding a note).[198]

In sum, a legal obligation dictating publicity for a specific purpose and/or in a specific context, installs a strong—though not insurmountable[199]—default against erasure or other obstructions to unfettered access. WP29 strongly recommends such legislation to be as specific as possible, in order to facilitate assessing the legality of further use of that data (eg by ISS providers) in terms of the data protection framework.[200] In the absence of the respective legal framework specifying conditions for such measures, these decisions will be very case-dependent. The right to object (Art 21), rather than the right to erasure (Art 17) will generally be the go-to provision to contest publicity, also offering more nuanced solutions (access restrictions, pseudonymization, etc) in light of the particular circumstances of the case.[201]

Public Registers v ISS Providers—In light of this book's overall focus, it is crucial to emphasize public registers maintained by official authorities do not qualify as ISS providers.[202] The lawfulness and (in)ability to invoke data subject rights (eg to object/erase) against the public register should clearly be distinguished from further processing by third parties such as ISS providers.[203] The CJEU has repeatedly made clear that each subsequent processing operation of the same personal data, but by a new actor needs to be in compliance with the GDPR in its own right.[204] This means that ISS providers facilitating access to personal data in public registers can still be targeted with data subject rights, as was endorsed by the ECtHR as well.[205] The lawfulness and/or ability to invoke data subject rights

[198] See the three decisions referred to in: Giusella Finocchiaro and Annarita Ricci, 'Quality of Information, the Right to Oblivion and Digital Reputation' in Bart Custers and others (eds), *Discrimination and Privacy in the Information Society—Data Mining and Profiling in Large Databases* (Springer 2013) 291.

[199] *Volker und Markus Schecke GbR and Hartmut Eifert v Land Hessen* (n 8) para 85; *ClientEarth* [2015] Court of Justice of the European Union C-615/13 P [51].

[200] Article 29 Working Party, 'Opinion 06/2014 on the Notion of Legitimate Interests of the Data Controller under Article 7 of Directive 95/46/EC' (n 5) 28. In the same vein, see also: *Rīgas satiksme* (n 71) paras 74–76.

[201] One example of such a nuance approach can be found in an Italian case involving the publication of decisions by the Antitrust Authority. In short it was said that that authority should: (a) create a restricted-access section on its website; and (b) define a period after which content should be moved to that restricted-access section. See: Finocchiaro and Ricci (n 198) 296.

[202] Not in the least because their operations cannot be considered 'economic activities', even if they charge for access to the register. *Compass-Datenbank GmbH v Republik Österreich* [2012] Court of Justice of the European Union C-138/11.

[203] 'Only processing of the first type is a manifestation of the exercise of official authority.' AG Opinion in: *Salvatore Manni* (n 183) para 59.

[204] eg *Satamedia* (n 106); *Google Spain* (n 2).

[205] In the *Satamedia* case, which the CJEU had already dealt with in 2008, after which it was decided on by the Finnish Supreme Administrative Court, whose ruling was confirmed by the ECtHR in 2017. The case concerned, a commercial service that facilitated access (via text messages) to officially published tax records of Finnish citizens. In short, the ECtHR confirmed that the national court had made a fair balance between information freedoms and privacy, in ruling that 'the publication of the taxation data in the manner and to the extent described did not contribute to a debate of public interest and that the applicants could not in substance claim that it had been done solely for a journalistic purpose within

against the public register directly in an individual case, may however still influence (both positively or negatively) the determination at the level of the ISS provider. The unrestricted availability of personal data in a public register, constitutes a strong presumption of legitimate interest in terms of Article 6(1)(f) GDPR for further processing by general purpose ISS providers. Such a presumption, however, only extends to *ex ante* balancing, and does not prevent reversal of the balance in specific situations where the right to erasure or to object is invoked *ex post*.

NEED FOR GUIDANCE—Finally, the issue of public registers also brings to the front a broader issue of regulating the accessibility and publicity of general interest information, considerate of the interests, freedoms, and rights of individuals involved. Provisions that install generalized, categorical information access restrictions may fail to capture important particularities in individual cases.[206] It is hard, and arguably even against the non-hierarchical nature of the Charter, to give automatic priority to transparency over data protection.[207] A casuistic approach, on the other hand, may not be ideal either, as it raises important questions regarding due process and legal certainty.[208] Overall, it is still advisable that whatever regulatory framework dictating transparency/publicity also specifies safeguards in light of individuals' privacy and data protection interests,[209] rather than exclusively relying on the GDPR to do so in individual cases.[210]

d) *What about Journalistic Content?*

JOURNALISTIC CONTENT IMPACTS BALANCE—Erasure requests against ISS providers may often involve journalistic content.[211] In the context of data protection law, journalistic content is generally only referred to in terms of the derogation regime specified in Article 85 GDPR. As such, entities generating and directly

the meaning of domestic and EU law'. *Satakunnan Markkinapörssi Oy et Satamedia Oy v Finland* (n 91) para 198. See also: Psychogiopoulou (n 1621) 48–49.

206 For example, in its *Manni* Ruling, the CJEU highlighted the impossibility to predetermine time limits on the full availability of public registers. *Salvatore Manni* (n 183) para 55.

207 See in this regard: Annex 2 in European Commission, 'Commission Staff Working Paper: Impact Assessment Accompanying the Proposals for General Data Protection Regulation and Directive on Data Protection in Police and Judicial Matters' (n 30).

208 The AG in *Manni* questioned public authorities' ability to determine on a case-by-case basis (a) the time after which access should be restricted and/or (b) whether people requesting access to personal data actually have a legitimate interest in doing so. AG Opinion in: *Salvatore Manni* (n 183) para 92 et seq.

209 *Volker und Markus Schecke GbR and Hartmut Fifert v Land Hessen* (n 293) paras 79–89. Similarly, the ECtHR has also decided that the inclusion of one's name in a sex offender database for 30 years does not disproportionately impact the right to privacy (Art 8 ECHR), because inter alia the consultation of such data by the court, police, and administrative authorities was subject to a duty of confidentiality and was restricted to precisely determined circumstances. See the ECtHR decision in *BB v France* (5335/06), *Gardel v France*, and *MB v France* (no 22115/06) 17 December 2009. <http://www.echr.coe.int/Documents/FS_New_technologies_ENG.pdf>.

210 Already recognized in the context of France's first data protection law. Holleaux (n 216) 38–39.

211 See in this regard, the heightened attention to safeguards for journalistic content within the GDPR (in comparison to Directive 95/46). See Chapters 3 and 4.

disseminating journalistic content are generally excluded from many data protection provisions (including data subject rights).[212] Based on an analysis of EU and Member-State case law Erdos observes that journalism is generally interpreted quite narrowly in the data protection context.[213] Importantly in light of this book, Member-State interpretations generally exclude ISS providers, which will thus not benefit from the derogatory regime for journalism.[214] Even though this seems to constitute the general status quo regarding the legal qualification of ISS providers, at least one Member-State court suggested a different interpretation.[215] According to the *Gerechtshof Den Haag*, it is not possible to categorically exclude ISS providers such as search engines from invoking the journalism derogation for their own activities.[216] It explains that the CJEU in *Google Spain* merely intended to clearly separate the legal status of the source, from that of the search engine itself. Because the former *can* benefit from the derogation and the latter may not, data subjects cannot be forced to first approach the source with a delisting request.[217] Yet, this does not imply—the Dutch court concludes—that search engines cannot rely on said derogation in a specific case.[218] This reading would remove the apparent contrast between the CJEU's findings in *Google Spain* and the earlier *Satamedia* ruling which seemed to suggest a wide interpretation of the journalistic exemption.[219] Increased scrutiny by regulators on the editorial control of powerful online platforms over the content they distribute, may also affect whether or not they can benefit from journalistic (or similar) derogations in the future. At the moment, the qualification of content as journalistic will at the very least still be a relevant factor in determining the interests at stake in a balancing act following an erasure request with the ISS controller.

[212] Erdos, 'EU Data Protection & Media Expression' (n 104); David Erdos, 'Statutory Regulation of Professional Journalism under European Data Protection: Down but Not Out?' (2016) 0 Journal of Media Law 229.

[213] Both at the EU level (*Satamedia* (n 106); *Google Spain* (n 2)). and at the Member-State level (see references to national cases regarding street mapping service, general search engines, and databases, referred to in Erdos, 'From the Scylla of Restriction to the Charybdis of Licence?' (n 25) 146).

[214] *Google Spain* (n 2) para 85. Seemingly contrasting with the findings in *Satamedia*. Erdos, 'From the Scylla of Restriction to the Charybdis of Licence?' (n 25) 131.

[215] At the time of writing, no other cases defending the same interpretation were identified.

[216] According to the Dutch Court, the applicability of said derogation to a search engine needs to be assessed independently on a case-by-case basis. *Google t X* [2017] Gerechtshof Den Haag ECLI:NL:GHDHA:2017:1360, Rechtspraak.nl [5.9.].

[217] *Google Spain* (n 2) paras 82–85.

[218] It should be pointed out that in the subsequent paragraphs, the Dutch court conflates determining the applicability of the derogation with actual balancing under the legitimate interests ground. The criteria put forward by the CJEU in para 81 (ie role of the individual in public life), relate to the *balancing* exercise and not to determining the applicability of the derogation per se.

[219] *Satamedia* (n 106) paras 56–61. Despite the seemingly wide interpretation of the journalistic derogation by the CJEU, the national (Finnish) court did not think the case at hand concerned journalism. This inapplicability of the journalistic derogation was then challenged before the ECtHR, which affirmed the national court's decision. *Satakunnan Markkinapörssi Oy et Satamedia Oy v Finland* (n 91).

FINDING THE RIGHT BALANCE—Information conflicts involving journalistic content have given rise to quite some case law[220] and scholarship already.[221] Even though data protection law is increasingly used to challenge journalistic content, these conflicts generally involve individuals' right to privacy more than their right to data protection.[222] With this in mind, much guidance can be found in ECtHR case law involving the balancing of Articles 8 and 10.[223] The role of the press as a 'public watchdog' in a democratic society constitutes the guiding criterion in these conflicts.[224] The nature of the content will also be critical, ranging from reporting facts (high protection), to articles concentrating on sensational news 'intended to titillate and entertain, […] satisfying the curiosity of a particular readership regarding aspects of a person's strictly private life'[225] (low protection).[226] It is also in this context that the ECtHR specified that assessing whether an Article 8 interference is justified, the 'focus must be on whether the publication is in the interest of the public and not whether the public might be interested in reading it' (see paragraph 71).[227] At several occasions, the ECtHR also pointed to the media's responsibility in sensibly dealing with the publication of private information.[228] Having said all that, the ECtHR did emphasize the importance of protecting the integrity of online (news) archives, opposing the expungement of articles as if they had never existed.[229] Finally, the inherently context-dependent nature of fair balancing was

[220] For an overview of relevant ECtHR case law, see: European Court of Human Rights—Press Unit, 'Factsheet on New Technologies' (2017) <http://www.echr.coe.int/Documents/FS_New_technologies_ENG.pdf> accessed 1 June 2019; European Court of Human Rights—Press Unit, 'Factsheet on Hate Speech' (2017) <www.echr.coe.int/Documents/FS_Hate_speech_ENG.pdf> accessed 1 June 2019.

[221] See, for example, the many references in: Joris van Hoboken, 'The Proposed Right to Be Forgotten Seen from the Perspective of Our Right to Remember' <www.law.nyu.edu/sites/default/files/upload_documents/VanHoboken_RightTo%20Be%20Forgotten_Manuscript_2013.pdf> accessed 1 June 2019; Erdos, 'Statutory Regulation of Professional Journalism under European Data Protection' (n 212).

[222] It is worth reiterating here that the fundamental right to data protection (Art 8 Charter) should be distinguished from the secondary framework in the GDPR, which defends a whole range of Charter rights (including privacy (Art 7) and freedom of expression (Art.11)).

[223] Noteworthy are the criteria (ie contribution to a debate of public interest; how well-known is the respective person; method of obtaining the information; prior conduct of the person; content, form, and consequences of the publication) developed in the *Von Hannover v Germany (No 2)* (n 134) paras 109–13; *Axel Springer AG v Germany* (n 134) paras 89–95; *Satakunnan Markkinapörssi Oy et Satamedia Oy v Finland* (n 91) para 165 et seq; *Fuchsmann v Germany* [2017] European Court of Human Rights 71233/13; *ML and WW v Germany* [2018] European Court of Human Rights 60798/10 & 65599/10. See also: Docksey (n 180) 206–07. For a recent case law overview, see: Directorate General Human Rights and Rule of Law, 'Case Law of the European Court of Human Rights Concerning the Protection of Personal Data' (Council of Europe 2018) T-PD(2018)15 3 <https://rm.coe.int/t-pd-2018-15-case-law-on-data-protection-may2018-en/16808b2d36> accessed 13 June 2018. For a list of relevant criteria drawn from policy documents and case law, specifically in the delisting context, see: Kuczerawy and Ausloos (n 100) Annex.

[224] Moosavian (n 134) 249. The author critically reflects on the rhetoric of using the 'watchdog trope' in this context.

[225] *Mosley v United Kingdom* (n 131) para 114 et seq. And the many case law references within.

[226] In this regard, see also: Petkova (n 179) 428.

[227] *Mosley v United Kingdom* (n 131) para 114 et seq.

[228] This, of course, may differ according to local sensibilities. *Couderc and Hachette Filipacchi Associés v France* [2015] European Court of Human Rights 40454/07. Expanded on in: Cariolou (n 167) 145.

[229] *Case of Times Newspapers Ltd (Nos 1 and 2) v The United Kingdom* [2009] European Court of Human Rights 3002/03 and 23676/03 para 27; *Wegrzynowski and Smolczewski v Poland* [2013]

illustrated quite well in two cases—with similar facts, but contrasting outcomes—before the Belgian and French supreme courts (*Cour de Cassation*).[230] Both cases concerned anonymization requests regarding online newspaper archives, by individuals who had been the subject of criminal proceedings. The French Court rejected the *droit à l'oubli*, whereas the Belgian one confirmed it. The relevant facts in the latter case dated back to 1994 already (in contrast to 2003 and 2006 in the French case), and also related less to the professional capacity of the individual.[231] Noteworthy as well is that the Belgian case explicitly did *not* rely on data protection law (but on tort law and the general right to privacy), whereas the French case did. By not relying on data protection law the journalistic and freedom of expression safeguards did not kick in.

Granularity—In conclusion, it should once more be emphasized that each 're-publication' or act in the chain of information-distribution should be assessed in its own right under the GDPR. Having said that, the lawfulness of specific content distribution by ISS providers will be impacted (not determined) by the fact that the source benefits from the journalistic derogation (Art 85 and national implementation). Separating different actions may be most evident when the ISS provider performs clearly distinct operations on the respective content (eg collating and ordering information in a personalized manner), but is equally important in less obvious cases. In a 2017 ECtHR ruling, for example, a company was prohibited from digitally republishing publicly available tax data.[232] The case had already been the subject of a 2008 CJEU ruling, where the Luxemburg court hinted that the company might benefit from the journalistic derogation.[233] The national court, however, ruled this not to be the case after which the company went to the ECtHR claiming its Art 11 ECHR rights were violated. The ECtHR explained that due to the lack of added value and scale of 'republishing', the impact on privacy was disproportionately amplified. The activities at hand cannot qualify as 'journalistic

European Court of Human Rights 33846/07 para 65; Oreste Pollicino, 'European Judicial Dialogue and the Protection of Fundamental Rights in the New Digital Environment: An Attempt at Emancipation and Reconciliation' in Sonia Morano-Foadi and Lucy Vickers (eds), *Fundamental Rights in the EU: A Matter for Two Courts* (Hart 2015) 12; Van Hoboken, 'The Proposed Right to Be Forgotten Seen from the Perspective of Our Right to Remember' (n 221) 24; Cécile de Terwangne, *The Right to Be Forgotten and the Informational Autonomy in the Digital Environment* (Publications Office 2013) 17–18<http://dx.publications.europa.eu/10.2788/54562> accessed 1 June 2019.

[230] Jef Ausloos, 'Vergetelheids-zaken voor de Hoven van Cassatie te België en Frankrijk—Contradictoir of Complementair? (noot onder Hof van cassatie 29 april 2016, nr C.15.0052.F)' (2017) 1 Computerrecht 31–35.

[231] The Belgian case related to a drunk-driving incident by a medical practitioner, whereas the French case involved misconduct in the financial sector by two individuals professionally active in that sector.

[232] *Satakunnan Markkinapörssi Oy et Satamedia Oy v Finland* (n 91) It is worth mentioning two earlier cases related to privacy-issues stemming from journalistic reuse of information available online (but not linked to data protection law): *Aleksey Ovchinnikov v Russia,* [2010] European Court of Human Rights 24061/04; *Editorial Board of Pravoye Delo and Shtekel v Ukraine* [2011] European Court of Human Rights 33014/05. See also: Benedek and Kettemann (n 92).

[233] *Satamedia* (n 106) para 61.

content' of public value but are merely 'a manifestation of the public's thirst for information about the private life of others and, as such, a form of sensationalism, even voyeurism'.[234] The Strasbourg Court further substantiated its judgment emphasizing the distinction between 'processing of data for journalistic purposes and the dissemination of the raw data to which the journalists were given privileged access'.[235]

2.2.5 ISS Providers Caught in the Middle?

POSITION ISS PROVIDERS—From what preceded, it appeared that ISS providers may often have some freedom of expression and information claims relating to the information (including personal data) they facilitate access to. So far, it does not seem to be a heavily relied upon (if at all) argument to fend off right to erasure/object requests in practice. Perhaps because it would contradict the much more frequently used line of arguments 'no knowledge, no intent, no humans' (see section on the 'automation fallacy' in Chapter 3). In cases where ISS providers would invoke their freedom of expression (eg ranking) and/or information (eg crawling), the GDPR and national implementations do offer some ammunition against right to erasure/object claims. The reason information freedoms are discussed here, however, is that they most importantly cover third party interests in the ISS context. This very fact also lies at the root of much criticism against the right to erasure online. It would make ISS providers—apparently mere middlemen in information transactions—responsible to adjudicate fair balances between interests, rights, and freedoms of third parties.

RESPONSIBLE MIDDLE-MEN—Yes, ISS providers are often positioned between persons imparting information and those receiving information; effectively bridging freedom of expression to freedom of information. But, as amply discussed before (Chapter 3), these activities entail the ISS provider wearing different hats with regard to different activities. What is of interest in the context of this chapter is their capacity as controllers—directly subject to data protection law—and *not* as mere intermediaries.[236] Put differently, this chapter concerns itself only with the responsibility of ISS providers over their *own* activities with regard to information (that might be provided by third parties).[237] Just like a traffic agent manages traffic, ISS providers regulate the flow of information and are responsible under the GDPR for the decisions they make in this regard. Apart from a swathe of national

[234] *Satakunnan Markkinapörssi Oy et Satamedia Oy v Finland* (n 91) para 177.

[235] ibid para 175.

[236] Which is not to say the liability/responsibility of ISS providers such as search engines in their capacity of 'intermediaries' is an important issue. See, for example: Van Hoboken, *Search Engine Freedom* (n 117) ch 9.

[237] This question should clearly be separated from that of traditional 'intermediary liability' and 'notice-and-takedown' debate, which is concerned about the liability over content and/or activities of third parties, not one's own. For a comprehensive analysis of the liability of intermediaries with regard to third party content/activities, see notably: Angelopoulos (n 61).

cases,[238] this also clearly appears from the CJEU's case law in *Telekabel*,[239] *eDate Advertising*,[240] and *Google Spain*[241] emphasizing the heightened impact of search engines and the internet in general on the ubiquity of information and thus also individuals' data protection and privacy interests. The ECtHR too has had to decide in cases where ISS providers are considered to have some duties and responsibilities with regard to the freedom of expression and information they enable on their platform or network (be it in order to protect rights in Art 8 or 10 ECHR).[242] UN special rapporteur on freedom of expression David Kaye, also recommended ICT companies to take a more human rights based approach to safeguarding information freedoms on their platforms.[243] As such, the right to erasure/object—ie a legal provision, which is subject to safeguards preventing abuse—constitutes a legitimate interference with Article 10 ECHR when invoked against ISS providers.

Power and Responsibility—The crucial role of ISS providers as enablers of freedom of expression/information, is not an acquired right of users. Even though they do not offer much safeguards for such freedoms in the first place,[244] this does not mean the impact of the right to erasure/object on third party interests is reduced. Any decision these entities make about information flows—whether on their own behalf, or when ordained by law—impacts the freedom of expression and information of third parties. This impact will be a function of the trust in and the size and power of the ISS provider, which in turn will also determine the responsibility for adequately considering third-party interests in relevant decisions.[245] The

[238] Involving for example so-called 'rating-websites' and street-mapping services, that cannot rely on the freedom of expression derogations. See the many references in: Erdos, 'From the Scylla of Restriction to the Charybdis of Licence?' (n 25) 132 et seq.

[239] In this case the CJEU importantly stated that addressees of an injunction (to block access to a website) *must ensure compliance with the fundamental right of internet users to freedom of information* when choosing the measures for implementing said injunction. *UPC Telekabel* (n 31) para 55.

[240] *Joined Cases eDate Advertising GmbH v X and Olivier Martinez and Robert Martinez v MGN Limited* [2011] Court of Justice of the European Union C-509/09 and C–161/10 para 45.

[241] *Google Spain* (n 2) para 80.

[242] These cases do not explicitly distinguish the different legal roles ISS providers have under EU law, ie 'intermediary' (Directive 95/46) v 'controller' (GDPR). *Delfi AS v Estonia (Grand Chamber Hearing)* [2015] European Court of Human Rights 64569/09; *Case of Magyar Tartalomszolgtatk Egyeslete and Index.hu ZRT v Hungary* [2016] European Court of Human Rights 22947/13.; but also: *Pihl v Sweden* [2017] European Court of Human Rights 74742/14; *Tamiz v the United Kingdom* [2017] European Court of Human Rights 3877/14; European Court of Human Rights—Press Unit, 'Factsheet on Hate Speech' (n 220) 12–13.

[243] David Kaye, 'Report of the Special Rapporteur on the Promotion and Protection of the Right to Freedom of Opinion and Expression' (United Nations (Human Rights Council) 2018) A/HRC/38/35 <http://ap.ohchr.org/documents/dpage_e.aspx?si=A/HRC/38/35>.

[244] Indeed, they offer little safeguards in this regard: Venturini and others (n 44) 96.

[245] See in this regard: Van Hoboken, *Search Engine Freedom* (n 117) 210–15; Peggy Valcke, Aleksandra Kuczerawy, and Pieter-Jan Ombelet, 'Did the Romans Get It Right? What Delfi, Google, EBay, and UPC TeleKabel Wien Have in Common' in Mariarosaria Taddeo and Luciano Floridi (eds), *The Responsibilities of Online Service Providers*, vol 31 (Springer 2017) <http://link.springer.com/10.1007/978-3-319-47852-4> accessed 1 June 2019. The ECtHR explicitly recognized the size of an ISS provider as a criterion in determining their liability over information it facilitated access to *Pihl v Sweden* (n 242); European Court of Human Rights—Press Unit, 'Factsheet on Hate Speech' (n 220) 14.

GDPR effectively channels ISS providers' decisional freedom so that the interests of all stakeholders (from data subjects to information providers and consumers) are taken into account when data subject rights are invoked.

Safeguarding Freedom of Expression and Information—In light of the above, ISS providers find themselves between different parties all pursuing fundamental rights and freedoms. Rather than being 'caught in the middle' of this complex net, however, they proactively position themselves as freedom of expression and information enablers.[246] As such, ISS providers—particularly large and powerful ones—can be expected to consider the different interests, rights, and freedoms involved *before* and *after* receiving right to erasure/object requests.[247,248] Inadequate decisions and abuse are inevitable in this context, though they are hardly issues that are unique to the right to erasure and should not be exploited as arguments against the right being used vis-à-vis ISS providers altogether.[249] Instead, the goal is to prevent bad decision-making and abuse as much as possible. The most straightforward way to do this *in casu*, is by ensuring legal certainty (eg through concrete guidance) and procedural safeguards (eg oversight mechanisms). Concretely, ISS providers-controllers are required to make an a priori balancing act, which will be subject to checks and balances such as oversight by public bodies.

Fine-Tuning the Law—The current status quo only seems to give a voice to data subjects disagreeing with the controller's balancing act (eg appealing a delisting case with a local DPA). In light of the potential impact on freedom of expression and information, there may be a positive obligation on the shoulders of the State to put in place a more fine-grained mechanism (eg of procedural safeguards) to prevent undue interference with third parties' rights in Article 10 ECHR[250] and Article 11 Charter. As a matter of fact, this is exactly what the GDPR already requires Member States to do in Article 85 (and enables in 23(1)(i)). Additionally, just as the development of ethical rules and codes of conduct in the

[246] Not in the least in the context of news and journalistic content. See, inter alia: Emily Bell, 'Who Owns the News Consumer: Social Media Platforms or Publishers?' (Tow Center 2016) <https://www.cjr.org/tow_center/platforms_and_publishers_new_research_from_the_tow_center.php> accessed 1 June 2019.

[247] Their responsibility to be considerate about how activities may affect others' interests, rights, and freedoms will be more abstract *before*, and more concrete *after* a specific erasure request (see Chapter 5).

[248] Also implicitly recognized by Van Hoboken when saying that 'major general-purpose search engines with a particular strong societal impact, would have enhanced duties and responsibilities based on their widespread use and their impact on the different value chains in which they operate. […] However, the need to respect the freedom of search engine providers to make their mediating choices freely would remain and interferences with their protected freedom would need to be both effective and proportional.' Van Hoboken, *Search Engine Freedom* (n 117) 215.

[249] Entirely deferring balancing acts onto the shoulders of ISS providers may be just as undesirable as exempting them from having to take any responsibility whatsoever. In this regard, see: ibid 270.

[250] This follows, inter alia, from *KU v Finland* [2009] European Court of Human Rights 2872/02 [49]. In this case, the ECtHR decided Finland failed in its positive obligation to provide the framework for reconciling competing claims based on Articles 8 and 10 in the Convention.

context of traditional media outlets,[251] (certain types of) ISS providers may be expected to establish common rules and standards as well.[252] This is not an easy, but nonetheless is a crucial, step to achieve a more sustainable fair balance overall.[253] In the medium-short term, judges, policy-makers, and administrative authorities will (have to) play a more prominent role in ensuring fair balances here. The ideal regulatory mix walks the line between on the one hand ISS providers' freedom and latitude to manage their services as they see fit, while on the other hand safeguard the fundamental rights exercised and affected through these services or platforms.[254]

2.2.6 Interim Conclusion

Different Levels of Safeguards—The right to erasure can trigger an important balancing act between the fundamental rights to freedom of expression and information (Art 11 Charter), data protection (Art 8 Charter), and/or privacy (Art 7 Charter). Any interference with information freedoms should be proportionate to the data subjects' rights and interests involved. As already mentioned in Chapter 5, a whole range of factors that may influence the impact on the data subject can be derived from CJEU and ECtHR case law (eg degree of publicity of the information, the data subject's age[255] or notoriety,[256] type of medium,[257] type of content,[258] and so on).[259] The ECtHR put down six criteria to assess the fair balance in the prototypical 'right to be forgotten' case, ie involving disproportionate media

[251] The ECtHR has already established that 'in order for the media to rely on the defence of contributing to a debate of public interest, they must act in good faith and comply with the duties and responsibilities attached to their exercise of the right to free expression, which govern their profession.' In: Cariolou (n 167) 145; 148. For a brief overview of some relevant ethical press codes, see: Valcke, Kuczerawy, and Ombelet (n 245) 112–13.

[252] eg Art 40 GDPR on Codes of Conduct.

[253] See notion of 'transitory jurisprudence' (*jurisprudence transitoire*), explained by Van Drooghenbroeck as a requirement for infusing more legal certainty into case-by-case fair balancing. Sébastien Van Drooghenbroeck, *La proportionnalité dans le droit de la Convention européenne des droits de l'Homme: prendre l'idée simple au sérieux* (FUSL 2001) 624ff.

[254] A useful theory worth further exploring is the public forum doctrine, as recently adopted by the German Federal Constitutional Court and highlighted in: Dissenting Opinion of Judge Pinto de Albuquerque *Case of Mouvement Ralien Suisse v Switzerland* [2012] European Court of Human Rights 16354/06 49–50. In the German case, freedom of expression was deemed to be breached when the administration of Frankfurt Airport prohibited the distribution of political leaflets in the check-in area because it wants to create 'a pleasant atmosphere for travellers, free from political or social debate'.

See 'the right to speech is only as good as the right to access to venues in which speech can be heard' Rebecca Tushnet, 'Power without Responsibility: Intermediaries and the First Amendment' (2007) 76 Geo Wash L Rev 986, 114.

[255] *Rīgas satiksme* (n 71) paras 31–33.

[256] *Buivids* (n 99) paras 63–68.

[257] *Case of Magyar Tartalomszolgtatk Egyeslete and Index.hu ZRT v Hungary* (n 242) para 56.

[258] Indeed, as frequently reiterated by the ECtHR, '[i]t is commonly acknowledged that the audiovisual media have often a much more immediate and powerful effect than the print media'. *Mosley v United Kingdom* (n 131) para 114 et seq.

[259] For a comprehensive overview of key criteria, see notably: Kuczerawy and Ausloos (n 100) Annex. See also: Evangelia Psychogiopoulou, 'The European Court of Human Rights, Privacy and Data Protection in the Digital Era' in Maja Brkan and Evangelia Psychogiopoulou, *Courts, Privacy and Data Protection in the Digital Environment* (Edward Elgar 2017) 61.

attention given to private information (see Chapter 2). This case in particular concerned the photographic coverage of criminal proceedings: (a) contribution to a debate of public interest; (b) degree to which the person affected was known; (c) influence on the criminal proceedings; (d) circumstances in which the photographs were taken; (e) the content, form, and consequences of the publication; (f) scope of the order and the severity of the sanction.[260]

This book, however, is primarily concerned with the right to erasure vis-á-vis ISS providers, which are oftentimes not the creators of the respective content. From this perspective, the most affected freedom of expression and information will be that of third parties. For this very reason—ie the fact that persons affected are not directly involved in the decision to process/erase personal data—the GDPR already foresees a swathe of information freedom safeguards at different levels. As a derogation (delegated to the Member States) in Arts 85 and 23(1)(i); an exemption in Article 17(3)(a); and finally a counterweighing interest in Article 6(1)(f)'s *ex ante* or Article 21's (right to object) *ex post* balancing acts. Whereas the derogations and exemption define situations where freedom of expression and information prevails by default, Article 6(1)(f) is more open-ended and a priori leaves it entirely up to the controller to balance.

Channelling Information Power—Delegating balancing acts involving fundamental rights and freedoms to private actors raises concerns. Affected individuals have no direct or actionable claim against ISS providers to safeguard their freedom of expression and information (or any other fundamental right/freedom for that matter). This becomes increasingly problematic in an environment where these private entities absorb almost all information channels, effectively supplanting the public sphere. It is not the right to erasure that challenges freedom of expression and information, it is private information-control in pursuit of economic—rather than democratic and fundamental rights-informed—goals.[261] States have a positive obligation to safeguard freedom of expression and information in the face of these developments.[262] The GDPR constitutes an important example in this regard, putting in place a legal infrastructure to channel control over (one important category of) information, in light of the Charter.

Need for Guidance—ISS providers effectively bridge the two key components of Article 11 Charter: freedom to *impart* and freedom to *receive* information. As the *de facto* (information) traffic agents online, it is important that their decisions to include/erase content are informed by fundamental rights.[263] Their duties and responsibilities in this regard will be a function of their ubiquity and overall power.

[260] *Axel Springer SE and RTL Television GmbH v Germany* (n 1683) para 43 et seq.

[261] Frank Pasquale, 'Platform Neutrality: Enhancing Freedom of Expression in Spheres of Private Power The Constitution of Information: From Gutenberg to Snowden' (2016) 17 Theoretical Inquiries in Law 487.

[262] Similarly, see: Van Hoboken, *Search Engine Freedom* (n 117) 73.

[263] *UPC Telekabel* (n 31) para 55.

The higher the (potential) impact on fundamental rights and freedoms, the more important it will be for the state to act,[264] notably through installing legal guidelines, procedural safeguards, and oversight mechanisms. The GDPR aims to achieve all three, but may still be too high-level in some contexts, requiring more fine-grained (legal) policies.[265] These should aim to create the right incentive structure so as to minimize chilling effects,[266] over- and under-compliance. Still, legitimate concerns remain as to the potential impact on information freedoms more broadly.[267] With this in mind, it is also crucial to keep in mind that in many cases where the right to erasure/object triggers a conflict with freedom of expression and information, other legal frameworks will be much better suited to tackle the balance at hand (eg tort, press, defamation, rehabilitation, or intellectual property law).[268]

Public Interest—The pivotal criterion for ISS providers to consider when evaluating third parties' freedom of expression and information in the face of an erasure request will be public interest. The contours of this concept are implicitly/explicitly defined in a rich body of case law (by ECtHR, CJEU, and national courts) and many legal frameworks.[269] When the source is considered to be in the public interest—eg public registers, journalistic content—this will generally install a presumption against erasure by ISS providers. Of course, it is important to emphasize once more the need for granularity, ie to assess the ISS provider's further processing activities in their own right. When these activities are not a function of the public interest goals of the source, there will be no default against the right to erasure/object. Indeed, one will need to evaluate whether the purpose(s) underlying the processing of the ISS provider itself (eg facial recognition, recommendations, or name-based search results) is/are in the public interest.

Granularity does not only play a key role in determining the scope of responsibilities and obligations, but also the response to right to erasure/object requests. Indeed, it is an enabler for finding least intrusive means to accommodate rights, in light of information freedoms. A whole range of 'in-between' solutions, tailored to the case at hand, may address the data subject's concerns while at the same time minimizing the impact on the freedom of expression and information.[270]

[264] Woods, 'Freedom of Expression and Information' (n 90) 324.

[265] The CJEU has highlighted that Member States may have to implement national laws in order to reconcile data subject interests with access to information interests. *Rīgas satiksme* (n 71). Article 40 GDPR also encourages the 'the drawing up of codes of conduct intended to contribute to the proper application of this Regulation'.

[266] In the context of search engines, see: Van Hoboken, *Search Engine Freedom* (n 117) 199.

[267] Tridimas (n 118) 376.

[268] Not in the least because these frameworks often have more established doctrines. See also: Van Hoboken, 'The Proposed Right to Be Forgotten Seen from the Perspective of Our Right to Remember' (n 221) 23 et seq. For an elaborate comparative study of relevant use cases, see: Aurelia Colombi Ciacchi, Gert Brüggemeier, and Patrick O'Callaghan, *Personality Rights in European Tort Law, The Common Core of European Private Law* (CUP 2010).

[269] Docksey (n 180) 206.

[270] Van Hoboken, 'The Proposed Right to Be Forgotten Seen from the Perspective of Our Right to Remember' (n 221) 26.

After all, in reality the data subject will often not be after total eradication of personal data but rather increasing the level of practical obscurity.[271] These 'fifty shades of erasure' (eg rectification, delisting, pseudonymization, access-restrictions, obfuscation, etc) will be discussed in more detail in the following chapters. In conclusion, a sustainable and holistic solution requires both a nuanced approach to data protection rights *and* a broader policy discussion on the information power of ISS providers.

2.3 Research and Security Interests

INTRODUCTION—The third and final balancing scenario relates to research and interests. Whereas the central interest(s) in the former two scenarios could generally be ascribed to either the controller *or* third parties, this last scenario deals with interests that serve both the controller and third parties simultaneously. Even more so, the distinctive feature of this third balancing scenario is that the interests pursued are of a more collective nature, not to be understood as a collection of individual interests, but as a public good benefitting (part of) society in general.[272] Research and/or security interests, may be a misnomer in this regard, as it is generally referred to as a processing *purpose* that can serve many different interests (eg public health, innovation, or commercial gain). Nonetheless, it is still used as an umbrella term here, referring to all processing for research purposes in the interest of both the controller *and* third parties (more or less) equally.[273] Going a step further even, research and security interests in this subsection can be considered as a placeholder for other 'joint interests' in the ISS context.

EXAMPLES—By way of illustrating the types of situations envisaged here, it is worth referring to a number of real-life examples. In 2014, Facebook scientists published a very controversial paper describing how social network users' emotions can be manipulated (see Facebook vignette).[274] Five years before, researchers at Google had claimed to be able to predict flu outbreaks based on monitoring

[271] Allen (n 70) 162 et seq; Woodrow Hartzog and Evan Selinger, 'Obscurity: A Better Way to Think About Your Data Than "Privacy"' *The Atlantic* (17 January 2013) <http://www.theatlantic.com/technology/archive/2013/01/obscurity-a-better-way-to-think-about-your-data-than-privacy/267283/> accessed 1 June 2019; Matt Bishop and others, 'Forgive and Forget: Return to Obscurity' (ACM Press 2013) <http://dl.acm.org/citation.cfm?doid=2535813.2535814> accessed 1 June 2019; Jones (n 171) 94.

[272] Mireille Hildebrandt, 'Balance or Trade-off? Online Security Technologies and Fundamental Rights' (2013) 26 Philosophy & Technology 357, 373; Alessandro Mantelero, 'From Group Privacy to Collective Privacy: Towards a New Dimension of Privacy and Data Protection in the Big Data Era' in Linnet Taylor, Luciano Floridi, and Bart van der Sloot (eds), *Group Privacy: New Challenges of Data Technologies*, vol 126 (Springer 2017).

[273] Excluding situations where processing primarily benefits the controller and only marginally third parties or vice versa.

[274] Adam DI Kramer, Jamie E Guillory, and Jeffrey T Hancock, 'Experimental Evidence of Massive-Scale Emotional Contagion through Social Networks' (2014) 111 Proceedings of the National Academy of Sciences 8788.

search behaviour.[275] In 2015 the UK's National Health Service shared the records of millions of patients suffering from acute kidney injury with Google DeepMind for the development of a smartphone app targeted at clinicians.[276] Also in 2015, the Belgian DPA sued Facebook inter alia for tracking non-users without consent, to which the social network responded having to do so for security reasons.[277] This brief selection of highly controversial real-world cases illustrates how certain uses of personal data by ISS providers are (allegedly) justified by being of a broader interest. Even if such processing operations can be deemed lawful[278] on an *ex ante* basis, this does not exclude the right to erasure/object from being applicable *ex post*. Put differently, a valid *ex ante* balance does not guarantee an *ex post* balance.

Abstract v Concrete, Ex Ante v Ex Post—As in the other balancing scenarios, it is important to distinguish between *ex ante* and *ex post* balances. The *ex ante* balancing act (in light of Article 6(1)(f) will operate at a more abstract level, relying on the average user as benchmark and general safeguards (albeit appropriate to the situation) for individuals' fundamental rights and freedoms.[279] The balancing exercise triggered by the right to erasure (and/or the right to object), will require a re-balancing in light of the particular, concrete circumstances of the data subject at hand. In the event of data being processed for any of the purposes in Article 89,[280] Article 17(3)(d) enables controllers to refuse accommodating the right to erasure when they can demonstrate that erasure would 'seriously impair the achievement of the objectives'. Overall, it should be re-emphasized that in light of the safeguards mentioned in Art 89(1), the data minimization principle (Art 5(1)(c)) and Article 11,[281] controllers should already anonymize or remove identification whenever not necessary to achieve the purposes at hand.[282] This may be impossible—as effective anonymization, apart from being a moving target itself, would strip most of the data's utility—or ineffective in a concrete situation.

[275] Jeremy Ginsberg and others, 'Detecting Influenza Epidemics Using Search Engine Query Data' (2009) 457 Nature 1012.

[276] Julia Powles and Hal Hodson, 'Google DeepMind and Healthcare in an Age of Algorithms' (2017) 7 Health and Technology 351.

[277] Commissie voor Bescherming van de Persoonlijke Levenssfeer, 'Aanbeveling uit eigen beweging met betrekking tot 1) Facebook, 2) de gebruikers van internet en/of Facebook alsook 3) de gebruikers en aanbieders van Facebook diensten, inzonderheid social plug-ins' (2015) Aanbeveling nr 04/2015 <https://www.gegevensbeschermingsautoriteit.be/sites/privacycommission/files/documents/aanbeveling_04_2015.pdf> accessed 1 June 2019.

[278] And thus, at the very least compliant with Article 6(1)(f). Most types of personal data processing for commercial research will require consent according to WP29. Article 29 Working Party, 'Opinion 03/2013 on Purpose Limitation' (n 41) 45–46.

[279] WP29 explicitly refers to reasonable expectations as well. This, of course, is not an argument against an erasure request in an individual case. Article 29 Working Party, 'Opinion 06/2014 on the Notion of Legitimate Interests of the Data Controller under Article 7 of Directive 95/46/EC' (n 5) 43.

[280] ie archiving purposes in the public interest, scientific or historical research purposes, or statistical purposes

[281] 'Processing which does not require identification.'

[282] Also see recommendations in: Article 29 Working Party, 'Opinion 03/2013 on Purpose Limitation' (n 41) 28 et seq.

Possible Defences—In the ISS context (and artificial intelligence and machine learning context more generally), much of data-driven research relies on the scale of the data available. With this in mind, it will be hard for a controller to justify the erasure of individual data points would *seriously impair* the outcome. This could change when the number of erasure requests reaches a critical mass. In such circumstances a policy response may be desirable, particularly when the processing occurs in light of public interest goals (eg public health research). Secondly, the controller may also establish that it would require a disproportionate burden to identify and erase the respective personal data (as long as this is not the result of lacking in its obligation to implement safeguards and a general ethos in light of data protection by design). Finally, there may always be situations where even the erasure of a specific piece of personal data would seriously impair the 'joint interest' objectives. This could be the case for example, with regard to security related processing (eg preventing identity theft and fraud) on a financial transactions platform. In any situation, such counter-arguments will always need to be grounded in the particular context of the right to erasure request.

Granularity—Mixed interests such as those underlying processing for research or security purposes, may be particularly susceptible to purpose creep. For example, in the case of the Belgian privacy commission against Facebook, the company initially argued that it tracked (non-)users across the web for security purposes only. Yet, during the trial, it updated its policies, plainly admitting that it was also tracking (non-)users for advertisement purposes.[283] It seems to be common strategy for ISS providers to present personal data processing for discrete purposes as bundles. Laudable goals such as security or research in the public interest, are grouped together with purposes primarily pursuing the ISS controller's economic interests.[284] Against this backdrop, it is of critical importance to insist on a granular approach. Grouping together purposes does not constitute a valid defence and goes against the logic of data subject rights, and the GDPR more broadly.

Sliding Scale—The third balancing scenario illustrates once again the temporal dimension to balancing tests. Even though *ex ante*, research interests may be sufficient to justify storing / further processing personal data overall (subject to safeguards), it will be harder to use it as an argument against an individual right to erasure/object request, especially when it cannot be established that the targeted personal data is not *actually* being used for said purposes. In other words, purely hypothetical, potential 'joint interests' are not sufficient to block data subject rights

[283] Belgian Privacy Commission, 'The Belgian Privacy Commission Publishes New Recommendation Relating to the Processing of Personal Data by Facebook through Cookies, Social Plug-Ins and Pixels' (16 May 2017) <https://www.privacycommission.be/en/news/belgian-privacy-commission-publishes-new-recommendation-relating-processing-personal-data> accessed 28 April 2018.

[284] Reading through the average ISS provider's privacy policy will already make this clear. At a hearing before the UK House of Commons, Facebook's CTO Mike Schroepfer even failed to mention the company's tracking operations also pursue commercial interests, only stressing the security purposes. Chair: Damian Collins and Mike Schroepfer, Chief Technical Officer, Facebook, Fake News 2018.

to erasure/object.[285] This also brings to mind the current 'perpetual beta' mode that most ISS providers operate in, constantly adjusting their service based on a permanent feedback loop of user-research.[286] Under this paradigm, personal data is always necessary for 'research' or 'optimization' purposes, albeit mainly in pursuit of the controller's commercial interests. Even though generally, the rights to erasure and to object should be available in this context, data subjects will often not be able to effectively invoke them without quitting the ISS altogether. One may question to what extent controllers can legitimately argue the way their systems operate effectively prevent data subject rights from being exercised.[287] A proper analysis of the dynamic nature of ISS providers' processing operations goes beyond the scope of this book. Suffice to say that it highlights the need for such providers to clearly and granularly define the different processing operations, in order to facilitate targeted exercises of the rights to erasure and to object.

PROPORTIONALITY—Just like in the other scenarios, the outcome of the balancing exercise will depend on the relative weight in each scale.[288] Recent ECtHR and CJEU case law has clamped down on mass surveillance by defining strict requirements in light of safeguarding fundamental rights and freedoms.[289] These requirements are formulated in the context of fighting terrorism and serious crime, target government agencies or policies, and generally only concern *ex ante* proportionality (eg functional separation, time limitation, access restrictions, etc). If such requirements are already deemed a minimum in the context of security of society as a whole, they certainly ought to apply to security of private entities and platforms (even if some of them constitute de facto public spheres). In order to be able to block a specific erasure request, the ISS provider/controller will essentially have to establish that further processing is effective, necessary, and proportionate to safeguard the security of its systems and/or other users.[290] In the same vein, an ISS provider processing for scientific research purposes, will have to demonstrate why the

[285] In this regard, see also: Peter Hustinx, 'How Practicable Is It to Apply Data Protection to Activities Involving Freedom of Expression?' (The 'Right to Be Forgotten' and Beyond: Data Protection and Freedom of Expression in the Age of Web 2.0, Oxford, UK, June 2012) <http://podcasts.ox.ac.uk/how-practicable-it-apply-data-protection-activities-involving-freedom-expression-3> accessed 1 June 2019.

[286] ENISA, 'Privacy Enhancing Technologies: Evolution and State of the Art' (2016) 16 <https://www.enisa.europa.eu/publications/pets-evolution-and-state-of-the-art>; Gürses and van Hoboken (n 6); Seda Gürses *Data Justice Conference: Keynote Plenary I* <https://cardiff.cloud.panopto.eu/Panopto/Pages/Viewer.aspx?id=547383b2-9d0a-4966-a4aa-a8e50178e2cf> accessed 16 June 2018 01:29:30.

[287] See Part III and Veale, Binns, and Ausloos, 'When Data Protection by Design and Data Subject Rights Clash' (n 28).

[288] Article 29 Working Party, 'Opinion 06/2014 on the Notion of Legitimate Interests of the Data Controller under Article 7 of Directive 95/46/EC' (n 5) 24.

[289] Sophie Stalla-Bourdillon, *Privacy vs. Security* (Springer 2014) 83; European Court of Human Rights—Press Unit, 'Factsheet—Mass Surveillance' (European Court of Human Rights 2016) <http://www.echr.coe.int/Documents/FS_Mass_surveillance_ENG.pdf> accessed 1 June 2019; *Digital Rights Ireland Ltd* (n 9); *Tele2 Sverige* (n 1709).

[290] On the requirements for online security technologies to constitute a legitimate tradeoff vis-à-vis freedoms and liberties, see: Hildebrandt, 'Balance or Trade-Off?' (n 272) 375 et seq.

respective data cannot be anonymized and/or erased *in casu*. This could be the case in the unlikely event that the interests in identification for achieving the research aims outweigh those of the data subject in having his/her data erased. Overall it seems reasonable to expect ISS providers following standard ethical guidelines for conducting research, even if they are not a scientific institution *stricto sensu*.[291]

Transparency Conundrum—An important practical limitation to the effective exercise of the right to erasure/object in the context of processing for research or security interests relates to transparency. This is especially so when considering the way in which data is generally processed in these contexts, ie dynamically and on a massive, automated and unpredictable scale (see machine learning and artificial intelligence).[292] The current *modus operandi* makes it particularly hard to define a concrete balance between the different interests at hand.[293] The difficulty of ensuring an adequate level of transparency in the context of processing for research purposes was already recognized in the 1970s, inter alia because of the potentially disproportionate costs it would entail (see proportionality).[294] Yet, in order to exercise one's data subject right to erasure (or to object), it is necessary to be able to identify the relevant personal data first (even if only by the controller itself). Practice suggests that this is an increasingly difficult thing to do, even if required by the GDPR.[295] Suffice to say at this stage that the transparency conundrum in the current ISS eco-system is already subject of a wider debate on 'algorithmic accountability'.[296]

Conclusion—Overall, it does not seem that processing in light of collective interests such as security and public interest research pose different issues than the ones already treated in the first two balancing scenarios. In the context of scientific research, the rights to erasure and to object can only realistically be blocked when identification is necessary, and the research is carried out in the public interest (see Arts 17(3)(d) and 21(6)). With regard to security interests, the controller will have to demonstrate the processing is necessary, effective, and proportionate. Taking a

291 For example, extending legal requirements for Institutional Review Boards (see many references in: Jane R Bambauer, 'All Life Is an Experiment. (Sometimes It Is a Controlled Experiment.)' (2015) 47 Loyola University Chicago Law Journal 15, 488; SATORI Project, 'Policy Brief. Industry and Research and Innovation (R&I): Towards Ethical, Responsible and Sustainable R&I' <http://satoriproject.eu/media/SATORI-policy-brief-_2017-Industry-_09-1-2017.pdf> accessed 28 April 2018) and the increase attention to the ethics of data-driven research and innovation at the EU policy level (eg The European Group on Ethics in Science and New Technologies (EGE), http://ec.europa.eu/research/ege).

292 Hildebrandt, 'Balance or Trade-Off?' (n 272) 377.

293 Daniel J Solove, *Nothing to Hide: The False Tradeoff between Privacy and Security* (Yale University Press 2012) 194.

294 Lindop (n 176) 240–41.

295 Ausloos and Dewitte (n 28); Veale, Binns, and Ausloos, 'When Data Protection by Design and Data Subject Rights Clash' (n 28).

296 See, for example: http://www.fatml.org/resources/relevant-scholarship; European Data Protection Supervisor, 'Meeting the Challenges of Big Data—A Call for Transparency, User Control, Data Protection by Design and Accountability' (EDPS 2015) Opinion 7/2015 <https://edps.europa.eu/sites/edp/files/publication/15-11-19_big_data_en.pdf> accessed 1 June 2019.

step back, it does appear that non-commercial interests and especially collective, public interests are more likely to override data subjects' interests in a particular case. This also follows from the fact that controller and third-party interests are better aligned, forming a stronger front against individual data subject rights.[297] Compared with the second scenario, third party interests are more likely to be defended by the controller in the balancing act. The difficulty resides in identifying all the relevant interests at stake and their relative weight. To what extent can the underlying interests be traced back to Charter rights and freedoms? How to compare a collective, societal interest—to be distinguished from a collection of individual interests—against that of data subjects in specific cases?

Section 3. Summary and Conclusion

Overview—Invoking the right to erasure/object against ISS providers essentially results in an individualized/context-dependent stress-test of the original balance relied upon to process the respective personal data in the first place. From a data protection perspective, this balance shifts in favour of the data subject by default upon invoking said right.[298] Article 6(1)(f) grants controllers—and controllers only—the ability to further process the personal data nonetheless if they establish their interests and/or those of third parties still override those of the data subject. These interests can take different shapes, but the most common ones in the ISS context relate to the controller's commercial interests, others' information freedom interests, and collective or shared interests (eg in security and scientific research). In general terms, the first scenario primarily challenges the rationale of the fundamental right to data protection (Art 8 Charter), namely autonomy. The second scenario especially challenges the fundamental right to privacy (Art 7 Charter) and the GDPR's instrumental role in safeguarding it. The third scenario potentially challenges data subjects' right to data protection (Art 8 Charter) and/or privacy (Art 7 Charter), but also other fundamental rights such as non-discrimination (Art 21 Charter). In practice, these balancing scenarios will rarely occur in isolation and generally overlap in different ways.

Inherent Open-Endedness—This chapter aimed to provide some guidance on how to go about balancing acts stemming from right to erasure/object requests vis-à-vis ISS providers. These rights inherently require a context-dependent and individualized assessment of the case at hand. The fair balancing mission of the

[297] As an interesting side-thought, one could also contemplate third parties to refer to shared interests such as security, (health) research, etc in order to compel controllers to share data. When there is a strong enough public interest, legal intervention ordering data sharing may be desirable.

[298] After all, it is a direct expression of their informational autonomy, implicating the fundamental right to data protection itself. See similarly: Gutwirth, 'De Toepassing van Het Finaliteitsbeginsel van de Privacywet' (n 13) 1447–48.

GDPR, but also CJEU and ECtHR case law, preclude categorical rules prioritizing one right or interest over the other in an absolute fashion. This also renders it unfeasible to devise comprehensive hierarchies or taxonomies of criteria for balancing. They are no check-box exercises. Indeed, due to the dynamic and vague nature of fair balancing it is impossible to fully automate the process (which might frustrate large ISS providers used to optimizing processes through automation). The legal uncertainty stemming from such a vague and flexible approach can be mitigated through procedural safeguards (ie the GDPR and satellite frameworks), a progressively growing body of case law and authoritative guidance.

McFadden Case Illustration—The CJEU's *McFadden* case offers a useful illustration summarizing some of the main points discussed throughout this chapter. In this case, the Court essentially put forward a five-prong test to assess whether requiring to password-protect an internet connection strikes a fair balance between the fundamental rights to intellectual property, freedom to conduct a business, and freedom of information.[299] The measure has to (a) respect the essence of the right to freedom to conduct a business; and (b) that of the right to freedom of information; (c) be strictly targeted; (d) be sufficiently effective to ensure genuine protection of the fundamental right at issue; and (e) there are no viable alternatives. It is easy to imagine how these five steps can also be applied to conflicts emerging from invoking the right to erasure/object as a tool to protect one's fundamental right to data protection, rather than requesting password-protection a network for safeguarding one's right to intellectual property protection.

Vignettes and McFadden Requirements—To illustrate, these five steps can be applied to erasure requests in the vignettes described in Chapter 1.[300] It is hard to see how *McFadden*'s first two steps would fail with regard to individual requests to erasure/object in any of the vignettes. Exercising these rights would not drive any of these actors out of business, nor effectively silence someone's ability to impart/receive information as protected under Article 11 Charter.[301] The third step requires the right to erasure or object to be specifically targeted. In the Google vignette, this implies delisting requests cannot be too generic (eg 'delist all information about me'), something which generally seems to align with post-*Google Spain* case law.[302] With regard to the remaining three vignettes (ie Uber, Facebook,

[299] *McFadden* (n 23) paras 90–100.

[300] As a reminder, the *first* vignette relates to Uber's psychological manipulation of drivers; the *second* vignette relates to Facebook's emotional manipulation and political advertisements; the *third* vignette concerns the Google Spain delisting case; and the *fourth* vignette relates to Apple's smart assistant Siri.

[301] If it would, that would mean that the respective ISS provider would effectively be constitutive of the essence of the relevant person's freedom of expression/information.

[302] It should be said that the limits of the specificity of requests is still being tested. The Belgian data protection authority, for example, issued a recommendation for Google to also delist contentious URLs when additional search terms are added to a search on the basis of the data subject's name. Belgian Privacy Commission, 'Advies 75/2017 Ingevolge Een Klacht Gericht Tegen Een Zoekmotor Betreffende de Modaliteiten Voor de Uitvoering En de Geografische Reikwijdte van Een Verwijdering van URL's Uit de Zoekresultaten (CO-A-2017-088)' (n 36).

and Apple), this third step might raise some practical difficulties for data subjects, as the respective data processing practices are often very complex and concealed. Controllers should therefore be more upfront about said practices, and more clearly and granularly offer data subjects the ability to target them individually. The fourth step requires sufficient effectiveness. It can therefore only be assessed in light of the respective data subject's actual goals when exercising the right to erasure/object. If this is simply as an extension of his/her right to data protection under Article 8 Charter (ie informational self-determination), then the mere exercise of that control over one's data can be considered 'effective'. If the goal is to not be unfairly discriminated against, mere erasure of a psychological/emotional profile in the Uber and Facebook vignettes might not be sufficiently effective. Data subjects might still be influenced on the basis of other elements. With regard to the Google vignette too, the 'effectiveness' will depend on whether the data subject wishes to obliterate personal data from the internet altogether or is contented with reducing findability through popular search engines. With regard to the fifth step, finally, there can be no viable alternatives to the right to erasure/object. When requesting the halt of psychological/emotional profiling and manipulation in the Uber and Facebook vignettes, there do not seem to be any viable alternatives (to the right to object). With regard to the Google vignette, one may question to what extent down ranking or adding clarifications to search results constitute effective and appropriate alternatives to actual delisting. In the Apple vignette, finally, a viable alternative to actual erasure of Siri voice data (and related data), might be effective and demonstrable anonymization. The last 'viable alternatives' step will be discussed further in Chapter 7, under 'fifty shades of erasure'.

Key Take-Aways—Overall, what is important to keep in mind is that balancing under the GDPR is inherently dynamic.[303] In order to validly oppose a right to erasure/object request, the interests involved should find their justification in the Charter (eg specific right or freedom, or a legislative measure in light of Article 52(1)). As such, Article 6(1)(f) as triggered by the data subject rights to erasure and to object, effectively constitutes a proxy for balancing fundamental rights. The interests involved should be actually pursued (ie not be purely hypothetical).[304] This does not mean all personal data without a clear and present purpose can simply be erased, but neither should the absolute openness and availability of information be fetishized (whether for public, economic, or freedom of expression interests).[305] 'Erasure versus publicity or free-to-use' is not a binary, there are 50 shades of erasure that may accommodate all interests at stake and effectuate a balance when implemented. A granular approach means that in principle, ISS

[303] See Lindop (n 176) 11; *Google Spain* (n 2) paras 69; 93.

[304] Article 29 Working Party, 'Opinion 06/2014 on the Notion of Legitimate Interests of the Data Controller under Article 7 of Directive 95/46/EC' (n 5) 24.

[305] See in the same vein, for example: Hustinx, 'How Practicable Is It to Apply Data Protection to Activities Involving Freedom of Expression?' (n 285).

providers should accommodate data subject rights with regard to any personal data and/or processing operations that are not in themselves strictly necessary to deliver the service requested by the data subject, *unless* doing so would disproportionately affect fundamental rights and freedoms of others. Commercial interests (Arts 16–17 Charter) alone will generally not be sufficient to block a right to erasure/object request, certainly not with regard to powerful ISS providers. In the unlikely event that individual requests would actually endanger their business, it is rather the business model that should be called into question.[306] The Charter protects people, citizens, individuals first. ISS providers' responsibility to ensure their information control is informed by the fundamental rights framework, will be a function of their size and overall power.

Despite having fleshed out some of the core issues emerging from right to erasure/object induced balancing in the ISS context, it must be acknowledged that key questions remain. The inherently context-dependent nature of said conflicts and the fact that they involve fundamental rights and freedoms, render it impossible to categorically define situations where the balance falls either way. Additionally, the balancing scenarios also pointed at some of the shortcomings in how GDPR balancing may be adjudicated in practice. Even though it nuances fear-mongers' worries of essentially having private entities balancing fundamental rights, some questions remain in this regard. Overall, it seems that both issues—private adjudication and the lack of determinative balancing criteria—can considerably be tackled through clear legal guidance and procedural safeguards. Both of which the GDPR already aims to pursue, at least in theory and at a high/horizontal level. In other words, much will depend on how the legal instrument will be fine-tuned, implemented, complemented, and applied in practice. Chapter 7 will tackle some remaining issues in light of the right to erasure.

306 Particularly when considering the predominant business model is based on behavioural marketing, against which data subjects have an unconditional right to object (Art 21(2)). See in this regard also: Information Commissioner's Office, 'Update Report into AdTech and Real Time Bidding' (n 49).

7

Open Questions on Balancing in the GDPR

In fleshing out the main complexities of fair balancing under the GDPR, the previous two chapters have laid bare several important questions. These relate to the vague and open-ended nature of fair balancing, the apparent priority of the right to data protection, and the role given to information society service (ISS) providers as de facto private adjudicators. This chapter purports to dissect and nuance these questions. It is not aimed at being comprehensive, but rather as a closing chapter to Part II on balancing, providing more context, and drawing together loose ends in an occasionally provocative manner. It is worth highlighting that fair balancing in the context of this book is interpreted broadly. I tend to follow Angelopoulos when she explains that

> balancing is to be approached merely as a metaphor intended to guide juridical thought—or perhaps more precisely, a formula for the investigation of what is ultimately a policy choice. The language of balancing can thus be seen simply as a way of explaining that no obvious solution to a given problem exists: the issue at stake is a complex one, comprised of multiple factors that must all be considered—'weighed', so to speak.[1]

Section 1. Fair Balancing, a Blessing and a Curse?

INTRODUCTION—As already made clear in the previous chapters, the very concept of fair balancing has been the subject of quite some criticism. Within the context of data protection law and *ex post* empowerment rights in particular, balancing plays a crucial role nonetheless. Indeed, as was amply explained in Chapters 2 and 5, the GDPR as a whole is a balancing framework by its very nature. It lays out an infrastructure to ensure data processing operations occur within a fair manner, pursuing a balance between all rights, freedoms, and interests at stake. Given its incredibly wide scope (see Chapter 3), the framework still remains quite abstract, leaving a lot of interpretative leeway to courts, data protection authorities,

[1] CJ Angelopoulos, 'European Intermediary Liability in Copyright: A Tort-Based Analysis' (PhD Thesis, University of Amsterdam 2016) <http://dare.uva.nl/record/1/527223> accessed 1 June 2019 285. Similarly see Smet, who also argues to look at balancing (of relative human rights) as *reasoning*. Stijn Smet, 'Resolving Conflicts between Human Rights: A Legal Theoretical Analysis in the Context of the ECHR' (PhD Thesis, Ghent University 2014) 321.

The Right to Erasure in EU Data Protection Law. First Edition. Jef Ausloos. Oxford University Press (2020). © Jef Ausloos
DOI: 10.1093/oso/9780198847977.001.0001

regulators, but also controllers and data subjects themselves. While this flexibility makes the GDPR quite versatile and sustainable, it may also result in subjective and diverging applications of the law.[2]

CURSE—Fair balancing is often an inherently frustrating legal exercise. Inevitably things will be lost in translation when legally interpreting a given case to distil the relevant rights, freedoms, and interests. It has also been argued that one cannot actually 'weigh' such abstract legal concepts.[3] In the context of human rights law, Van Drooghenbroeck explains that an overreliance on proportionality may lead to a 'government by judges' (*gouvernement des juges*).[4] Translated to the GDPR, this would mean an overreliance on 'balancing' could result in a 'government by controllers' (who do the *prima facie* balancing, see Chapter 5). All of the above is conducive to perhaps the most important criticism against fair balancing: legal uncertainty. This may be remedied to some extent by a growing body of cases, which in turn will help identify a mean (not unlike the principle of big data, where more data enables to more easily identify commonalities). But the aforementioned author also warns against what he calls 'hypercontextualization', where each case is particularized so much, making it almost impossible to identify a common interpretation.[5]

BLESSING—While certainly raising valid concerns, a lot of the criticism against fair balancing (in the GDPR) can be nuanced, as will be done throughout this chapter. In general terms, fair balancing recognizes the cognitive inability to foresee all potential situations that might be regulated by a rule.[6] It allows 'humanizing' the law, actively pushing to think in terms of the impact one's actions might have on others and enables considering each case on its own merits. Of course, it does not suffice to simply require 'a fair balance to be sought'. Solid safeguards and refinements should be installed. The GDPR is a considerable step forward in providing such safeguards but should be complemented with additional refinements in specific contexts.

RULES V PRINCIPLES—The discussion on the merits and drawbacks of fair balancing can be tied back to the debate on rules versus principles (or standards). Put very briefly, 'a rule sets forth the outcome in advance, while a standard allows greater discretion and decision making on a case-by-case basis'.[7] Whereas rules are

[2] See in the same vein, but with regard to fair balancing of human rights: Sébastien Van Drooghenbroeck, *La proportionnalité dans le droit de la Convention européenne des droits de l'Homme: prendre l'idée simple au sérieux* (FUSL 2001) 13 et seq.

[3] See, for example: Bart van der Sloot, 'Editorial' (2017) 3 European Data Protection Law Review 1.

[4] Van Drooghenbroeck (n 2) 16.

[5] eg when each fair balancing decision includes phrases such as '*all things considered*' or '*taking into account all circumstances at hand*', rather than defining clear sets of determinative factors, its value as a precedent diminishes considerably. Van Drooghenbroeck (n 2) 297.

[6] ibid 213–14.

[7] Edward Lee, 'The Right to Be Forgotten v. Free Speech Internet Freedom' (2015) 12 I/S: A Journal of Law and Policy for the Information Society 85, 10.

binary, principles are relative and have different degrees.[8] Summarizing the relevant literature, Van Alsenoy explains that

> rules are likely to be preferable over standards if the primary behaviour (i.e. the regulated activity) is factually homogenous, stable, and occurs frequently. Standards, on the other hand, are likely to be preferable in situations where the primary behaviour is heterogeneous, evolves rapidly over time, or occurs infrequently. The underlying rationale is that the benefits of detailing a rule will be greater the more often it is applied. The cost of detailing a rule, however, is likely to be higher as the heterogeneity or complexity of the regulated activity increases. Moreover, if the social, economic or technical factors shaping the problem evolve rapidly over time, crafting detailed rules may yield insufficient return on investment. Finally, (certain) rules are more likely to create risks of over- or under-inclusion than standards. Standards, on the other hand, are less likely to be affected by changes over time in the circumstances to which they are applied.[9]

Most legal provisions find themselves somewhere on the continuum with, on the one end, rules and, on the other, principles/standards.[10] Given its wide scope, data protection law's core provisions seem to be located more at the 'principles' extremity (notably Article 5 GDPR). Some provisions gravitate more towards the other end, installing obligations under clearly delineated situations (eg Art 9 on sensitive data). The rights to erasure (Art 17) and to object (Art 21) may give the appearance of being 'rules' because they are defined as 'if condition A is fulfilled, then perform action X (ie erase/stop processing)'. In reality, however, they lean much more towards the principle/standard extremity. Indeed, as demonstrated in Chapter 5, all of the right-to-erasure triggers (Art 17(1)) and exemptions (Art 17(3)) incorporate/defer balancing acts, or at the very least require a context-dependent evaluation. Van Drooghenbroeck explains that even the most clearly defined rules are simply balancing acts in disguise.[11] After all, defining a rule (notably its application trigger) is a subjective exercise where the legislator will perform a balancing act as well (even if only implied and/or simply in order to respect the ECHR).[12] This was also made clear with regard to the first five lawful grounds in Chapter 5 already.

[8] Van Drooghenbroeck (n 2) 625–29, referring to: Robert Alexy, *Theorie der Grundrechte, Suhrkamp Taschenbucher Wissenschaft* 582 (Suhrkamp 1985).

[9] Brendan Van Alsenoy, *Data Protection Law in the EU: Roles, Responsibilities and Liability* (Intersentia. 2019).

[10] One author has aimed to project different types of legal provisions on this continuum: trumps (ie rules) > presumptions > catalogs > case-by-case (ie fair balancing). See: Lee (n 7) 10–15.

[11] Van Drooghenbroeck (n 2) 288–90.

[12] Van Drooghenbroeck explains that the main difference between rules and principle lies in their temporal effect. The former is much more persistent or long term, whereas the latter is less impactful given its ad hoc nature. He then continues, explaining that the bigger impact of rules might induce deeper reflexivity and thus a 'better' and more thoughtful outcome then having to rely on

Pushing Interpretation Costs Downstream—Because they gravitate more towards the end of principles/standards, many GDPR provisions effectively push the 'burden of fair balancing' downstream. The legislator has defined the broad strokes, but essentially leaves much of the actual balancing to be done by others. As amply described in previous chapters, this can be done by deferring to other legal frameworks[13] or requiring controllers to do the balancing.[14] The legal uncertainty this may initially bring about, is hoped to fade away in the mid-long term, through the adoption of codes of conduct, standards, and regulatory guidelines. Ideally, the gradual development of a substantial body of balancing decisions—whether by controllers or judges—may also bring about more coherence.[15] When De Schutter and Tulkens talk about balancing in the context of human rights, they might as well have been speaking about data protection law:

> [A]s comparable situations of conflicting rights develop, and as a pattern emerges from their repetition, certain standards will develop as to how to address them. It is one of the roles of the ECtHR [and the CJEU, DPAs or even controllers] to progressively identify such standards as they emerge from local experiences, since a purely ad hoc approach addressing situations of conflict on a case-to-case basis provides too little guidance […]. [S]uch standards, however, should not rigidify into rules, closed to revision […]. Just like scientific hypotheses may be tested against physical phenomena, such standards should be tested against the reality of conflicts which occur.[16]

Conclusion—In sum, fair balancing in the GDPR is both a blessing and a curse. It is a necessary corollary of the framework's wide scope, ensures sustainability, safeguards, and that each data subject gets an opportunity to be treated as an individual, taking into account his/her particular situation. The flipside of such a

judicial prudence in a more casuistic approach. See also: Antonin Scalia, 'The Rule of Law as a Law of Rules Essay' (1989) 56 University of Chicago Law Review 1175, 1179–80. As referred to in: Van Drooghenbroeck (n 2) 290.

[13] eg Articles 6(1)(f), 17(1)(e) and derogations in Articles 23, 85.

[14] eg Article 6(1)(f) or 21(1).

[15] Also recognized by the ECtHR in: *Satakunnan Markkinapörssi Oy et Satamedia Oy v Finland* [2017] European Court of Human Rights 931/13 paras 143–44. 'Whilst certainty is desirable, it may bring in its train excessive rigidity, and the law must be able to keep pace with changing circumstances. Accordingly, many laws are inevitably couched in terms which, to a greater or lesser extent, are vague, and whose interpretation and application are questions of practice.' See also: Serge Gutwirth, 'De Toepassing van Het Finaliteitsbeginsel van de Privacywet van 8 December 1992 Tot Bescherming van de Persoonlijke Levenssfeer Ten Opzichte van de Verwerking van Persoonsgegevens' [The Application of the Purpose Specification Principle in the Belgian Data Protection Act of 8 December 1992] (1993) 1993 Tijdschrift voor Privaatrecht—TPR 1466. See concept of '*jurisprudence transitoire*', Van Drooghenbroeck (n 2).

[16] Olivier De Schutter and Françoise Tulkens, 'Rights in Conflict: The European Court of Human Rights as a Pragmatic Institution' (Université Catholique de Louvain 2007) Working Paper 44–45.

flexible approach is that the necessarily vague language pushes the burden of interpretation downstream to actors that may be more or less well-equipped to deal with this. Recognizing this to some extent, the GDPR does put in place certain obligations qualifying more as strict 'rules' and calls for interpretative guidance. The rights to erasure and object in particular, ensure that balances pre-defined by the legislator or controller, can be challenged from the data subject's perspective.

Section 2. How Far Does the Responsibility to Balance Reach?

RESPONSIBILITY AND LIABILITY—Chapter 2 already distinguished between *responsibility* and *liability* in the context of data protection law. In short, the GDPR installs a framework of *responsibility*, while *liability* is primarily kept as a stick behind the door in case of 'irresponsible' behaviour. In light of the vagueness of many provisions, this may render it particularly hard to demonstrate such 'irresponsibility' in practice. This is especially true with regard to the open-ended balancing provisions, where non-compliance (and liability) will often only be demonstrable in blatant cases. In this context, it will be easier to establish liability for (not) incorporating certain procedural safeguards (eg not giving data subjects an opportunity to be heard, not responding to a request within one month).

BURDEN—Exercising data subject rights will by definition require proactive steps by the data subject. Put differently, data subjects will have to take the initiative to challenge existing balances.[17] Article 17(1) GDPR does not explicitly require data subjects to motivate their erasure requests. Yet, it seems fair to argue that unmotivated requests will only be granted when the controller does not oppose erasure. Additionally, it should be kept in mind that all right to erasure triggers in Article 17(1) refer to other provisions, which may in turn require some sort of motivation. This is implicitly true for the first (purpose expiration) and fourth (unlawful processing) triggers, explicitly for the third trigger (right to object)[18] and potentially for the fifth trigger (legal obligation). Upon receiving a request, the controller (wishing to continue processing personal data, even if only for limited subset of purposes), will have to assess the legitimacy of the request and re-evaluate the balance. Such reassessment can only be done in light of the information available to the controller. Pursuant to Article 12 (on the modalities for exercising data subject rights)—and the fairness principle more broadly—controllers do have an obligation to ask data subjects for more information in case they cannot adequately re-assess the balance. In practice, a dialogue may emerge between controller and

[17] That is, unless the controller itself challenges the balance and/or offers a re-evaluation of the balance to data subjects at regular intervals.

[18] Following Article 21(1), data subjects can object *on grounds relating to their particular situation*. No such burden exists when the data subject objects to personal data being processed for direct marketing purposes.

data subject, resulting in the final decision.[19] Helberger et al. propose the notion of 'cooperative responsibility', which involves a 'multi-stakeholder process of public deliberation and exchange, in which agreement can be reached between platforms, users, and public institutions on how important public values can be advanced'.[20] In sum, whereas the prima facie burden for triggering a re-balancing act may lie with the data subject wishing to exercise the right to erasure/object, the eventual burden will be on the controller's shoulders.[21]

Obligation of Means—The act of balancing rights, freedoms, and interests is inherently subjective. The GDPR purports to install a procedural framework to ensure fairness. With this in mind, one could say that from a formal perspective, balancing in the GDPR is an obligation of result, ie the controller needs to go through the motions of balancing as dictated by the respective GDPR provisions. Substantially, however, *fair* balancing is in essence an obligation of means (see the mechanics of fair balancing as described in Chapter 5). What this entails in practice is that a controller cannot be held liable for the outcome of fair balancing (respecting all GDPR requirements), when a data protection authority comes to a different conclusion.[22] As mentioned before, the burden on controllers' shoulders will be a function of their 'responsibilities, powers and capabilities'.[23] This means that the required effort to be put in the fair balancing act will scale depending on the controller (eg size,[24] involvement,[25] what is technically/realistically possible).[26] As described by Bygrave and Schartum, 'the proportionality principle must inevitably be observed by both DPAs and data controllers when exercising their respective decision-making competence'.[27]

19 Which may also entail a compromise solution (see 'Fifty Shades of Erasure').

20 Natali Helberger, Jo Pierson, and Thomas Poell, 'Governing Online Platforms: From Contested to Cooperative Responsibility' (2018) 34 Information Society 10.

21 This is also true with regard to the establishment of liability under the GDPR. See in this regard: Brendan Van Alsenoy, 'Liability under EU Data Protection Law: From Directive 95/46 to the General Data Protection Regulation' (2017) 7 JIPITEC para 43<http://www.jipitec.eu/issues/jipitec-7-3-2016/1506>.

22 eg after the data subject challenged the controller's re-balance, filing a complaint with the data protection authority.

23 *Google Spain SL, Google Inc v Agencia Española de Protección de Datos (AEPD), Mario Costeja González* [2014] Court of Justice of the European Union C-131/12, paras 38, 83.

24 David Erdos, 'Delimiting the Ambit of Responsibility of Intermediary Publishers for Third Party Rights in European Data Protection: Towards a Synthetic Interpretation of the EU Acquis' (University of Cambridge, Faculty of Law 2017) Legal Studies Research Paper 31/2017 21<https://papers.ssrn.com/abstract=2993154> accessed 1 June 2019.; Brendan Van Alsenoy, 'The Evolving Role of the Individual Under EU Data Protection Law' (KU Leuven—CiTiP 2015) Working Paper 23 5<http://papers.ssrn.com/abstract=2641680> accessed 1 June 2019.

25 For an elaborate analysis in the context of intermediaries, see: Erdos, 'Delimiting the Ambit of Responsibility of Intermediary Publishers for Third Party Rights in European Data Protection' (n 24) 28.

26 Brendan Van Alsenoy, *Data Protection Law in the EU: Roles, Responsibilities and Liability* (Intersentia 2019) 581ff.

27 Lee Bygrave and Dag Wiese Schartum, 'Consent, Proportionality and Collective Power' in Serge Gutwirth and others (eds), *Reinventing Data Protection?* (Springer Netherlands 2009) 163<http://link.springer.com/10.1007/978-1-4020-9498-9> accessed 1 June 2019.

FAIRNESS—The controller's 'obligation of means' to balance should be read in light of the fairness principle (Art 5(1)(a)).[28] In short, the controller should be able to demonstrate the respective balancing is done in good faith and in line with the GDPR's overall system of checks and balances.[29] Fully complying with all GDPR provisions (let alone demonstrating it) may be more or less difficult in practice.[30] Instilling fairness in the (data processing) operations of large-scale ISS providers presents particular challenges, extending beyond the realms of data protection law, such as relating to discrimination, freedom of expression, competition, and so on.[31] WP29 has listed a number of measures to be taken by controllers in order to ensure fair balances under the GDPR:[32]

- *Purpose limitation* (strict limitations on how much data are collected; immediate deletion of data after use; ensure functional separation; extra care to data minimization principle and storage limitation principle (which offer different degrees of compliance).
- *Technical and organizational measures* (ensure functional separation; anonymization techniques; aggregation of data; privacy-enhancing technologies; privacy by design; local v centralized processing).
- *Accountability* (increased transparency; privacy and data protection impact assessments; training and guidance on the people doing the processing; transparency, specifically regarding 'free' services online, it will have to be made very clear that they are not in fact free, but consumers 'pay' with their data).
- *Increase Empowerment* (provide an easily workable and accessible mechanism to ensure an unconditional possibility for data subjects to opt-out of the processing; data portability; and related measures to empower data subjects).

[28] Damian Clifford and Jef Ausloos, 'Data Protection and the Role of Fairness' (2018) 37 Yearbook of European Law 130; European Group on Ethics in Science and New Technologies (n 33).

[29] Notably the data quality principles in Article 5(1); data protection by design and by default in Article 25; and the designation of a data protection officer in Article 37.

[30] eg data may be rendered pseudonymous with no easy way for the controller to re-identify and accommodate data subject rights. Michael Veale, Reuben Binns, and Jef Ausloos, 'When Data Protection by Design and Data Subject Rights Clash' International Data Privacy Law <https://academic.oup.com/idpl/advance-article/doi/10.1093/idpl/ipy002/4960902> accessed 5 April 2018); Reuben Binns, 'Tweet' (*Twitter*, 2 May 2018) <https://twitter.com/RDBinns/status/991622955561046017> accessed 7 May 2018.

[31] Which explains broader policy initiatives such as European Commission, 'Building a European Data Economy' (10 January 2017) <https://ec.europa.eu/digital-single-market/en/policies/building-european-data-economy> accessed 28 April 2018; European Commission, Proposal for a Regulation on Promoting Fairness and Transparency for Business Users of Online Intermediation Services 2018 [COM(2018) 238 final].

[32] Guidance on several of these has already been drafted by 29WP in the past. See references in: Article 29 Working Party, 'Opinion 06/2014 on the Notion of Legitimate Interests of the Data Controller under Article 7 of Directive 95/46/EC' (European Commission 2014) Opinion WP 217 42 <http://ec.europa.eu/justice/article-29/documentation> accessed 1 June 2019.

Apple Vignette—It is possible now to look more closely at how far the fair balancing responsibility of Apple extends, as a controller vis-a-vis Siri data.[33] As a reminder, in the operation of the Siri voice assistant, Apple collects voice recordings and adds it to a profile associated with a unique and persistent 'voice identifier' (also including other information such as playlists, reminders lists, names and relationships of contacts).[34] In the name of data protection by design, the company claims this identifier is disassociated from other identifiers and 'they do not have a technical means to access the Siri identifier on the device, nor to search the data by identifier, as they have chosen not to build one'.[35] Evidently this information is personal data, and could even contain sensitive data (eg depending on what is being asked/said to Siri). The vignette demonstrates how a controller's data protection by design measures may prevent the individual exercise of data subject rights (access, erasure, portability). In fact, Apple designed its infrastructure so that it does not even get to the point of performing individualized balancing acts following an erasure request. It has effectively made such a balance *ex ante* for all of its customers (and anyone else whose personal data might be caught up in the system).[36] Whereas the company may have valid reasons for doing so (ie data protection by design, security, thwarting access requests by intelligence services), the practice does raise important issues. All the more considering how 'easy' it could be to re-identify data subjects in case a hacker would get access to (some of) the information and/or there would be a data breach.[37] Requesting controllers to reconsider their overall data processing infrastructure in light of improving data protection aligns with CJEU case law, for as long as it would not entail 'an excessive burden'.[38] In the case at hand, it seems hard for Apple to argue such an excessive burden, not least considering the company's resources. Several options seem to be

[33] See Apple Vignette as described in Chapter 1.

[34] The voice-recording is stored together with the identifier for six months, after which the identifier is removed and the information can be retained for another two years. Apple Inc, 'IOS Security (IOS 10)' 49–50 <https://perma.cc/8EQE-TFW5> accessed 7 May 2018.

[35] Veale, Binns, and Ausloos, 'When Data Protection by Design and Data Subject Rights Clash' (n 30) 8.

[36] eg contact details or others speaking to Siri.

[37] The risk of re-identification seems relatively trivial, even to non-experts. Not only can the information connected to the voice recordings be highly revealing (ie contact details and relationship to the data subject), technological advances in stylometry and voice recognition render re-identification fairly easy as well.

[38] *College van burgemeester en wethouders van Rotterdam v MEE Rijkeboer* [2009] Court of Justice of the European Union C-553/07. In this case, the controller applied a different retention policy for 'basic data' (ie the personal data it used for its own purposes) and information relating to how the personal data was used, its source, and time. The latter type was removed after one year, whereas the 'basic data' could be stored for longer. This meant that data subjects could not exercise their access right (Art 15 GDPR) regarding who their data had been shared with and/or how it was used exactly more than a year ago. The Court essentially ruled that any time limit upon this 'metadata' should constitute 'a fair balance between, on the one hand, the interest of the data subject in protecting his privacy, in particular by way of his rights to object and to bring legal proceedings and, on the other, the burden which the obligation to store that information represents for the controller' (para 64). Explained in: Veale, Binns, and Ausloos, 'When Data Protection by Design and Data Subject Rights Clash' (n 30) 11.

available that would enable individual exercises of data subject rights, while at the same time ensuring a high level of data protection.[39] In sum, effectively preventing data subjects from challenging balancing acts individually (pursuant to the right to erasure/object) only seems permissible in exceptional cases where the controller can demonstrate enabling this would constitute an excessive burden. Such argumentation will in itself constitute some sort of balancing act, as the controller will have to weigh different interests as well (eg its own resourcefulness and the merits of its data protection by design strategy versus the potential impact on the data subject of a breach and/or benefit in exercising the right).

Conclusion—Clearly, the full extent of a controller's responsibility in fair balancing is impossible to capture in the abstract. Even in individual cases it will be hard to objectively delineate such responsibility. What can be said is that controllers are not expected to do the impossible. Their duty to balance is an obligation of means, which essentially means they have to make a best effort in ensuring a fair balance is achieved. The level of responsibility to balance will be a function of a number of environmental variables such as size and resources of the controller, magnitude of processing, impact, etc. As demonstrated in the Apple vignette, blocking *ex post* balancing acts altogether, even if for legitimate reasons, can only be accepted in exceptional cases.

Section 3. Biased Balancing?

Problem—Data protection law has been criticized for overprotecting individuals, to the detriment of other fundamental rights and freedoms (notably economic and information freedoms, see Chapter 6). Such criticism might appear justified in light of the *Google Spain* ruling[40] (where the CJEU posited that data subjects' interests when exercising their rights to erasure/object override the search engine's economic interests and the interests of internet users by default) or the right to object (which puts the burden on controllers to establish they do *not* have to accommodate the right). The previous chapter also suggested that economic freedoms alone will hardly ever be sufficient in overriding data subjects' interests in *ex post* balancing acts. Information freedoms stand a better chance, but will often still require some level of public interest determination. With this in mind, is it possible to say that the GDPR balancing is biased towards data subjects?

[39] eg installing a parallel system with the specific purpose of upholding data subject rights, either by retaining relevant data in such a separate database *or* allowing for the provision of additional information provided by the data subject so as to enable re-identification. Both options can be made so that the data can still not be readily re-identified by Apple itself (as it claims is now the case) and requires the data subject's input (eg through providing a decryption key). For a complete explanation, see: Veale, Binns, and Ausloos, 'When Data Protection by Design and Data Subject Rights Clash' (n 30) 10 et seq.

[40] *Google Spain* (n 23) para 81.

And does this not go against the goal of the GDPR to lay down an infrastructure for balancing *all* fundamental rights and freedoms in the context of personal data being processed (see Chapter 5)? Several important points nuance the apparent bias in the GDPR.

Unfair to Begin With—Often overlooked or disregarded is the fact that the current status quo already massively favours the processing of (personal) data. As described in Chapter 1, technological advancements and the exponential growth in Internet usage has resulted in a golden age for information processing. 'Big data' is still expanding, with growing popularity of AI, machine learning, and data markets. It is also incontestable that the unprecedented communication abilities offered by the Internet have been a boon for freedom of expression and information globally.[41] There is no doubt that these developments have brought tremendous benefits to individuals, businesses, and society at large. This is also recognized in the GDPR's open approach to *ex ante* balancing (including the exemptions and derogations) and flexibility offered to controllers in defining said balance. Yet, it is important to keep in mind this broader context when evaluating the alleged 'bias' of *ex post* balancing under the GDPR.[42] As powerfully stated by Rodotà, '[t]he fundamental right to data protection is continuously eroded or downright overridden by alleging the prevailing interests of security and market logic'.[43] Against this backdrop, the GDPR installs defaults in favour of data subjects when they challenge the status quo. One could say that the default in favour of processing is reversed when comparing *ex ante* and *ex post* balances. It is up to the controller (initially, and potentially a DPA and/or court after that) to justify processing against the clear wishes of the data subject. In sum, while economic, technological, and societal reality has swung the pendulum forcefully towards data processing, some pushback favouring data subject's rights, freedoms, and interests seems warranted.

Safeguarding Data Protection In Particular—Even if the GDPR purports to install a fair balance between all fundamental rights, freedoms, and interests involved in data processing operations, it safeguards the right to data protection *in particular*. Article 1 puts data subjects at the centre of the GDPR's protective cloak. This importance given to data subjects and their rights, freedoms,

[41] Also recognized by the ECtHR, notably in: *Case of Times Newspapers Ltd (Nos 1 and 2) v The United Kingdom* [2009] European Court of Human Rights 3002/03 and 23676/03 para 27.

[42] For example, a 2016 empirical study demonstrated how the majority of online platforms explicitly do not commit to data minimization principles, track users outside of their platform, and allow for third-party tracking on their own platforms. Jamila Venturini and others, *Terms of Service and Human Rights: An Analysis of Online Platform Contracts* (Revan 2016) 61–74<http://internet-governance.fgv.br/sites/internet-governance.fgv.br/files/publicacoes/terms_of_services_06_12_2016.pdf> accessed 1 June 2019. See generally: M Jozwiak, 'Balancing the Rights to Data Protection and Freedom of Expression and Information by the Court of Justice of the European Union: The Vulnerability of Rights in an Online Context' (2016) 23 Maastricht Journal of European and Comparative Law (MJ) 404, 419.

[43] Stefano Rodotà, 'Data Protection as a Fundamental Right' in Serge Gutwirth and others (eds), *Reinventing Data Protection?* (Springer 2009) 80 <http://link.springer.com/10.1007/978-1-4020-9498-9> accessed 1 June 2019.

and interests does not constitute a bias, but a deliberate policy choice in the face of asymmetric information society realities.

RED HERRING—It was highlighted in the previous chapter already, the alleged 'imbalance' resulting from data protection rights in the ISS context is at least in part a red herring.[44] Such concerns appear to ignore the deeper, structural problem which is the position of powerful ISS providers. As described amply before, these entities have tremendous power over how information is accessed, shared, and exploited. Data protection rules essentially place this power under democratic control, ensuring safeguards based in law rather than shareholder value. While such a system is certainly not fool-proof, it would be unfortunate to consider that as the main issue at hand. The so-called 'trade-offs' between privacy and data protection versus security, innovation, or freedom of expression often make data protection the scapegoat for furthering the vested interests of powerful stakeholders.

BIG DATA GLORIFICATION—The erasure of personal data (Art 17) or prohibitions to further process personal data for a certain purpose (Art 21) is often represented as negative to everyone who is not the data subject. But is this really the case? A lot of commentary assumes the inherent value of maximizing data collection and processing. Yet a more critical appraisal of the actual net-benefit is necessary. What is in fact the value of easily finding information—from embarrassing pictures to the fact someone was a victim of rape—upon a mere name search on a popular search engine?[45] What is in fact the value of mass-scale tracking, monitoring, and profiling of Internet users? Sure, these operations may serve curiosity and/or commercial interests, but should value not be determined on a more holistic level? This is what fair balancing in the GDPR purports to do; not *just* to consider the immediate value to certain actors, but to critically assess the net-benefit, considering all interests and actors at stake.

GOOGLE VIGNETTE—The 'right to be delisted' from search engines has been widely criticized for being a tool for censorship and rewriting history. Looking at the statistics that are available, such claims seem absurdly overblown.[46] Even

[44] 'As an informal fallacy, the red herring falls into a broad class of relevance fallacies. Unlike the straw man, which is premised on a distortion of the other party's position, the red herring is a seemingly plausible, though ultimately irrelevant, diversionary tactic. According to the Oxford English Dictionary, a red herring may be intentional, or unintentional.' 'Red Herring', *Wikipedia* (2018) <https://en.wikipedia.org/wiki/Red_herring> accessed 9 May 2018.

[45] 'Simply because people desire to know everything about a person does not grant them the right to circumvent that individual's rights to privacy. […] now that a public searchable database exists, some feel that it is their right to know any and all private information regarding another, regardless if it contradicts the UDHR right to privacy and reputation. To live in an unforgiving world that allows unrestricted access to all personal information would be detrimental to society.' Andrew Neville, 'Is It a Human Right To Be Forgotten? Conceptualizing The World View' (2017) 15 Santa Clara Journal of International Law 17, 171.

[46] Sylvia Tippmann and Julia Powles, 'Google Accidentally Reveals Data on "right to Be Forgotten" Requests' *The Guardian* (14 July 2015) <http://www.theguardian.com/technology/2015/jul/14/google-accidentally-reveals-right-to-be-forgotten-requests> accessed 1 June 2019; Bertram and others (n 1700).

more, they take the 'red herring' bait in focusing on a side-issue of what is really at stake: search engines' position as powerful information gatekeepers.[47] Given their crucial impact on fundamental rights and freedoms, having some legal safeguards certainly seems in place.[48] If delisting something from Google or Facebook is seen as effectively removing it from the Internet, the issue at hand is first and foremost those companies' impact over information flows. Criticism that claims delisting amounts to 'altering history' assume that search engines constitute *the* historical record. If that were to be the case, or if it is considered they should be entrusted with such a goal, then certainly even stronger legal safeguards should be put in place on how these entities control information flows. Some also argue data subject rights such as delisting install incentives to over-comply.[49] Even if this were to be true,[50] how problematic is this from an information freedoms perspective and is this not simply restoring a perturbed balance?[51] Indeed, what impact does the right to be delisted actually have on information freedoms, considering that such freedoms are essentially at the mercy of opaque and dynamic search engine practices already?[52]

CONCLUSION—The particular attention paid to the right to data protection in the GDPR's fair balancing mission does raise some valid concerns. Yet, it is important to look at this apparent 'bias' in light of the broader context against which the GDPR operates. What is seen as bias by some, is in fact a corrective regulatory measure in order to recalibrate power asymmetries over data. As amply illustrated in the previous chapters, the GDPR already incorporates important safeguards

[47] Julia Powles, 'The Case That Won't Be Forgotten' (2015) 47 Loy U Chi LJ 583, 598.

[48] See the many case law references in Chapter 6 and also the Commission's European Commission Proposal for a Regulation on Promoting Fairness and Transparency for Business Users of Online Intermediation Services (n 31).

[49] eg Zingales and Janczuk-Gorywoda in: Olivia Tambou (ed), *Le Droit à l'oubli En Europe et Au-Delà / The Right to Be Forgotten in Europe and Beyond* (Blogdroiteuropéen 2018) 89 <https://wp.me/p6OBGR-2OK> accessed 1 June 2019.

[50] Admittedly it is very hard to 'prove' an incentive to over-comply. At the very least, comprehensive transparency is an important first step. Detailed search engine transparency reporting will not just enable third parties to verify the scale and impact, but also installs counter-incentives for over-compliance.

[51] The emergence of search engines and thus the easy findability of any information about individuals at the search engine's whims, has massively shifted the balance against data subjects in the first place. See also: Hielke Hijmans, 'The European Union as a Constitutional Guardian of Internet Privacy and Data Protection' (PhD Thesis, University of Amsterdam 2016) 196, 232–33<http://dare.uva.nl/document/2/169421> accessed 1 June 2019.

[52] An entertaining illustration of Google's position regarding delisting information occurred in 2014, only three months after the *Google Spain* Ruling against which the company reacted with a whole PR campaign. A British bakery chain tweeted to @GoogleUK asking them to delist a satirical picture of their logo. After being promised donuts for 'fixing it', GoogleUK had adjusted search results within the hour. This demonstrates how easy and potentially randomly search results may be altered at the whims of the search engine operator. See: Greggs, 'Hey @GoogleUK, Fix It and They're Yours!!! #FixGreggs Pic.Twitter.Com/D5Ub7qtrLG' (*@GreggstheBakers*, 19 August 2014) <https://twitter.com/GreggstheBakers/status/501730930311331840/photo/1> accessed 28 August 2014; Joe McNamee, 'Google Now Supports AND Opposes the "Right to Be Forgotten"' (*EDRi*, 27 August 2014) <http://edri.org/google-now-supports-and-opposes-right-forgotten/> accessed 1 June 2019.

against over-privileging the right to data protection in the face of other fundamental rights, freedoms, and interests.

Section 4. Privatized Balancing?

BASICS—The GDPR requires controllers to take responsibility for their actions, and *their* actions only. In essence, the situations at hand can be brought back to simple private law relation between controller and data subject. The former determines a balance in its favour *ex ante* and the latter challenges that balance *ex post*.[53] Fears and criticism that the GDPR requires entities such as ISS providers to become private adjudicators of balancing rights, freedoms, and interests of others can be nuanced considerably. Any actor in society can in principle be expected to evaluate the legality of its actions and take responsibility for them. The GDPR simply fleshes out the requirements for legality of such actions that concern the processing of personal data. What often raises confusion and concerns in the ISS context is the scale and the multiplicity of interests/actors.

SCALE—Modern-day ISS providers often operate at an enormous scale. This scale also explains and justifies the basic mechanics of *ex ante* (generalized) and *ex post* (contextualized) balancing as explained in Chapter 5. In other words, *ex ante* balancing weighs lighter on controllers' shoulders than *ex post* balancing upon data subject request. In light of the scale at which they operate, the number of data subject requests ISS controllers receive may appear large (though are generally quite small in proportion).[54]

MULTIPLICITY OF INTERESTS AND ACTORS—As illustrated in the vignettes and previous chapters, data processing in the ISS context rarely relates to just one interest and/or only the relationship between ISS provider and data subject. Moreover, fundamental rights and freedoms are often affected as well,[55] tying in the discussion on direct horizontal effect (see Chapters 5 and 6).[56] The multiplicity of actors and interests certainly complexifies fair balancing in this context, but should in no way be taken as a justification not to balance at all. As explained in Chapter 3, it is important to take a functional and granular approach, so as to clearly separate the different data processing operations at hand. Doing so will enable pinpointing the operations for which the ISS provider is (not) the controller and thus (not) responsible for balancing (see 'Functional and Granular Approach'

[53] See also: Herbert Burkert, 'Institutions of Data Protection—An Attempt at a Functional Explanation of European National Data Protection Laws' (1981) 3 Computer/LJ 174.

[54] Even more so when one compares the number of data protection motivated requests with requests based on copyright law for example. See: Powles (n 47).

[55] Notably information freedoms, non-discrimination, privacy, and data protection

[56] See also: Eleni Frantziou, 'The Horizontal Effect of the Charter of Fundamental Rights of the EU: Rediscovering the Reasons for Horizontality' (2015) 21 European Law Journal 674–75.

below). Having said that, even if the ISS provider's balancing duty only extends to operations for which it is in fact controller, its decisions might still affect the interests of others (not in the least due to the scale at which they operate, eg *Google Spain* vignette). That is also why the GDPR installs certain safeguards to force ISS controllers to also take into account these broader interests.[57]

Last Mile—Another important consideration to take into account is that when it comes to fair balancing, the law can only take us so far. Requirements and safeguards are laid out, but in the end, these need to be applied by the actors involved. Put differently, the last mile of translating abstract legal rules to a concrete situation is to be done first and foremost by the ones that are targeted by those rules.[58] Arguably, this last mile is particularly long in the GDPR, because of the framework's wide scope and high level of abstraction.[59] Yet, this does not change the basic premise that an ISS provider bears that interpretative responsibility with regard to the processing operations it is the controller for. Because of this long last mile, and the interpretative flexibility that comes with it, controller decisions may have a more or less important impact on third parties. Especially in the context of the large and complex ISS data processing ecosystem. Importantly, however, this potential impact on third parties is not a result of the GDPR per se, but of the position in which these entities have placed themselves (ie de facto information gatekeepers). The GDPR purports to mitigate negative impact by a number of safeguards, exemptions, and derogations that pre-define balance when certain conditions are met. Whether it does so adequately is a different question.

Responsibility v Private Enforcement—There is a noticeable trend of policymakers wishing to enlist large ISS providers to effectively enforce public policy objectives (notably combating hate speech, terrorist content, copyright infringement, etc).[60] It is important to distinguish what these initiatives call for, from what the GDPR requires.[61] An ISS provider who is also a controller, defines

[57] For example, through exemptions and derogations (eg Art 17(3)), the legislator defines situations where the balance should tip in favour of processing by default, in light of the broader interests at stake.

[58] It would be unworkable (even undesirable) to have any decision with legal implications be made by a judge. The role of courts (and administrative authorities) should be limited to specific problem-cases. Policymakers should also maintain general oversight and react if systematic issues are identified.

[59] The GDPR calls for interpretative guidance (eg through EDPB opinion, standard-setting, and other co-regulatory initiatives) to shorten the last mile.

[60] Peggy Valcke, Aleksandra Kuczerawy, and Pieter-Jan Ombelet, 'Did the Romans Get It Right? What Delfi, Google, EBay, and UPC TeleKabel Wien Have in Common' in Mariarosaria Taddeo and Luciano Floridi (eds), *The Responsibilities of Online Service Providers*, vol 31. Law, Governance and Technology Series (Springer 2017) 101–16; Giancarlo Frosio, 'The Death of "No Monitoring Obligations": A Story of Untameable Monsters' (2017) <https://papers.ssrn.com/abstract=2980786> accessed 10 February 2018. See also: John Naughton, 'Facebook and Twitter Could Pay the Price for Hate Speech' *The Guardian* (19 March 2017) <https://www.theguardian.com/commentisfree/2017/mar/19/john-naughton-germany-fine-social-media-sites-facebook-twitter-hate-speech> accessed 1 June 2019.

[61] See in this regard also: Giancarlo Frosio, 'Why Keep a Dog and Bark Yourself? From Intermediary Liability to Responsibility' (2017) <https://papers.ssrn.com/abstract=3053995> accessed 10 February 2018.

the balance in favour of processing *ex ante*, and thus can also be expected to re-evaluate that balance when it is challenged by data subjects invoking their right to erasure/object. This is different from 'private enforcement of public policy' initiatives, that essentially demand of ISS providers to perform balancing acts over content or activities of third parties, that they are not directly involved in. Looking at user-generated-content platforms in particular, it is important to distinguish between the content of information shared by users, and the platform's management of that content. A priori, ISS providers will only be responsible with regard to the latter. Things get more complex in reality, especially considering the increased involvement of ISS providers in managing content flows, on the basis of personal data processing. Another relevant example concerns the ongoing discussion on the responsibility of platforms such as App stores, for ensuring available apps are GDPR compliant.[62] While it is easy to see the appeal of enlisting these actors—essentially being central information gatekeepers or chokepoints—such policies raise a lot of complicated questions that require further research.[63]

PROCESSOR RESPONSIBILITIES—In light of their size and impact on processing operations, ISS providers can still have some role to play in the *ex post* fair balancing act following a right to erasure/object. When they act in a capacity as *processor* (see Chapter 3), ISS providers are responsible for facilitating the exercise of data subject rights between data subject and controller (Art 28). For example, a social network is a processor when enabling controller X to upload a picture of person Y and making it publicly available.[64] In light of its position, the social network could be expected to facilitate a dialogue between data subject (Y) and controller (X), to essentially do the balancing. Some have suggested that social network operators (or video-hosting platforms for example), should ask users to set an expiration date and/or include an extra step in the uploading process asking users 'are you sure to submit?'.[65] These are essentially steps to introduce some friction in the

[62] eg through performing data protection impact assessments and/or ensuring the technical infrastructure allows for GDPR compliance. See inter alia: Kristina Irion and others, 'A Roadmap to Enhancing User Control via Privacy Dashboards' (IViR 2017) <https://www.ivir.nl/publicaties/download/PrivacyBridgesUserControls2017.pdf>; Nicolo Zingales, 'The Rise of "Infomediaries" in Support of Individual Autonomy: A Matter of Trust and (Joint) Responsibility' (2018).

[63] eg Broad-sweep obligations to remove content, to proactively monitor traffic, or notice-and-staydown requirements are especially problematic from a freedom of expression perspective, but also raise privacy and data protection questions. For an excellent analysis in this regard, see notably: Aleksandra Kuczerawy, *Intermediary Liability and Freedom of Expression in the EU: From Concepts to Safeguards* (Intersentia 2018). See also: C Angelopoulos and others, 'Study of Fundamental Rights Limitations for Online Enforcement through Self-Regulation' <https://pure.uva.nl/ws/files/8763808/IVIR_Study_Online_enforcement_through_self_regulation.pdf>; Angelopoulos (n 1).

[64] This activity should be separated from all other activities the social network performs on said picture on its own behalf (eg facial recognition, profiling, determining relevance to push it in users' timelines, etc).

[65] Bruno Rasle, 'Droit à l'oubli: Quel rôle pour le délégué à la protection des données personnelles?' in David Dechenaud (ed), *Le droit à l'oubli numérique: Données nominatives—Approche comparée* (Larcier 2015) 354.

process and thus force more reflexivity by the uploader. It has also been suggested that the social network operator itself might be responsible for erasing the picture on data protection grounds itself, when 'it is sufficiently clear that the interests of the data subject outweigh the interests of others'.[66] Others yet have proposed a co-regulatory approach, putting in place a specialized public agency to review decisions and empowered to take necessary action.[67]

CONCLUSION—The GDPR provides a basic infrastructure for fair balancing in the context of personal data processing. The main responsible for doing said balancing is also the one determining the purpose and means of the respective processing operation, ie the controller. In other words, the GDPR *does not* require actors to perform balancing acts regarding activities they are not responsible for (ie processing activities they did not determine purpose and means for). Given the scale and complexity of ISS providers, it may often seem these entities are effectively enlisted as private adjudicators. Indeed, the balancing the GDPR requires them to do, may have a wide impact reaching beyond the mere controller-data subject relationship (see *Google Spain* vignette). Yet, this impact is not the result of the GDPR, but of the size and power of these ISS providers themselves (and society's reliance on them). In fact, the GDPR safeguards *against* privatized balancing, by installing minimum requirements aimed at defending the interests of data subjects, third parties, and society more broadly.

Section 5. Qualifying the Debate

Having discussed some of the oft-recurring questions related to data subject rights in the context of large ISS providers, this section will further qualify the debate. Indeed, given the fact that virtually everyone in modern-day western society comes in contact with these actors on a daily basis, opinions on their impact and role are legion. This sub-section aims to highlight some key elements that I believe to be important in having an informed debate on ISS providers' responsibility in the area of data subject rights.

5.1 Calling a Spade, a Spade

> [W]e have come to rely, comprehensively and largely unwittingly, on privately-owned, culturally biased, black box services in navigating the digital ecosystem and discovering and reconstructing information. We have outsourced the raw material, design and execution of multilayered

[66] Van Alsenoy (n 26) 458.
[67] Tambou (n 49) 90 et seq.

search strategies, in return for easy, efficient interfaces and mysterious algorithms.[68]

Size Matters—It was said in Chapter 3 already that not all controllers are equal. Because of its wide scope, the GDPR captures a huge variety of controllers within its regulatory cloak. Both the duty of fair balancing as well as the outcome inherently depends on the size of the controller and processing operations at hand.[69] As explained by AG Bot, 'there ought to be, perhaps not always an exact match, but at least a reasonable correlation between power, control, and responsibility'.[70] Due to the scale and impact of their (personal data processing) operations, as key interfaces for how people interact with the world, ISS providers bear considerable responsibility reaching far beyond data protection. Indeed, in light of many ISS providers' powerful gatekeeper roles online, there is a broader debate to be had on increased responsibilization of these actors.[71]

Context Matters—When assessing the extent of responsibilities and balancing duties, one cannot ignore the broader context of the ISS landscape. Powerful operators are penetrating ever more aspects of daily life with increasingly sophisticated technology (see Uber vignette). When it comes to public facing personal data (see *Google Spain* vignette), ISS providers do not follow the same codes and standards adopted by more traditional information gatekeepers (eg news organizations, archives, libraries, etc),[72] even if the impact of their processing is potentially much larger.[73] Without much a priori restraints on how they should rank or filter information, search engines, social networks, or e-commerce platforms may (deliberately or not) 'undermine democratic values, economic efficiency, fairness, and

[68] Powles (n 47) 17.

[69] Illustrated in Google Spain (*Google Spain* (n 23) para 86). The ECtHR has also recognized that (small) size and good faith matter when it comes to reacting to privacy-motivated takedown requests: *Pihl v Sweden* [2017] European Court of Human Rights 74742/14, para 31. See more generally on how data protection distributes responsibility: Van Alsenoy (n 26).

[70] AG Bot in: *Fashion ID* Court of Justice of the European Union C-40/17, para 91.

[71] Peggy Valcke, Aleksandra Kuczerawy, and Pieter-Jan Ombelet (n 60); Friso Bostoen, 'Neutrality, Fairness or Freedom? Principles for Platform Regulation' (2018) 7 Internet Policy Review <https://policyreview.info/articles/analysis/neutrality-fairness-or-freedom-principles-platform-regulation> accessed 12 April 2018; Kuczerawy (n 63); European Commission Proposal for a Regulation on Promoting Fairness and Transparency for Business Users of Online Intermediation Services (n 31).

[72] 'The seemingly dominant criteria for the valuation of information and ideas in commercial Web search engines, namely relevancy, popularity and marketing, can be contrasted with quality, independence, and institutional legitimacy, i.e. the traditional professional standards for the ordering of knowledge, information and ideas.' Joris Van Hoboken, *Search Engine Freedom: On the Implications of the Right to Freedom Expression for the Legal Governance of Web Search Engines* (First edn, Kluwer Law International 2012) 202. See also: Frank Pasquale, 'Platform Neutrality: Enhancing Freedom of Expression in Spheres of Private Power The Constitution of Information: From Gutenberg to Snowden' (2016) 17 Theoretical Inquiries in Law 512; Erin C Carroll, 'Making News: Balancing Newsworthiness and Privacy in the Age of Algorithms' (Georgetown University Law Center 2016) <https://papers.ssrn.com/abstract=2877335> accessed 1 June 2019.

[73] See also for example (doctor, teacher, lawyer) rating websites. David Erdos, 'Confused? Analysing the Scope of Freedom of Speech Protection Vis-à-Vis European Data Protection' (Oxford University 2012) 48/2012 10–14<http://papers.ssrn.com/abstract=2119187> accessed 1 June 2019.

individual autonomy'.[74] The opacity of ISS providers' processing operations further complicates and exacerbates their impact and thus the fair balancing act.[75] These elements all influence the burden on ISS providers' shoulders to ensure fair balances under the GDPR.

Dilemma—The fact that many ISS providers effectively constitute central nodes in data processing ecosystems, raises a regulatory dilemma. On the one hand, they offer a great focal point for enforcing data protection on a wide scale (ie with regard to data processing operations they are not controllers over, but are somehow facilitating—see the mobile App store example mentioned in 403–4). On the other hand, it might not be appropriate to effectively enlist these actors as private adjudicators of data protection law. The dilemma is somewhat resolved by taking a functional and granular approach, considering the actual involvement of the relevant ISS provider in the respective data processing operations. In that sense, the GDPR does not conflict with intermediary liability exemptions that essentially imply the respective entity is not involved in the activity/information, let alone determine the purpose and means (see Chapter 3). What complicates matters is that today, 'intermediaries' are seldom 'just intermediaries'.[76] As illustrated in the Facebook/Cambridge Analytica saga,[77] a social network bears some responsibility over how personal data is processed by Apps on its platform. Indeed, when a user installs an App, the App-provider and the social network might be considered co-controllers or in a controller-processor relationship.[78] Their responsibility will be a function of their involvement. This has important implications for the ISS provider's duty to balance upon receiving a right to erase/object.[79]

What this section purports to convey is that ISS providers' fair balancing responsibility under the GDPR will be a function of their involvement in the respective processing operation and their position in the broader ecosystem.

[74] Oren Bracha and Frank Pasquale, 'Federal Search Commission? Access, Fairness, and Accountability in the Law of Search' (2008) 93 Cornell Law Review 1171. Similarly, see: Powles (n 47) 591.

[75] This opacity may be deliberate or not. The GDPR does put in place minimum transparency requirements yet providing such transparency may be hard to provide in practice. This also explains the growing body of interdisciplinary research on how to increase transparency in this context: see notably the FAT/ML society and the work of Pasquale. See also: Orla Lynskey, 'Regulating "Platform Power"' (LSE 2017) Working Paper 1/2017 18 <https://papers.ssrn.com/abstract=2921021> accessed 1 June 2019.

[76] The current modus operandi of most 'intermediaries' and ISS providers more broadly, is through constant iterations and improvements of the platform. See: ENISA, 'Privacy Enhancing Technologies: Evolution and State of the Art' (2016) 16 <https://www.enisa.europa.eu/publications/pets-evolution-and-state-of-the-art>; Seda Gürses and Joris Van Hoboken, 'Privacy after the Agile Turn' in Jules Polonetsky, Omer Tene, and Evan Selinger (eds), *Cambridge Handbook of Consumer Privacy* (CUP 2017) <https://osf.io/preprints/socarxiv/9gy73> accessed 1 June 2019.

[77] https://www.theguardian.com/uk-news/cambridge-analytica.

[78] The exact relationship (and thus the distribution of responsibilities) will depend on the circumstances at hand. It would go beyond the scope of this book to flesh this out in detail here, but readers may want to go back to Chapter 3 to get a better sense. See also: Van Alsenoy (n 26) 395–466.

[79] See notably: Erdos, 'Delimiting the Ambit of Responsibility of Intermediary Publishers for Third Party Rights in European Data Protection' (n 1029); Van Alsenoy (n 26).

With this in mind, procedural safeguards play a critical role, extensively laid out Chapters 3, 4, and 5. It goes without saying that the GDPR alone is not sufficient—nor appropriate—to tackle all the complex issues stemming from ISS' information power. Policy actions such as the Proposal for a Regulation on promoting fairness and transparency for business users of online intermediation services,[80] and ambitious enforcement investigations,[81] should be encouraged. These initiatives may kick up a lot of dust in the short term, but are necessary to ensure the development of a fair and sustainable status quo in the long run. Such revamped status quo may involve the translation of fundamental human rights protections to the operations of ISS providers who have a much deeper impact in individuals' daily lives than States (some effectively constituting quasi-public spheres).[82]

5.2 Functional and Granular Approach

Introduction—It has been said time and again throughout this book: fair balancing under the GDPR requires a functional and granular approach.[83] This means that fair balances need to be made with regard to specifically delineated processing purposes, taking into account the concrete facts and context. This approach benefits both controller, data subjects, and society at large, as it enables challenging each individual processing operation on its own merits, considerate of all the relevant stakeholders and their interests. It is worth highlighting that a functional and granular approach to fair balancing in the GDPR also aligns with both the CJEU and ECtHR's case law on fair balancing of fundamental/human rights.[84]

[80] European Commission Proposal for a Regulation on Promoting Fairness and Transparency for Business Users of Online Intermediation Services (n 31).

[81] ; European Data Protection Supervisor, 'Opinion on Coherent Enforcement of Fundamental Rights in the Age of Big Data' (EDPS 2016) Opinion 8/2016 3 <https://secure.edps.europa.eu/EDPSWEB/webdav/site/mySite/shared/Documents/EDPS/Events/16-09-23_BigData_opinion_EN.pdf> accessed 1 June 2019; Sarah Lyall, 'Who Strikes Fear Into Silicon Valley? Margrethe Vestager, Europe's Antitrust Enforcer' *The New York Times* (8 May 2018) <https://www.nytimes.com/2018/05/05/world/europe/margrethe-vestager-silicon-valley-data-privacy.html> accessed 12 May 2018.

[82] Wolfgang Benedek and Matthias C Kettemann, *Freedom of Expression and the Internet* (Council of Europe 2013) 102; Powles (n 47).

[83] Confirmed by WP29 in the context of consent particularly. Yet the warning against conflating different purposes is relevant with regard to all lawful grounds in Article 6. Article 29 Working Party, 'Guidelines on Consent under Regulation 2016/679' (2018) WP 259 11 <http://ec.europa.eu/justice/article-29/documentation>. See similarly: Article 29 Working Party, 'Opinion 15/2011 on the Definition of Consent' (Article 29 Working Party 2011) WP187 18<http://ec.europa.eu/justice/article-29/documentation>.

[84] In a variety of cases, the CJEU has emphasized conflicts between fundamental rights/freedoms cannot be resolved wholesale and generically. There should always be an opportunity to tip the default of a balance. See notably: *Scarlet Extended v Sabam* [2011] Court of Justice of the European Union C-70/10; *SABAM v Netlog* [2012] Court of Justice of the European Union C-360/10.; *SABAM v Netlog* [2012] Court of Justice of the European Union C-360/10.; *Salvatore Manni* [2017] Court of Justice of the European Union C-398/15; Orla Lynskey, *The Foundations of EU Data Protection Law* (OUP 2016) 158. The ECtHR ruled similarly that even if journalists benefit from particular protection and/or the fact that personal information has already been published before installs strong presumptions, this

TEMPORAL DIMENSION—There is also a temporal dimension to the granular/functional approach. Especially in the ISS context, data processing is highly dynamic (with evolving sets of purposes, transforming personal data, etc).[85] This is recognized by the *ex ante* v *ex post* fair balancing divide as explained in Chapter 5. The former is defined at the start of a processing operation, on the basis of the narrowest purposes possible, considering categories of data subjects. The latter requires taking into account maximum level of detail of a very concrete and specific situation as raised by one or more data subjects.

BALANCING CASCADE—There is another important element that emerges from the temporal dimension of functional and granular fair balancing. It allows to more clearly discern how different processing purposes may follow, and/or build upon, one another. As a result, the granular/functional approach enables to observe some sort of cascade effect in GDPR fair balancing, especially in complex data processing environments. One can think, for example, of someone uploading a video containing personal data onto YouTube, after which that video is analysed for copyright-infringement, pushed to other users, added to playlists and/or remixed by other users. Even though each processing operation should be assessed in its own right, such assessments will be impacted by the ones preceding it. It does raise the question how much all these processing operations inter-depend on one another. Granularly rebalancing specific operations may break the symbiosis and result in effectively blocking all processing in the cascade.

VIGNETTES—The previous paragraph is perhaps most clearly illustrated by the *Google Spain* vignette. Imagine a picture of Alice is uploaded to a personal blog for the purposes of exposing illegal activities Alice was involved in. Google shows the picture when entering Alice's name in the search bar, for the purposes of offering its search services to users. This picture may then be picked up by a reporter who publishes a story about it, for journalistic purposes. Each processing needs to be evaluated on its own merits, but will impact the fair balancing of the subsequent assessments.[86] Depending on the circumstances at hand, Google may, for example, be required to delist Alice's picture, while the journalist may still remain using it. This is also the case when all the different processing operations are performed by one and the same controller. Ad hoc purposes such as security or service improvement may emerge only after (and because of) personal data are already collected for a specific processing purpose. This is true for example, in the Facebook and

cannot result in effectively preventing the protection of private or family life. See notably: *A Aleksey Ovchinnikov v Russia,* [2010] European Court of Human Rights 24061/04; *Satakunnan Markkinapörssi Oy et Satamedia Oy v Finland* (n 15); Benedek and Kettemann (n 82) 52.

[85] See in this regard: Lokke Moerel and Corien Prins, 'Privacy for the Homo Digitalis: Proposal for a New Regulatory Framework for Data Protection in the Light of Big Data and the Internet of Things' 7 <http://papers.ssrn.com/abstract=2784123> accessed 1 June 2019.

[86] The fair balancing of Google will be impacted by the one regarding the source page, but not determined.

Uber vignettes, where the impetus for processing and central purpose is the delivery of the service as requested by data subjects (ie social networking or transportation). The additional processing purposes initiated by the respective controllers should be assessed individually, but also hinge on the initial purpose. This ties back to the discussion in Chapter 6 on the extent to which data subjects may challenge the ad hoc processing operations while still continuing to use the service.

DRAWBACKS—The granular and functional approach also has considerable drawbacks. Firstly, an overemphasis on the particular may diminish foreseeability and as a result legal certainty. Van Drooghenbroeck's criticism against *hypercontextualization*—effectively thwarting 'precedent potential'—in the realm of human rights balancing,[87] is equally relevant to fair balancing within the GDPR. Secondly, an overly granular and/or casuistic approach may also overburden data subjects wishing to challenge fair balances. Should data subjects, for example have to invoke their right to be delisted every time the same information pops up on the basis of a name search, but under a different URL?[88] Thirdly, the flexibility offered by the granular/functional approach may not only reduce legal certainty, but also fail to effectively empower data subjects. Especially in situations characterized by strong power asymmetries, it is important to have bright lines set out in law (eg the general prohibition to process sensitive data in Art 9 GDPR).[89,90] Fourthly, granularity may require a fundamental shift in the operations of many ISS providers, whose business model is currently built around extracting value from personal data. Chapter 6 made clear that there is a strong argument to be made that data subjects should be able to fully use ISS *without* being tracked and profiled for purposes other than those explicitly requested.

SOLUTIONS—Some of the drawbacks can be resolved more easily than others. For example, soft law instruments may draw clear(er) lines in the sand, so as to

[87] Essentially, the author explains that the more factors that are added to a fair balancing act, the more its value as a precedent will diminish. Van Drooghenbroeck (n 2) 297.

[88] The Belgian DPA advised Google to essentially install a notice-and-staydown mechanism. See: Belgian Privacy Commission, 'Advies 75/2017 Ingevolge Een Klacht Gericht Tegen Een Zoekmotor Betreffende de Modaliteiten Voor de Uitvoering En de Geografische Reikwijdte van Een Verwijdering van URL's Uit de Zoekresultaten (CO- A-2017-088)' (2017) Advies 75/2017 <https://www.privacycommission.be/sites/privacycommission/files/documents/advies_75_2017.pdf> accessed 17 April 2018. The French *Cour de Cassation* ruled the opposite way in: *Google v M X* (Cour de Cassation, 1ère ch civile (France)).

[89] Itself the subject of a CJEU case involving the right to be delisted, not yet decided at the time of writing (C-136/17).

[90] As highlighted by WP29 in the context of the GDPR trilogue: 'the rights granted to data subjects by EU law should be respected regardless of the level of the risks which the latter incur through the data processing involved (eg right of access, rectification, erasure and objection, transparency, right to be forgotten, right to data portability). Therefore, some references in the Council of the EU position to the necessity of "taking into account the circumstances" or "having regard to the purposes" when granting rights to the data subjects, are creating uncertainty and potentially room for interpretation that could lead to lowering the level of protection for data subjects.' Article 29 Working Party, 'Appendix: Core Topics in View of the Trilogue' Brussels (17 June 2015) <https://ec.europa.eu/justice/article-29/documentation/other-document/files/2015/20150617_appendix_core_issues_plenary_en.pdf> accessed 1 June 2019.

more easily assess fair balances in particular circumstances. A minimum level of transparency regarding the growing number of balancing decisions—by controllers, DPAs, or courts—should also enable identifying a common thread. Such transparency might for example cover (percentage-rates of) the determinative criteria. This will also allow for a broader discussion on the adequacy of fair balancing and refinement if desirable. Indeed, such broader societal debate is also necessary to determine the appropriate level of granularity. Most notably, can the data subject object to any and all processing operations that are not directly necessary for the purpose he/she asked for? In order for the granular and functional approach to have a practical relevance, ISS providers also have a responsibility to design their user interface so as to enable easy retrospection and reflection by data subjects.[91]

5.3 Deferring Balances

As explained in Chapter 5, the GDPR provides an infrastructure for fair balancing (rights, freedoms, and interests) in the context of personal data processing. An important part of that infrastructure consists of *deferring* balancing. This is crucial to keep in mind, as it nuances oft-heard criticism that the GDPR is not clear enough and/or would overburden controllers to balance. Whenever the GDPR does not predefine the balancing default,[92] it generally defers fair balancing to the legislator. This became particularly clear with regard to *ex post* balancing pursuant to the right to erasure in Article 17 (Chapter 4). Many 'right-to-erasure triggers' (Art 17(1)) and exemptions (Art 17(3)) implicitly/explicitly refer to sources outside the GDPR. Such 'outsourcing' of fair balancing can be found in other GDPR provisions as well, notably in the lawful grounds provision (Art 6(1)) or the deference to Member-State (or EU) laws installing derogations (Arts 23 and 85).[93] Moreover, it is important to keep in mind that the law does not operate in a vacuum, and a progressively growing body of case law[94] and soft-law

[91] See in this regard: Chris Elsden and others, 'Fitter, Happier, More Productive: What to Ask of a Data-Driven Life' (2016) 23 Interactions 46; Luke Hutton and Tristan Henderson, 'Beyond the EULA: Improving Consent for Data Mining' [2017] arXiv:1701.07999 [cs] <http://arxiv.org/abs/1701.07999> accessed 1 June 2019.

[92] eg the first five lawful grounds in Article 6(1), as explained in Chapter 5; or the general prohibition for processing sensitive data in Article 9.

[93] See also the CJEU's case law evaluating such externa legal frameworks in light of data protection law: *Joined ASNEF and FECEMD Cases* [2011] Court of Justice of the European Union Joined Cases C-468/10 and C-469/10 [42] para 43; *Michael Schwarz v Stadt Bochum* [2013] Court of Justice of the European Union C-291/12 para 33; Court of Justice of the EU, C-473/12, *Institut professionnel des agents immobiliers (IPI) v Geoffrey Englebert & Ors*, [3 July 2019]; *Salvatore Manni* (n 84).

[94] Since the early 2010s, there has been a noticeable increase in data protection cases being decided by the CJEU. See also: M Eliantonio, F Galli, and M Schaper, 'A Balanced Data Protection in the EU: Conflicts and Possible Solutions' (2016) 23 Maastricht Journal of European and Comparative Law (MJ) 391, 203–04. Pollicino warns for an overreliance on the judiciary though. See: Oreste Pollicino, 'European Judicial Dialogue and the Protection of Fundamental Rights in the New Digital

instruments[95] may further clarify the practical operation of GDPR fair balancing in specific situations.[96]

Pre-defining what side the balance should tip over to in specific circumstances (either within the GDPR, or in external legal frameworks), is crucial to provide legal certainty, but also to safeguard important rights, freedoms, or interests that might otherwise be ignored. This is especially true regarding the freedom of expression and information safeguards in Article 17(3)1, Article 23(1)I, and Article 85. The predecessors of the latter two provisions in Directive 95/46 (Articles 13(1)(g) and 9) have already been the subject of CJEU rulings.[97] It is interesting to note that these cases concerned provisions mandating/enabling balances in Member-State law, and so the CJEU simply referred the actual balancing back to the national courts. This is in contrast to the *Google Spain* ruling, for example, where the CJEU did balance itself as the provisions at hand (notably lawful ground (Art 7), right to erasure (Art 12(b)), and right to object (Art 14) in Directive 95/46) did not include such external balancing references.[98] Based on this observation, ISS controllers may wish to invoke legal freedom of expression/information exemptions to fend off right to erasure/object requests. This would seemingly offload the responsibility to 'balance' onto another entity (ie court or DPA).[99] It is doubtful though, whether courts or DPAs would accept categorical denial of data subject rights by ISS providers simply invoking freedom of expression/information exemptions.

In conclusion, one of the most important questions to consider, from a broader policy perspective, is where fair balancing should occur. To some, fair balancing should always be done by an absolutely neutral and independent court with the highest ethical standards. This is not only unrealistic, but also undesirable as it would risk eroding the moral responsibilities that come with participating in a society. Such responsibility, essentially to (micro-)balance, is given shape through 'the law'. The law can ensure fair balances in roughly two manners, either by defining what side the balance should tip in advance or leaving it up to the parties to do the fair balancing themselves. The first case basically puts in place a 'syllogism'[100] and may be most appropriate in obvious

Environment: An Attempt at Emancipation and Reconciliation' in Sonia Morano-Foadi and Lucy Vickers (eds), *Fundamental Rights in the EU: A Matter for Two Courts* (Hart 2015) 18.

[95] See notably: Articles 40 and 57.

[96] See in this regard also: Article 29 Working Party, 'Opinion 06/2014 on the Notion of Legitimate Interests of the Data Controller under Article 7 of Directive 95/46/EC' (n 32) 57.

[97] *Satamedia* (n 15) para 50 et seq; *IPI v Englebert* (n 93) para 48.

[98] *Google Spain* (n 23). See also: Hijmans, *The EU as Guardian of Internet Privacy* (n 51) 234.

[99] In fact, such a scenario rather concerns assessing the applicability of the exemption, which itself is in fact a pre-defined balance by the legislator.

[100] Consisting of a *majeure* (eg all men are mortal), *mineure* (Socrates is a man), and conclusion (Socrates is mortal).

cases (eg criminal behaviour). The second case, is more flexible and considerate of practical realities. One of the main differences between these approaches is that with the former 'subjectivity' occurs upstream and has a long-term effect, while with the latter it occurs downstream and in principle without long-term effect.[101] The GDPR comprises both approaches. Especially in situations that occur very frequently or involve strong interests (eg freedom of expression, public health), it pre-defines balances (or at least requires the EU or Member-State legislator to intervene). The considerable leeway it gives to private actors to do the fair balancing stems from the framework's tremendously broad scope and relevance in rapidly evolving sectors (that require high adaptability to new practical realities). That is also why a lot of attention should be given to the procedural safeguards which aim to ensure such case-by-case balancing occurs *fairly*. Situations characterized by strong power asymmetries, such as the ones discussed in this book, may require predefined balances and at the very least a sturdy procedural framework.[102]

5.4 Fifty Shades of Erasure

Fair balancing following the exercise of a right to erasure/object does not simply relate to the validity of that request itself. It can also extend to the actual implementation of the right. In short, this comes down to a dynamic 'least restrictive means' test which can calibrate the original erasure request in light of other rights, freedoms, or interests at stake. This observation is especially important in the context of ISS providers and with regard to digital information in general. The complexity of the data processing ecosystem—involving many different processing operations, interests, and controllers/processors—may render an all-or-nothing right to erasure/object quite hard in practice (whether for technical reasons or because of the many conflicting interests). It will therefore often be more realistic to only object to certain specific processing operations and/or constraining others. Moreover, the very nature of *digital* information also allows for a plethora of alternatives to fully fledged erasure. It is important to be aware of the differences between accommodating the right to erasure/object in a digital environment versus in an offline/analogue/paper context. While in the latter, options are rather constrained, the former enables many more in-between solutions.

[101] Van Drooghenbroeck (n 2) 288–90. The author adds to this that the long-term effect of syllogisms may also imply a deeper reflexivity when defining the balance. See also the reference to: Scalia (n 12) 1179–80.

[102] Norman Lindop, *Report of the Committee on Data Protection, Chairman: Norman Lindop* (HMSO 1978) 11.

One could think of the 50 shades of erasure as a spectrum, with free and unrestrained processing on one side and full erasure at the other end. Rather than oscillating between the two, solutions will generally lie in shifting the needle along this spectrum so as to find the most balanced solution.[103] From CJEU case law on copyright-injunctions one can derive that ISS providers have a certain degree of flexibility in determining what measures to take to accommodate rights.[104] A useful conceptual tool to do so will be by tweaking parameters of the personal data equalizer as described in Chapter 3. It seems recommendable for controllers to thoroughly think about the alternative ways for implementing the right to erasure/object in the context of their operations, and proactively offer these to data subjects. This is also recognized in the Human Computer Interaction (HCI) community: 'Importantly, the meaning, relevance, and use of data shifts over time, and we must look for design opportunities beyond a present-focused and analytic relationship to include a longer retrospective and more reflective or performative experience.'[105]

VIGNETTE—One could imagine a blog, for example, to allow for pseudonymizing personal data in posts, installing access-restrictions (for post altogether or visitors with different credentials, would see anonymized/identifiable post),[106] prevent searches on personal attributes, add a corrigendum or note,[107] and so on.[108] Especially with regard to the processing of public-facing personal data, information freedoms will almost always be at stake. In light of Article 85 GDPR, it will therefore be important for national legislators to sufficiently consider erasure alternatives in their implementing laws[109] and also for EU/national legislators to

[103] In the context of public-facing personal data, the question will often be to identify the optimal degree of practical obscurity. On practical obscurity, see notably: Anita L Allen, *Unpopular Privacy: What Must We Hide?* (OUP 2011) 162ff; Hartzog and Selinger (n 111); Meg Leta Jones, 'Privacy without Screens & the Internet of Other People's Things' (2014) 51 Idaho Law Review 94.

[104] Measures should be 'sufficiently effective to ensure genuine protection of the fundamental right at issue, that is to say that they must have the effect of preventing unauthorised access to the protected subject matter or, at least, of making it difficult to achieve and of seriously discouraging internet users who are using the services of the addressee of that injunction from accessing the subject matter made available to them in breach of that fundamental right'. *McFadden* [2016] Court of Justice of the European Union C-484/14 [95]; *UPC Telekabel* (n 60) para 62.

[105] Elsden and others (n 91) 46.

[106] See in this regard CJEU case law in: *Huber v Germany* [2008] Court of Justice of the European Union C-524/06 para 61; *ClientEarth* [2015] Court of Justice of the European Union C-615/13 para 47; *Salvatore Manni* (n 84) para 60 et seq. See also the section on Public Registers in Chapter 6.

[107] The ECtHR 'does not consider that the requirement to publish an appropriate qualification to an article contained in an Internet archive, where it has been brought to the notice of a newspaper that a libel action has been initiated in respect of that same article published in the written press, constitutes a disproportionate interference with the right to freedom of expression. *Case of Times Newspapers Ltd. (Nos 1 and 2) v The United Kingdom* (n 41) para 47. Also later recognized in: *Wegrzynowski and Smolczewski v Poland* [2013] European Court of Human Rights 33846/07 paras 66–67.

[108] Cécile de Terwangne, *The Right to Be Forgotten and the Informational Autonomy in the Digital Environment* (Publications Office 2013) 9–10<http://dx.publications.europa.eu/10.2788/54562> accessed 1 June 2019.

[109] See in this regard also: Joris van Hoboken, 'The Proposed Right to Be Forgotten Seen from the Perspective of Our Right to Remember' 26 <www.law.nyu.edu/sites/default/files/upload_documents/VanHoboken_RightTo%20Be%20Forgotten_Manuscript_2013.pdf> accessed 1 June 2019.

consider it in legal frameworks more broadly.[110] Oftentimes it will simply be a matter of increasing practical obscurity.[111] Regarding controllers processing personal data that is not public-facing (eg Uber, Facebook, Apple vignettes), the 50 shades of erasure will in fact come down to a granular approach in conjunction with the right to object. Uber drivers, for example, may wish to erase their star rating, while still being able to provide their services. If erasing the score altogether would be considered disproportionate in light of riders' interests, one could consider that the rating can henceforth only be used for informing those riders (and not, for example, to use it as a variable in Uber's algorithms aimed at subliminally influencing drivers' behaviour). What is in fact done in this vignette-illustration is picking apart the different operations performed on the same personal data and retaining only some, while blocking others.

In sum, there are 50 shades of erasure. There is no one-size-fits-all practical application of the right to erasure/object.[112] Different mutations may arise depending on the context. A fair balance should be sought between the data subject's interests underlying his/her request and the respective rights, freedoms, and interests at stake.[113] In that sense, one could draw a parallel with the doctrine of *concordance pratique / Praktische Konkordanz* in human rights law (see Chapter 5). Rather than sacrificing one right (or freedom/interest) for another, the goal should be to find a compromise between them, keeping both as intact as possible in the circumstances at hand.[114] The very nature of *digital* data offers many opportunities in this regard.

Section 6. Conclusion

Fair balancing in the GDPR brings about a complicated set of issues. Part II of this book aimed to clarify and nuance these issues from the perspective of *ex post* empowerment measures. After Chapter 5, which dissecting the mechanics of such balancing, Chapter 6 concretized this abstract legal exercise by applying it to three prototypical 'balancing scenarios' in the ISS context. This final chapter has aimed

[110] Clear examples are laws covering public registers (see Chapter 6) or national archives. See also: Article 29 Working Party, 'Opinion 03/2013 on Purpose Limitation' (n 41) 29; André Holleaux, 'La Loi Du 6 Janvier 1978 Sur Informatique et Les Libertés — II —' (1978) 31 La Revue administrative 38–39.

[111] Ie by creating challenges to the accessibility of information. See: Jones (n 103) 94; de Terwangne (n 108) 20; Woodrow Hartzog and Frederic D Stutzman, 'The Case for Online Obscurity' (2012) 101 California Law Review 1.

[112] Maryline Boizard, 'Le Droit Au Respect de La Vie Privée, Un Instrument Effectif Du Droit à l'oubli?' (2015) 1 Montesquieu Law Review 149.

[113] See Florent Thouvenin and others, 'Remembering and Forgetting in the Digital Age—A Position Paper' (2016) 21 Information Research <http://www.informationr.net/ir/21-1/memo/memo2.html#ric13> accessed 1 June 2019.

[114] Smet, 'Resolving Conflicts between Human Rights' (n 1) 124 et seq and the many references contained within.

to tackle some of the questions left unanswered but also to summarize and pinpoint key considerations for an informed debate in this field. Put differently, it is not aimed at answering questions, but at guiding the right questions to be asked in the first place. An informed debate will be critical in the further interpretation, elaboration, and implementation of the GDPR and satellite frameworks.

PART III
EFFECTIVENESS

8
The Right to Erasure in Practice

Voyez-vous, Robineau, dans la vie, il n'y a pas de solutions. Il y a des forces en marche: il faut les créer et les solutions suivent.[1]

Section 1. Introduction

Individuals, and society at large, increasingly interact with the world mediated through information communication technology. Every interaction through information technology generates data, which in turn is monetized or valorized in some way. This trend has produced strong power asymmetries between those to whom the data relates, ie the data subject, and those valorizing the personal data, ie the controllers. This is especially evident with regard to information society services (ISS).

Power asymmetries in the ISS context are intensifying in a vicious cycle. The sector is characterized by quasi-monopolies dominating their respective market segments. Finding, accessing, sharing, or distributing information has to a large extent become dependent on these platforms. Most of these entities have access to the vast amounts of information flowing through their platforms (as well as the expansive metadata related to it), as their service is often based on helping users to manage information in the first place (from organizing one's social/professional friends and connections, to arranging content or filtering relevant news). By their very nature, these entities are also able to capture and commodify any interaction an individual has with the service. All this information is then fed back to the system, further solidifying their dominance.

Data protection law provides for a regulatory framework aimed at ensuring responsible and accountable data processing. As such it purports to safeguard *all* fundamental rights and freedoms, and in particular the right to data protection. This book in particular, set out to assess the ability of the right to erasure to contribute to such a goal—and effectively counter power asymmetries—in the context described above. Specifically, the guiding question throughout was: Does the right to erasure meaningfully contribute to safeguarding the fundamental right to data protection in the face of online power asymmetries?

The answer to this question will be formulated in this chapter. To do so, links will be made with previous chapters throughout. *Firstly*, the rationale and normative

[1] Antoine de Saint-Exupéry, *Vol de nuit* (Gallimard 1991) 159.

The Right to Erasure in EU Data Protection Law. First Edition. Jef Ausloos. Oxford University Press (2020). © Jef Ausloos
DOI: 10.1093/oso/9780198847977.001.0001

foundation of the fundamental right of data protection and how it relates to the GDPR will be reiterated (see Chapter 2). Put briefly, this will entail setting out control, autonomy, and informational self-determination as core values underlying Article 8 Charter, with the GDPR pursuing fair balances more broadly (regarding any fundamental right freedom or interest). *Secondly*, this chapter will evaluate whether Article 17 GDPR—and data subject empowerment tools more broadly—effectively contribute to the rationales as previously identified. This will also include critical thinking about the potential downsides of data subject empowerment on fundamental rights, freedoms, and/or interests (see Part II on balancing), and the many practical difficulties/issues that may arise when invoking/applying Article 17 GDPR. It will be concluded that the right to object (Art 21) will often be a much more effective empowerment tool. *Thirdly*, based on the insights gathered throughout the previous chapters, this chapter will briefly enumerate key requirements for achieving data subject empowerment in practice.

Section 2. Positioning Data Protection

2.1 Control v Fair Balancing

CONTROL IN THE CHARTER—The fundamental right to data protection in Article 8 of the Charter is first and foremost about safeguarding control over one's personal data (see Chapter 2). Its positioning as a fundamental right can be explained by the emergence of information technologies. The 'datafication of everything' has led to society increasingly being governed through data.[2] The right to data protection purports to safeguard individual freedom and autonomy in the face of such 'government through data'. It has both a positive (actively empowering individuals) and negative (protecting from control being negated) dimension. With this in mind, the right to data protection's goal should be interpreted broadly, ie as an architecture of control designed in function of individuals.

FAIR BALANCING IN THE GDPR—Whereas Article 8 Charter is about safeguarding *control* over one's personal data, the GDPR is about ensuring fair balances between rights, freedoms, and interests whenever personal data is being processed. The GDPR is of particular importance in light of the fact that the above-mentioned 'government through data' to a large extent occurs through private, commercial actors. Whereas direct horizontal effect of fundamental rights (and how they interact, see Art 52(1) Charter) is contested, the GDPR regulates the interaction between private actors. Put briefly, the GDPR puts in place an infrastructure of

[2] See in this regard: Lina Dencik, Arne Hintz, and Jonathan Cable, 'Towards Data Justice? The Ambiguity of Anti-Surveillance Resistance in Political Activism' (2016) 3 Big Data & Society 8–10 <http://journals.sagepub.com/doi/abs/10.1177/2053951716679678> accessed 2 January 2017.

checks and balances for safeguarding rights, freedoms, and interests in the context of data processing.

Data Subject Empowerment in the GDPR—The fact that the GDPR is essentially a fair balancing framework, does not preclude it from incorporating several important empowerment measures as well. As explained previously, the framework protects the right to data protection in particular and does so inter alia through strong data subject rights (Chapter III in the GDPR). Key empowerment measures such as the right to erasure and object in fact trigger a balancing act incorporating relevant rights, freedoms, and interests, demonstrating the intertwined nature of 'control' and 'fair balancing'.

Flexibility—In light of its broad scope, the GDPR's provisions should be interpreted with some level of flexibility (see Chapter, 3).[3] This allows for a more adaptable and sustainable framework, focused more on *responsibility* than *liability* (see Chapter 2).[4] The flipside of such flexibility is legal uncertainty and that it may result in precipitating power asymmetries, where controllers effectively determine the interpretation of the rules *in casu*.[5,6] This stresses all the more the importance of having strong *ex post* empowerment measures in place that enable data subjects to challenge controllers' interpretation. From a controller's perspective, legal uncertainty is hoped to be resolved through regulatory guidance (notably the EDPB)[7] and co-regulatory initiatives (eg standardization).

Autonomy—One of the red threads throughout this book relates to the importance of autonomy and informational self-determination in the face of intensifying power asymmetries. The GDPR purports to safeguard these prerogatives as laid down in Article 8 Charter, with due respect to, and in light of, the broader spectrum of rights, freedoms, and interests. Autonomy, in a data processing environment, can be expressed in terms of *control* over personal data. Individuals need

[3] As explained in Part II, fixing specific criteria or strict requirements for fair balancing can be quite problematic. *Joined ASNEF and FECEMD Cases* [2011] Court of Justice of the European Union Joined Cases C-468/10 and C-469/10 [42] para 43; *Michael Schwarz v Stadt Bochum* [2013] Court of Justice of the European Union C-291/12; Serge Gutwirth, 'De Toepassing van Het Finaliteitsbeginsel van de Privacywet van 8 December 1992 Tot Bescherming van de Persoonlijke Levenssfeer Ten Opzichte van de Verwerking van Persoonsgegevens' [The Application of the Purpose Specification Principle in the Belgian Data Protection Act of 8 December 1992] (1993) 1993 Tijdschrift voor Privaatrecht—TPR 1466. 1466.

[4] Article 29 Working Party, 'Opinion 06/2014 on the Notion of Legitimate Interests of the Data Controller under Article 7 of Directive 95/46/EC' (n 105) 52.

[5] ibid 5; 12; 43; 50; Ferretti (n 437) 858.

[6] This interpretational flexibility, and ensuing confusions, is also illustrated by the extensive debate on the so-called 'right to explanation' (stemming from a combined reading of Arts 15 and 22), starting with: Goodman and Flaxman (n 115); Wachter, Mittelstadt, and Floridi (n 115); Andrew Selbst and Julia Powles, 'Meaningful Information and the Right to Explanation' (2017) 7 International Data Privacy Law 233; Lilian Edwards and Michael Veale, 'Slave to the Algorithm: Why a Right to an Explanation Is Probably Not the Remedy You Are Looking For' (2017) 16 Duke Law & Technology Review 18, 67.

[7] See, for example: Article 29 Working Party, 'Annex 2: Proposals for Amendments Regarding Exemption for Personal or Household Activities' 7 <http://ec.europa.eu/justice/article-29/documentation> accessed 1 June 2019.

to be empowered and have a minimum level of 'control' over what happens with their personal data (even if only passive). Such control is challenged by the growing asymmetries between individuals and ISS providers. Two important catalysts driving these power asymmetries are (increasingly powerful and ubiquitous) technology and economic forces. The main technologies which constitute our interfaces to interact with the world are privately-owned and managed in the interest of the corporations behind them. This creates an 'architecture of control' constraining individual freedom if left unchecked.[8] Such 'architectures of control' become particularly impactful when concentrated in the hands of a few actors. Whereas human rights law developed exactly to constrain the concentration of power in the hands of the State, a lot of power in today's 'data processing ecosystem' is concentrated in the hands of private, economic actors. These actors have rational incentives to amplify their power, by processing growing amounts of personal data.[9] Against this backdrop, Daly explains that

> autonomy should be safeguarded against 'the undue influence of concentrations of power which may manipulate or coerce choices and choice-making, and can have both public (i.e. state-controlled) and private (i.e. corporate) character. The malign influence of power with either of these provenances on individuals' autonomy ought to be viewed as suspect.[10]

2.2 Hold to Account the Powerful

MORE POWER, MORE RESPONSIBILITY—With great power comes great responsibility, the saying goes. This is especially true in light of the power asymmetries described in the previous paragraphs. The digital or technological interface through which these asymmetries manifest and propagate, implies the right to data protection (Art 8 Charter) is generally triggered.[11] The GDPR, in turn, constitutes an important regulatory framework to constrain such power asymmetries. Reigning in large organizations processing data has been a central prerogative of data protection law from the start (see Chapter 2).[12] In short, and as

[8] Lawrence Lessig, *Code: Version 2.0* (Basic Books 2006) 216; Julie E Cohen, *Configuring the Networked Self: Law, Code, and the Play of Everyday Practice* (Yale UP 2012) ch 7.

[9] A worrying example of the mindset of large companies in this context can be found in: Vlad Savov, 'Google's Selfish Ledger Is an Unsettling Vision of Silicon Valley Social Engineering' (*The Verge*, 17 May 2018) <https://www.theverge.com/2018/5/17/17344250/google-x-selfish-ledger-video-data-privacy> accessed 30 May 2018.

[10] Angela Daly, *Private Power, Online Information Flows and EU Law: Mind the Gap* (Hart 2016) 22.

[11] As is the right to freedom of expression and information (Art 11 Charter) and other fundamental rights and freedoms. The focus of this book, however, is on the right to data protection in particular.

[12] Brendan Van Alsenoy, 'The Evolving Role of the Individual Under EU Data Protection Law' (KU Leuven—CiTiP 2015) Working Paper 23 <http://papers.ssrn.com/abstract=2641680> accessed 1 June 2019; Brendan Van Alsenoy, *Data Protection Law in the EU: Roles, Responsibilities and Liability* (Intersentia 2019) 612ff.

appeared throughout this book, the extent of obligations and general responsibility of a controller will be a function of the scale of its operations.[13] This scale can relate to different elements such as userbase, amount of personal data, or the type of processing.

DEFINING POWER—Talking about power asymmetries, implies a conceptualization of what power is. From a legal perspective, it may not be sufficient to simply resort to 'you know it when you see it'. Yet, defining power and/or its parameters remains particularly difficult, even only within the confines of the information society. Chapter 2 (paragraph 34) alluded to several scholars, in different fields, that have tried to frame models for identifying and evaluating power in the digital realm.[14] Different conceptualizations are useful for different purposes, but what seems to be lacking is a metric for defining power in terms of impact on fundamental rights and freedoms (if possible at all). For the purposes here, an important indicator is the 'central node' nature of certain actors, constituting inevitable infrastructures for certain activities (whether navigating the internet, interacting with one's smart home, transportation, commerce). Power is further exacerbated by the 'architectures of control' erected by information society services (ISS), effectively conditioning human activity (see Uber and Facebook vignettes). Despite these useful indicators for identifying power (asymmetries), it remains hard—perhaps even impossible—to devise a comprehensive definition and/or scale of measurement. Some also wonder to what extent such a definition is actually necessary from a legal perspective, as it may be more feasible (and sufficient) for regulation to target the vices of power (asymmetries) directly.[15] Throughout this book, power asymmetries are primarily understood as being composed of information and control asymmetries. The former referring to a clear imbalance in the amount of knowledge and information available to controllers versus individual data subjects. The latter referring to the actual capacity to manipulate (personal) data. Combined, these two have an important impact on 'data autonomy' or informational self-determination, and as a result individual freedom.

GDPR, AUTONOMY, AND POWER—The GDPR purports to safeguard autonomy in the face of power asymmetries over personal data. It essentially democratizes

[13] This also appears from ECtHR case law. See (references in): *Pihl v Sweden* [2017] European Court of Human Rights 74742/14, para 31ff; *Satakunnan Markkinapörssi Oy et Satamedia Oy v Finland* [2017] European Court of Human Rights 931/13 paras 136; 181.

[14] eg Emily Laidlaw, 'A Framework for Identifying Internet Information Gatekeepers' (2010) 24 International Review of Law, Computers & Technology 263, 268; Paul Bernal, *Internet Privacy Rights: Rights to Protect Autonomy* (CUP 2014); Shoshana Zuboff, 'Big Other: Surveillance Capitalism and the Prospects of an Information Civilization' (2015) 30 Journal of Information Technology 75); Daly (n 10); Martin Moore, 'Tech Giants and Civic Power' (King's College (Policy Institute) 2016) <www.kcl.ac.uk/sspp/policy-institute/CMCP/Tech-Giants-and-Civic-Power.pdf>; Inge Graef, *EU Competition Law, Data Protection and Online Platforms: Data as Essential Facility* (Kluwer 2016); Orla Lynskey, 'Regulating "Platform Power"' (LSE 2017) Working Paper 1/2017 10; 27 <https://papers.ssrn.com/abstract=2921021> accessed 1 June 2019.

[15] Lynskey, 'Regulating "Platform Power"' (n 14) 10; 27.

control over how personal data is processed by constraining the power of controllers and safeguarding a minimum level of autonomy for data subjects.[16] The bigger the power imbalance, the stronger such safeguards will have to be.[17] Paradoxically, large ISS providers often argue that exactly *because* of their size and the scale at which they process (personal) data, makes it impossible to comply with legal provisions aimed at empowering individuals.[18] Stricter enforcement (combined with high fines and collective action opportunities) might appear necessary to make sure great power results in great responsibility.

Bigger Picture—What complicates matters in the ISS context is that the interaction between rights, freedoms, and interests often goes beyond the controller-data subject relationship. Put differently, protecting the data subject's autonomy in the face of power asymmetries, may impact others as well (perhaps most evident in the *Google Spain* vignette). The interpretation and application of empowerment measures aimed at safeguarding data subject autonomy, should therefore clearly consider potential negative externalities beyond the asymmetric (controller-data subject) relationship at hand. Indeed, data protection cannot be looked at in isolation. The ongoing debate on platform responsibility requires a broader perspective and rethinking of notions such as 'diligent economic operator' and '*bonus pater familias*'.[19]

In the face of intensifying power asymmetries, I share Hildebrandt's concern on whether (and how)

> the data driven architecture of platforms can afford individual human flourishing, autonomy, meaningful choice, agonistic democratic decision making, fair distribution of risk and opportunities and balanced growth of public and private

[16] This is, Gutwirth explains, the very idea behind the rule of law in general. See: Gutwirth, 'De Toepassing van Het Finaliteitsbeginsel van de Privacywet' (n 3) 1419–20.

[17] ibid 1425–27; *Google Spain SL, Google Inc v Agencia Española de Protección de Datos (AEPD), Mario Costeja González* [2014] Court of Justice of the European Union C-131/12 para 83; European Data Protection Supervisor, 'Opinion on Coherent Enforcement of Fundamental Rights in the Age of Big Data' (EDPS 2016) Opinion 8/2016 7 <https://secure.edps.europa.eu/EDPSWEB/webdav/site/mySite/shared/Documents/EDPS/Events/16-09-23_BigData_opinion_EN.pdf> accessed 1 June 2019.

[18] Facebook, for example, claims it is too time-consuming and resource-heavy to accommodate individual data subject access requests regarding all personal data collected through its plugins on third party websites. See: Jef Ausloos, 'Paul-Olivier Dehaye and the Raiders of the Lost Data' (*CITIP blog*, 10 April 2018) <www.law.kuleuven.be/citip/blog/paul-olivier-dehaye-and-the-raiders-of-the-lost-data> accessed 23 April 2018. Similarly, Twitter refused to accommodate an access request regarding interaction with hyperlinks on the platform, because 'it would involve a disproportionate effort' (email in response to personal data subject access request, *de dato* 31 May 2018, on file with the author).

[19] Peggy Valcke, Aleksandra Kuczerawy, and Pieter-Jan Ombelet, 'Did the Romans Get It Right? What Delfi, Google, EBay, and UPC TeleKabel Wien Have in Common' in Mariarosaria Taddeo and Luciano Floridi (eds), *The Responsibilities of Online Service Providers*, vol 31 (Springer 2017) <http://link.springer.com/10.1007/978-3-319-47852-4> accessed 4 June 2017; Lynskey, 'Regulating "Platform Power"' (n 14); Friso Bostoen, 'Neutrality, Fairness or Freedom? Principles for Platform Regulation' (2018) 7 Internet Policy Review <https://policyreview.info/articles/analysis/neutrality-fairness-or-freedom-principles-platform-regulation> accessed 12 April 2018.

welfare. This requires keen attention to the relationship between their technical and corporate architecture on the one hand and what Julie Cohen has described as semantic discontinuity on the other hand, taking into account the mathematical underpinnings of their operations.[20]

While the GDPR as a whole lays out requirements for such technical/corporate architecture, data subject rights (to erasure and to object) in particular offer the tools for realizing Cohen's semantic discontinuity.[21] These rights can contribute breaking the vicious circle of datafication, commodification, and conditioning of humans. At least, in theory.

Section 3. Evaluating Data Subject Empowerment

In the past few decades, there has been an important discrepancy between data protection in theory versus data protection in practice. This is not different for the right to erasure. It does not come as a surprise therefore, that the European Commission stressed its intention to render the right to erasure more effective when proposing the GDPR in 2012.[22] Two years later, the Court of Justice of the European Union (CJEU) also emphasized the importance of effectiveness of data protection law and more broadly 'of the effective and complete protection of the fundamental rights and freedoms of natural persons'.[23] It is still too early to comprehensively assess whether the GDPR—and the broader socio-economic reality surrounding it—achieves these goals. Still, based on the insights gained throughout the previous chapters, this section purports to make a modest evaluation already. First by analysing how the exercise of the right to erasure is challenged in a growingly complex data processing eco-system. Secondly, by summarizing the findings of empirical work testing data subject rights in the field. And thirdly, by comparing the effectiveness of the right to erasure with the right to object.

[20] Mireille Hildebrandt, 'Primitives of Legal Protection in the Era of Data-Driven Platforms' (2018) II Georgetown Law Technology Review 252, 7.

[21] As explained by Cohen, '[s]emantic discontinuity helps to separate contexts from one another, thereby preserving breathing room for personal boundary management and for the play of everyday practice'. Cohen, *Configuring the Networked Self* (n 8); Julie Cohen, 'What Privacy Is for' (2013) 126 Harvard Law Review 1931–32; Hildebrandt, 'Primitives of Legal Protection in the Era of Data-Driven Platforms' (n 20) 260.

[22] European Commission, 'Communication from the Commission to the European Parliament, the Council, the European Economic and Social Committee and the Committee of the Regions Safeguarding Privacy in a Connected World. A European Data Protection Framework for the 21st Century', 25 January 2012.

[23] AG Opinion, paragraph 26 in: *František Ryneš v Úřad pro ochranu osobních údajů* [2014] Court of Justice of the European Union C-212/13.

3.1 Complex Ecosystem

The increasing complexity of the data processing ecosystem in the context of ISS providers has been illustrated throughout this book. The multitude of actors and purposes involved in processing operations severely challenges the effectiveness of data subject rights in practice. It is worth to briefly recap some of the most important obstacles emerging from the ecosystem's complexity.

EXAMPLE—In January 2017, Paul-Olivier Dehaye filed an access request with Facebook to gain access, inter alia, to all data points the company gathers in tracking him across the Web.[24] Obtaining no response after several reminders, Dehaye escalated the matter to the Irish data protection commissioner (DPC) in April 2017. The Irish DPC only undertook steps in October 2017, asking Facebook for a comment. It was only on 7 March 2018—more than a year after his initial request for additional information—that Dehaye received a response from the company. Alas, the response was not quite what was hoped for:

> In both cases, your requests were for information that is not available through our self-service tools which we explained to you (including DYI and Ads Preferences). Instead, this information is stored in 'Hive', which is Facebook's log storage area where data is stored primarily for back-up purposes and data analytics. [. . .] an individual's data in Hive is not readily accessible. This is because it is not stored on a per user basis. Facebook simply does not have the infrastructure capacity to store log data in Hive in a form that is indexed by user in the way that it can for production data used for the main Facebook site.[25]

Essentially, Facebook's argument comes down to (a) yes, we do retain all web tracking data; (b) we use it for 'data analytics'; but (c) we cannot give you access (and as a consequence also cannot erase) your personal data on a granular level. Why? Because we designed our systems in such a way that we do not have the capacity to accommodate your requests at scale.

[24] It is no secret that Facebook—as does Google—tracks users and non-users across the Web. See for example: Arnold Roosendaal, 'Digital Personae and Profiles in Law: Protecting Individuals' Rights in Online Contexts' (PhD Thesis, Tilburg University 2013); Brendan Van Alsenoy and others, 'From Social Media Service to Advertising Network—A Critical Analysis of Facebook's Revised Policies and Terms' (KU Leuven & VUB 2015) 1.3 <www.law.kuleuven.be/icri/en/news/item/icri-cir-advises-belgian-privacy-commission-in-facebook-investigation>; Günes Acar and others, 'Facebook Tracking Through Social Plug-Ins. Technical Report Prepared for the Belgian Privacy Commission' (KU Leuven–COSIC 2015) <https://securehomes.esat.kuleuven.be/~gacar/fb_tracking>; Reuben Binns and others, 'Third Party Tracking in the Mobile Ecosystem' [2018] arXiv:1804.03603 [cs] <http://arxiv.org/abs/1804.03603> accessed 12 April 2018.

[25] Paul-Olivier Dehaye, 'Written Evidence to House of Commons DMCS Committee' (March 2018) <http://data.parliament.uk/writtenevidence/committeeevidence.svc/evidencedocument/digital-culture-media-and-sport-committee/fake-news/written/80117.html#_ftn3> accessed 29 March 2018.

NOT A SOLITARY EXAMPLE—Unfortunately, similar types of responses were received in access requests to other tech giants such as Apple (regarding Siri data)[26] and Twitter (regarding hyperlinking activity).[27] Essentially, the main argument of many of these controllers can be summarized as 'too big to comply'. The complexity of the data processing eco-system, even internally within those respective entities, allegedly renders it too difficult or resourceful for them to accommodate the rights. This might frustrate data subjects (but also other stakeholders such as policy-makers) wishing to gain better insights into the breadth and depth of data processing. Anecdotes like these demonstrate that in practice, the complexity of data processing raises hurdles to enabling data subject empowerment, whether justified or not.

CONTROLLERS' PERSPECTIVE—Controllers often have a radically different perspective on the breadth of data subject rights and how they ought to be accommodated. Simply rejecting data subject rights, claiming that it would be too costly to accommodate them, is certainly not ok from a legal perspective. An oil refinery also cannot negate environmental protection laws simply because they are 'too costly'. Having said that, in some situations accommodating data subject rights might be quite challenging indeed. This may be due to the general landscape in which the controller finds itself,[28] and/or due to deliberate security and data protection by design measures to make re-identification harder for example.[29] The turn to agile software development—especially by ISS providers—further complicates matters for controllers.[30] In 'perpetual *beta*', user behaviour is massively captured and directly fed into the further development of the services (eg A/B testing).[31] In such a scenario, it might not always be straightforward to determine what exactly the

[26] See Michael Veale, Reuben Binns, and Jef Ausloos, 'When Data Protection by Design and Data Subject Rights Clash' (2018) 8 International Data Privacy Law 4.

[27] In an initial email exchange with the author (31 May 2018)), Twitter explains that 'we are unable to provide the specific information you have requested because it would involve a disproportionate effort as envisioned under Article 15 of the General Data Protection Regulation'. After explaining inter alia that no 'disproportionate effort' derogation applies *in casu*, Twitter responded again (14 June 2018): 'Our systems are built in such a way as to make this information unavailable without disproportionate effort, consistent with the GDPR.'

[28] For example, the way the online advertisement currently looks like makes it hard to impossible for publishers (eg a newspaper website) to know exactly which third party has processed what personal data of a specific visitor.

[29] Resulting in a careful balancing act to be performed between the actual security provided by these measures and the stripping away of empowerment measures on the other hand. See more elaborately: Veale, Binns, and Ausloos, 'When Data Protection by Design and Data Subject Rights Clash' (n 26).

[30] Seda Gürses and Joris Van Hoboken, 'Privacy after the Agile Turn' in Jules Polonetsky, Omer Tene, and Evan Selinger (eds), *Cambridge Handbook of Consumer Privacy* (CUP 2017) <https://osf.io/preprints/socarxiv/9gy73> accessed 1 June 2019.

[31] Researchers at Princeton University uncovered literally the entire interaction with a website (including mouse movements, etc) can be captured. Steven Englehardt, 'No Boundaries: Exfiltration of Personal Data by Session-Replay Scripts' (*Freedom to Tinker*, 15 November 2017) <https://freedom-to-tinker.com/2017/11/15/no-boundaries-exfiltration-of-personal-data-by-session-replay-scripts> accessed 1 June 2019.

right to erasure would target. The growing use of artificial intelligence and machine learning further renders it hard for controllers to effectively explain certain decisions, let alone enable data to be erased.[32] Importantly, this does not mean controllers can simply throw their hands up claiming it is too hard to accommodate rights. Instead, the GDPR requires an inclusive and proactive approach, as apparent from the fairness principle (Art 5(1)(a)), data protection by design and by default (Art 25) and data protection impact assessments (Art 35).

DATA SUBJECTS' PERSPECTIVE—From data subjects' perspective it has become virtually impossible to grasp the full extent of how personal data is processed. Since at least the early 2000s, scholars have been pointing to how '*problems of consensual exhaustion, laxity and apathy—in addition to ignorance and myopia—can reduce the amount of care that data subjects invest in*' controlling their personal data.[33] This trend is only exacerbated by data processing penetrating ever more facets of life (see 'smart-' home, car, city, school) and the complexification of the ecosystem behind it. This apathy often also stems from the fact that it is hard to observe the direct impact of a singular processing activity or piece of personal data on one's life. People commonly lack the tools to appreciate the cumulative effect—on themselves or society—of seemingly innocuous and/or unrelated data processing activities, let alone who is responsible for it.[34] In some situations data protection empowerment measures might not even be available, even though data processing is evidently impacting individuals. This is the case, for example, where a navigation app decides to re-route a high number of users via an otherwise quiet street; or when your insurance premium increases because you refuse to install a driving-behaviour monitoring app used by the majority of other insurance-holders.[35]

CONTRADICTORY POSITION OF DATA SUBJECTS—Further complexifying the scope and meaning of data subject empowerment is the apparently contradictory behaviour of individuals. A growing number of people 'self-track' (eg through dedicated devices or through their smartphones/watches), freely sharing large quantities of personal data with ISS providers.[36] In a continuous feedback-loop—with

[32] See more broadly: Mireille Hildebrandt, *Smart Technologies and the End(s) of Law: Novel Entanglements of Law and Technology* (Edward Elgar Publishing 2015) 91.

[33] See, inter alia, references in: Bygrave and Wiese Schartum (n 1421) 161. A 2018 survey in the UK also pointed out that '[t]he data ecosystem is invisible to consumers, limiting their knowledge of it'. Britain Thinks, 'Control, Alt or Delete? Consumer Research on Attitudes to Data Collection and Use' (*Which?* 2018) 5 <http://britainthinks.com/pdfs/Consumer-Data-Research-report.pdf> accessed 13 June 2018.

[34] Article 29 Working Party, 'Opinion 06/2014 on the Notion of Legitimate Interests of the Data Controller under Article 7 of Directive 95/46/EC' (European Commission 2014) Opinion WP 217 37 <http://ec.europa.eu/justice/article-29/documentation> accessed 1 June 2019.

[35] These issues of course raise broader questions (than data protection) and policy approaches regarding the responsibility of the actors behind these decisions. Yet they are worth mention here because the decisions are—to a large extent—based on the processing of (other people's) personal data. See also: Seda Gürses, Rebekah Overdorf, and Ero Balsa, 'POTs: The Revolution Will Not Be Optimized?' [2018] arXiv:1806.02711 [cs] <http://arxiv.org/abs/1806.02711> accessed 11 June 2018.

[36] eg: Sarah Pink and others, 'Mundane Data: The Routines, Contingencies and Accomplishments of Digital Living' (2017) 4 Big Data & Society 2053951717700924.

data being provided and 'insights' sent in return—such data-processing is deeply incorporated into individuals' lives.[37] Individuals may not wish to fully erase all of this data. Yet, it is important not to lose sight of the broader ecosystem, notably ISS providers' incentives to further monetize the personal data. Even if protective measures such as purpose limitation theoretically constrain said actors from freely selling that personal data for example, processing activities may still affect data subjects in more intricate manners (eg data-driven sponsored or promoted suggestions, predictions, and user design). How can user autonomy and oversight be maintained in such systems?[38]

Data Hurdles—The amorphous nature of personal data further complexifies the way in which data subject rights should be interpreted (see Chapter 3). Even a seemingly straightforward 'advertising profile' held by Facebook or Google is constantly changing based on individuals' behaviour and the inferences those companies make. Data is also increasingly interconnected. Posting a video online results in a plethora of additional personal data being generated such as comments, tags, and viewer behaviour metrics. The CJEU's *Rijkeboer* Ruling also emphasized how separating 'basic data' from 'metadata' (eg when it was collected, the source and who it was shared with) may severely impact data subjects' rights.[39] Furthermore, while anonymization may be used to fend off data subject rights, many have pointed out the ease with which data can be re-identified.[40] Finally, in the context of group profiles, data subject rights may only be of limited use,[41] ie at the moment personal data is collected and at the moment the group profile is actually applied to a data subject.[42] Of course, this is not to say

[37] Often with added incentives to share more data, eg using gamification methods.

[38] Chris Elsden and others, 'Fitter, Happier, More Productive: What to Ask of a Data-Driven Life' (2016) 23 Interactions 47.

[39] *In casu*, the controller had stored 'basic data' (ie 'personal data kept by the local authority on a person, such as his name and address') while it had deleted the 'information on recipients or categories of recipient to whom [the] basic data are disclosed'. The data subject, therefore, could no longer gain access to who had obtained his personal data in the past. *College van burgemeester en wethouders van Rotterdam v MEE Rijkeboer* [2009] Court of Justice of the European Union C-553/07.

[40] See for example (the references in): Mario Viola de Azevedo Cunha, 'Review of the Data Protection Directive: Is There Need (and Room) For a New Concept of Personal Data?' in Serge Gutwirth and others (eds), *European Data Protection: In Good Health?* (Springer 2012); Yves-Alexandre de Montjoye and others, 'Unique in the Crowd: The Privacy Bounds of Human Mobility' (2013) 3 Scientific Reports <http://www.nature.com/srep/2013/130325/srep01376/full/srep01376.html> accessed 1 June 2019; Yves-Alexandre de Montjoye and others, 'Unique in the Shopping Mall: On the Reidentifiability of Credit Card Metadata' (2015) 347 Science 536; Sophie Stalla-Bourdillon and Alison Knight, 'Anonymous Data v. Personal Data—A False Debate: An EU Perspective on Anonymization, Pseudonymization and Personal Data' (2017) 34 Wisconsin International Law Journal 284; Michael Veale, Reuben Binns, and Lilian Edwards, 'Algorithms That Remember: Model Inversion Attacks and Data Protection Law' [2018] arXiv:1807.04644 [cs] <http://arxiv.org/abs/1807.04644> accessed 17 August 2018.

[41] Edwards and Veale (n 6) 68ff.

[42] When it is applied to groups of people at the same time (eg in a smart city environment), data subject rights may not be available at all.

other legal tools may be more appropriate to tackle issues emerging from group profiling.[43]

Opaque Processing Hotchpotch—This book is concerned first and foremost with the interaction between data subjects and ISS providers. This implies a relationship, or at the very least knowledge about the existence of the ISS provider. Beneath the surface however, there is an incalculable number of entities—most of which data subjects will never even have heard of—that process personal data as well.[44] These can be processors acting on behalf of the ISS provider, third parties (eg trackers), or a combination of both. Personal data may also be shared in different mutations with different entities, in a complex chain of processing. This raises complicated questions regarding who to approach with the right to erasure and how far said right reaches. From a data subject's perspective, it might be desirable to have single points-of-attack, for example an App Store, or video-hosting platform. Yet, responsibilizing such 'platforms' over the personal data processing operations of its users (eg app developers or video-uploaders) raises a number of other issues.[45]

Technical Hurdles—Even if all entities involved agree upon the erasure of personal data, there might still be considerable *technical* hurdles challenging actual erasure.[46] A priori, erasure applies to any storage medium and copies of the personal data (eg backups in different locations). WP29 has stressed each instance of the respective personal data should be erased irretrievably, including 'temporary files and even file fragments'.[47] Secure erasure, WP29 continues, 'requires that either the storage media be destroyed or demagnetised or the stored personal data is deleted effectively through overwriting'.[48] Cloud providers (and users thereof) should also make sure that personal data is physically erased by all other processors down the processing chain. Something which may be impossible to verify technically without having full access to the respective infrastructure.[49] Even if the only

[43] eg property law, personality rights, or tort law. See: Mireille Hildebrandt, 'Who Is Profiling Who? Invisible Visibility' in Serge Gutwirth and others (eds), *Reinventing Data Protection?* (Springer 2009) 250<www.springerlink.com/index/P7710R0760613778.pdf> accessed 1 June 2019.

[44] A clear example would be the Real Time Bidding sector in online advertisement. See: Information Commissioner's Office, 'Update Report into AdTech and Real Time Bidding' (ICO 2019) <https://ico.org.uk/media/about-the-ico/documents/2615156/adtech-real-time-bidding-report-201906.pdf> accessed 20 June 2019.

[45] See notably the intermediary liability debate discussed in Chapters 2 and 6–7, as well as the analysis of the right to erasure's second paragraph in Chapter 4.

[46] This was also a concern raised during the legislative process. Council of the European Union, 'Working Party on Information Exchange and Data Protection (DAPIX). Summary of Discussion on 23–24 February 2012'.

[47] Article 29 Working Party, 'Opinion 05/2012 on Cloud Computing' (Article 29 Working Party 2012) WP 196 11–12 <http://ec.europa.eu/justice/article-29/documentation> accessed 1 June 2019.

[48] 'For the overwriting of personal data, special software tools that overwrite data multiple times in accordance with a recognised specification should be used.' ibid.

[49] Kristina Irion, 'Your Digital Home Is No Longer Your Castle: How Cloud Computing Transforms the (Legal) Relationship between Individuals and Their Personal Records' [2015] International Journal of Law and Information Technology 9 <http://ijlit.oxfordjournals.org/content/early/2015/09/25/ijlit.eav015> accessed 1 June 2019.

way of guaranteeing absolute and irretrievable erasure of personal data is by destroying the physical storage-medium, requiring this in each individual case appears unreasonable, if not unfeasible (see Chapter 6).[50] Moreover, erasing all the various generations and/or associated log data raises several data security issues as well.[51] Regarding *published* personal data, erasure has been said to be impossible to achieve, or even observe, through technical means (as it is virtually impossible to trace its propagation).[52] Realistic solutions, therefore, should be based on a combination of technical and legal measures.

Legal Hurdles—As is amply illustrated throughout this book (in particular Chapters 4 and 6), data subjects wishing to invoke the right to erasure face numerous legal hurdles as well. The most obvious examples in this regard are the exemptions to the GDPR overall and to the right to erasure in particular, as well as the open-ended balancing provisions. The delegation of derogatory regimes to Member States (eg Arts 23(1) and 85(1)) and the potentially diverging interpretation by national courts and data protection authorities may further complicate matters for data subjects.

3.2 Data Subject Empowerment in Practice

The GDPR purports to facilitate the exercise of data subject rights (Art 12 and Recital 59). This is all the more important considering the already quite complex data processing eco-system as well as the substantial power asymmetries characterizing data subject-ISS provider relationships. Indeed, rendering data subject empowerment[53] effective hinges on clear and easily accessible/exercisable legal rights. Technology should follow the law, not *vice versa*.

Empirical Research—In the run-up to the entry into force of the GDPR, I organized empirical research so as to test data subject rights in the field. The main impulse for this was the lack of evidence supporting general assumptions about

[50] Concerns as to the technical feasibility of some data subject rights including the right to erasure, were also voiced by several delegations during the GDPR negotiations. See: Council of the European Union, 'Note to the Working Party on Information Exchange of Data Protection. Council Revised Version of the Proposal for a Regulation of the European Parliament and of the Council on the Protection of Individuals with Regard to the Processing of Personal Data and on the Free Movement of Such Data (General Data Protection Regulation)' (n 667) n 138.

[51] ACM Nugter, *Transborder Flow of Personal Data within the EC: A Comparative Analysis of the Privacy Statutes of the Federal Republic of Germany, France, the United Kingdom and The Netherlands and Their Impact on the Private Sector* (Kluwer Law and Taxation Publ 1990) 52; André Holleaux, 'La Loi Du 6 Janvier 1978 Sur Informatique et Les Libertés—II—' (1978) 31 La Revue administrative, 165.

[52] Peter Druschel, Michael Backes, and Rodica Tirtea, 'The Right to Be Forgotten—Between Expectations and Practice' (ENISA 2012) 8ff <https://www.enisa.europa.eu/activities/identity-and-trust/library/deliverables/the-right-to-be-forgotten/> accessed 1 June 2019.

[53] This section is based on published work: Jef Ausloos and Pierre Dewitte, 'Shattering One-Way Mirrors—Data Subject Access Rights in Practice' (2018) 8 International Data Privacy Law 4.

problematic compliance with data subject rights.[54] The initial goal was to test the right of erasure in the ISS context. In order to do so, roughly four steps were identified. Firstly, participants would register with a service and perform some basic interactions so as to generate data. Secondly, they would file access requests to gain insight in what personal data was actually processed by the respective ISS provider. Thirdly, an erasure request would be filed. Fourthly, a new access request would be filed after a certain time, in order to verify whether personal data had in fact been erased. Due to time constraints, the research was stopped somewhere between steps three and four. The only conclusive findings therefore, relate to the right of access. Still, most findings are still very relevant with regard to compliance with the right to erasure. After all, accessing personal data is an important first step to erasure, and the way in which controllers respond to one right will generally also translate to other rights.

METHODOLOGY—After a preparatory phase, the actual collection of information took place between February 2017 and July 2017. Three students following an advanced master's program (in IT & IP Law) at the KU Leuven[55] were recruited to participate in this research as part of their thesis-writing project. In deliberation with these students, a selection of 66 commonly used (across the EU) ISS providers was made.[56] The findings were gathered through online surveys which the students had to fill in after completing each step for every single service provider. These surveys contained both quantitative (eg how many clicks to find access request instructions, how many days until a reply?) and qualitative (eg how satisfied are you with the process of filing the access request and why?). Even if some answers can be considered subjective (eg using a 1–5 Likert scale to rate the ease of filing one's access request), they still serve as useful indicators. All the

[54] Some notable exceptions exist though: Clive Norris and others, *The Unaccountable State of Surveillance: Exercising Access Rights in Europe* (Sprinter International Publishing 2017); Antonella Galetta, Chiara Fonio, and Alessia Ceresa, 'Nothing Is as It Seems. The Exercise of Access Rights in Italy and Belgium: Dispelling Fallacies in the Legal Reasoning from the "Law in Theory" to the "Law in Practice"' (2015) 6 International Data Privacy Law 16; Dominik Herrmann and Jens Lindemann, 'Obtaining Personal Data and Asking for Erasure: Do App Vendors and Website Owners Honour Your Privacy Rights?' [2016] arXiv:1602.01804 [cs] <http://arxiv.org/abs/1602.01804> accessed 11 June 2019.

[55] Organized by KU Leuven Centre for IT & IP Law (CiTiP): http://www.law.kuleuven.be/brussel/en/education/intellectual_property_rights/intellectual_property_rights.

[56] These were spread across the following sectors: sharing economy (22 per cent); social media (26 per cent); eCommerce (22 per cent); user generated content (UGC) platforms (12 per cent); email providers (6 per cent); online publishers (5 per cent); online hosting and file storage (3 per cent); Internet of Things (IoT) services (3 per cent); online games (1 per cent). In light of the constant metamorphosis of many online service providers and relevant sectors, it was decided to base this categorization on examples rather than strict definitions. Despite many service providers being active in several of these sectors simultaneously, they were each only categorized into one, according to their core functionality to end-users. The unequal spread can be explained by different market constellations in each of these sectors. It was also decided to leave the selection to the students, so as to best represent the main services they frequently use. The selection can therefore be considered indicative of the broader landscape and as such adequate for the purposes of an explorative study. Having said that, it is also acknowledged that the modest nature of the list should be further enriched in future initiatives, ensuring a wider spread.

more, taking into account the fact that they were provided by advanced master's in law students that are arguably much more knowledgeable and motivated than the average data subject wishing to exercise data subject rights. Moreover, the students were asked to clarify their answers so that subjective findings were generally also further substantiated by other quantifiable factors (eg number of clicks to get to access request, word-count of privacy policy). Regular meetings between me and the students (on average >2 times a month) ensured proper follow-up and completion of the surveys.

FINDINGS REGARDING THE SUBMITTING OF REQUESTS—Only two thirds of the investigated services provided clear instructions on how to exercise the right of access in their privacy policy. In the remainder of cases, it was unclear what means of communication had to be used (27 per cent did not clearly mention contact details). While the electronic form was always used whenever available, on four occasions (6 per cent) postal letters had to be sent as it was the only option to effectively exercise the right of access. Two eCommerce platforms only offered electronic support via contact forms to data subjects who had a pending or a past order on their website. Without a valid order number, it was therefore practically impossible to contact them other than through regular mail. Such a requirement may be considered quite restrictive, discouraging, and disproportionate, especially in light of the service being exclusively offered online. Only 29 per cent of controllers responded (even if only a mere acknowledgment of receipt) within 10 days and 36 per cent took more than 30 days. In 87 per cent of cases, it was necessary to take extra steps (ie sending reminders) to even receive a mere acknowledgment of the request. Despite the fact reminders were sent about every two or three weeks for five months in a row, 26 per cent of providers did not bother to respond at all. Unsurprisingly, requests received faster support when privacy-dedicated contact points were approached.

FINDINGS RECEIVING REQUESTS—Not one of the initial responses received were satisfactory. This necessitated further interaction with the respective controller, making the whole process quite time-consuming. Whether as a deliberate avoidance strategy or due to simple ignorance, initial responses often only contained very basic information and/or asked further clarifications as to what data was requested exactly (even if the request already referred to all information listed in Article 12(a) Directive 95/46). Trying to engage in a constructive and in-depth dialogue was also considerably complicated by the fact that some controllers redirected follow up emails to different officers; or spontaneously closed ongoing requests. Some controllers showed suspicion, irritation, reluctance, and even bad faith in follow-up correspondence to access requests. In some instances, data subjects were given the feeling that their demands were not welcome or even illegitimate.[57] It also

[57] Answers included, for example: 'We really don't have time for this; please look at our privacy policy, all your questions are answered. If you wish to erase your data, you are perfectly entitled to'; 'I can't manage to motivate the developers'; 'This type of legislation is the reason we incorporated ***** in

appeared very hard to assess the completeness of responses. Without having access to the actual systems of the controller, the only way (apart from blindly trusting the controller) to verify completeness seems by cross-referencing responses with what is described in the privacy policy and checking the activity of third-party trackers when visiting the respective websites. Overall, it appeared that in practice, a considerable burden rests on data subjects' shoulders wishing to invoke their right of access (and by extension the right to erasure). With long waiting times, necessity of back-and-forth interaction, and little to no tools to even verify full compliance, it is safe to assume many data subjects would be discouraged to actively pursue their rights until the end.

General Findings—Some good practices and positive experiences aside, the empirical study suggests an important gap between theory and practice when it comes to accommodating data subject rights in the ISS sector. Answers provided were indeed rated satisfactory in only 22 per cent of instances. Correspondence with controllers throughout the empirical study (eg questioning the reasons behind incomplete answers, etc) did give an indication as to the reasons behind the many issues, the most important of which can be summarized as a lack of awareness; organization; and motivation. Firstly, the empirical findings laid bare a worrying lack of awareness among controllers as to the existence and scope of data subject rights. A good portion of controllers completely ignored or at least showed general discomfort when confronted with access requests. Secondly, substantial deficiencies regarding the internal organization of controllers in light of data subject rights were observed. Most of the small- and medium-sized ISS providers contacted did not have any department, team, or even person in charge of managing privacy- and data protection-related issues. From a more technical perspective, some controllers struggled to identify and locate the personal data requested, simply because their storage methods fell short of offering clear and reliable ways to accommodate data subject rights. Thirdly, a general lack in motivation to comply could also be observed. Indicators of this were, for example, the number of days it took controllers to respond (with 71 per cent not providing any response within 10 days) and the necessity to take extra steps before even obtaining a simple reaction in 87 per cent of cases. Additionally, the amount of suspicion, bad faith, irritation, and disrespect encountered throughout, further suggest a general unwillingness to accommodate data subject rights. It is unclear (and hard to establish) to what extent this apparent lack of motivation is symptomatic of deeper, systematic issues regarding non-compliance with data protection rules more broadly. Combined, these hurdles obstruct an effective exercise of data subject rights. Either data subjects are effectively denied access to their data (26 per cent of the access requests filed during the empirical study were not answered at all), or they face considerable obstacles

the US and not in Belgium. In reality, real users never ask for this type of information.' See: Ausloos and Dewitte (n 53) 11–12.

trying to obtain a satisfying answer from controllers. This, in turn, often prevents (or at the very least curtails) data subjects' ability to exercise other key rights (eg correct, object, erasure).

Privacy Dashboards—It is also worth mentioning that both in the empirical research, but also when filing ad hoc requests myself, controllers often defer data subjects to their user-profiles and/or 'privacy dashboards'.[58] While it is certainly to be encouraged that controllers invest in easily accessible visualizations of what personal data is processed and how, such dashboards are rarely comprehensive. As a general observation, such dashboards often only give users basic information such as personal details directly provided by the user or observed data. Users may be able to see, for example, when they listened to a certain song, watched a video or made a certain search. But they will generally not see what inferences the controller has made on the basis of that information and how it has subsequently used those inferences.[59] What is more, these dashboards are only available to data subjects who have registered with the respective service provider. Data subjects without an account may still find their personal data being processed, but with no means of accessing and managing said data via these 'privacy dashboards'.[60]

The dating App Tinder[61] offers an interesting illustration of the points in the previous paragraph. Whenever you 'match' with a person, Tinder looks for common Facebook-friends, even if those friends are not on Tinder themselves. Having filed multiple access requests myself (with the eventual goal of exercising my right to erasure and/or to object), Tinder keeps on saying I have to log in and use the 'download my data tool', even though I have explained not being a registered user. Moreover, even if I were to be a user, Tinder's 'download my data' tool is still not comprehensive. Indeed, in 2017 it appeared the company algorithmically attributes a 'hotness'-factor to each user in order to only match people with others who are 'in the same league'.[62] Such information is not shared in response to access requests. In sum, the adoption of privacy dashboards is often being used by controllers to shape the scope of their legal obligations. Any pushback is met with the hurdles mentioned before (irritation, unresponsiveness, denials).

[58] Perhaps the most obvious example would be Google's My Activity dashboard, which includes users' search, maps, YouTube history, and much more. See: myactivity.google.com.

[59] Let alone several other categories listed in Article 15 GDPR (eg source of personal data, who it is shared with, the right to lodge a complaint with the DPA) or, for example, the risks involved in certain personal data processing operations.

[60] See in this regard: '[Facebook] also doesn't want to be regulated by governments—which is why it's rushing out its own set of self-crafted 'transparency' tools, rather than waiting for rules to be imposed on it'. Natasha Lomas, 'Facebook's Dark Ads Problem Is Systemic' (*TechCrunch*, 28 April 2018) <http://social.techcrunch.com/2018/04/28/facebooks-dark-ads-problem-is-systemic/> accessed 15 May 2018.

[61] https://tinder.com.

[62] Judith Duportail, 'I Asked Tinder for My Data. It Sent Me 800 Pages of My Deepest, Darkest Secrets' *The Guardian* (26 September 2017) <http://www.theguardian.com/technology/2017/sep/26/tinder-personal-data-dating-app-messages-hacked-sold> accessed 1 June 2019.

Future—It should be acknowledged that the same empirical research would probably yield different results if done today, *after* the entry into force of the GDPR. Still, it would be naïve to assume no practical hurdles to data subject requests remain whatsoever. Throughout this book, several references have already been made to unsuccessful access requests, made by highly motivated and knowledgeable individuals with resourceful tech companies (eg Apple,[63] Facebook,[64] Twitter[65]). Difficulties with obtaining access to personal data also leads to a strong presumption of similar difficulties in obtaining erasure. Data subjects will generally have to jump through the same hurdles and controllers will likely use the same arguments to fend off requests.

3.3 Abusing the Right to Erasure

Just like any other (data subject) right, the right to erasure is susceptible to being abused.[66] The potential for data protection law to be abused has already been recognized by several Advocate Generals.[67] It is not unimaginable that people infringing intellectual property rights, performing terrorist activities online, or spreading child pornography, may use the right to erasure to cover their tracks (eg by requesting their access provider to delete all personal data).[68] Legal obligations may

[63] Access requests to Siri voice recordings, see Veale, Binns, and Ausloos, 'When Data Protection by Design and Data Subject Rights Clash' (n 26).

[64] Access requests to Facebook's cross-websites tracking practices, see Dehaye (n 25); Ausloos, 'Paul-Olivier Dehaye and the Raiders of the Lost Data' (n 18).

[65] Access requests with regard to Twitter's processing of hyperlink-interaction data. Correspondence of the author with Twitter and the Belgian Gegevensbeschermingautoriteit.

[66] In a 2018 Dutch ruling, an individual was said to have abused his right of access under data protection law, because he would simply have invoked it in order to obtain 'damages imposed on a daily basis in case of non-compliance' (*dwangsom*). See: RCK van Andel and MW van Nijendaal, 'Misbruik Wbp en incasseren dwangsommen' (*Nysingh*, 22 January 2018) <https://www.nysingh.nl/actueel/misbruik-wbp-en-incasseren-dwangsommen/> accessed 30 January 2018. There is a rich body of scholarship (and case law) on abuse of rights, both at EU and Member-State level For an analysis of the relevant Article 54 of the Charter, see notably: Lorna Woods, 'Abuse of Rights' in Steve Peers and others (eds), *The EU Charter of Fundamental Rights: A Commentary* (Hart 2014) <https://www.bloomsburycollections.com/book/the-eu-charter-of-fundamental-rights-a-commentary/>. For an extensive and comparative analysis of abuse of rights in the context of European patent law, see: Amandine Léonard, 'Abuse of Rights in European Patent Law— Testing the Theory of Abuse to Patent Assertion Entities' Litigation Strategies' (PhD Thesis, KU Leuven—Faculty of Law 2019).

[67] See notably AG Kokott in: *Peter Nowak v Data Protection Commissioner* (n 51) paras 42ff; AG Bobek in: *Rīgas satiksme* [2017] Court of Justice of the European Union C-13/16 paras 97–99.

[68] In this regard, it is also worth referring to an increased uptake of end-to-end encrypted communications and self-destructing messages services, by heavily regulated sectors (eg banking). This trend may effectively prevent accountability of the relevant actors. See for example: Edward W Felten, 'On Encryption, Archiving, and Accountability' (*Freedom to Tinker*, 7 July 2017) <http://freedom-to-tinker.com/2017/07/07/on-encryption-archiving-and-accountability/> accessed 1 June 2019; 'Cambridge Analytica's Board Suspends CEO Nix Amid Inquiry' *Bloomberg.com* (20 March 2018) <https://www.bloomberg.com/news/articles/2018-03-20/cambridge-analytica-s-board-suspends-ceo-nix-pending-inquiry> accessed 4 June 2018.

be required to ensure the respective controllers have an incentive not to accommodate such requests.[69] Indeed, the exemptions in Article 17(3) and derogations to the GDPR more broadly, should safeguard specific types of processing which can be deemed valuable (eg for criminal prosecution or health research). This is not to say, of course, that erasure requests will always be invalid in such context. Just that there will be a more or less strong default against erasure. As a matter of fact, these situations are in fact already dealt with in Part II of this book. The GDPR aims to prevent abuse of the right to erasure by installing pre-defined or open balancing acts. Indeed, also other legal frameworks may have to step in, in order for the right to erasure not to be abused for nefarious purposes (eg fraud in the financial sector).[70]

The GDPR also foresees situations where 'requests from a data subject are manifestly unfounded or excessive, in particular because of their repetitive character' (Art 12(5)). If the controller manages to prove this is the case, it can either charge a reasonable fee (in light of the actual administrative costs of accommodating the request) or refuse to act altogether. In any case, the controller will have to substantiate its decision. This provision may prove to be the battleground for effectuating data subject rights in the future. Indeed, what exactly constitutes an 'excessive' (repetition of) request(s)? If a data subject is permanently tracked across the web, his/her profile is constantly changing. Would a daily resubmission of an access and/or erasure request (or even more frequent than that) be *excessive*? A teleological reading of the GDPR (also considering Article 8 Charter and the impact of such tracking) suggests this does not constitute 'abuse'. Similarly, in principle I would not consider automating the exercise of data subject rights and/or relying on a third-party service to do so, to be excessive. Yet, in light of what is at stake for some controllers, this question may eventually have to be decided by the courts.

Overall, abuse will never be entirely eradicated. The point is to create the right incentive structures for controllers not to follow abusive requests and make it less attractive for individuals to file such requests in the first place. In the mid-long term, substantial transparency on controllers' erasure policies and actual decisions will be critical in identifying the problem areas (eg what is the number of public officials requesting Google to be delisted and what is Google's assessment-procedure?).

[69] See *mutadis mutandis*: Orla Lynskey, *The Foundations of EU Data Protection Law* (OUP 2016) 154ff.

[70] Council of the European Union, 'Note to the Working Party on Information Exchange of Data Protection. Council Revised Version of the Proposal for a Regulation of the European Parliament and of the Council on the Protection of Individuals with Regard to the Processing of Personal Data and on the Free Movement of Such Data (General Data Protection Regulation)', Council of Europe, June 21, 2013.

3.4 To Erase or to Object, That's the Question

Article 17 as a Central Hub in the GDPR—Chapter 4 clearly demonstrated how the right to erasure in Article 17 constitutes more of central joint in the overall GDPR infrastructure, rather than an autonomous provision or 'right'. Both its triggers and exceptions all (in)directly refer to other provisions in- and outside the GDPR. With that in mind, a cynic could argue that Article 17 is in fact superfluous.[71] Yet, in this book, it appears that Article 17 does have added value. This stems from how the right reemphasizes, clarifies, and centralizes key data protection components from a data subject's perspective.[72] It *reemphasizes* how many existing data protection elements already imply a right (and obligation) to erasure. It *clarifies* by unambiguously specifying how other provisions may (not) result in erasure. And it *centralizes*, as it effectively constitutes a central node in the GDPR drawing together the key provisions that are relevant in light of *ex post* empowerment. In light of this, the provision offers a great starting point for data subjects interested in reclaiming control over their personal data.

Issues with Erasure—The right to erasure does raise a number of important issues, as is clearly demonstrated throughout this book. Ranging from the vagueness of its actual field of application (Chapters 3 and 4), to the ensuing balancing (Part II), and a number of practical hurdles that complicate the actual implementation of the right (see above, subsection 3.2, paragraphs 33–42). Indeed, it was mentioned before that more pragmatic solutions will often impose themselves as alternatives to 'erasure *stricto sensu*' (eg access-restrictions, pseudonymization, abstention from further dissemination, correction, etc).[73] With that in mind, does the right to erasure actually constitute the *empowerment tool by excellence* as was suggested at the start of this book? The answer to this question is more about managing expectations. As a centralized hub for data subject empowerment more broadly, it certainly serves as an important safeguard for Article 8 Charter. Moreover, the rhetorical power in the public debate of the 'right to erasure'—and 'the right to be forgotten' even more—cannot be underestimated, sending a clear normative message to all stakeholders.

Right to Object as Ultimate Empowerment Measure—Substantially and pragmatically, the right to object might in fact be a more empowering GDPR provision. As was explained before (subsection 3.2.1, paragraphs 41–47), the right

[71] As a matter of fact, the consultative committee for the modernization of Convention 108 considered the introduction of a 'right to oblivion' unnecessary, considering it was already comprised in other safeguards. See: Lilian Mitrou and Maria Karyda, 'EU's Data Protection Reform and the Right to Be Forgotten: A Legal Response to a Technological Challenge?' (2012) 11–12 <http://papers.ssrn.com/abstract=2165245> accessed 1 June 2019.

[72] As opposed to from the perspective of controllers.

[73] See also in this regard: Cécile de Terwangne, *The Right to Be Forgotten and the Informational Autonomy in the Digital Environment* (Publications Office 2013) 19ff <http://dx.publications.europa.eu/10.2788/54562> accessed 1 June 2019.

to object (Art 21) is an autonomous provision enabling data subjects to address problematic processing operations much more granularly (see Chapter 4, subsections 2.3 and 2.4.4). Such a surgical approach is much more realistic in the complex ISS data processing ecosystem, with many simultaneous processing operations pursuing different purposes, on the basis of different lawful grounds. As such, it also enables the 'fifty shades of erasure' (see Chapter 7), finding a compromise solution that suits everyone's rights, freedoms, and interests.[74] The ability to only target specific processing operations also ensures data subjects are not confronted with a de facto all-or-nothing choice under the right to erasure. For example, erasing one's profile information may render impossible further normal use of a social network, whereas a right to object offers individuals the opportunity to maintain that data while simply preventing specific processing operations (eg advertisement profiling or analytics). Indeed, the right to object may also be more appropriate to target the application of specific group profiles on particular data subjects for example. This ties back to the 'right to be delisted', which constitutes some sort of a hybrid between the rights to erasure and to object. The data subject *objects* to the specific processing operation of linking one set of information (eg a group profile, or a picture on a blog) with him-/herself. To the extent such 'links' are pre-determined (as opposed to being created on the spot), the result is that they are to be *erased*. Finally, it is of course important to recall that a successful right to object may also lead to actual erasure (see Art 17(1)(c)) if there are no (more) lawful grounds to continue processing the personal data.[75] In fact, one can conclude that the right to object and the right to erasure complement, rather than compete with, each other.

RIGHT TO RESTRICTION OF PROCESSING—It is worth, finally, referring to an often-overlooked data subject right. The right to restriction of processing in Article 18 GDPR is available to data subjects whenever: (a) the data subject contests the accuracy; (b) the processing is unlawful and the data subject requests restriction rather than erasure; (c) the purpose has expired, but the personal data is required by the data subject for the establishment, exercise or defence of legal claims; (d) the data subject has objected, pending the controller's assessment.[76] Generally, this

[74] *Salvatore Manni* [2017] Court of Justice of the European Union C-398/15. In this case, erasure from a 'companies register' maintained by a local chamber of commerce, was not deemed acceptable, whereas the availability of a right to object cannot be excluded.

[75] As appears from Chapter 4, a successful right to object may indirectly affect the lawfulness of other processing operations on the same personal data as well.

[76] The actual wording of Article 18(1) is: 'The data subject shall have the right to obtain from the controller restriction of processing where one of the following applies: (a) the accuracy of the personal data is contested by the data subject, for a period enabling the controller to verify the accuracy of the personal data; (b) the processing is unlawful and the data subject opposes the erasure of the personal data and requests the restriction of their use instead; (c) the controller no longer needs the personal data for the purposes of the processing, but they are required by the data subject for the establishment, exercise or defence of legal claims; (d) the data subject has objected to processing pursuant to Article 21(1) pending the verification whether the legitimate grounds of the controller override those of the data subject.'

measure should be seen as a temporary one. During the period of 'restricted processing' the controller may not process the personal data, apart from mere storage, unless 'the data subject consents or for the establishment, exercise or defence of legal claims or for the protection of the rights of another natural or legal person or for reasons of important public interest of the Union or of a Member State' (Art 18(2)). This data subject right is interesting because it effectively blocks the controller from processing the personal data—even if only temporarily—without the need for an a priori balancing act. Merely invoking the right to object, for example, is already sufficient to claim processing should be restricted, up until the moment the validity of the right to object is determined. As such, the provision can be seen as a tool to challenge power asymmetries. Having said that, at the moment it seems this provision will only have limited practical relevance.

Interim Conclusion—The practical issues involved with the exercise of the right to erasure are legion.[77] Yet I would not go so far as to suggest they render the provision useless altogether. The right to erasure's most important contribution is how it strongly affirms and centralizes data subject empowerment. It allows data subjects to put controllers on the spot and enforce *ex ante* obligations such as purpose limitation or data minimization principles. The importance of such a role cannot be underestimated in the face of under-resourced data protection authorities and over-resourced controllers.

Section 4. Making Data Subject Empowerment Effective

Overview—This section will specify certain key requirements for making the right to erasure—and data subject empowerment more broadly—effective in practice. The analyses of the mechanics both of Article 17 (Part I) and the ensuing balancing (Part II) have enabled putting the finger on some essential prerequisites for ensuring effective control over personal data pursuant to Article 8 Charter. Importantly, the CJEU has repeatedly emphasized the need for *effective and complete* protection of individuals' right to privacy (Art 7

[77] A useful overview of key issues with regard to empowerment measures in data protection law can be found in: Tuukka Lehtiniemi and Yki Kortesniemi, 'Can the Obstacles to Privacy Self-Management Be Overcome? Exploring the Consent Intermediary Approach' (2017) 4 Big Data & Society 1. In short, the authors list the following eight categories of 'obstacles to privacy self-management': *Timing and duration* (estimating harms is difficult due to timing of decisions and the typically unlimited duration of the consent); *Non-negotiability* (the terms are not negotiable enough); *Scale* (privacy self-management does not scale well enough); *Aggregation* (Data is aggregated and analysed to produce new data, leading to implicit disclosure of latent data); *Downstream uses* (Data flows to parties and purposes not foreseen at the time of consenting); *Cognitive demands* (The cognitive limitations of all human decision making hamper cost-benefit analysis); *Social norms* (Pressure to conform can strongly affect the decisions people make); *Social data* (Privacy decisions are framed as individual choices, but the data and the decisions also affect others).

Charter) and data protection (Art 8 Charter) and has interpreted data protection law accordingly.[78]

Structure—A comprehensive overview of all necessary requirements for effective empowerment is impossible to deliver. In light of the GDPR's wide scope, there are simply too many situations in which empowerment may play a role. With that caveat in mind, it is still possible to list some foundational building blocks without which empowerment would come down like a house of cards. These will be discussed in the first subsection. Data subject empowerment, however, does not operate in a 'GDPR vacuum'. That is why the last two subsections will take a broader perspective, also exploring relevant components for ensuring effective empowerment in other legal frameworks (3.2) and beyond the law per se (3.3).

What is Effectiveness?—Before moving on to these subsections, it is worth briefly considering the notion of effectiveness in the first place. What does it mean for data subject empowerment, or the right to erasure, to be 'effective'? Different fields may have different conceptualizations of what is effective data erasure (see Section 3). From a legal perspective, the notion of effectiveness ties back to the first step of the proportionality test (also called 'suitability'). Essentially, effectiveness means a measure is reasonably likely to achieve its objectives.[79] Given the many dimensions involved in implementing a legal provision, absolute effectiveness can never be guaranteed.[80]

The CJEU's *Google Spain* case offers a useful illustration. During the hearings, it was argued that delisting information—ie removing specific results when searching on the basis of a person's name—is not very effective, because the information can still be reached otherwise (through different search terms, search engines and/or directly on the website itself).[81] But, as I have explained with others elsewhere:

[78] *Google Spain* (n 17); *Unabhängiges Landeszentrum für Datenschutz Schleswig-Holstein v Wirtschaftsakademie Schleswig-Holstein GmbH* [2018] Court of Justice of the European Union C-210/16 [46; 62]. This can also be tied back to Article 47 Charter, safeguarding the right to an effective remedy and to a fair trial. See in this regard: *Maximillian Schrems v Data Protection Commissioner* [2015] Court of Justice of the European Union C-362/14.

[79] Gérard Cornu and Association Henri Capitant, *Vocabulaire juridique, Publié sous la dir. de Gérard Cornu.* (PUF 1987). Cited in: Sébastien Van Drooghenbroeck, *La proportionnalité dans le droit de la Convention européenne des droits de l'Homme: prendre l'idée simple au sérieux* (FUSL 2001) 619–20; *UPC Telekabel* [2014] Court of Justice of the European Union C-314/12 [618]. Also see: Brendan Van Alsenoy, Aleksandra Kuczerawy, and Jef Ausloos, 'Search Engines after "Google Spain": Internet@ Liberty or Privacy@Peril?' (2013) 70–71 <http://papers.ssrn.com/abstract=2321494> accessed 1 June 2019.

[80] Van Drooghenbroeck (n 79) 619–620; *UPC Telekabel* [2014] Court of Justice of the European Union C-314/12 [55]; para 60.

[81] For a summary of the main arguments during the hearing, see: Jef Ausloos, 'Google v Spain at the Court of Justice of the EU' (*Tech, Policy & Society*, 5 March 2013) <https://jefausloos.wordpress.com/2013/03/05/google-v-spain-at-the-european-court-of-justice/> accessed 28 March 2018.

> In order to assess the effectiveness of a measure, however, one must first establish its aim. What exactly might an individual hope to achieve when requesting the removal of a search engine result? In many cases, the individual would like to see the content erased from the Internet entirely. In other cases, however, the individual may merely want to decrease the visibility of this content. Given search engines' crucial role in accessing information on the Internet, one could argue that the removal of a search engine reference might NOT be as ineffective as it first seems. The outcome of the effectiveness test depends on how one articulates the 'legitimate' aim that is being pursued. If the aim is complete deletion of the content at issue, removal of a single search engine reference is arguably ineffective. If, on the other hand, the aim is to decrease the visibility of content, one might consider the removal of references reasonably effective to achieve that goal, particularly where the search engine in question assumes a dominant role on the relevant market.[82]

Need for Regulatory Infrastructure—There is a positive obligation on the legislator's shoulders to safeguard the effectiveness of the right to data protection in Article 8 Charter.[83] The GDPR is the most important manifestation of this, and the data subject rights comprised within contribute in no small part to such effectiveness. In fact, the CJEU has even ruled that the lack of any opportunity for an individual to pursue legal remedies in order to obtain access and/or erasure of personal data, compromises the essence of the fundamental right to effective judicial protection.'[84]

The right to erasure in Article 17 GDPR essentially formalizes and democratizes a key component of controlling one's personal data. It formalizes, by laying down a legal infrastructure—subject to safeguards taking into account other rights, freedoms, and interests—to empower data subjects. Embedded in a broader legal infrastructure, it puts the tools in data subjects' hands ('front-end') and puts into place minimum requirements for ensuring effectiveness in the back-end (notably modalities for the exercise of data subject rights in Art 12 and data protection by design and by default in Art 25). It democratizes 'data empowerment' as it is easily accessible to anyone. This is in sharp contrast with, for example, the US where a whole industry of reputation managers has emerged who operate in a legal vacuum and offer their services to whomever can afford it. Even if flawed to some extent, at least data subject empowerment in the GDPR is a product of the rule of law, subject to democratic safeguards, and not only accessible to those with the (financial or technical) resources.

82 Van Alsenoy, Kuczerawy, and Ausloos (n 79) 71.
83 'Legal instruments must ensure that individuals are able to effectively protect themselves, be in control.' Hielke Hijmans, *The European Union as Guardian of Internet Privacy: The Story of Art 16 TFEU* (Springer International Publishing 06) 159.
84 *Maximillian Schrems v Data Protection Commissioner* (n 78) para 95.

4.1 No Empowerment Without Protective Measures

The main provisions in the GDPR can roughly be qualified into four different categories. The 'data protection matrix' described in Chapter 2, is composed of four quadrants: (*ex ante* protective measures; *ex ante* empowerment measures; *ex post* protective measures; and *ex post* empowerment measures). Given its central subject-matter, this book has primarily focused on *ex post* empowerment measures in the GDPR. These are the tools that allow data subjects to actively *control* their personal data. Yet of course, these empowerment measures would not have much practical impact or effectiveness without a solid system of safeguards in place.[85] Indeed, when the European Commission announced its proposal for the GDPR in 2012, it explained that

> [a]s regards deletion of data, clarifications as to the duties of the data controller would be included in order to strengthen the right of the data subject to have his/her data deleted when there are no longer lawful grounds to retain them ('right to be forgotten'), also clarifying that the burden of proving the need for further conservation of the data lies with the data controller.[86]

This quote illustrates that the intention of empowering data subjects goes hand in hand with a strengthening of protective measures such as compelling controllers to behave more responsibly. The present subsection will highlight the main protective measures in the GDPR, that are necessary for ensuring the right to erasure is effective.

4.1.1 Responsibility

RATIONALE—It may be self-evident that an effective right to erasure—and data subject rights more broadly—requires controllers to behave responsibly. As summarized by Ferretti, data protection law enforces accountability, 'thus regulating an accepted exercise of power'.[87] Yet, as over two decades of Directive 95/46 have

[85] See in this regard: Marion Albers, 'Realizing the Complexity of Data Protection' in Serge Gutwirth, Ronald Leenes, and Paul De Hert (eds), *Reloading Data Protection—Multidisciplinary Insights and Contemporary Challenges* (Springer 2014) 231–32<http://www.springer.com/law/international/book/978-94-007-7539-8> accessed 1 June 2019; European Data Protection Supervisor, 'Opinion on Online Manipulation and Personal Data' (EDPS 2018) Opinion 03/2018 21 <https://edps.europa.eu/sites/edp/files/publication/18 03 19_online_manipulation_en.pdf> accessed 5 April 2018.

[86] European Commission, 'Commission Staff Working Paper: Impact Assessment Accompanying the Proposals for General Data Protection Regulation and Directive on Data Protection in Police and Judicial Matters' (European Commission 2012) Commission Staff working Paper SEC (2012) 72 final 53.

[87] Federico Ferretti, 'Data Protection and the Legitimate Interest of Data Controllers: Much Ado about Nothing or the Winter of Rights?' (2014) 51 Common Market Law Review 849. Referring to: Paul De Hert and Serge Gutwirth, 'Data Protection in the Case Law of Strasbourg and Luxemburg: Constitutionalisation in Action' in Serge Gutwirth and others (eds), *Reinventing Data Protection?* (Springer Science 2009).

demonstrated, being too vague and concise about what such responsibility entails will often not result in *actual* responsible behaviour over personal data processing in practice. The GDPR emphasizes responsibility of controllers, notably in Articles 5(2) and 24, but then goes on to specify more specific components of such responsibility (see following paragraph). Of course, it cannot be denied that one of the key motivations to take responsibility more seriously today are the increased powers of DPAs (Art 58) and the risk of considerable fines (Art 83).[88] The elaboration on responsibility in the GDPR (combined with the threats in case of irresponsible behaviour), is a clear boon to a more effective exercise of data subject rights.

Relevant Provisions—The responsibility of entities involved in the processing of personal data is emphasized throughout the GDPR. Controllers, as the pivotal actors in this regard, are clearly tasked with the responsibility to ensure the data quality principles are fully complied with (Art 5). Adequate and proactive compliance with the principles in Article 5(1) bears clear links with the triggers for the right to erasure (see Chapter 4). Article 12 lists modalities for exercising data subject rights that need to be provided by the controller. Articles 24(1) and 25 jointly require the controller to put in place the appropriate technical and organizational measures to ensure full compliance with data subject rights. The responsibility to maintain a full record of processing activities (see Art 30), will clearly also impact the ease with which a right to erasure can swiftly and fully be accommodated. Then there is a range of other provisions reinforcing the general accountability and responsibility of controllers, indirectly benefitting data subject empowerment as well, notably the data protection impact assessment (Art 35); designation of a data protection officer (Arts 37–39);[89] and the adoption of codes of conduct (Arts 40–41) or certification mechanisms (Arts 42–43).

Modalities for Erasure—The effectiveness of Article 17—and the other data subject rights in Articles 15–22, greatly hinges on Article 12. This provision sets out the modalities for data subject rights, laying down obligations for controllers in order to ensure effective data subject empowerment. Pursuant to the first paragraph, the option to erase personal data—as well as any interactions following a request—should be 'concise, transparent, intelligible and easily accessible form, using clear and plain language, in particular for any information addressed specifically to a child'. The second paragraph emphasizes controllers should facilitate the right to erasure and cannot refuse a request unless they demonstrate not to be

[88] Up to 20 million euros or 4 per cent of total worldwide annual turnover, whichever is highest.

[89] From the empirical research on data subject access rights (see subsection 2.2), it also clearly appeared that requests received faster support when the respective controller had a dedicated contact point for privacy and data protection related questions. Ausloos and Dewitte (n 53). See also: Bruno Rasle, 'Droit à l'oubli: Quel rôle pour le délégué à la protection des données personnelles?' in David Dechenaud (ed), *Le droit à l'oubli numérique: Données nominatives—Approche comparée* (Larcier 2015) 354.

'in a position to identify the data subject', even after the data subject has provided additional information.[90] The third paragraph sets a time-limit of one month (after receipt of the request), which can exceptionally be extended by two months if the controller can justify this (within one month) due to the complexity or number of requests. The fourth paragraph requires that any rejection should occur within one month, be motivated, and mention the possibility of lodging a complaint with the DPA or before the courts. The fifth paragraph stresses that exercising the right to erasure should be free of charge unless the request is manifestly unfounded and/or excessive.

RESPONSIBILITY PRE-EMPTS EMPOWERMENT—As highlighted throughout this book already, ideally the right to erasure and other data subject rights would only play a marginal role. To put it in González Fuster's words, these rights 'are actually mirrors that data subjects can, when they wish, place in front of data controllers so the latter are forced to examine their own compliance (or lack of) with data protection obligations. Responsibility for such compliance had always fallen on their shoulders, irrespective of whether somebody was looking, or whether somebody complains.'[91] Responsibility in the context of processing biometric data for example, may require technical safeguards to ensure automated erasure after specific timeframes.[92]

PLATFORM RESPONSIBILITY—The more impactful a controller, the larger their responsibility under the GDPR. Central nodes in the personal data processing ecosystem are particularly appealing targets of regulation. For example, a lot of personal data processing is essentially enabled by platforms such as App stores, social networks, or browsers. Even if these entities are not controllers *stricto sensu*, one might still expect them to bear some responsibility with regard to the processing they facilitate or enable. This is a particularly complex and much broader discussion which is being debated by policy-makers and academics for years already.[93] From a GDPR perspective in particular, I would at least argue that such platforms might under some circumstances be considered *processors* and as such should assist 'the controller by appropriate technical and organisational measures [. . .] for the fulfilment of the controller's obligation to respond to requests for exercising the data subject's rights' (Art 28(3)(e)). This could take the shape, for example, of a mediation tool to resolve conflicts between the data subject and actual controller; and/or scrutiny of the data processing practices of third parties allowed on the platform. In cases where they cannot be considered controller or processor, but still

[90] See Article 11(2) GDPR.
[91] González Fuster, 'Beyond the GDPR, above the GDPR' (n 302).
[92] Article 29 Working Party, Article 29 Working Party, 'Opinion 03/2013 on Purpose Limitation' (Article 29 Working Party 2013) WP 03/2013 33 <http://ec.europa.eu/justice/article-29/documentation> accessed 1 June 2019.
[93] Aleksandra Kuczerawy, *Intermediary Liability and Freedom of Expression in the EU: From Concepts to Safeguards* (Intersentia 2018).

have a considerable impact, some level of responsibility might still be implied,[94] but broader policy initiatives may be required.[95]

4.1.2 Transparency

Rationale—It has been said before: effective empowerment hinges on transparency.[96] Without knowing the extent of data processing taking place—or even the existence of it—it is impossible for data subjects to evaluate and exercise their rights.[97] Transparency therefore constitutes a 'natural precondition' for data subjects to exercise their rights.[98] It also offers a tool (eg to data subjects individually, collectively, or to data protection authorities) for monitoring compliance with the GDPR more broadly.[99] In this regard, two important levels of transparency can be distinguished. Firstly, controllers ought to be open about their decision-making processes (for how they manage information on their own behalf, as well as their decision-procedures for complying with the law, such as accommodating data

[94] See notably Recital 78: 'When developing, designing, selecting and using applications, services and products that are based on the processing of personal data or process personal data to fulfil their task, producers of the products, services and applications should be encouraged to take into account the right to data protection when developing and designing such products, services and applications and, with due regard to the state of the art, to make sure that controllers and processors are able to fulfil their data protection obligations.' See also: N Van Dijk and others, 'Right Engineering? The Redesign of Privacy and Personal Data Protection' [2018] International Review of Law, Computers & Technology 250 <https://www-tandfonline-com.kuleuven.ezproxy.kuleuven.be/doi/abs/10.1080/13600869.2018.1457002> accessed 14 June 2018.

[95] It is also possible the relevant industry players act on their own behalf. For example, in 2018 Apple announced how it would block third party trackers (notably Facebook's like- and share-buttons), as well as make device-fingerprinting much harder. 'Apple Jams Facebook's Web-Tracking Tools' *BBC News* (4 June 2018) <https://www.bbc.com/news/technology-44360273> accessed 9 June 2018.

[96] Hildebrandt, 'Who Is Profiling Who?' (n 43) 248ff; Article 29 Working Party, 'Guidelines on Consent under Regulation 2016/679' (2018) WP 259 9 <http://ec.europa.eu/justice/article-29/documentation>; European Commission, 'Communication from the Commission to the European Parliament, the Council, the European Economic and Social Committee and the Committee of the Regions Safeguarding Privacy in a Connected World. A European Data Protection Framework for the 21st Century' (n 596) 6; Brendan Van Alsenoy, Eleni Kosta, and Jos Dumortier, 'Privacy Notices versus Informational Self-Determination: Minding the Gap' (2013) 28 International Review of Law, Computers & Technology 185, 2–3; Article 29 Working Party, 'Opinion 03/2013 on Purpose Limitation' (n 92) 13–14; Hijmans, 'The European Union as a Constitutional Guardian of Internet Privacy and Data Protection' (n 83) 159; Directorate General Human Rights and Rule of Law, 'Case Law of the European Court of Human Rights Concerning the Protection of Personal Data' (Council of Europe 2018) T-PD(2018)15 1 <https://rm.coe.int/t-pd-2018-15-case-law-on-data-protection-may2018-en/16808b2d36> accessed 13 June 2018.

[97] As such, an interesting parallel can be drawn with the notion of 'foreseeability' comprised within the 'prescribed by law' requirement in human rights case law. Foreseeability of a legal rule, according to the ECtHR, 'applies not only to a course of conduct, of which an applicant should be reasonably able to foresee the consequences, but also to "formalities, conditions, restrictions or penalties"'. *Editorial Board of Pravoye Delo and Shtekel v Ukraine* [2011] European Court of Human Rights 33014/05 para 52. Similarly, one may expect from controllers, who effectively lay down a policy regulating the behavior and personal data of individuals, to make sure its operations are sufficiently foreseeable as well.

[98] Xavier Duncan L'Hoiry and Clive Norris, 'The Honest Data Protection Officer's Guide to Enable Citizens to Exercise Their Subject Access Rights: Lessons from a Ten-Country European Study' (2015) 5 International Data Privacy Law 190, 190; Ausloos and Dewitte (n 53) 7.

[99] Ausloos and Dewitte (n 53) 8.

subject rights). Secondly, they need to be transparent about past decisions made (ie give detailed statistics and relevant information about the types of data subject requests received and how they were dealt with).[100] Ideally, such transparency would be standardized across the industry, so as to enable comparisons and a more holistic perspective.

Forcing proper transparency—ie by requiring controllers to explain the nature and implications of their processing operations at different levels of detail[101]—may also bring to light unexpected/unforeseen issues. Sunlight, after all, is said 'to be the best of disinfectants; electric light the most efficient policeman'.[102] Indeed, a lack of transparency may precipitate power asymmetries and challenge individual autonomy (see Chapter 2).[103] In light of all this, transparency bears a strong link with responsibility and accountability see above).[104] Importantly, transparency should not be seen as sufficient in and on itself. Its main function is to enable the exercise of data subject rights and assess the controller's processing operations. Put differently, transparency 'is a necessary condition to enable the debate […], not a sufficient condition for the justification'.[105]

Relevant Provision—Article 5(1)(a) posits transparency as one of the key data protection principles. Different mutations of transparency exist throughout the GDPR. For example, Articles 6(2), 13, and 14 are clear examples of the *ex ante* protective role transparency plays. Controllers are not just required to shine a light on their processing operations but should also be open about their data retention policies and inform data subjects about their rights under the GDPR. A joined reading of Articles 4(11), 6(1)(a) and 7 also make very clear that consent is only valid if the controller can demonstrate the data subject was fully informed.

100 In order to ensure data protection and privacy of those involved, such information can be anonymized and/or made only accessible to DPA's for example. For an extensive take, see: Julia Powles, 'The Case That Won't Be Forgotten' (2015) 47 Loy U Chi LJ 583, 598.

101 See also in this regard: Simone Fischer-Hübner and others, 'Online Privacy: Towards Informational Self-Determination on the Internet' in M Hildebrandt and others (eds), *Digital Enlightenment Yearbook 2013: The Value of Personal Data*, vol 1 (IOS Press 2013) 127 <http://ssrn.com/abstract=2468200> accessed 1 June 2019.

102 Louis D Brandeis, *Other People's Money and How the Bankers Use It* (Stokes 1914) ch V.

103 'When citizens have no way of knowing, when they lack relevant knowledge, their choices are rendered meaningless, a problem that is only compounded further if the very fact of secrecy, of concealing things from others, is itself hidden: "To have no insight into what others conceal is to lack power as well"'. Lawrence Quill, *Secrets and Democracy from Arcana Imperii to Wikileaks* (Palgrave Macmillan 2014) 54. Referring to: Sissela Bok, *Secrets: On the Ethics of Concealment and Revelation* (Pantheon Books 1982) 19. See also: Eike Gräf, 'When Automated Profiling Threatens Our Freedom: A Neo-Republican Perspective' (2017) 3 European Data Protection Law Review 446.

104 Van Alsenoy, Kosta and Dumortier (n 96) 8; Article 29 Working Party, 'Opinion 06/2014 on the Notion of Legitimate Interests of the Data Controller under Article 7 of Directive 95/46/EC' (n 34) 43–44.

105 European Group on Ethics in Science and New Technologies (n 33) 75; Jakko Kemper and Daan Kolkman, 'Transparent to Whom? No Algorithmic Accountability without a Critical Audience' [2018] Information, Communication & Society 1. Hoepman also explains the issues with over-reliance on transparency: Jaap-Henk Hoepman, 'Transparency Is the Perfect Cover-up (If the Sun Does Not Shine)', *Transparency Theory for Data Driven Decision Making* (2018) 1–2.

None of the other lawful grounds in Article 6(1) can be relied on without properly informing the data subject either.[106]

COMPLEXITY IS NO EXCUSE—Complex data processing eco-systems may render transparency difficult.[107] Many have written about the problems involved in providing transparency in the context of 'screen-less devices',[108] Internet of Things,[109] 'smart technologies and pre-emptive environments',[110] and more. Technology is often configured so as to easily single people out for the delivery of a service or tracking behaviour, but not for the exercise of data subject rights. Be that as it may, it is worth reiterating that potential difficulties in accommodating transparency do not a priori absolve controllers from having to do so nonetheless.[111]

In sum, for the GDPR to have any significance, it is critical that controllers are fully transparent. Such transparency extends from information about general operations, to the very detailed, individual level. This also includes comprehensive information about their strategies for accommodating data subject rights (eg what are decision criteria, response rates, etc). Ideally, controllers—especially those receiving high numbers of requests—should also be as open as possible about the cases they have dealt with. Without such insights, a huge body of case law is essentially developing behind closed doors.[112]

[106] Especially the last (legitimate interests) lawful ground. See Article 29 Working Party, 'Opinion 06/2014 on the Notion of Legitimate Interests of the Data Controller under Article 7 of Directive 95/46/EC' (n 34) 34.

[107] Bart W Schermer, 'The Limits of Privacy in Automated Profiling and Data Mining' (2011) 27 Computer Law & Security Review 47; Matthias Leese, 'The New Profiling: Algorithms, Black Boxes, and the Failure Of Anti-Discriminatory Safeguards in the European Union' (2014) 45 Security Dialogue 494, 500.

[108] Meg Leta Jones, 'Privacy without Screens & the Internet of Other People's Things' (2014) 51 Idaho Law Review 639, 647.

[109] Gilad Rosner and Erin Kenneally, 'Clearly Opaque: Privacy Risks of the Internet of Things' (The Internet of Things Privacy Forum 2018) <https://www.iotprivacyforum.org/wp-content/uploads/2018/06/Clearly-Opaque-Privacy-Risks-of-the-Internet-of-Things.pdf?d8bd54&d8bd54> accessed 9 June 2018.

[110] Hildebrandt, *Smart Technologies and the End(s) of Law* (n 32) 97.

[111] Different options are often available to controllers to reconcile transparency requirements with data protection by design measures. For example, controllers could maintain parallel systems to enable the accommodating data subject rights, while still having strong security in place. More concretely, with regard to Apple Siri data, for example, this could entail that data subjects should have easy access to the Siri identifier (which is separate from one's Apple's ID) on their device, and use it to request access to the pseudonymized Siri data processed by Apple for delivering and improving its Siri service. See: Veale, Binns, and Ausloos, 'When Data Protection by Design and Data Subject Rights Clash' (n 26) 10ff.

[112] Powles (n 100); Julia Powles and Enrique Chaparro, 'How Google Determined Our Right to Be Forgotten' *The Guardian* (London, 18 February 2015) <http://www.theguardian.com/technology/2015/feb/18/the-right-be-forgotten-google-search> accessed 1 June 2019; Ellen Goodman, 'Open Letter to Google From 80 Internet Scholars: Release RTBF Compliance Data' (*Medium*, 14 May 2015) <https://medium.com/@ellgood/open-letter-to-google-from-80-internet-scholars-release-rtbf-compliance-data-cbfc6d59f1bd> accessed 1 June 2019; Eerke Boiten, 'Not Transparent, Certainly Not Accountable: Google and the Right To Be Forgotten' (*Eerke Boiten's blog*, 13 October 2016) <https://blogs.kent.ac.uk/eerke/2016/10/13/not-transparent-certainly-not-accountable-google-and-the-right-to-be-forgotten/> accessed 1 June 2019.

4.1.3 Enforcement

RATIONALE—Valuable as they are, transparency and responsibility alone will generally not be sufficient to safeguard data subject empowerment in practice. This was also recognized by the European Commission when it proposed the first draft of the GDPR. Most notably, the powers of data protection authorities were considerably strengthened, not least by empowering them to impose large fines in case of violations.[113] In other words, you need a strong stick to compel actual transparency, responsibility, and ultimately individual empowerment.[114] This appears especially true vis-à-vis large, multi-national entities who have very strong incentives to maximize data processing.[115] Enforcement in this context, comprises different elements, ranging from proactive supervision by independent authorities, to the easy ability for individuals to (collectively) challenge certain processing practices. Indeed, just as is the case in labour law, consumer or environmental protection, collective empowerment measures may also be stronger and more effective in ensuring effective data protection.[116]

RELEVANT PROVISIONS—Compliance with the GDPR, including all quadrants of the data protection matrix (see Chapter 2)—is monitored and enforced by data protection authorities (Art 57(1)(a)). These authorities can either act on their own initiative, or on the basis of data subject(s) complaints (Art 57(1)(f)). But, GDPR enforcement does not solely hinge on data protection authorities.[117] As amply discussed throughout this book, data subject rights also enable individuals to challenge controllers' practices themselves. Transparency requirements (including information obligations in Arts 13–14 and the right of access in Art 15) offer the necessary tools for data subjects to investigate such practices. Apart from the rights in Chapter III of the GDPR, data subjects have the right to compensation from

[113] European Commission, 'Press Release: Commission Proposes a Comprehensive Reform of Data Protection Rules to Increase Users' Control of Their Data and to Cut Costs for Businesses' <http://europa.eu/rapid/press-release_IP-12-46_en.htm?locale=en> accessed 1 June 2019; European Commission, 'Communication from the Commission to the European Parliament, the Council, the European Economic and Social Committee and the Committee of the Regions Safeguarding Privacy in a Connected World. A European Data Protection Framework for the 21st Century' (n 596) 7ff.

[114] '[L]aws that lack the means of being enforced undermine the legal system'. Dan Jerker B Svantesson, *Extraterritoriality in Data Privacy Law* (Ex Tuto Publishing 2013) 233. See also: Hijmans, 'The European Union as a Constitutional Guardian of Internet Privacy and Data Protection' (n 83) 161ff.

[115] As is clear from a comprehensive empirical analysis: Jamila Venturini and others, *Terms of Service and Human Rights: An Analysis of Online Platform Contracts* (Revan 2016) 67 ff <http://internet-governance.fgv.br/sites/internet-governance.fgv.br/files/publicacoes/terms_of_services_06_12_2016.pdf> accessed 1 June 2019.

[116] Alessandro Mantelero, 'From Group Privacy to Collective Privacy: Towards a New Dimension of Privacy and Data Protection in the Big Data Era' in Linnet Taylor, Luciano Floridi, and Bart van der Sloot (eds), *Group Privacy: New Challenges of Data Technologies*, vol 126 (Springer 2017). Especially page 149ff.

[117] This is important in light of the systematic lack of sufficient resources with most data protection authorities, but also because overreliance on these entities may counterintuitively lead to 'the prospering of surveillance societies, because the public has a false sense of security, and the data protectors themselves, have or have used, limited power'. Flaherty (n 1489) 11.

the controller/processor for any (non-)material damages (Art 82).[118] Data subjects can also lodge a complaint with the DPA, (Art 77), and have a right to effective judicial remedy against DPA decisions (Art 78), as well as controllers or processors (Art 79).[119] Because of the potentially very limited *individual* impact (or at least the difficulty in measuring it) and the apparent high threshold for taking legal action, data subjects might 'have little incentive to denounce or sue a data controller'.[120] The GDPR tries to remedy this by enabling representation of data subjects and collective action in relation to Articles 77–79 (Art 80).

Data Protection Authorities—The importance of independent and proactive bodies has been recognized as fundamental to effective data protection from the early start (see Art 8(3) Charter and 16(2) TFEU).[121] Citing CJEU case law, AG Bot has made clear that data protection authorities constitute the guardians of fundamental rights and freedoms.[122] To ensure data protection authorities are taken seriously, the GDPR foresees substantial fines of up 20 million euros or 4 per cent of total worldwide turnover, whichever is higher (Art 83). Though not explicitly required by the GDPR, it is very advisable for data protection authorities to have adequate inhouse technical expertise.[123] Importantly, the GDPR requires that DPAs exercise their powers subject to appropriate safeguards, including effective judicial remedy and due process (Art 58(4)).

4.1.4 Granularity

Rationale—A recurring theme throughout this book was the need for granularity in effectuating the right to erasure/object. Put briefly, data subjects should be able to target very specific processing operations and/or personal data with their requests, while leaving others (mostly) untouched. Making use of an ISS should essentially not be an all-or-nothing choice.[124] Indeed, without such

[118] Brendan Van Alsenoy, 'Liability under EU Data Protection Law: From Directive 95/46 to the General Data Protection Regulation' (2017) 7 JIPITEC para 43<http://www.jipitec.eu/issues/jipitec-7-3-2016/4506>.

[119] For an overview of categories of litigation in the field of data protection, see: Maja Brkan, 'The Concept of Essence of Fundamental Rights in the EU Legal Order: Peeling the Onion to Its Core' (2018) 14 European Constitutional Law Review 259ff.

[120] Ferretti (n 87) 861.

[121] Frits W Hondius, *Emerging Data Protection in Europe* (North-Holland 1975) 146. For an extensive overview of the role and importance of data protection authorities, see notably: Hijmans, 'The European Union as a Constitutional Guardian of Internet Privacy and Data Protection' (n 83) ch 7.

[122] Opinion AG Bot: *Maximillian Schrems v Data Protection Commissioner* (n 78) para 70. Independent oversight is generally seen as a criterion for ensuring the effectiveness of fundamental rights protection (Van Drooghenbroeck (n 79) 619–20). It can be expected, therefore, that such oversight is also ensured in the context of fundamental rights protection in the context of personal data processing (ie the GDPR).

[123] Charles D Raab and Ivan Szekely, 'Data Protection Authorities and Information Technology' (2017) 33 Computer Law & Security Review 421; Fischer-Hübner and others (n 101) 132–33.

[124] Article 29 Working Party, 'Opinion 06/2014 on the Notion of Legitimate Interests of the Data Controller under Article 7 of Directive 95/46/EC' (n 34) Annex 2, example 26.

granular options available to data subjects, their empowerment would be an empty promise.[125]

Relevant Provision—The need for granularity is apparent from several key GDPR provisions. Most importantly perhaps, in the purpose limitation, data minimization and storage limitation principles in Article 5(1). The use of the word *necessary* in all but the first lawful ground in Article 6(1) further implies processing operations should be approached granularly.[126] Article 7(4) also emphasizes that *freely* given consent precludes making the provision of a service conditional on consenting to personal data processing that is not necessary for the performance of the contract. Transparency provisions (Arts13–15; 30) are also aimed at facilitating the granular exercise of data subject rights, by requiring controllers to very specifically define all processing operations and their respective lawful ground. Finally, granularity also appears from the exemptions and derogations to (parts of) the GDPR. This is notably the case for the exemptions to the right to erasure (ie qualified by a necessity requirement) in Article 17(3) and the derogation for ASHRS purposes where it is clearly specified that '[w]here processing referred to in paragraphs 2 and 3 serves at the same time another purpose, the derogations shall apply only to processing for the purposes referred to in those paragraphs' (Art 89(4)).

4.1.5 Interim Conclusion

In sum, effective empowerment necessitates a clear regulatory framework of protective measures, especially in contexts characterized by strong power asymmetries.[127] The GDPR constitutes a checks and balances instrument that safeguards fundamental rights and freedoms both by setting baseline protections as well as by empowering individuals. Protective and empowerment measures in the GDPR reinforce each other in safeguarding rights, freedoms, and interests that are affected by the processing of personal data. Whereas the focus of the GDPR is certainly on data subjects, it is important to also consider its relevance with regard to collective interests. As a whole, the framework contributes to the societal dimensions of fundamental rights such as privacy, information freedoms, and non-discrimination, but also constitutional values such as autonomy, freedom, solidarity, pluralism,

[125] Made most evident in the *Google Spain* ruling, where it was clearly emphasized the legitimacy of processing by a website publisher, does not prevent data subjects from exercising data subject rights with regard to search engines referring to that website. *Google Spain* (n 17) paras 35–38; 83–85; Lynskey, *The Foundations of EU Data Protection Law* (n 69) 149.

[126] In the context of IoT, WP29 has explained '[t[his necessity test must be carried out by each and every stakeholder in the provision of a specific service on the IoT, as the purposes of their respective processing can in fact be different.'. Article 29 Working Party, 'Opinion 8/2014 on the on Recent Developments on the Internet of Things' (2014) Opinion WP 223 17<http://ec.europa.eu/justice/article-29/documentation> accessed 1 June 2019.

[127] Daly (n 10) 22; Joseph Raz, *The Morality of Freedom* (Clarendon Press 1986) 425. Referring to RAZ's conception of personal autonomy, Daly explains that positive action by the State to enhance freedom may be required.

and democracy.[128] This is clearly illustrated by the Facebook vignette, where solid data protection contributes to safeguarding election integrity and thus democratic society in general.

4.2 Beyond the GDPR

Overview—It goes without saying that data subject empowerment in the GDPR does not operate in a vacuum. It should be understood within a broader body of law that (in)directly impacts the effectiveness of such empowerment. Indeed, the GDPR does not hold a monopoly on defending the 'control-rationale' of the right to data protection in Article 8 Charter. General tort law may be the most straightforward legal remedy sought for in case an individual suffers damages from how his/her personal data is (ab)used. It can be used to stop or require certain processing operations and as such offers some level of control to data subjects.[129] One can of course also think of the right to the protection of private life (ie the 'general right to privacy'), which is often used to effectively safeguard control over personal data (also referred to as 'informational privacy').[130] Beyond these specific legal instruments, there are a number of other legal regimes (at EU level) that might safeguard empowerment over one's personal data.

Competition Law—Especially in the context of powerful economic actors in the digital economy, competition law offers an appealing legal regime. Data protection law and competition law are both aimed at protecting individuals and tackling power asymmetries.[131] Put very briefly, competition law prohibits undertakings from colluding to restrict competition (Art 101 TFEU), abuse their dominant position (Art 102 TFEU), or engage 'in a concentration that significantly impacts upon effective competition pursuant to the EU Merger Regulation ("EUMR")'.[132] Up until now, the European Commission has notoriously *not* considered data protection in its enforcement actions, even if data subject control was effectively diminished as a direct consequence.[133] More recently, there is a noticeable trend of

[128] Lokke Moerel and Corien Prins, 'Privacy for the Homo Digitalis: Proposal for a New Regulatory Framework for Data Protection in the Light of Big Data and the Internet of Things' 42 <http://papers.ssrn.com/abstract=2784123> accessed 1 June 2019.

[129] A notable example is provided by a 2016 Belgian supreme court case, where an individual achieved the anonymization of a digitized old newspaper-article, by explicitly *not* relying on data protection law but on general tort law instead. See: Ausloos, Jef, 'Vergetelheids-zaken voor de Hoven van Cassatie te België en Frankrijk—Contradictoir of Complementair?' (noot onder Hof van cassatie 29 april 2016, nr. C.15.0052.F) (2017) Computerrecht 1, 31–35.

[130] For an overview of relevant ECtHR case law, see: European Union Agency for Fundamental Rights (FRA), 'Opinion on the Proposed Data Protection Reform Package' (2012) FRA Opinion 2/2012 379ff; Directorate General Human Rights and Rule of Law (n 96).

[131] Francisco Costa-Cabral and Orla Lynskey, 'Family Ties: The Intersection between Data Protection and Competition in EU Law' (2017) 54 Common Market Law Review 11, 22.

[132] ibid 17.

[133] Graef (n 14) pt III; Lynskey, 'Regulating "Platform Power"' (n 14) 16. Referring in particular to the Google/DoubleClick and Facebook/WhatsApp mergers.

pushing towards better integration of data protection concerns into competition law.[134] Costa-Cabral and Lynskey convincingly argue for better alignment between the two frameworks, pointing out 'the normative coherence of EU law and the internal and external influence of data protection on competition law'.[135] Importantly, the European institutions are not just constrained by the Charter when adopting legally binding measures, they have a positive obligation to promote its application (Art 51(1) Charter).[136] As such, competition law decisions should respect (and promote) Article 8 Charter and thus individual control over personal data.[137] Self-regulatory efforts on personal data collection, sharing or other processing practices, may also run afoul of Article 101 TFEU.[138] Assessing 'abuse' under Article 102 TFEU, may be impacted by effectively limiting or constraining data subject rights.[139] In sum, EU competition law has great potential to boost data subject empowerment vis-à-vis powerful ISS providers, albeit on a more collective than individual level. It is not well-suited however, to deal with the non-economic—or non-consumer-welfare related—facets of data subject empowerment.[140]

Consumer Protection Law—Consumer protection law is another legal field that has been increasingly discussed in terms of data protection for the last few

[134] Even including some initiatives by official Member-State and EU bodies: Autorité de la concurrence and Bundeskartellamt, 'Competition Law and Data' (2016) <http://www.autoritedelaconcurrence.fr/doc/reportcompetitionlawanddatafinal.pdf> accessed 1 June 2019; European Data Protection Supervisor, 'Opinion on Coherent Enforcement of Fundamental Rights in the Age of Big Data' (EDPS 2016) Opinion 8/2016 3 <https://secure.edps.europa.eu/EDPSWEB/webdav/site/mySite/shared/Documents/EDPS/Events/16-09-23_BigData_opinion_EN.pdf> accessed 1 June 2019; Orla Lynskey, 'Non-Price Effect of Mergers' (OECD 2018) JT03432756 <https://one.oecd.org/document/DAF/COMP/WD(2018)70/en/pdf> accessed 17 June 2018; Online Manipulation and Personal Data, 'Online Manipulation and Personal Data. Intervention by Giovanni Buttarelli' (Committee Meeting on Civil Liberties, Justice and Home Affairs, Brussels, 25 June 2018) <http://www.europarl.europa.eu/ep-live/en/committees/video?event=20180625-1430-COMMITTEE-LIBE> accessed 26 June 2018; Inge Graef, Damian Clifford, and Peggy Valcke, 'Fairness and Enforcement: Bridging Competition, Data Protection and Consumer Law' [2018] International Data Privacy Law (Forthcoming); Jacques Crémer, Yves-Alexandre de Montjoye, and Heike Schweitzer, 'Competition Policy for the Digital Era' (European Commission 2019) <http://ec.europa.eu/competition/publications/reports/kd0419345enn.pdf> accessed 4 April 2019.

[135] Data protection law can, for example, constitute a normative yardstick in competition law analyses of non-price discrimination. Costa-Cabral and Lynskey (n 131) 6; 15.

[136] *Volker und Markus Schecke GbR and Hartmut Eifert v Land Hessen* [2010] Court of Justice of the European Union Joined Cases C-92/09 and C-93/09; Costa-Cabral and Lynskey (n 131) 39ff.

[137] This is more of an external constraint, as it limits the way in which a decision can be rather than allowing to trigger the application of competition law in the first place. See: Costa-Cabral and Lynskey (n131) 15.

[138] ibid 31.

[139] '[A] legal decrease in control over personal data or an increase in the extent of processing—for example, a wholesale change to the initial data processing conditions offered to individuals that users must accept in order to continue using an online service—might be considered exploitative'. European Data Protection Supervisor, 'Opinion on Coherent Enforcement of Fundamental Rights in the Age of Big Data' (EDPS 2016) Opinion 8/2016 3 <https://secure.edps.europa.eu/EDPSWEB/webdav/site/mySite/shared/Documents/EDPS/Events/16-09-23_BigData_opinion_EN.pdf> accessed 1 June 2019. Costa-Cabral and Lynskey (n 131) 34.

[140] Daly (n 10) 23–25; Costa-Cabral and Lynskey (n 131) 18; Lynskey, 'Regulating "Platform Power"' (n 14) 16; Orla Lynskey and others, 'The Internet: To Regulate or Not to Regulate?' 2018 <https://parliamentlive.tv/Event/Index/cc7d5d3b-c7cb-47a6-a423-c0e9918059dd>.

years.[141] Indeed, just like data protection and competition law, consumer protection aims to safeguard individuals from (the negative externalities of) power asymmetries.[142] Consumer protection in the EU is guaranteed in a variety of policy frameworks, from aviation, to retail banking, and the telecom sector. Three of the most often discussed documents in relation to data protection law are probably the unfair contract terms directive,[143] consumer rights directive,[144] and the unfair commercial practices directive.[145] A core element which all of these frameworks share with the GDPR and data subject empowerment requirements more broadly, relates to transparency. They emphasize the importance of transparency by laying down information requirements aimed at empowering consumers.[146] To the extent a data protection case falls within the scope of consumer protection law as well, a considerable body of scholarship and case law may further data subjects' rights.[147] For example, Helberger et al. explain that 'a company could breach that provision [ie Art 7(2)Unfair Commercial Practices Directive][148] if it fails to inform consumers that its "free" app captures the consumer's personal data'.[149] WP29 explains that a controller hiding important information regarding further use (eg in legalese and/or small print), 'this may infringe consumer protection rules concerning unfair contractual terms'.[150] Consumer protection law is also expected to play an increasingly important

[141] Consumer protection also features in the Charter, Article 38 of which says that '[u]nion policies shall ensure a high level of consumer protection'. For an analysis, see: Steve Weatherill, 'Consumer Protection (Article 38)' in Steve Peers and others (eds), *The EU Charter of Fundamental Rights: A Commentary* (Hart 2014) <https://www.bloomsburycollections.com/book/the-eu-charter-of-fundamental-rights-a-commentary/>.

[142] European Data Protection Supervisor, 'Opinion on Coherent Enforcement of Fundamental Rights in the Age of Big Data' (n 17); Article 29 Working Party, 'Opinion 06/2014 on the Notion of Legitimate Interests of the Data Controller under Article 7 of Directive 95/46/EC' (n 34) 40.

[143] Council Directive 93/13/EEC of 5 April 1993 on unfair terms in consumer contracts. The GDPR makes an explicit reference to this Directive in Recital 42 on data subject consent.

[144] Directive 2011/83/EU of the European Parliament and of the Council of 25 October 2011 on consumer rights, amending Council Directive 93/13/EEC and Directive 1999/44/EC of the European Parliament and of the Council and repealing Council Directive 85/577/EEC and Directive 97/7/EC of the European Parliament and of the Council.

[145] Directive 2005/29/EC of the European Parliament and of the Council of 11 May 2005 concerning unfair business-to-consumer commercial practices in the internal market and amending Council Directive 84/450/EEC, Directives 97/7/EC, 98/27/EC and 2002/65/EC of the European Parliament and of the Council and Regulation (EC) No 2006/2004 of the European Parliament and of the Council ('Unfair Commercial Practices Directive').

[146] See in this regard: Natali Helberger, Frederik Zuiderveen Borgesius, and Agustin Reyna, 'The Perfect Match? A Closer Look at the Relationship between EU Consumer Law and Data Protection Law' (2017) 54 Common Market Law Review 1427, 1437.

[147] eg detailing the meaning of 'plain, intelligible language'. See: *Árpád Kásler, Hajnalka Káslerné Rábai v OTP Jelzálogbank Zrt* [2014] Court of Justice of the European Union C-26/13; Damian Clifford, Inge Graef, and Peggy Valcke, 'Pre-Formulated Declarations of Data Subject Consent—Citizen-Consumer Empowerment and the Alignment of Data, Consumer and Competition Law Protections' (KU Leuven 2018) CiTiP Working Paper 33/2017 13ff<https://papers.ssrn.com/abstract=3126706> accessed 18 April 2018.

[148] According to this provision 'it is a misleading omission if a company fails to identify the commercial intent of a commercial practice (if not already apparent from the context)'.

[149] Helberger, Borgesius, and Reyna (n 146) 1443.

[150] Article 29 Working Party, 'Opinion 06/2014 on the Notion of Legitimate Interests of the Data Controller under Article 7 of Directive 95/46/EC' (n 34) 44.

role in an Internet of Things environment, where transparency and empowerment may not be straightforward to accomplish.[151] In April 2018, the Commission issued two ambitious policy initiatives—'New Deal for Consumers'[152] and 'Artificial Intelligence for Europe'[153]—both of which tackle issues at the intersection of consumer and data protection law. In sum, there is a considerable overlap in scope and ambition of consumer and data protection frameworks, especially when it comes to the empowerment of individuals.[154] Putting the finger on the key issues and how to resolve them remains particularly challenging in such a highly dynamic commercial environment (and with policy-developments currently in full motion).[155]

Sector-Specific Rules—Data subject empowerment in the ISS context can further be effectuated by a number of other regulatory frameworks.[156] One could think, for example, of regulation in the medical (research), financial, or media sectors. It is also worth exploring new legal frameworks that might (in)directly affect data empowerment as well, such as the 2018 EC proposal for a Regulation on B2B platform fairness,[157] or the older and more radical academic proposal of a 'privacy tax', to be levied on controllers' profits.[158] When it comes to published personal data, Chapter 6 already alludes to other legal instruments that may be much more appropriate to tackle the issue at hand (eg defamation[159] or right to image).[160,161] EU and Member-State legislators also

151 Jones (n 107); Natali Helberger, 'Profiling and Targeting Users in the Internet of Things—A New Challenge for Consumer Law' in Reiner Schulze and Dirk Staudenmayer (eds), *Digital Revolution: Challenges for Contract Law in Practice* (Nomos 2016) <http://hdl.handle.net/11245/1.519095>; Helberger, Borgesius, and Reyna (n 146) 1456.

152 European Commission, 'Communication. A New Deal for Consumers' (2018) COM(2018) 183 final <https://eur-lex.europa.eu/legal-content/EN/TXT/?qid=1523866913149&uri=COM:2018:183:FIN> accessed 11 June 2018. The Commission's plans include amending some of the before-mentioned Directives.

153 European Commission, 'Communication. Artificial Intelligence for Europe' (2018) COM(2018) 237 final <https://ec.europa.eu/digital-single-market/en/news/communication-artificial-intelligence-europe>.

154 Helberger, Borgesius, and Reyna (n 146) 1442; Manon Oostveen, 'Protecting Individuals Against the Negative Impact of Big Data: The Potential and Limitations of the Privacy and Data Protection Law Approach' (PhD Thesis, University of Amsterdam 2018) 162–64.

155 Further analysis is certainly recommended, regarding all the different roles personal data plays in the consumer context (eg as assets used to develop services, to categorize consumers, or to influence them). See: Helberger, Borgesius, and Reyna (n 146) 1430. One of the most complicated issues the authors also refer to is how to approach personal data as the 'price paid' or 'counter-performance' in so-called free online services. On this point, also see: European Data Protection Supervisor, 'Opinion on the Proposal for a Directive on Certain Aspects Concerning Contracts for the Supply of Digital Content' (n 1299); Clifford, Graef, and Valcke (n 147).

156 See for instance: Oostveen (n 154) 166ff.

157 European Commission, Proposal for a Regulation on Promoting Fairness and Transparency for Business Users of Online Intermediation Services 2018 [COM(2018) 238 final].

158 Lilian Edwards, 'Reconstructing Consumer Privacy Protection On-line: A Modest Proposal' (2004) 18 International Review of Law, Computers & Technology 313.

159 On relevant ECtHR case law, see: Stijn Smet, 'Freedom of Expression and the Right to Reputation: Human Rights in Conflict' (2010) 26 American University International Law Review 183, 192ff.

160 Ellen Wauters, Eva Lievens, and Peggy Valcke, 'Towards a Better Protection of Social Media Users: A Legal Perspective on the Terms of Use of Social Networking Sites' 22 International Journal of Law and Information Technology 254, 270–71.

161 See in this regard also: Joris van Hoboken, 'The Proposed Right to Be Forgotten Seen from the Perspective of Our Right to Remember' 23 <www.law.nyu.edu/sites/default/files/upload_documents/VanHoboken_RightTo%20Be%20Forgotten_Manuscript_2013.pdf> accessed 1 June 2019.

have a duty to make sure legal frameworks regulating the publicity of certain information—eg public interest archiving, company registers, freedom of information laws—strike an appropriate balance between all relevant rights, freedoms, and interests at stake.[162] In sum, the right to data protection (as any other Charter provision) should be considered in each regulatory initiative. As appears throughout this book, it will often be more appropriate for subject-/sector-specific frameworks (eg labour or non-discrimination laws) to regulate data protection issues directly, rather than deferring to the GDPR with its generic approach.

Thinking Outside the Box—The challenges raised by information and power asymmetries in the information society have provoked creative legal thinking. Especially in the US—in the absence of an omnibus data protection framework and its first amendment primacy—there have been a variety of suggestions on how to tweak existing legal concepts so as to promote data protection and empowerment. Balkin introduces the concept of *Information Fiduciaries* in an attempt to instil more responsible data processing.[163] Zittrain proposed 'reputation bankruptcy'[164] and Froomkin 'identity bankruptcy'[165] as sort of 'right to be forgotten lite'-versions. Hirsch has been drawing parallels between data protection and environmental protection for over a decade already.[166] Pasquale has focused more broadly on inducing responsibility among powerful platforms (not just in processing personal data, but in controlling information flows generally).[167] Pasquale's work also ties back to the burgeoning field of algorithmic transparency and accountability, ensuring increased reliance on automated decision-making occurs fairly.[168] The EU legislator is developing a range of initiatives that are aimed at ensuring fairness, and as a result also individual

[162] See, for instance, the CJEU's case law in: *Bavarian Lager* [2010] Court of Justice of the European Union C-28/08 P [115] para 78; *Salvatore Manni* (n 74).

[163] Jack M Balkin, 'Information Fiduciaries and the First Amendment' (2016) 49 UC Davis Law Review 1183.

[164] Zittrain, *The Future of the Internet—And How to Stop It* (n 34) 228ff.

[165] A Michael Froomkin, 'Towards Identity Bankruptcy' (CPDP (Senior Academic Session), January 2017) <https://www.youtube.com/watch?v=N_t18gL7i3E> accessed 16 May 2018.

[166] Dennis D Hirsch, 'Protecting the Inner Environment: What Privacy Regulation Can Learn from Environmental Law' (2006) 41 Georgia Law Review 1; Dennis D Hirsch and Jonathan H King, 'Big Data Sustainability: An Environmental Management Systems Analogy' (2015) 72 Washington and Lee Law Review Online 409.

[167] Frank Pasquale, *The Black Box Society: The Secret Algorithms That Control Money and Information* (Harvard UP 2014) 8; Frank Pasquale, 'Platform Neutrality: Enhancing Freedom of Expression in Spheres of Private Power The Constitution of Information: From Gutenberg to Snowden' (2016) 17 Theoretical Inquiries in Law 512.

[168] France has been particularly proactive in taking regulatory action in this regard. See notably: Loi pour une République numérique 2016; CNIL, 'Comment Permettre à l'homme de Garder La Main? Les Enjeux Éthiques Des Algorithmes et de l'intelligence Artificielle. Synthèse Du Débat Public Animé Par La CNIL Dans Le Cadre de La Mission de Réflexion Éthique Confiée Par La Loi Pour Une République Numérique' (2017) <www.cnil.fr/sites/default/files/atoms/files/cnil_rapport_garder_la_main_web.pdf> accessed 10 June 2018.

autonomy, in the context of artificial intelligence and online information/power asymmetries.[169]

Delegating Regulation—As mentioned before, the GDPR pushes a lot of the interpretative burden downstream.[170] While this may constitute a considerable onus on controllers' shoulders, it also gives them the freedom to apply their own expertise to the issues at stake. Binns tries to capture this dynamic by applying the concept of meta-regulation.[171] Meta-regulation is a specific form of co-regulation, holding companies to account for self-regulating corporate responsibility (eg enforced press ethics).[172] Following this theory, it is possible to expect from (powerful) ISS controllers, to put in place the necessary infrastructure to enable data subject control over their personal data (without the GDPR having to dictate the specifics of such implementation). The growing adoption of privacy dashboards are one example of this, offering data subjects abilities to access, correct, or erase personal data. It is important in this context, that there is sufficient evaluation and oversight over such interpretations and implementations by corporate actors.[173] As explained before, these dashboards enable controllers to define how individuals can(not) control their personal data, and as such fail to fully *empower* them. Indeed, extreme caution should be exercised not to over-rely on private entities to enforce public policy objectives.[174] Such overreliance may further inflate the power of corporations, eg by endorsing the constitutional aspirations of terms of service;[175] and reinforcing Cohen's 'architectures of control'.[176]

Interim Conclusion—In sum, it is clear that data subject empowerment can be effectuated by many other legal means than simply the GDPR. In fact, other

[169] Ranging from network and information systems security, the development of AI ethics guidelines and a framework for safety and liability. European Commission, 'Communication. Artificial Intelligence for Europe' (n 153) 14–17. The Commission's Proposal for a 'Regulation on promoting fairness and transparency for business users of online intermediation services' targets B2B relationships but is expected to positively affect consumers. European Commission Proposal for a Regulation on Promoting Fairness and Transparency for Business Users of Online Intermediation Services (n 157).

[170] As the result of being an omnibus regime, covering a huge variety of situations, GDPR provisions are generally quite vague.

[171] In fact the author discusses this concept particularly in relation to data protection impact assessments in Article 35 GDPR. Reuben Binns, 'Data Protection Impact Assessments: A Meta-Regulatory Approach' (2017) 7 International Data Privacy Law 22.

[172] Christine Parker, 'Meta-Regulation: Legal Accountability for Corporate Social Responsibility' in Doreen McBarnet, Aurora Voiculescu, and Tom Campbell, *The New Corporate Accountability: Corporate Social Responsibility and the Law* (CUP 2009). The concept allows for a more rigorous organization and assessment of co-regulatory approaches. A similar concept is developed in: Kenneth A Bamberger, 'Regulation as Delegation: Private Firms, Decisionmaking, and Accountability in the Administrative State' (2006) 56 Duke Law Journal 377.

[173] Indeed, this is something which the theoretical framework of meta-regulation requires. Binns, 'Data Protection Impact Assessments' (n 171).

[174] See Kuczerawy (n 93); Edoardo Celeste, 'Terms of Service and Bills of Rights: New Mechanisms of Constitutionalisation in the Social Media Environment?' (2018) 0 International Review of Law, Computers & Technology 1.

[175] Celeste (n 174).

[176] Cohen, *Configuring the Networked Self* (n 8) 2.

regimes may often be better suited to promote collective empowerment, ie enable control and autonomy at a larger and more systematic scale. It is not the goal of this section to elaborate on regulation theory questions, though a closer investigation would certainly be useful in further uncovering how to render data subject control more effective in practice. More work is also required on the mutually beneficial/detrimental effects of different legal regimes. The growing interaction between experts in data protection, consumer protection, and competition law certainly constitutes a step in the right direction.

4.3 Beyond the Law

The law plays a crucial role in enforcing individual empowerment (over data) in the face of power asymmetries encountered in the ISS context. Yet, individual empowerment is by no means at the mercy of the law alone. It seems fair to say that the general impotence of the law in effectuating data empowerment and countering asymmetries over the past few decades, has led to many alternatives being explored. This subsection will point to some of the most relevant ones in light of the right to erasure in the ISS context in particular. It will do so by looking at proposed solutions to data empowerment from a technological, market-based, and cultural or societal perspective.

4.3.1 Technology

PERSPECTIVES—Data subject empowerment cannot be achieved by the law alone, it needs to be effectuated through technology.[177] This is recognized throughout the GDPR—most notably in Article 25 on data protection by design and by default—with ample references to 'technology' and 'technical measures' in relation to implementing rights and obligations. Having said that, there is a notorious disconnect between how computer scientists or engineers understand privacy and data protection versus how lawyers understand it.[178] Aligning approaches and expectations as to what it actually means to *control* and *erase* one's personal data are necessary in order to develop effective technical tools.[179] A strict interpretation of

[177] Adamantia Rachovitsa, 'Engineering and Lawyering Privacy by Design: Understanding Online Privacy Both as a Technical and an International Human Rights Issue' (2016) 24 International Journal of Law and Information Technology 374, 374; Bryce Clayton Newell, 'Forewords—Privacy as Antipower: In Pursuit of Non-Domination' (2018) 4 European Data Protection Law Review 12, 15.

[178] George Danezis and others, 'Privacy and Data Protection by Design—from Policy to Engineering' (ENISA 2014); Van Dijk and others (n 94).

[179] A year before the European Commission issued its GDPR proposal, the Council had already emphasized the need to consider the technical feasibility of a potential right to be forgotten. Council of the European Union, 'Council Conclusions on the Communication from the Commission to the European Parliament and the Council—A Comprehensive Approach on Personal Data Protection in the European Union' (n 605) 11. Questions as to the technical feasibility remained throughout the legislative process. See for example also: Council of the European Union, 'Working Party on Information Exchange and Data Protection (DAPIX). Summary of Discussion on 23–24 February 2012' (n 46) 6. See also: Irion and others (n 49) 11–12.

data erasure implies the destruction of all physical media on which (copies of) the respective data have been stored.[180] Yet Chapter 6 already makes clear that such a rigorous interpretation would not strike a fair balance. Making personal data unrecognizable by 'superimposing other data' may be the next best thing.[181] Still, one may wonder how erasure should operate in environments where full deletion would compromise the integrity of a system (eg social network profile)[182] or be technically impossible (eg blockchain). The GDPR encourages (interdisciplinary) industry dialogues to identify operational technical solutions to inter alia the right to erasure (see Art 40(2)). Indeed, the rather vague and open-ended nature of provisions in the GDPR allows controllers some flexibility in how to interpret and implement rights such as access, erasure, or portability.

Solutions—Even before the GDPR solidified the call for effective tools to ensure data empowerment and erasure, there had been many technological initiatives to achieve these goals. According to Daly, technical tools offer a much more pragmatic short(er) term solution to ensure autonomy online.[183] These tools range from rather modest to very ambitious projects. For the purposes here, three types of tools are worth pointing out. Firstly, a range of technical solutions require active cooperation of those processing personal data. This is the case, for example, with so-called privacy dashboards,[184] adding meta-data (eg robots.txt,[185] expiration dates,[186] creative commons like licenses,[187] and/or DRM-like protections[188]), or decentralizing personal data architectures.[189] Secondly, there are tools that are

[180] Druschel, Backes, and Tirtea (n 52). See also: Nugter (n 51) 52. Talking about the 1977 German BDSG (see Chapter 2), the author explains that '*Obliteration of stored data* is every process that irretrievably ensures that particular information is no longer recoverable from a data file. The simple refusal of access or the imposition of a prohibition on use are consequently not sufficient, for such measures can be reversed at any time.'

[181] Synthesis Report by Hans Peter Gassmann and G Russel Pipe (OECD Secretariat): *Policy Issues in Data Protection and Privacy: Concepts and Perspectives: Proceedings of the OECD Seminar, 24th to 26th June 1974* (Paris: Organisation for Economic Co-operation and Development 1976) 161.

[182] When it was audited in 2012, Facebook explained it solves the issue by de-identifying logfile entries when a user requests their account to be deleted. This means that the company deletes 'the relationship between a user ID and the associated replacement ID whenever a user deletes the account', making it allegedly impossible to 'associate the log records with the deleted account'. Findings of FTR Solutions in: Irish Data Protection Commissioner, 'Report of Re-Audit (Facebook Ireland Ltd)' (2012) 47 <dataprotection.ie/documents/press/Facebook_Ireland_Audit_Review_Report_21_Sept_2012.pdf> accessed 18 October 2012.

[183] Daly (n 10) 11; 39–40.

[184] Irion and others (n 49).

[185] 'Robots Exclusion Standard', *Wikipedia* (2018) <https://en.wikipedia.org/w/index.php?title=Robots_exclusion_standard&oldid=844679166> accessed 14 June 2018.

[186] MViktor Mayer-Schönberger, 'Generational Development of Data Protection in Europe' in Philip E Agre and Marc Rotenberg (eds), *Technology and Privacy: The New Landscape* (MIT Press 1998) 171ff.

[187] Jonathan Zittrain, *The Future of the Internet—And How to Stop It* (Yale UP 2008) 225ff.

[188] Digital Rights Management has traditionally been referred to in relation to copyright protection, but might also be relevant for personal information suggests Mayer-Schönberger in: Mayer-Schönberger (n 186) 144–54.

[189] Arvind Narayanan and others, 'A Critical Look at Decentralized Personal Data Architectures' [2012] arXiv preprint arXiv:1202.4503 <http://arxiv.org/abs/1202.4503> accessed 1 June 2019.

specifically designed with a zero-trust threat model in mind (ie where data subjects do not have to rely on others to enforce control). Such tools are primarily aimed at *preventing* personal data from being collected in the first place, as it is quite hard to enforce erasure without at least some cooperation from the entity with whom the personal data resides. Examples include a variety of encryption strategies,[190] self-managed databoxes (eg that interface with ISS providers on a need-to-know basis),[191] Privacy Enhancing Technologies (PETs),[192] or Protective Optimization Technologies (POTs).[193] Thirdly, some technological tools fostering data empowerment, require a certain level of trust in another entity, in order to effectuate empowerment vis-à-vis third parties. Examples of such 'meta-tools' include ephemeral messaging apps (eg Snapchat, ProtonMail)[194] and platform operators more broadly (eg social networks,[195] mobile operating systems).

ISSUES—Even if technology is unavoidably part of the solution in empowering data subjects, it also brings with it some issues and pitfalls. Firstly, and as mentioned before, data protection by design may be used in perverse ways so as to deny data subject rights.[196] Controllers who strictly silo datasets in order to render re-identification harder, may find it hard to verify the identity of a data subject wishing to exercise rights.[197] Blockchain technology might offer great security features, while at the same time making it virtually impossible to erase personal

[190] See, for example, the many resources at: 'CryptoParty'. <https://www.cryptoparty.in/connect/resources> accessed 14 June 2018.

[191] Hamed Haddadi and others, 'Personal Data: Thinking Inside the Box' [2015] arXiv:1501.04737 [cs] <http://arxiv.org/abs/1501.04737> accessed 1 June 2019.

[192] 'Defined as technologies designed to provide privacy protection from untrusted and potentially adversarial data controllers' in: Claudia Diaz, Omer Tene, and Seda Gurses, 'Hero or Villain: The Data Controller in Privacy Law and Technologies.(The Second Wave of Global Privacy Protection)' (2013) 74 Ohio State Law Journal 923, 939ff. One category of PETs are obfuscation tools. See generally in this regard: Finn Brunton and Helen Nissenbaum, *Obfuscation: A User's Guide for Privacy and Protest* (MIT Press 2015).

[193] 'POTs analyze how events (or lack thereof) affect users and environments, then manipulate these events to influence system outcomes, eg, by altering the optimization constraints and poisoning system inputs.' Gürses, Overdorf and Balsa (n 35). The authors clearly distinguish POTs from PETs, because the latter 'focus on privacy and not the protection of populations and environments from optimization'. As mentioned throughout this book, data protection and data empowerment are not just about privacy either. To the extent optimization strategies are based on (personal) data processing, the GDPR may therefore constitute a useful toolbox for achieving the aims pursued.

[194] These services effectuate erasure, and thus 'empower' users, vis-à-vis third parties but not necessarily vis-à-vis themselves.

[195] eg Cheol Ho Sin and others, 'Realizing the Right to Be Forgotten in an SNS Environment' in Hwa Young Jeong and others (eds), *Advances in Computer Science and its Applications*, vol 279 (Springer 2014) <http://link.springer.com/10.1007/978-3-642-41674-3_201> accessed 1 June 2019.

[196] See Apple Siri Vignette and: Veale, Binns, and Ausloos, 'When Data Protection by Design and Data Subject Rights Clash' (n 26); Ausloos, 'Paul-Olivier Dehaye and the Raiders of the Lost Data' (n 18).

[197] Reuben Binns, 'Ideally We Want Architectures Where Its Easy for DS to Provide a Key to Reconnect, but Difficult for DC / Attacker to Do on Their Own. As @podehaye Goes on to Say in That Panel, Many DCs Haven't Grasped That DSs Could Provide Additional Info to Make Pseudonymous Data Identifiable' (*@RDBinns*, 13 February 2018) <https://twitter.com/RDBinns/status/963411691022311427> accessed 14 June 2018.

data.[198] Secondly, technology (in combination with psychological insights) may also be used to circumvent individual autonomy, deliberately or not.[199] Indeed, one should be vigilant that the adoption of technical tools to 'give users control over their data' do not exploit individuals' bounded rationality, cognitive and behavioural biases.[200] Thirdly, due to the scale at which most ISS controllers operate, technological tools to empower individuals will probably be automated to some extent. Especially when the respective processing operations affect the rights, freedoms, or interests of others, extra care should be taken that such automated accommodation of rights is proportionate.[201] Automation also stresses the importance for adequate identity verification mechanisms, preventing fraudulent requests (eg persons claiming to be their ex-partner in order to access their location data).[202] Fourthly, overreliance on technical tools may exclude a great number of data subjects, eg that do not have the resources, time, or know-how to use them.[203] Moreover, such tools may only be offered to registered users of a service, effectively rendering them unavailable to non-users whose personal data is equally processed. Fifthly, it may be hard to enforce and/or verify the effectiveness of technological tools, especially those that rely on other actors (see previous paragraph). Finally, even if technically feasible to 'erase' personal data, controllers may have little incentives to fully accommodate such a right.[204] Which leads back to the 50 shades of erasure explained in Chapter 7. Rather than full-fledged erasure, there may be many in-between technical fixes (eg access-restrictions, obscuring information)[205] that form a compromise between all rights, freedoms, and interests at stake. In sum,

[198] Michèle Finck, 'Blockchains and Data Protection in the European Union' (2018) 4 European Data Protection Law Review 17; Olga Kharif, 'Is Your Blockchain Business Doomed?' *Bloomberg.com* (22 March 2018) <https://www.bloomberg.com/news/articles/2018-03-22/is-your-blockchain-business-doomed> accessed 14 June 2018.

[199] See Facebook and Uber vignettes. See also: Laura Brandimart, Alessandro Acquisti, and George Loewenstein, 'Misplaced Confidences: Privacy and the Control Paradox', *Privacy and Controversial Social Issues* (2010) <http://www.futureofprivacy.org/wp-content/uploads/2010/09/Misplaced-Confidences-acquisti-FPF.pdf> accessed 1 June 2019.

[200] Irion and others (n 49) 15.

This also relates to how Lessig (Lessig, *Code* (n 8)), Cohen (Cohen, *Configuring the Networked Self* (n 8)), and Hildebrandt (Hildebrandt, 'Legal and Technological Normativity' (n 410)) warn against technology regulating—or even becoming constitutive of—our behaviour.

[201] This ties back to the discussion on automated takedowns in the intermediary liability debate. See notably: Jennifer M Urban, Joe Karaganis, and Brianna L Schofield, 'Notice and Takedown in Everyday Practice' (UC Berkeley and Columbia University 2016) <http://papers.ssrn.com/abstract=2755628> accessed 1 June 2019; Kuczerawy (n 93).

[202] Chris Norval and others, 'Reclaiming Data: Overcoming App Identification Barriers for Exercising Data Protection Rights' [2018] arXiv:1809.05369 [cs] <http://arxiv.org/abs/1809.05369> accessed 20 September 2018; Coline Boniface and others, 'Security Analysis of Subject Access Request Procedures How to Authenticate Data Subjects Safely When They Request for Their Data' (2019) <https://hal.inria.fr/hal-02072302/document> accessed 4 April 2019.

[203] See, for example, in the context of 'privacy-dashboards': Irion and others (n 49) 27–28.

[204] Sophie Guicherd, Marie-Laurence Caron-Fasan, and Nicolas Lesca, 'Droit à l'oubli numérique: Quel alignement entre chartes et pratique?' in David Dechenaud (ed), *Le droit à l'oubli numérique: Données nominatives—Approche comparée* (Larcier 2015) 326.

[205] Jones (n 107) 94; de Terwangne (n 73) 20.

technology should not be seen as a *deus ex machina* for data subject empowerment, but rather as an important component of it.[206]

4.3.2 Market

Perspectives—One perspective would be to leave data empowerment to the market. Tech giants often argue competition is only one click away. If individuals—or rather consumers—really care about privacy and data protection, the argument goes, they are free to move to a different service. Such rationalization does not hold up today, for many reasons that cannot be discussed here.[207] In fact, current market dynamics install very strong incentives to maximize (personal) data processing,[208] extracting value wherever possible (eg by converting information into marketable commodities).[209,210] This status quo contrasts with the rationale of the right to data protection (see Chapter 2) and renders it unlikely that effective control will arise from within the tech industry establishment. Certainly not without political and legal pressure. Having said that, alternative business models are emerging that either try to substitute existing services, or that are specifically designed at assisting individuals in effectuating control over their personal data.

Solutions—For the purposes here, three types of market-based tools for 'data empowerment' can be distinguished. Firstly, increased awareness and pressure (whether legal, political, or from users), may drive established ISS providers to incorporate certain control-features (eg privacy dashboards, strong encryption/anonymization, installing authoritative ethics review boards).[211] Companies whose business models hinge less on the processing of personal data also started using privacy and data protection as a competitive edge in recent years (eg Apple). Secondly, a number of new businesses has emerged that try to constitute 'privacy/data protection-friendly alternatives' to existing services (eg Mastodon for social

[206] See Morozov's 'solutionism': Evgeny Morozov, *To Save Everything, Click Here: Technology, Solutionism, and the Urge to Fix Problems That Don't Exist* (PublicAffairs 2013) ch 8.

[207] For example, network effects leading to quasi-monopolies and dark patterns rendering it incredibly hard to effectively sign off, delete information, or move elsewhere. See also Chapter 2.

[208] Katherine J Strandburg, 'Free Fall: The Online Market's Consumer Preference Disconnect' [2013] University of Chicago Legal Forum 79, 130ff.

[209] Ejan Mackaay, *Economics of Information and Law* (Kluwer 1982) 115; Adam Arvidsson, 'Facebook and Finance: On the Social Logic of the Derivative' (2016) 33 Theory, Culture & Society 3; Oscar H Gandy Jr, and Selena Nemorin, 'Toward a Political Economy of Nudge: Smart City Variations' [2018] Information, Communication & Society <https://doi.org/10.1080/1369118X.2018.1477969> accessed 30 May 2018.

[210] Zuboff, 'Big Other' (n 14); Shoshana Zuboff, 'Google as a Fortune Teller: The Secrets of Surveillance Capitalism' *Frankfurter Allgemeine Zeitung* (5 March 2016) <http://www.faz.net/aktuell/feuilleton/debatten/the-digital-debate/shoshana-zuboff-secrets-of-surveillance-capitalism-14103616-p2.html?printPagedArticle=true#pageIndex_2> accessed 1 June 2019); M Poon, 'Corporate Capitalism and the Growing Power of Big Data: Review Essay' (2016) 41 Science, Technology & Human Values 1088, 1100–01.

[211] Ryan Calo, 'Consumer Subject Review Boards: A Thought Experiment' (2013) 66 Stanford Law Review Online 6; Polonetsky and Hirsch (n 1149); Omer Tene and Jules Polonetsky, 'Beyond IRBs: Ethical Guidelines for Data Research' (2016) 72 Washington and Lee Law Review Online 458; Irion and others (n 49) 16.

networking, DuckDuckGo for search). Thirdly, a whole range of new business models is emerging that specifically position themselves in-between data subjects and controllers, assisting the former in controlling their personal data. For example, 'personal data stores' (eg Mydex,[212] HubofAllThings[213]) enable individuals to have all their personal data in one place and manage access by third parties (from banks to social networks) in a centralized and secure manner.[214] More ambitious are so-called Personal Information Management Systems (PIMs),[215] or infomediaries,[216] that may offer a number of added functionalities such as verification services or data analytics.[217] More radical ideas involve the creation of 'data trusts',[218] or requiring 'nano-payments' to be made for each processing operation of personal data.[219] Finally, there are a number of commercial actors focusing on niche data subject empowerment tools (eg assisting in exercising access or portability rights,[220] browser plugins and smartphone apps that block third-party tracking,[221] or so-called 'reputation managers').[222]

Issues—Market-based solutions, cutting across the 'mere compliance mentality', may certainly contribute to effective data subject empowerment. Yet, several important issues emerge when taking a closer look. Firstly, one may be rather sceptical of any market-based solution for as long as there is no shift in the predominant 'surveillance/informational capitalism' mindset among most tech giants today.[223] Indeed, comprehensive individual control would undercut many existing business-models and seems to be quite antithetical to an information economy that relies on maximizing value-extraction from data.[224] Just like with

[212] https://mydex.org.

[213] https://hubofallthings.com.

[214] See generally: Guillaume Brochot and others, 'Study on Personal Data Stores, Commissioned by the European Commission (DG Connect)' (Cambridge University 2015) Study <https://ec.europa.eu/digital-single-market/en/news/study-personal-data-stores-conducted-cambridge-university-judge-business-school> accessed 1 June 2019.

[215] European Data Protection Supervisor, 'EDPS Opinion on Personal Information Management Systems' (EDPS 2016) Opinion 9/2016.

[216] Nicolo Zingales, 'The Rise of "Infomediaries" in Support of Individual Autonomy: A Matter of Trust and (Joint) Responsibility' (2018).

[217] See also, more broadly, research on what is called 'Vendor Relationship Management (VRM) tools', in: Doc Searls, *The Intention Economy: When Customers Take Charge* (Harvard Business Review Press 2012) pt III.

[218] Neil Lawrence, 'Data Trusts Could Allay Our Privacy Fears' *The Guardian* (3 June 2016) <http://www.theguardian.com/media-network/2016/jun/03/data-trusts-privacy-fears-feudalism-democracy> accessed 22 February 2018. As referred to in: Julia Powles and Hal Hodson, 'Google DeepMind and Healthcare in an Age of Algorithms' (2017) 7 Health and Technology 351.

[219] Jaron Lanier, *Who Owns the Future?* (Allen Lane 2013).

[220] eg <https://personaldata.io>

[221] eg <https://better.fyi>

[222] eg <https://www.reputationvip.com> See also: Jones (n 107) 74–75.

[223] Zuboff, Shoshana, *The Age of Surveillance Capitalism: The Fight for a Human Future at the New Frontier of Power* (London: Profile Books 2019); Cohen, Julie E, *Between Truth and Power: The Legal Constructions of Informational Capitalism* (Oxford, New York: Oxford University Press 2019).

[224] See similarly: Serge Gutwirth, *Privacy and the Information Age* (Raf Casert tr, Rowman & Littlefield 2002) 84; Jonathan Cave and others, 'Data Protection Review: Impact on EU Innovation and Competitiveness (Study Drafted for European Parliament's Committee on Industry, Research and

environmental protection, regulation has become necessary because of a market failure resulting from negative externalities and power asymmetries.[225] Secondly, an important caveat when relying on 'the market' to empower individuals over their data relates to resources. These tools may end up offering data protection 'for a price', only to those who can afford it, without legal safeguards and ignoring the fundamental rights dimension.[226] Indeed, reputation management services may be used by anyone willing to pay to suppress certain information and do not have anti-censorship safeguards built-in.[227]

4.3.3 Culture

Perspectives—Confronted with modern-day technical capabilities—ie cheap sensors, storage, and networks—some people believe there to be a moral duty to maximize data collection and preservation.[228] Somewhat caricatural, one writer contrasted this 'school of thought' of preservationists with that of the deletionists.[229] In between these extremes, however, there is a more nuanced reality. As was mentioned in previous chapters already, the nature of digital information—especially in an ISS context—is not static, nor objective, or permanent. While it is not the purpose here to describe the literature on the nature of information and data,[230] at the very least I wish to emphasize its amorphousness and potentiality.[231] Additionally, it is crucial to consider digital information within the broader social, political, and economic landscape. When talking about 'data empowerment', it is crucial to appreciate the fact that virtually all such data is intermediated by a handful of private entities.[232] The web, let alone search engines like Google, should not be seen as

Energy)' (2012) IP/A/ITRE/ST/2011-17 10 <http://www.europarl.europa.eu/RegData/etudes/etudes/join/2012/492463/IPOL-ITRE_ET(2012)492463_EN.pdf> accessed 1 June 2019; Strandburg (n 208); Zuboff, 'Google as a Fortune Teller' (n 209).

[225] Frederik Zuiderveen Borgesius, 'Improving Privacy Protection in the Area of Behavioural Targeting' (PhD Thesis, University of Amsterdam 2014) 165ff<http://hdl.handle.net/11245/1.434236> 281ff; Bruce Schneier, 'Click Here to Kill Everyone' [2017] *NY Mag* <http://nymag.com/selectall/2017/01/the-internet-of-things-dangerous-future-bruce-schneier.html> accessed 1 June 2019.

[226] See also in this regard: Jones (n 107) 74–75.

[227] Making them even more appealing to exactly those people that would not be able to achieve the same result through data protection rights.

[228] Mayer-Schönberger and Cukier (n 186); Florent Thouvenin and others (eds), *Remembering and Forgetting in the Digital Age* (Springer International Publishing 2018) <//www.springer.com/gp/book/9783319902296> accessed 1 May 2018.

[229] Sumit Paul-Choudhury, 'Digital Legacy: The Fate of Your Online Soul' (2011) 210 New Scientist 41, 41.

[230] See for instance: Floridi (n 828).

[231] Many different disciplines have many different interpretations of the nature of information. One relevant example from the field of media studies explores a state of information in between erasure and preservation, namely: lost/found. This conceptualization may also be useful to think in more practical terms about how to implement the right to erasure in practice, ie by making it irretrievable, or hard to find (see Chapter 7, Fifty Shades of Erasure). Ella Klik and Diana Kamin, 'Between Archived, Shredded, and Lost/Found: Erasure in Digital and Artistic Contexts' (*NMC Media-N*, 11 April 2015) <http://median.newmediacaucus.org/the_aesthetics_of_erasure/between-archived-shredded-and-lostfound-erasure-in-digital-and-artistic-contexts/> accessed 30 May 2018.

[232] Victoria Nash and others, 'Public Policy in the Platform Society' (2017) 9 Policy & Internet 368.

'digital libraries or archives', for they lack integrity, persistence, or a public interest vocation.[233] One should be careful not to blindly accept the deterministic view that unconstrained datafication is both inevitable and welcome.[234] The balance between forgetting and remembering, deletion or preservation is not a binary one. It requires a continued, inclusive debate and a framework of values underpinning what is to be remembered, preserved, or stored versus what is not, and who gets to decide so.[235]

Solutions—Effectuating data subject empowerment requires human and social engagement. There needs to be an appetite to actually exercise control over one's personal data.[236] Especially over the last years, a number of civil society organizations have emerged or re-calibrated their focus on empowering data subjects.[237] Increased attention in the media and politics may promote general awareness among society more broadly about data subject rights and how to enforce them. Such an awareness, or 'literacy' is also crucial in order to better understand the 'data economy', the nature of digital information and how it is managed differently by different actors.[238] This has led Morozov, for example, to suggest (personal) data should be seen as an 'essential, infrastructural good that should belong to all of us; it should not be claimed, owned or managed by corporations'.[239]

[233] See also: Wallace Koehler, 'Digital Libraries and World Wide Web Sites and Page Persistence' (1999) 4 Information Research <http://www.informationr.net/ir/4-4/paper60.html> accessed 1 June 2019; Jon Baines, 'Google Is Not a Library, Dr Cavoukian' (*informationrightsandwrongs*, 27 June 2014) <http://informationrightsandwrongs.com/2014/06/27/google-is-not-a-library-dr-cavoukian/> accessed 1 June 2019; Noble (n 489).

[234] Danah Boyd and Kate Crawford, 'Critical Questions for Big Data: Provocations for a Cultural, Technological, and Scholarly Phenomenon' (2012) 15 Information, Communication & Society 662; Kate Crawford, Mary L Gray, and Kate Miltner, 'Critiquing Big Data: Politics, Ethics, Epistemology' (2014) 8 International Journal of Communication 10; Hildebrandt, *Smart Technologies and the End(s) of Law* (n 32) 210–21; Poon (n 2367).

[235] Something which lawmakers have been struggling with for a long time already (eg laws on wiping of criminal records, credit history reporting, archiving, etc). See notably: Liam J Bannon, 'Forgetting as a Feature, Not a Bug: The Duality of Memory and Implications for Ubiquitous Computing' (2006) 2 CoDesign 3; Mayer-Schonberger (n 186); Jones (n 107); Thouvenin and others (n 228).

[236] Surveys in both the EU and the US point to a clear desire among the general public to be able to control one's personal data. See: European Commission, 'Data Protection Eurobarometer out Today' (*Data Protection Newsroom*, 24 June 2015) <https://web.archive.org/web/20150702003030/http://ec.europa.eu/justice/newsroom/data-protection/news/240615_en.htm> accessed 1 June 2019; Shahin (n 653) 17; European Commission, 'Special Eurobarometer: The General Data Protection Regulation' (2019) 487a.

[237] The most notable recent example probably being NOYB.eu, set up by Max Schrems.

[238] A commercial social network or search engine should be approached differently than a public interest research or archival organization, yet different than a news organization, and so on. Bannon (n 2392); Joris Van Hoboken, *Search Engine Freedom: On the Implications of the Right to Freedom Expression for the Legal Governance of Web Search Engines* (First edn, Kluwer Law International 2012) 202; Wasim Ahmed, 'The Ethics of Memory in a Digital Age: Interrogating the Right to Be Forgotten' (2017) 20 Information, Communication & Society 1.; and De Terwagne in: Alessia Ghezzi, Ângela Guimarães Pereira, and Lucia (eds), *The Ethics of Memory in a Digital Age* (Palgrave Macmillan 2014) 85 <http://www.palgrave.com/gp/book/9781137428448> accessed 1 June 2019.

[239] Evgeny Morozov, 'Data Populists Must Seize Our Information—for the Benefit of Us All' *The Guardian* (4 December 2016) <https://www.theguardian.com/commentisfree/2016/dec/04/data-populists-must-seize-information-for-benefit-of-all-evgeny-morozov> accessed 1 June 2019. This relates to the legal concept of 'essential facility', as explored in: Graef (n 14).

Mayer-Schönberger, explores a number of responses—digital abstinence,[240] cognitive adjustment,[241] and perfect contextualization[242]—each flawed but constituting useful thought-exercises nonetheless.[243] Crucial however, is to humanize the debate.[244] Indeed, looking at *actual* cases rather than sterile statistics demonstrates more clearly the merits of strong empowerment rights (as well as helps delineating abuses).[245] In sum, the human and social component to effectuating 'data empowerment' requires first and foremost critical thinking and an openness to adjust one's social/data practices and attitudes.[246] The emerging research field of 'data justice' may constitute a fertile ground for having this discussion.[247]

Issues—As already explored in Chapter 2, there are a lot of forces working against actual individual data empowerment. People's bounded rationality, combined with strong incentives to capitalize on it,[248] may well be one of the biggest impediments.[249] Over-responsibilizing 'humans' to effectuate empowerment might also be exploited to shun regulation and tougher forms of effectuating empowerment (see arguments such as 'competition is only one click away' or 'we offer control through a privacy dashboard'). In sum, effective empowerment over personal data requires more than simply leaving individuals to their own devices. Especially

240 Expecting people to refrain from, or be more cautious when, releasing information. While caution and awareness about one's digital footprint is certainly to be lauded, it is nonsensical to advocate for digital abstinence in modern Western society.

241 Assuming a gradual rewiring of people's minds, adjusting to the new digital data ecosystem's status quo.

242 Pushing for even more transparency so that all data is interpreted and used with due consideration of its full context. See similarly: Brin (n 205); Bart van Der Sloot, 'From Data Minimization to Data Minimummization' in Bart Custers and others (eds), *Discrimination and Privacy in the Information Society—Data Mining and Profiling in Large Databases* (First, Springer 2013); Jonathan Zittrain, 'The Ten Things That Define You' (*Future of the Internet—And How to Stop It*, 14 May 2014) <http://blogs.law.harvard.edu/futureoftheinternet/2014/05/15/the-ten-things-that-define-you/> accessed 1 June 2019.

243 Mayer-Schönberger (n 186) ch 5.

244 Powles (n 100) 602.

245 This is not to advocate for an exclusively anecdotal approach either of course. It is simply to make clear that concrete cases will bring to light the many cases where vulnerable (groups of) individuals can effectively be protected through strong empowerment tools, while the impact on other interests, rights, or freedoms is much more nuanced that one might expect in the abstract. See in this regard also: Article 29 Working Party, 'Opinion 06/2014 on the Notion of Legitimate Interests of the Data Controller under Article 7 of Directive 95/46/EC' (n 34) 56; Jones (n 107) 157; Jenny Afia, 'The Internet: To Regulate or Not To Regulate?' 2018 <https://parliamentlive.tv/Event/Index/cc7d5d3b-c7cb-47a6-a423-c0e99918059dd>.

246 Indeed, it may not be a coincidence that most of the criticism against strong data subject empowerment tools comes from privileged social groups (ie mostly white, Western, male, and middle-class).

247 The interdisciplinary research field of 'data justice' investigates 'the implications that data-driven processes at the core of surveillance capitalism have for the pursuit of substantive social and economic justice claims' and 'how society is and ought to be organized in relation to digital infrastructures—on social, political, economic, cultural and ecological terms'. Dencik, Hintz and Cable (n 2) 9; Seda Gürses, *Data Justice Conference: Keynote Plenary I* <https://cardiff.cloud.panopto.eu/Panopto/Pages/Viewer.aspx?id=547383b2-9d0a-4966-a4aa-a8e50178e2cf> accessed 16 June 2018 01:29:30.

248 Strandburg (n 208).

249 This also appeared from a 2018 survey in the UK: *Which?* Britain Thinks (n 33) 5.

in a complex eco-system characterized by massive power/information asymmetries with many factors actively working against such empowerment.

4.4 Summary

Transversal Empowerment—Rendering the right to erasure, and data subject empowerment more broadly, effective is a complex endeavour in the ISS environment. It requires strong legal backing. Not just through data protection law per se, but also other legal disciplines that might equally contribute to achieving Article 8 Charter's prerogative. Moreover, it was explained that data subject empowerment is not something that should exclusively be looked at through a legal lens. Even if it only scratched the surface, the last subsection gave a taste of the many different considerations and ways in which such empowerment may be effectuated. Effective data subject empowerment is composed of many moving parts that need to work together. Privacy-dashboards constitute a useful demonstration of this interaction. A market in the development of such dashboards is already emerging.[250] Depending on the controller, these tools will require considerable technical resources. Of course, such dashboards also need to be as user-friendly as possible for them to have any impact on rendering data subject empowerment more accessible and effective. The field of Human Computer Interaction (HCI) may be of particular use here.[251] Responsible design, with the data subject at the centre, 'should enable users to practice privacy management as a natural consequence of their ordinary use of the system'.[252]

Effective Empowerment—Van Drooghenbroeck lists three criteria that need to be met for guaranteeing the effectiveness of rights: (a) they should be *actually* exercised by rights-holders; (b) respected by those against whom the rights are guaranteed; and (c) there should be an impartial arbiter.[253] It is hard to get a comprehensive overview of the numbers for the *first criterion*. The available numbers on

[250] OneTrust, for example, already has a 'Data Subject Access Rights Portal' in its products catalogue: https://www.onetrust.com/products/data-subject-access-requests-portal/.

[251] HCI is defined as: 'Human-computer interaction is a discipline concerned with the design, evaluation and implementation of interactive computing systems for human use and with the study of major phenomena surrounding them.' SIGCHI (Group: U.S.) and Curriculum Development Group, *ACM SIGCHI Curricula for Human-Computer Interaction* (Association for Computing Machinery 1992) <http://old.sigchi.org/cdg/index.html> accessed 16 June 2018. For concrete examples of how HCI can contribute to effectuate data subject empowerment, see: Pierre Dewitte, 'GDPR and HCI, a Perfect Match? A Data Protection Lawyer's Perspective on CHI 2018' (*CITIP blog*, 12 June 2018) <https://www.law.kuleuven.be/citip/blog/gdpr-and-hci-a-perfect-match-a-data-protection-lawyers-perspective-on-chi-2018/> accessed 17 June 2018.

[252] Scott Lederer and others, 'Personal Privacy through Understanding and Action: Five Pitfalls for Designers' (2004) 8 Personal and Ubiquitous Computing 440, 447; Irion and others (n 49) 23ff.

[253] Van Drooghenbroeck (n 79) 619–20. Even if the author was talking about provisions in the ECHR, the same requirements apply to Article 8 Charter *mutadis mutandis*.

delisting requests[254] as well as several surveys[255] do suggest a considerable number of individuals actually (wish to) give effect to their data subject rights. In order to ensure the *second criterion*, it remains to be seen whether the GDPR (notably through its fines) will sufficiently alter incentives so that data subject empowerment is taken more seriously than it has in the past. Increased awareness—from developers to corporate boards and the public at large—may prove to effectuate even more profound change.[256] With regard to the *third criterion*, data protection authorities and the judicial system constitute the most straightforward guarantees for impartial enforcement of data subject empowerment. Time and resource constraints may render their impact in practice less substantial, increasing the importance of, for example, alternative dispute resolution mechanisms (eg ODR),[257] DPA-approved standards for data subject rights, and sectoral ethics-bodies.[258] In the end, effectuating data subject empowerment requires efforts from everyone in the data processing ecosystem.[259]

Section 5. Conclusion

Overview—This chapter explored the effectiveness of the right to erasure, and data subject empowerment tools more broadly, in the ISS context. It did so, first by setting the scene, summarizing some of the key threads running throughout this book: ie the control rationale of the right to data protection in the Charter and its relation to the GDPR; and the importance of the GDPR in constraining power asymmetries. Against this backdrop, the second section evaluated how data subject empowerment currently operates in the field. It explained how the ecosystem's

[254] Theo Bertram and others, 'Three Years of the Right to Be Forgotten' (*Google*, 26 February 2018) <https://drive.google.com/file/d/1H4MKNwf5MgeztG7OnJRnl3ym3gIT3HUK/view> accessed date 1 June 2019; 'Updating Our "Right to Be Forgotten" Transparency Report' (*Google*, 26 February 2018) <https://www.blog.google/topics/google-europe/updating-our-right-be-forgotten-transparency-report/> accessed 28 February 2018.

[255] European Commission, 'Data Protection Eurobarometer out Today' (n 236); *Which?* Britain Thinks (n 33); European Commission, 'Special Eurobarometer: The General Data Protection Regulation' (n 236).

[256] Christopher Hodges, 'Discussion. Delivering Data Protection: Trust and Ethical Culture' (2018) 4 European Data Protection Law Review 65, 70.

[257] Damian Clifford and Yung Shin Van Der Sype, 'Online Dispute Resolution: Settling Data Protection Disputes in a Digital World of Customers' [2015] Computer Law & Security Review <http://linkinghub.elsevier.com/retrieve/pii/S026736491500179X> accessed 1 June 2019.

[258] eg as there have been in the press sectorErin C Carroll, 'Making News: Balancing Newsworthiness and Privacy in the Age of Algorithms' (Georgetown University Law Center 2016) <https://papers.ssrn.com/abstract=2877335> accessed 1 June 2019; Pasquale, 'Platform Neutrality' (n 167).

[259] See Natali Helberger, Jo Pierson, and Thomas Poell, 'Governing Online Platforms: From Contested to Cooperative Responsibility' (2018) 34 Information Society 11. The authors summarize what they call 'cooperative responsibility' can take many different forms, such as: 'a) organizational and design responsibility for platforms, b) active participation, empowerment, and real responsibility for users, and c) creating frameworks for shared responsibility and shared values for governments, considering platforms and users as partners in regulation rather than as subjects'.

complexity raises considerable hurdles; presented the results of empirical research; and, based on an adversarial evaluation, concluded that the right to object may be a more effective 'data subject empowerment' tool. Building on what came before, the third section highlighted key requirements for effectuating data subject empowerment in the ISS context. It was emphasized that the GDPR's protective and *ex ante* measures are absolute requirements in order for *ex post* empowerment measures to have any practical effect. This section also made clear that the right to data protection does not hinge on the GDPR alone but is (should be) safeguarded through a wide variety of mechanisms inside and outside the legal domain.

Effectuating Data Subject Empowerment—In short, data subject empowerment requires awareness and real freedom of choice.[260] Currently, data subjects are essentially left at the mercy of others when it comes to effectuating their data protection rights. Whether personal data is *actually* erased or not used for specific purposes anymore is entirely in the hands of the controller. This, in itself, curbs individuals' freedom and autonomy.[261] The GDPR purports to put safeguards in place so that data subjects are not simply left with having to trust controllers. In order for the right to erasure/object (Arts 17, 21 GDPR) to contribute to Article 8 Charter's prerogative, data subjects need to be genuinely free in using them to challenge controllers' decisions. The frequent all-or-nothing 'choice' in the ISS context does not provide freedom.[262]

The Business Model Is the Problem—All or nothing choices are often concealed with cosmetic options to 'control' one's personal data.[263] Many processing operations remain effectively unchallengeable,[264] even if the GDPR requires otherwise. This is not surprising as accommodating data subject rights in full goes against the very business model of many large ISS providers. In an economic environment dominated by a 'grow fast and break things' mantra, many ISS providers are in fact caught in a catch-22 situation, where they are always pushed towards more data processing in order to pre-empt competition.[265] A 2016 study showed

[260] Directorate General of Human Rights and Rule of Law (n 96) 1.

[261] JEJ Prins and others, *De Staat van Informatie* (Amsterdam University Press 2011) 178 <http://www.oapen.org/download?type=document&docid=375125> accessed 1 June 2019.

[262] This ties back to Pettit's theory of liberty as non-domination. Arbitrary control over data constitutes a form of domination, arguably the case when powerful ISS providers present data subjects with take it or leave it options. Gräf (n 103) 446.

[263] Privacy dashboards, for example, often allow adjusting levels of visibility (eg of posts on a social network) or whether you will *receive* personalized advertisements.

[264] eg requesting the erasure of personal data and/or objecting to further processing regarding the tracking of (non-)users across the web, capturing of every aspect of interaction with an ISS (including mouse movements, scrolls, searches, unfinished posts), personalization of information, etc.

[265] 'Internet companies face an interesting, if also morally questionable, imperative: either they hijack neuroscience to gain market share and make large profits, or they let competitors do that and run away with the market.' Bill Davidow, 'Exploiting the Neuroscience of Internet Addiction' [2012] *The Atlantic* <https://www.theatlantic.com/health/archive/2012/07/exploiting-the-neuroscience-of-internet-addiction/259820/> accessed 17 June 2018; Richard Freed, 'The Tech Industry's Psychological War on Kids' (12 March 2018) <https://medium.com/@richardnfreed/the-tech-industrys-psychological-war-on-kids-c452870464ce> accessed 20 April 2018.

that two thirds of online platforms admit tracking people outside of their platforms, while 80 per cent allowed for third-party tracking on its own platform.[266] This is not even mentioning the prevalent coding/development paradigm today, which requires permanent surveillance and tweaking of user-behaviour.[267] Data protection rules form a critical threat to such an environment.[268]

It is easy to be swept away by the argument that the law should keep up with technology and innovation. Yet that is not the argument I would like to pursue here. Fundamental rights and freedoms are democratic products that represent the foundations of society. As a general rule, technology, and how it is mainstreamed commercially, should be moulded around the law and norms, not *vice versa*. Technological progress, while producing tremendous social good, should still be assessed critically, especially when pushed by powerful actors with vested interests. For centuries economic imperatives have resulted in mass-scale environmental pollution. This does not justify such practices today, now that society has finally come to realize its impact. Even if it means certain businesses are no longer viable. Similarly, banks cannot offer their services for a better price if customers sign up to a Ponzi-scheme. If perhaps a bit extreme, these examples demonstrate that business-models should operate within the confines of the law and established norms. This is no different when new technology enables profitable new economic opportunities. To say that the law hampers technological innovation is often, I would argue, disingenuous. Ultimately, technological and economic progress should be at the service of society as a whole. This is an incredibly value-laden discussion without conclusive answers, but one we should all take part in (and policy-makers especially being agents of democracy). I do not believe, however, that the surveillance-based business-model and software-development paradigm predominant in today's ISS environment constitutes such a laudable contribution to society.

Conclusion—This chapter started by asking whether the right to erasure contributes to achieving data protection's rationale in the ISS-context? Based on the insights gained throughout this chapter and the preceding chapters, the short answer to this question is *yes*. At least in theory. In order for the right to have any *practical* meaning, there are some substantial practical hurdles to overcome. Increased awareness, the emergence of technical solutions, and grass-roots initiatives to 'take back control' may complement the GDPR in reshuffling commercial incentives so as to restore autonomy in the face of online power asymmetries. A more truthful answer to the main research question therefore might be: it's complicated.

[266] Venturini and others (n 115) 67ff.

[267] ie the 'agile turn' in software development has resulted in a constant feedback-loop of users' interaction behaviour data into further refining the software. See: Gürses and Van Hoboken (n 30).

[268] Cave and others (n 224) 10.

9
Summary and Conclusion

Section 1. Goal of this Book

CONTEXT—It is not without a sense of irony that the Internet—originally designed to make it very hard to monitor or control individual behaviour[1]—has become the breeding ground for some of the most important information and power asymmetries of our time. One of the main elements enabling these asymmetries, primarily playing out between individuals and commercial entities, is the processing of (personal) data. That was the main starting point of this book. With technology infiltrating ever more aspects of our daily lives, data processing by the economic operators driving the information society have an increasing impact on individuals and society at large. Golden cages are constructed around us, that anticipate and govern how we interact with the world.[2] As such, these growing, data-driven asymmetries are affecting core values such as individual autonomy, dignity, and freedom. Because a constant influx of data is what keeps the information society running, data protection law constitutes the go-to legal framework to resist and break down these golden cages.

RESEARCH QUESTION—Against this backdrop, I set out to investigate the role of individual *empowerment* over personal data in countering power asymmetries online. This book's modest aim was to dissect 'data empowerment' in the information society through the lens of the right to erasure. Indeed, it was never the ambition to come up with a grand new theory, or innovative recommendations for legislators. Instead, its starting point is a legal framework that just entered into force, ie the GDPR, and to unravel its complexities and explain how it can meaningfully contribute to data subject empowerment in the face of information and power asymmetries in the online environment. In this quest, I attempted to frame answers to the following question(s):

Does the right to erasure meaningfully contribute to safeguarding the fundamental right to data protection in the face of online power asymmetries?

- What is the rationale of the right to erasure and when does it apply?

[1] Wendy Hui-Kyong Chun, *Control and Freedom: Power and Paranoia in the Age of Fiber Optics* (MIT Press 2006) 69.

[2] Mireille Hildebrandt, 'The Dawn of a Critical Transparency Right for the Profiling Era' *Digital Enlightenment Yearbook 2012* (IOS Press 2012) 54 <https://works.bepress.com/mireille_hildebrandt/40> accessed 12 July 2016.

The Right to Erasure in EU Data Protection Law. First Edition. Jef Ausloos. Oxford University Press (2020). © Jef Ausloos
DOI: 10.1093/oso/9780198847977.001.0001

- How to balance rights, freedoms, and interests when accommodating the right to erasure?
- What are the practical challenges to realizing the right to erasure and how might they be overcome?

These questions are arranged in such a way as to reflect the logical sequence of analyses to be followed when applying the right to erasure. Firstly, one needs to know if the right can be invoked in the first place. In case the answer is yes, secondly, one needs to evaluate how the right to erasure can be applied in a balanced way, ie considering all interests, rights, and freedoms at stake. Thirdly, if the right to erasure *is* applicable, and if a balance *can* be identified, one still needs to consider how to make it work in practice. These three steps determined the structure of this book, each one being comprehensively tackled in a corresponding part. The following section provides a brief description of each of these parts and the chapters comprised within. The main research question will be answered in the section after that.

Section 2. Summary of Findings

OVERVIEW—This book can be subdivided into three substantive parts, each corresponding to the research sub-questions mentioned above. After the introductory Chapter 1, Part I fleshes out the right to erasure as such. This is done by looking at its relation to the fundamental right to data protection in Article 8 Charter (Chapter 2), its scope of application within the GDPR (Chapter 3), and the conditions for its application (Chapter 4). Part II investigates the balancing acts that are generally implied within the exercise of the right to erasure. This part explores the mechanics of balancing within the GDPR (Chapter 5), how such balancing operates in three discrete and representative balancing scenarios in the information society (Chapter 6), and ends with a critical look at some of the key remaining issues regarding data protection balancing. Part III, finally, looks more closely at the practical operationalization of data subject empowerment, exploring key hurdles to effectuating the right to erasure and how to tackle them. A more narratively pleasing way for looking at this book might be by framing it within the 'three-act structure'. From Chapter 1 until Chapter 4 constitutes the *set-up* of the story; Chapters 4 to 8 the *confrontation*; and Chapters 8 and Conclusion the *resolution*.

DATA PROTECTION—Chapter 2 lays the groundwork for the rest of the book, clearly delineating the fundamental right to data protection, its relation to the GDPR, and the right to erasure in it. The historical overview demonstrates that the emergence of data protection is inherently tied to technological developments and how these may amplify power asymmetries. It was also made clear that informational self-determination or control over personal data lies at the heart of the fundamental right to data protection as proclaimed in Article 8 Charter. This is a clear difference with the GDPR that has a much wider prerogative, ie protecting *all* fundamental rights and freedoms whenever personal data is being processed. Put differently, whereas Article 8 Charter safeguards a minimum level of control over one's personal data, the GDPR installs a fair balancing framework that safeguards any and all fundamental rights and freedoms as they are affected by the processing of personal data. The substantive provisions of the GDPR can be divided into four categories along the lines of *ex ante* v *ex post* and protective v empowerment measures (see data protection matrix). Chapter 2 ends with positioning the right to erasure within the GDPR's arsenal of *ex post* empowerment measures, describing its legislative history as well as its main benefits and drawbacks.

SCOPE OF THE GDPR—Having laid the foundation of data protection empowerment in Chapter 2, Chapter 3 zooms in on the GDPR's scope of application in particular. It examines the territorial, material, and personal scope respectively, with a focus on the latter two because of their particular relevance in light of the book's overall focus. What becomes very clear is how malleable and dynamic the nature of (personal) data is, something which will prove to be important with regard to the operationalization of the right to erasure. This third chapter also fleshes out the concept of controller, particularly in the ISS context with many different actors involved in processing the same personal data. It appears that from data subjects' perspective, ISS providers will practically always be approachable with a right to erasure/object, even if not ultimately responsible or liable. Chapter 3 ends with describing four key derogations and exemptions in the GDPR, which may effectively lead to the inapplicability of the right to erasure. What appears from this chapter overall, is the importance of a granular and functional approach when determining the GDPR's scope of application. This is all the more important in light of the growing complexity of the ecosystem, with many moving elements.

THE RIGHT TO ERASURE—Chapter 4 zooms even further in on one specific provision in the GDPR: Article 17 on the right to erasure ('right to be forgotten'). The chapter meticulously dissects the three paragraphs of this provision. The first paragraph lists six right to erasure triggers which can be summarized as: (a) purpose expiration; (b) withdrawal of consent; (c) right to object; (d) unlawful processing; (e) legal obligation; and (f) withdrawal of consent by minors in the online environment. The second paragraph comprises an odd extension of the right to erasure, enabling data subjects to request that controllers who have made the personal data public, communicate potential erasure to anyone else processing that same personal data. The third paragraph lists five exemptions to the right to erasure, summarized as: (a) freedom of expression and information; (b) legal obligation or task carried out in the public interest or official authority; (c) public interest in the area of public health; (d) public interest archiving, scientific and historical research, or statistical purposes; and (e) legal claims. What becomes clear right away is how both the right to erasure's triggers *and* exemptions all refer to other legal provisions in/outside the GDPR. As such, the right to erasure can be seen as a central hub in the GDPR, bringing together key data protection principles from the perspective of data subject empowerment.

Balancing in the GDPR—Part II of the book takes a step back and looks at balancing acts induced by invoking the right to erasure. Chapter 5 sets the scene for the coming two chapters. It starts with comparing balancing of fundamental rights and freedoms in the Charter with balancing in the GDPR. Indeed, it re-emphasizes how the GDPR as a whole, essentially constitutes a framework for fair balancing of rights, freedoms, and interests in the context of personal data processing. The chapter then lays out the actual blueprint for such fair balancing in the GDPR. It becomes clear how fair balancing in the GDPR is an iterative process, with *ex ante* and *ex post* balancing acts. The former need to be performed before processing initiates, and the latter refer to subsequent balances as triggered by data subject rights for example. Overall, the very nature of fair balancing does not allow for clear-cut, categorical answers to conflicts of rights, freedoms, and/or interests. Instead the GDPR should be looked at as defining the basic infrastructure for ensuring fair balancing, further to be refined by relevant stakeholders. This can notably happen through standards or certification mechanisms, guidance by authorities, and by controllers themselves.

Balancing Scenarios—Having defined the mechanics of balancing in Chapter 5, Chapter 6 explores how this applies in three concrete balancing scenarios. The three scenarios are selected based on their prevalence in the ISS context, and on the different types of entities they generally represent: (a) commercial interests, mainly relating to the ISS provider; (b) information freedoms, mainly relating to third parties such as users of the ISS provider; and (c) research and security interests, mainly representing a shared or common interest. It appears from a combined reading of the GDPR, policy documents, and CJEU case law that as a general rule, commercial interests cannot trump data subjects' interests when exercising their right to erasure or to object. When these rights affect the information freedoms of third parties, the GDPR requires powerful ISS providers to take up their responsibility, but only insofar as they actually *control* the respective information processing operations. This emphasizes the need for a granular approach, where ISS providers should not be seen as judge and jury for third-party content, but rather as responsible actors for the deliberate actions they take to distribute information. Having said, further guidance is certainly desirable and would benefit from transparency by ISS providers on their internal decision-mechanisms as well as details on the actual cases dealt with. In order for research interests to be able to override data subject rights, it will generally have to be carried out in the public interest and severely hampered by anonymization. With regard to security interests, finally, the processing will have to be strictly necessary, effective, and proportionate. Overall, Chapter 6 clearly demonstrates how fair balancing is an inherently open-ended legal exercise. The GDPR tries to provide some structure, inter alia by setting clear defaults in favour of different rights, freedoms, or interests that might be particularly at risk in certain situations.

BALANCING ISSUES—Chapter 7 discusses some of the loose ends that remain after the previous two chapters in Part II on Balancing. In particular, it tries to frame answers or at the very least nuances to key open questions arising from the right to erasure induced balancing acts in the ISS context. After a critical appraisal of open-ended fair balancing in the data protection context, Chapter 7 tackles questions such as how far ISS controllers' responsibility to balance goes; whether the GDPR defines a balance that is biased towards data subjects; and whether the framework is not essentially 'privatizing' fair balancing. The last half of the chapter is dedicated to some important elements that nuance the aforementioned questions, and the debate on GDPR balancing by ISS controllers more broadly. It emphasizes the importance of taking into account the size and broader context in which large ISS providers operate; makes a critical appraisal of the merits and pitfalls of a granular and functional approach; shows how the GDPR essentially defers fair balancing; and explains the right to erasure should not be looked at as a binary (ie full erasure v unrestrained processing).

EFFECTUATING ERASURE—The last substantial Part III takes a more practical approach, looking at challenges to accommodating the right to erasure and how to resolve them. Indeed, assuming the right to erasure applies (see Part I) *and* that a fair balance can be drawn (see Part II), the right still needs to be operationalized *on the ground*, Chapter 8 roughly has two main parts. The first one identifies and evaluates the key hurdles to operationalizing data subject empowerment in the ISS context. This is done by pinpointing complexities, describing the results of empirical research testing data subject rights, and a critical appraisal of potential abuses of the right to erasure. It is concluded that, in practice, the right to object will often be much more realistic and effective in empowering data subjects. Secondly, Chapter 8 lists the key requirements for effective data subject empowerment. It does so by building on all the previous chapters and the practical evaluation in the previous section. Effectuating data empowerment—and the fundamental right to data protection (Art 8 Charter)—does not solely hinge on the GDPR, but requires a holistic approach considering other legal frameworks as well. Technical tools and reshuffled incentive structures for dominant market players will also prove fundamental in rendering data empowerment effective.

CONCLUSION—In the face of massive power asymmetries online, a sound regulatory framework is critical in ensuring data subject empowerment. Ideally, such a framework should render the actual exercise of data subject rights superfluous, or at least only a last resort solution. The norm should be that individuals can move freely both physically and digitally. Values such as autonomy and informational self-determination should not be constrained by, but rather inform, technological development and business-practices.

Section 3. So, Does the Right to Erasure Contribute to Informational Self-Determination in the Information Society?

YES—All things considered, the right to erasure in the GDPR can be expected to contribute to informational self-determination in the information society. But perhaps not in the way one might think at first. Indeed, the right's main added value is how it emphasizes, clarifies, and centralizes key data protection safeguards into one provision. Rather than being an autonomous provision that data subjects can invoke against a controller, it is a convenient proxy through which individuals can 'exercise control'. Put differently, the right to erasure constitutes a central hub for data subject empowerment in the GDPR. As such, the right to erasure has two concrete functions: firstly, it gives shape to the control imperative of Article 8 Charter, being an evocative and accessible tool in data subjects' hands. This may prove particularly useful in an increasingly datafied environment where many rights, freedoms, and interests are affected. Secondly, as an *ex post* empowerment measure, the right to erasure also constitutes a crucial check on whether the GDPR is safeguarded throughout the processing lifecycle. This 'compliance-monitoring' function might prove particularly useful in light of under-resourced data protection authorities.

NO—Of course the right to erasure is no silver bullet to data subject empowerment. The right to erasure and data subject empowerment measures more broadly are often criticized for over-responsibilizing individuals. Moreover, it is not the toolbox that defines the craftsmanship. What is more, as individual measures, one may question their capability of guaranteeing the right to data protection in society more broadly. Of course, one cannot look at such empowerment measures in isolation, but needs to consider the GDPR as a whole, including the strong protective measures as well. A right or freedom should also not be actively exercised to be meaningful or enjoyed. Still, when implemented badly, the right to erasure may result in potential under- or over-compliance, which in turn might negatively affect other fundamental rights, freedoms, and interests. Such circumstances should be avoided via interpretative guidance through co-regulatory and/or DPA initiatives but also strict enforcement.

Having reached the end of this book, it is worth revisiting the vignettes described in Chapter 1.

UBER VIGNETTE—The Uber vignette illustrates how insights from social sciences, advanced data processing techniques, and a permanent feedback-loop with drivers is used to manipulate their behaviour in the company's interests. The right of access (Art 15 GDPR) should enable drivers to get detailed information on how their personal data is processed exactly. This should in turn make it possible for them to very granularly exercise the right to erasure—and perhaps the right to object even more so—in order to oppose to very specific processing operations, without being kicked off the platform. After all, Uber will only be able to rely on consent (Art 6(1)(a) GDPR) or legitimate interests (Art 6(1)(f) GDPR) to perform such processing. With regard to the former, the data subject has an unconditional right to withdraw consent (Art 7(3) GDPR) and with regard to the latter a right to object (Art 21), both of which can lead to erasure (see Art 17(1)(b)–(c) GDPR). Data subject rights, in this context, can also be used as tools to enforce other goals such as anti-discrimination rules or workers' rights.

FACEBOOK VIGNETTE—The Facebook vignette dealt with the social network's potential impact on election integrity, for example through emotional manipulation. Similar to the previous vignette, the only lawful ground that can legitimately be relied on would be consent (Art 6(1)(a) GDPR) or legitimate interests (Art 6(1)(f) GDPR). In both cases, the rights to erasure and/or to object should be freely exercisable. The vignette demonstrates how data subject rights in fact contribute to safeguarding multiple Charter provisions as well as democracy more broadly. Actually, in some situations the respective processing operations should not have occurred in the first place. But in case non-compliance with the GDPR is left unenforced, the right to erasure/object gives a clear legal hook for motivated individuals to challenge said practices nonetheless. A priori, data subject rights will only affect the data subjects invoking them, eg only they will no longer be politically profiled and targeted. That being said, once a critical mass of data subjects exercises their rights, and/or it appears these operations do not comply with the GDPR in the first place, individual data subject rights may in fact constitute a watershed, triggering a change in processing practices (see Schrems's 2011 access request as recounted in Chapter 1).

GOOGLE VIGNETTE—When personal data has been made public, the rights to erasure and object constitute a clear and straightforward tool for individuals to maintain some level of control over their personal data. What makes them especially effective is that they can also be invoked against every controller down the 'processing-chain'. This is most clearly illustrated in the Google vignette, where data subjects can target central chokepoints. This is important from an individual empowerment perspective, as it renders the rights to erasure/object much more effective in safeguarding data subjects' right to privacy.

APPLE VIGNETTE—The fourth and final vignette relates to Apple's smart voice assistant Siri. In order to be useful, the service uses a lot of information streams about users' connections, apps, behaviour, and so on. Some of this information is stored on Apple's servers where it is analysed for improving the service. Due to 'data protection by design' measures, the company claims it cannot accommodate access or erasure rights. Even if one was to stop using Siri right now, that user's voice recordings may be stored for up to two years. This vignette demonstrates compatibility issues between data subject empowerment tools and actual technology. Technology should align with the law and not vice versa. As a general rule, controllers cannot claim it would be too burdensome to accommodate data subject rights if they are clearly applicable in a given case.

Conclusion—In sum, the answer to the main research question is *yes, but*. The 'but' refers to several potential hurdles that might obstruct an effective exercise of the right to erasure. These may range from legitimate legal measures safeguarding other fundamental rights, freedoms, and interests; more complicated technical operationalization issues; or illegitimate obstructions such as controller avoidance strategies. An important take-away is that data subject rights can be powerful tools not just to safeguard the fundamental right to data protection, but many other Charter provisions as well. This also emphasizes yet again how the GDPR should clearly be distinguished from Article 8 Charter. The former being a fair balancing instrument safeguarding many rights, freedoms, and interests in the context of personal data processing, the latter defending a fundamental value in and on itself, ie informational self-determination.

Section 4. Outlook

Data protection law is often scorned for being the 'law of everything', appearing to be applicable to almost every aspect of our lives. Yet, is this not turning things on its head? Information technology is penetrating every aspect of our lives, and this is why the GDPR becomes omni-relevant as well. A sound regulatory infrastructure is absolutely necessary to ensure the expansion of ICTs occurs in a manner that respects fundamental rights, freedoms, and interests. Given the fact that (personal) data is the fuel that makes ICTs operate, it is only natural that it is the go-to framework for defining the rules of the game. Moreover, growing data-driven power asymmetries (catalysed by commercial and technological factors) have a considerable impact on the control-imperative of the fundamental right to data protection in Article 8 Charter. The right to data protection not only implies the freedom to proactively control one's personal data, but also safeguards that freedom from being effectively usurped, whether by commercial, technological, or bureaucratic forces. The GDPR contributes to this aim both through concrete empowerment tools, as well as by turning the processing of personal data into a liability. In explaining the importance and operationalization of data empowerment, this book provides a modest contribution to the broader debate we ought to have on the challenges faced in an increasingly datafied society.

Bibliography

Abrams M, '"The Origins of Personal Data and Its Implications for Governance"', *OECD Expert Roundtable Discussion Protecting Privacy in a Data-Driven Economy: Taking Stock of Current Thinking* (2014) <http://informationaccountability.org/wp-content/uploads/Data-Origins-Abrams.pdf> accessed 14 November 2014

Acar G, 'Preserving Privacy in Belgium' (*COSIC*, 26 October 2015) <https://www.esat.kuleuven.be/cosic/preserving-privacy-in-belgium/> accessed 10 November 2017

Acar G and others, 'The Web Never Forgets: Persistent Tracking Mechanisms in the Wild' (ACM Press 2014) <http://dl.acm.org/citation.cfm?doid=2660267.2660347> accessed 8 April 2015

Acar G and others, 'Facebook Tracking Through Social Plug-Ins. Technical Report Prepared for the Belgian Privacy Commission' (KU Leuven—COSIC 2015) <https://securehomes.esat.kuleuven.be/~gacar/fb_tracking/>

'Advances in AI Are Used to Spot Signs of Sexuality' [2017] *The Economist* <https://www.economist.com/news/science-and-technology/21728614-machines-read-faces-are-coming-advances-ai-are-used-spot-signs> accessed 22 February 2018

Ahmed W, 'The Ethics of Memory in a Digital Age: Interrogating the Right to Be Forgotten' (2017) 20 Information, Communication & Society 1

AI B, 'Anonymized Data Is Not Subject to Privacy Regulations' (*Medium*, 19 February 2019) <https://medium.com/generate-vision/anonymized-data-is-not-subject-to-privacy-regulations-9e4667856261> accessed 25 February 2019

Akrivopoulou C and Garipidis N (eds), *Human Rights and Risks in the Digital Era: Globalization and the Effects of Information Technologies* (Information Science Reference 2012)

Albers M, 'Realizing the Complexity of Data Protection' in Serge Gutwirth, Ronald Leenes, and Paul De Hert (eds), *Reloading Data Protection—Multidisciplinary Insights and Contemporary Challenges* (1st edn, Springer 2014) <http://www.springer.com/law/international/book/978-94-007-7539-8> accessed 26 May 2014

Alexy R, *Theorie der Grundrechte* (Suhrkamp 1986)

——, *A Theory of Constitutional Rights* (OUP 2002)

Allen AL, *Unpopular Privacy: What Must We Hide?* (OUP 2011)

Alter A, 'Your E-Book Is Reading You' *Wall Street Journal* (29 June 2012) <http://online.wsj.com/article/SB10001424052702304870304577490950051438304.html> accessed 2 July 2012

Amberhawk, 'Council's Exceptions from the Data Protection Regulation Degrade the Privacy Protection below Directive 95/46/EC' (*Hawktalk*, 3 August 2015) <http://amberhawk.typepad.com/amberhawk/2015/08/councils-exceptions-from-the-data-protection-regulation-degrade-the-privacy-protection-below-directive-9546ec.html> accessed 2 May 2016

Ambrose ML, 'You Are What Google Says You Are: The Right to Be Forgotten and Information Stewardship' (2012) 17 International Review of Information Ethics 07

Ambrose ML, 'It's About Time: Privacy, Information Life Cycles, and the Right to Be Forgotten' (2013) 16 Stanford Technology Law Review 371

Ambrose ML, 'Speaking of Forgetting: Analysis of Possible Non-EU Responses to the Right to Be Forgotten and Speech Exception' (2014) 38 Telecommunications Policy 800

Ambrose ML and Ausloos J, 'The Right to Be Forgotten Across the Pond' (2012) 3 Journal of Information Policy 1

Andrade N, 'Oblivion: The Right to Be Different from Oneself—Reproposing the Right to Be Forgotten' (2012) 13 Revista de Internet, Derecho Y Política 122

Andrejevic M, 'Exploitation in the Data Mine' in Christian Fuchs and others (eds), *Internet and Surveillance: the Challenges of Web 2. 0 and Social Media.* (Routledge 2012)

Angelopoulos C and others, 'Study of Fundamental Rights Limitations for Online Enforcement through Self-Regulation' <https://pure.uva.nl/ws/files/8763808/IVIR_Study_Online_enforcement_through_self_regulation.pdf>

Angelopoulos CJ, 'European Intermediary Liability in Copyright: A Tort-Based Analysis' (PhD Thesis, University of Amsterdam 2016) <http://dare.uva.nl/record/1/527223> accessed 22 April 2016

Angwin J, *Dragnet Nation: A Quest for Privacy, Security, and Freedom in a World of Relentless Surveillance* (Times Books, Henry Holt and Company 2014)

'Another Game of Thrones' [2012] *The Economist* <http://www.economist.com/news/21567361-google-apple-facebook-and-amazon-are-each-others-throats-all-sorts-ways-another-game> accessed 20 July 2015

Anthony S, 'Ashley Madison, an Online Dating Website for Cheaters, Gets Hacked [Updated]' (*Ars Technica*, 21 July 2015) <https://arstechnica.com/information-technology/2015/07/ashley-madison-an-dating-website-for-cheaters-gets-hacked/> accessed 18 March 2018

Apple Inc, 'IOS Security (IOS 10)' <https://perma.cc/8EQE-TFW5> accessed 7 May 2018

'Apple Jams Facebook's Web-Tracking Tools' *BBC News* (4 June 2018) <https://www.bbc.com/news/technology-44360273> accessed 9 June 2018

Article 19 and others, 'Written Observations in Case C-507/17 Google, Inc v CNIL' <https://cippic.ca/uploads/C507_17-A19-CJEU_EN.pdf> accessed 28 May 2018

Article 29 Working Party, 'Recommendation 1/97 Data Protection Law and the Media' (1997) Recommendation 1/97 <http://ec.europa.eu/justice/article-29/documentation> accessed 19 May 2016

——, 'Working Document on Determining the International Application of EU Data Protection Law to Personal Data Processing on the Internet by Non-EU Based Web Sites' (Article 29 Working Party 2002) WP 56 <http://ec.europa.eu/justice/article-29/documentation>.

——, 'Opinion on the Use of Location Data with a View to Providing Value-Added Services' (European Commission 2005) Opinion WP 115 <http://ec.europa.eu/justice/article-29/documentation>.

——, 'Opinion 10/2006 on the Processing of Personal Data by the Society for Worldwide Interbank Financial Telecommunication (SWIFT)' (Article 29 Working Party 2006) Opinion WP 128 <http://ec.europa.eu/justice/article-29/documentation> accessed 7 March 2017

——, 'Working Document on the Processing of Personal Data Relating to Health in Electronic Health Records (EHR)' (2007) WP 131 <http://ec.europa.eu/justice/article-29/documentation> accessed 4 February 2016

——, 'Opinion 4/2007 on the Concept of Personal Data' (Article 29 Working Party 2007) WP 136 <http://ec.europa.eu/justice/article-29/documentation> accessed 9 December 2012

——, 'Working Document 1/2008 on the Protection of Children's Personal Data' (Article 29 Working Party 2008) WP 147 <http://ec.europa.eu/justice/article-29/documentation> accessed 25 October 2012

——, 'Opinion 1/2008 on Data Protection Issues Related to Search Engines' (Article 29 Working Party 2008) WP 148 <http://ec.europa.eu/justice/article-29/documentation> accessed 22 April 2016

——, 'Opinion 5/2009 on Online Social Networking' (Article 29 Working Party 2009) WP 136 <http://ec.europa.eu/justice/article-29/documentation> accessed 24 October 2012

——, 'Opinion 1/2010 on the Concepts of "Controller" and "Processor"' (Article 29 Working Party 2010) WP 169 <http://ec.europa.eu/justice/article-29/documentation> accessed 19 April 2015

——, 'Opinion 02/2010 on Online Behavioural Advertising' (Article 29 Working Party 2010) WP 171 <http://ec.europa.eu/justice/article-29/documentation> accessed 2 November 2012

——, 'Opinion 3/2010 on the Principle of Accountability' (European Commission 2010) Opinion WP 173 <http://ec.europa.eu/justice/article-29/documentation> accessed 1 August 2017

——, 'Opinion 5/2010 on the Industry Proposal for a Privacy and Data Protection Impact Assessment Framework for RFID Applications' (2010) WP 175 <http://ec.europa.eu/justice/article-29/documentation> accessed 5 February 2016

——, 'Opinion 8/2010 on Applicable Law' (Article 29 Working Party 2010) WP 179 <http://ec.europa.eu/justice/article-29/documentation> accessed 20 April 2016

——, 'Opinion 13/2011 on Geolocation Services on Smart Mobile Devices' (Article 29 Working Party 2011) WP 185 <http://ec.europa.eu/justice/article-29/documentation> accessed 24 October 2012

——, 'Opinion 15/2011 on the Definition of Consent' (Article 29 Working Party 2011) WP187 <http://ec.europa.eu/justice/article-29/documentation>.

——, 'Opinion 01/2012 on the Data Protection Reform Proposals' (Article 29 Working Party 2012) WP 191 <http://ec.europa.eu/justice/article-29/documentation> accessed 12 October 2016

——, 'Opinion 3/2012 on Developments in Biometric Technologies' (Article 29 Working Party 2012) Opinion WP 193 <http://ec.europa.eu/justice/article-29/documentation> accessed 2 February 2017

——, 'Opinion 05/2012 on Cloud Computing' (Article 29 Working Party 2012) WP 196 <http://ec.europa.eu/justice/article-29/documentation> accessed 13 September 2012

——, 'Letter Addressed to Google' (16 October 2012) <http://ec.europa.eu/justice/article-29/documentation> accessed 8 September 2016

——, 'Annex 2: Proposals for Amendments Regarding Exemption for Personal or Household Activities' <http://ec.europa.eu/justice/article-29/documentation> accessed 7 January 2015

——, 'Opinion 03/2013 on Purpose Limitation' (Article 29 Working Party 2013) WP 03/2013 <http://ec.europa.eu/justice/article-29/documentation> accessed 11 April 2013

——, 'Opinion 01/2014 on the Application of Necessity and Proportionality Concepts and Data Protection within the Law Enforcement Sector' (2014) Opinion WP 211 <http://ec.europa.eu/justice/article-29/documentation> accessed 27 October 2016

——, 'Opinion 06/2014 on the Notion of Legitimate Interests of the Data Controller under Article 7 of Directive 95/46/EC' (European Commission 2014) Opinion WP 217 <http://ec.europa.eu/justice/article-29/documentation> accessed 10 September 2014

——, 'Opinion 05/2014 on Anonymisation Techniques' (Article 29 Working Party 2014) WP 05/2014 <http://ec.europa.eu/justice/article-29/documentation> accessed 4 February 2016

——, 'Statement on the Role of a Risk-Based Approach in Data Protection Legal Frameworks' (2014) WP 218 <http://ec.europa.eu/justice/article-29/documentation>.

——, 'Opinion 8/2014 on the on Recent Developments on the Internet of Things' (Article 29 Working Party 2014) Opinion WP 223 <http://ec.europa.eu/justice/article-29/documentation> accessed 9 April 2015

——, 'Guidelines on the Implementation of the Court of Justice of the European Union Judgment on "Google Spain and Inc. v Agencia Española de Protección de Datos (AEPD) and Mario Costeja González" C-131/12' (Article 29 Working Party 2014) Guidelines WP 225 <http://ec.europa.eu/justice/article-29/documentation>

——, 'Opinion 01/2015 on Privacy and Data Protection Issues Relating to the Utilisation of Drones' (2015) Opinion WP 231 <http://ec.europa.eu/justice/article-29/documentation> accessed 1 April 2018

——, 'Appendix: Core Topics in View of the Trilogue' (2015) <http://ec.europa.eu/justice/article-29/documentation> accessed 12 May 2016

——, 'Update of Opinion 8/2010 on Applicable Law in Light of the CJEU Judgment in Google Spain' (Article 29 Working Party 2015) Opinion WP 179 update <http://ec.europa.eu/justice/article-29/documentation> accessed 18 January 2016

——, 'Guidelines on Automated Individual Decision-Making and Profiling for the Purposes of Regulation 2016/679' (Article 29 Working Party 2018) Guidelines WP 251 <http://ec.europa.eu/justice/article-29/documentation>.

——, 'Guidelines on Consent under Regulation 2016/679' (2018) WP 259 <http://ec.europa.eu/justice/article-29/documentation>.

—— to Larry Page, 'Google Privacy Policy' (23 September 2014) <http://ec.europa.eu/justice/article-29/documentation>.

—— to Paul Timmers (DG Connect), 'Letter to the European Commission, DG CONNECT on MHealth' (5 February 2015) <http://ec.europa.eu/justice/article-29/documentation>.

Arvidsson A, 'Facebook and Finance: On the Social Logic of the Derivative' (2016) 33 Theory, Culture & Society 3

Ash TG, *The File* (Atlantic Books 2009)

Ausloos J, 'The "Right to Be Forgotten"—Worth Remembering?' (2012) 28 Computer Law & Security Review 143

——, 'Google v Spain at the Court of Justice of the EU' (*Tech, Policy & Society*, 5 March 2013) <https://jefausloos.wordpress.com/2013/03/05/google-v-spain-at-the-european-court-of-justice/> accessed 28 March 2018

——, 'The Interaction between the Rights to Object and to Erasure in the GDPR' (*CITIP blog*, 25 August 2016) <https://www.law.kuleuven.be/citip/blog/gdpr-update-the-interaction-between-the-right-to-object-and-the-right-to-erasure/> accessed 11 October 2017

——, 'Vergetelheids-zaken voor de Hoven van Cassatie te België en Frankrijk—Contradictoir of Complementair? (noot onder Hof van cassatie 29 april 2016, nr C.15.0052.F' [2017] Computerrecht: Tijdschrift voor Informatica, Telecommunicatie en Recht 31

——, 'Balancing in the GDPR: Legitimate Interests v. Right to Object' (*CITIP blog*, 28 February 2017) <https://www.law.kuleuven.be/citip/blog/balancing-in-the-gdpr-legitimate-interests-v-right-to-object/> accessed 4 June 2017

——, 'Paul-Olivier Dehaye and the Raiders of the Lost Data' (*CITIP blog*, 10 April 2018) <https://www.law.kuleuven.be/citip/blog/paul-olivier-dehaye-and-the-raiders-of-the-lost-data/> accessed 23 April 2018

——, *How Internet Censorship Works* (2012) <https://youtu.be/HfS_2oXVch0> accessed 19 November 2015

Ausloos J and Dewitte P, 'Shattering One-Way Mirrors—Data Subject Access Rights in Practice' (2018) 8 International Data Privacy Law 4

——, 'Shattering One-Way Mirrors. Data Subject Access Rights in Practice' (KU Leuven—CiTiP 2018) CiTiP Working Paper 31/2018 <https://papers.ssrn.com/abstract=3106632> accessed 15 February 2018

Autorité de la concurrence and Bundeskartellamt, 'Competition Law and Data' (2016) <http://www.autoritedelaconcurrence.fr/doc/reportcompetitionlawanddatafinal.pdf> accessed 24 May 2016

Ayenson M and others, 'Flash Cookies and Privacy II: Now with HTML5 and ETag Respawning' <ssrn.com/abstract=1898390> accessed 23 October 2012

Baines J, 'Google Is Not a Library, Dr Cavoukian' (*informationrightsandwrongs*, 27 June 2014) <http://informationrightsandwrongs.com/2014/06/27/google-is-not-a-library-dr-cavoukian/> accessed 7 August 2014

Balboni P and others, 'Legitimate Interest of the Data Controller New Data Protection Paradigm: Legitimacy Grounded on Appropriate Protection' (2013) 3 International Data Privacy Law 244

Balkin JM, 'Information Fiduciaries and the First Amendment' (2016) 49 UC Davis Law Review 1183

——, 'Free Speech in the Algorithmic Society: Big Data, Private Governance, and New School Speech Regulation' (2017) Working Draft <https://papers.ssrn.com/abstract=3038939> accessed 20 September 2017

Bambauer JR, 'All Life Is an Experiment (Sometimes It Is a Controlled Experiment.)' (2015) 47 Loyola University Chicago Law Journal 15

Bamberger KA, 'Regulation as Delegation: Private Firms, Decisionmaking, and Accountability in the Administrative State' (2006) 56 Duke Law Journal 377

Bankston K and Stepanovich A, 'When Robot Eyes Are Watching You: The Law & Policy of Automated Communications Surveillance' (2014)

Banning ME, 'Shared Entanglements—Web 2.0, Info-Liberalism & Digital Sharing' (2016) 19 Information, Communication & Society 489

Bannon LJ, 'Forgetting as a Feature, Not a Bug: The Duality of Memory and Implications for Ubiquitous Computing' (2006) 2 CoDesign 3

Barlow JP, 'A Declaration of the Independence of Cyberspace' (*Electronic Frontier Foundation*, 8 February 1996) <https://www.eff.org/cyberspace-independence> accessed 18 April 2016

Barocas S and Nissenbaum H, 'Big Data's End Run around Anonymity and Consent' in Julia Lane and others (eds), *Privacy, Big Data, and the Public Good: Frameworks for Engagement* (1st edn, CUP 2014)

Bartolini C and Siry L, 'The Right to Be Forgotten in the Light of the Consent of the Data Subject' [2016] Computer Law & Security Review <http://www.sciencedirect.com/science/article/pii/S026736491630019X> accessed 1 March 2016

BBC Academy, 'Journalism Law/Privacy' (2013) <http://www.bbc.co.uk/academy/journalism/article/art20130702112133653> accessed 26 May 2017

'BBC Editorial Guidelines' <www.bbc.co.uk/editorialguidelines/guidelines> accessed 17 November 2015

Beer D, *Metric Power* (Palgrave Macmillan UK 2016) <http://link.springer.com/10.1057/978-1-137-55649-3> accessed 24 February 2018

Belgian Privacy Commission, 'Own-Initiative Recommendation Relating to 1) Facebook, 2) Internet and/or Facebook Users as Well as 3) Users and Providers of Facebook Services, Particularly Plug-Ins' (2015) Recommendation no 04/2015 <https://www.gegevensbeschermingsautoriteit.be/sites/privacycommission/files/documents/recommendation_04_2015_0.pdf> accessed 21 May 2015

——, 'The Belgian Privacy Commission Publishes New Recommendation Relating to the Processing of Personal Data by Facebook through Cookies, Social Plug-Ins and Pixels' (16 May 2017) <https://www.privacycommission.be/en/news/belgian-privacy-commission-publishes-new-recommendation-relating-processing-personal-data> accessed 28 April 2018

——, 'Advies 75/2017 Ingevolge Een Klacht Gericht Tegen Een Zoekmotor Betreffende de Modaliteiten Voor de Uitvoering En de Geografische Reikwijdte van Een Verwijdering van URL's Uit de Zoekresultaten (CO- A-2017-088)' (2017) Advies 75/2017 <https://www.privacycommission.be/sites/privacycommission/files/documents/advies_75_2017.pdf> accessed 17 April 2018

——, 'Frequently Asked Questions—Google Street View' <https://www.dataprotectionauthority.be/faq-themes/the-internet/google-street-view> accessed 20 October 2016

Bell E, 'Who Owns the News Consumer: Social Media Platforms or Publishers?' (Tow Center 2016) <https://www.cjr.org/tow_center/platforms_and_publishers_new_research_from_the_tow_center.php> accessed 22 May 2017

Belli L and Venturini J, 'Private Ordering and the Rise of Terms of Service as Cyber-Regulation' (2016) 5 Internet Policy Review <https://policyreview.info/articles/analysis/private-ordering-and-rise-terms-service-cyber-regulation> accessed 3 January 2017

Benedek W and Kettemann MC, *Freedom of Expression and the Internet* (Council of Europe 2013)

Bennett CJ, *Regulating Privacy: Data Protection and Public Policy in Europe and the United States* (Cornell University Press 1992)

Bennett SC, 'The Right to Be Forgotten: Reconciling EU and US Perspectives' (2012) 30 Berkeley J Int'l L 161

Bergkamp L, 'EU Data Protection Policy: The Privacy Fallacy: Adverse Effects of Europe's Data Protection Policy in an Information-Driven Economy' (2002) 18 Computer Law & Security Review 31

Berlin I and Hardy H, *Liberty: Incorporating Four Essays on Liberty* (OUP 2008)

Bernal P, 'Collaborative Consent: Harnessing the Strengths of the Internet for Consent in the Online Environment' (2010) 24 International Review of Law, Computers & Technology 287

——, *Internet Privacy Rights: Rights to Protect Autonomy* (CUP 2014)

Bernitz U, Groussot X, and Schulyok F (eds), *General Principles of EU Law and European Private Law* (Kluwer Law International 2013)

Bertram T and others, 'Three Years of the Right to Be Forgotten' (Google 2018) <https://drive.google.com/file/d/1H4MKNwf5MgeztG7OnJRnl3ym3gIT3HUK/view>.

Bignami F, 'The Case for Tolerant Constitutional Patriotism: The Right of Privacy before the European Courts' (2008) 41 Cornell International Law Journal 211

Bing J, 'Classification of Personal Information, with Respect to the Sensitivity Aspect', *The First International Oslo Symposium on Data Banks and Society, Presented by Klaus Lenk ea* (Universitetsførlaget 1972)

Binns R, 'How to Be Open about Being Closed' [2016] Limn <http://limn.it/how-to-be-open-about-being-closed/> accessed 14 May 2017

Binns R, 'Data Protection Impact Assessments: A Meta-Regulatory Approach' (2017) 7 International Data Privacy Law 22

——, 'Ideally We Want Architectures Where Its Easy for DS to Provide a Key to Reconnect, but Difficult for DC / Attacker to Do on Their Own. As @podehaye Goes on to Say in That Panel, Many DCs Haven't Grasped That DSs Could Provide Additional Info to Make Pseudonymous Data Identifiable' (*@RDBinns*, 13 February 2018) <https://twitter.com/RDBinns/status/963411691022311427> accessed 14 June 2018

——, 'Tweet' (*Twitter*, 2 May 2018) <https://twitter.com/RDBinns/status/991622955561046017> accessed 7 May 2018

——, 'Third Party Tracking in the Mobile Ecosystem' [2018] arXiv:1804.03603 [cs] <http://arxiv.org/abs/1804.03603> accessed 12 April 2018

Birnhack MD and Elkin-Koren N, 'The Invisible Handshake: The Reemergence of the State in the Digital Environment' (2003) 8 Virginia Journal of Law and Technology 57

Bishop M and others, 'Forgive and Forget: Return to Obscurity' (ACM Press 2013) <http://dl.acm.org/citation.cfm?doid=2535813.2535814> accessed 15 July 2014

Black E, *IBM and the Holocaust the Strategic Alliance between Nazi Germany and America's Most Powerful Corporation* (Crown Publishers 2001)

Blume P, 'The Inherent Contradictions in Data Protection Law' (2012) 2 International Data Privacy Law 26

——, 'Will It Be a Better World? The Proposed EU Data Protection Regulation' [2012] International Data Privacy Law <http://idpl.oxfordjournals.org/content/early/2012/04/14/idpl.ips007> accessed 18 April 2012

——, 'The Data Subject' (2015) 1 European Data Protection Law Review 258

Boehme-Neßler V, 'Privacy: A Matter of Democracy. Why Democracy Needs Privacy and Data Protection' (2016) 6 International Data Privacy Law 222

Bogard W, 'Welcome to the Society of Control: The Simulation of Surveillance Revisited' in Richard Victor Ericson and Kevin D Haggerty (eds), *The New Politics of Surveillance and Visibility* (University of Toronto Press 2006)

Boiten E, 'Not Transparent, Certainly Not Accountable: Google and the Right To Be Forgotten' (*Eerke Boiten's blog*, 13 October 2016) <https://blogs.kent.ac.uk/eerke/2016/10/13/not-transparent-certainly-not-accountable-google-and-the-right-to-be-forgotten/> accessed 17 October 2016

Boizard M, 'Le Droit A L'Oubli' (Faculté de droit et de science politique, Rennes 1 2015) IODE UMR CNRS 6262

——, 'Le Droit Au Respect de La Vie Privée, Un Instrument Effectif Du Droit à l'oubli?' (2015) 1 Montesquieu Law Review 8

Bok S, *Secrets: On the Ethics of Concealment and Revelation* (Pantheon Books 1982)

Bond RM and others, 'A 61-Million-Person Experiment in Social Influence and Political Mobilization' (2012) 489 Nature 295

Boniface C and others, 'Security Analysis of Subject Access Request Procedures How to Authenticate Data Subjects Safely When They Request for Their Data' (2019) <https://hal.inria.fr/hal-02072302/document> accessed 4 April 2019

Borgesius FJZ, 'Personal Data Processing for Behavioural Targeting: Which Legal Basis?' [2015] International Data Privacy Law ipv011

Bostoen F, 'Neutrality, Fairness or Freedom? Principles for Platform Regulation' (2018) 7 Internet Policy Review <https://policyreview.info/articles/analysis/neutrality-fairness-or-freedom-principles-platform-regulation> accessed 12 April 2018

Boulanger M and others, 'La Protection Des Données à Caractère Personnel En Droit Communautaire: Deuxième Partie' [1997] Journal des Tribunaux—Droit Européen 145

boyd danah and Crawford K, 'Critical Questions for Big Data: Provocations for a Cultural, Technological, and Scholarly Phenomenon' (2012) 15 Information, Communication & Society 662

Bracha O and Pasquale F, 'Federal Search Commission? Access, Fairness, and Accountability in the Law of Search' (2008) 93 Cornell Law Review 1149

Brandeis LD, *Other People's Money and How the Bankers Use It* (Stokes 1914)

Brandimart L, Acquisti A, and Loewenstein G, 'Misplaced Confidences: Privacy and the Control Paradox', *Privacy and Controversial Social Issues* (2010) <http://www.futureofprivacy.org/wp-content/uploads/2010/09/Misplaced-Confidences-acquisti-FPF.pdf> accessed 11 February 2012

Brandimarte L and Acquisti A, 'The Economics of Privacy' in Martin Peitz and Joel Waldfogel (eds), *The Oxford Handbook of the Digital Economy* (OUP 2012)

Brewster T, 'CIA Security Luminary: "Right to Be Forgotten Is Not Enough"' *The Guardian* (15 August 2014) <http://www.theguardian.com/technology/2014/aug/15/cia-security-dan-geer-right-to-be-forgotten> accessed 8 September 2014

Brin D, *The Transparent Society: Will Technology Force Us To Choose Between Privacy And Freedom?* (1st edn, Basic Books 1999)

Brkan M, 'Data Protection and European Private International Law: Observing a Bull in a China Shop' (2015) 5 International Data Privacy Law 257

——, 'The Concept of Essence of Fundamental Rights in the EU Legal Order: Peeling the Onion to Its Core' (2018) 14 European Constitutional Law Review 332

Brochot G and others, 'Study on Personal Data Stores, Commissioned by the European Commission (DG Connect)' (CUP 2015) Study <https://ec.europa.eu/digital-single-market/en/news/study-personal-data-stores-conducted-cambridge-university-judge-business-school> accessed 23 March 2017

Brown I, 'The Economics of Privacy, Data Protection and Surveillance' (2013) <http://papers.ssrn.com/abstract=2358392> accessed 9 May 2016

Brownsword R, 'Consent in Data Protection Law: Privacy, Fair Processing and Confidentiality' in Serge Gutwirth and others (eds), *Reinventing Data Protection?* (Springer Netherlands 2009) <http://link.springer.com/10.1007/978-1-4020-9498-9> accessed 16 January 2015

Brunton F and Nissenbaum H, *Obfuscation: A User's Guide for Privacy and Protest* (MIT Press 2015)

Büllesbach A, Poullet Y, and Prins C (eds), *Concise European IT Law* (Kluwer Law International 2006)

Burdick A, 'The A.I. "Gaydar" Study and the Real Dangers of Big Data' [2017] *The New Yorker* <https://www.newyorker.com/news/daily-comment/the-ai-gaydar-study-and-the-real-dangers-of-big-data> accessed 24 July 2018

Burkert H, 'Institutions of Data Protection-An Attempt at a Functional Explanation of European National Data Protection Laws' (1981) 3 Computer/LJ 167

——, 'Privacy-Data Protection: A German/European Perspective', *2nd Symposium of the Max Planck Project Group on the Law of Common Goods and the Computer Science and Telecommunications Board of the National Research Council* (1999) <http://www.coll.mpg.de/sites/www/files/text/burkert.pdf> accessed 20 October 2015

Bygrave L and Wiese Schartum D, 'Consent, Proportionality and Collective Power' in Serge Gutwirth and others (eds), *Reinventing Data Protection?* (Springer 2009) <http://link.springer.com/10.1007/978-1-4020-9498-9> accessed 16 January 2015

Bygrave LA, 'Data Protection Pursuant to the Right to Privacy in Human Rights Treaties' (1998) 6 International Journal of Law and Information Technology 247

Bygrave LA, *Data Protection Law: Approaching Its Rationale, Logic and Limits* (Kluwer law international 2002)

Cadwalladr C, '"I Made Steve Bannon's Psychological Warfare Tool": Meet the Data War Whistleblower' *The Guardian* (18 March 2018) <http://www.theguardian.com/news/2018/mar/17/data-war-whistleblower-christopher-wylie-faceook-nix-bannon-trump> accessed 29 March 2018

Cadwalladr C and Campbell D, 'Revealed: Facebook's Global Lobbying against Data Privacy Laws' *The Observer* (2 March 2019) <https://www.theguardian.com/technology/2019/mar/02/facebook-global-lobbying-campaign-against-data-privacy-laws-investment> accessed 5 March 2019

Calo R, 'Consumer Subject Review Boards: A Thought Experiment' (2013) 66 Stanford Law Review Online 6

——, 'Code, Nudge, or Notice?' (2014) 99 Iowa L Rev 773

——, 'Digital Market Manipulation' (2014) 82 Geo Wash L Rev 995

Calo R and Rosenblat A, 'The Taking Economy: Uber, Information, and Power' (2017) 117 Columbia Law Review 1623

'Cambridge Analytica's Board Suspends CEO Nix Amid Inquiry' *Bloomberg.com* (20 March 2018) <https://www.bloomberg.com/news/articles/2018-03-20/cambridge-analytica-s-board-suspends-ceo-nix-pending-inquiry> accessed 4 June 2018

Camenisch J, Fischer-Hübner, S and Rannenberg K (eds), *Privacy and Identity Management for Life* (Springer; Dordrecht 2011)

Cariolou L, 'The Developing Law of Privacy and the Limits to the Public Interest Defence: The Grand Chamber Judgment in Couderc and Hachette Filipacchi Associés v France' (2016) 8 Journal of Media Law 138

Carroll EC, 'Making News: Balancing Newsworthiness and Privacy in the Age of Algorithms' (Georgetown University Law Center 2016) <https://papers.ssrn.com/abstract=2877335> accessed 5 December 2016

Caspar J, 'The CJEU Google Spain Decision' (2015) 39 Datenschutz und Datensicherheit—DuD 589

Castells M, *Communication Power* (OUP 2009)

Castelluccia C, 'Behavioural Tracking on the Internet: A Technical Perspective' in Serge Gutwirth and others (eds), *European Data Protection: In Good Health?* (Springer 2012)

Cate FH, Cullen P, and Mayer-Schönberger V, 'Data Protection Principles for the 21st Century - Revising the 1980 OECD Guidelines' <https://www.repository.law.indiana.edu/facbooks/23>.

Cate FH and Mayer-Schönberger V, 'Notice and Consent in a World of Big Data' (2013) 3 International Data Privacy Law 67

Cave J and others, 'Data Protection Review: Impact on EU Innovation and Competitiveness (Study Drafted for European Parliament's Committee on Industry, Research and Energy)' (2012) IP/A/ITRE/ST/2011 17 <http://www.europarl.europa.eu/RegData/etudes/etudes/join/2012/492463/IPOL-ITRE_ET(2012)492463_EN.pdf> accessed 11 December 2017

Celeste E, 'Terms of Service and Bills of Rights: New Mechanisms of Constitutionalisation in the Social Media Environment?' (2018) 0 International Review of Law, Computers & Technology 1

Chambers C, 'Facebook Fiasco: Was Cornell University's Study of "Emotional Contagion" a Breach of Ethics?' *The Guardian* (1 July 2014) <http://www.theguardian.com/science/

head-quarters/2014/jul/01/facebook-cornell-study-emotional-contagion-ethics-breach> accessed 1 August 2017

Chandler JA, 'A Right to Reach an Audience: An Approach to Intermediary Bias on the Internet Reclaiming the First Amendment: Constitutional Theories of Media Reform' (2006) 35 Hofstra Law Review 1095

Cheney-Lippold J, *We Are Data: Algorithms and the Making of Our Digital Selves* (New York University Press 2017)

Chowdhry A, 'Uber: Users Are More Likely To Pay Surge Pricing If Their Phone Battery Is Low' (*Forbes*, 25 May 2016) <https://www.forbes.com/sites/amitchowdhry/2016/05/25/uber-low-battery/> accessed 20 April 2018

Christl W, 'How Companies Use Personal Data Against People' (Cracked Labs 2017) <http://crackedlabs.org/dl/CrackedLabs_Christl_DataAgainstPeople.pdf> accessed 12 October 2017

Chun WH-K, *Control and Freedom: Power and Paranoia in the Age of Fiber Optics* (MIT Press 2006)

Chung WJ, Patwa P, and Markov MM, 'Targeting Advertisements Based on Emotion (United States Patent Application: 0120143693)' <http://appft1.uspto.gov/netacgi/nph-Parser?Sect1=PTO1&Sect2=HITOFF&d=PG01&p=1&u=%2Fnetahtml%2FPTO%2Fsrchnum.html&r=1&f=G&l=50&s1=%2220120143693%22.PGNR.&OS=DN/20120143693&RS=DN/20120143693> accessed 15 July 2015

Citron DK and Pasquale F, 'The Scored Society: Due Process for Automated Predictions' (2014) 89 Washington Law Review 1

Clarke R, 'Information Technology and Dataveillance' (1988) 31 Communications of the ACM 498

Clifford D and Ausloos J, 'Data Protection and the Role of Fairness' (2018) 37 Yearbook of European Law 130

Clifford D, Graef I, and Valcke P, 'Pre-Formulated Declarations of Data Subject Consent—Citizen-Consumer Empowerment and the Alignment of Data, Consumer and Competition Law Protections' (KU Leuven 2018) CiTiP Working Paper 33/2017 <https://papers.ssrn.com/abstract=3126706> accessed 18 April 2018

Clifford D and Van Der Sype YS, 'Online Dispute Resolution: Settling Data Protection Disputes in a Digital World of Customers' [2015] Computer Law & Security Review <http://linkinghub.elsevier.com/retrieve/pii/S026736491500179X> accessed 8 March 2016

CNIL, 'CNIL Review of Google's New Privacy Policy: Incomplete Information and Uncontrolled Combination of Data across Services' (16 October 2012) <www.cnil.fr/english/news-and-events/news/article/googles-new-privacy-policy-incomplete-information-and-uncontrolled-combination-of-data-across-ser/> accessed 16 October 2012

——, 'Comment Permettre à l'homme de Garder La Main? Les Enjeux Éthiques Des Algorithmes et de l'intelligence Artificielle. Synthèse Du Débat Public Animé Par La CNIL Dans Le Cadre de La Mission de Réflexion Éthique Confiée Par La Loi Pour Une République Numérique' (2017) <www.cnil.fr/sites/default/files/atoms/files/cnil_rapport_garder_la_main_web.pdf> accessed 10 June 2018

Cohen J, 'What Privacy Is For' (2013) 126 Harvard Law Review 1904

Cohen JE, 'Examined Lives: Informational Privacy and the Subject as Object' (2000) 52 Stanford Law Review 1373

——, *Configuring the Networked Self: Law, Code, and the Play of Everyday Practice* (Yale University Press 2012)

——, 'The Biopolitical Public Domain: The Legal Construction of the Surveillance Economy' (2017) 31 Philosophy & Technology 213

Colburn B, *Autonomy and Liberalism* (Routledge, Taylor & Francis Group 2010)

Colin C and Poullet Y, 'Du Consommateur et de Sa Protection Face à de Nouvelles Applications Des Technologies de l'information: Risques et Opportunités' (2010) 2010/3 DCCR 94

Coll S, 'Power, Knowledge, and the Subjects of Privacy: Understanding Privacy as the Ally of Surveillance' (2014) 17 Information, Communication & Society 1250

College Bescherming Persoonsgegevens, 'Investigation into the Combining of Personal Data by Google—Report of Definitive Findings' (Dutch Data Protection Authority 2013) z2013-00194 <https://cbpweb.nl/sites/default/files/downloads/mijn_privacy/en_rap_2013-google-privacypolicy.pdf>.

Comité des Sages, *For a Europe of Civic and Social Rights* (Office for Official Publications of the European Communities 1996)

Commissie voor Bescherming van de Persoonlijke Levenssfeer, 'Aanbeveling uit eigen beweging met betrekking tot 1) Facebook, 2) de gebruikers van internet en/of Facebook alsook 3) de gebruikers en aanbieders van Facebook diensten, inzonderheid social plug-ins' (2015) Aanbeveling nr. 04/2015 <https://www.gegevensbeschermingsautoriteit.be/sites/privacycommission/files/documents/aanbeveling_04_2015.pdf> accessed 21 May 2015

Committee of Experts on Internet Intermediaries (MSI-NET), 'Draft Recommendation CM/Rec(2017)Xxx of the Committee of Ministers to Member States on the Roles and Responsibilities of Internet Intermediaries' <https://rm.coe.int/draft-recommendation-on-internet-intermediaries-7th-revised-version-/1680770c37> accessed 10 March 2018

Committee on Civil Liberties, Justice and Home Affairs (Rapporteur Albrecht JP), 'Draft Report on the Proposal for a Regulation of the European Parliament and of the Council on the Protection of Individual with Regard to the Processing of Personal Data and on the Free Movement of Such Data (General Data Protection Regulation)' (European Parliament (Committee on Civil Liberties, Justice and Home Affairs) 2012) 2012/0011(COD)

——, 'Draft Report on the Proposal for a Regulation of the European Parliament and of the Council on the Protection of Individual with Regard to the Processing of Personal Data and on the Free Movement of Such Data (General Data Protection Regulation). Amendments (4) 1189–1492' (European Parliament (Committee on Civil Liberties, Justice and Home Affairs) 2013) 2012/0011(COD)

——, 'Report on the Proposal for a Regulation of the European Parliament and of the Council on the Protection of Individuals with Regard to the Processing of Personal Data and on the Free Movement of Such Data (General Data Protection Regulation)' (European Parliament (Committee on Civil Liberties, Justice and Home Affairs) 2013) A7-0402/2013

Comparato G and Micklitz H-W, 'Regulated Autonomy between Market Freedoms and Fundamental Rights in the Case Law of the CJEU' in Ulf Bernitz, Xavier Groussot, and Felix Schulyok (eds), *General Principles of EU Law and European Private Law* (Kluwer Law International 2013)

Conseil de déontologie journalistique, 'Code de Déontologie Journalistique' (16 October 2013) <http://codededeontologiejournalistique.be/> accessed 17 November 2015

Corfield G, 'Info Commissioner Tears into Google's "Call Us Journalists" Trial Defence' (*The Register*, 8 March 2018) <https://www.theregister.co.uk/2018/03/08/ico_declares_war_google/> accessed 10 March 2018

Cornu G and Association Henri Capitant, *Vocabulaire juridique, Publié sous la dir. de Gérard Cornu* (PUF 1987)

Costa-Cabral F and Lynskey O, 'Family Ties: The Intersection between Data Protection and Competition in EU Law' (2017) 54 Common Market Law Review 11

Couldry N and Hepp A, *The Mediated Construction of Reality* (Polity Press 2017)

Council of Europe, 'Recommendation on the Protection of Individuals with Regard to Automatic Processing of Personal Data in the Context of Profiling CM/Rec(2010)13'

——, 'Modernisation of the Data Protection "Convention 108"' (May 2018) <https://www.coe.int/en/web/portal/28-january-data-protection-day-factsheet> accessed 22 June 2018

Council of Europe—Committee of Ministers, 'Resolution (73) 22 on the Protection of the Privacy of Individuals Vis-à-Vis Electronic Data Banks in the Private Sector' <https://rm.coe.int/CoERMPublicCommonSearchServices/DisplayDCTMContent?documentId=0900001680502830>.

——, 'Resolution (74) 29 on the Protection of the Privacy of Individuals Vis-a-Vis Electronic Data Banks in the Public Sector'

Council of Europe—Parliamentary Assembly, 'Recommendation 509 (1968)—Human Rights and Modern Scientific and Technological Developments'

Council of the European Union, 'Council Conclusions on the Communication from the Commission to the European Parliament and the Council—A Comprehensive Approach on Personal Data Protection in the European Union' <http://www.statewatch.org/news/2011/feb/eu-council-draft-conclusion-dp-17923-rev1-11.pdf> accessed 16 March 2018

——, 'Working Party on Information Exchange and Data Protection (DAPIX). Summary of Discussion on 23–24 February 2012'

——, 'Note to the Working Party on Information Exchange of Data Protection. Council Revised Version of the Proposal for a Regulation of the European Parliament and of the Council on the Protection of Individuals with Regard to the Processing of Personal Data and on the Free Movement of Such Data (General Data Protection Regulation)'

——, 'Presidency De-Briefing on the Outcome of the Data Protection Trilogue on 16/17 September 2015 and Preparation for Trilogue (Chapter III)' (2015) 12733/1/15 <http://www.statewatch.org/news/2015/oct/eu-council-dp-reg-Chap-III-12733-re01-15.pdf> accessed 13 October 2015

Council of the European Union—Working Group on Information Exchange and Data Protection (DAPIX), 'Note to the Working Group on Information Exchange and Data Protection (DAPIX) on the Proposal for a General Data Protection Regulation—the Right to Be Forgotten and the Google Judgment' (2014) 11289/14 <http://register.consilium.europa.eu/doc/srv?l=EN&f=ST%2011289%202014%20INIT>.

Craig PP and De Búrca G, *EU Law: Text, Cases, and Materials* (OUP 2011)

Crawford K, 'The Hidden Biases in Big Data' (*Harvard Business Review*, 1 April 2013) <http://blogs.hbr.org/2013/04/the-hidden-biases-in-big-data/> accessed 18 June 2014

Crawford K, Gray ML, and Miltner K, 'Critiquing Big Data: Politics, Ethics, Epistemology' (2014) 8 International Journal of Communication 10

Crawford K and Schultz J, 'Big Data and Due Process: Toward a Framework to Redress Predictive Privacy Harms' (2014) 55 Boston College Law Review 93

Crémer J, de Montjoye Y-A, and Schweitzer H, 'Competition Policy for the Digital Era' (European Commission 2019) <http://ec.europa.eu/competition/publications/reports/kd0419345enn.pdf> accessed 4 April 2019

'CryptoParty.' <https://www.cryptoparty.in/connect/resources> accessed 14 June 2018

Cuijpers C, Purtova N, and Kosta E, 'Data Protection Reform and the Internet: The Draft Data Protection Regulation' in Andrej Savin and Jan Trzaskowski (eds), *Research Handbook on EU Internet Law* (Edward Elgar Publishing 2014)

Cullen International, *A Business Guide to Changes in European Data Protection Legislation* (Kluwer Law International (IS), Kluwer Law International 1999)

Curren L and Kaye J, 'Revoking Consent: A "Blind Spot" in Data Protection Law?' (2010) 26 Computer Law & Security Review 273

Curtin D and Mendes J, 'Right of Access to Documents (Article 42)' in Steve Peers and others (eds), *The EU Charter of Fundamental Rights: A Commentary* (Hart 2014) <https://www.bloomsburycollections.com/book/the-eu-charter-of-fundamental-rights-a-commentary/>.

Custers B, 'Click Here to Consent Forever: Expiry Dates for Informed Consent' (2016) 3 Big Data & Society 1

—— (eds), *Discrimination and Privacy in the Information Society - Data Mining and Profiling in Large Databases* (1st edn, Springer Berlin Heidelberg 2013)

Custers B, van der Hof S, and Schermer B, 'Privacy Expectations of Social Media Users: The Role of Informed Consent in Privacy Policies' (2014) 6 Policy & Internet 268

Dalenius T, Klevmarken A, and Statens råd för samhällsforskning (Sweden) (eds), *Proceedings of a Symposium on Personal Integrity and the Need for Data in the Social Sciences, Held at Hässelby Slott, Stockholm March 15–17, 1976 and Sponsored by the Swedish Council for Social Science Research* (Swedish Council for Social Science Research [Statens råd för samhällsforskning]: [Humanistisk-samhällsvetenskapliga forskningsrådet, distr 1976)

Daly A, *Private Power, Online Information Flows and EU Law: Mind the Gap* (Hart 2016)

Danezis G and others, 'Privacy and Data Protection by Design—from Policy to Engineering' (ENISA 2014)

Data Justice Conference: Keynote Plenary I <https://cardiff.cloud.panopto.eu/Panopto/Pages/Viewer.aspx?id=547383b2-9d0a-4966-a4aa-a8e50178e2cf> accessed 16 June 2018

Davidow B, 'Exploiting the Neuroscience of Internet Addiction' [2012] *The Atlantic* <https://www.theatlantic.com/health/archive/2012/07/exploiting-the-neuroscience-of-internet-addiction/259820/> accessed 17 June 2018

Davis RM, 'Technologist's View of Privacy and Security in Automated Information Systems, A' (1974) 4 Rutgers J Computers & L 264

De Been W, Arora P, and Hildebrandt M (eds), *Crossroads in New Media, Identity, and Law: The Shape of Diversity to Come* (Palgrave Macmillan 2015)

De Bot D, *Gegevensverwerking in de publieke sector: een verkennend onderzoek van de relatie tussen privacy-, gegevensbeschermings-, administratief en grondwettelijk recht aan de hand van de uitwisseling van gegevens tussen besturen* (Politieia 2015)

De Hert P, 'Consumer Protection and Personal Data Protection' (Data Protection Conference (organised by the European commission as part of its open consultation), 20 May 2009) <http://ec.europa.eu/justice/newsroom/data-protection/events/090519_en.htm>.

De Hert P and Gutwirth S, 'Data Protection in the Case Law of Strasbourg and Luxembur g: Constitutionalisation in Action' in Serge Gutwirth and others (eds), *Reinventing Data Protection?* (Springer Science 2009)

De Hert P and Papakonstantinou V, 'The Proposed Data Protection Regulation Replacing Directive 95/46/EC: A Sound System for the Protection of Individuals' (2012) 28 Computer Law & Security Review 130

de Montjoye Y-A and others, 'Unique in the Crowd: The Privacy Bounds of Human Mobility' (2013) 3 Scientific Reports <http://www.nature.com/srep/2013/130325/srep01376/full/srep01376.html> accessed 2 April 2013

De Schutter O and Tulkens F, 'Rights in Conflict: The European Court of Human Rights as a Pragmatic Institution' (Université Catholique de Louvain 2007) Working Paper

de Terwangne C, *The Right to Be Forgotten and the Informational Autonomy in the Digital Environment* (Publications Office 2013) <http://dx.publications.europa.eu/10.2788/54562> accessed 11 November 2015

Defreyne E, 'Le droit à l'oubli et les archives journalistiques' (2013) 2013 Revue Du Droit Des Technologies De L'Information 75

Dehaye P-O, 'Written Evidence to House of Commons DMCS Committee' (March 2018) <http://data.parliament.uk/writtenevidence/committeeevidence.svc/evidencedocument/digital-culture-media-and-sport-committee/fake-news/written/80117.html#_ftn3> accessed 29 March 2018

Dencik L, Hintz A, and Cable J, 'Towards Data Justice? The Ambiguity of Anti-Surveillance Resistance in Political Activism' (2016) 3 Big Data & Society <http://journals.sagepub.com/doi/abs/10.1177/2053951716679678> accessed 2 January 2017

Dewitte P, 'GDPR and HCI, a Perfect Match? A Data Protection Lawyer's Perspective on CHI 2018' (*CITIP blog*, 12 June 2018) <https://www.law.kuleuven.be/citip/blog/gdpr-and-hci-a-perfect-match-a-data-protection-lawyers-perspective-on-chi-2018/> accessed 17 June 2018

DG Justice, 'Summary of Replies to the Public Consultation about the Future Legal Framework for Protecting Personal Data' (European Commission 2010)

Di Iorio CT and Carinci F, 'Privacy and Health Care Information Systems: Where Is the Balance?' in Carlisle George, Diane Whitehouse, and Penny Duquenoy (eds), *eHealth: Legal, Ethical and Governance Challenges* (Springer 2012)

Diakopoulos N, 'Algorithmic Accountability Reporting: On the Investigation of Black Boxes' <http://towcenter.org/wp-content/uploads/2014/02/78524_Tow-Center-Report-WEB-1.pdf>

Diaz C, Tene O, and Gurses S, 'Hero or Villain: The Data Controller in Privacy Law and Technologies.(The Second Wave of Global Privacy Protection)' (2013) 74 Ohio State Law Journal 923

Digital, Culture, Media and Sport Committee, 'Disinformation and "Fake News": Interim Report' (House of Commons 2018) 5

——, 'Disinformation and "Fake News": Final Report' (House of Commons 2019) 8

Directorate General Human Rights and Rule of Law, 'Case Law of the European Court of Human Rights Concerning the Protection of Personal Data' (Council of Europe 2018) T-PD(2018)15 <https://rm.coe.int/t-pd-2018-15-case-law-on-data-protection-may2018-en/16808b2d36> accessed 13 June 2018

Directorate General of Human Rights and Rule of Law, 'Guidelines on the Protection of Individuals with Regard to the Processing of Personal Data in a World of Big Data' (Council of Europe 2017) T-PD(2017)01

DLA Piper, 'Data Protection Laws of the World' <https://www.dlapiperdataprotection.com/index.html?t=world-map> accessed 12 June 2019

Docksey C, 'Articles 7 and 8 of the EU Charter: two distinct fundamental rights' in Alain Grosjean (ed), *Enjeux européens et mondiaux de la protection des données personnelles: Ouvrage de synthèse* (Primento Digital Publishing 2016)

——, 'Four Fundamental Rights: Finding the Balance' (2016) 6 International Data Privacy Law 195

Doctorow C, 'NYC Will Cease Retaining Data That Trump Could Use for Mass Deportations' (*Boing Boing*, 8 December 2016) <https://boingboing.net/2016/12/08/nyc-will-cease-retaining-data.html> accessed 9 December 2016

Döhmann IS genannt and others, 'The Regulation of Commercial Profiling—A Comparative Analysis' (2016) 2 European Data Protection Law Review 535

Dowty T and Korff D, 'Protecting the Virtual Child—The Law and Children's Consent to Sharing Personal Data' (ARCH 2009) <nuffieldfoundation.org/sites/default/files/Protecting%20the%20virtual%20child.pdf> accessed 7 February 2013

dpa, 'Google Street View: Bilder Aus "Blurmany"' *Die Zeit* (Hamburg, 18 November 2010) <http://www.zeit.de/digital/internet/2010-11/start-google-street-view> accessed 20 October 2016

Druschel P, Backes M, and Tirtea R, 'The Right to Be Forgotten—Between Expectations and Practice' (ENISA 2012) <https://www.enisa.europa.eu/activities/identity-and-trust/library/deliverables/the-right-to-be-forgotten/> accessed 21 November 2012

Dumortier J and others, 'EPrivacy Directive: Assessment of Transposition, Effectiveness and Compatibility with Proposed Data Protection Regulation' (European Commission DG Communications Networks, Content & Technology 2015) Study SMART 2013/0071 <https://ec.europa.eu/digital-agenda/en/news/eprivacy-directive-assessment-transposition-effectiveness-and-compatibility-proposed-data>.

Duportail J, 'I Asked Tinder for My Data. It Sent Me 800 Pages of My Deepest, Darkest Secrets' *The Guardian* (26 September 2017) <http://www.theguardian.com/technology/2017/sep/26/tinder-personal-data-dating-app-messages-hacked-sold> accessed 26 September 2017

Dworkin G, *The Theory and Practice of Autonomy* (CUP 1988)

Dwoskin E, 'What's Driving Silicon Valley to Become "Radicalized"' *Washington Post* (24 May 2016) <https://www.washingtonpost.com/news/the-switch/wp/2016/05/24/what-is-driving-silicon-valley-to-become-radicalized/> accessed 26 May 2016

EDRi, 'Italian Supreme Court: Google's Youtube Is Just a Hosting Provider' (*EDRi*, 12 February 2014) <http://edri.org/italian-supreme-court-search-engines-just-hosting-providers/> accessed 13 February 2014

Edwards L, 'Reconstructing Consumer Privacy Protection On-line: A Modest Proposal' (2004) 18 International Review of Law, Computers & Technology 313

——, 'Keynote Address on the Right to Be Forgotten' (Bileta, Hertfordshire, UK, 12 April 2016)

Edwards L and Harbina E, 'Protecting Post-Mortem Privacy: Reconsidering the Privacy Interests of the Deceased in a Digital World' (2013) 32 Cardozo Arts & Entertainment Law Journal 83

Edwards L and Veale M, 'Slave to the Algorithm: Why a Right to an Explanation Is Probably Not the Remedy You Are Looking For' (2017) 16 Duke Law & Technology Review 18

Eliantonio M, Galli F, and Schaper M, 'A Balanced Data Protection in the EU: Conflicts and Possible Solutions' (2016) 23 Maastricht Journal of European and Comparative Law (MJ) 391

Elsden C and others, 'Fitter, Happier, More Productive: What to Ask of a Data-Driven Life' (2016) 23 interactions 45

Elsden C, Kirk DS, and Durrant AC, 'A Quantified Past: Toward Design for Remembering With Personal Informatics' (2016) 31 Human–Computer Interaction 518

Englehardt S, 'No Boundaries: Exfiltration of Personal Data by Session-Replay Scripts' (*Freedom to Tinker*, 15 November 2017) <https://freedom-to-tinker.com/2017/11/15/

no-boundaries-exfiltration-of-personal-data-by-session-replay-scripts/> accessed 1 December 2017

ENISA, 'Privacy Enhancing Technologies: Evolution and State of the Art' (2016) <https://www.enisa.europa.eu/publications/pets-evolution-and-state-of-the-art>.

Erdos D, 'Confused? Analysing the Scope of Freedom of Speech Protection Vis-à-Vis European Data Protection' (OUP) 48/2012 <http://papers.ssrn.com/abstract=2119187> accessed 4 April 2013

——, 'Filling Defamation's "Gaps": Data Protection and the Right to Reputation' (OUP) 69/2013 <http://papers.ssrn.com/abstract=2283284> accessed 17 January 2014

——, 'From the Scylla of Restriction to the Charybdis of Licence? Exploring the Scope of the "Special Purposes" Freedom of Expression Shield in European Data Protection' (2015) 52 Common Market Law Review 119

——, 'European Union Data Protection Law and Media Expression: Fundamentally Off Balance' (2016) 65 International and Comparative Law Quarterly 139

——, 'Statutory Regulation of Professional Journalism under European Data Protection: Down but Not Out?' (2016) 0 Journal of Media Law 229

——, 'Communicating Responsibilities: The Spanish DPA Targets Google's Notification Practices When Delisting Personal Information' (*Inforrm's Blog*, 21 March 2017) <https://inforrm.wordpress.com/2017/03/21/communicating-responsibilities-the-spanish-dpa-targets-googles-notification-practices-when-delisting-personal-information-david-erdos/> accessed 22 March 2017

——, 'Delimiting the Ambit of Responsibility of Intermediary Publishers for Third Party Rights in European Data Protection: Towards a Synthetic Interpretation of the EU Acquis' (University of Cambridge, Faculty of Law 2017) Legal Studies Research Paper 31/2017 <https://papers.ssrn.com/abstract=2993154> accessed 12 October 2017

——, 'Beyond "Having a Domestic"'? Regulatory Interpretation of European Data Protection Law and Individual Publication' Computer Law & Security Review <http://www.sciencedirect.com/science/article/pii/S0267364917300730> accessed 16 May 2017

Espeland WN and Stevens ML, 'A Sociology of Quantification' (2008) 49 European Journal of Sociology 401

Eubanks V, *Automating Inequality: How High-Tech Tools Profile, Police, and Punish the Poor* (St Martin's Press 2018)

European Commission, 'Green Paper on Services of General Interest' (2003) COM(2003) 270 final <http://eur-lex.europa.eu/legal-content/EN/TXT/PDF/?uri=CELEX:52003DC0270&from=EN> accessed 15 December 2016

——, 'Communication from the Commission to the European Parliament, the Council, the European Economic and Social Committee and the Committee of the Regions A Comprehensive Approach on Personal Data Protection in the European Union' (2010) COM(2010)609 final

——, 'Special Eurobarometer 359: Attitudes on Data Protection and Electronic Identity in the European Union' (European Commission 2011) <http://ec.europa.eu/public_opinion/archives/ebs/ebs_359_en.pdf>

——, 'Leaked Proposal for a General Data Protection Regulation'

——, 'Commission Staff Working Paper: Impact Assessment Accompanying the Proposals for General Data Protection Regulation and Directive on Data Protection in Police and Judicial Matters' (European Commission 2012) Commission Staff working Paper SEC(2012) 72 final

——, 'Communication from the Commission to the European Parliament, the Council, the European Economic and Social Committee and the Committee of the Regions

Safeguarding Privacy in a Connected World. A European Data Protection Framework for the 21st Century'
——, 'Press Release: Commission Proposes a Comprehensive Reform of Data Protection Rules to Increase Users' Control of Their Data and to Cut Costs for Businesses' <http://europa.eu/rapid/press-release_IP-12-46_en.htm?locale=en> accessed 11 January 2016
——, 'Proposal for a Regulation of the European Parliament and of The Council on the Protection of Individuals with Regard to the Processing of Personal Data and on the Free Movement of Such Data (General Data Protection Regulation)'
——, 'Green Paper: Preparing for a Fully Converged Audiovisual World: Growth, Creation and Values' (2013) COM(2013) 231 final <https://ec.europa.eu/digital-single-market/sites/digital-agenda/files/convergence_green_paper_en_0.pdf> accessed 2 May 2016
——, 'Special Eurobarometer: Data Protection' (European Commission 2015) 431
——, 'Data Protection Eurobarometer out Today' (*Data Protection Newsroom*, 24 June 2015) <https://web.archive.org/web/20150702003030/http://ec.europa.eu/justice/newsroom/data-protection/news/240615_en.htm> accessed 25 June 2015
——, 'Building a European Data Economy' (10 January 2017) <https://ec.europa.eu/digital-single-market/en/policies/building-european-data-economy> accessed 28 April 2018
——, 'Ex-Post REFIT Evaluation of the EPrivacy Directive 2002/58/EC Accompanying the Proposal for a Regulation of the European Parliament and the Council on the Protection of Privacy and Confidentiality in Relation to Electronic Communications and Repealing Directive 2002/58/EC (Regulation on Privacy and Electronic Communications)' (European Commission 2017) Commission Staff working document
——, 'Communication on Tackling Illegal Content Online—Towards an Enhanced Responsibility of Online Platforms' (2017) COM(2017) 555 final
——, 'Communication. A New Deal for Consumers' (2018) COM(2018) 183 final <https://eur-lex.europa.eu/legal-content/EN/TXT/?qid=1523866913149&uri=COM:2018:183:FIN> accessed 11 June 2018
——, 'Communication. Artificial Intelligence for Europe' (2018) COM(2018) 237 final <https://ec.europa.eu/digital-single-market/en/news/communication-artificial-intelligence-europe>.
——, 'Special Eurobarometer: The General Data Protection Regulation' (2019) 487a
——, 'Impact Assessment (Explanation)' <http://ec.europa.eu/smart-regulation/impact/index_en.htm> accessed 12 January 2016
European Court of Human Rights—Press Unit, 'Factsheet—Mass Surveillance' (European Court of Human Rights 2016) <http://www.echr.coe.int/Documents/FS_Mass_surveillance_ENG.pdf> accessed 30 May 2017
——, 'Factsheet on Hate Speech' (2017) <www.echr.coe.int/Documents/FS_Hate_speech_ENG.pdf> accessed 4 May 2017
——, 'Factsheet on New Technologies' (2017) <http://www.echr.coe.int/Documents/FS_New_technologies_ENG.pdf> accessed 23 May 2017
European Court of Human Rights—Research Division, 'Internet: Case-Law of the European Court of Human Rights' (European Court of Human Rights 2011) <www.echr.coe.int/Documents/Research_report_internet_ENG.pdf> accessed 23 December 2014
European Data Protection Board, 'Work Program 2019-2020' <https://edpb.europa.eu/sites/edpb/files/files/file1/edpb-2019-02-12plen-2.1edpb_work_program_en.pdf> accessed 14 February 2019
——, 'Opinion 5/2019 on the Interplay between the EPrivacy Directive and the GDPR, in Particular Regarding the Competence, Tasks and Powers of Data Protection Authorities'

(EDPB 2019) Opinion 5/2019 <https://edpb.europa.eu/sites/edpb/files/files/file1/201905_edpb_opinion_eprivacydir_gdpr_interplay_en_0.pdf> accessed 22 March 2019

——, 'Draft Guidelines 2/2019 on the Processing of Personal Data under Article 6(1)(b) GDPR in the Context of the Provision of Online Services to Data Subject' (EDPB 2019) <https://edpb.europa.eu/sites/edpb/files/consultation/edpb_draft_guidelines-art_6-1-b-final_public_consultation_version_en.pdf> accessed 19 April 2019

European Data Protection Supervisor, 'Public Access to Documents Containing Personal Data after the Bavarian Lager Ruling' (EDPS 2011) <https://edps.europa.eu/data-protection/our-work/publications/papers/public-access-documents-and-data-protection_en> accessed 23 May 2017

——, 'Opinion of the European Data Protection Supervisor (EDPS) on the Data Protection Reform Package' <www.edps.europa.eu/EDPSWEB/webdav/site/mySite/shared/Documents/Consultation/Opinions/2012/12-03-07_EDPS_Reform_package_EN.pdf> accessed 16 September 2012

——, 'Opinion of the EDPS on the Communication from the Commission—"European Strategy for a Better Internet for Children"' (2012) <edps.europa.eu/EDPSWEB/webdav/site/mySite/shared/Documents/Consultation/Opinions/2012/12-07-17_Better_Iternet_Children_EN.pdf> accessed 14 February 2013

——, 'Meeting the Challenges of Big Data - A Call for Transparency, User Control, Data Protection by Design and Accountability' (EDPS 2015) Opinion 7/2015 <https://edps.europa.eu/sites/edp/files/publication/15-11-19_big_data_en.pdf> accessed 28 March 2017

——, 'Case Law Overview 1 December 2014—31 December 2015' (EDPS 2016) Working document <https://secure.edps.europa.eu/EDPSWEB/webdav/site/mySite/shared/Documents/EDPS/MembersMission/Members/Documents/16-03-15_Case_Law_Overview_2015_EN.pdf> accessed 15 March 2016

——, 'Developing a "Toolkit" for Assessing the Necessity of Measures That Interfere with Fundamental Rights. Background Paper' <https://secure.edps.europa.eu/EDPSWEB/webdav/site/mySite/shared/Documents/Consultation/Papers/16-06-16_Necessity_paper_for_consultation_EN.pdf> accessed 5 February 2017

——, 'Preliminary EDPS Opinion on the Review of the EPrivacy Directive (2002/58/EC)' (EDPS 2016) Opinion 5/2016 <https://edps.europa.eu/sites/edp/files/publication/16-07-22_opinion_eprivacy_en.pdf> accessed 11 April 2017

——, 'Opinion on Coherent Enforcement of Fundamental Rights in the Age of Big Data' (EDPS 2016) Opinion 8/2016 <https://secure.edps.europa.eu/EDPSWEB/webdav/site/mySite/shared/Documents/EDPS/Events/16-09-23_BigData_opinion_EN.pdf> accessed 25 October 2016

——, 'EDPS Opinion on Personal Information Management Systems' (EDPS 2016) Opinion 9/2016

——, 'Opinion on the Proposal for a Directive on Certain Aspects Concerning Contracts for the Supply of Digital Content' (EDPS 2017) Opinion 4/2017 <https://edps.europa.eu/sites/edp/files/publication/17-03-14_opinion_digital_content_en_0.pdf> accessed 11 April 2017

——, 'Assessing the Necessity of Measures That Limit the Fundamental Right to the Protection of Personal Data: A Toolkit' (EDPS 2017) <https://edps.europa.eu/sites/edp/files/publication/17-04-11_necessity_toolkit_en_0.pdf> accessed 16 April 2017

——, 'Opinion on Online Manipulation and Personal Data' (EDPS 2018) Opinion 03/2018 <https://edps.europa.eu/sites/edp/files/publication/18-03-19_online_manipulation_en.pdf> accessed 5 April 2018

European Group on Ethics in Science and New Technologies, 'Citizens Rights and New Technologies: A European Challenge. Report on the Charter on Fundamental Rights Related to Technological Innovation as Requested by President Prodi (Reproduced in: Draft Charter of Fundamental Rights of the European Union, CHARTE 4370/00)' (European Commission 2000) CONTRIB 233

——, 'Ethics of Security and Surveillance Technologies' (European Commission 2014) Opinion 28

European Parliament, Council and Commission, 'Explanations Relating to the Charter of Fundamental Rights (2007/C 303/02)' <http://eur-lex.europa.eu> accessed 15 April 2014

European Union Agency for Fundamental Rights (FRA)), 'Opinion on the Proposed Data Protection Reform Package' (2012) FRA Opinion 2/2012

European Union Agency for Fundamental Rights (FRA), 'Surveillance by Intelligence Services: Fundamental Rights Safeguards and Remedies in the EU. Volume I: Member States' Legal Frameworks' (Fundamental Rights Agency 2015) <http://fra.europa.eu/en/publication/2015/surveillance-intelligence-services>.

——, 'Surveillance by Intelligence Services: Fundamental Rights Safeguards and Remedies in the EU Volume II: Field Perspectives and Legal Update' (2017) <http://fra.europa.eu/en/publication/2017/surveillance-intelligence-socio-lega>.

European Union Agency for Fundamental Rights (FRA) and Council of Europe, *Handbook on European Non-Discrimination Law* (First, Publications Office of the Euroepan Union 2011)

——, *Handbook on European Data Protection Law* (1st edn, Publications Office of the European Union 2018) <http://www.coe.int/t/dghl/standardsetting/dataprotection/TPD_documents/Handbook.pdf>.

Everson M and Rui Correia G, 'Freedom to Conduct a Business' in Steve Peers and others (eds), *The EU Charter of Fundamental Rights: A Commentary* (Hart 2014) <https://www.bloomsburycollections.com/book/the-eu-charter-of-fundamental-rights-a-commentary/>.

Executive Office of the President, 'White House Report on Big Data and Differential Pricing' (2015) <https://obamawhitehouse.archives.gov/sites/default/files/whitehouse_files/docs/Big_Data_Report_Nonembargo_v2.pdf>.

Ezrachi A, *Virtual Competition: The Promise and Perils of the Algorithm-Driven Economy* (Harvard University Press 2017) <https://doi.org/10.4159/9780674973336> accessed 22 February 2018

Facebook Support to Jef Ausloos, 'Data Policy Questions #1789301 39475103' (15 June 2018)

Federal Trade Commission, 'Facing Facts—Best Practices for Common Uses of Facial Recognition Technologies' (Federal Trade Commission 2012) <http://www.ftc.gov/os/2012/10/121022facialtechrpt.pdf>.

——, 'Internet of Things—Privacy & Security in a Connected World' (Federal Trade Commission 2015) FTC Staff Report <www.ftc.gov/system/files/documents/reports/federal-trade-commission-staff-report-november-2013-workshop-entitled-internet-things-privacy/150127iotrpt.pdf>.

Felten EW, 'On Encryption, Archiving, and Accountability' (*Freedom to Tinker*, 7 July 2017) <http://freedom-to-tinker.com/2017/07/07/on-encryption-archiving-and-accountability/> accessed 7 July 2017

Ferraris V, Bosco F, and D'Angelo E, 'The Impact of Profiling on Fundamental Rights' (2013) <http://profiling-project.eu/wp-content/uploads/2013/10/PROFILINGproject_WS1_Fundamental_1110.pdf>.

Ferretti F, 'Data Protection and the Legitimate Interest of Data Controllers: Much Ado about Nothing or the Winter of Rights?' (2014) 51 Common Market Law Review 843

Finck M, 'Blockchains and Data Protection in the European Union' (2018) 4 European Data Protection Law Review 17

——, 'Tweet' (*@finck_m*, 13 February 2019) <https://twitter.com/finck_m/status/1095593826436202496?s=11> accessed 14 February 2019

Finocchiaro G and Ricci A, 'Quality of Information, the Right to Oblivion and Digital Reputation' in Bart Custers and others (eds), *Discrimination and Privacy in the Information Society—Data Mining and Profiling in Large Databases* (1st edn, Springer 2013)

Fischer-Hübner S and others, 'Online Privacy: Towards Informational Self-Determination on the Internet' in M Hildebrandt and others (eds), *Digital Enlightenment Yearbook 2013: The Value of Personal Data*, vol 1 (IOS Press 2013) <http://ssrn.com/abstract=2468200> accessed 13 July 2015

Flaherty DH, *Protecting Privacy in Surveillance Societies: The Federal Republic of Germany, Sweden, France, Canada, and the United States* (University of North Carolina Press 1989)

Fleischer P, 'Peter Fleischer: Privacy... ?: The Right to Be Forgotten, or How to Edit Your History' (*Peter Fleischer*, 29 January 2012) <http://peterfleischer.blogspot.com/2012/01/right-to-be-forgotten-or-how-to-edit.html> accessed 23 June 2018

Floridi L, *Information: A Very Short Introduction* (OUP 2010)

Flyverbom M, Deibert R, and Matten D, 'The Governance of Digital Technology, Big Data, and the Internet: New Roles and Responsibilities for Business' [2017] Business & Society

Forbruker Rådet, 'Deceived By Design. How Tech Companies Use Dark Patterns to Discourage Us from Exercising Our Rights to Privacy' (2018) <https://fil.forbrukerradet.no/wp-content/uploads/2018/06/2018-06-27-deceived-by-design-final.pdf> accessed 28 June 2018

Foucault M, *Surveiller et punir: naissance de la prison* (Gallimard 2004)

Frantziou E, 'The Horizontal Effect of the Charter of Fundamental Rights of the EU: Rediscovering the Reasons for Horizontality' (2015) 21 European Law Journal 657

Fraser N, 'Foucault on Modern Power: Empirical Insights and Normative Confusions' in Stuart Henry (ed), *Social Control: Aspects of Non-state Justice* (Aldershot Dartmouth 1994)

Freed R, 'The Tech Industry's Psychological War on Kids' (*Richard Freed*, 12 March 2018) <https://medium.com/@richardnfreed/the-tech-industrys-psychological-war-on-kids-c452870464ce> accessed 20 April 2018

Froomkin AM, 'Towards Identity Bankruptcy.' (CPDP (Senior Academic Session), January 2017) <https://www.youtube.com/watch?v=N_t18gL7i3E> accessed 16 May 2018

Frosio G, 'The Death of "No Monitoring Obligations": A Story of Untameable Monsters' (2017) <https://papers.ssrn.com/abstract=2980786> accessed 10 February 2018

——, 'Why Keep a Dog and Bark Yourself? From Intermediary Liability to Responsibility' (2017) <https://papers.ssrn.com/abstract=3053995> accessed 10 February 2018

Fuchs C, *Social Media: A Critical Introduction* (Sage 2014)

—— (eds), *Internet and Surveillance: The Challenges of Web 2.0 and Social Media.* (Routledge 2012)

Fuster GG and Gellert R, 'The Fundamental Right of Data Protection in the European Union: In Search of an Uncharted Right' (2012) 26 International Review of Law, Computers & Technology 73

Galetta A, Fonio C, and Ceresa A, 'Nothing Is as It Seems. The Exercise of Access Rights in Italy and Belgium: Dispelling Fallacies in the Legal Reasoning from the "Law in Theory" to the "Law in Practice"' (2015) 6 International Data Privacy Law 16

Gamino Garcia A and others, 'Mass Surveillance: Part 1—Risks and Opportunities Raised by the Current Generation of Network Services and Applications' (European Parliament Research Service 2014) Science and Technology Options Assessment (STOA) IP/G/STOA/FWC-2013-1/LOT 9/C5/SC1 <http://www.europarl.europa.eu/stoa/webdav/site/cms/shared/0_home/STOA%20Study%20Mass%20Surveillance%20Part%201.pdf> accessed 15 January 2015

Gandy Jr OH and Nemorin S, 'Toward a Political Economy of Nudge: Smart City Variations' [2018] Information, Communication & Society <https://doi.org/10.1080/1369118X.2018.1477969> accessed 30 May 2018

Gandy OH, 'Toward a Political Economy of Personal Information' (1993) 10 Critical Studies in Mass Communication 70

——, *The Panoptic Sort: A Political Economy of Personal Information* (Westview 1993)

——, 'Data Mining, Surveillance, and Discrimination in the Post-9/11 Environment' in Richard Victor Ericson and Kevin D Haggerty (eds), *The New Politics of Surveillance and Visibility* (University of Toronto Press 2006)

——, 'Engaging Rational Discrimination: Exploring Reasons for Placing Regulatory Constraints on Decision Support Systems' (2010) 12 Ethics and Information Technology 29

Garcia FJ, 'Bodil Lindqvist: A Swedish Churchgoer's Violation of the European Union's Data Protection Directive Should Be a Warning to U.S. Legislators' (2005) 15 Fordham Intell Prop Media & Ent LJ 1205

Ge Y and others, 'Racial and Gender Discrimination in Transportation Network Companies' (National Bureau of Economic Research 2016)

Gellert R, 'We Have Always Managed Risks in Data Protection Law': (2016) 2 European Data Protection Law Review 481

——, 'Discussion—On Risk, Balancing, and Data Protection: A Response to van Der Sloot' (2017) 3 European Data Protection Law Review 180

——, 'A Comparative Analysis of Anti-Discrimination and Data Protection Legislations' in Bart Custers and others (eds), *Discrimination and Privacy in the Information Society—Data Mining and Profiling in Large Databases* (Springer 2013)

Gellert R and Gutwirth S, 'The Legal Construction of Privacy and Data Protection' (2013) 29 Computer Law & Security Review 522

Gelman A, Mattson G, and Simpson D, 'Gaydar and the Fallacy of Decontextualized Measurement' (2018) 5 Sociological Science 270

Gerlitz C and Helmond A, 'The Like Economy: Social Buttons and the Data-Intensive Web' (2013) 15 New Media & Society 1348

Ghezzi A, Guimarães Pereira Â and Lucia V-A (eds), *The Ethics of Memory in a Digital Age* (Palgrave Macmillan 2014) <http://www.palgrave.com/gp/book/9781137428448> accessed 3 August 2017

Gibbs S, 'Facebook "Tracks All Visitors, Breaching EU Law"' *The Guardian* (31 March 2015) <https://www.theguardian.com/technology/2015/mar/31/facebook-tracks-all-visitors-breaching-eu-law-report> accessed 15 December 2016

Gillespie T, 'Facebook Can't Moderate in Secret Any More.' (*Data & Society: Points*, 24 May 2017) <https://points.datasociety.net/facebook-cant-moderate-in-secret-any-more-ca2dbcd9d2> accessed 28 May 2017

Ginsberg J and others, 'Detecting Influenza Epidemics Using Search Engine Query Data' (2009) 457 Nature 1012

Gitelman L, *'Raw Data' Is an Oxymoron* (MIT Press 2013)

Gitelman L and Jackson V, 'Introduction' in Lisa Gitelman, *'Raw Data' Is an Oxymoron* (2013)

González Fuster G, 'How Uninformed Is the Average Data Subject? A Quest for Benchmarks in EU Personal Data Protection' [2014] IDP. Revista de Internet, Derecho y Política

——, *The Emergence of Personal Data Protection as a Fundamental Right of the EU* (Springer 2014)

——, 'Curtailing a Right in Flux: Restrictions of the Right to Personal Data Protection' in Artemi Rallo Lombarte and Rosario García Mahamut (eds), *Hacia un nuevo derecho europeo de protección de datos = Towards A New European Data Protection Regime* (Tirant lo Blanch 2015)

——, 'Beyond the GDPR, above the GDPR' (*Internet Policy Review*, 30 November 2015) <http://policyreview.info/articles/news/beyond-gdpr-above-gdpr/385> accessed 7 December 2015

González Fuster G and Hijmans H, 'The EU Rights to Privacy and Personal Data Protection: 20 Years in 10 Questions' <https://brusselsprivacyhub.eu/events/20190513.Working_Paper_González_Fuster_Hijmans.pdf>.

Goodin D, 'Beware of Ads That Use Inaudible Sound to Link Your Phone, TV, Tablet, and PC' (*Ars Technica*, 13 November 2015) <http://arstechnica.com/tech-policy/2015/11/beware-of-ads-that-use-inaudible-sound-to-link-your-phone-tv-tablet-and-pc/> accessed 15 November 2015

Goodman B and Flaxman S, 'EU Regulations on Algorithmic Decision-Making and a "Right to Explanation"' (2016) <http://arxiv.org/pdf/1606.08813v1.pdf> accessed 12 July 2016

Goodman E, 'Open Letter to Google From 80 Internet Scholars: Release RTBF Compliance Data' (*Medium*, 14 May 2015) <https://medium.com/@ellgood/open-letter-to-google-from-80-internet-scholars-release-rtbf-compliance-data-cbfc6d59f1bd> accessed 20 May 2015

Graef I, *EU Competition Law, Data Protection and Online Platforms: Data as Essential Facility* (Kluwer Law International 2016)

Graef I, Clifford D, and Valcke P, 'Fairness and Enforcement: Bridging Competition, Data Protection and Consumer Law' [2018] International Data Privacy Law (Forthcoming)

Gräf E, 'When Automated Profiling Threatens Our Freedom: A Neo-Republican Perspective' (2017) 3 European Data Protection Law Review 441

Graham-Harrison E and Cadwalladr C, 'Revealed: 50 Million Facebook Profiles Harvested for Cambridge Analytica in Major Data Breach' (*The Guardian*, 17 March 2018) <http://www.theguardian.com/news/2018/mar/17/cambridge-analytica-facebook-influence-us-election> accessed 19 March 2018

Granick J, 'Convicted Murderer To Wikipedia: Shhh!' (*Electronic Frontier Foundation*, 10 November 2009) <https://www.eff.org/deeplinks/2009/11/murderer-wikipedia-shhh> accessed 17 November 2015

Granieri G, 'Algorithmic Culture. "Culture Now Has Two Audiences: People and Machines"—Futurists' Views' (*Medium*, 30 April 2014) <https://medium.com/futurists-views/algorithmic-culture-culture-now-has-two-audiences-people-and-machines-2bdaa404f643> accessed 19 July 2015

Graux H, Ausloos J, and Valcke P, 'The Right to Be Forgotten in the Internet Era' in Jorge Pérez, Enrique Badía, and Rosa María Sáinz Peña (eds), *The Debate on Privacy and Security over the Network: Regulation and Markets*, vol 36 (1st edn, Ariel 2012) <publicpolicy.telefonica.com/blogs/wp-content/uploads/2011/01/net_privacy.pdf> accessed 18 April 2013

Greenleaf G, 'Global Data Privacy Laws 2017: 120 National Data Privacy Laws, Including Indonesia and Turkey' (Social Science Research Network 2017) SSRN Scholarly Paper ID 2993035 <https://papers.ssrn.com/abstract=2993035> accessed 12 June 2019

——, 'Global Data Privacy Laws: 89 Countries, and Accelerating' SSRN eLibrary <http://papers.ssrn.com/sol3/papers.cfm?abstract_id=2000034> accessed 8 February 2012

Greenwald G, *No Place to Hide: Edward Snowden, the NSA, and the Surveillance State* (Hamish Hamilton 2014)

Greggs, 'Hey @GoogleUK, Fix It and They're Yours!!! #FixGreggs Pic.Twitter.Com/D5Ub7qtrLG' (*@GreggstheBakers*, 19 August 2014) <https://twitter.com/GreggstheBakers/status/501730930311331840/photo/1> accessed 28 August 2014

Grimmelmann J, 'An Offer You Can't Understand' (*Jotwell: The Journal of Things We Like (Lots)*, 15 May 2015) <http://cyber.jotwell.com/an-offer-you-cant-understand/> accessed 29 June 2015

Guicherd S, Caron-Fasan M-L, and Lesca N, 'Droit à l'oubli numérique: Quel alignement entre chartes et pratique?' in David Dechenaud (ed), *Le droit à l'oubli numérique: Données nominatives—Approche comparée* (Larcier 2015)

Gürses S, 'The Spectre of Anonymity' in Renée Turner (ed), *Sniff, Scrape, Crawl … {On Privacy, Surveillance and Our Shadowy Data-Double}* (Mute Publishing Ltd 2012)

——, 'Can You Engineer Privacy?' (2014) 57 Commun ACM 20

Gürses S, Overdorf R, and Balsa E, 'POTs: The Revolution Will Not Be Optimized?' [2018] arXiv:1806.02711 [cs] <http://arxiv.org/abs/1806.02711> accessed 11 June 2018

Gürses S and van Hoboken J, 'Privacy after the Agile Turn' in Jules Polonetsky, Omer Tene, and Evan Selinger (eds), *Cambridge Handbook of Consumer Privacy* (CUP 2017) <https://osf.io/preprints/socarxiv/9gy73/> accessed 12 November 2017

Gutwirth S, 'De Toepassing van Het Finaliteitsbeginsel van de Privacywet van 8 December 1992 Tot Bescherming van de Persoonlijke Levenssfeer Ten Opzichte van de Verwerking van Persoonsgegevens' [The Application of the Purpose Specification Principle in the Belgian Data Protection Act of 8 December 1992]' (1993) 1993 Tijdschrift voor Privaatrecht—TPR 1409

——, *Privacy and the Information Age* (Raf Casert tr, Rowman & Littlefield Publishers 2002)

——, 'Short Statement about the Role of Consent in the European Data Protection Directive' <http://works.bepress.com/serge_gutwirth/80/>.

Gutwirth S and De Hert P, 'Regulating Profiling in a Democratic Constitutional State' in Mireille Hildebrandt and Serge Gutwirth (eds), *Profiling the European Citizen: Cross-Disciplinary Perspectives* (Springer 2008)

Haddadi H and others, 'Personal Data: Thinking Inside the Box' [2015] arXiv:1501.04737 [cs] <http://arxiv.org/abs/1501.04737> accessed 28 July 2015

Hanson JD and Kysar DA, 'Taking Behavioralism Seriously: Some Evidence of Market Manipulation' [1999] Harvard Law Review 1420

——, 'Taking Behavioralism Seriously: The Problem of Market Manipulation' (1999) 74 NYUL Rev 630

Harbo T-I, *The Function of Proportionality Analysis in European Law* (Brill Nijhoff 2015)

Harris D, 'The One-Night Stand, Quantified and Visualized by Uber' (26 March 2012) <https://gigaom.com/2012/03/26/uber-one-night-stands/> accessed 8 December 2014

Harris J, 'Our Phones and Gadgets Are Now Endangering the Planet' *The Guardian* (17 July 2018) <https://www.theguardian.com/commentisfree/2018/jul/17/internet-climate-carbon-footprint-data-centres> accessed 30 August 2018

Hartzog W, 'There Is No Such Thing as "Public" Data' [2016] *Slate* <http://www.slate.com/articles/technology/future_tense/2016/05/okcupid_s_data_leak_shows_there_s_no_such_thing_as_public_data.html> accessed 19 May 2016

——, *Privacy's Blueprint: The Battle to Control the Design of New Technologies* (Harvard University Press 2018)

Hartzog W and Selinger E, 'Obscurity: A Better Way to Think About Your Data Than "Privacy"' *The Atlantic* (17 January 2013) <http://www.theatlantic.com/technology/archive/2013/01/obscurity-a-better-way-to-think-about-your-data-than-privacy/267283/> accessed 22 January 2013

Hartzog W and Stutzman FD, 'The Case for Online Obscurity' (2012) 101 California Law Review 1

Haucap J and Heimeshoff U, 'Google, Facebook, Amazon, EBay: Is the Internet Driving Competition or Market Monopolization?' (Düsseldorf Institute for Competition Economics (DICE) 2013) <http://nbn-resolving.de/urn:nbn:de:101:1-201301155754> accessed 22 July 2015

Haynes Stuart A, 'Google Search Results: Buried If Not Forgotten' (2014) 15 North Carolina Journal of Law & Technology 463

Helberger N, 'Profiling and Targeting Users in the Internet of Things—A New Challenge for Consumer Law' in Reiner Schulze and Dirk Staudenmayer (eds), *Digital Revolution: Challenges for Contract Law in Practice* (Nomos 2016) <http://hdl.handle.net/11245/1.519095>.

——, 'Form Matters: Informing Consumers Effectively' (University of Amsterdam) 2013-10 <http://papers.ssrn.com/abstract=2354988> accessed 3 August 2016

Helberger N, Borgesius FZ, and Reyna A, 'The Perfect Match? A Closer Look at the Relationship between EU Consumer Law and Data Protection Law' (2017) 54 Common Market Law Review 1427

Helberger N, Pierson J, and Poell T, 'Governing Online Platforms: From Contested to Cooperative Responsibility' (2018) 34 The Information Society 1

Helberger N and Van Hoboken J, 'Little Brother Is Tagging You—Legal and Policy Implications of Amateur Data Controllers' (2010) 4 Computer Law International 101

Hemminki S, Nurmi P, and Tarkoma S, 'Accelerometer-Based Transportation Mode Detection on Smartphones', *11th ACM Conference on Embedded Networked Sensor Systems* (ACM Press 2013) <http://dl.acm.org/citation.cfm?doid=2517351.2517367> accessed 29 November 2013

Hendel J, 'Why Journalists Shouldn't Fear Europe's "Right to Be Forgotten"' (*The Atlantic*, 25 January 2012) <http://www.theatlantic.com/technology/archive/2012/01/why-journalists-shouldnt-fear-europes-right-to-be-forgotten/251955/> accessed 25 January 2012

Hern A, 'I Read All the Small Print on the Internet and It Made Me Want to Die' (*The Guardian*, 15 June 2015) <www.theguardian.com/technology/2015/jun/15/i-read-all-the-small-print-on-the-internet> accessed 19 July 2015

——, 'How Your Smartphone's Battery Life Can Be Used to Invade Your Privacy' *The Guardian* (4 August 2015) <http://www.theguardian.com/technology/2015/aug/03/privacy-smartphones-battery-life> accessed 5 October 2015

Herrmann D and Lindemann J, 'Obtaining Personal Data and Asking for Erasure: Do App Vendors and Website Owners Honour Your Privacy Rights?' [2016] arXiv:1602.01804 [cs] <http://arxiv.org/abs/1602.01804> accessed 16 October 2017

Hesseldahl A, 'Moore's Law Hits 50, but It May Not See 60' (*Re/code*, 15 April 2015) <http://recode.net/2015/04/15/moores-law-hits-50-but-it-may-not-see-60/> accessed 16 April 2015

Heyman R and Van Dijk N, 'Who Can Afford Users as Targets? Interfaces, Transparency and the Commodification of Relations in Online Social Networks' (iMinds—SMIT—VUB 2013) Research Report <http://emsoc.be/wp-content/uploads/2013/11/D322-SMIT-and-LSTS.pdf> accessed 19 December 2013

High Level Expert Group on Artificial Intelligence, 'Policy and Investment Recommendations for Trustworthy AI' (European Commission 2019)

Hijmans H, *The European Union as Guardian of Internet Privacy: The Story of Art 16 TFEU* (Springer International Publishing 06)

——, *The European Union as Guardian of Internet Privacy: The Story of Art 16 TFEU* (Springer 2016)

——, 'The European Union as a Constitutional Guardian of Internet Privacy and Data Protection' (PhD Thesis, University of Amsterdam 2016) <http://dare.uva.nl/document/2/169421> accessed 6 February 2016

Hildebrandt M, 'Legal and Technological Normativity: More (and Less) than Twin Sisters' (2008) 12 Techné: Research in Philosophy and Technology 169

——, 'Who Is Profiling Who? Invisible Visibility' in Serge Gutwirth and others (eds), *Reinventing Data Protection?* (First, 2009) <http://www.springerlink.com/index/P7710R0760613778.pdf> accessed 12 February 2013

——, 'The Dawn of a Critical Transparency Right for the Profiling Era', *Digital Enlightenment Yearbook 2012* (IOS Press 2012) <https://works.bepress.com/mireille_hildebrandt/40/> accessed 12 July 2016

——, 'Slaves to Big Data. Or Are We?' (2013) 16 IDP Revista de Internet, Derecho Y Política <http://works.bepress.com/mireille_hildebrandt/52> accessed 22 April 2014

——, 'Balance or Trade-off? Online Security Technologies and Fundamental Rights' (2013) 26 Philosophy & Technology 357

——, *Smart Technologies and the End(s) of Law: Novel Entanglements of Law and Technology* (Edward Elgar Publishing 2015)

——, 'Primitives of Legal Protection in the Era of Data-Driven Platforms' (2018) II Georgetown Law Technology Review 252

Hill K, 'Facebook Wants To Listen In On What You're Doing' (*Forbes*, 22 May 2014) <www.forbes.com/sites/kashmirhill/2014/05/22/facebook-wants-to-listen-in-on-what-youre-doing/> accessed 14 July 2015

——, 'Ok Cupid Lied To Users About Their Compatibility As An Experiment' [2014] *Forbes* <www.forbes.com/sites/kashmirhill/2014/07/28/okcupid-experiment-compatibility-deception/> accessed 1 August 2014

Hirsch DD, 'Protecting the Inner Environment: What Privacy Regulation Can Learn from Environmental Law' (2006) 41 Georgia Law Review 1

Hirsch DD and King JH, 'Big Data Sustainability: An Environmental Management Systems Analogy' (2015) 72 Washington and Lee Law Review Online 409

Hodges C, 'Discussion. Delivering Data Protection: Trust and Ethical Culture' (2018) 4 European Data Protection Law Review 65

Hodson H, 'Google Knows Your Ills' (2016) 230 New Scientist 22

Hoepman J-H, 'Transparency Is the Perfect Cover-up (If the Sun Does Not Shine)', *Transparency Theory for Data Driven Decision Making* (2018)

Holleaux A, 'La Loi Du 6 Janvier 1978 Sur Informatique et Les Libertés—II—' (1978) 31 La Revue administrative 160

——, 'La Loi Du 6 Janvier 1978 Sur l'informatique et Les Libertés-I' (1978) 31 la Revue administrative 31

Hon WK, Millard C and Walden I, 'The Problem of "Personal Data" in Cloud Computing: What Information Is Regulated?—The Cloud of Unknowing' (2011) 1 International Data Privacy Law 211

——, 'Who Is Responsible for "Personal Data" in Cloud Computing?—The Cloud of Unknowing, Part 2' (2012) 2 International Data Privacy Law 3

Hondius FW, *Emerging Data Protection in Europe* (North-Holland 1975)

Hornung G and Schnabel C, 'Data Protection in Germany I: The Population Census Decision and the Right to Informational Self-Determination' (2009) 25 Computer Law & Security Review 84

Horten M, *Closing of the Net* (Polity Press 2016)

'How to Tame the Tech Titans' [2018] *The Economist* <https://www.economist.com/news/leaders/21735021-dominance-google-facebook-and-amazon-bad-consumers-and-competition-how-tame> accessed 22 February 2018

Humphries C, 'Ireland Asks Europe's Top Court to Rule on EU-U.S. Data Transfers' *Reuters* (3 October 2017) <https://www.reuters.com/article/us-eu-privacy-facebook/ireland-refers-key-eu-u-s-data-transfer-mechanism-to-europes-top-court-idUSKCN1C80XQ> accessed 13 February 2018

Hustinx P, 'Data Protection in the European Union' (2005) 2 Privacy & Informatie 62

——, 'How Practicable Is It to Apply Data Protection to Activities Involving Freedom of Expression?' (The 'Right to be Forgotten' and Beyond: Data Protection and Freedom of Expression in the Age of Web 2.0, Oxford, UK, June 2012) <http://podcasts.ox.ac.uk/how-practicable-it-apply-data-protection-activities-involving-freedom-expression-3> accessed 20 April 2017

——, 'EU Data Protection Law: The Review of Directive 95/46 EC and the Proposed General Data Protection Regulation' <https://secure.edps.europa.eu/EDPSWEB/webdav/site/mySite/shared/Documents/EDPS/Publications/Speeches/2014/14-09-15_Article_EUI_EN.pdf>.

Hutton L and Henderson T, 'Beyond the EULA: Improving Consent for Data Mining' [2017] arXiv:1701.07999 [cs] <http://arxiv.org/abs/1701.07999> accessed 6 February 2017

Ilshammar L, 'When Computers Became Dangerous: The Swedish Computer Discourse of the 1960s' (2007) 9 Human IT 6

Information Commissioner's Office, 'Anonymisation: Managing Data Protection Risk Code of Practice' <http://eprints.soton.ac.uk/345821/> accessed 24 February 2016

——, 'Democracy Disrupted? Personal Information and Political Influence' (2018) <https://ico.org.uk/media/action-weve-taken/2259369/democracy-disrupted-110718.pdf> accessed 23 July 2018

——, 'Investigation into the Use of Data Analytics in Political Campaigns' (2018) <https://ico.org.uk/media/action-weve-taken/2259371/investigation-into-data-analytics-for-political-purposes-update.pdf> accessed 23 July 2018

——, 'Update Report into AdTech and Real Time Bidding' (ICO 2019) <https://ico.org.uk/media/about-the-ico/documents/2615156/adtech-real-time-bidding-report-201906.pdf> accessed 20 June 2019

Information Commissioner's Office (ICO), 'Deleting Your Data from Computers, Laptops and Other Devices' <https://ico.org.uk/for-the-public/online/deleting-your-data/> accessed 7 April 2017

International Commission of Jurists, 'The Protection of Privacy' (1972) XXIV International Social Science Journal 413

International Institute for the Unification of Private Law, *Unidroit Principles of International Commercial Contracts* (2010) <https://www.unidroit.org/english/principles/contracts/principles2010/integralversionprinciples2010-e.pdf> accessed 15 March 2018

Irion K, 'Your Digital Home Is No Longer Your Castle: How Cloud Computing Transforms the (Legal) Relationship between Individuals and Their Personal Records' [2015] International Journal of Law and Information Technology <http://ijlit.oxfordjournals.

org.kuleuven.ezproxy.kuleuven.be/content/early/2015/09/25/ijlit.eav015> accessed 28 September 2015

——, 'A Roadmap to Enhancing User Control via Privacy Dashboards' (IViR 2017) <https://www.ivir.nl/publicaties/download/PrivacyBridgesUserControls2017.pdf>.

Irish Data Protection Commissioner, 'Report of Audit (Facebook Ireland Ltd)' (2011) <http://europe-v-facebook.org/Facebook_Ireland_Audit_Report_Final.pdf> accessed 11 May 2015

——, 'Report of Re-Audit (Facebook Ireland Ltd)' (2012) <dataprotection.ie/documents/press/Facebook_Ireland_Audit_Review_Report_21_Sept_2012.pdf> accessed 18 October 2012

Jarvis J, *Public Parts: How Sharing in the Digital Age Improves the Way We Work and Live* (Simon & Schuster 2011)

Jasmontaite L and Hert PD, 'The EU, Children under 13 Years, and Parental Consent: A Human Rights Analysis of a New, Age-Based Bright-Line for the Protection of Children on the Internet' (2015) 5 International Data Privacy Law 20

Jay R, *Data Protection: Law and Practice.* (Sweet & Maxwell 2012)

Johnson DR and Post D, 'Law and Borders: The Rise of Law in Cyberspace' (1996) 48 Stanford Law Review 1367

Jones ML, 'Privacy without Screens & the Internet of Other People's Things' (2014) 51 Idaho Law Review 639

——, *Ctrl + Z: The Right to Be Forgotten* (New York University Press 2016)

Jozwiak M, 'Balancing the Rights to Data Protection and Freedom of Expression and Information by the Court of Justice of the European Union: The Vulnerability of Rights in an Online Context' (2016) 23 Maastricht Journal of European and Comparative Law (MJ) 404

Kaltheuner F and Bietti E, 'Data Is Power: Towards Additional Guidance on Profiling and Automated Decision-Making in the GDPR' (2018) 2 Journal of Information Rights, Policy and Practice <https://jirpp.winchesteruniversitypress.org/articles/abstract/10.21039/irpandp.v2i2.45/> accessed 11 February 2018

Kaminski M, 'Reading Over Your Shoulder: Social Readers and Privacy Law' (*Wake Forest Law Review*, 9 March 2012) <http://wakeforestlawreview.com/2012/03/reading-over-your-shoulder-social-readers-and-privacy-law/> accessed 9 April 2015

Karapapa S and Borghi M, 'Search Engine Liability for Autocomplete Suggestions: Personality, Privacy and the Power of the Algorithm' (2015) 23 International Journal of Law and Information Technology 261

Karst KL, '"The Files": Legal Controls over the Accuracy and Accessibility of Stored Personal Data' (1966) 31 Law and Contemporary Problems 342

Kaye D, 'Report of the Special Rapporteur on the Promotion and Protection of the Right to Freedom of Opinion and Expression' (United Nations (Human Rights Council) 2018) A/HRC/38/35 <http://ap.ohchr.org/documents/dpage_e.aspx?si=A/HRC/38/35>.

Kemper J and Kolkman D, 'Transparent to Whom? No Algorithmic Accountability without a Critical Audience' [2018] Information, Communication & Society 1

Kerr I, Steeves V, and Lucock C (eds), *Lessons from the Identity Trail Anonymity, Privacy, and Identity in a Networked Society* (OUP 2009) <http://site.ebrary.com/id/10476908> accessed 15 January 2014

Kharif O, 'Is Your Blockchain Business Doomed?' *Bloomberg.com* (22 March 2018) <https://www.bloomberg.com/news/articles/2018-03-22/is-your-blockchain-business-doomed> accessed 14 June 2018

Kindt EJ, *Privacy and Data Protection Issues of Biometric Applications: A Comparative Legal Analysis* (Springer 2013)

Kirby M, 'The History, Achievement and Future of the 1980 OECD Guidelines on Privacy' (2011) 1 International Data Privacy Law 6

Kitchin R, *The Data Revolution: Big Data, Open Data, Data Infrastructures & Their Consequences* (Sage Publishing 2014)

Klein A, 'The Cost of Hard Drives Over Time' (*Backblaze Blog | Cloud Storage & Cloud Backup*, 11 July 2017) <https://www.backblaze.com/blog/hard-drive-cost-per-gigabyte/> accessed 20 February 2018

Klik E and Kamin D, 'Between Archived, Shredded, and Lost/Found: Erasure in Digital and Artistic Contexts' (*NMC Media-N*, 11 April 2015) <http://median.newmediacaucus.org/the_aesthetics_of_erasure/between-archived-shredded-and-lostfound-erasure-in-digital-and-artistic-contexts/> accessed 30 May 2018

Koehler W, 'Digital Libraries and World Wide Web Sites and Page Persistence' (1999) 4 Information Research <http://www.informationr.net/ir/4-4/paper60.html> accessed 9 January 2017

——, 'A Longitudinal Study of Web Pages Continued: A Consideration of Document Persistence' (2004) 9 Information Research <http://www.informationr.net/ir/9-2/paper174.html> accessed 9 January 2017

Kohl U, 'The Rule of Law, Jurisdiction and the Internet' (2004) 12 International Journal of Law and Information Technology 365

——, *Jurisdiction and the Internet: A Study of Regulatory Competence over Online Activity* (CUP 2007)

Kokott J and Sobotta C, 'The Charter of Fundamental Rights of the European Union after Lisbon' (2010) Working Paper <http://cadmus.eui.eu//handle/1814/15208> accessed 22 September 2017

——, 'The Distinction between Privacy and Data Protection in the Jurisprudence of the CJEU and the ECtHR' (2013) 3 International Data Privacy Law 222

Kolb A, 'Data Protection—Germany: The Creation of Legislation for Data Protection in the New States of the Federal Republic of Germany' (1991) 7 Computer Law & Security Review 123

Konarski X and others, 'Reforming the Data Protection Package (Study Drafted for EP Committee on Internal Market and Consumer Protection)' (EP Committee on Internal Market and Consumer Protection 2012) IP/A/IMCO/ST/2012-02 <http://www.europarl.europa.eu/document/activities/cont/201209/20120928ATT52488/20120928ATT52488EN.pdf>.

Koops B-J, 'Forgetting Footprints, Shunning Shadows: A Critical Analysis of the "Right to Be Forgotten" in Big Data Practice' (2011) 8 SCRIPTed 229

——, 'The Trouble with European Data Protection Law' (2014) 4 International Data Privacy Law 250

Korenhof P, 'Forgetting Bits and Pieces: An Exploration of the "Right to Be Forgotten" as Implementation of "Forgetting" in Online Memory Processes' (TILT 2013) Paper for the IFIP Summer School 4/2013 <http://papers.ssrn.com/abstract=2326475> accessed 27 January 2014

——, 'Timing the Right to Be Forgotten: A Study into "Time" as a Factor in Deciding About Retention or Erasure of Data' in Serge Gutwirth, Ronald Leenes, and Paul De Hert (eds), *Reforming European Data Protection Law*, vol 20 (Springer 2015) <www.springer.com/law/international/book/978-94-017-9384-1> accessed 7 January 2015

Korff D, 'Study on the Protection of the Rights and Interests of Legal Persons with Regard to the Processing of Personal Data Relating to Such Persons' (European Commission 2000)

Study ETD/97/B5-9500/78 <http://ec.europa.eu/justice/data-protection/document/studies/files/20000202_rights_interests_legal_en.pdf> accessed 8 March 2016

——, 'EC Study on Implementation of Data Protection Directive: Comparative Summary of National Laws' (2002) <https://ssrn.com/abstract=1287667>.

——, 'Data Protection Laws in the EU: The Difficulties in Meeting the Challenges Posed by Global Social and Technical Developments' (European Commission - DG Justice 2010) Working Paper No.2 <http://ssrn.com/abstract=1638949> accessed 10 February 2016

Korff D and Brown I, 'Comparative Study on Different Approaches to New Privacy Challenges, in Particular in the Light of Technological Developments' (European Commission—DG Justice Final Report 2010)

Kosinski M, Stillwell D, and Graepel T, 'Private Traits and Attributes Are Predictable from Digital Records of Human Behavior' (2013) 110 Proceedings of the National Academy of Sciences 5802

Kosta E, *Consent in European Data Protection Law* (Martinus Nijhoff 2013)

Kramer ADI, Guillory JE, and Hancock JT, 'Experimental Evidence of Massive-Scale Emotional Contagion through Social Networks' (2014) 111 Proceedings of the National Academy of Sciences 8788

Kranenborg H, 'Protection of Personal Data' in Steve Peers and others (eds), *The EU Charter of Fundamental Rights: A Commentary* (Hart 2014) <https://www.bloomsburycollections.com/book/the-eu-charter-of-fundamental-rights-a-commentary/>.

Kuchler H, 'Facebook Blocks Belgian Users after Privacy Ruling over Cookies' *Financial Times* (3 December 2015) <https://www.ft.com/content/9c9bf084-994f-11e5-95c7-d47aa298f769> accessed 15 December 2016

Kuczerawy A, *Intermediary Liability and Freedom of Expression in the EU: From Concepts to Safeguards* (Intersentia 2018)

——, 'Private Enforcement of Public Policy: Freedom of Expression in the Era of Online Gatekeeping' (PhD Thesis, KU Leuven—Faculty of Law 2018) <http://limo.libis.be>.

Kuczerawy A and Ausloos J, 'NoC Online Intermediaries Case Studies Series: European Union and Google Spain' (2015) <http://ssrn.com/abstract=2567183> accessed 28 August 2015

——, 'From Notice-and-Takedown to Notice-and-Delist: Implementing Google Spain' (2016) 14 Colorado Technology Law Journal 219

Kuner C, *European Data Protection Law: Corporate Compliance and Regulation* (OUP 2007)

——, 'Proportionality in European Data Protection Law And Its Importance for Data Processing by Companies' (2008) 7 Privacy & Security Law Report 1615

——, 'The European Commission's Proposed Data Protection Regulation: A Copernican Revolution in European Data Protection Law' (2012) 11 Privacy & Security Law Report 15

La Rue F, 'Report of the Special Rapporteur on the Promotion and Protection of the Right to Freedom of Opinion and Expression' (United Nations (Human Rights Council) 2013) A/HRC/23/40

Laba JT, 'If You Can't Stand the Heat, Get out of the Drug Business: Thermal Imagers, Emerging Technologies, and the Fourth Amendment' (1996) 84 California Law Review 1437

Laidlaw E, 'A Framework for Identifying Internet Information Gatekeepers' (2010) 24 International Review of Law, Computers & Technology 263

Lane J and others, *Privacy, Big Data, and the Public Good: Frameworks for Engagement* (CUP 2014)

Lanier J, *Who Owns the Future?* (Allen Lane 2013)

Lapowsky I, 'How Facebook Knows You Better Than Your Friends Do' (*WIRED*, 13 January 2015) <www.wired.com/2015/01/facebook-personality-test/> accessed 14 January 2015

Lawrence N, 'Data Trusts Could Allay Our Privacy Fears' *The Guardian* (3 June 2016) <http://www.theguardian.com/media-network/2016/jun/03/data-trusts-privacy-fears-feudalism-democracy> accessed 22 February 2018

Lawton G, 'Emerging Technologies Promise to Quantify Emotions' (*Torque*, 15 September 2014) <http://torquemag.io/emerging-technologies-promise-quantify-emotions/> accessed 30 September 2014

Lazaro C and Le Métayer D, 'Control over Personal Data: True Remedy or Fairytale?' (2015) 12 SCRIPTed <http://script-ed.org/?p=1927> accessed 6 November 2015

Lederer S and others, 'Personal Privacy through Understanding and Action: Five Pitfalls for Designers' (2004) 8 Personal and Ubiquitous Computing 440

Lee E, 'The Right to Be Forgotten v. Free Speech Internet Freedom' (2015) 12 I/S: A Journal of Law and Policy for the Information Society 85

Leese M, 'The New Profiling: Algorithms, Black Boxes, And The Failure Of Anti-Discriminatory Safeguards In The European Union' (2014) 45 Security Dialogue 494

Lehtiniemi T and Kortesniemi Y, 'Can the Obstacles to Privacy Self-Management Be Overcome? Exploring the Consent Intermediary Approach' (2017) 4 Big Data & Society 1

Lenaerts K, 'Opening Address: Limit to Limitations: The Essence of Fundamental Rights in the EU' (Conference—The Essence of Fundamental Rights in EU Law, Leuven, Belgium, 17 May 2018)

Lenaerts K and Gutiérrez-Fons JA, 'The Place of the Charter in the EU Constitutional Edifice' in Steve Peers and others (eds), *The EU Charter of Fundamental Rights: A Commentary*, vols 1559–1594 (Hart 2014) <https://www.bloomsburycollections.com/book/the-eu-charter-of-fundamental-rights-a-commentary/>

Lenk K, *The First International Oslo Symposium on Data Banks and Society, Presented by Klaus Lenk e a* (Oslo: Universitetsforlaget 1972)

Léonard A, 'Abuse of Rights in European Patent Law—Testing the Theory of Abuse to Patent Assertion Entities' Litigation Strategies' (PhD Thesis, KU Leuven—Faculty of Law 2019)

Lessig L, 'The Zones of Cyberspace' (1996) 48 Stanford Law Review 1403

——, 'The Architecture of Privacy' (1999) 1 Vand J Ent L & Prac 56

——, *Code: And Other Laws of Cyberspace* (Basic Books 1999)

——, *Code: Version 2.0* (Basic Books 2006)

L'Hoiry XD and Norris C, 'The Honest Data Protection Officer's Guide to Enable Citizens to Exercise Their Subject Access Rights: Lessons from a Ten-Country European Study' (2015) 5 International Data Privacy Law 190

Lievens E and Vander Maelen C, 'A Child's Right to Be Forgotten: Letting Go of the Past and Embracing the Future?' [2019] Latin American Law Review 61

Lievens E and Verdoodt V, 'Looking for Needles in a Haystack: Key Issues Affecting Children's Rights in the General Data Protection Regulation' (2018) 34 Computer Law & Security Review 269

Lindh M and Nolin J, 'Information We Collect: Surveillance and Privacy in the Implementation of Google Apps for Education' (2016) 15 European Educational Research Journal 644

Lindop N, *Report of the Committee on Data Protection, Chairman: Norman Lindop* (HMSO 1978)

Lindsay D, 'The "Right to Be Forgotten" by Search Engines under Data Privacy Law: A Legal Analysis of the Costeja Ruling' (2014) 6 Journal of Media Law 159

Livingston S, 'Book Review: Communication Power by Manuel Castells' (2010) 27 Political Communication 471

Lobba P, 'Holocaust Denial before the European Court of Human Rights: Evolution of an Exceptional Regime' (2015) 26 European Journal of International Law 237

Lomas N, 'Facebook's Dark Ads Problem Is Systemic' (*TechCrunch*, 28 April 2018) <http://social.techcrunch.com/2018/04/28/facebooks-dark-ads-problem-is-systemic/> accessed 15 May 2018

Luebke DM and Milton S, 'Locating the Victim: An Overview of Census-Taking, Tabulation Technology and Persecution in Nazi Germany' (1994) 16 IEEE Annals of the History of Computing 25

Luma Partners, 'Display LumaScape' (Luma Partners LLC 2019) <https://lumapartners.com/content/lumascapes/display-ad-tech-lumascape/> accessed 1 June 2019.

Lyall S, 'Who Strikes Fear Into Silicon Valley? Margrethe Vestager, Europe's Antitrust Enforcer' *The New York Times* (8 May 2018) <https://www.nytimes.com/2018/05/05/world/europe/margrethe-vestager-silicon-valley-data-privacy.html> accessed 12 May 2018

Lynskey O, 'Deconstructing Data Protection: The "Added-Value" Of A Right To Data Protection In The EU Legal Order' (2014) 63 International & Comparative Law Quarterly 569

——, *The Foundations of EU Data Protection Law* (OUP 2016)

——, 'In the Shadows of the Data Protection Juggernaut: Bara and Weltimmo' (*European Law Blog*, 28 January 2016) <http://europeanlawblog.eu/?p=3083> accessed 6 February 2016

——, 'Regulating "Platform Power"' (LSE 2017) Working Paper 1/2017 <https://papers.ssrn.com/abstract=2921021> accessed 17 April 2017

——, 'Non-Price Effect of Mergers' (OECD 2018) JT03432756 <https://one.oecd.org/document/DAF/COMP/WD(2018)70/en/pdf> accessed 17 June 2018

Lyon D, *Surveillance as Social Sorting: Privacy, Risk, and Digital Discrimination* (Routledge 2003)

——, *Theorizing Surveillance: The Panopticon and Beyond* (Willan Publishing 2006)

Macenaite M, 'From Universal towards Child-Specific Protection of the Right to Privacy Online: Dilemmas in the EU General Data Protection Regulation' (2017) 19 New Media & Society 765

Macenaite M and Kosta E, 'Consent for Processing Children's Personal Data in the EU: Following in US Footsteps?' (2017) 26 Information & Communications Technology Law 146

Machkovech S, 'Report: Facebook Helped Advertisers Target Teens Who Feel "Worthless" [Updated]' (*Ars Technica*, 1 May 2017) <https://arstechnica.com/information-technology/2017/05/facebook-helped-advertisers-target-teens-who-feel-worthless/> accessed 30 October 2017

Mackaay E, *Economics of Information and Law* (Kluwer 1982)

MacKinnon R, *Consent of the Networked: The Worldwide Struggle for Internet Freedom* (Basic Books 2012)

Macovei M, 'Freedom of Expression: A Guide to the Implementation of Article 10 of the European Convention on Human Rights' [2004] Human Rights Handbooks <http://www.supremecourt.ge/files/upload-file/pdf/article10eng.pdf> accessed 24 July 2013

Maldoff G, 'How GDPR Changes the Rules for Research' (*IAPP*, 19 April 2016) <https://iapp.org/news/a/how-gdpr-changes-the-rules-for-research/> accessed 20 May 2016

Malgieri G, 'Trade Secrets v Personal Data: A Possible Solution for Balancing Rights' (2016) 6 International Data Privacy Law 102

Malgieri G and Comandé G, 'Sensitive-by-Distance: Quasi-Health Data in the Algorithmic Era' (2017) 26 Information & Communications Technology Law 229

Manovich L, *The Language of New Media* (MIT Press 2002)

Mantelero A, 'The EU Proposal for a General Data Protection Regulation and the Roots of the "Right to Be Forgotten"' (2013) 29 Computer Law & Security Review 229

——, 'The Future of Consumer Data Protection in the E.U. Re-Thinking the "Notice and Consent" Paradigm in the New Era of Predictive Analytics' (2014) 30 Computer Law & Security Review 643

——, 'From Group Privacy to Collective Privacy: Towards a New Dimension of Privacy and Data Protection in the Big Data Era' in Linnet Taylor, Luciano Floridi, and Bart van der Sloot (eds), *Group Privacy: New Challenges of Data Technologies*, vol 126 (Springer International Publishing 2017)

Maras M-H, 'Internet of Things: Security and Privacy Implications' (2015) 5 International Data Privacy Law 99

Markou C, 'The "Right to Be Forgotten": Ten Reasons Why It Should Be Forgotten' in Serge Gutwirth, Ronald Leenes, and Paul de Hert (eds), *Reforming European Data Protection Law* (Springer Netherlands 2015) <http://link.springer.com/chapter/10.1007/978-94-017-9385-8_8> accessed 26 January 2015

Marx GT, 'Personal Information as Influences on Attitudes towards Surveillance' in Richard Victor Ericson and Kevin D Haggerty (eds), *The New Politics of Surveillance and Visibility* (University of Toronto Press 2006)

——, 'Soft Surveillance: The Growth of Mandatory Volunteerism in Collecting Personal Information—"Hey Buddy Can You Spare a DNA?"' in Torin Monahan (ed), *Surveillance and Security: Technological Politics and Power in Everyday Life* (Routledge 2006)

Masnick M, 'Why Can't Europe Just Forget The Ridiculous Idea Of A "Right To Be Forgotten"' (*Techdirt*, 31 January 2012) <www.techdirt.com/articles/20120129/23085517583/why-cant-europe-just-forget-ridiculous-idea-right-to-be-forgotten.shtml> accessed 30 July 2014

Mathews L, 'Equifax Data Breach Impacts 143 Million Americans' (*Forbes*, 7 September 2017) <https://www.forbes.com/sites/leemathews/2017/09/07/equifax-data-breach-impacts-143-million-americans/> accessed 18 March 2018

Mayer-Schönberger V, 'Generational Development of Data Protection In Europe' in Philip E Agre and Marc Rotenberg (eds), *Technology and Privacy: The New Landscape* (First, MIT Press 1998)

——, *Delete: The Virtue of Forgetting in the Digital Age* (1st edn, Princeton University Press 2009)

Mayer-Schönberger V and Cukier K, *Big Data: A Revolution That Will Transform How We Live, Work and Think* (Houghton Mifflin Harcourt 2013)

McCullagh K, 'Data Sensitivity: Resolving the Conundrum', *British & Irish Law, Education and Technology Association Annual Conference, Hertfordshire* (2007) <http://bileta.ac.uk/content/files/conference%20papers/2007/Data%20Sensitivity%20-%20resolving%20the%20conundrum.pdf> accessed 22 February 2016

——, 'The Social, Cultural, Epistemological and Technical Basis of the Concept of "Private Data"' (PhD Thesis, University of Manchester—Faculty of Humanities 2011) <https://www.escholar.manchester.ac.uk/api/datastream?publicationPid=uk-ac-man-scw:157750&datastreamId=FULL-TEXT.PDF> accessed 3 March 2016

McChesney RW, *Digital Disconnect: How Capitalism Is Turning the Internet against Democracy* (The New Press 2013)

McClay W, 'On the Need for Erasure' (2015) 17 The Hedgehog Review <http://www.iasc-culture.org/THR/THR_article_2015_Spring_McClay.php> accessed 26 July 2016

McDermott Y, 'Conceptualising the Right to Data Protection in an Era of Big Data' (2017) 4 Big Data & Society 2053951716686994

McDonagh M, 'Balancing Disclosure of Information and the Right to Respect for Private We in Europe' (2012) 16 Journal of Internet Law; New York 3

McDonald AM and Cranor LF, 'The Cost of Reading Privacy Policies' (2008) 4 I/S: A Journal of Law and Policy for the Information Society 543

McNamee J, 'Google Now Supports AND Opposes the "Right to Be Forgotten"' (*EDRi*, 27 August 2014) <http://edri.org/google-now-supports-and-opposes-right-forgotten/> accessed 28 August 2014

——, 'ENDitorial: Is "Privacy" Still Relevant in a World of Bastard Data?' (*EDRi*, 9 March 2016) <https://edri.org/enditorial-is-privacy-still-relevant-in-a-world-of-bastard-data/ > accessed 18 April 2016

——, 'Is "Privacy" Still Relevant in a World of Bastard Data?' (10 March 2016) <https://www.scl.org/articles/3616-is-privacy-still-relevant-in-a-world-of-bastard-data> accessed 22 February 2018

Menn J, 'Google Admits That Street View Project Cars Accidentally Gathered WiFi Data from Homes' *Financial Times* (London (UK), United Kingdom, 15 May 2010)

Metcalf S, 'Neoliberalism: The Idea That Swallowed the World' *The Guardian* (18 August 2017) <http://www.theguardian.com/news/2017/aug/18/neoliberalism-the-idea-that-changed-the-world> accessed 6 September 2017

Meyer M, 'Everything You Need to Know About Facebook's Controversial Emotion Experiment' (*WIRED*, 30 June 2014) <www.wired.com/2014/06/everything-you-need-to-know-about-facebooks-manipulative-experiment/> accessed 1 July 2014

Mik E, 'The Erosion of Autonomy in Online Consumer Transactions' (2016) 8 Law, Innovation and Technology 1

Mill JS, *On Liberty* (Dover Publications 2002)

Miller AR, 'Personal Privacy in the Computer Age: The Challenge of a New Technology in an Information-Oriented Society' (1969) 67 Michigan Law Review 1089

Mitrou L and Karyda M, 'EU's Data Protection Reform and the Right to Be Forgotten: A Legal Response to a Technological Challenge?' (2012) <http://papers.ssrn.com/abstract=2165245> accessed 14 January 2013

Moerel L, 'The Long Arm of EU Data Protection Law: Does the Data Protection Directive Apply to Processing of Personal Data of EU Citizens by Websites Worldwide?' (2011) 1 International Data Privacy Law 28

Moerel L, 'Back to Basics: When Does EU Data Protection Law Apply?' (2011) 1 International Data Privacy Law 92

Moerel L and Prins C, 'On the Death of Purpose Limitation' (*IAPP*, 2 June 2015) <https://privacyassociation.org/news/a/on-the-death-of-purpose-limitation/> accessed 25 June 2015

——, 'Privacy for the Homo Digitalis: Proposal for a New Regulatory Framework for Data Protection in the Light of Big Data and the Internet of Things' <http://papers.ssrn.com/abstract=2784123> accessed 13 July 2016

Montero E and Van Enis Q, 'Les métamorphoses du droit à l'oubli sur le net' (2016) 2016 Tijdschrift voor Belgisch Burgerlijk Recht 243

Montjoye Y-A de and others, 'Unique in the Shopping Mall: On the Reidentifiability of Credit Card Metadata' (2015) 347 Science 536

Moore M, 'Tech Giants and Civic Power' (King's College (Policy Institute) 2016) <https://www.kcl.ac.uk/sspp/policy-institute/CMCP/Tech-Giants-and-Civic-Power.pdf>

Moosavian R, 'Deconstructing "Public Interest" in the Article 8 vs Article 10 Balancing Exercise' (2014) 6 Journal of Media Law 234

Morozov E, *To Save Everything, Click Here: Technology, Solutionism, and the Urge to Fix Problems That Don't Exist* (PublicAffairs 2013)

——, 'Facebook Invades Your Personality, Not Your Privacy' *Financial Times* (10 August 2014) <http://www.ft.com/intl/cms/s/2/dd5e5514-198d-11e4-8730-00144feabdc0.html> accessed 19 May 2015

——, 'Data Populists Must Seize Our Information—For the Benefit of Us All' *The Guardian* (4 December 2016) <https://www.theguardian.com/commentisfree/2016/dec/04/data-populists-must-seize-information-for-benefit-of-all-evgeny-morozov> accessed 5 December 2016

——, 'Moral Panic over Fake News Hides the Real Enemy—The Digital Giants' *The Guardian* (8 January 2017) <https://www.theguardian.com/commentisfree/2017/jan/08/blaming-fake-news-not-the-answer-democracy-crisis> accessed 8 January 2017

——, 'To Tackle Google's Power, Regulators Have to Go after Its Ownership of Data' *The Guardian* (2 July 2017) <https://www.theguardian.com/technology/2017/jul/01/google-european-commission-fine-search-engines> accessed 3 July 2017

Mowbray AR, *The Development of Positive Obligations under the European Convention on Human Rights by the European Court of Human Rights* (Hart 2004)

Narayanan A, 'When the Business Model *is* the Privacy Violation' (*Freedom to Tinker*, 12 April 2018) <https://freedom-to-tinker.com/2018/04/12/when-the-business-model-is-the-privacy-violation/> accessed 16 April 2018

——, 'A Critical Look at Decentralized Personal Data Architectures' [2012] arXiv preprint arXiv:1202.4503 <http://arxiv.org/abs/1202.4503> accessed 17 October 2016

Narayanan A and Felten EW, 'No Silver Bullet: De-Identification Still Doesn't Work' [2014] White Paper <http://randomwalker.info/publications/no-silver-bullet-de-identification.pdf> accessed 24 February 2016

Narayanan A, Huey J, and Felten EW, 'A Precautionary Approach to Big Data Privacy' <http://randomwalker.info/publications/precautionary.pdf> accessed 2 April 2015

Narayanan A and Shmatikov V, 'Myths and Fallacies of "Personally Identifiable Information"' (2010) 53 Communications of the ACM 24

Narayanan M and others, 'How Do Humans Understand Explanations from Machine Learning Systems? An Evaluation of the Human-Interpretability of Explanation' [2018] arXiv:1802.00682 [cs] <http://arxiv.org/abs/1802.00682> accessed 11 February 2018

Nash V and others, 'Public Policy in the Platform Society' (2017) 9 Policy & Internet 368

Naughton J, *From Gutenberg to Zuckerberg: What You Really Need to Know about the Internet* (Quercus 2012)

——, 'Facebook and Twitter Could Pay the Price for Hate Speech' *The Guardian* (19 March 2017) <https://www.theguardian.com/commentisfree/2017/mar/19/john-naughton-germany-fine-social-media-sites-facebook-twitter-hate-speech> accessed 22 March 2017

——, 'Extremism Pays. That's Why Silicon Valley Isn't Shutting It down | John Naughton' (*The Guardian*, 18 March 2018) <http://www.theguardian.com/commentisfree/2018/mar/18/extremism-pays-why-silicon-valley-not-shutting-it-down-youtube> accessed 18 March 2018

Nauwelaerts W, 'Practitioner's Corner—GDPR—The Perfect Privacy Storm: You Can Run from the Regulator, but You Cannot Hide from the Consumer' (2017) 3 European Data Protection Law Review 251

Nemitz P, 'No Reason for AI and GAFAM to Escape Democratic Oversight' (2019) 11 The Progressive Post 50

Neville A, 'Is It a Human Right To Be Forgotten? Conceptualizing The World View' (2017) 15 Santa Clara Journal of International Law 17

Newell BC, 'Forewords—Privacy as Antipower: In Pursuit of Non-Domination' (2018) 4 European Data Protection Law Review 12

Newlands G, Lutz C, and Fieseler C, 'Power in the Sharing Economy' (BI Norwegian Business School 2017) <https://papers.ssrn.com/abstract=2960938> accessed 5 May 2017

Nissenbaum H, *Privacy in Context: Technology, Policy, and the Integrity of Social Life* (Stanford University Press 2009)

Noble SU, *Algorithms of Oppression: How Search Engines Reinforce Racism* (New York University Press 2018) <https://www.overdrive.com/search?q=50344CBA-F46F-46D8-AED3-8E55ACCAEC93> accessed 16 March 2018

Nora S and Minc A, *L'informatisation de la société: rapport a M. le President de la Republique* (La Documentation française 1978)

Norris C and others, *The Unaccountable State of Surveillance: Exercising Access Rights in Europe* (Sprinter International Publishing 2017)

Norte JC, 'Advanced Tor Browser Fingerprinting' (6 March 2016) <http://jcarlosnorte.com/security/2016/03/06/advanced-tor-browser-fingerprinting.html> accessed 9 March 2016

Norval C and others, 'Reclaiming Data: Overcoming App Identification Barriers for Exercising Data Protection Rights' [2018] arXiv:1809.05369 [cs] <http://arxiv.org/abs/1809.05369> accessed 20 September 2018

Nugter ACM, *Transborder Flow of Personal Data within the EC: A Comparative Analysis of the Privacy Statutes of the Federal Republic of Germany, France, the United Kingdom and The Netherlands and Their Impact on the Private Sector* (Kluwer Law and Taxation 1990)

OECD, 'The OECD Privacy Framework' (OECD 2013) <www.oecd.org/sti/ieconomy/oecd_privacy_framework.pdf> accessed 9 May 2014

Ohm P, 'Broken Promises of Privacy: Responding to the Surprising Failure of Anonymization' (2010) 57 UCLA Law Review 1701

Ohm P, 'Sensitive Information' (2014) 88 S Cal L Rev 1125

Oliver P, 'The Protection of Privacy in the Economic Sphere before the European Court of Justice' (2009) 46 Common Market Law Review 1443

——, 'What Purpose Does Article 16 of the Charter Serve?' in Ulf Bernitz, Xavier Groussot, and Felix Schulyok (eds), *General Principles of EU Law and European Private Law* (1st edn, Kluwer Law International 2013)

Olsen T and Mahler T, 'Identity Management and Data Protection Law: Risk, Responsibility and Compliance in "Circles of Trust"—Part II' (2007) 23 Computer Law & Security Review 415

O'Neil C, *Weapons of Math Destruction: How Big Data Increases Inequality and Threatens Democracy* (Penguin Books 2017)

Online Manipulation and Personal Data, 'Online Manipulation and Personal Data. Intervention by Giovanni Buttarelli' (Committee Meeting on Civil Liberties, Justice and Home Affairs, Brussels, 25 June 2018) <http://www.europarl.europa.eu/ep-live/en/committees/video?event=20180625-1430-COMMITTEE-LIBE> accessed 26 June 2018

Oostveen M, 'Protecting Individuals Against the Negative Impact of Big Data: The Potential and Limitations of the Privacy and Data Protection Law Approach' (PhD Thesis, University of Amsterdam 2018)

Oostveen M and Irion K, 'The Golden Age of Personal Data: How to Regulate an Enabling Fundamental Right?' in Bakhoum and others (eds), *Personal Data in Competition,*

Consumer Protection and IP Law—Towards a Holistic Approach? (Springer 2017) <https://papers.ssrn.com/abstract=2885701> accessed 19 January 2017

Ost F and van de Kerchove M, *Entre la lettre et l'esprit: les directives d'interprétation en droit* (Bruylant 1989)

Oswald M, 'Data Anonymisation and Managing Risk—The ICO's New Code' (2012) 13 Privacy & Data Protection 3

Pan SB, 'Get to Know Me: Protecting Privacy and Autonomy under Big Data's Penetrating Gaze Notes' (2016) 30 Harvard Journal of Law & Technology (Harvard JOLT) 239

Pariser E, *The Filter Bubble: What The Internet Is Hiding From You* (Penguin Books 2012)

Parker C, 'Meta-Regulation: Legal Accountability for Corporate Social Responsibility' in Doreen McBarnet, Aurora Voiculescu, and Tom Campbell, *The New Corporate Accountability: Corporate Social Responsibility and the Law* (CUP 2009)

Pasquale F, 'Privacy, Antitrust, and Power' (2013) 20 George Mason Law Review 1009

——, *The Black Box Society: The Secret Algorithms That Control Money and Information* (Harvard University Press 2014)

——, 'Platform Neutrality: Enhancing Freedom of Expression in Spheres of Private Power The Constitution of Information: From Gutenberg to Snowden' (2016) 17 Theoretical Inquiries in Law 487

——, 'Two Narratives of Platform Capitalism' (2016) 35 Yale L & Pol'y Rev 309

Paul-Choudhury S, 'Digital Legacy: The Fate of Your Online Soul' (2011) 210 New Scientist 41

Peacock SE, 'How Web Tracking Changes User Agency in the Age of Big Data: The Used User' (2014) 1 Big Data & Society <https://doi.org/10.1177/2053951714564228> accessed 21 July 2015

Peers S and others (eds), *The EU Charter of Fundamental Rights: A Commentary* (Hart 2014) <https://www.bloomsburycollections.com/book/the-eu-charter-of-fundamental-rights-a-commentary/>

Peers S and Prechal S, 'Scope and Interpretation of Rights and Principles' in Steve Peers and others (eds), *The EU Charter of Fundamental Rights: A Commentary* (Hart 2014) <https://www.bloomsburycollections.com/book/the-eu-charter-of-fundamental-rights-a-commentary/>.

Peguera M, 'In the Aftermath of Google Spain: How the "Right to Be Forgotten" Is Being Shaped in Spain by Courts and the Data Protection Authority' (2015) 23 International Journal of Law and Information Technology 325

——, 'No More Right-to-Be-Forgotten for Mr. Costeja, Says Spanish Data Protection Authority' (*Center for Internet and Society (CIS) at Stanford University*, 3 October 2015) <https://cyberlaw.stanford.edu/blog/2015/10/no-more-right-be-forgotten-mr-costeja-says-spanish-data-protection-authority> accessed 7 October 2015

Peppet SR, 'Regulating the Internet of Things: First Steps toward Managing Discrimination, Privacy, Security and Consent' (2014) 93 Texas Law Review 85

Petkova B, 'Towards an Internal Hierarchy of Values in the EU Legal Order: Balancing the Freedom of Speech and Data Privacy' (2016) 23 Maastricht Journal of European and Comparative Law (MJ) 421

Pettit P, *Republicanism: A Theory of Freedom and Government* (Clarendon Press 2002)

Pfitzmann A and Hansen M, 'A Terminology for Talking about Privacy by Data Minimization: Anonymity, Unlinkability, Undetectability, Unobservability, Pseudonymity, and Identity Management' <https://dud.inf.tu-dresden.de/literatur/Anon_Terminology_v0.34.pdf> accessed 24 February 2016

Picard RW, *Affective Computing* (MIT Press 2000)

Pink S and others, 'Mundane Data: The Routines, Contingencies and Accomplishments of Digital Living' (2017) 4 Big Data & Society 2053951717700924

Policy Issues in Data Protection and Privacy: Concepts and Perspectives: Proceedings of the OECD Seminar, 24th to 26th June 1974 (OECD 1976)

Pollicino O, 'European Judicial Dialogue and the Protection of Fundamental Rights in the New Digital Environment: An Attempt at Emancipation and Reconciliation' in Sonia Morano-Foadi and Lucy Vickers (eds), *Fundamental Rights in the EU: A Matter for Two Courts.* (Hart 2015)

Polonetsky J and Hirsch DD, 'The Emerging Ethical Standards for Studying Corporate Data' (*Recode*, 14 June 2016) <https://www.recode.net/2016/6/14/11923286/facebook-emotional-contagion-controversy-data-research-review-policy-ethics> accessed 2 April 2018

Poon M, 'Corporate Capitalism and the Growing Power of Big Data: Review Essay' (2016) 41 Science, Technology & Human Values 1088

Poullet Y and Léonard T, 'Les libertés comme fondement de la protection des données nominatives' in François Rigaux, *La vie privée: une liberté parmi les autres?* (Larcier 1992)

Powles J, 'The Case That Won't Be Forgotten' (2015) 47 Loy U Chi LJ 583

——, 'DeepMind's Data Deals Raise Some Serious Questions' *Financial Times* (4 December 2016) <https://www.ft.com/content/ddd1478e-b70d-11e6-961e-a1acd97f622d> accessed 9 December 2016

Powles J and Chaparro E, 'How Google Determined Our Right to Be Forgotten' *The Guardian* (London, 18 February 2015) <http://www.theguardian.com/technology/2015/feb/18/the-right-be-forgotten-google-search> accessed 2 April 2015

Powles J and Floridi L, 'A Manifesto for the Future of the "right to Be Forgotten" Debate' *The Guardian* (22 July 2014) <http://www.theguardian.com/technology/2014/jul/22/a-manifesto-for-the-future-of-the-right-to-be-forgotten-debate> accessed 23 July 2014

Powles J and Hodson H, 'Google DeepMind and Healthcare in an Age of Algorithms' (2017) 7 Health and Technology 351

Powles J and Singh J, 'Why the Internet of Things Favours Dominance' (*The Guardian*, 24 July 2015) <www.theguardian.com/technology/2015/jul/24/internet-of-things-centralisation-dominance> accessed 28 July 2015

Premier Ministre de la République Française, 'Charte Du Droit a l'Oubli Dans Les Sites Collaboratifs et Les Moteurs de Recherche'

Prins JEJ and others, *De Staat van Informatie* (Amsterdam University Press 2011) <http://www.oapen.org/download?type=document&docid=375125> accessed 30 May 2016

'Privacy, Privatisation and Self-Determination', in John Young and Christopher GA Bryant, *Privacy* (Wiley 1978)

Psychogiopoulou E, 'The European Court of Human Rights, Privacy and Data Protection in the Digital Era' in Maja Brkan and Evangelia Psychogiopoulou, *Courts, Privacy and Data Protection in the Digital Environment* (Edward Elgar 2017)

Purtova N, *Property Rights in Personal Data : A European Perspective*, vol 24 (First, Kluwer Law International 2012)

——, 'The Illusion of Personal Data as No One's Property' (2015) 7 Law, Innovation and Technology 83

——, 'The Law of Everything. Broad Concept of Personal Data and Overstretched Scope of EU Data Protection Law' (2017) <https://papers.ssrn.com/abstract=3036355> accessed 21 September 2017

Quelle C, 'Not Just User Control in the General Data Protection Regulation', *Privacy and Identity Management. Facing up to Next Steps* (Springer International Publishing

2016) <https://link-springer-com/chapter/10.1007/978-3-319-55783-0_11> accessed 27 February 2018

Quill L, *Secrets and Democracy from Arcana Imperii to Wikileaks* (Palgrave Macmillan 2014)

Raab CD and Szekely I, 'Data Protection Authorities and Information Technology' (2017) 33 Computer Law & Security Review 421

Raad voor de Journalistiek, 'Journalistieke Code' <http://www.rvdj.be/sites/default/files/pdf/code-rvdj.pdf> accessed 26 May 2017

Rachovitsa A, 'Engineering and Lawyering Privacy by Design: Understanding Online Privacy Both as a Technical and an International Human Rights Issue' (2016) 24 International Journal of Law and Information Technology 374

Rallo Lombarte A and Centro de Estudios Políticos y Constitucionales (Espanya), *El Derecho al olvido en Internet: Google versus España* (Centro de Estudios Políticos y Constitucionales 2014)

Rasle B, 'Droit à l'oubli: Quel rôle pour le délégué à la protection des données personnelles?' in David Dechenaud (ed), *Le droit à l'oubli numérique: Données nominatives—Approche comparée* (Larcier 2015)

Rauhofer J, 'Of Men and Mice: Should the EU Data Protection Authorities' Reaction to Google's New Privacy Policy Raise Concern for the Future of the Purpose Limitation Principle?' (2015) 1 European Data Protection Law Review 5

Raz J, *The Morality of Freedom* (OUP; Clarendon Press 1986)

——, *From Normativity to Responsibility* (OUP 2011)

'Red Herring', *Wikipedia* (2018) <https://en.wikipedia.org/wiki/Red_herring> accessed 9 May 2018

Reding V, 'Building Trust in the Digital Single Market: Reforming the EU's Data Protection Rules (SPEECH/11/814)' (Conference organised by the Industry Coalition for Data Protection—American Chamber of Commerce to the European Union, Brussels, 28 November 2011)

——, 'The EU Data Protection Reform 2012: Safeguarding Privacy in a Connected World' (Press Conference on the Presentation of the New Proposals, Brussels, 25 January 2012) <http://ec.europa.eu/archives/commission_2010-2014/reding/pdf/speeches/data-protection-reform2012_en.pdf> accessed 18 January 2016

Regan PM, *Legislating Privacy: Technology, Social Values, and Public Policy* (University of North Carolina Press 1995)

Reidenberg JR and others, 'Disagreeable Privacy Policies: Mismatches between Meaning and Users' Understanding' (2015) 30 Berkeley Technology Law Journal 1

Reidenberg JR and others, 'Ambiguity in Privacy Policies and the Impact of Regulation' (2016) 45 Journal of Legal Studies S163

Richards N, *Intellectual Privacy: Rethinking Civil Liberties in the Digital Age* (2015)

Richards NM, 'The Dangers of Surveillance' (2013) 126 Harvard Law Review 1934

Rigaux F, *La vie privée: une liberté parmi les autres?* (Larcier 1992)

'Robots Exclusion Standard', *Wikipedia* (2018) <https://en.wikipedia.org/w/index.php?title=Robots_exclusion_standard&oldid=844679166> accessed 14 June 2018

Rodotà S, 'Data Protection as a Fundamental Right' in Serge Gutwirth and others (eds), *Reinventing Data Protection?* (1st edn, Springer Netherlands 2009) <http://link.springer.com/10.1007/978-1-4020-9498-9> accessed 6 April 2015

Roosendaal A, 'Digital Personae and Profiles in Law: Protecting Individuals' Rights in Online Contexts' (PhD Thesis, Tilburg University 2013)

Rosen J, 'The Right to Be Forgotten' (2012) 64 Stanford Law Review Online 88

Rosenblat A and others, 'Discriminating Tastes: Customer Ratings as Vehicles for Bias' [2016] Data & Society <https://datasociety.net/output/discriminating-tastes-customer-ratings-as-vehicles-for-bias/> accessed 27 July 2018

Rosenblat A and Stark L, 'Algorithmic Labor and Information Asymmetries: A Case Study of Uber's Drivers' (*Data & Society*, 15 October 2015) <https://datasociety.net/output/ubers-drivers-information-asymmetries-and-control-in-dynamic-work/> accessed 21 June 2018

Rosner G and Kenneally E, 'Clearly Opaque: Privacy Risks of the Internet of Things' (The Internet of Things Privacy Forum 2018) <https://www.iotprivacyforum.org/wp-content/uploads/2018/06/Clearly-Opaque-Privacy-Risks-of-the-Internet-of-Things.pdf?d8bd54&d8bd54> accessed 9 June 2018

Rouvroy A, 'The End(s) of Critique: Data-Behaviourism vs. Due-Process' in Mireille Hildebrandt and Katja de Vries, *Privacy, Due Process and the Computational Turn: The Philosophy of Law Meets the Philosophy of Technology* (Routledge 2013)

——, '"Of Data and Men". Fundamental Rights and Freedoms in a World of Big Data' (Council of Europe 2016) T-PD-BUR(2015)09REV <www.coe.int/t/dghl/standardsetting/DataProtection/TPD_documents/T-PD-BUR(2015)09REV_Big%20Data%20report_A%20%20Rouvroy_Final_EN.pdf> accessed 1 February 2016

Rouvroy A and Poullet Y, 'The Right to Informational Self-Determination and the Value of Self-Development: Reassessing the Importance of Privacy for Democracy' in Serge Gutwirth and others (eds), *Reinventing Data Protection?* (Springer Netherlands 2009) <http://link.springer.com/10.1007/978-1-4020-9498-9> accessed 16 January 2015

Rubinstein IS, 'Big Data: The End of Privacy or a New Beginning?' (2013) 3 International Data Privacy Law 74

Rushkoff D, 'How Facebook Exploited Us All' (*latimes.com*) <http://www.latimes.com/opinion/op-ed/la-oe-rushkoff-leaving-facebook-20180325-story.html> accessed 28 March 2018

Rustad ML and Kulevska S, 'Reconceptualizing the Right to Be Forgotten to Enable Transatlantic Data Flow' (2015) 28 Harv J Law & Tec 349

Rutkin A, 'Facebook Can Recognise You in Photos Even If You're Not Looking' (*New Scientist*, 22 June 2015) <www.newscientist.com/article/dn27761-facebook-can-recognise-you-in-photos-even-if-youre-not-looking.html#.VYkeo0a4HEIcc> accessed 30 June 2015

Saint-Exupéry A de, *Vol de nuit* (Gallimard 1991)

Salom JA, '"A Third Party to Whom Data Are Disclosed": A Third Group among Those Processing Data' (2014) 4 International Data Privacy Law 177

Samuelson P, 'Privacy As Intellectual Property?' (2000) 52 Stanford Law Review 1125

Sandoval M, 'A Critical Empirical Case Study of Consumer Surveillance on Web 2.0' in Christian Fuchs and others (eds), *Internet and Surveillance: The Challenges of Web 2.0 and Social Media* (Routledge 2012)

Sandvig C and others, 'Can Algorithms Be Unethical?' (2015)

SATORI Project, 'Policy Brief. Industry and Research and Innovation (R&I): Towards Ethical, Responsible and Sustainable R&I' <http://satoriproject.eu/media/SATORI-policy-brief-_2017-Industry-_09-1-2017.pdf> accessed 28 April 2018

Savov V, 'Google's Selfish Ledger Is an Unsettling Vision of Silicon Valley Social Engineering' (*The Verge*, 17 May 2018) <https://www.theverge.com/2018/5/17/17344250/google-x-selfish-ledger-video-data-privacy> accessed 30 May 2018

Scalia A, 'The Rule of Law as a Law of Rules Essay' (1989) 56 University of Chicago Law Review 1175

Scheiber N, 'How Uber Uses Psychological Tricks to Push Its Drivers' Buttons' *The New York Times* (2 April 2017) <https://www.nytimes.com/interactive/2017/04/02/technology/uber-drivers-psychological-tricks.html> accessed 25 October 2017

Schermer B, 'Risks of Profiling and the Limits of Data Protection Law' in Bart Custers and others (eds), *Discrimination and Privacy in the Information Society—Data Mining and Profiling in Large Databases* (1st edn Springer 2013)

Schermer BW, 'The Limits of Privacy in Automated Profiling and Data Mining' (2011) 27 Computer Law & Security Review 45

Schmidt E and Cohen J, *The New Digital Age: Reshaping the Future of People, Nations and Business* (Alfred A Knopf 2013)

Schneier B, *Data and Goliath: The Hidden Battles to Capture Your Data and Control Your World* (W W Norton 2015)

——, 'The Security of Data Deletion' (*Schneier on Security*, 15 January 2015) <https://www.schneier.com/blog/archives/2015/01/the_security_of_10.html> accessed 9 April 2015

——, 'Click Here to Kill Everyone' [2017] *NY Mag* <http://nymag.com/selectall/2017/01/the-internet-of-things-dangerous-future-bruce-schneier.html> accessed 1 March 2017.

Scholz T, *Digital Labor: The Internet as Playground and Factory* (Routledge 2013)

Schreurs W and others, 'Cogitas, Ergo Sum. The Role of Data Protection Law and Non-Discrimination Law in Group Profiling in the Private Sector' in Mireille Hildebrandt and Serge Gutwirth (eds), *Profiling the European Citizen: Cross-Disciplinary Perspectives* (Springer 2008)

Schroeder R, 'Big Data and the Brave New World of Social Media Research' (2014) 1 Big Data & Society 2053951714563194

Schwartz J, 'Two German Killers Demanding Anonymity Sue Wikipedia's Parent' *The New York Times* (12 November 2009) <http://www.nytimes.com/2009/11/13/us/13wiki.html> accessed 17 November 2015

Schwartz PM, 'Property, Privacy, and Personal Data' (2004) 117 Harvard Law Review 2056

Schwartz PM and Solove DJ, 'PII Problem: Privacy and a New Concept of Personally Identifiable Information, The' (2011) 86 New York University Law Review 1814

Scott M, 'Europe's Highest Court Sides with Facebook in Privacy Class-Action Lawsuit' *POLITICO* (Europe, 25 January 2018) <https://www.politico.eu/article/facebook-ecj-european-court-justice-max-schrems-austria-lawsuit-classaction-privacy-data-protection-max-schrems/> accessed 13 February 2018

Searls D, *The Intention Economy: When Customers Take Charge* (Harvard Business Review Press 2012)

Selbst A and Powles J, 'Meaningful Information and the Right to Explanation' (2017) 7 International Data Privacy Law 233

Selbst AD and Barocas S, 'The Intuitive Appeal of Explainable Machines' (2018) 87 Fordham Law Review 1085

Selinger E, 'Opinion: If Predictive Algorithms Craft the Best e-Mails, We're All in Big Trouble' [2015] *Christian Science Monitor* <http://www.csmonitor.com/World/Passcode/Passcode-Voices/2015/0427/Opinion-If-predictive-algorithms-craft-the-best-e-mails-we-re-all-in-big-trouble> accessed 15 July 2015

Selvadurai N, 'Not Just a Face in the Crowd: Addressing the Intrusive Potential of the Online Application of Face Recognition Technologies' (2015) 23 International Journal of Law and Information Technology 187

Shahin S, 'Right to Be Forgotten How National Identity, Political Orientation, and Capitalist Ideology Structured a Trans-Atlantic Debate on Information Access and Control' (2016) 93 Journalism & Mass Communication Quarterly 360

SIGCHI (Group: U.S.) and Curriculum Development Group, *ACM SIGCHI Curricula for Human-Computer Interaction* (Association for Computing Machinery 1992) <http://old.sigchi.org/cdg/index.html> accessed 16 June 2018

Simitis S, 'Revisiting Sensitive Data' <https://www.coe.int/t/dghl/standardsetting/dataprotection/Reports/Report_Simitis_1999.pdf> accessed 8 February 2016

——, 'Privacy—An Endless Debate' (2010) 98 California Law Review 1989

Simmonds NE, *Central Issues in Jurisprudence: Justice, Law and Rights* (Sweet & Maxwell 2006)

Sin CH and others, 'Realizing the Right to Be Forgotten in an SNS Environment' in Hwa Young Jeong and others (eds), *Advances in Computer Science and its Applications*, vol 279 (Springer 2014) <http://link.springer.com/10.1007/978-3-642-41674-3_201> accessed 24 November 2014

Singh J and others, 'Big Ideas Paper: Policy-Driven Middleware for a Legally-Compliant Internet of Things', *Proceedings of the 17th International Middleware Conference* (ACM 2016) <http://doi.acm.org/10.1145/2988336.2988349> accessed 12 April 2017

Sloot B van der, 'Legal Fundamentalism: Is Data Protection Really a Fundamental Right?' in Ronald Leenes and others (eds), *Data Protection and Privacy: (In)visibilities and Infrastructures* (Springer 2017) <https://link-springer-com.kuleuven.ezproxy.kuleuven.be/chapter/10.1007/978-3-319-50796-5_1> accessed 12 March 2018

Smedt SD, 'Data Protection May Have to Yield in IP Infringement Cases (Case C580/13, Coty Germany)' (2015) 1 European Data Protection Law Review 316

Smet S, 'Freedom of Expression and the Right to Reputation: Human Rights in Conflict' (2010) 26 American University International Law Review 183

——, 'Resolving Conflicts between Human Rights: A Legal Theoretical Analysis in the Context of the ECHR' (PhD Thesis, Ghent University 2014)

——, *Resolving Conflicts Between Human Rights: The Judge's Dilemma.* (CRC Press 2018)

Society of American Archivists, 'Core Values Statement and Code of Ethics' <http://www2.archivists.org/statements/saa-core-values-statement-and-code-of-ethics> accessed 26 May 2017

Solove D, *The Digital Person: Technology and Privacy in the Information Age* (New York University Press 2004)

Solove D, 'A Taxonomy of Privacy' (2006) 154 University of Pennsylvania Law Review 477

Solove D, '"I've Got Nothing to Hide" and Other Misunderstandings of Privacy' (2007) 44 The San Diego Law Review 745

Solove DJ, *Nothing to Hide: The False Tradeoff between Privacy and Security* (Yale University Press 2012)

Solove DJ, 'Introduction: Privacy Self-Management and the Consent Dilemma' (2013) 126 Harvard Law Review 1880

Song S, 'Multiculturalism' in Edward N Zalta (ed), *The Stanford Encyclopedia of Philosophy* (Spring 2017, Metaphysics Research Lab, Stanford University 2017) <https://plato.stanford.edu/archives/spr2017/entries/multiculturalism/> accessed 18 January 2017

Stahl T, 'Indiscriminate Mass Surveillance and the Public Sphere' (2016) 18 Ethics and Information Technology 33

Stalla-Bourdillon S, *Privacy vs. Security* (Springer, 2014)

Stalla-Bourdillon S and Knight A, 'Anonymous Data v. Personal Data—A False Debate: An EU Perspective on Anonymization, Pseudonymization and Personal Data' (2017) 34 Wisconsin International Law Journal 284

Statement, 'Common Statement by the Contact Group of the Data Protection Authorities of The Netherlands, France, Spain, Hamburg and Belgium' (4 December 2015) <www.

privacycommission.be/sites/privacycommission/files/documents/Common%20 Statement%20Facebook%20-%20final%20-withOUT%20signatures.pdf> accessed 12 September 2016

Sterling B, 'Dispatches From the Hyperlocal Future' (*WIRED*, 26 June 2007) <https://www.wired.com/2007/06/local/> accessed 18 July 2017

Strandburg KJ, 'Free Fall: The Online Market's Consumer Preference Disconnect' [2013] University of Chicago Legal Forum 79

'Streisand Effect', *Wikipedia* (2018) <https://en.wikipedia.org/w/index.php?title=Streisand_effect&oldid=835810997> accessed 12 April 2018

Svantesson DJB, *Extraterritoriality in Data Privacy Law* (Ex Tuto Publishing 2013)

——, 'The Extraterritoriality of EU Data Privacy Law—Its Theoretical Justification and Its Practical Effect on U.S. Businesses' (2013) 50 Stanford Journal of International Law 53

Svantesson DJB, 'A "Layered Approach" to the Extraterritoriality of Data Privacy Laws' (2013) 3 International Data Privacy Law 278

——, 'Extraterritoriality and Targeting in EU Data Privacy Law: The Weak Spot Undermining the Regulation' (2015) 5 International Data Privacy Law 226

——, 'The (Uncertain) Future of Online Data Privacy' (2015) 9 Masaryk University Journal of Law and Technology 129

Sweeney L, 'Uniqueness of Simple Demographics in the U.S. Population' (Carnegie Mellon University, School of Computer Science, Data Privacy Laboratory 2000) Technical Report LIDAP-WP4

Swisher K, Interview with Nicole Wong, 'Is It Time for a "Slow Food" Movement for the Internet?' (12 September 2018) <https://www.recode.net/2018/9/12/17848384/nicole-wong-cto-lawyer-google-twitter-kara-swisher-decode-podcast-full-transcript> accessed 13 September 2018

Tambou O (ed), *Le Droit à l'oubli En Europe et Au-Delà / The Right to Be Forgotten in Europe and Beyond* (Blogdroiteuropéen 2018) <https://wp.me/p6OBGR-2QK> accessed 30 April 2018

Taylor M, 'The EU's Human Rights Obligations in Relation to Its Data Protection Laws with Extraterritorial Effect' (2015) 5 International Data Privacy Law 246

Tene O and Polonetsky J, 'A Theory of Creepy: Technology, Privacy and Shifting Social Norms' (2013) 16 Yale Journal of Law & Technology 59

——, 'Beyond IRBs: Ethical Guidelines for Data Research' (2016) 72 Washington and Lee Law Review Online 458

The Berkman Klein Center for Internet & Society, *Jonas Kaiser on The Dark Side of the Networked Public Sphere* <https://www.youtube.com/watch?v=bhiA6pg4ohs> accessed 7 February 2018

The Dark Side of Data (2012) <http://www.ted.com/playlists/130/the_dark_side_of_data> accessed 16 November 2015

The Guardian, 'Community Standards and Participation Guidelines' *The Guardian* (7 May 2009) <https://www.theguardian.com/community-standards> accessed 22 May 2017

Thierer A, 'Europe's "Right to Be Forgotten": Privacy as Internet Censorship' (*The Technology Liberation Front*, 23 January 2012) <http://techliberation.com/2012/01/23/europes-right-to-be-forgotten-privacy-as-internet-censorship/> accessed 23 October 2012

Thouvenin F and others, 'Remembering and Forgetting in the Digital Age—A Position Paper' (2016) 21 Information Research <http://www.informationr.net/ir/21-1/memo/memo2.html#ric13> accessed 7 April 2017

—— (eds), *Remembering and Forgetting in the Digital Age* (Springer International Publishing 2018) <//www.springer.com/gp/book/9783319902296> accessed 1 May 2018

Tippmann S and Powles J, 'Google Accidentally Reveals Data on "right to Be Forgotten" Requests' *The Guardian* (14 July 2015) <http://www.theguardian.com/technology/2015/jul/14/google-accidentally-reveals-right-to-be-forgotten-requests> accessed 27 August 2015

Tridimas T, 'Fundamental Rights, General Principles of EU Law, and the Charter' (2014) 16 Cambridge Yearbook of European Legal Studies 361

——, *The General Principles of EU Law* (New Edition, 3rd edn, OUP 2018)

Tsormpatzoudi P, 'Eksistenz D7.4 Intermediate Report for D7.5' (CiTiP 2015) Deliverable D7.4 <http://eksistenz.eu/>

Tufekci Z, 'Engineering the Public: Big Data, Surveillance and Computational Politics' (2014) 19 First Monday <http://firstmonday.org/ojs/index.php/fm/article/view/4901> accessed 25 November 2014

Turn R, 'Classification of Personal Information for Privacy Protection Purposes', *Proceedings of the June 7–10, 1976, National Computer Conference and Exposition* (ACM 1976) <http://doi.acm.org/10.1145/1499799.1499846> accessed 22 February 2016

Tushnet R, 'Power without Responsibility: Intermediaries and the First Amendment' (2007) 76 Geo Wash L Rev 986

Tzanou M, 'Data Protection as a Fundamental Right next to Privacy? "Reconstructing" a Not So New Right' (2013) 3 International Data Privacy Law 88

United Nations Conference on Trade and Development, 'Data Protection and Privacy Legislation Worldwide' <https://unctad.org/en/Pages/DTL/STI_and_ICTs/ICT4D-Legislation/eCom-Data-Protection-Laws.aspx> accessed 12 June 2019

Untersinger M, 'Le Conseil d'Etat face au casse-tête du "droit à l'oubli"' *Le Monde.fr* (2 February 2017) <http://www.lemonde.fr/pixels/article/2017/02/02/le-conseil-d-etat-face-au-casse-tete-du-droit-a-l-oubli_5073709_4408996.html> accessed 6 February 2017

'Updating Our "Right to Be Forgotten" Transparency Report' (*Google*, 26 February 2018) <https://www.blog.google/topics/google-europe/updating-our-right-be-forgotten-transparency-report/> accessed 28 February 2018

Urban JM, Karaganis J, and Schofield BL, 'Notice and Takedown in Everyday Practice' (UC Berkeley and Columbia University 2016) <http://papers.ssrn.com/abstract=2755628> accessed 6 April 2016

Valcke P, Kuczerawy A, and Ombelet P-J, 'Did the Romans Get It Right? What Delfi, Google, EBay, and UPC TeleKabel Wien Have in Common' in Mariarosaria Taddeo and Luciano Floridi (eds), *The Responsibilities of Online Service Providers*, vol 31 (Springer International Publishing 2017) <http://link.springer.com/10.1007/978-3-319-47852-4> accessed 4 June 2017

Van Alsenoy B, 'Allocating Responsibility among Controllers, Processors, and "Everything in between": The Definition of Actors and Roles in Directive 95/46/EC' (2012) 28 Computer Law & Security Review 25

——, '"Who's Who?" Mapping the Relevant Actors in a Social Networking Context' Publisher and date needed

——, 'Rights and Obligations of Actors in Social Networking Sites' (KU Leuven - CiTiP 2014) Deliverable D.6.2 <https://lirias.kuleuven.be/handle/123456789/453689> accessed 16 March 2016

——, 'The Evolving Role of the Individual Under EU Data Protection Law' (KU Leuven—CiTiP 2015) Working Paper 23 <http://papers.ssrn.com/abstract=2641680> accessed 4 November 2015

——, 'Regulating Data Protection: The Allocation of Responsibility and Risk among Involved in Personal Data Processing' (PhD Thesis, KU Leuven—Faculty of Law 2016)

——, 'Liability under EU Data Protection Law: From Directive 95/46 to the General Data Protection Regulation' (2017) 7 JIPITEC <http://www.jipitec.eu/issues/jipitec-7-3-2016/4506>

——, *Data Protection Law in the EU: Roles, Responsibilities and Liability* (Intersentia 2019)

Van Alsenoy B and others, 'Cultures of Accountability: A Cross-Cultural Perspective on Current and Future Accountability Mechanisms' (University of Leuven—CiTiP 2014) Report of Expert Workshop <www.law.kuleuven.be/citip/en/news/item/coa-workshop-report.pdf>.

——, 'From Social Media Service to Advertising Network—A Critical Analysis of Facebook's Revised Policies and Terms' (KU Leuven & VUB 2015) 1.3 <www.law.kuleuven.be/icri/en/news/item/icri-cir-advises-belgian-privacy-commission-in-facebook-investigation>.

Van Alsenoy B and Koekkoek M, 'Internet and Jurisdiction after Google Spain: The Extraterritorial Reach of the "Right to Be Delisted" ' (2015) 5 International Data Privacy Law 105

Van Alsenoy B, Kosta E, and Dumortier J, 'Privacy Notices versus Informational Self-Determination: Minding the Gap' (2013) 28 International Review of Law, Computers & Technology 185

Van Alsenoy B, Kuczerawy A, and Ausloos J, 'Search Engines after "Google Spain": Internet@Liberty or Privacy@Peril?' (2013) <http://papers.ssrn.com/abstract=2321494> accessed 21 January 2014

van Andel RCK and van Nijendaal MW, 'Misbruik Wbp en incasseren dwangsommen' (*Nysingh*, 22 January 2018) <https://www.nysingh.nl/actueel/misbruik-wbp-en-incasseren-dwangsommen/> accessed 30 January 2018

Van Calster G and others, 'Not Just One, but Many "Rights to Be Forgotten". A Global Status Quo' (Foundation for European Progressive Studies 2016) <https://lirias.kuleuven.be/handle/123456789/559109> accessed 6 December 2016

Van Calster G, Arreaza AG, and Apers E, 'Not Just One, but Many "Rights to Be Forgotten" ' (2018) 7 Internet Policy Review <https://policyreview.info/articles/analysis/not-just-one-many-rights-be-forgotten> accessed 27 July 2018

van den Hoven J, 'Information Technology, Privacy, and the Protection of Personal Data', *Information Technology and Moral Philosophy* (CUP 2008)

van Der Sloot B, 'From Data Minimization to Data Minimummization' in Bart Custers and others (eds), *Discrimination and Privacy in the Information Society - Data Mining and Profiling in Large Databases* (First, Springer 2013)

——, 'Do Data Protection Rules Protect the Individual and Should They? An Assessment of the Proposed General Data Protection Regulation' (2014) 4 International Data Privacy Law 307

——, 'Do Privacy and Data Protection Rules Apply to Legal Persons and Should They? A Proposal for a Two-Tiered System' (2015) 31 Computer Law & Security Review 26

——, 'The Practical and Theoretical Problems with "Balancing": Delfi, Coty and the Redundancy of the Human Rights Framework' (2016) 23 Maastricht Journal of European and Comparative Law (MJ) 439

——, 'Editorial' (2017) 3 European Data Protection Law Review 1

Van Dijk N and others, 'Right Engineering? The Redesign of Privacy and Personal Data Protection' [2018] International Review of Law, Computers & Technology

<https://www-tandfonline-com.kuleuven.ezproxy.kuleuven.be/doi/abs/10.1080/13600869.2018.1457002> accessed 14 June 2018

Van Drooghenbroeck S, *La proportionnalité dans le droit de la Convention européenne des droits de l'Homme: prendre l'idée simple au sérieux* (FUSL 2001)

Van Eecke P and Truyens M, 'Privacy and Social Networks' (2010) 26 Computer Law & Security Review 535

Van Hoboken J, '9 Reasons Why a "Right to Be Forgotten" Is Really Wrong' (8 December 2011) <http://www.jorisvanhoboken.nl/?m=201112> accessed 19 September 2012

——, 'Search Engine Freedom: On the Implications of the Right to Freedom Expression for the Legal Governance of Web Search Engines' (PhD Thesis, University of Amsterdam 2012) <http://dare.uva.nl/document/357527> accessed 15 November 2012

——, *Search Engine Freedom: On the Implications of the Right to Freedom Expression for the Legal Governance of Web Search Engines* (1st edn Kluwer Law International 2012)

——, 'The Proposed Right to Be Forgotten Seen from the Perspective of Our Right to Remember' <www.law.nyu.edu/sites/default/files/upload_documents/VanHoboken_RightTo%20Be%20Forgotten_Manuscript_2013.pdf> accessed 15 July 2014

van Hoboken J and Zuiderveen Borgesius F, 'Scoping Electronic Communication Privacy Rules: Data, Services and Values' (2015) 6 JIPITEC <http://www.jipitec.eu/issues/issue.2016-01-12.5219458400/4316>.

Van Malleghem P-A, 'Proportionality and the Erosion of Formalism' (PhD Thesis, KU Leuven—Faculty of Law 2016)

Veale M, Binns R, and Ausloos J, 'When Data Protection by Design and Data Subject Rights Clash' (2017) ID 3081069 <https://papers.ssrn.com/abstract=3081069> accessed 9 February 2018

——, 'When Data Protection by Design and Data Subject Rights Clash' (2018) 8 International Data Privacy Law 4

——, 'When Data Protection by Design and Data Subject Rights Clash' International Data Privacy Law <https://academic.oup.com/idpl/advance-article/doi/10.1093/idpl/ipy002/4960902> accessed 5 April 2018

Veale M, Binns R, and Edwards L, 'Algorithms That Remember: Model Inversion Attacks and Data Protection Law' [2018] arXiv:1807.04644 [cs] <http://arxiv.org/abs/1807.04644> accessed 17 August 2018

Veldkamp JT, *Het Amsterdamse Bevolkingsregister in Oorlogstijd (on File with the Author)* (Unpublished monograph available at the Amsterdam Resistance Museum 1954)

Venturini J and others, *Terms of Service and Human Rights: An Analysis of Online Platform Contracts* (Revan 2016) <http://internet-governance.fgv.br/sites/internet-governance.fgv.br/files/publicacoes/terms_of_services 06_12_2016.pdf> accessed 29 December 2016

Verdoodt V, Clifford D, and Lievens E, 'Toying with Children's Emotions, the New Game in Town? The Legality of Advergames in the EU' (2016) 32 Computer Law & Security Review 599

Viola de Azevedo Cunha M, 'Review of the Data Protection Directive: Is There Need (and Room) For a New Concept of Personal Data?' in Serge Gutwirth and others (eds), *European Data Protection: In Good Health?* (Springer 2012)

Voss WG and Castets-Renard C, 'Proposal for an International Taxonomy on the Various Forms of the Right to Be Forgotten: A Study on the Convergence of Norms' (2015) 14 J. on Telecomm. & High Tech L 281

Voytek B, 'Uberdata: The Ride of Glory' (*Uber Blog*, 26 March 2012) <http://blog.uber.com/2012/03/26/uberdata-the-ride-of-glory/> accessed 21 March 2018

Wachter S, Mittelstadt B, and Floridi L, 'Why a Right to Explanation of Automated Decision-Making Does Not Exist in the General Data Protection Regulation' (2017) 7 International Data Privacy Law 76

Wang Y and Kosinski M, 'Deep Neural Networks Are More Accurate than Humans at Detecting Sexual Orientation from Facial Images' [2017] Open Science Framework <https://osf.io/zn79k/> accessed 22 February 2018

Ward A, 'Field of Application (Article 51)' in Steve Peers and others (eds), *The EU Charter of Fundamental Rights: A Commentary* (Hart 2014) <https://www.bloomsburycollections.com/book/the-eu-charter-of-fundamental-rights-a-commentary/>Accessed & date needed ??

Warso Z, 'There's More to It than Data Protection—Fundamental Rights, Privacy and the Personal/Household Exemption in the Digital Age' (2013) 29 Computer Law & Security Review 491

Watters A, 'Pigeons, Operant Conditioning, and Social Control' (*Hack Education*, 15 June 2018) <http://hackeducation.com/2018/06/15/pigeons> accessed 18 June 2018

Wauters E, Lievens E, and Valcke P, 'Towards a Better Protection of Social Media Users: A Legal Perspective on the Terms of Use of Social Networking Sites' 22 International Journal of Law and Information Technology 254

Weatherill S, 'Consumer Protection (Article 38)' in Steve Peers and others (eds), *The EU Charter of Fundamental Rights: A Commentary* (Hart 2014) <https://www.bloomsburycollections.com/book/the-eu-charter-of-fundamental-rights-a-commentary/>.

Weaver M, 'UK Public Must Wake up to Risks of CCTV, Says Surveillance Commissioner' (*The Guardian*, 6 January 2015) <www.theguardian.com/world/2015/jan/06/tony-porter-surveillance-commissioner-risk-cctv-public-transparent> accessed 7 April 2015

Weber RH, 'The Right to Be Forgotten More Than a Pandora's Box?' (2011) 2 jipitec <http://www.jipitec.eu/issues/jipitec-2-2-2011/3084>.

Weinberger C, 'Records, Computers and the Rights of Citizens' (US Department of Health, Education and Welfare 1973)

Weitzner DJ and others, 'Information Accountability' (2008) 51 Commun ACM 82

Werbach K, 'Centripetal Network: How the Internet Holds Itself Together, and the Forces Tearing It Apart (2008) 42 UC Davis L Rev 343

Werro F, 'The Right to Inform v. The Right to Be Forgotten: A Transatlantic Clash' in Aurelia Colombi Ciacchi, *Haftungsrecht im dritten Millennium—Liability in the Third Millennium* (1st edn Nomos Verlagsges 2009) <http://papers.ssrn.com/sol3/papers.cfm?abstract_id=1401357> accessed 18 September 2012

Wery E, 'Les cookies peuvent coûter très cher ...' (*Droit & Technologies*, 18 June 2018) <https://www.droit-technologie.org/actualites/cookies-peuvent-couter-cher-tres-cher/> accessed 31 July 2018

Westin AF, *Privacy and Freedom* (Atheneum 1967)

Which and Britain Thinks, 'Control, Alt or Delete? Consumer Research on Attitudes to Data Collection and Use' (2018) <http://britainthinks.com/pdfs/Consumer-Data-Research-report.pdf> accessed 13 June 2018

Whitwam R, 'Facebook Developing Way to Fingerprint the Camera You Used to Take a Photo' (*@geekdotcom*, 20 September 2015) <http://www.geek.com/news/facebook-developing-way-to-fingerprint-the-camera-you-used-to-take-a-photo-1634542/> accessed 22 September 2015

Wollenschläger F, 'Right to Property' in Steve Peers and others (eds), *The EU Charter of Fundamental Rights: A Commentary* (Hart 2014) <https://www.bloomsburycollections.com/book/the-eu-charter-of-fundamental-rights-a-commentary/>.

Wong R, 'Data Protection Online: Alternative Approaches to Sensitive Data?' (2007) 2 Journal of International Commercial Law and Technology 9

Woods L, 'Abuse of Rights' in Steve Peers and others (eds), *The EU Charter of Fundamental Rights: A Commentary* (Hart 2014) <https://www.bloomsburycollections.com/book/the-eu-charter-of-fundamental-rights-a-commentary/>

——, 'Freedom of Expression and Information' in Steve Peers and others (eds), *The EU Charter of Fundamental Rights: A Commentary* (Hart 2014) <https://www.bloomsburycollections.com/book/the-eu-charter-of-fundamental-rights-a-commentary/>.

——, 'Big Brother's Little Brother? The Scope of the "Household Exception" to EU Data Protection Law' (*EU Law Analysis*, 10 July 2014) <http://eulawanalysis.blogspot.co.uk/2014/07/big-brothers-little-brother-scope-of.html> accessed 12 February 2015

Wopereis L, 'David vs Googliath: Het Recht Om Vergeten Te Worden' (*Advocatie*, 18 January 2017) <http://www.advocatie.nl/david-vs-googliath-het-recht-om-vergeten-te-worden> accessed 4 February 2017

Wright D and others, 'Privacy, Trust and Policy-Making: Challenges and Responses' (2009) 25 Computer Law & Security Review 69

Wu T, *The Master Switch* (Atlantic Books 2011)

——, *The Attention Merchants: From the Daily Newspaper to Social Media, How Our Time and Attention Is Harvested and Sold* (Atlantic Books 2017)

Yakowitz J, 'More Crap From the E.U.' (*Info/Law*, 25 January 2012) <http://blogs.law.harvard.edu/infolaw/2012/01/25/more-crap-from-the-e-u/> accessed 15 October 2012

Youyou W, Kosinski M, and Stillwell D, 'Computer-Based Personality Judgments Are More Accurate than Those Made by Humans' [2015] Proceedings of the National Academy of Sciences 201418680

Zanfir G, 'Tracing the Right to Be Forgotten in the Short History of Data Protection Law: The "New Clothes" of an Old Right' in Serge Gutwirth, Ronald Leenes, and Paul de Hert (eds), *Reforming European Data Protection Law* (Springer Netherlands 2015) <http://link.springer.com/chapter/10.1007/978-94-017-9385-8_8> accessed 26 January 2015

Zarsky T, 'Mine Your Own Business: Making the Case for the Implications of the Data Mining of Personal Information in the Forum of Public Opinion' (2002) 5 Yale JL & Tech 1

Zarsky TZ, 'Desperately Seeking Solutions: Using Implementation-Based Solutions for the Troubles of Information Privacy in the Age of Data Mining and the Internet Society' (2004) 56 Maine Law Review 13

Zeit Online, 'Verräterisches Handy' *Zeit Online* (February 2011) <http://www.zeit.de/datenschutz/malte-spitz-data-retention> accessed 23 October 2012

Zheng N, Paloski A, and Wang H, 'An Efficient User Verification System via Mouse Movements', *Proceedings of the 18th ACM Conference on Computer and Communications Security* (ACM 2011) <http://dl.acm.org/citation.cfm?id=2046725> accessed 7 April 2015

Zingales N, 'The Rise of "Infomediaries" in Support of Individual Autonomy: A Matter of Trust and (Joint) Responsibility' (2018)

Zittrain J, *The Future of the Internet—And How to Stop It* (Yale University Press 2008)

——, 'The Ten Things That Define You' (*Future of the Internet—And How to Stop It*, 14 May 2014) <http://blogs.law.harvard.edu/futureoftheinternet/2014/05/15/the-ten-things-that-define-you/> accessed 9 July 2014

——, 'Facebook Could Decide an Election Without Anyone Ever Finding Out' [2014] *The New Republic* <http://www.newrepublic.com/article/117878/information-fiduciary-solution-facebook-digital-gerrymandering> accessed 10 June 2014

Zuboff S, 'Big Other: Surveillance Capitalism and the Prospects of an Information Civilization' (2015) 30 Journal of Information Technology 75

——, 'Google as a Fortune Teller: The Secrets of Surveillance Capitalism' *Frankfurter Allgemeine Zeitung* (5 March 2016) <http://www.faz.net/aktuell/feuilleton/debatten/the-digital-debate/shoshana-zuboff-secrets-of-surveillance-capitalism-14103616-p2.html?printPagedArticle=true#pageIndex_2> accessed 9 March 2016

——, *The Age of Surveillance Capitalism: The Fight for a Human Future at the New Frontier of Power* (2019)

Zuiderveen Borgesius F, 'Consent to Behavioural Targeting in European Law - What Are the Policy Implications of Insights from Behavioural Economics?' (2013) <http://papers.ssrn.com/abstract=2300969> accessed 29 April 2014

——, 'Improving Privacy Protection in the Area of Behavioural Targeting' (PhD Thesis, University of Amsterdam 2014) <http://hdl.handle.net/11245/1.434236>.

——, 'Het "right to be forgotten" en bijzondere persoonsgegevens' (2016) 126 Computerrecht

Zuiderveen Borgesius FJ, 'Singling out People without Knowing Their Names—Behavioural Targeting, Pseudonymous Data, and the New Data Protection Regulation' 32 Computer Law & Security Review 256

Index

Note: *For the benefit of digital users, indexed terms that span two pages (e.g., 52–53) may, on occasion, appear on only one of those pages.*

The manufacturer's authorised representative in the EU for product safety is Oxford University Press España S.A. of el Parque Empresarial San Fernando de Henares, Avenida de Castilla, 2 – 28830 Madrid (www.oup.es/en or product.safety@oup.com). OUP España S.A. also acts as importer into Spain of products made by the manufacturer.

www.ingramcontent.com/pod-product-compliance
Lightning Source LLC
Chambersburg PA
CBHW071158260726
48726CB00019B/26
9780198847977